# YUKON WILD

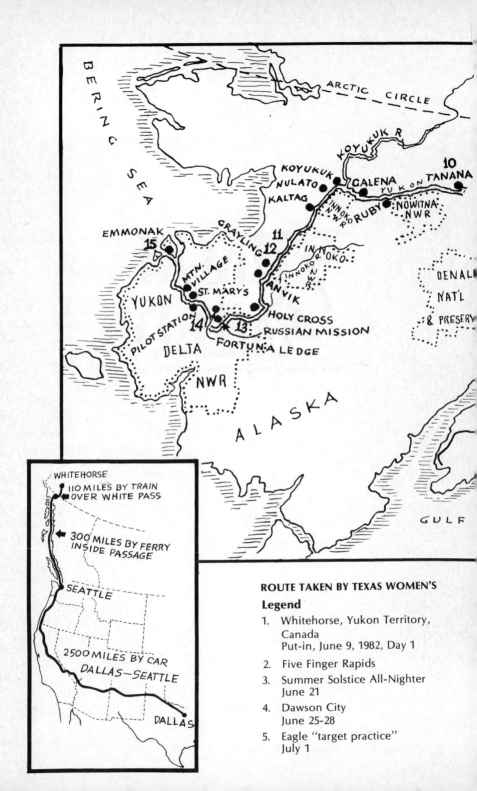

BERING SEA

ARCTIC CIRCLE

KOYUKUK R.

KOYUKUK
NULATO
KALTAG
GALENA
TANANA 10
RUBY
NOWITNA NWR
INNOKO NWR
YUKON

EMMONAK 15

GRAYLING 11 12
MTN. VILLAGE
ST. MARY'S
ANVIK
INNOKO NWR
DENALI NATL & PRESERV

YUKON
PILOT STATION
14 13
HOLY CROSS
RUSSIAN MISSION
FORTUNA LEDGE

DELTA NWR

ALASKA

GULF

WHITEHORSE
110 MILES BY TRAIN OVER WHITE PASS

300 MILES BY FERRY INSIDE PASSAGE

SEATTLE

2500 MILES BY CAR
DALLAS—SEATTLE

DALLAS

**ROUTE TAKEN BY TEXAS WOMEN'S**
**Legend**

1. Whitehorse, Yukon Territory, Canada
   Put-in, June 9, 1982, Day 1

2. Five Finger Rapids

3. Summer Solstice All-Nighter
   June 21

4. Dawson City
   June 25-28

5. Eagle "target practice"
   July 1

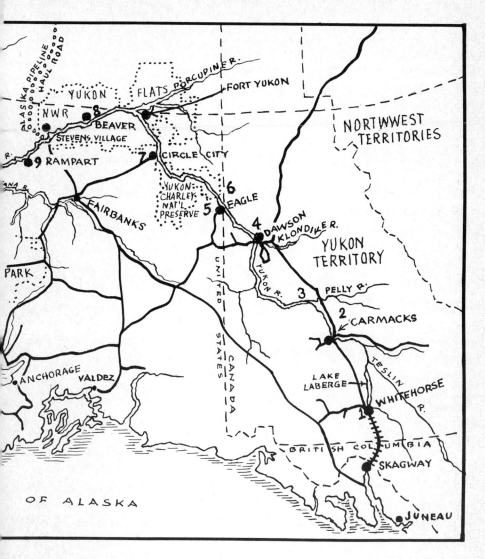

# YUKON RIVER EXPEDITION

*To Anne,*
*who believed and who understood.*
*To Bill,*
*who never quite understood but who accepted.*
*And to the love between them.*

# YUKON WILD

The Adventures of Four Women Who Paddled
2,000 Miles Through America's Last Frontier

## Beth Johnson

With Yukon River Guide and Logistics Summary

THE BERKSHIRE TRAVELLER PRESS
Stockbridge, Massachusetts

OTHER TITLES FROM BERKSHIRE TRAVELLER PRESS

Country Inns & Back Roads, North America
Country Inns & Back Roads, Britain & Ireland
Country Inns & Back Roads, Continental Europe
Bed & Breakfast, American Style

Grateful acknowledgment is made to the following publishers for permission to use material from:

*The Yukon* by Richard Mathews. Copyright 1968 by Richard Mathews. Reprinted by permission of Holt, Rinehart & Winston.
*The Collected Poems of Robert Service.* Copyright 1940 by Robert Service. Quoted by permission of Dodd, Mead & Company, Inc.
*John Muir Travels in Alaska* by John Muir. Houghton Mifflin Co., 1915.
*The Klondike Fever* by Pierre Berton. Copyright 1958 by Pierre Berton. Reprinted by permission of Alfred A. Knopf, Inc.
*Exploring the Yukon* by Archie Satterfield. Copyright 1975 and 1979, The Mountaineer Books.
"Poem II" by Yamabe no Akahito. In *One Hundred Poems from the Japanese,* copyright 1976 by Kenneth Rexroth. Reprinted by permission of New Directions Publishing Corp.

Book Design: Janice Lindstrom and Virginia Rowe
Maps: Janice Lindstrom

Library of Congress Catalog Card No. 83-71367
ISBN 0-912944-78-1

Printed in the United States of America by The Studley Press, Inc., Dalton Mass.
Published by Berkshire Traveller Press, Stockbridge, Mass. 01262. 413-298-3636

# contents

[illustrations following page 208]

*When I went out*
*In the Spring meadows*
*To gather violets,*
*I enjoyed myself*
*So much that I stayed all night.*

Yamabe no Akahito
A.D. 734-748

# preface

What is it, you ask, that would lure four Texas women, who'd never seen the Yukon River, away from their jobs, their homes, their families and friends for three months to paddle canoes 2,000 miles through the wilderness of Canada's Yukon Territory and across the breadth of Alaska—America's last frontier? What would drive us to spend months of preparation and thousands of dollars, risk marriages, jeopardize careers, in order to enjoy months of muddy feet, sweat-stained T-shirts, chapped hands and lips, sand-gritted food, wind, rain, living under mosquito headnets, and being on constant alert for grizzlies?

Oh, we had our reasons. And after all, why not?

"I am going to save the earth," said fifty-one-year-old Evelyn, "starting with me. The Yukon River is an important part of the earth, and I want to experience it. And there's something about the sheer size of this endeavor that intrigues me."

Sue, forty years old, had always wanted to take a long trip, and the Yukon certainly qualified. She would head for the North one day after completing a year of the chemotherapy and radiation treatment that followed her surgery for breast cancer. For her, paddling the Yukon meant "the completion of therapy, a celebration of hopefully whipping cancer."

"My whole life basically has been structured," said Jude, twenty-seven years old. "You go to high school, you go to college, you get a job, and find your apartment. Everything has its own rules. Paddling the Yukon is something that's breaking all the rules. . . . I think I'm doing it more or less to rebel."

At age twenty-eight, I had several reasons: to do something I'd never done . . . to discover how our views of what's important might change over time on the river . . . to experience something as big as a whole continent, from beginning to end, in one continuous effort, in the muscle-powered mode of travel by which America was explored . . . to memorize the words to a bunch of songs I'd been trying to learn for years . . . to meet a king salmon, a grizzly bear, an Arctic tern, a moose, an Eskimo, an Athapascan Indian, and maybe a caribou and a whale . . . to know the subtleties of how rivers and land change as they move toward the sea . . . to practice my photography and my trumpet and my harmonica and catch up on some reading . . . to see what it would be like putting up with mosquitoes and each other and myself for that long . . . for the hell of it (not necessarily in order of importance).

Humans have a profound need for wilderness—and I thank God, environmental activists, and some farsighted elected representatives, that a few wild places remain in this world—for those of us who must go there, for those who take comfort in knowing the places are there, for those who enrich their lives in some small measure by reading of the places, and most of all, for the bacteria and tundra flowers and geese and foxes and waterfalls and clouds of mountains and glaciers and claybanks, whose right it is to be there.

¡Salud!

August, 1983
beneath a midnight moon
on a Brazos River sandbar

# acknowledgments

I wish to thank the biggest and most frenetic stubborn dreamer I will ever hope to know—my boss and mentor and exasperation and inspiration—Ned Fritz. In addition, Elizabeth Hittson showed me long ago that one way or another, sooner or later, you can get yourself anywhere in the world you want to be. Beverly Hayes had the sense of humor and the wonderful temerity to get in the same boat with me on a whitewater river on my first—and her first—canoe trip. David Conrad taught me to draw, ferry, pry, and lean downstream when you hit the rock; he also gave excellent back rubs.

Many thanks to the following people who gave us advice, encouragement, seat pads, dehydrators, fishing poles . . . : Tom Anderson, Jim Bridges, Jim Brittin, J.C. and Arlene Pendleton Foster, Barbara Franklin, Suzanne Greer, Chuck Hummer, Neely Kerr, Ed Lyles, Sid Rucker, John Ryan, Gloria Shone, Nancy Webber (all of the Dallas/Fort Worth area); Richard O. Albert of Alice, Texas; Martha McCalspin Boyd of Seattle; Paul Gray of Corpus Christi; Bev Feldspauch of Kalamazoo, Michigan; Jack Hession of Anchorage; Verlen and Jenny Kruger of Lansing, Michigan; Bryna Millman of New York. Thanks also to Steve Runnels and Walt Davis of the Dallas Museum of Natural History, who sought funds and served as press agents and photography advisors before, during, and long after the trip. Thanks also to the families of the Texas Women's Yukon River Expedition, who worried for us while we paddled. A big, big thanks to my parents, Anne and Bill, whose unfaltering freedom and tolerance and support through the years happily produced a stubborn dreamer like me. For the Yukon they endured potato bits in the kitchen carpet and onion gas through the house, designed mosquito headnets and sewed custom stuff sacks, paid phone bills and floated loans, designed trumpet cases, fastened/painted/glued equipment, lugged supplies to the post office each week—in short, placed at our utter disposal their home, their every waking hour, and their Mastercard. . . .

Our very special gratitude and admiration goes to Twelve Baskets Distributors of Bellevue, Washington, for their extremely generous support and their high-quality, chemical-free, dehydrated, and freeze-dried foods. We are also indebted to the following firms for tangible support of the expedition: Arrowhead Mills, Barry's Cameras, Broadway Reprographics, Camp 7, Coleman Co., Early Winters, High Trails Canoe Outfitters, Illes Spice Co., International Mountain Equipment, Lowe Alpine Systems, Mesquite Boat Works, Minolta Corporation, Northwest River Supply, Southwest Canoe and Trail, The North Face.

For their wealth of historical information and the delicious way they present it, I am indebted to Richard Mathews's *The Yukon* and Pierre Berton's *The Klondike Fever*, both of which I have drawn upon in the following pages.

My special thanks to Kathy Rucker, an angel who volunteered to transcribe endless hours of tapes and type endless pages of manuscript; and to Bob Edens for his hours of toil at the copying machine.

A very warm thanks to editor Virginia Rowe for nurturing the manuscript to sensibility; and to Norman Simpson of the Berkshire Traveller Press, who believed in having fun, taking risks, and an unpublished writer who'd never seen the Yukon, but claimed she'd canoe its length and write a book about it.

I wish to thank especially all those warm, wonderful souls who live on the Yukon who gave us their laughter, the shelter of their cabins and the heat from their wood stoves, their salmon strips and beer; and Sybil Brittin and David Gile and Bing Ahlering, who sometimes shared the river and its sandbars with us, and who could always be counted on for a smile, a joke, and a keen observation of the Yukon's special world.

And finally, my most profound appreciation goes to my fellow paddlers:

Jane Kittleman and Barbara Martin, whose boundless energies helped ensure that there was never a dull nor entirely sane moment during the 4,000-mile journey to the river and the 460 miles they paddled with us on the Yukon;

Sue Sherrod and Jude Hammett, who believed in the dream and—despite broken bones and intestinal viruses—paddled 2,000 miles to the Bering Sea; and

Evelyn Edens, my partner, who never doubted. Not only did she paddle 2,000 miles to the Bering Sea, but she cheerfully tolerated my endless singing and fidgeting with cameras and trumpets in the bow; found humor in the strangest of circumstances; was equally content sleeping in the boat in the sun or paddling for ten hours straight in the rain; and was ready, willing, and gleefully able to meet whatever or whomever might appear 'round that next bend.

# PART I

*A journey of a thousand miles began with a single step.*

Lao-Tsze
550 B.C.

# 1 tequila sunrises and dreams

"What in the hell am I doing here?" I asked myself as my tent collapsed on top of me one night on a sandbar in the middle of the Yukon River in a forty-mile-an-hour gale. I thrashed my way, half-dressed, into the darkness and the storm, shivering under pelting raindrops.

Crawling on all fours, I dragged the nylon jumble through the wet sand toward my partner's tent. I smiled at how I must look wrestling a bucking tent.

"Evelyn!" I shouted over the bashing of waves against the shore. "My tent won't stay up!"

"Come on in!" came the wide-awake reply. "I'm sitting here holding up mine!"

I slithered into the little A-frame shelter and collapsed into the puddle of water seeping up through the floor. Huddled in our wet long johns and sleeping bags, we each supported a pole against the roaring wind. We had paddled our overloaded canoe fifty miles through the rain that day. Just as we had pitched the tents, the windstorm had exploded, so we had retreated without supper. We were exhausted, hungry, wet, cold. And now two grown women were launching a Yukon slumber party. We giggled at the prospect of crouching there all night holding up a tent.

We joked. Our boat would be swept away. The river would rise and we'd battle five-foot waves in a desperate bid for shore. But beneath the light chatter, we knew there was a real danger of hypothermia, the deadly loss of body heat that strikes when you're too cold, or exhausted, or hungry. We reprimanded ourselves for pushing so to catch our partners Sue and Jude, for having no high-energy, ready-to-eat-food, and for camping on this unprotected sandbar.

Cocooned in her sleeping bag, Evelyn tugged at the sheet she always used. "I am not animal," she muttered. "I am wet and I haven't had a bath in three weeks and I am miserable, but I am human because I have a sheet. . . . Animals do not have sheets." Brightening, she suggested, "At least we're not getting hypothermia. We seem to be rational."

"Sure," I tittered, "thinking you're rational is the first sign. . . ."

In the morning, our canoe sat half-buried in sand and full of water. Two days would drip by before slackening wind and rain would allow our escape to shore across the mile-wide channel.

Exactly what *were* four women from Dallas, Texas, who had never before seen the Yukon River, doing there?

We were attempting the first non-motorized descent of the river, as far as we knew, by an all-female group. The Yukon flows about 2,000 miles through Canada's Yukon Territory and all of Alaska to the Bering Sea, not far from Russia. What we were attempting was like paddling from Washington, D.C., to Utah.

*      *      *

The idea had bobbed to the surface a year before. I was in a kayak, paddling the muddy rapids of the Green River that flows through Dinosaur National Monument in the Colorado-Utah desert. The day I turned twenty-eight we had climbed massive Steamboat Rock, where the Yampa rushes into the Green. (From Steamboat, the one-armed Major John Wesley Powell had hung high above the river, quite unintentionally, for some minutes during his historic 1869 exploration of the Colorado River system. A companion had jumped out of his long johns and dangled them over the precipice, whereupon Powell grabbed them and scrambled to safety.)

We paddled through Whirlpool Canyon to a shady grove where Jones Hole Creek gurgled from the hills and over our wine bottles and into the Green. In the icy trout stream where we had bathed that afternoon, the guys had made red Jello in a bowl, then stuck a fat candle into the half-set wiggle. They sang "Happy Birthday" as a huge July sun dipped behind the mesa.

It was our last night on the river, and we wallowed in heavenly freeze-dried pork chops and amaretto-laced dehydrated fruit cocktail. Among the cottonwoods, in the hot, dry dusk, we watched stars bloom across the desert night. We passed the tequila canteen for "instant tequila sunrises." You stuff an orange slice into your mouth, chomping it into a pulp, and swallow orange and tequila in one gulp. My lips stung and my stomach flipped, but suddenly I remembered the words to "Faded Love" by Bob Wills and the Texas Playboys.

A grand birthday tradition, I thought—running a river every July. On my previous birthday I had camped from a canoe on a river for the first time on a three-day trip down Virgina's Rappahannock River, a few hours from where I lived in Washington, D.C. The hot July sun, the cool water, the shady green corridor through the mountains, dining at night by candlelight on an overturned canoe, the banana omelet David made to put the bruised bananas out of their misery—all had suited me fine, and I had decided to make it a tradition. On that trip I sat in a kayak for the first time when we traded our canoe for our friends' kayaks for a few hours. Now, a year later, I was living back in my home state of Texas, had my own kayak "Flipper," and found myself running one of the great wilderness rivers of the West.

This evening, sitting on a log in the desert, I was feeling triumphant; Flipper and I had dumped ourselves into the water only once yesterday, once the day before, and not at all today. I could now snap my helmet chin-strap without assistance nine times out of ten, and after only a few minutes I could walk on the cramped legs I withdrew from the kayak at day's end. This was all right.

The next day we snaked our way down a liquid ribbon that flowed through the sturdy desert crust, between giant sandstone shoulders, ever headed toward the sea. I became enamored of the idea of continuing what we were doing beyond the planned four days, onward to the sea, for as long as it took. Paddle, eat, sleep; paddle, eat, sleep; day after day in the Utah sun. Or beneath some other sun—the Arctic sun, the Amazon jungle sun. . . .

But you can't paddle down a river from the Utah desert to the sea. Water hustlers have dammed and redammed the mighty Colorado until it is no longer a living river system, but a series of deadwater reservoirs. Majestic desert canyons sculpted by millions of years of wind and water and time have been drowned in a geologic instant by humans. In exchange, desert residents can have lush lawns and golf courses, backyard swimming pools, electric dishwashers, and frosty summer air conditioning. If you wanted to canoe down the Colorado to the sea, you'd have to portage around a lot of dams, and you'd subject yourself to hordes of motorboats and weekend campers and radios.

That wasn't what I had in mind. I wanted to flow down an entire, natural river—experience everything from headwaters to mouth. I wanted to see how the river and the animals and the vegetation and the people interact. I wanted to witness how the river forms and is formed by the earth through which it pushes. I wanted a river unshackled by dams—a wild river, free of roads, bridges, and developments.

And I wanted it to be long. Long enough so that halfway down the river, you'd forget whatever it was you used to do every day and would know only what you were doing—floating a river. Long enough so that you'd attain a simple peace in being there, doing, each day as it came.

I like to dream, and that's what I began to do as I stroked that muddy Utah water through the ancient desert. I had taken dozens of weekend canoe trips, but at forty-eight river miles and four days long, the Green was my first "long" river trip. And it was my first wilderness river where help, if needed, might be more than a few hours' walk. But something was beginning to tell me I was ready for more. (Two weeks earlier I had never heard of the Green River, but as we rafted the flooded Guadalupe in Texas, Betsy Butler had suggested I go with the guys to Utah; something had told me I was ready, and here I was.) This trip seemed to be nothing more than what I always did on weekend trips, only doing it longer.

The following day, I lay outstretched on the warm rubber tube of Joe Butler's raft as we headed into Westwater Canyon of the Colorado.

"Let's all do a long river trip," I said, opening my eyes.

"Yeah," he smiled, "like a month."

"No, I'm talking about a *long* trip, like three to six months." Suddenly, I blurted, "The whole Yukon River!"

There, I'd said it. The dream had expressed itself aloud, which meant I was more than half serious. I didn't quite know where the thought came from; I didn't know much about the Yukon. I liked rivers, I wanted a long trip, and I'd always wanted to see Alaska; the Yukon seemed to offer all three. Maybe it was a process of elimination: The Missouri-Mississippi system has suffered the same fate as the Colorado and is full of locks and dams and motorized boats and barges. The Saint Lawrence is full of sea traffic. If you want your river really long, halfway wild, and in North America, you're pretty well limited to rivers in Alaska and Canada, and even then, the logging companies and the mining companies and the oil companies and the dam-builders are not letting wild, clean rivers stand between them and dollars.

I suppose we carry things filed in the back of our brains, and maybe in mine lots of Yukon bits floated around waiting to gel. Once, as I jounced in a jeep through the mesquite pastures of the Texas Hill Country with a South Texas birder named Richard O. Albert, he told me he'd once paddled for a month down some other river and into the Yukon, and the trip had pleased him tremendously. I'd seen a *National Geographic* special on TV, in which four young guys chopped down big trees, built a raft, and played poker all the way down the Yukon. (Just as I always do when I see something like that, or like *The African Queen,* on TV, I had shed tears of admiration for them.) When an Alaskan had come to Texas to generate support for the Alaska lands bill that would preserve a hunk of our public lands there, I had made a speaking tour with him around the state in connection with citizens' environmental organizations. Between stops he had filled my ears with tales of Alaska's wild beauty and the arrogant greed that threatens it. Later, I had spent more than a year in Washington, D.C., working with the Alaska Coalition and the Wilderness Society to pass that bill. Every day as I talked on the phone with an editorial writer from Lawrence, Kansas, or a reporter from Seattle, I would stare at the big map above my desk, with all the boundaries of the refuges and parks and rivers we were trying to save, none of which I had ever seen. And every day, smack dab across the middle of it all, had wiggled the mighty Yukon. Once or twice, during particularly long phone conversations, I may have absently traced the great river's course across the last frontier with the fly-swatter we used to smush desktop roaches. . . .

Joe's voice penetrated my musings, and he was talking about jobs and vacation allotments and house payments and. . . . It was the same with the others: a smile, a brief, faraway look in their eyes, a comment on what kind of gear to take, then another smile, and the discussion would end. They did not dare to dream this dream.

# 2 an itch, a bathtub orgy, a decision

An itch had developed and I meant to attend to it. Monday morning, back in Dallas, I carted home all three books the library had about the Yukon River. The new dream took another step.

The Yukon! As a little girl I had known its hardships and cruelty and courage through Buck, in *The Call of the Wild*. In junior high school, I had thrilled to the adventure, the pain, and the joy of being a Canadian Mountie's wife in *Mrs. Mike*. The North meant fireplaces and bearded woodchoppers, and I'd always had a weakness for both.

Now, in the still July evenings in my one-room apartment, I curled up in bed, beneath the ceiling fan's gentle creaking. I lost myself in *The Yukon*, a delightful history of Eskimos and Russians and English fur-traders and Klondike stampeders; or *Yukon Passage*, an account of the poker-players' escapades in their bulky wooden raft; or *99 Days on the Yukon*, a light-hearted diary of a young novice's trip down most of the Yukon with a not-quite-seventy-year-old veteran canoeist.

Gradually it seeped in that the Yukon is big. She's the fifth longest river in North America, a giant who gushes more water, farther, faster, than anything I had ever paddled. She pushes through part of Canada and across the entire breadth of Alaska until finally, not far from Russia, she eases her glacially-silted self into the Bering Sea. She roils along her tons of silt at a fast clip, and yet, except for a couple of places where she kicks up her heels, she's a flatwater river. She's often more than a mile wide and flows through everything from abrupt, snowcapped mountains to soggy delta marshlands. She's wild, knows but one bridge and one pipeline crossing below Whitehorse, Canada. From there, she flows free and undammed almost 2,000 miles to the sea. And yet, she's been subjected to a degree of "civilization." A couple of dozen villages squat along her banks. Motorboats and airplanes flit through her big valley. Upstream from Whitehorse in the headwaters lakes are a highway bridge and a railroad. A dam at Whitehorse has choked the river and drowned some once-thrilling rapids.

The Yukon is the only river that crosses the entire state of Alaska. To paddle its length might be like paddling across a continent, as Lewis and Clark had done, to glimpse what it was like for the early explorers whose only way to discover North America's secrets was to paddle through its wildness on rivers. To flow down its length would be to meet Indians and Eskimos, to encounter moose and foxes and wolves and bears, to follow the path of one of the most exciting gold rushes in history. If you paddled through this big piece of what's left of wild America, you might spend some time with yourself, discover what thoughts you might think if your head were free from appointments, deadlines, commitments, money, and time.

On a Friday afternoon in late July, Suzanne Greer and I threw two kayaks, some bean dip and Doritos into the car and headed for the Guadalupe River in the Texas Hill Country.

"You wanna float the Yukon?" I asked, as casually as I could, and for five hours down the Interstate we talked of Alaska, fish, and Alaskan mosquitoes.

"But I've got house payments to make," she finally said. "I'd have to sell the press." She had just quit her sales job to launch her own printing business.

"So sell it," I shrugged.

She talked about floating the river for only two weeks. "That's hardly worth going up there for," I said.

"But what about my kids?" she said, grinning. "What would they think if their mother went off down the Yukon?"

"Aw, they're in high school," I said. "They can take care of themselves until you get back."

The next day we kayaked the Guadalupe. After running Waco Springs Rapid with style, we sat on a warm rock, nibbled our lunch, and watched thousands of other idiots in inner tubes and canoes dump in the river. People who couldn't swim washed over the drop in inner tubes, without life jackets, and looked frantic when the hole behind Big Rock sucked their tubes from them; people who'd never canoed were running dangerous Waco, their knuckles clenched white on the gunnels, mouths agape in helpless fear. Down the river bobbed a thick debris of swamped canoes, riderless tubes, ice chests, and people. The Guadalupe on a midsummer weekend was not very relaxing, and I decided I'd seek less-congested rivers for my future entertainment.

That evening at the crowded campground on the banks of the Guadalupe, Suzanne's boyfriend, Tom Anderson, drove up. He was sick of missing all the river trips because he worked every Saturday, so he'd quit his job that morning, grabbed Suzanne's other kayak, and tracked us down. We laughed and went for a swim. "By the way, you wanna float the Yukon?" I eyed him speculatively.

Veggies sputtered in the wok on the propane stove; locusts sang in the late afternoon light; we talked of Alaska. Tom had a book called *Yukon Summer* about a guy who paddled a kayak solo halfway down the Yukon.

Tom mentioned with a grin that although the Yukon was mostly flatwater, the guy had routinely made fifty miles a day because the current was so fast. I was astounded; fifty miles on Texas's sluggish, flatland rivers was a respectable three-day paddle.

"Well, he did say the water was a little high that year," Tom added.

The next day we had the clear, green waters of the Lampasas River to ourselves. In the shade of the thick floodplain forest, three kayaks slithered through a lazy Sunday afternoon. I leaned back against the cockpit, closed my eyes, sang "Summertime," and drifted. We stopped at a gravel bar, and while Suzanne and Tom fished, I took off my clothes and cavorted, porpoiselike, in a little riffle near the shore. The only sounds were an occasional dive-bombing kingfisher, a cow's mooing. This, not the crowded madness of the Guadalupe, was what a river should be.

In the evening, we sat in our lawn chairs among the high grasses and chiggers and grasshoppers beside the highway bridge, shared the little fish Tom had caught, drank wine from tin cups, and talked of the Yukon. But already, I detected that "it-would-be-nice-but . . . " look in their eyes.

"Hey, you wanna float the Yukon?" I asked my younger brother, Steve, the following weekend as we fried okra in a cast-iron skillet in my mother's kitchen. I was getting used to saying this out loud.

"The Yukon?!" he looked disgusted. (That didn't necessarily mean he wasn't all for the idea. He and I had tolerated each other for a couple of thousand miles on a car-camping trip once, and I believe he liked it. But all he usually said when asked if he'd like to do a given thing was that it was better than a poke in the eye with a sharp stick.)

"You'd freeze your tail up there," he said. "Are the rapids any good?"

"Mostly flatwater," I admitted, "but it moves. You can do fifty miles a day." He didn't believe me.

"How long would it take?" he asked.

"I figure about three months," I smiled.

"Three months? Flatwater? Mosquitoes? Nah," he said, wrinkling his nose. I dropped the invitation with a "you-had-your-chance" shrug.

After I borrowed *Yukon Summer* from Tom, every night in my imagination I'd paddle a little farther through the Arctic with a guy from California who, on a whim, bought a kayak and decided to float the Yukon for a month. He knew next to nothing about rivers and kayaks before he headed north. The other books had told delightful tales about groups of people going down the river; this one told equally humorous tales about a solo voyage.

Now *there* was a thought. . . .

One lazy August afternoon I ran a tubful of steaming water, as I often do when I'm recovering from some mess I'm in or dreaming up a new one to get into. The tub, one of those old ones with ball-and-claw feet, was deep enough with a perfect curve on its smooth sides for resting my elbows with a beer in one hand and a book in the other. So I sat in the hot water and pondered the past and the future and the faucet drip. I read about Arctic mosquitoes, Arctic grizzlies, wild mountain ranges from which tumble pristine waters.

According to the books, the Yukon is very big and flat. If I really did decide to paddle it, would I be bored by so many miles with so few rapids? Aw, who *couldn't* hear the word "Yukon" without itching to dash off to the mysterious land of the midnight sun? Besides, I couldn't think of a river or a swamp or a natural lake I hadn't liked; something about them imparts a joy and a magic sensuality to the most ordinary activities. Sinking deeper into the water, I closed my eyes and slipped into an orgy of memories . . . skinny-dipping under a hot May sun where cold water cascaded over the rocks of the Llano River . . . moonlight floats on the Brazos, when we drank margaritas and swung from the bank on a big knotted rope to plunge into the river's warm depths. . . . lying in a canoe, staring at stars above the wondrous swampy expanses of Caddo Lake in East Texas . . . the faint voice of my mother, from the bow, saying, "But I don't *do* waterfalls" as I steered us over one. Flatwater or whitewater, each river was lovable in its own way, and I was addicted to paddling them.

. . . I opened my eyes. But would the Yukon's grizzlies and moose be dangerous? I had met a few wild animals in my time. I remembered a misty morning hike when four deer whistled in a Florida meadow . . . a black bear crashing from the woods across my path in Shenandoah National Park . . . the great lips of a moose munching underwater salad at the edge of a pond in Maine . . . fearless, dog-sized skunks in the Smokies who swarmed into the campground the minute the sun went down . . . hordes of devilish Georgia raccoons who'd steal the food from your table as Coke-bottle missiles merely glanced off their shoulders. Meeting animals eyeball to eyeball was one of the main attractions, wasn't it?

. . . But what would it involve to get the money to buy the food and equipment and to lose three months' salary, to choose and collect and pack the equipment and food, and to get myself almost 4,000 miles up to the Yukon, not to mention paddling almost 2,000 miles down its length? To say the least, it would be quite a little undertaking. But if I'm anything, I'm stubborn. When I was fourteen I announced I was going to Europe. I joined some Campfire Girls who were earning Europe money by washing ceilings and windows, selling lawn fertilizer, building floats for the Christmas parade; dollar by dollar, I built my war chest. When I was sixteen I toured the Continent, all with an infected ingrown toenail that required surgery upon my return to the States. Ever since, I'd known that I would always come up with the money for whatever I wanted to do. The key was first to make the decision—to fix the dream—then somehow the means would follow.

. . . I had one leg shaved now. A dog yapped in a neighbor's yard, charcoal smoke drifted from somebody's barbecue. But was my outdoor experience adequate for the Yukon? I had done lots of camping while I was growing up and during college. Last fall I had camped out of my van "Oscar" for three months and 8,500 miles, traveling alone from Nova

Scotia to Key West. And yet, most of my experience had been with the comforts of all the paraphernalia that an automobile can bring to your campsite. I had backpacked only a dozen times, the longest trip a mere three days. I had camped from a boat only five times. I had been canoeing for only four years.

I smiled as I remembered the first time I had set foot in a canoe. The person who was supposed to teach us had gotten sick at the last minute, but Beverly and Susan and I, who'd never been in a canoe, rented one anyway. As we floated through riffles and dodged trees in the Medina River, we labored under the misconception that it was the front person who steered, like a car. As we would ram accidentally into the bank, the current would whip the stern around so that the bow pointed upstream, at which point we'd simply shout "Switch!" and the three of us would swivel in our seats to face downstream again. That worked pretty well until we capsized on the third swivel, but we did finally make our way five miles down the river. It came as quite a revelation later when I learned that the back person could do something called a J-stroke, or a rudder, that would control the direction of the bow. Amazing!

I became hooked on canoeing my first Saturday in Washington, D.C., when Dave Conrad of the American Rivers Conservation Council dragged me off to West Virginia to paddle some mild rapids on the Potomac. Later, I took a notion to learn how to solo a canoe, amongst the alligators of Georgia's Okefenokee Swamp. I spent hours going in circles before I figured out the intricacies of the slight headwind and subtle current of the flooded swamp, but I finally made it the few miles to my island goal and strolled triumphantly through the moss-draped forest. Afterwards, I took a couple of Red Cross canoeing courses, read technique books and tried to comprehend all those strange drawings with the little arrows, and learned about riffles, leaning downstream, eddies, draws, pries, and ferrying. I took some guided trips and ran sections of several dozen rivers. I had to admit, I probably was ready to live on a river for three months.

. . . But would paddling 2,000 miles be *work*? I was certainly no athlete. I had bought a kayak not particularly to be a whitewater daredevil, but because at 5 feet 5 inches tall and 130 pounds, I could tote a 30-pound kayak down to the river more easily than an 80-pound canoe. My physical abilities were rather unimpressive. I remembered how once, I had backpacked a meager two-and-a-half miles when I had such a ridiculous pain in my thigh that I just knew I had thrombosis, that there was a blood clot and I would expire at any moment. I lay motionless in the tent all afternoon and night, too much in pain to shift positions. But in the morning I limped back to the trailhead and in a few days the pain subsided. I decided later that I'd loaded the pack incorrectly, or it had been much too heavy, or I'd been out of shape, or all of the above.

One Labor Day I had hopped on a bicycle and set out for an easy twenty miles among the fishing villages of Maryland's flat Eastern Shore. I had to stop every few minutes for water, and once I even lay down in the shade. I kicked myself for being so out of shape; this was absurd, I thought.

I had a good laugh at day's end when I learned the thermometer had hit 104°.

There was that clear defeat when I had tried to walk up Mount Katahdin in Maine. I'd heard that senior citizens and kids had climbed it, so I looked forward to an easy one-day stroll. I got a late start, and I'm a slow walker anyway (three summers of corrective foot surgery when I was young failed to improve my speed much). The boulder-strewn path tortured my ankles, and eventually I found myself scrambling hand over hand up some iron rungs imbedded in the granite. Looking over my shoulder at the sheer drop and the thunderheads rumbling up the valley toward me, I thought, "What in the hell am I doing here?" A twisted ankle could mean spending the night alone on the mountain with no tent in the unpredictable fall weather. Feeling wise and defeated, I walked down the mountain as darkness settled. No sense in pushing your luck.

But I had to admit, I was better in the water than on land. Paddling the Yukon might involve some effort, but I'd probably get where I was going, sooner or later.

. . . I got another cold beer, ran more hot water; a blur of intro-spections swirled through my steamed brain. If I really did float the Yukon, how would her trappers and fishermen—Indians, Eskimos, whites—react to me? What if they were unfriendly? I'd heard about people taking potshots at canoes for entertainment. What if they were a little *too* friendly? Being a woman, traveling, had always meant meeting men, sometimes when I felt like it, sometimes when I didn't. But I usually coped fairly well. There had been that sweet seventy-year-old Bostonian, about four feet eleven inches tall, who invited me to stay with him so he could show me around. I took him up on it, relieved to learn that when he said he had a casual lifestyle he meant only that he had lawn chairs for furniture. And he was a great tour guide.

When I had visited with a group in the Okefenokee, a big lunk with whom I'd hardly spoken during the evening motioned toward my tent and said, "Well, would you like some company tonight?" I couldn't help smiling; his approach was so . . . so . . . forthright. I said, "I guess not." He shrugged and said, "O.K.," and we waved good night.

Once, after a month's search through Florida, I had finally spotted an endangered West Indian manatee in the warm effluent waters of a power plant. An old fisherman started talking to me as I watched the sea cow surface for air every few minutes, rising from the depths like some ephemeral vision. The nearly extinct porpoiselike mammals are six to fifteen feet long and weigh up to a ton. Propelled by two flippers and a flattened tail, they amble sluggishly through the water, pausing to graze on underwater vegetation. I wanted to watch this magnificent, harmless creature quietly, reverently, knowing I was looking at approximately one-thousandth of the entire number of these beings. (We've killed the rest by hunting them in the past, and today we kill them by accidentally chopping them up with motorboat propellers.) But the fisherman had been joined by his thirtyish son, and the old man was intent on fixing me up with him. I tried to pass it off as a joke and concentrate on my manatee, but he was serious, and they would not leave me alone. All I wanted to do was watch a manatee and eat a peanut butter sandwich in peace in the Sunday morning sun. I finally just got in my van and drove off, saddened for the old man and his horny son and me.

On the other hand, there had been that nice bearded guy who'd just motorcycled from Alaska through Mexico to Florida. At a bar in town, we watched the 1980 presidential election returns and talked of Alaskan spruce forests and Mexican pueblos, of manatees and whales. Back at the campground, I considered asking if he'd like some company that night, but I was too depressed by the election returns.

All in all, there's not much to be afraid of; people are just people. As much as I'm addicted to paddling rivers, I'm equally addicted to meeting the world's colorful characters, and I figured the Yukon would probably harbor its share.

. . . I shaved my other leg. Sweat ran down my face and hair. I sucked my now-warm beer. But what about the little fact that I'd never camped in the Arctic or in grizzly country or even set foot in Alaska? Well, isn't it good for the soul occasionally to have no idea what in the hell is going on? "I don't know what I'm doing but I'm an expert at it!" said a plaque my mother gave me as I headed for California alone one summer, and that philosophy had served me pretty well so far. It feels good to be perplexed, to confront little problems—to round a bend and hear whitewater ahead and wonder, in those four-and-a-half instants that you've got before you hit the drop, whether to back-ferry and head down the left chute or barrel straight through the middle.

Aren't life's little gambles necessary to keep things interesting? Like the time in West Virginina when I met three guys who needed a fourth raft paddler for the rambunctious Lower Gauley River. I didn't hesitate to join them, but I wondered if I'd made a bad decision when we accidentally washed into a boulder and ran the first rapid backwards. Our coordination improved during the day, except that the big whitewater kept tossing people from the raft. Pure Screaming Hell was the rapid to worry about, since running it wrong meant possible loss of equipment or life. As we headed into it, my bow partner paddled so frantically away from a big undercut rock on the right that he swung the whole boat broadside to the big drop he hadn't noticed. My heart pounded, for I knew that if we went over the six-foot drop broadside we'd flip and very likely get pinned under the big undercut rock dead ahead. "Paddle, Beth, paddle!" was the command screamed from the back of the boat; it was my corner that must swing around. The bucking waves had tossed me to the floor of the raft, but I did the biggest, hardest sweeps—straining at the paddle with all my weight—that I've ever done in my life. As we plunged over the drop, the corner of the raft angled just enough. We wallowed through, a ton of water dashing in our faces, and made it past the killer rock amid our victorious whoops. In town that night there was pizza and cold beer; they'd never tasted better.

After all, "If you ain't scared, you ain't havin' fun," kayakers always say. I remembered having so much fun I could hardly stand it a few weeks ago when I kayaked the Guadalupe with Suzanne. At Slumber Falls, the river pours over a dangerous and useless little human-made dam, a submerged structure that sets up a powerful hydraulic recirculating current behind it. Someone was supposedly poised ashore there with a rescue line, just in case, and I had run Slumber before with no problem, so I paddled on into it.

I plowed easily through the squirrelly wave at the top. But suddenly there were dozens of inner tubers in the short stretch between the first drop and the falls. Just as I lined up for my final surge to gain critical momentum, a boy in a tube, dead ahead, went over the drop and flipped head over heels. To avoid spearing him in the nape of the neck with Flipper's pointed bow, I was forced to angle slightly, and that was not good.

Not good at all. Maybe I hesitated a fraction of a second too long after I plunged over the drop, maybe there were bodies and inner tubes in my way, maybe it just wasn't my day. The river seized Flipper and whipped us parallel to the drop, in the predictable, sickening way of hydraulics. For endless, helpless seconds I wobbled in the frothing whitewater, trying to stay upright. The river poured over the two-foot drop at my elbow, roaring in my ears. Flipper's bow rammed two or three times into the rocks at the bank, from which people stared at me and I at them. No throw lines arced through the air toward me. There were bare feet and hands inches from my bow, but neither they nor I could decide if it would make matters better or worse if a hand reached for Flipper's nose.

In a split second the question was moot; I was underwater, caught in the hydraulic that yearly drowns a dozen people—some with life jackets. Through my head went a panicked jumble of thoughts. Someone had said once that if you dump in Slumber in a kayak, try to stay in your boat, because the river will have a hard time sucking the whole air-filled boat to the bottom. If you're out of your boat and get driven downward by the tons of water, you can wait until you touch bottom and push back up to the surface for a gulp of air before you're pulled under again, and by repeating this process, you might stay alive until someone throws you a rope. Or, you can push off the side of the dam underwater—if you can find it—and with luck, overcome the current's power.

I seem to have decided to stay in my boat. Amid the thundering turbulence, I had no idea whether I was just on the surface or deep underwater. I released my grip on my paddle; I didn't know the Eskimo roll to right myself with it, and it might not have worked in this mess anyway. Theories aside, though, I needed some air.

Somehow, my life jacket brought my face to the surface and I grabbed some air. From the corner of my eye I saw looming over the drop a huge rubber raft, with tennis-shoed feet draped over it, wallowing onto Flipper's backside.

I was jerked underwater again, wondering how I would ever get some air if I had not only to untangle myself from the hydraulic and the kayak, but also to surface beneath a big raft!

The next thing I remember is that I was breathing air, the sky and the bald cypress trees were above me, the banks were moving past; I knew I was free of the hydraulic and floating downstream. Much as I cursed that raft, its momentum could well have shoved me clear of the hydraulic's grip. Coughing up water, I wiggled out of Flipper and swam him to shore; Suzanne paddled up and asked me where I'd been; someone handed me my paddle. When my legs stopped shaking enough for me to stand, I dumped the water from Flipper and we headed downstream for the next rapid.

"Damned inner tubers," I muttered.

. . . Yes, I usually pulled through, one way or another, and the Yukon probably would be no exception. Besides, what's the worst that could happen? Drowning or being eaten by a grizzly were both pretty unlikely . . . right?

Actually, I had to admit there was no good reason *not* to float the entire Yukon. The itch was intensifying, I was working myself into something of a frenzy. I felt some inner clock winding itself tighter and tighter toward an alarm, and I realized I have this hopeless little habit of quitting my job every eighteen months to go traveling. Did I quit jobs to get better ones or as an excuse to travel in between them? Did it matter?

Maybe I'd float the entire length of a different river every eighteen months, from now on. Maybe the Yukon was just a warm-up, with easy logistics. After all, it's in English-speaking territory, there isn't much whitewater to it, there aren't even any snakes or ticks up there. . . .

"Oh, Lord," I said to myself, suddenly realizing that all afternoon in the bathtub, my conniving brain had been working hard to convince me that paddling the Yukon was no big deal, coaxing me into feeling rational as I succumbed to a wild dream. "You're gonna do this, aren't you? Admit it." The familiar rush was like the friendly cold froth that slaps you in the face as you slither over a ledge in a kayak. I'd felt the same spark of decision many times before, but never on so grand a scale. "Mother's not gonna believe this one," I thought.

It was settled; I would experience America's last frontier from the bow of a canoe. If I'd been a dog I'd have wagged my tail. I stared at the pile of Yukon books through a teary blur of excitement that kept coming for some time. "I've never done anything like this," I smiled.

That, after all, was the very best reason to do it.

# 3 go for it!

Next morning I wrote Jack Hession and Sally Kabisch, the Sierra Club representatives in Anchorage, with whom I'd worked on the Alaska lands bill. The dream was now bedrock.

I told them my plan and invited them to come. "Obviously," I wrote, "it's going to be hard for me to find a partner, because everybody I know claims that they're either (a) broke; (b) can't take off work for one to three months; (c) not interested; or (d) they don't know how to canoe or kayak. And obviously, a minimum of two boats is desirable for safety reasons. But (and please don't think me crazy), I'm *considering* doing it alone if necessary. I found out a long time ago that if you wait around to do something until someone else wants to or can, you spend all your time waiting and never doing. . . . "

I presented them with a list entitled "Dumb Questions about the Yukon," including: Are there so many motorboats that the Yukon wouldn't be a wilderness trip? What about bears (should I carry a gun)? Is it true that you can easily get lost in the Yukon delta? (In the books no one had gone all the way through the delta, referring to mosquitoes, the "sluggishness" of the river, and the "boring" landscape.) What about the high winds and endless days of rain the books talked about? Will you get diarrhea if you drink the glacially silted Yukon water? What supplies are available at the villages en route? How would I get myself and my equipment back to the Lower 48 from the river's mouth?

It was inevitable that I'd go to the Yukon the following summer, and the question now became not whether I should try to do it alone, but whether I should even bother inviting others. If I went alone I'd be breaking the first rule of canoeing. But I'd broken that rule before. It would be so simple, too, with only my own whims to consider. I could sleep when I wanted, eat when I wanted, read all day long, sit silently for hours soaking in the sounds of nature. There'd be a certain flair about not only paddling the whole damned Yukon River, but in doing it alone—and a woman at that! Maybe no woman had ever paddled the whole river alone. For that matter, not all that many men had paddled the whole river. Maybe

I'd make history. . . .

Good Lord, I thought, just who did I think I was? The purpose of the trip was to have fun, and I'd have more fun—not to mention safety—if I could share it with some fun person. Besides, alone on a big river for three months, maybe I'd go quite literally crazy. Would I run into enough characters to keep me entertained? Would I run into the wrong characters?

And yet, if I chose to go with someone else, who in the world would it be? Of those I thought I could put up with (and vice versa) for three months, would any of them be willing to quit their jobs? But if I went alone, would I get bored and not finish the river? (On my three-month East Coast trip I had enjoyed my own company for awhile, but after about six weeks the "routine" began to bore me. Though I would wake up in a different forest or city every few days, I knew that I would eat my oatmeal with raisins and strawberry jam, drink my orange spice tea, then I'd hike down a trail or two; in the afternoon I'd doze in my hammock for awhile, maybe read about Alaska or Patagonia or the Himalayas, then I might wash my hair or some clothes in the big green plastic bucket; then I might bicycle around the campground a few times or see a slide show at the visitors' center; I'd probably play "King of the Road" on my guitar, then go to sleep between the filing cabinet and the bicycle tire in my van. But what the heck, I had figured—I was bored living in the city and working and eating vegetable soup and an onion bagel at the deli every day, so I might as well be bored in the hills and swamps.)

Maybe it would be better to float the Yukon alone, with my own company, which I enjoyed, than to choose the wrong partner and risk bickering on the river. Besides, the fun campers and good paddlers I knew all had a standard array of excuses why they couldn't go.

Two days later, on September 2, all these dilemmas became moot.

Evelyn Edens, a fifty-one-year-old free spirit whom I'd known for years, called about saving the Brazos River from a dam or going paddling over Labor Day or something. We had a rambling talk about environmental politics, men, bars, and kayaks; suddenly it struck me.

"Hey," I said, "who do you know who wants to paddle the Yukon River?"

"I do, I do!" came the exuberant reply.

"I mean the *whole* Yukon River, like three months," I said, still hopeful.

"When?"

"Next summer."

"Well, why not?" she chuckled, "I'll just fly up there for two months—I have a break between two markets that I have to do—and meet you on the river."

"I'm serious," I said.

"So am I," she said. "I was just thinking the other day—really—that the Arctic is one area of the world that I need to get up to and spend some time in. Now I do have this job, you understand, where I'm supposed to be a sales representative, and I'm supposed to show up every now and then, like at the July market and the Labor Day market, or I really would lose my job. But other than that, I'm free to come and go. So maybe I can't do the whole river with you, but I could do two months."

I mumbled something about the complicated logistics of her finding me on the Yukon. I didn't even know if planes flew to the Yukon.

"Now look, Beth," she said, "ya gotta have a little faith. If I say I'm gonna meet you on a given date, anywhere in the world, you just wait where you're supposed to; *somehow,* I will get myself there and I will find you. Period."

Evelyn and I had first met in 1978 when we rode together for four hours to East Texas to hike with other environmentalists through our proposed Upland Island wilderness area. Evelyn was a little shorter and a little sturdier than me, with dark, shoulder-length hair. She was very much at home in jeans and workman's boots, with a pair of binoculars around her neck. She was married and had two daughters in their twenties. She was a talker, with a keen sense of the absurd, and as we sped down the highway in the August heat, her stories had greatly entertained me. She had a titty collection, started with a body mask of a hairy-chested gorilla that she bought in 1975 as she entered the hospital for her mastectomy. There was the time she'd left the Cancer Society building with a grocery bag full of those silicon-filled fake boobs they give to breast cancer victims; she had just known that then, of all times, she'd be run down by a bus and titties would go flying all over downtown Portland, Oregon. And did I think, she asked, that her marriage would suffer just because she had a bumper sticker on the wall above the bed that said "I'd Rather Be Birding?"

On that weekend in 1978, Evelyn and I had camped out, hiked through pitcher-plant seeps and long-leaf pine uplands, lost our way on muddy back roads, had a flat tire, waded into two different lakes with all our clothes on, and generally had a great time together.

In the three years since, Evelyn had backpacked through Australia, tramped across Europe, and paddled the wild lakes of Canada's Quetico wilderness. Now she drove all over West Texas as a sales representative for a gift company, usually camping out of her van, and each time after she'd sold her crystal perfume bottles to big department stores, she'd return to the manure and the rattlesnakes of the farm where she lived near Santo. Her husband was an insurance executive and lived in their house in Dallas, a hundred miles away. When she wasn't gardening or digging pit toilets or organizing the statewide Texas Meeting on the Outdoors she held every year, she would nail a few boards into place on the salvaged-materials-only house she was building at the farm for her older daughter. Or she'd sledge-hammer the caked cement off a few more cinder blocks she'd found for the prickly-pear cactus jelly factory she was building in her mesquite pasture.

The last time I'd run into Evelyn had been at a campground in mid-May when she'd thrown her annual Guadalupe River birthday float for her younger daughter. As I walked back from the bathroom to where I was camped with another group, her unmistakable laugh had rung through the campground. I followed it and found Evelyn and about thirty other canoeists of all ages weaving around her van, drinking from plastic champagne glasses. We drove a vanload of revelers in circles for hours under a full moon until we finally found the town of Gruene, where we ended up in the oldest dance hall in Texas.

And now it was September 2, and we had just agreed to paddle part of the Yukon together. I smiled at the wonderful absurdity of paddling the Yukon with someone almost twice my age, with whom I'd never shared a canoe. I didn't really know Evelyn well enough to be sure whether she was serious, but I suspected she was. A trip down the Yukon would be in no way inconsistent with her past escapades.

The next morning I grabbed the phone that awakened me at the crack of dawn. "Hello!" I barked.

"Well, so I called Richard Albert down in Alice and he's sending his journal from when he paddled the Yukon with a bunch of kids from Whitman College in Washington State a few years ago, and I'm waiting to hear back from my travel agent about where the planes fly to on the Yukon, but I realized I didn't know which towns are even on the Yukon, and I've checked with my boss to get the exact dates of that July market. . . ."

It was Evelyn, calling from the market center at 7:30 A.M. As I crawled back into bed for a few more moments' rest after our conversation, I smiled. Evelyn was serious, and I now had as a Yukon co-conspirator one of the zaniest people I knew!

\*    \*    \*

To me, there is almost as much adventure and humor and joy in planning a long journey as in taking the journey itself. If that's true, then we had a helluva lot of joy during the next nine months. For a long time there were more questions than answers, but solving all the minor mysteries that comprised the big puzzle was a fun challenge in itself. The only certainty was that sooner or later, one way or another, we'd figure it all out. The path that led us from that phone conversation on that September morning in 1981 to our bon voyage party on May 28, 1982, was long, sometimes difficult, and always crazy:

## SEPTEMBER, 1981

**September 5**—J.C. Foster and I stood on the bank of the rain-swollen Little River in central Texas. Floating trees lurched through the narrow channel. As we peered at the first bend, we wondered what would be the likelihood of our being swept into dangerous fallen or overhanging trees—"strainers" or "sweepers" that trap people or boats.

J.C., a decade or so older than me, was an experienced canoeist, but was unfamiliar with the new kayak he intended to paddle. He puffed on his cigarette and stared at the river; I dug the toe of my tennis shoe into the mud.

"Well, the only slight problem I can possibly foresee," he said in slow, gravelly tones, "is my drowning."

"Oh, well," I sighed.

"Go for it," he shrugged, gulping the last of his Lone Star beer. "It's 1981."

As it turned out, the river posed no real problems and took us a million wonderful miles away. Graceful great blue herons glided above the river around each bend. Raccoons splashed at the edges of gravel bars. An orange moon bobbed over a clay cutbank. Among the thick branches of an old willow a barred owl called. Turtles plopped from logs into the water, red-tailed hawks soared on the hot September winds. I napped on smooth, warm, round pebbles of a gravel bar. A spring trickled down a fern-lined limestone bank. Eight big black turkey vultures squatted on a hot sandbar. Thirty-two miles and forty-eight hours later, when we reached the take-out, I felt more strongly than ever that I wanted to do a trip forty or fifty times longer than this.

**September 9**—Over a plate of barbecue, Evelyn and I scrutinized her Alaska maps and my U.S. atlas and tried to figure out how one would get oneself and one's gear from Dallas, Texas, to the Yukon River, and back. Then we went across the street to the Sierra Club meeting. Afterward, at M.D's Saloon, I spotted Evelyn and Barbara Martin and Jane Kittleman huddled deep in conversation at a far table. They waved me over with big smiles; I knew we had two more recruits.

"Well, are you coming?" I feigned casualness, reaching for the beer pitcher.

"We were already going!" they screamed and laughed.

They had been planning a trip to Alaska for the coming summer which would include backpacking, day-hiking, and routine tourist stuff all around the state. They hadn't planned to canoe, but they were intrigued by the notion of throwing in a little canoe trip.

Jane was fifty-two, with short, wavy black hair, a Mississippi drawl, and a quick smile. She had recently retired from classroom teaching and was now tutoring in her home. She was married, mother of three grown children, and had just become a grandmother. Her husband taught math at a Dallas private school. Barbara, thirty-seven, taught music appreciation and outdoor education at a Dallas middle school. She had short, straight brown hair and boisterous, rapid-fire speech, punctuated with many gestures and wide-eyed reactions. Like me, she had never been married. Jane and Barbara were slim and fit. They ran regularly, backpacked several times a year, and did a fair amount of paddling, although they jokingly admitted they operated as a team a lot more effectively on flatwater than whitewater.

I had met them both on a Sierra Club trip on a Halloween weekend in 1977. We had paddled through the lily pads and bald cypress trees and quiet, glassy waters of Caddo Lake to Goat Island, where we camped among the pine trees and Spanish moss. In the afternoon, as Jane and Barbara paddled back from a short birding expedition, my friend Mac and I had waved from the bushy confines of a duck blind where we'd spent the afternoon. Jane was jealous because we'd seen ducks and she hadn't.

That night we sat around the campfire nibbling the cattail roots Jane had gathered. "I heard they're edible," she said matter-of-factly. The boiled ones were bitter and the fried ones were tasteless, but the ones they threw onto the coals looked and—I swear this is true—tasted like the kind of barbecued chicken that has a thick black crust. I admired Jane's and Barbara's casual spirit of adventure and the ease with which they camped in the woods. After dinner, we all sat around the campfire drinking, playing the harmonica, singing, and telling ghost stories. After that first encounter, I had run into Jane and Barb at various Audubon and Sierra Club meetings.

And now, here we were in M.D.'s Saloon, plotting. "Here's a vital one," said Evelyn, pulling a pamphlet from her well-worn Alaska file for a cruise- and bus-tour she once took to Alaska. "How to skin a moose." We laughed and toasted moose.

"I can't *wait* to catch a big king salmon!" Jane sighed, casting an imaginary fishing rod. We toasted salmon.

We moaned and toasted mosquitoes. "Well, nothing could be worse than those damn black flies in Maine," said Barbara. "At least Jane and I already have our mosquito headnets—they look like space helmets."

"Which bird books should I take?" Jane asked. "Oh, don't you just know we're gonna see a million birds?!"

"I know! I can't wait," I said. "Let me see if I can remember what we always used to say during the Alaska lands fight: The Yukon Flats is one of the most productive waterfowl breeding areas in North America, with snow geese, Arctic terns that fly 10,000 miles from Antarctica to raise one or two downy chicks in Alaska. . . ."

"Now what kind of money are we talking about?" Barbara grabbed my arm.

"I don't know," I grinned. "I haven't wanted to think about it. I think the transportation up there and back will be the main expense. If we take our own canoes that won't cost anything, and the food—well, we'd have to eat even if we stayed here all summer. As much as I eat out, it'll probably be cheaper on the river! 'Course, we'll want to have some money to blow on the way up there and probably in Dawson."

"Dawson!" Evelyn raised her glass and we joined in the toast. "To the best hell-raisin' city in the North!"

"Oh Lord," I clucked my tongue with a smile. "When these Texas women hit town, those folks in Dawson won't know what hit 'em!"

This was shaping up to be a heck of a good group, I thought. I felt the main prerequisite for being happy on the Yukon was the ability to be comfortable outdoors. I believed such adaptability to be far more important than canoeing experience, although that was helpful. Evelyn and Jane and Barbara each possessed an endless curiosity about and affinity for nature, a ready sense of humor, and a commitment to create good times wherever they went. We all had extensive backpacking and car-camping experience, had a fair amount of canoeing experience, and above all, had traveled the world enough to be able to accept and handle whatever situation might arise.

"Well, let's see now," Jane said. "If Barb and I didn't paddle the whole river—'cause we wouldn't have time for that—if we just wanted to go for a week or two or three, is there some place you can take out, like a town or something?" I said I thought Whitehorse to Dawson was a fairly standard run of about two to four weeks on the river.

They nodded. "How far is that on the river?"

"Oh, just about five hundred miles," I grinned.

"Well, sure, Janie," said Barbara with a shrug and a smile, "let's throw that in." We laughed and wondered if M.D.'s patrons suspected the crazy adventure being plotted by the four women in the corner.

**September 30**—Yukon planning had now become a routine part of my life, like taking out the garbage or watching the evening news on TV. It seemed normal to finish a day's work, then write several letters seeking Alaska information. One night I looked more closely at the map and discovered that four roads touched the river in the roughly-1,000 miles between Whitehorse and the oil pipeline crossing, which lay halfway down the river. I was disappointed that so many links with "civilization" intruded, but I realized that the roads might be useful for Evelyn and Jane and Barbara who would be coming and going from the Outside, rather than doing the whole river as I would be. It occurred to me, too, looking at the map, that if I were to paddle the second half of the river, I would more than likely be doing it alone, because the easy-access points would be behind me.

One Saturday I bought a green wool army shirt and a pair of forty-percent wool, double-layered long johns to replace my all-cotton ones that offered little insulation when wet. I would use these on the Lower Canyons of the Rio Grande River in a few weeks, but they were really for Alaska. I lovingly brought them home and spread them on the floor in a rite of passage; I was now moving from the thinking-about-it phase to the purchasing phase of my Yukon preparations. Then I hauled all my backpacking and canoeing gear from the closet into piles on the living-room floor: shelter-related stuff here, food and cooking stuff there, clothing over there, boat stuff here. . . . I'm an absolutely hopeless list-maker (it runs in the family), and I spent the rest of the day happily weighing and listing every item from spoons and underwear to fuel bottles and tent. A common ailment afflicting backpackers and canoeists is equipment-itis, a preoccupation with what kinds, for what uses, at what cost, weight, and size. Through the years, the more I used my gear the more important became its durability, efficiency, and suitability for its purpose. And now that the Yukon was on my agenda—joy supreme—I could incorporate my lifelong addiction to making lists with my preoccupation with equipment. I began to wonder if I made lists to better plan my camping and kayaking, or if I kayaked and camped just so I could make lists. It didn't matter; I loved both.

## OCTOBER, 1981

**October 9**—We had just cleared Fort Worth's rush-hour traffic and were headed across West Texas for a week-long trip through the Lower Canyons of the Rio Grande, where we would join other Dallas Downriver Club members for eighty-four miles of desert whitewater.

I sat beside Jim Bridges, a fiftyish, grey-haired kayaker who had encouraged me and helped me with my kayaking. In the back seat was Sue Sherrod, a forty-year-old physician specializing in anesthesiology. She was about my height, a little heavier than I. She had been married for several years and was now divorced. I'd heard of Sue from fellow members of the club. I knew that about six months before, she and her roommate, Jude Hammett, had been on the verge of quitting their jobs to travel around the United States, run rivers and camp out for a year. Sue had a permit for rafting the Colorado River through the Grand Canyon (the premier whitewater of the Lower 48 states, with rapids so overwhelming it has its own rating scale of I to X rather than the standard I to VI). To round out their trip, Sue and Jude had planned to do a little backpacking in the Himalayas.

But on the eve of their departure, Sue discovered she had breast cancer and suddenly found herself in the hospital having a mastectomy. The women paddlers in the Downriver Club had been stunned, terribly saddened, and angered. For months I'd been hearing from them about this Sue Sherrod and what a helluva lady and top-notch paddler she was. Before cancer had struck, she had rafted and canoed all sorts of big whitewater rivers in the West, and smaller ones in Texas, Oklahoma, and Arkansas. Several times she had canoed the Lower Canyons, where we were now headed.

After the mastectomy, though, she gave away her one-time permit for the Grand Canyon; she hadn't been strong enough to do a three-week whitewater trip only a few months after her surgery. In fact, we were now headed for her first big trip since the operation. The women and men of the Downriver Club had cheered when they heard Sue was back on the big rivers and was refusing to be slowed down by a mastectomy.

I'd known her for a couple of hours now; we'd joked as we loaded the car, and we'd talked rivers as we crawled through Fort Worth traffic. Several Downriver Club people had suggested she'd be the perfect candidate for a Yukon trip, and I found her likable.

"Hey, we're gonna float the Yukon next summer," I threw out the general invitation. Jim already had that I'd-like-to-but-I-can't smile. I turned to Sue in the back seat, who was staring at me intently.

"You interested in a three-month trip 2,000 miles down the Yukon?" I asked.

"I'd be interested," she nodded slowly, a smile growing. "I'd be very, very interested."

Sue had just undergone one of her monthly post-surgery chemotherapy sessions. The treatments made her very weak for a few days and exacerbated an existing problem with digestion in her esophagus. They also robbed her of her hair, and she wore an attractive, sandy-colored, short wig. As we drove through the endless miles of mesquite trees and sagebrush, she ate handfuls of antacid tablets and napped every hour or so. I admired her gumption. Was it wise, I wondered, to count on somebody for a 2,000-mile Yukon trip who had so recently been subjected to such extreme mental and physical trauma? But I believed that she had the stamina to do it, if she believed she did. If anything, during the coming week on the Lower Canyons, she proved that even on the heels of her monthly chemotherapy treatment, she had more endurance than I. Besides, I had no intention of making the Yukon trip a speed contest; I envisioned endless days of drifting in the sun on a big, fast river.

The Lower Canyons were a week of glorious sunshine, big water (the Rio Grande surged at two or three times its normal height), serene hikes through beautiful isolated canyons, soaking in hot springs, popcorn and hot chocolate around the campfire, and full moons above dark canyon walls. I paddled my kayak solo, but I often shared dinner with Sue and Jim, who were canoe partners.

We had a grand time, though Sue wrenched a previously-injured knee from its socket in the deep sticky mud the first night on the river and had to wear an Ace bandage for the rest of the trip. We camped every night in mud, mud, mud. And one day we had to make a three-hour portage in 100° heat, lugging a week's worth of gear for twenty-two people up the side of a mountain and around a rapid.

And there were little adventures, to be sure: a rattlesnake, sunning in a rocky path, refused to budge when our party of ten slipped nervously past him. Jerry overturned in a squirrelly eddy at the riffle at the top of rocky Burro Bluff Rapid, ended up swimming three miles down the flooded Rio to catch his boat, and camped alone that night downstream. Jim and Darrell unintentionally ran a rapid while trying to cross the river and they too ended up camping alone downstream one night. During the tequila bash, J.C. slipped beneath the soporific waters of the hot spring and turned a little blue before we dragged him onto the bank. And after we left the river, the Goodmans' car hit one too many rocky washouts on the twenty-mile dirt road leaving the river; we got them to town by sticking an apple slice in the hole in the ruptured gas tank, patching it with some duct tape, and filling the tank with our leftover Coleman fuel.

One moment on the trip stuck in my mind. It was a warm October morning, the fifth day out. I had just watched Tommy's and Linda's canoe accidentally ride the Rio Grande over a boulder and plunge into the vast hole behind it. Their entire boat disappeared beneath the frothing brown waters, but somehow, unbelievably, they emerged right-side-up. Then the current whipped them around and they ran the entire mess of four-foot waves through New Rapid backwards.

Then it was my turn. With my heart beating ridiculously, Flipper and I swung into the rain-swollen Rio Grande. Determined to avoid Tommy's error, I aimed for the "V" of the rapid where the current squished and accelerated into standing waves. I hit the tongue *precisely* where I wanted to, and the craziest thing happened.

At that moment, the heart-pounding and nervousness melted into a supreme serenity. As I slid down the drop and faced a couple of dozen yards of angry brown choppers, I grinned. I was *exactly* where I wanted to be on that rapid's tongue and *exactly* where I wanted to be in the world. I hummed a little. I had intended to ride the "foothills" just to the right of the main waves, but I got sucked into the "mountains." Flipper bucked and was underwater a lot, and I madly flailed the waves with my paddle, but still upright, we emerged from the waves and crossed the swirling eddy line into calm water. Cheers went up from shore.

During the following months of endless, sometimes frustrating, Yukon preparations, I would sometimes close my eyes and remember the peace and victory that came from having gotten myself exactly where I wanted to be, of being completely absorbed in the moment. I knew the Yukon would evoke that same feeling.

The week-long Lower Canyons trip was the kind that makes you feel like you've been gone a month, which of course was its purpose. When I returned, I itched more than ever to spend thirteen times as many weeks on the Yukon.

**October 19—**Monday morning back in Dallas, my mind was sucked from the serenity of the Lower Canyons into its usual turbulence of being a professional environmentalist. The governor and the speaker of the house were water-hustling again, threatening the few free-flowing stretches of river left in Texas with a constitutional amendment "water trust fund" (meaning "water slush fund") that would automatically divert state monies to unspecified "water projects" (meaning river-killing and often unnecessary dams and reservoirs, channelization projects, and levees). I had phonebank operations to launch and news conferences to organize. (We beat the scheme at the polls, saving a few rivers and their bottomland forests, for awhile.)

In the midst of the election-eve chaos, I unexpectedly faced an important decision. My boss, chairman Ned Fritz of the Texas Committee on Natural Resources, offered me a new role as executive director of our statewide citizens' organization. Accepting increased responsibilities would mean more pressures and frustrations (if that were possible), but also greater creative opportunity and challenge. The job would be invaluable experience for someone twenty-eight years old. I was willing, but not if it meant sacrificing the Yukon trip.

Sitting across from me at my kitchen table, Ned wanted an answer.

"You're aware that I'm going to paddle the Yukon next summer?" I asked him.

"Yes," he nodded and smiled paternally. "I'm sure we could let you off for a few weeks."

"No, uh, you see—I'm going to paddle the *whole* Yukon." I had mentioned little of the trip to Ned because I had been committed to work for TCONR only through March. I had been vaguely looking forward to finding some "normal" job with merely a forty-hour work week and higher pay during April and May to save money for the Yukon.

"The *whole* Yukon?" Ned began to pay attention; his bushy eyebrows joined in a frown. "How long would that take?"

"We don't really know," I shrugged. "Probably about three months."

He thought for a minute. "Well, we need you. Go on and go, I guess, and start your new job the minute you get back."

**October 31**— A couple of dozen canoe-loads of Dallas Downriver Club members had paddled to a Caddo Lake island for our annual Swamp-Monster Halloween Campout. Some (mostly kids who didn't know better) spent the afternoon exploring the woods in the rain. We more hard-core outdoorspeople, including Sue and her roommate, Jude, spent the day in lawn chairs beneath a giant cozy tarp, pondering the sound of rain on canvas, telling jokes, having a bump-and-grind jam session on kazoos, and devouring jar after jar of jalapeño jelly that Jude pulled from a duffel bag.

Like Sue, Jude was pretty willing to paddle the whole Yukon the next summer. She was twenty-seven, stood several inches taller than I at about five feet nine, and had short, black hair. She had a sturdy, athletic build with powerful-looking shoulders and legs. As head nurse of orthopedic surgery at Dallas's Saint Paul Hospital, she had crossed paths with Sue in the operating room. Like Barb and me, she had never been married.

Night fell, kids trick-or-treated from tent to tent, and horror stories swirled around the campfire. At intervals, the ghostly, illuminated figure of a woman draped in Spanish moss floated among the bald cypress trees. Her screams echoed over the dark waters. (Soon Tom tired of paddling into cypress knees in the dark; Suzanne waded ashore in a long white gown, chased kids through the woods for awhile, then spent the rest of the evening plucking moss from her blond hair.)

Late that night, I was sleeping soundly, as rain beat the tent and wind whipped the forest. But I suddenly found myself awake. Had the earth just shaken? Mother and I looked at each other. I unzipped the front flap: a foot from our doorway lay an eight-foot-long, six-inch-thick, lethal-looking limb that had thudded to earth from the top of a thirty-foot pine tree.

Next morning, a slightly-hungover line of paddlers snaked its way toward shore. Most of us poked along, enjoying the sun that had finally come out. Jude, however, wanted to do some real paddling. But about halfway through the swamp, stern-paddler Sue lay back on the stern deck to think about the whole thing awhile. Jude soon became disenchanted with trying to steer from the bow. "Get up here!" she snapped playfully. As the rest of us whooped and cheered, Sue and Jude executed the most laughable canoe maneuver I've seen. Sue, with an "I'm-in-for-it-now" expression, flopped forward face down amidships on the mountain of gear strewn in the boat. "Not on the guitar, you fool!" shouted Jude, as she herself crawled gingerly toward the stern. Meanwhile, their two mischievous white spitzes, Gonzo and Wendy, yapped and joined in the general laughter. The boat rocked, dogs skittered from bow to stern, Jude picked her way over Sue leapfrog fashion to the stern seat, where she steered and soloed the canoe to the take-out. Sue grinned, pulled her cowboy hat over her eyes, and napped.

These two promised to be an entertaining pair to float the Yukon with, I thought to myself. As we parted, I shouted out the van window, "Remember, we're all meeting Saturday at Janie's to pool our ignorance on the Yukon!" Beside me in the front seat, Mother looked puzzled and gazed off into space.

## NOVEMBER, 1981

**November 7**—Gathered together for the first time were what would become the Texas Women's Yukon River Expedition. I introduced Jane and Barbara and Evelyn to Sue and Jude. We sat cross-legged on the carpet before the crackling flames of Jane's woodburning stove. Evelyn, wearing her trademark tuxedo T-shirt, was tackling the steak and potatoes and peas Jane had heated up when Evelyn mentioned she hadn't eaten all day. Jane held in her lap her new baby granddaughter. In the corner sat a friend of Jane's and Barbara's who was considering paddling part of the Yukon. Her hair was meticulously coifed, she wore what seemed to me a lot of makeup for a Saturday afternoon meeting with a bunch of women, and her long fingernails were carefully manicured and painted. Somehow I couldn't picture her on the Yukon. With us, also, was a friend of mine who wanted to float the Yukon for a few weeks. He smoked cigarettes and talked a lot about guns, and I was having a hard time picturing him on the Yukon, too.

I shuffled through my fledgling Yukon file. "O.K., ladies—and gentleman—let's begin."

"Can anybody figure out why my prickly-pear jelly turned to sugar?" interrupted Evelyn, her brain characteristically flowing in patterns of its own. "And don't forget, Beth, when you go to East Texas next month, I want you to find me a bunch of places where I can gather mayhaws to make jelly." A full-blown discussion about jelly erupted, and between that and the oohs and aaahs over Jane's granddaughter, I couldn't believe what a bunch of cackling hens we seemed.

"Now come on, ya'll," I pleaded, "we need to talk about who's gonna paddle with whom, for how long, with what gear; how we're gonna get ourselves and our gear to the Yukon; and how we'll get back." We decided that an hour after Barb finished teaching on May 28, we'd head for the

North. We'd heard that the Yukon was ice-free only four months or so a year, and since we didn't know how long it would take to paddle it, we wanted to start as early as possible. "Of course," I noted, "a guy in one of the books had to battle great big ice jams in the lakes when he first put in, and that was in June." That was amazing news to a bunch of Texans accustomed to swimming in the rivers almost year-round.

"Well," said Evelyn, "if the river's still frozen we'll just have to party in Whitehorse until the ice moves out." We heartily agreed.

"I think the Alaska state ferry starts at Seattle," I said, "and you can take that to Skagway. Then I think you can get on that train that goes over that famous pass where all the gold miners went." We agreed we'd take our own canoes (Jane and Barb would change their minds a dozen times and finally end up renting), if we could ship them on the ferry and the train at a reasonable cost.

We agreed we'd drive my van to Seattle, but we had no idea where we could leave it for three months while we were on the river.

We also decided to forgo paddling the hundred miles or so of the Yukon's natural and human-made headwaters lakes. Since dams, a highway, a railroad, and a bridge degraded the river's natural character there, and since we weren't particularly fond of windy flatwater lakes, we agreed to put in at Whitehorse where the Yukon proper emerges from the dam.

Talk turned to signal flares and radio transmitters and other ways to call for help if we needed it on the river.

"Well, I don't think the Yukon is really all *that* isolated," I said. "You know, there are barges that go up and down every now and then, and the people probably have motorboats, and there are villages. Why, I bet the longest you'd go without running into somebody would be a week and a half."

But for every item we knew enough about to make a tentative decision, there were a dozen items about which we knew very little. We didn't know if permits would be required to camp and build fires and fish in the newly-created preserves and refuges through which we would paddle. (We would find out later that only Canadian and Alaskan fishing licenses, and a fire permit from the Mounties when we checked in at Whitehorse, were required.)

We didn't know how cold or wet the weather would be (finally decided to take gear for everything from subfreezing nights and monsoons to scorching days, and were glad we did).

We didn't know how tricky it would be to paddle the Yukon's fast current.

We didn't know how to camp with grizzlies. (We would research, argue, and lose sleep over this issue for months.) To my male friend, guns and more guns were the answer.

**November 14**—It was a quiet Saturday night on a sandbar. My gun-happy friend and I had spent the day battling Brazos River wind. Since he was interested in the Yukon I wanted to see how much he enjoyed the scenery on this wild stretch (threatened by a dam) and how much he disliked hard flatwater paddling on a big wide river, which I expected the Yukon to be. After dinner, he built an embarrassingly huge bonfire that wasted wood and polluted unnecessarily. I breathed in the sweet damp night air; he lit a cigarette. I enjoyed the peaceful mourning doves' song across the water; he pulled from his pack a loud transistor radio. Then he mentioned that a guy he knew had emphatically encouraged him to go with us down the Yukon.

"He said that as a man it's my duty to take care of you on the river," he explained.

"Hah," I chuckled, "that's a good one—the jerk. You don't agree with that bull, do you?"

"Well, he might be right," he said. "I mean, I *know* about guns; I've used 'em all my life." I smiled weakly; that was not a particular plus with me. He continued, "You don't know what you might run into out there. If you had to kill a grizzly, or hunt rabbits or catch fish to survive. . . . "

I didn't know with whom I was more exasperated—his friend, who knew nothing about the women's backgrounds but automatically assumed we were in need of protection, or my friend, who had never canoed or backpacked, but assumed he was going to take care of a group of women, who, together, had decades of experience. And among the very last things I felt like doing for three months on the Yukon were smelling cigarette smoke, hearing loud electronic music, and watching someone blast rabbits' heads off.

I realized my friend and I had incompatible ideas about how to enjoy the wild, but before I could gracefully disinvite him on the Yukon, I noticed our sandbar was sinking into the water. Someone at the dam upstream was releasing water, and within ten minutes the river rose about a foot and inundated what had been our camp. We cut short our sexism argument to scramble with gear to higher ground. The water spared us at the last minute, providing a merely humorous adventure to an otherwise irritating evening.

By the time we got back to Dallas the following evening we were at each other's throats about everything from red meat to identifying cottonwoods, and it was probably a relief for both of us that we never again mentioned the Yukon after our little shakedown cruise on the Brazos.

I knew Evelyn a lot better than I knew this guy, and I suspected and hoped that her philosophies about paddling and camping would be much more in tune with mine, but I realized after that Brazos run that you never know until you get out there.

Meanwhile, through one twist of fate or another, Evelyn and I would find ourselves in the same canoe together only twice before we would become partners on a three-month trip down the Yukon.

**November 26**—At six o'clock on a nippy Thanksgiving morning, Evelyn and I stood in a parking lot in Austin at a Texas Ornithological

Society gathering. We grilled our friend Richard O. Albert, the eccentric and lovable birder from Alice, Texas, who'd once floated the Canadian Yukon. Yes, the air got cold, he said, tugging on his earring—sometimes down in the 30s at night. And yes, the water was cold—47° according to his thermometer. (The farthest a good swimmer could swim in 50° water, said my hypothermia brochure, is about eight-tenths of a mile, and the Yukon would be wider than a mile for much of its length.) And yes, we'd see moose. Richard said not to worry much about bears, just to keep our food away from our tents.

Evelyn and I and a friend of hers spent the day birding and gabbing about the Yukon. We drove through the hills seeking warblers and hawks and listing our favorite vegetables and beans to take on the Yukon.

"Well," I finally asked Evelyn, "are you thinking that you'll do the whole trip, rather than just two months between markets?"

"Yeah, why not?" she said. "It's the mammoth quality of this thing that intrigues me. I mean, if you're gonna float the Yukon, you might as well do it right and float the *whole* Yukon!"

"Right on!" I smacked her outstretched palms. "But what about your job?"

"Well," she threw up her hands, "if they can't take a joke . . . no, actually when I tell them I'm going to miss that July market they'll probably fire me. But I'll get another job when I get back."

Her friend planned to float the Yukon with us, but said that when she told her husband he'd probably throw a really big fit. "Mine too," sighed Evelyn.

I had a dark thought. "What are the chances," I asked Evelyn, "that when he throws his fit you'll decide not to go?" I was counting on Evelyn's companionship—and also her boat.

"None!" she and her friend stated emphatically.

"Well, I'm not even going to tell him until a month before we leave," Evelyn shrugged. My mouth fell open. "If I tell him now, we'll have a big fight, then he'll forget all about it 'cause he won't believe me, then when it comes time to go he'll act like he never heard about it and he'll throw a fit all over again. If I wait, I just have to go through one knock-down-drag-out fight instead of two."

I turned to Evelyn's friend. "Well, what's the big deal with your husband? Your kids are grown and he can feed himself for three months, or he can come with us if he wants."

"No, he'd never do that," she laughed. "But he won't want *me* to go either. He still hasn't gotten over my traipsing off to Australia, but I think he thought that'd be the end of it. When I tell him we're going down the Yukon, he may say I shouldn't bother to come back."

Three days later, on the eve of my sending in our group's ferry reservations, her husband presented her with precisely that painful ultimatum. She withdrew from our trip, and we were back down to the original six. I felt saddened that selfish spouses hold their partners' dreams hostage; perplexed that people let their dreams die. And I admired more than ever Evelyn's absolute resolve that neither spouse nor employer would stand between her and the Yukon.

## DECEMBER, 1981

By now my apartment was one big pile of Yukon, Alaska, and Canada literature. Every day the mail brought more natural history books and Arctic true-adventure books and Robert Service poetry and brochures from departments of tourism or the Mounties or fish and game departments. Piecing together the logistics puzzle had taken on the dimensions of a regular part-time job. There were topographical maps of the river to be ordered from the U.S. Geological Survey. From the U.S. Postal Service, I had to find out how much it would cost to ship food to villages along the river, how far ahead of time we had to ship it, and what packaging peculiarities applied. And it was loads of fun phoning through the maze of the postal bureaucracy to discover whether the food would go by air, and if so, whether the cargo compartment was pressurized, and if not, whether all the bags of dehydrated food would burst. (An Alaskan airline finally said everything would be fine.)

One morning I spotted an alarming item in a Canadian customs brochure that said only two days' food per person could be imported duty-free. Did that mean we would have to pay duty on the other twenty-eight days' worth we'd be carrying into Canada (we'd pick up more at the first Alaskan post office on the river), and how much would it cost? Surely such a rule couldn't exist, I thought, in a territory such as the Yukon that relies heavily on the tourism of backpackers and canoeists. A series of phone calls all over Dallas, Seattle, and Canada finally revealed that yes, indeedy, we should show up at the border with receipts to prove how much all the food was worth, unless we wanted to be charged an arbitrary sum by whatever inspector happened to be working that day. (We decided to ignore the whole issue and hope for the best when we got up there.)

Meanwhile, replies from two sets of Seattle friends still hadn't yielded a safe spot to leave a car for three months.

One Saturday morning I ate a grilled cheese sandwich at my mother's kitchen table and scribbled numbers on a piece of notebook paper. I had to figure out how I could lose three months' pay and still pay for ferries and trains and hotels and equipment and three months' worth of dehydrated food on my salary of $10,000 a year.

"How much can I borrow on my life insurance?" I asked my father.

"About $300," he said.

"Mo-ther," I said in a wheedling tone. She looked up from the stove. "Can I move back home for a few months to save rent?"

She shrugged and nodded absently as if to say, "Don't you always?"

"Well, and, uh," I cleared my throat. "What's your credit line on your Mastercard these days?" She looked at me with a sigh of resignation and a "so-we're-gonna-go-through-that-again" shake of her head.

"Well," she said, "no one has used it since I took it away from you after your last trip to Mexico, so I guess there's about $1700 worth of credit on it." That would go a long way toward covering equipment costs and return air fare.

"I'll pay you back as soon as I can," I said. She rolled her eyes, smiled, and continued stirring soup.

"My kayak loan will be paid for in a couple of months," I said. "Do you think they'd give me another loan with my van as collateral?" I knew my salary didn't look too impressive on a loan application. Mother said she'd talk to the loan officer at the bank where she worked.

I figured if it came down to it, I'd moonlight in addition to my TCONR job during April and May.

During these increasingly frenetic Yukon preparations, one faint disappointment tugged at me: I had no intimate male soul mate with whom to share the wondrous insanity. The only thing more exciting than floating the whole Yukon River, I thought, would be to float it with my love. There were certain advantages to having a warm, cuddly, hairy partner in your tent on a cold rainy night. I was dating several backpackers and canoeists, but their minds seemed confined within the same tight boxes. When I told them of my Yukon plans, they first said they thought they'd get bored on a trip that long (didn't they get bored working eight to five in Dallas, eleven-and-a-half months a year?!), then they usually mentioned house payments, and last they'd say something about careers. In all my years and relationships, I hadn't yet run across a male companion who believed in flitting around the world quite like I did. Society had certainly hung one helluva security trip on the poor dears. Perhaps it was no coincidence that so far, the only people willing to quit their jobs for three months to paddle the Yukon were women.

**December 12**—On a cold Saturday afternoon, the six of us gathered in Evelyn's farmhouse for a weekend of planning and carousing. Jane and Barbara simmered chowder on the stove, Evelyn tossed wood into the fireplace. Sue and Jude examined the Australian aborigine spears on Evelyn's wall.

"Now, I want you all to sample this for lunch," I said, holding up a baggie of brown crumbs left over from the Lower Canyons trip. They all booed. "No, really, dehydrated food is ten times better than that freeze-dried stuff you're used to. I dried this myself in J.C.'s dehydrator."

"What the hell is it?" Evelyn looked disgusted.

"Refried beans, of course," I said. "I bought a can at the store and just spread 'em out on the tray in his dehydrator and this is the result. Let's try 'em." To everyone's amazement, with a little water, a little heat from the stove, and a little picante sauce, the dried cow-pattylike mess became a tasty bean dip. Jane was already plotting how to make tortillas to accompany it on the river.

We spent the afternoon chopping up the first of our Yukon food—carrots and yellow squash—and spreading it on trays in Evelyn's dehydrator. One canoe will scarcely contain gear and whole fresh food for two people for three months. And, of course, fresh food will spoil. To dramatically reduce its size and weight and maintain its freshness almost indefinitely, you can dehydrate your own food or buy it commercially dehydrated or freeze-dried. Even with these methods, we'd still have to ship in food to pick up along the river. We planned to carry a month's worth with us at a time. With a home dehydrator, about the size of a microwave oven, you can dry vegetables and fruits and meats in six to twenty-four hours and package them in airtight heat-sealed bags. When you add water they take on pretty much the consistency they had when they were fresh. The dehydrator, which circulates dry heated air around trays of food, costs between $100 and $200. By dehydrating your own food, you can prepare your camping meals more cheaply, with better control over the combinations and quantities, and without the chemicals of prepackaged backpackers' food.

"O.K., now," Evelyn announced. "I volunteer to plan the menus, calculate the amounts, and buy all the food for this voyage, and to cook it most of the time on the river." We looked at her as if she'd gone mad.

"You've gotta be crazy," said Jane, "but if you want to do it, that's wonderful. Just give us assignments and we'll help."

Evelyn unfurled her lists. "If we assume ninety days on the river for four of us," she said, "plus about twenty days for Barb and Jane, that's about a hundred days for four people." We nodded slowly.

"Then, if you assume about 1 cup of something per person for breakfast, 2 cups for lunch, and 3 cups for dinner, that's 6 cups per day per person or 2,400 cups for a hundred days." We nodded more slowly.

"Then, if you assume that 2 cups equals a pound of real food—not dehydrated—that comes to 1,200 pounds of food." Our eyes got big.

"That's not counting the condiments and stuff like coffee, tea, sugar, and so forth. Now, if you assume that dehydrating, plus throwing in the extras, will bring that down to about 600 pounds, that's 200 pounds per month, or about 50 pounds of food a week. If we carry a month's worth with us at a time, that's 200 pounds—100 pounds in Sue's and Jude's canoe, and 100 in Beth's and mine. Of course, when Jane and Barbara are with us we can spread that out a little. . . . "

It boggled the mind. We looked at each other sheepishly. Evelyn moved on to specifics.

". . . so that's 13 pounds of rice, 8 pounds of sugar, 4 pounds each of pinto beans, navy beans, split peas, black-eyed peas, lima beans, lentils, black beans. . . ."

"Oh Lord!" gasped Jude.

"She won't touch a bean," said Sue.

" . . . 30 pounds of flour, 10 pounds of cornmeal, 2 pounds of tabouli—that's cracked wheat—12 heads of cabbage, 50 cups each of broccoli, asparagus, carrots, yellow squash, corn. . . . "

We offered hurrahs or boos to the different items as Evelyn moved through her incredible roster.

" . . . 13 dehydrated chickens, 13 pounds of beef jerky, 400 powdered eggs, 100 quarts of powdered milk, same of hot chocolate, 1200 cups of coffee, 400 cups of orange drink, 400 cups of lemonade, 800 cups of instant tea. . . . "

Evelyn finished, and we fell silent.

"You know," said Sue, "those amounts of food . . . and when you think that our gear and our clothes are going to have to last three months in constant use . . . and shipping all that stuff half a continent away . . . none of us has ever done *anything* like this, have we?"

"Well," I said, "I took a three-month trip alone in a van once, but my longest river trip was six days."

"I paddled around lakes and islands in Canada for ten days once," said Evelyn.

Sue held the group record; once, she had been on a river for two weeks.

By now we had settled that Jane and Barbara would paddle together from Whitehorse to Dawson and leave the river there. Sue and Jude would paddle together, and Evelyn and I would paddle together, all the way to the Bering Sea. However, we said, anybody was free to leave the river by whatever means she wanted, at any time, if she became disenchanted for any reason. (We were pretty well convinced that mail planes that carried a few passengers went to the river villages at least once a week.) The purpose of the whole thing was to have fun, after all, and if someone wasn't having fun, there was no reason for her to continue.

"What are you going to do about your jobs?" I asked Sue and Jude.

"Well, Sue's the senior partner of her firm," smiled Jude. "So she just tells 'em 'bye!' She might lose a few clients if they can't cover for her while she's gone, but it'll be O.K. As for me, I'll just have to quit."

I reached for my Alaska file, which now bulged from two large boxes, and pulled out the evening's agenda. There were lots of decisions to be made. We agreed that in the boats we'd wear life jackets at all times; on land we'd wear a whistle around our neck and bells on our person to warn bears; each boat would have plenty of waterproof duct tape and spare rivets for aluminum boat repairs and liquid plastic for plastic boat repairs; each woman would have within reach in the boat a small emergency pack she could grab if she capsized and got stranded alone ashore. Each boat would be self-sufficient with maps and compass, tent, candles and water-proof matches, water purification tablets, backpacker stove, cooking utensils, sleeping bags, one gallon of fuel, two-to-five gallons of water-carrying capacity in collapsible water jugs, food, and one deck of water-proof cards. In short, we would each have whatever we needed to survive if we got separated from the others for any length of time.

We pored over equipment catalogs and talked about every item of clothing from waterproof boots to gloves to belts. We discussed the relative percentage of Deet (the mosquito-repelling ingredient) in various brands of stick, spray, and squeeze-bottle repellents.

We easily agreed not to take radios, pets (bear bait), tin cans if we could help it (a hassle to dispose of), cigarettes, or lanterns. We knew to avoid anything sweet-smelling, because of bears' attraction to it—but what constituted sweet-smelling was the subject of a spirited debate. "No toothpaste," somebody said. "Oh, that's ridiculous," somebody retorted. "A bear's not gonna eat toothpaste." "Yes they will! They don't know it has no caloric value." "Well, O.K., then, if I can't take toothpaste you can't take deodorant." "Mine is unscented." "Maybe unscented to people, but I bet a bear can smell it. Why, I think I read they can smell salmon a mile away." "Well, what about Jane's makeup then, I bet they can smell that." "Oh, who would eat makeup?" "Which reminds me of Evelyn's coffee in the morning—you're not to bring that in our tent. . . . "

"Well, you know what the *real* problem is," said Barbara, smirking at Jude and me. We rolled our eyes to the ceiling in anticipation of the discussion. We were the only two still-menstruating women of the bunch, and we'd heard and tried to dismiss all those stories about how grizzlies are attracted to women who are having their period.

"Now, now, don't look at me that way," I said. "I read that all that stuff about menstruating women and grizzlies is a bunch of bull; some study showed there were just as many women who were attacked who weren't having their period as those who were."

"Oh, great," said Sue.

Evelyn was laughing. "You mean you're gonna make me take my life in my hands by sleeping in the same tent with *her* (she pointed an accusing finger), the perfect bait for a raving grizzly?!!"

"Aw, come on y'all," Jude and I squirmed. But Evelyn had conjured up an image she was having fun with, and we all began to smile.

"Yeah," she imitated a crazed grizzly ripping open the tent flap and looking wildly about the tent. "So, he goes right for the crotch!" she growled, opened her mouth and bared her teeth. We all howled with laughter. "Now, that's what I call pretty heavy-duty oral sex!"

"Yeah, but what a way to go!" I said, smiling and feigning a swoon.

Jude said she'd take the Pill straight through for the entire trip so she wouldn't have a period, but I thought that would foul up our systems in some way. We left the matter unresolved for the time being, but it would continue to be the source of much ribbing and merriment.

The discussion turned from grizzlies to guns, as usual. We agreed we'd take every precaution against inviting bears into camp, but the question was whether to carry guns as a last resort. "Jack Hession just answered my letter," I said, "and he had some interesting thoughts about bears and guns." Jack, who is the Sierra Club Alaska representative and who has been kayaking Alaskan rivers ever since he arrived there just prior to the oil strike in '68, had pointed out that Alaska's wilderness rivers are uniquely valuable in large part because of the opportunity to see bears, moose, water birds, and other critters that concentrate in and along them. His advice put him in the take-along-protection camp: "Assume that you will see bears and will camp in bear country. I recommend a 12-gauge shotgun with shortest barrel and 00 buckshot. Take it into the tent with you."

I commented, however, that in most of the true bear-attack stories I'd read, people seemed to get themselves into more trouble when they had guns, and often the guns didn't help them much. For instance, a hunter accidentally got himself between a grizzly and her cubs, and the mother grizzly was making noises for him to get lost, fast. The man used the few seconds available to him to stand his ground and aim his gun, but it misfired and the grizzly cuffed him around a little. She left him then, having made her point, and he died not so much from the bear injuries as from hypothermia after spending the night on a freezing mountain without the slightest emergency shelter. Would he have been better off using those few seconds to retreat? Would he have sent less hostile signals to the grizzly if he had had no gun? Would he have been more careful in the first place if he knew in his bones that he had no protection other than his own caution and alertness?

The larger question, though, was whether any of us knew the first thing about guns. Barbara taught gun safety with B-B guns in her outdoor education class, but she said she didn't really know much about grizzly-duty guns. Evelyn had fired a shotgun a few times at the farm, "And my shoulder still hurts," she said.

"Well, I think anybody's free to take one if she wants," said Sue, "but all I can say is she better damn well know what she's doing with it."

"Yeah," I said, "if Evelyn, for instance, had a big gun lying between us in the tent, I'd be a lot more scared of that gun than a grizzly."

"And you might overreact and shoot somebody who'd gone out to go to the bathroom," said Evelyn. We all laughed. "Well, really," she said. "One night in the Quetico, my daughter Nancy had slipped outside the tent, and I woke up as she crawled back through the door. I thought she was a bear and kicked the crap out of her. Now, what would have happened if I'd had a gun?"

Since none of us was interested in learning about guns in addition to all the other things we had to do between then and May 28, we made a pact that no one would carry one. Jude pointed out, though, that we shouldn't advertise that fact, just in case we ran into any unsavory characters on the river.

The "meeting" ended and we began to drink and laugh about everything from prickly-pear jelly to various Sierra Club men we'd known.

Sue, sitting on the floor before the fireplace, began to scratch at the knit hat she'd worn all day. As the party atmosphere built, she finally removed the hat. The chemotherapy had robbed her head of all but the finest light brown fuzz of hair. No one reacted, and we kept telling jokes and parading back and forth with more food and wine and equipment catalogs.

"Doesn't anyone want to know why I don't have any hair?" Sue finally asked.

"Well, we know you had a mastectomy and you're having chemo-therapy," said Janie, matter-of-factly.

"I had mine seven years ago!" Evelyn called from the kitchen. "We'll have to compare scars!" Evelyn never shied away from coming right to the point. "By the way," she asked, "are you gonna take your fake titty on the Yukon?"

"Well I . . . I," Sue was deep in thought.

"I'm not about to wear that thing out in the wilderness for three months," said Evelyn. "If the fishermen don't like it, tough."

You all may not have known it," said Jane, "but I had cancer, too. When I was thirty-one I found out I had cancer of the cervix. I had to have a hysterectomy. Look at us; three women out of six have had cancer. Makes you wonder what we're doing to ourselves and this world, doesn't it?"

I pulled out the trumpet I had brought along. "Now, I hope y'all won't mind," I said, "but I really want to take this on the river. Ever since I quit playing in college, I've wanted some free time to get my lip back, and I figure the Yukon'll be the perfect time, right?" They looked at me in amazement.

"Let me see that," said Sue with a smile. She began to play it, rather well.

"You play the trumpet?" I asked, astonished. There were very few female trumpet players when I was in school, and even fewer, I felt sure, when Sue was in school.

"Let *me* see it," Barbara grabbed the horn, and she, too, began to play.

I couldn't believe it. Turned out they had both played trumpet in high school. "Good grief, this is a weird bunch of women," I said.

I passed around some harmonicas, a kazoo, and my old belly-dancing finger cymbals, and we jammed with the trumpet about fifteen times through "Swing Low, Sweet Chariot," dancing and singing and clapping around the room, as the beer flowed and the old spiritual took on a Dixieland beat.

Almost in mid-song, though, Sue seemed to fall into a drunken sleep, or maybe a chemotherapy sleep, and the party wound down quickly. We spread our sleeping bags on the floor. As I gazed into the fire's coals before drifting to sleep, I marveled at the incredibly diverse and fun-loving bunch of women we had gathered to float the Yukon.

Next morning, Evelyn asked, "Say, where's your friend who was at the last meeting? Is he still planning to come?"

"Well, I kind of didn't tell him about this meeting," I said. "I took him down the Brazos and I think that cured him of any desire to paddle a big flat river, at least with me. In fact, I've been thinking, we're far enough along in the planning now that it would be kind of awkward for somebody to join the group after this. They wouldn't know everybody, and we've already sent in our ferry reservation and stuff. And especially if one or more men came along, I think we could get into some touchy group dynamics. You know how couples always seem to fight more than anybody on a river.

"Besides, I think maybe we'd be the first women—without men— who have ever paddled the whole river in a non-motorized boat," I added softly. It sounded funny out loud. "None are mentioned in any of the books."

"Maybe we could get some sponsors or something and help defray some of our costs," Jude suggested.

"Yeah, let's go for it!" said Sue enthusiastically. "You know, you hardly ever go wrong by thinking big. What have we got to lose?"

"I know a guy with the Fish and Wildlife Service who's been flying the Rio Grande this week with a photographer from a big national magazine," said Evelyn. "I'll call him and ask him to ask the photographer to ask his editor to get in touch with these crazy Texas women who're gonna make history by paddling the whole Yukon."

**December 19**— Evelyn, Sue, Jude, and I went to one of those survival companies that peddles freeze-dried and dehydrated foods. First we had to sit through their spiel about how, when the Big Boom comes, everything will be hunky-dory if you have provided for your family by buying a year's worth of their emergency food and storing it in your home (presumably along with the five-and-a-half tons of uncontaminated water that I figured it would take to keep your family of four alive for a year). But then we sampled all sorts of soups and casseroles they had cooked with dehydrated food, and they were delicious.

In the corner sat their fifteen-case "essential food reserve"—complete food for one year for one person.

"Hey," whispered Sue, "that's the same as a fourth of a year for four people. That's how much we'll need on the Yukon, plus enough for Barb and Jane for a few weeks."

We stared in awe. The fifteen cases would more than fill an entire canoe, and together they weighed 369 pounds. The suggested retail price was $979.00.

**December 23**— "Mother, there's an expeditions editor on the phone!" Evelyn's daughter called to her from the screened porch of the farmhouse. Evelyn stood up from the pile of mesquite wood she was splitting and rushed inside. Sure enough, it was the "Expeditions Editor" (we were flattered to be thought of as an "expedition") with a national magazine in Washington, D.C., and he said that if we sent them thirty of our best color slides after the trip, they'd review them. Evelyn said we'd be delighted to. The rest of us could hardly contain ourselves when we heard. Of course, none of us was an expert photographer, and the challenge of taking extremely high-quality photographs was almost overwhelming, but we vowed to do our best.

This courtesy call gave us hope that somewhere, somebody would help us pay for this mammoth undertaking. And it made us realize that the journey we half-jokingly considered significant might be considered pretty much so by some people.

**December 31**— It was a cold, dark, damp New Year's Eve on a Neches River sandbar, and Sue and Jude and my friend Tommy and I were halfway into a forty-four-mile canoe trip through the wilds of the Big Thicket

National Preserve in southeast Texas. Like the Little River Labor Day trip, the Rio Grande trip, and the Brazos trip, it was another mini-shakedown cruise for the Yukon. In our lawn chairs, we huddled before a wonderful fire. We had already finished off the Bailey's Irish Cream and the sherry and were now drinking peppermint schnapps in hot chocolate. Each drink seemed more wonderful, each joke more witty, than the last. The little spitzes, Wendy and Gonzo, scurried around the campfire, we strummed the guitar, a heavy fog settled; though we were surely freezing to death, we didn't know it. Finally, we declared it midnight (the only timepiece we had on the five-day trip was Sue's sundial watch, and it didn't work at night) and sang "Auld Lang Syne" at the top of our lungs. Then we waltzed and stumbled in the deep sand as we sang "Good Night, Irene." I had a feeling 1982 would be one hell of an interesting year.

We had been on the big, wide Neches for three days, during which we had perfected a technique we called "thwarting," which we hoped to use extensively on the Yukon. While floating along on the current, we would pull the canoes together side by side, then we'd stretch bungy cords (thick elasticized woven cords with hooks on each end) between thwarts (crosspieces between gunnels) to fasten the boats together. If there were no downed trees in our way we could float for hours like this, and we enjoyed leisurely lunches, singing, drinking, and joking while moving downstream.

The technique wasn't without risks, though. It was pretty hard to maneuver both boats tied together like that, and we had a few near-collisions with trees. Once, around noon on New Year's Eve when we'd just popped the cork on our second bottle of champagne, Sue leaned over to sample more crackers and cheese from our boat and we all nearly took a swim.

Tommy and I were experienced campers, but we had never camped together. We couldn't anticipate each other's moves. There's a certain amount of stress, adjustment, and awkward communication that has to take place with a new partner—on everything from how to load the boat to where to set up the tent to how to cook the black-eyed peas. But we coped quite well, and I admired Tommy's willingness not only to learn canoeing, but to choose as his second-ever trip a five-day voyage in the dead of winter. Once again, I wondered how Evelyn and I would feel launching not merely a five-day trip, but a three-month trip, with a brand new partner.

The trip offered further insight into Sue's and Jude's personalities. Sue and I seemed to share much the same canoeing philosophy. We tended toward slow-paced breakfasts, long periods of thwartation on the river, and pulling out early to make camp each evening. Jude, on the other hand, was much more of a go-getter. She liked to putz around camp, tidying up the gear, chopping firewood, fishing, arranging the cookstoves and the lawn chairs. She much preferred fast current to flatwater, and I wondered if she would like the wide Yukon with its scarcity of rapids. Though she grumbled about flatwater, when her powerful shoulders laid into paddling, her boat would surge through the water far ahead of Tommy and me.

## JANUARY, 1982

**January 3**—Jane and Barbara and I gathered in Dallas at the home of Jane's friend Nancy Webber, whose father had professionally explored various parts of the world from the Arctic to Africa. He was in town visiting and was kind enough to show us some of his films. We saw gyrfalcons swoop upon their prey and Eskimo children play tag in their pajamas in the bright midnight sun. With us was Sid Rucker of Dallas, who had spent several summers in the North and had hiked the Chilkoot Trail that had ushered most of the Klondike stampeders into the Yukon's headwaters. We picked their brains about everything from mosquitoes to grizzlies, both of which they said not to worry about much. They both said we probably needn't bother to take a gun. My mother, who sat beside me eating popcorn during the discussion, was strangely quiet on the drive home.

**January 4**—In the morning I moved out of my Dallas apartment, loaded up my van with clothes, camping gear, a few dishes, filing cabinets, typewriter, and mimeograph machine, and took up residence 150 miles away in Nacogdoches to begin a project not quite like anything I'd ever done. I was to direct a three-month, twelve-county public education campaign on the wholesale clearcut logging of our East Texas national forests and on the alternative of designating some of those public lands as wilderness. I would live in an unfamiliar town in the heart of Texas's timber industry, which opposed almost everything I advocated.

My life was not simple. On a typical day I might hit the road at 5:45 A.M. to present our slide show to the men of the Lions Club in Center; in the afternoon I'd debate a timber company spokesperson on Lufkin TV; that night at a cafe somewhere I'd pass around petitions and try to enlist the support of the local loggers, maybe ending up sharing a little nip in the back room and nearly beating one of them at eight-ball pool. Then I'd drive fifty miles back home, dodging deer on the back roads and making sure I wasn't followed by some over-zealous timber company type, and before going to sleep I might read a little further in a book called *Tracks*, about a woman who walked across the entire Australian desert with a couple of camels. Just before turning out the light, I'd follow the course of the Yukon one more time on the big map of Alaska tacked on the wall above my rollaway bed.

Communications with the Yukon crew weren't so easy, what with Evelyn's living on her farm 100 miles west of Dallas and my living 150 miles east of Dallas. There were long-distance calls about everything from birth control pills to a music festival in Sitka, Alaska. I took great pains to deluge the others with every tidbit of interest, because I believed the one thing that would jeopardize our group's emotional stability on the river would be if someone got herself into a situation she didn't like and hadn't expected. I felt that I myself had read enough to know the range of possible adverse circumstances to expect, and I was prepared to meet them cheerfully. I could only hope that the others, too, were reading; if anyone thought the Yukon might not be what she wanted, I hoped she'd find out now rather than halfway down the river.

**January 12**—For days, something had been wrong with the central heating system and there was no heat in the 12′ x 12′ apartment where I worked and lived. The pipes had burst and there was no water either. It was 12° outside; inside, I could see my breath. I slept in my wool long johns, inside my sleeping bag, in a knit hat. I had wanted to test my gear for cold weather, but I hadn't planned to do it inside my home.

With several inches of snow on the ground, and a quarter-inch of ice *inside* my windowpane, I was inspired to read through some of the old editorials from the Alaska lands battle. " . . . the most far-reaching conservation legislation ever devised in the United States," said the *Arkansas Gazette,* adding that "never again will this nation have the opportunity to set aside such vast expanses of relatively untouched natural wonders as those of the Udall bill."

Interior Secretary Cecil Andrus called Alaska's public lands "the crown jewels of our nation." Said the Palestine, Texas, *Herald Press,* "The lands include majestic snow-clad mountains, huge glaciers, sprawling ice fields, gloomy rain forests, lonely tundra, rushing rivers, deep fjords, barren ocean beaches, lakes teeming with fish, and the habitat of caribou, bears and other wildlife."

"We owe it to ourselves, to those Americans yet to be born and to the world community to do all we can to preserve some of the priceless and irreplaceable wilderness and wildlife resources on this continent," said the Corpus Christi, Texas, *Caller-Times.* "Every congressman should be put on notice by his constituents that Americans want and deserve this legislation; the national interest must take precedence over commercial interests in exploiting and destroying our heritage."

I had heard Alaska's praises sung—and helped sing them—for years. Now I had only five months to go before I would see what all that singing was about!

**January 15**—I drove into Dallas to see an Audubon film about Alaska. Jane and Barbara and I watched two hours of grizzlies ripping open bright red salmon. The narrator also mentioned in passing that a female moose with a calf was just about the most dangerous and unpredictable critter alive; full-grown male grizzlies had been known to flee from them.

By now I had a hopeless case of equipment-itis. I could cope with any old setup for a mere weekend canoe trip, but I would have to get along with my Yukon equipment morning, noon, and night for three months, so I took extreme pains to think everything through.

I combed Dallas's hardware, army surplus, and camping stores; today's fixations were fasteners and a mosquito headnet. The problem was what kind of fastener to use at the end of the rope that I would run through the handles of all the gear in the boat. I knew I didn't want to be tying and untying wet, dirty knots several times a day. The fasteners should be quick and easy, but reliable; they would be the only thing holding in our gear if we turned over. But there were so many to choose from. There were spring-loaded carabiners that mountain climbers use, at $5.95 each, or you could get locking carabiners at $6.95 each, or there were the metal fasteners like you find at the end of a dog leash (but I heard that the button can get stuck when sand gets in the track), or. . . . And as for the mosquito headnet, there were ready-made ones available, but that would be too easy. I wanted the headnet to descend from a sturdy, waterproof, broad-brimmed hat, and, naturally, to close tightly around the chin to keep out mosquitoes, but also to remove easily from the hat when it wasn't needed. And, of course, the hat itself should have a chin-strap so it wouldn't blow off. My mother and brother and I sat around the kitchen with a bunch of mosquito netting, some drawstring cord, some seam tape, and an old cowboy hat and plotted. . . .

Back in Nacogdoches, each day's mail brought some new piece to the giant puzzle. Here was a catalog with the wool sweater I wanted. Here was a letter from a friend of a friend who had paddled a river near the Inside Passage; she wrote that we should be sure our tent and headnet netting had mesh small enough to keep out no-see-ums (tiny biting gnats or mites), and that she and her partner carried Freon compressed-air horns to scare away bears. Here was a letter from Mother saying the bank would loan me $3,000 on a two-year loan (hallelujah!).

I went to camera shops to learn what all those millimeter numbers on the different lenses meant. I looked at waterproof cameras and waterproof boxes for cameras and waterproof bags to take pictures through. I looked at filters and extenders and converters and lens shades and lens caps and automatic drives and shutter-release cables. It was all so bewildering, and none of it was cheap.

O.K., sometimes I carried all this equipment stuff a little far. One day I got to wondering how much toilet paper I'd need on the river (as with any other item in the cramped boats, you don't want to take too much, and you sure don't want to take too little). So I set up a meticulous record-keeping procedure at home and gauged that in three months I'd use about four rolls of two-ply paper (barring, of course, any unforeseen increase in demand).

From equipment catalogs and the ads in outdoor magazines, Sue and I compiled a list of potential sponsors. I wrote a background sheet about the women and the trip and typed "Texas Women's Yukon River Expedition" across the top of it. We sent it to dozens of canoe and equipment manufacturers, along with a cover letter that described our wilderness expedition, pointing out that, according to our research, this would be the first time an all-women's group would travel the 2,000-mile length of the legendary Yukon River in non-motorized craft, and inviting the participation of the firms "in this historic venture. We are all working women, with few cash reserves, who are quitting our jobs or taking unpaid leave to paddle the river. We would be most grateful for any cash contribution or for any equipment that you could make available." It all sounded a little pretentious set down in cold black and white, but no matter how many times I read it, it was true.

## FEBRUARY, 1982

**February 26**—Wrapped in a sheet, I perched on the examination table after my annual checkup. My gynecologist is an older man, with white hair and a gentle manner, who looks remarkably like Richard Widmark. For weeks I had pictured in my mind the upcoming moment that, were it not so embarrassing, would be funny.

"Uh," I began, "I'm going to paddle a canoe down the Yukon River this summer, and—"

"How nice," the doc smiled in his kindly way. "I bet you're looking forward to that."

"Yes, well, I was wondering if it would be possible to take the Pill straight through so I wouldn't have a period, or whether that would throw off my system in some way?"

"That would be fine," he nodded, unsurprised. "Lots of women do that when they're going on vacation. It won't hurt anything to delay your period for a couple of weeks."

"No you see, I'm canoeing the *whole* Yukon River," I explained. He looked up in surprise. "It'll take about three months."

He shook his head and frowned. "Oh, well, that's a different story. I wouldn't recommend delaying your period for that long. Besides, you'd probably have it anyway, even though you took a Pill every day."

That meant I had to ask an even stranger question. "Uh, I suppose you're not really the one to ask about this, but I thought maybe from your medical readings or something. . . . Do you think grizzlies can smell the, uh, well you know, when women are having their period?"

Intrigued by the biological puzzle, he thoughtfully rubbed his chin. His nurse clearly thought me loony for going into grizzly country in the first place. "I think it's quite possible grizzlies can smell the blood," the doc nodded. "After all, sharks can home in on blood from a long way off, and dogs can track an injured animal by its trail of blood."

We shrugged at each other. "Them's the breaks," I thought.

The doctor said to see him after the trip so he could check a minor problem, and he said to douche twice a week. I suppressed a laugh, envisioning the Yukon's freezing, silt-laden waters.

"Well, take disposable douches," he said. The man had obviously never packed for a 2,000-mile canoe trip. I could just see me lugging onto the ferry in Seattle—in addition to all our other gear—whole duffel bags full of nothing but douches. The douching would have to wait, thank you very much.

**February 28**—So here I was, laying groundwork for new long-term responsibilities as TCONR's executive director; pioneering a wilderness campaign on timber industry turf; groping through the logistics of a trip twenty times longer than I'd ever paddled, to a river with climate and animals foreign to me; and recovering from a week-long stay in bed with the flu.

As if that weren't enough, I thought I might launch a writing career. It was something I'd always wanted to do, and as initiator of the first all-female expedition down the length of the Yukon River, I now had a pretty catchy story to offer, I thought. A month before, Sue and I had divided up a list of magazines to contact. I decided that if I were going to pursue this aspect of the trip, I might as well do it right, so I drove to Dallas and plunked down $95 of my mother's Mastercard credit for an all-day workshop on how to sell free-lance travel and adventure articles to newspapers and magazines. The seminar confirmed my notion that, like planning the trip itself, the answer to getting published was simple diligence.

"Go for it!" I pledged.

During the long drive back to Nacogdoches that evening, my mind buzzed with enthusiasm for the happy challenge of the coming months of preparation and the epic adventure down North America's fifth longest river. It was a rare moment, for I seldom contemplated this broad picture. When I confronted the likelihood of the thousands of decisions we faced, the endless hours of shopping and evaluating gear, the volume of money that I'd spend, the interminable hours on the phone coordinating with the troops, the 4,000-mile trip to the river, and the months on the river in the company of the same three women morning, noon, and night, I felt a little overwhelmed. On the one hand, I couldn't believe I was really doing all this; on the other hand, it seemed a perfectly normal way to spend the spring and summer. Generally, I tucked the larger dreams and worries away and tackled one day at a time.

## MARCH, 1982

**March 6**—"Well, here we are," I mumbled dourly, staring into the bleak morning through the window of Evelyn's van. Rain poured from grey skies and washed in sheets across pine needles into the rising Neches River. My breath formed clouds of steam in the 40° air. A clap of thunder rattled the van's foggy windows.

It was ten o'clock on a Saturday morning, and the six of us had gathered in the proposed Big Slough wilderness area for a shakedown cruise and campout. Inside the van, we lingered over breakfast, catching up on news of the past few months, talking equipment and food, hoping the rain would stop and the day would warm up about 20°.

"Maybe some wine would help," suggested Evelyn, over the pounding of rain on the roof. Out came wine and amaretto; breakfast took on a party atmosphere. Sue pulled out her new mini tape recorder for recording her Yukon journal, and we sang for posterity a rousing version of "Drop-Kick Me, Jesus, Through the Goal-Posts of Life."

"Why, these aren't bad at all," declared Cook Evelyn, swallowing a spoonful of precooked powdered eggs mixed with dehydrated onions and Parmesan cheese. She plopped a lump of the gruel into each of our Sierra cups.

"Blaaaah!" we choked down the grainy, white, wet stuff with the strange smell and wondered aloud about having a camp cook who admittedly would eat anything that wouldn't eat her first.

A group poll split three to three on whether to call off the whole shakedown cruise and spend the weekend planning and carousing in nearby Nacogdoches in my dry, warm apartment. But I knew that, with our crazy schedules, this was the only chance for the six of us to paddle together before shoving into the big waters of the Yukon. During a meeting I had missed, the others had elected me leader of the group; they now explained that the post included breaking tie votes.

"Well, finish your wine then, ladies," I announced cheerily, rain cascading off the brim of my cowboy hat as I stepped from the van, "it's eleven A.M., forty degrees, and time to paddle!" They rolled their eyes, but agreed there'd be days like this on the Yukon and we might as well test our rain gear and our tempers now.

Into the boats we threw a rough approximation of the amount of gear we'd take on the Yukon; to our relief, it did fit (more or less) into the boats and they did float. Then we paddled upstream a few miles through narrow, tree-lined Big Slough, drifted downstream a few miles on the faster waters of the Neches, and pulled out early in the afternoon on the banks of a big island. By now the rain had stopped, and though it was still cold, the day was quite pleasant.

Sue and Jane and I pitched the tents; I got my first inkling of Evelyn's approach to camping when I discovered hers was a mass of tangled, knotted ropes and tent stakes that were old rusted nails. Jude and Barbara chopped wood, and Evelyn started a fire.

A big pot of soup boiled merrily over the fire on a new $5 backpacker's grill I had bought, until the grill's legs melted and the whole affair collapsed into the fire. Such are the reasons for shakedown cruises.

After dinner, as we settled around the fire—I in my short-legged lawn chair and they on wet logs—Barbara led us in every song she could think of from "Old Man River" to "Don't Cry for Me, Argentina" to "Mame." She and Jude discovered they had both attended Texas Women's University, albeit about ten years apart, and they reminisced about old professors and class rivalries. By the time the moon and stars had peeked through the woods and unseen barred owls had begun to answer each other's lonely echoing hoots, the conversation had turned to men and how few good ones there were. Except for Jane, who—knocking on a log for her luck in having found him—had nothing but praise for her husband, Wesley, the rest of us had our lighthearted complaints. I mentioned one guy I had lived with who was really nice, but he never wanted to do anything or go anywhere; other men had had some get-up-and-go, but wanted to fit me into stereotyped roles. We talked about the problems of finding long-term romances in today's mobile society in which women and men have their own careers. I commented that on the one hand, I didn't relate well to men (nor they to me) who wanted to live their whole lives in one place, but that on the other hand, the ones who believed in getting a taste of every part of the world weren't around long enough (nor was I) for me to get to know them. As we joked on the subject, I concluded that while long-term romances would be nice, in the meantime it was perhaps the prudent course to take what you could get while you could get it. To which the others exploded with everything from shocked embarrassment to head-shaking to enthusiastic applause. We all laughed, toasted the concept, and threw another log on the fire. The merriment, harmonica-playing, and philosophizing continued far into the night. Such are the joys of a shakedown cruise.

During the night I woke up shivering several times, though I wore a knit hat and my long johns. I wondered whether my synthetic fiber bag had finally lost its lofting/insulating ability after several years of use, and whether I'd have to buy a new one for the Yukon.

A flurry of screams from Jane's tent finally brought me wide awake first thing in the morning. Evelyn had coaxed Jane into taking the plastic jar of sourdough bread starter to bed with her to keep it warm so it would rise for our breakfast crêpes, and "Doughboy" had rudely exploded wet goo throughout Jane's sleeping bag. Such are the reasons for shakedown cruises. Everybody but Jane had a good laugh about it.

The water in my bottle was frozen, and Jane's thermometer said the air was 25°, which meant that during the night the temperature had dipped several degrees below my sleeping bag's temperature rating, so my dear old bag redeemed its right to accompany me on the Yukon. I assumed a Yukon summer wouldn't get any colder than this.

After breakfast, as we packed up Evelyn's tent, I asked her, "By the way, since we're using your tent and your boat, if for some reason you decide not to finish the river, do I get to use them?"

"Yes," she answered, "but believe me, I'm gonna finish that river. By the same token, if you decide to leave the river for a few weeks to go hike Denali National Park or something, and if I'm gonna wait with the canoes on the river, don't plan to take my tent with you." Sue and Jude had talked about flying away from the river briefly to see some other parts of Alaska.

"Fair enough," I grinned. "I don't think there'll be much time to throw in sightseeing. I think you can either canoe the whole Yukon River or you can jump around the state sightseeing, but you can't do both in one summer. I'll go back up there someday for the other. Besides, leaving the river for more than a short backpack trip near the river would ruin it for me; I want to do the whole river, and nothing but the river, from beginning to end."

We paddled upstream through Big Slough to the van and loaded the gear while Evelyn cooked a lunch of macaroni and cheese. Jane modeled her new Gore-Tex rain suit and showed us its features. Gore-Tex is a relatively new fabric that has swept the outdoor clothing market during the past several years. Although much more expensive than traditional nylon or rubberized rain suits, the fabric has "breathing" holes just big enough to allow moisture vapor (sweat) to escape, but not big enough to let raindrops enter. The fabric thus gives rain protection while avoiding transforming your clothing into a sweatbox—a very important consideration when you're paddling or hiking. We all knew we wanted Gore-Tex or one of the few other breathable fabrics, but there were so many different kinds and prices and weights of rain suits to choose from. The only drawback (other than price) that we'd heard about was that Gore-Tex doesn't breathe too well when it is dirty.

I modeled my "booties" made of black wetsuit material that I wore like socks inside my tennis shoes. As with a diver's full-body wetsuit, when you walk in water the tiny air pockets of the spongy nylon material (inside the neoprene outer covering) fill with water, are heated by body heat to the temperature of your blood, and serve as a warm second skin to keep your feet warm. Sue and Jude had wetsuit booties with stiff soles that served as full-fledged boots. I also showed off my new orange wool balaclava, a long wool knit hat that pulled over my head and tucked into my shirt collar, with an opening for my face and a little bill above the eyes to protect them from blowing snow or rain. It could be rolled up to cover just my head and ears or pulled down to my shoulders; it promised to be great for windy days.

Envious of me as I enjoyed my lunch above the mud in the comfort of my squatty lawn chair, Sue and Jude and Barbara decided to order chairs for themselves. Jane and Evelyn still wanted to go the martyr route. "That would be like taking a pillow!" they cried in disgust.

We passed around equipment catalogs; we'd just gotten our first offer of a discount from a manufacturer who'd received one of our sponsorship letters, so we had to get a group order together. We looked at some sample maps of one segment of the Yukon and, after recovering from the shock of seeing the hundreds of tiny islands they depicted, voted to order for each boat only twenty-four big-scale maps at $61.50 a set, rather than hundreds of more detailed ones at who-knows-how-much a set.

The others each wrote a $155 check for their Alaska state ferry tickets up the Inside Passage. Jane smiled as she handed me hers and said, "There's no turning back now!"

We decided to take Evelyn's van (bigger and more powerful than mine) to Seattle, with the six of us inside, two boats on top, maybe a trailer behind with the gear. As we bounced over the sandy road leaving Big Slough, Evelyn's roof rack jumped its moorings and the canoes slid all over the place. Evelyn and Sue and Jude wrestled the thing into place and retied the canoe ropes, grumbling about what might have happened if the roof rack had done that on the way to Seattle at sixty miles an hour. Such are the reasons for shakedown cruises.

During the rest of March, publicizing the expedition, attracting sponsors, and landing writing assignments consumed as many hours a week as preparing the equipment and the food and communicating with the crew. But, after all, I had pledged to go whole hog on this thing. I sent Yukon story proposals to a dozen magazines. I researched the needs of about 800 book publishers, narrowed my prospective market to about fifty, and sent a four-page book outline to them. I had written news releases and fact sheets through the years, but I had never taken a journalism course and had no real writing background. "Who the heck do I think I am?" I sometimes asked myself, but then I'd read the book outline and think, "I'd want to read a book like that." I figured it was worth the $50 I spent in copying, paper, and postage to see if anyone agreed.

One day a woman with a film company in Dallas called and asked permission to seek funding for a documentary about our expedition. "Go right ahead," I said, when I regained my speech.

Meanwhile, equipment companies were calling and writing from all over the country to offer price discounts. Each offer meant, in turn, that we had to circulate the company's catalog among the six of us so we could choose what we wanted. This thing was getting wonderfully out of hand.

**March 26**—Five minutes before my dinner date was to arrive one Friday night, as I flew around my apartment trying to make it presentable, my bare foot got tangled in a bedsheet on the floor and down I stumbled, whamming my big toe into the floor with a loud crack. I limped to dinner that night and to a speech I had to give the next morning, then went to the hospital for an X-ray. It wasn't broken, they said; I spent the last hectic week of my East Texas campaign limping in tennis shoes and hoping everything would be mended by the time I headed for the Yukon.

## APRIL, 1982

I concluded my Nacogdoches project and moved my office, my Yukon gear, and my personal belongings into one room—"Y-Day" launch site— of my parents' house in Garland, a Dallas suburb. Through the years, I had run lots of strange operations from this house, but neither my parents nor I anticipated the full insanity this little project would evoke during those eight weeks until May 28.

### Eight Weeks and Counting . . .

The morning after I "settled in," I was taking a bath when the phone rang. Dripping, I wrapped a towel around myself and stood shivering in the hallway to answer it. It was a publisher in Chicago, and he wanted to sign a book contract before I left for the Yukon! He would send me a sample contract. I had sent out the book outline only a week before; I couldn't believe anyone had even had time to read it, let alone decide to go for it. Still dripping in my towel, I called Mother at the bank to break the incredible news. We laughed and cried a few minutes, then she blurted, "Goodbye, I gotta go tell everybody!"

I had been back in the bathtub all of five minutes when the phone rang again. This time I was dripping not only water, but also shampoo, and as I stood shivering in my towel again, I found myself talking to a friendly and happy-go-lucky publisher named Norman Simpson of the Berkshire

Traveller Press in Massachusetts, who also wanted to sign a contract before I left for the Yukon, and who also would send the information. I called Mother, we laughed and cried some more, and she hung up again to flash word on the bank grapevine. Back in the tub, I was overwhelmed. I couldn't believe one, let alone two, publishers were willing to put up a little money and sign a contract for a book by someone who'd never published anything, about a journey that hadn't begun, to a place she'd never been!

Through the week continued the phone calls and letters to clothing and camera manufacturers. Bundles of maps were arriving by mail, as were more equipment catalogs. Jane and I were spending hours on the phone talking about rain pants. During the week, when I wasn't poring over equipment catalogs to choose gear by mail, I drove all over town to pick up what I could locally: spare paddles, a daypack, canvas river shoes, vinyl "waterproof" pouches, nylon for Mother to sew stuff sacks for organizing my gear inside the big "waterproof" bags.

Sue and I were receiving tentative writing assignments from some magazines and rejection slips from others. Local newspapers were calling for interviews. And now that I had the happiest and most unexpected of problems—choosing between publishers—I began a crash course in book publishing.

In the midst of this wonderful chaos, I was supposed to be working full-time for TCONR in the little room in my parents' house. Among the boxes of TCONR wilderness files and forestry brochures sprawled all manner of tents and backpacks and ropes and paddles and boots. Mother gave up entering the room for any reason, lest she disturb some pile that signified something. If she wanted to talk to me, she stood warily at the door. If she needed to deliver clean clothes, she gingerly placed them on the floor just inside the door. Each night I simply made a flying leap over the mass to reach the bed, where I'd read a page from John Muir's *Travels in Alaska* or Margaret Murie's *Two in the Far North* before closing my weary eyes.

### Seven Weeks and Counting . . .

Mother and I spent Easter morning sewing a little mesh bag for a bar of soap (I was determined to make one bar last three months on the Yukon), with a cord to slip around my wrist so I wouldn't lose the soap in the river. Then we cut up and hemmed washcloths and towels to make smaller washcloths and towels.

There were calls to be made to food companies, seventy pieces of sheet music to be copied, cut up, and coated with clear contact paper for waterproofing. My new $91 backpack arrived (the United Parcel Service delivery person and I were good friends by now). There were calls to California about rain pants, calls to Maine about rain pants, calls all over Dallas about rain pants. The "waterproof" box I'd ordered for my tape recorder had no way to fasten into the boat, and the fifty pounds of peanuts that Jane was running through her food processor were emerging more peanut than butter.

One night at the Dallas Downriver Club meeting, I was offered two dehydrators, beef jerky, a fishing lesson and a fishing rod, and ethafoam knee pads and seats for the canoe.

Evelyn received word from a friend in Japan, to whom she'd written, that they do manufacture dehydrated beer over there but they sell it only overseas; Evelyn vowed to track it down if it took contacting everybody from the Texas Alcoholic Beverage Commission to the Sierra Club national headquarters in San Francisco.

I went to the dentist ("A toothache can really ruin a trip," Sue had said at one meeting), who said I had three cavities—one of which was fairly major—that I'd have to come back to have filled. He also said I needed to buy several brushes, so that no matter how often a day I brushed my teeth, I'd always have a dry brush for my gums. The conversation reminded me of the gynecologist and the douches.

A woman named Bryna Millman, an Outward Bound alumna now with the New York public relations firm handling the Minolta Corporation account, was very interested in our women's trip. When she wasn't trying to obtain camera equipment loans for us from Minolta, she was stirring up film-producer friends in New York and Florida to do a documentary about us. Meanwhile, the two women with the film company back in Dallas were contacting beer companies to fund their proposed documentary. "If they go for it," I said, "see if they'll airlift beer for us to the Yukon." (We could just see the commercial we'd film at the Bering Sea: "You mean we paddled 2,000 miles down the Yukon River and all you brought is *light* beer?!")

A literary agent said we should take a professional photographer along. "Look," I sputtered, "we have no money for that sort of thing. We can barely get ourselves up there. No one has given us a dime. I just signed a $3,000 loan that I'll still be paying nineteen percent interest on two years from now. We've gotten some price discounts on equipment, but there comes a point at which you don't need more equipment, you need money—*money!* For 1,200 pounds of food, and gasoline for 2,500 miles to Seattle, and ferry fares and train fares for another 1,400 miles to the river, and air fares to fly back to Dallas from the Bering Sea, and a hundred rolls of film, not to mention the developing. . . ."

Meanwhile, decision-making was not simple: Evelyn was somewhere in West Texas selling perfume bottles and prickly-pear jelly, Jane was backpacking for a week in the Grand Canyon, and Sue and Jude were watching whales in Hawaii.

## Six Weeks and Counting . . .

Jane returned from Arizona, and every morning she and I chopped bell peppers or onions or potatoes and spread them on the dehydrators' trays; every night Mother and I bagged them up and labeled them. The first time the overpowering onion smell hit Mother as she walked in the door, she almost closed up my base of operations, but it helped some to move the dehydrators to the garage. Other than that, the dehydrating went well, if slowly, except when one entire load of potatoes turned black.

Meanwhile, I combed the stores for Kentucky Wonder beans, yet more powdered eggs, quick-drying cotton-polyester pants with big pockets, folding scissors, and mesh paddling gloves. I calculated that I'd need at least $1,500 for food en route, lodging, freight fees, and return transportation for myself. There were bright spots, though: Sue had finagled three months' worth of free vitamins for all of us.

Every night Mother and I would put waterproof sealer on tarp and tent seams, hash over publishing contracts, dunk waterproof matches into a sinkful of water to see if they'd light (they did), or discuss once again how we might get my tape recorder box to stop smelling like a diaper pail.

The dentist filled one cavity and started talking root canal on another.

Several book publishers had now expressed various levels of interest. I pored over sample contracts and read library books on how to get published.

One day when I went to the bookstore to buy some paperbacks for my on-the-river library, I ran into the news anchor-person for a local TV station. As I was showing him the Yukon River on a big globe, another guy walked up and said he was from Alaska and had paddled half the Yukon River. Practically seizing him bodily, I picked his brain. He said we'd constantly have to be on the alert for sweepers—trees and debris extending from the banks, hung up on sandbars in the middle of the river or floating down the river—and for the whirlpool-like boils in the river that would try to turn us over. He said, though, that he had no trouble finding his way in the Yukon Flats. He said there was usually one phone in each village and that we should have no problem receiving our food if we shipped it to post offices. On the final 150 miles of the river, he'd heard, the wind is always against you and it's hard to find a dry place to camp. He said the tide comes in against you for about fifty miles.

We held another planning meeting at Sue's, where the new floorless dining-and-happy-hour tent of mosquito netting that Sue and Jude had bought was displayed on the front lawn. "That's really fine, I think we could take in boarders along the Yukon," said Evelyn as she walked in with thirteen bags of dehydrated broccoli. The meeting was five hours of chaos: "Are you sure this works out to a hundred pounds of food in each canoe?!" . . . "Should we order some Bill's Bags?" "You wrote me a check two weeks ago and I already ordered 'em." "Oh, good." . . . "Anybody want to say anything about clothes and shoes?" "I will have clothes and I will have shoes, I'm tired of worrying about what kind." . . . "We've still gotta buy a frying pan with a humped-up lid." . . . "Do we really need sixty empty plastic jars for food?" "We're not really gonna keep our spices in specimen bottles, are we?" . . . "I *know* I read an article that said if you eat bananas the mosquitoes will eat you alive." . . . "And Lord, let's don't take sunflower seeds whatever we do—they make you horny." "They *do,*too!" . . . "I still haven't found out if bears can smell thirteen Gouda cheeses and thirteen salamis inside a waterproof bag."

**Five Weeks and Counting . . .**

I went backpacking in Angelina National Forest in East Texas with a friend, to test my new backpack and relax, but the Neches River was rising out of its high banks and we had to turn back about a mile into the flooded woods. On top of that, my sleeping bag zipper came apart, which was the last thing I needed. At least it did it here and not the first day on the Yukon, I thought. First thing the next day I shipped it to the manufacturer in Colorado to be repaired and hoped like hell it would return in time. (Amazingly, it was back in a week.)

One day I jogged at the park to begin getting in shape for the Yukon; it would turn out to be the last time I had thirty minutes to get in shape for anything.

The Dallas Museum of Natural History was now seeking funding for an exhibition of our photography after the trip, with maybe some funding thrown in for the trip itself. "It's kind of late to be approaching foundations for this trip," said Walt Davis and Steve Runnels, "but once you finish this expedition, they'll really believe you on the next one." Meanwhile, I spent hours on the phone checking local river levels and put-in sites for a canoe trip so we could be filmed by the Dallas film company. Publishers were calling for decisions on book contracts, and I was studying how-to photography books.

I had another cavity filled, a phone bill arrived that said Mother owed the phone company $132.70 for the first seventeen days since I had hit town, and Evelyn's new $100 dehydrator quit working.

I measured and sawed styrofoam for a trumpet case, finally decided to roll the trumpet up inside my sleeping pad and let it go at that; Mother shortened sleeves on workshirts, cut off jeans to make shorts, designed waterproof backpack covers, and patched the hole a Greek mouse once chewed through Evelyn's tent.

As a waterproof floatable housing for camera and lenses, I bought a green 12" x 7" x 6" army-surplus ammunition, or "ammo," can. I then painted it white so it would reflect the sun's heat and would be less likely to be forgotten in some campsite as it blended into the greens and grays of the landscape. Then I glued ethafoam padding into the box to guard the camera equipment against damage from knocks and bumps.

A friend of Sue's showed her slides from twenty years' residence in Alaska. "I was so excited afterwards I couldn't go to sleep all night!" Sue said. She had now completed her chemotherapy treatments and was beginning radiation.

A company that had offered us a discount had $150 of Jane's and my money for rain suits, but the rain suits were missing-in-action somewhere between California and Nacogdoches, where they weren't supposed to go in the first place, and we discovered during the many phone calls that when and if the rain pants ever showed up, they'd be the wrong size.

Evelyn got a solid offer of free food from the owner of an organic dehydrated and freeze-dried food company in Washington State called Twelve Baskets, as well as a substantial free sample of flours and grains from the owner's brother, who works at Arrowhead Mills in Texas. This gracious gesture would turn out to be one of the most significant contributions of any company to our expedition. We never did figure out just how the quantities in the donated packages compared to the quantities on Evelyn's master food list, but we seemed to have been offered about $500 worth of food from Twelve Baskets and $50 to $100 from Arrowhead Mills, which seemed to be at least a third of what we'd need for the whole trip. As she relayed the great news to me by phone, Evelyn said there was only one hitch: Twelve Baskets was new and their food wasn't quite packaged yet and we'd have to pick it up in Seattle on our way through to the Yukon.

"Aw, c'mon, Beth," Evelyn chuckled, "it'll be O.K. . . . probably."

So, what else was new . . . ?

One day Mother walked in after work and stood at attention, as usual, awaiting her assignments for the evening. I held up my hand for silence as I concentrated on the mass of food and baggies on the kitchen table, talking to myself and counting on my fingers: "I've got eight trays of green peas dehydrated and that's supposed to be four meals for six people, but I'm supposed to package it in bags for four people, so two trays would be one meal for six people, so one-and-a-third trays would be one meal for four people, and then two-thirds of a tray would be one meal for two people. . . ."

The dog continued grazing on the dehydrated food bits imbedded in the kitchen carpet. ". . . Eight trays of English peas is four meals for six people, or six meals for four people, or six bags!"

Mother looked at me with a worried expression and asked if there was anything she could do to help. "Well, yes," I motioned to the counter. "I need you to package up these dried zucchinis. Now Evelyn says nine zukes are one meal for six people, so you see we've got eighteen zukes. But only fourteen of them would fit into the dehydrator. But I think nine is really too many for six people anyway, so let's say one zuke to a person. So if we've got fourteen zukes on nine trays, that's one-and-a-half zuke per tray. Packaging it up one meal for four people, at one zuke each, and one-and-a-half zukes per tray, that's two-and-two-thirds trays for one meal for four people, so that's what you put in the bag. Got it?"

One night Sid Rucker and I got to talking about Dawson, the home of the Klondike gold rush, which would await us 460 miles downstream from our put-in. "I can just see it when you six women hit town on a Saturday night," he laughed. "Three things there's no shortage of in Dawson City: wild times, beer, and gold miners."

"We'll probably sample a little of each," I said.

## MAY, 1982

### Four Weeks and Counting . . .

On Saturday, Evelyn and I met for lunch, then climbed into her boat in John Ryan's back yard and got measured for placement of foam rubber kneepads that John would glue into the bottom of the boat; then we threw the boat onto my van and drove to my house, where we painted "Bering

Sea or Bust" in big red letters in marine paint on both sides of the aluminum canoe. "Well," said Evelyn, "there's really no turning back now."

At nine o'clock on a rainy Sunday morning, all of us but Barbara (who was leading a backpack trip in Arkansas) stood in the mud beside White Rock Lake in Dallas. The film crew for the nationwide ESPN cable network "SportsWoman" program showed up and strapped inside my rain jacket a wireless microphone that picked up sound for several dozen feet. This was the first time we'd piled into the boats the real amount of gear and food we'd be taking, and the crew shot some crazy footage of Evelyn and me grunting and struggling to shove our loaded boat into the water. "One, two, three!" I would holler, and we would heave with all our weight. The boat would move one inch and our feet would slide out from under us through the mud. It was hard, watching the sequence later on TV, to imagine these two women on the Yukon.

Jim Bridges paddled the camera crew around in Sue's rubber raft, while the rest of us paddled our loaded canoes up and down flooded White Rock Creek. Several snakes hung from each tree and, forgetting the microphone in her astonishment, Jude cried out a few choice epithets at the slithering beasts.

The highlight of the day for the film crew was our ill-fated attempts to practice throwing the new rescue bag that Jane and Sue had made. The idea was to throw the rope-filled bag to anyone swimming after a capsize. But there was too much rope, too much bag, and try as we might, we could throw the bag only about twenty feet. So if we planned to turn over on the Yukon, we joked, we'd better do it within a canoe-length of our companions.

The crew wanted film footage of us unloading the boats, so we each heaved a duffel bag onto our shoulders and walked toward the camera. Each time something was slightly wrong, in the crew's eyes. About the third time we were ordered back through the mud for a rerun, somebody said, "Lady, these damn things weigh fifty pounds!" Then, for the camera, we unfurled one map of the mouth of the river, where hundreds of islands and sloughs and tiny channels splayed out across the delta. It was sort of intimidating and conjured up images of being lost for days on flat, mosquito-filled waters.

"Look down here at the end," I said, "it splits into two or three main channels." Jude asked which one we'd take. "Well, we don't know yet," I said offhandedly. Jude stared at me in disbelief and Sue smiled. I shrugged, "Well, we'll just have to ask the Eskimos when we get down there."

After some of Evelyn's husband Bob's delicious spaghetti in Evelyn's back yard after the filming, we joked about the morning's film session and changed our minds yet again about who was driving what cars to Seattle. We'd now go in Sue's pickup truck, for which she'd buy a camper shell, and in Barbara's little hatch-back.

After the others had left, Evelyn and I discussed with Bob the finer points of dehydrating chili and laughed about this whole mess. "You know," Evelyn told me with mock seriousness, "you've contracted what I call 'stuff-sack syndrome.' It's a serious disorder that strikes many backpackers and canoeists. You want to organize and categorize all your little odds and ends of equipment, so you put some into stuff sacks, then you put those stuff sacks into bigger stuff sacks, then you put those—"

"I know, I know," I admitted. I had inherited my father's zeal for detail, for getting things right, for pondering problems for the sheer joy of problem-solving. I knew I actively sought order.

I knew, too, that Evelyn actively sought chaos. She adamantly avoided stuff sacks or anything that smacked of organization. She was one of those who dumped out her entire duffel bag of gear each time she needed her toothbrush.

"If I want to make stuff sacks and worry about carabiners," I chuckled, "let me do it; I'm having fun."

"Fair enough, just don't try to organize *me*," she pointed a finger for emphasis. "Well, I gotta go," she said, "I've got thirteen cabbages to dehydrate."

I finally traced the missing rain suits to Lufkin, only to discover that they had already been shipped back to California in anticipation of a nationwide UPS strike. "Oh great," I thought, "I've got ninety-nine pieces of equipment scattered from Idaho to Maine coming to me by UPS." (Luckily, the strike was short-lived.)

Jane returned from a week of birding in the Everglades and the Dry Tortugas with the news that the people there believed that taking massive doses of vitamin B1 really did keep mosquitoes from biting you, and that a doctor there had said B1 is water-soluble and the excess will be passed out and it can't hurt you. So I added B1 tablets to my shopping list.

One day Walt Davis at the Museum and I calculated that if you counted all the gear—like boats—that we had before we started buying new gear, the expedition was costing the six of us between $10,000 and $15,000.

One night Sid Rucker showed us his slide show of the Chilkoot Trail, the historic route by which 30,000 gold-crazed miners made their way into the Yukon in 1896-98. I had seen the show before, but once again felt inspired. I also felt that what we were about to do was a Sunday picnic compared to the hardships those stampeders faced. During the evening Sid finally answered the burning question about drinking glacially-silted water: Yes, it would give you the trots. Jim Brittin, a friend of Sue's and Jude's from the hospital, who'd been a doctor in the village of Tanana on the Yukon for five years, showed us his slides. In addition to his interesting narrative about river life, he had several boating comments: First, be very careful of landslides and huge blocks of earth that can crash into the river from its high banks. Once a whole fish camp had been wiped out by the tidal wave from one of those chunks. Another danger is that canoeists ("pilgrims" the river folk call them) drift down the river asleep and sometimes get caught up in fish nets stretched out from shore. If their boat turns over and they get swept into the net, they can be held underwater and drown. Then, there's the three-foot wave the barges create in their wake—a wave that can roll a boat over near shore and dump all its belongings into the silty Yukon.

"Weren't those slide shows wonderful?" I asked Mother on the way home. "I'm so excited!!"

"I'm so worried," she mumbled.

## Three Weeks and Counting . . .

Evelyn was washing a bathtubful of her garden lettuce that she was going to palm off on fifty people who'd gathered at her farm for her annual Texas Meeting on the Outdoors. I modeled the new full-price $182 rain suit I had just bought—a rain suit made by the same company that had offered us a forty percent discount but never seemed to have in stock what we wanted or to be able to ship us what they said they'd sent. Meanwhile, they still had Jane's and my money. (We finally received a refund a few days before we left.)

Evelyn and I were having a funny little tug of war over equipment. I was presenting her with little gifts I thought she'd need—a little folding stool, an elasticized band made from wetsuit material to keep her glasses from falling off—which she was rejecting. And I had decided not to take deodorant (back to nature and all that), so she was presenting me with little deodorant bottles, which I was refusing.

Meanwhile, based on my lack of several hundred dollars for a root canal operation, as well as an informal poll Mother took at the bank about root canal experiences, I decided to take my chances with a possible severe toothache on the river, rather than risk complications from having a root canal done just before I was to leave.

The "SportsWoman" show on ESPN cable telecast a seven-minute segment entitled "Six Texas Women" on national cable television. "Today," said the commentator, "we'll take a look at six women who are embarking on an expedition that's sure to make history. The Yukon, one of the longest rivers in North America, winds its way from Whitehorse, Canada, over two thousand miles across Alaska, and into the Bering Sea. During the Klondike gold rush of the 1890s, it brought more than 40,000 adventurers into the region to prospect for gold. Today, the Yukon region is very sparsely populated. The rugged terrain and abundance of wild creatures are what will make an adventure through this vast wilderness so challenging for six Texas women. . . .

"Each canoe must be packed perfectly," the commentator claimed. "The heavier items are packed on the bottom to reduce the tendency of a capsize in rough water. Every pound counts, and it's necessary for each woman to reduce her load as much as possible." Watching the show, I snickered as I thought of my load of three pounds of sheet music.

"These women, as a group, aren't setting out to research anything, discover anything, or even to prove anything," the commentator continued. "But individually, they have their personal motives. Three of them have overcome cancer. Sue Sherrod has only recently completed treatment." We were shown sitting in our boats, in our cowboy hats, with birds singing along the banks of White Rock Creek. Sue talked about floating the Yukon as a way to celebrate whipping cancer; Jude saw it as a way to rebel a little and escape the routine structure of her life; Jane would watch birds and pick wild greens for salad.

After showing our failed attempts to toss the rescue line, the commentator said, "Well, apparently there are just a couple of things that still have to be worked out before they leave. But these brave adventurers aren't worried. Their combined years of canoeing, backpacking, and camping experience have prepared them for this unique adventure. Will the sacrifice of thousands of hours and thousands of dollars in preparation for this expedition be worth it?"

"I think so," answered Jude on the film. "With the river going ten miles an hour, it's not gonna be all that much hard work."

"Boredom would probably be the only reason for not making it," said Sue, "but I don't think that'll happen—we're gonna make it. Bering Sea or bust!"

"But when Beth Johnson, originator of this trip, was asked how she would feel if they don't make it to the Bering Sea . . . " said the commentator.

". . . well, then, we won't make it," I said on camera with a shrug. I obviously thought the world would go on as usual whether we made it or not. And throughout all the preparations, I always believed that the purpose of the trip was to have fun, not just to get to the end of the river, so I never locked myself into feeling that I *had* to finish the river. At the same time, though, I could foresee absolutely no circumstance that would cause me to want to leave the river early.

"Oh, we're gonna do it," said Evelyn on the film. "We're gonna do it."

"Well more power to ya, Evelyn!" said the commentator. "While most of us will spend the summer at home, wishing we were doing something more interesting, these six women—a retired classroom teacher, a head nurse, a sales representative, an anesthesiologist, an environmentalist, and a music teacher—will be making history, and loving every minute of it."

**Two Weeks and Counting . . .**
The whole affair had now taken on the proportions of a space launch. I got up at six every morning to begin rooting through the piles of Yukon junk between the piles of TCONR junk. As Mother left each day for work, she planted herself in the doorway and asked, "Well?" I'd give the day's status: "Lookin' good," "Lookin' bad," or "Iffy," and Mother duly carried official word to my fans at the bank.

One day I stood laughing hysterically beneath the garage rain spout during an afternoon rainstorm, in my new rain suit, making sure there was no truth to the rumor about "leaky Gore-Tex."

Then I hopped in the car and went to the camera store and put $748 worth of film and developing on my mother's Mastercard and wrote a check for another $500 worth of camera lenses and accessories. The loaned

Minolta camera and lenses arrived a few days later. Since I didn't have time to become familiar with the new set, we'd use it as a backup camera that would remain loaded with black-and-white film.

Barbara Franklin, a friend from the Downriver Club, threw a bon voyage brunch for us. After five hours of drinking champagne and playing with our new cameras (Sue had also bought a full array of camera lenses and equipment), I drove myself home (barely), slept off the champagne for a couple of hours, then made it through another going-away dinner with my family that evening. It was rough being a celebrity.

The week degenerated from there. On Tuesday morning, in the dark at 6:30 A.M., my father and brother and I loaded the canoe into the van. I drove into Dallas, picked up Evelyn and her backpack, duffel bags, fifty pounds of food, and drove to White Rock Lake where a TV news crew from one of the local channels was supposed to meet us. We stood around in the mud and rain, examining Sue's and Jude's new camper shell and discussing which Mitch Miller songs to bring on the Yukon. At eight o'clock we admitted we'd been stood up and adjourned to Sue's for a breakfast of Chili-Mac and coffee. Sue complained to the station about their standing us up after they'd asked us to meet them with all our gear and boats at such an ungodly hour. Then Sue went on to work, and Evelyn and Jude and I negotiated over how we'd split any monies we got from magazine sales. Several publishers and a couple of members from other expeditions had warned us emphatically to work out all such agreements before the trip if we wanted to remain friends. It all seemed rather presumptuous, though, since no one had offered us a dime.

I dropped Evelyn off at home and helped her lug the fifty pounds of food and all her gear back into the house. I got home at one o'clock in the afternoon, threw the canoe out of the van, threw off my muddy clothes, threw on some others, ate a piece of cake and studied a position paper about a local water project, raced back into Dallas and met a TV news reporter at two o'clock at the TCONR office to be interviewed about that issue.

When I walked back into my parents' house at three o'clock, the phone was ringing. It was Jude, laughing hysterically. "You're not gonna believe this," she said. "Another channel just called, and they want to film us at White Rock Lake at six o'clock tonight."

"You're making this up," I said. But she wasn't.

"I told them," she said, "that we'd been stood up once today and that if we set this up they sure better be there." I knew Evelyn was out buying food and couldn't be reached, so I took a nap.

The alarm woke me at five, and I called Evelyn. "What are you doing at six o'clock tonight? How'd you like to go paddle your boat at White Rock Lake for another TV station?"

I threw on my muddy clothes again, dragged the boat back into the van, stuffed some ham and cheese into my mouth, drove into Dallas to Evelyn's where the same fifty pounds of food and backpack and duffel bags again sat in her driveway. Her in-laws had just arrived and were flitting around excitedly, ready to watch the filming, wondering why we seemed less than enthusiastic about the whole thing.

So once again we stood in the mud on the bank of White Rock Lake, where we'd stood twelve hours before, and this time the film crew did show up. We paddled a camera person around in our canoes, then at eight o'clock, as we concluded the interview, the van from the morning's station pulled up. Their producer had been trying to work out another interview time with us all day, and when we agreed to come for the second station, we let the first know they could film afterwards.

As the light faded and black stormclouds moved in across the lake, we slid our boats back through the mud and paddled another photographer out over the waters. Ten minutes out, his camera quit working, so we called the whole thing off. This station—the same one that had stood us up in the morning—really knew how to endear itself to its interviewees. Back on shore, their producer was asking for us to come down yet another time to paddle around the lake.

I suggested that the crew could film us at Evelyn's during our upcoming food-packaging session. I knew Sue couldn't be there, but I figured she'd be grateful not to have to deal with the media anymore. All day long, Sue had been unable to shake her anger at being stood up at seven in the morning, and she had joined the rest of us in wondering why we were doing all this media stuff anyway. The original premise had been that publicity might bring us some sponsors, but stories were appearing so late that there was probably no time for anyone to contact us. So, as we made the arrangements with this crew to meet us at Evelyn's, Sue voiced no objection. But after the crew left, I realized the arrangement had upset her. I had been loading and unloading boats, hauling gear, paddling around lakes, and being interviewed not only about the Yukon, but about Dallas environmental issues for at least fifteen hours today, after about five hours' sleep; this was the last thing I needed.

Maybe the radiation treatments were affecting Sue. Besides, we were all tired and grumpy and probably on the verge of something equally crazy ourselves. And Sue, after all, was finishing a year of tremendous physical and emotional trauma, still undergoing radiation treatments, and trying to work full time, all while trying to prepare for a mammoth expedition that would drive anybody crazy.

I said I'd change the interview time, and we passed the whole thing off to the strain we'd all been under. We parted with a laugh, then Evelyn and I went to the store for more chickens.

On Wednesday, from noon until six o'clock, Evelyn and I spread five quarts of Bob's chili and bits from thirteen chopped chickens in the dehydrators, talked about men and marriage and carabiners and whole-wheat flour and the future of the world, and stuffed 2,000 letters into 2,000 envelopes for a TCONR mailing. At six, Jane and I copied sheet music at Tom's and Suzanne's print shop, then learned how to cast a fishing rod in their back yard. At nine I had dinner with a friend I hadn't seen in awhile. I supposed we might renew an old glimmer of a romance, but he seemed a little aloof. I mean, just because I had been in East Texas for three months in the spring and would be gone for three more months on the Yukon in the summer. . . . Men today just have no patience.

Thursday was another fifteen-hour Yukon day, which began at 9 A.M. at Evelyn's, ended at midnight at Evelyn's, and included one newspaper interview, ten hours of scooping peanut butter or flour or corn into a million plastic baggies, two hours of packing and taping food boxes for shipment to Alaska, and one fight with a TV producer.

A local station was seeking money to send themselves to the Yukon to film us. Thus, they joined at least two other crews who were trying to do the same thing. I was beginning to think our entire "vacation" would be nothing but posing for pictures and baby-sitting one film crew after another. We had been advised by publishers and independent film producers who specialized in covering expeditions that it was the usual practice for the expedition to be paid something by the film company. "Don't let anyone come near you with a camera for less than $250 a day," one producer had said. So, as I stood among several hundred pounds of food in Evelyn's kitchen, talking on the phone to this local TV producer, I asked if there was a possibility that we might recoup some of our expedition costs. The producer seemed morally offended and appeared reluctant to even raise the question with the sources from whom she was seeking money to send herself to the Yukon.

Late into the night, long after the others had gone, Evelyn and I were still labeling boxes. Evelyn's brother-in-law, Roy, who since seven that morning had patiently stood at the kitchen counter sealing and labeling hundreds of bags of food, finally had the good sense to cook some delicious ham and green beans and force us to sit down for dinner. That, and packing into boxes the four bottles of champagne that we were shipping illegally to ourselves to the last village on the Yukon, were the only pleasurable moments in the exhausting day. By the time Evelyn and I wearily dragged the food boxes out to my van, I had completely lost my voice from the combination cold and sinus infection that I had been fighting for two weeks.

"Don't forget, you're paddling the Guadalupe with me this week-end!" Evelyn ordered as I coughed a goodbye.

First thing Friday morning, Sue called to say she was worried that my raising the question of money was making the TV and film crews back off from doing documentaries on our trip. She said that she and Jude would abide by whatever decision I made as leader, but that she wanted to let the film companies come for free, let them stay with us on the river for as long as they wanted, and not to mention the question of money anymore.

Afterwards, for long minutes, I sat with my head buried in my hands, crying. My throat hurt, I could barely talk. I had to blow my nose every three seconds, I was exhausted (hadn't gotten to bed before midnight for three nights), I didn't particularly enjoy having to become an overnight expert on film company deals, let alone satisfy the feelings of three other women in the process. The longer I blubbered into my shirtsleeves and the more I thought about it, the madder I got. These media people would have their way paid to Alaska, would probably receive free a whole camping outfit from the finest sleeping bag to the finest tent and Gore-Tex rain suits, and would undoubtedly make some money by selling their films. And though we had been advised by separate professional concerns on both coasts that it was appropriate for us to receive at least a percentage of what they would make from film sales, they seemed outraged at the mere question of money. One of our main reasons for seeking publicity had been the hope that it might bring forth a sponsor, but what good would it do us to have the publicity after the trip, after all our money had been spent? Furthermore, this was *my* trip. I didn't necessarily want to spend it with motorboats and helicopters, or with people who smoked cigarettes in my camp or carried radios or guns or who didn't know how to camp around bears; I wanted to lay down a few ground rules if anyone was to accompany us.

Half the stress I had undergone and the time I had spent in the last few months had been because I had to coordinate others' thoughts and plans, not just my own. The added strain was like the difference between planning a weekend trip alone and planning it with someone else— multiplied by fifty times.

As I sat there crying, feeling so very tired and so very sick of everything from Gore-Tex to chopped chicken to strapping tape to film crews, the phone rang. It was Evelyn. I told her what I was doing at that moment, and why, and after we swore and laughed awhile, I felt better. Evelyn had some sage advice: "You can either be a doormat and everyone stays happy, or you can rock the boat every now and then and stand up for yourself and make some people mad. Go ahead and make a decision. We'll all abide by your decision, and the decision will be no worse today than if you had agonized all weekend over it."

So I told the producer we were sorry if we seemed less than thrilled with her offer, that it had been a bad week. I said if she wanted to join us she was welcome to do so, that we were spending between $10,000 and $15,000 to make this little jaunt that she was so interested in, and that if she made some money by selling her films of us and wanted to give us a little of it, we'd probably take it.

It was Friday afternoon, time to drive five hours to the Guadalupe for Evelyn's daughter's birthday canoe float, and I thought neither my health nor my mood could get any worse.

I was wrong.

**One Week and Counting . . .**

It was a rainy Sunday morning in a campground on the bank of the Guadalupe, and we were drinking birthday champagne and eating french toast. Evelyn had rounded up food and boats and forty people for her daughter Kay's annual river birthday party. The day before, Evelyn and I had paddled together and made a start at getting our communications down for paddling as a team in whitewater. And now we were discussing the rapids we'd paddle today.

Holding my plate in one hand, I adjusted the position of the full-sized lawn chair in which I was sitting so that it wouldn't lean at such a precarious angle on the bumpy, grassy slope. As I settled into it, it toppled sideways and I caught my weight with my legs. Suddenly I found myself on the ground, experiencing a sickening sensation I'd felt only twice in my life: My knee was dislocated. The top part of my leg was pointed in one direction and the bottom part in another, but nobody could see it inside my voluminous Gore-Tex rain pants.

"Steve! Steve!" I called between clenched teeth to my brother, who had just been handed his breakfast after an hour's wait. "My knee's gone out! Get over here and lift up my heel!" He set his plate on a car hood, said "Don't anybody eat that," bent over me, and quickly and gently popped the joint back into place.

As the hot flash of pain flowed up my neck and face, I felt faint and lay back on the ground. "The fire, the fire!" everyone began to scream. "Well, sonofabitch!" my brother exclaimed impatiently and pulled me a few feet away. Not only had I wrenched my knee out of socket, but I had collapsed into the smoldering coals of last night's campfire in my new $120 Gore-Tex rain jacket.

"I think it's gonna be one of those days," I mumbled.

I lay there on my back in the wet grass, wiping involuntary tears from my eyes, trying to keep from fainting or throwing up. Mercifully, the others ate their breakfast and drank their champagne and no one asked me how I felt. "More toast, y'all!" Evelyn announced cheerfully, waving her spatula in the air.

All I could think was that my knee has picked a helluva time to do this. It had done it only twice before, under equally unexpected circumstances. After the first time, eight years ago when I was doing nothing more strenuous than potting plants, the doctor had put a hip-to-ankle cast on it for a month, saying if it popped out again I'd have to have surgery. It had worked O.K. for a couple of years until it popped out again as I hopped into my van to go to a job interview; for some reason, that time, I could walk on it, carefully, without a cast.

Now, lying here on the bank of the Guadalupe, less than a week before I was to leave on a three-month trip down the Yukon, I was scared. It had been five years since the knee had done this; why had it waited until now? If it wouldn't hold my weight, I'd have to wear a cast or risk forever ruining the ligaments. If I had to have a straight-leg cast from ankle to hip, how could I sit in a canoe or kneel to build a campfire or go hiking? And casts weren't supposed to get very wet. How could I wade ashore in the water and mud?

Lying there, I knew that sooner or later I had to answer the question that would determine whether the months of planning and the thousands of dollars that I'd spent were all for naught: could I walk?

I sat up, rubbed the swelling joint, gingerly flexing it. "O.K., now, I'd better see how this little maneuver works," said Evelyn, motioning to my brother to show her the technique for replacing dislocated knees. She shook her head and smiled, "If I'm gonna have a Yukon partner whose—"

"I don't think your partner can walk," I interrupted, tersely. Evelyn frowned and stared at me for a moment. I shrugged as if to say, "I'm sorry for you *and* me." Then Evelyn ignored the remark and continued the discussion with my brother.

Finally they hoisted me up, and ever so carefully, I put my weight on the wobbly, aching joint. I could stand on it (with some assistance)! It was all systems go (with caution) for the Yukon! Even my Gore-Tex jacket survived.

Our last week would prove to be no less frantic than all the others, but I began to feel a sense of relief. One by one, loose ends were being tied up. Soon, mercifully, we'd be on our way, ready or not.

On Monday, I realized I had studied book contracts and publishers all I could and that it was time to make a decision. I called up Norman Simpson at Berkshire Traveller Press. Alone, among the others, he had been direct and specific from the first moment we talked. He was willing to sign a contract before the trip even started, and he would put up a small cash advance to show his good faith. Because his was a small, personal publishing house, he could make such decisions over the phone, and he already had a publishing timetable worked out. It had been clear from the start that he was enthusiastic and pleasantly tickled with the idea of someone who'd never seen the North setting out to paddle the whole Yukon, with three other women, yet. And he was willing to gamble on an unpublished writer who had the *chutzpah* to claim she could write a book about it. In short, he *believed,* and he thought the whole thing would be a lot of fun.

"Norman," I said, when he answered the phone, "let's do it!"

"O.K.," he laughed, "when do you leave?"

"In four days," I said. He said he'd put a check in the mail immediately. I was halfway there to becoming an author. Now all I had to do was paddle 2,000 miles down the Yukon and return to write the book on nights and weekends as I began a new job as TCONR's executive director.

There were traveler's checks and hospitalization and theft insurance to buy. There was diarrhea medicine to be bought. There were food boxes to be weighed and $93 in shipment fees to be left with my parents, who would ship the stuff to us through the mails at the appropriate times. There was still the unfinished TCONR mailing, whose completion finally required drafting into service my entire family, plus in-laws. Mother's washing machine was broken and all the clothes I planned for the Yukon were still muddy from White Rock Lake. Something was wrong with the starter on my van, so that every time I had to limp into someplace to buy film or return somebody's dehydrator, I had to leave the car running with the keys in it.

All the while, I exercised my knee by flexing it while wearing ankle weights, and avoided making sudden turns when walking (er, limping) around.

There were calls from all sorts of old and new friends who'd heard about the trip. They all professed the same desire to do something like this, someday, and the same excuses for why they couldn't right now. We had come to realize that they really didn't want to do it, or they'd be doing it. One acquaintance, who made twice as much money as I did, said it must be nice to be able to afford to take off work for three months. None of us could "afford" to do this. But you do what you have to do; you jeopardize your job, move out of your apartment, sell your car (Sue had sold one of hers to get some cash), take out a loan, or whatever it takes. Only one fellow, a friend from the Downriver Club, seemed to admit his own feelings about our undertaking. "I know I'd enjoy the river," he said, "but I'm not sure I'd want to go through all the preparations for something like that."

"There *are* some preparations," I grinned understatedly. "And you suppose you've got all the gear you'd need until you start thinking it'll have to last three solid months; then you begin to order this and that and pretty soon you've replaced and doubled the volume of everything you started out with."

"Think of it this way," somebody else said. "You're doing nothing more than researching and buying the same amount of equipment you'd buy during a lifetime of canoeing and backpacking, but you're doing it all in a two-month span!"

"But be grateful," still another suggested. "Now you've got everything you'll ever need. You'll be all set for the Amazon!"

There was radio interview after newspaper interview after TV interview. The reporters always asked why we wanted to do the trip. If they had to ask, I thought, they probably wouldn't understand the answer, but we tried to be patient. They usually tried to play up the grizzly bear angle, whereupon we usually claimed we'd be more likely to receive bodily injury from a rattlesnake in Texas than a grizzly on the Yukon. (Evelyn had had plenty of rattlesnakes on her front porch at the farm, but never a single grizzly.) They often asked whether we had any fears or worries, at which point Jude sometimes mentioned that the hardest thing on the trip would be getting along with each other in close quarters for 2,000 miles. It was a concern, certainly, but I wondered whether, if Jude expected not to get along with us, she might behave in such a way as to cause her expectation to come true. She always added that she thought we could handle any personality difficulties we might encounter, though, so I pushed the statement to the back of my mind. I had plenty of other things to worry about right now.

The reporters usually asked us if we were trying to make any particular statement or prove anything. No, we said. We didn't think anything needed to be proved. "We would like to invite others, though," I added in one interview, "to realize that you *can* take off for three months and go do whatever you want to do, if you just put your mind to it. . . . A lot of people are envious of us; they see this trip as something they could never do. But anybody can do it. Just make up your mind and go do it."

Invariably, both male and female reporters seemed to express through their questions some doubt about whether we knew what we were doing. Maybe that was because we were so flip and upbeat about the whole thing. The reporters seemed so serious about it all.

"What's the longest river trip you've ever taken?" they'd ask.

"Two weeks," we'd chuckle.

"Have you ever seen the Yukon?"

"No. Evelyn's the only one who's ever set foot in Alaska."

"Have you ever camped in grizzly country?"

"Not so's you could tell it."

The clincher, though, was always, "How have you trained for this grueling expedition? Have you established a daily schedule of running, paddling, calisthenics . . . ?"

We'd knit our brows, look the reporter intently in the eye and say, "We've been taking a lot of naps in the sun." That pretty well summed up what we intended to do on the Yukon, we told them, but they never believed us.

They'd usually wind up the interview by asking if we planned any big trips in the future. "Personally, no," Jude made it clear in one interview, shaking her head and grinning at Sue and me, "but from the rumor mill, I understand there's discussion of South America."

"I want to do the Amazon in South America," I said, "Evelyn wants the Nile in Africa, and Sue's got her eye on a river in Australia, but Evelyn says you can only run Australian rivers during monsoon season or some such. We might have to compromise."

"I still haven't seen the Trinity below downtown Dallas," Jude concluded the interview, amid laughter from Sue and me and the reporter.

Now that the media had gotten interested, we were real, we had legitimacy. Thus, one night after watching us on the evening news, my father decided I really was going to the Yukon. He had been painting boats and fastening handles on boxes and designing floating trumpet cases for weeks, but not until now did it dawn on him that I was going really far from home, down a really long river, to a place where there might be a tiny bit of danger. The same thing had dawned on Evelyn's husband. They began to raise all sorts of questions as if we'd never thought of them. How would we purify our water? Were we taking a gun? Did we have enough food? What if somebody got sick? (Never mind that we had a doctor and a nurse with us.) As they became more worried, they became more impressed and began proudly telling the people at their offices. Evelyn and I had both appeared on TV about environmental issues dozens of times, but somehow this had really caught their attention.

People's reactions to the journey fell along predictable lines. Everybody we talked to, including the media, was a little impressed and thought what we were doing was a little crazy, a little fun, a lot of hard work, and very admirable. There was a tad of disbelief in their voices— even as we packed to go—but they sincerely wished us luck, and we could tell they intended to do some worrying for us. And they wanted to help, to be in some small way a part of the trip.

"Beth," said Tom Anderson, one day, "I want you to come over and go through our garage, and if there's anything at all you need—a fishing rod, life jackets, paddles, a boat, anything at all—I'd be honored if you'd take it."

In the end, I had no idea how much I'd spent on equipment or food, or how much my gear or the food weighed, or whether it would all fit into the boat. I did know that I had lost about one month's salary, in addition to the three months' I'd planned on losing, because Yukon stuff had taken up so much of my time during April and May that I worked only half time. Jude, like me, had told her superiors she wanted to quit so she could paddle the Yukon for three months, and as happened with me, they said they valued her work enough that she could have her job back when she returned. Evelyn, too, would have her job when she returned.

In the end, none of the TV stations or independent film companies or newspapers who wanted to accompany us on parts of the river came up with money to send themselves. None of the magazines who were interested in a story offered to send a photographer to meet us on the river. Although we received quite a few price discount offers, no company or person came forward with any cash. And we never did find any dehydrated beer.

Finally, it was Friday afternoon, and the weight of nine months' preparation began to ease off my back. Whatever hadn't been done wasn't going to be done; whatever had been forgotten was going to stay forgotten; whoever was trying to reach me wouldn't do so for three months. I felt giddy.. Mother had taken off work early to help with the last-minute crises she knew I'd be embroiled in, and now she sat at the kitchen table madly sticking clear contact paper onto yet more sheet music, mumbling once again that she couldn't believe I really wanted to take seventy songs. We were due at Sue's in ten minutes.

"Head 'em up, move 'em out," I said. "I think I'll go float the Yukon."

# 4 as far as bolivia . . .

At 5 P.M. on May 28, 1982, Mother and I drove to the Texas Women's Yukon River Expedition launch site—the alley behind Sue's house—which writhed with friends and family who'd come to see us off. There were the canoes tied on top of Sue's ancient orange pickup truck, "Big Orange," and Jude was cramming the last of the gear into its camper shell. Barbara's hatch-back, "The Little Spook," would carry people and a little gear. As we tied the last ropes, discovered forgotten paddles, and claimed riding places, our pal Jim Bridges kept a cold beer in everyone's hand. My father, who had taken off work early to meet us, checked every knot on every rope and peered with awe at the incredible amount of gear that master-packer Jude had successfully stuffed into one vehicle. There was even a rollaway double bed in there, atop the gear. Mother had made a butcher-paper banner that said, "Good luck, Pilgrims!" We stretched it across Big Orange and posed for pictures.

"I thought there'd be a photographer from the paper here," said Evelyn.

"Well," said Jude, "for a half-hour there's been one standing in the bushes in the front yard peering into our living room."

We asked the photographer inside and posed for yet another picture. Jim Bridges, beaming excitement and well-wishing, presented us with a bottle of Bailey's Irish Cream. "To six women with balls," said the card. We laughed and accepted the slightly sexist compliment, which was offered with the highest affection. We toasted "six women with balls!" as the photographer clicked away. Wendy and Gonzo raced around the living room, perhaps sensing that something was up and they'd be cared for by a neighbor for three months. My parents hovered on the fringe of the chaos shaking their heads and smiling.

There were kisses and hugs, tears from my mother and a "y'all be careful" from my father, then we lumbered out of the driveway—six women, two canoes, two cars, and about a half-ton of gear.

Evelyn and I sprawled gleefully on the bed inside the hot pickup camper, where two full ice chests sat within reach, and popped the tops of the first of many, many cold beers.

"I'm so glad to get the hell out of Dodge!" Evelyn toasted at passing motorists.

"Here we are, partner!" I held up a beer. Floating the whole Yukon River had to be a cinch compared to what we'd been through for the past nine months.

Evelyn picked up the little Magic Slate that Jude had placed in the camper for communicating with the occupants of the cab. "Sue, did you bring your titty?" Evelyn wrote and held the slate against the glass, as the two of us giggled like schoolgirls. Sue smiled and nodded. Evelyn scribbled, "Chicken!" and held it against the glass.

After a few hours Evelyn and I joined Barbara and Jane in the Little Spook. We had gone through quite a few beers by this time and were feeling mischievous. Sue and Jude were behind us in Big Orange, and as we sped down the highway through the darkness, a thought occurred to me. I suggested to Evelyn, beside me in the back seat, that we "moon" our cohorts.

"I am fifty-one years old and I've never mooned anyone in my life," slurred Evelyn, with as much indignation as she could muster.

"Good Lord, it's high time you learned!" I countered.

"O.K.," she tittered.

With Big Orange right behind us, Evelyn and I stood in the seat, dropped our drawers, and stuck our behinds up in the hatch-back window, laughing so hard we could scarcely breathe. Over the citizens' band radio came a flurry of laughter from Sue and Jude.

"Congratulations," I shook Evelyn's hand when we'd gotten our pants back up. "I told you we'd learn all kinds of new things on this trip."

By the time we pulled into a Mexican restaurant in Wichita Falls for dinner, Evelyn and I were staggering ever so slightly from the couple of six-packs we'd consumed, and Sue and Jude weren't much better off. We slid into a booth and caused a minor scene with our loud laughter.

"Hey, where are Jane and Barb?" Sue asked. Evelyn and I rolled our eyes, grinned, and said they were out in the parking lot jogging, which they were. We couldn't believe it either.

"Well, to heck with that," I said, lofting a margarita, "I'm gonna sit here and gorge on tortillas and tostados and enchiladas!"

We took turns driving through the night, stopped for breakfast with friends of Sue's in New Mexico, and ended up in the afternoon picnicking on the lawn of a forlorn gas station beside the highway in Arizona. As we passed around barbecued brisket left over from one of Evelyn's gatherings, Jude's spinach balls and popcorn cake, and Jane's party mix of pretzels and crackers and nuts, we studied the map to pick a route to Seattle. Someone suggested a brief fling in Las Vegas. Jude, who'd never been there, let out an excited whoop, and Jane and Barbara seemed thrilled at the prospect of Vegas's cheap food. So we piled into the cars and headed for The Strip.

Into the glittering city we whizzed about ten o'clock. All the cheap motels were full, and the expensive ones had a two-night minimum that we thought was positively unAmerican. So we decided to explore the town and worry later about where we'd sleep. We split up: Jane and Barbara headed for the $1.49 cafeteria special, Sue and Jude set out for the nearest casino, and Evelyn and I strolled proudly in our wool pants and T-shirts into an expensive Chinese restaurant, where we were seated in the far corner. When we met back at Big Orange at midnight, as agreed, the others had the mattress and half the gear strung out all over the parking lot. One ice chest had overturned, and water had soaked through the mattress, through two or three layers of baggage, and was now dripping out the tailgate opening. Jude was in a surly mood, as if it were our fault; it had been a long thirty hours since we'd left Dallas. A few miles down the highway we pulled off the road into the desert, threw our sleeping bags down on the rocky earth beneath the stars, and went to sleep.

At 6 A.M., Evelyn dragged me from my sleep to show her how to work my stove to make her morning coffee, to which she was an avowed addict. Then I crawled back into my bag for a few moments' rest. Evelyn wiggled into her bag beside me on the groundcloth we shared and spilled some coffee on my bag, drawing a mild outburst about bears from me. Barbara, meanwhile was proclaiming loudly the virtues of her air-filled sleeping pad.

"This thing is wonderful!" she said. "Look, I'm here on these rocks and I slept like a *baby!*" She sat up and realized that during the night she'd slid off the pad and had been sleeping directly on the rocks. We laughed at her lavish praise for a pad she hadn't slept on. "Guess I was really tired," she shrugged.

We sat on the ground and nibbled leftover sausage and biscuits and peanut butter. Jude's mood was much improved. She smiled and admitted, "Well, I've gotten my snit out of the way; who'll be next?" We laughed it off and hit the road.

Through Death Valley National Monument we drove, enjoying the hazy purple hues of the mountains and the bright flowers that waved in the desert breeze, marveling at the long vistas over glaring white saltpans. Somehow, we couldn't synchronize our pit stops. Between the coffee-drinkers and the beer-drinkers, every few miles we were obliged to make a quick stop beside some cactus or sagebrush. About halfway through the valley in the afternoon heat, some of us could no longer resist riding shirtless down the semi-deserted highway. Every time we came to a crossroads, though, there was a mad scramble to don our apparel.

Soon we had climbed from the glassy below-sea-level heat of the lowest place in the United States, up to the frozen lakes and 10,000-foot peaks of Yosemite National Park. The Tioga Pass road had been open but a few days, and a solid wall of snow higher than Big Orange loomed, tunnel-like, on either side of us. Most of the campgrounds were closed; those open were full. The sun had already dipped behind the mountains and there was no time to hike the minimum required mile down a back-country trail to camp. So we pulled off onto a still-closed branch road, grabbed whatever gear was handy, and carried it a hundred feet or so up a steep snowbank behind some big rocks that we pretended would hide our illegal campsite. We figured we'd set up camp, eat, and sleep, and if a ranger spotted us, we'd move. We ducked behind the rocks when cars went by. Evelyn gallantly carried my pack to spare my still-swollen knee, but even so, I feared another dislocation as I slipped and slid on the snow and ice. We each claimed a niche between some rocks for our sleeping bags; we would forgo tents to escape discovery by park officials.

"Remember, we're in bear country," I mother-henned. "No food near the sleeping bags."

"If they've got any sense they're probably still hibernating!" somebody muttered, shivering. But we did set up the stoves and "kitchen" a token few dozen yards from the "bedroom." At first my stove refused to light, but when it did it began to spout flames ominously from its side.

"Oh, it always does that," I said, trying to remain nonchalant, as the others crept away. Barbara's stove finally got the stew boiling.

"Where's Jane—jogging over the pass through the snow?" I asked.

"You're not gonna believe this," somebody answered. "She's down in the snowbank beside the trout stream—the one that still has ice lining its banks—taking a bath and washing her hair!"

"You know," Jane smiled meekly, when she trudged up the hill to join us, "I got to thinking as I sort of stood on a log that was kind of sticking out over the stream—what if I fell in? That water is really rushing through that creek; you all might not hear me. So I took a real quick bath."

We weren't really set up for camping and cooking—most of our gear was still packed away—so the six of us ate dinner using one flashlight, two forks, two spoons, and two cups. Nor were most of our cold-weather clothes accessible; when we'd left Dallas in 100° heat, it hadn't occurred to us that forty-eight hours later we'd be camping in the snow without a tent. In the dark, we shivered, drank Bailey's Irish Cream in hot coffee and thought of Jim Bridges, admired the rising moon, and watched silver sparkles creep across the snowbanks. Evelyn finally dug the last chunk of cork from a wine bottle with a pocket knife and triumphantly took a hearty swallow, only to discover that the wine had turned to vinegar.

We stumbled down the hill to the bedroom, where everyone but me had spread their sleeping bags out hours before. Now they were covered with a cold, thick coat of dew; Evelyn had turned back the top of hers a few feet, and the *inside* of hers was soaking wet. I had always supposed there was some rational reason why I never spread my bag out before I was ready to get into it, but I thought it had more to do with snakes and scorpions and ticks than dew. Evelyn's warm clothes were still buried somewhere in Big Orange, so she slept in jeans, T-shirt, and life jacket. She and I were wedged into a severely sloping nook between two big rocks that we hoped had retained a little of the sun's heat and would block the wind. As I drifted to sleep, trying to maintain my uphill position without completely crushing Evelyn against the boulder, the forest seemed incredibly quiet and peaceful. Directly above us, through the dark branches of a stout lodgepole pine, peeked a creamy half-moon and a few distant stars.

In the morning, I hoped the ice coating Evelyn's sleeping bag might keep her in bed a little longer, but no such luck. At the crack of dawn she was clinking and thumping and muttering around with the stove for coffee water. About the time I poked my frozen face from the sleeping bag, she set the stove two feet from me and held a match to it. She planned to get back into her sleeping bag to await hot coffee, and she wanted the stove within arm's reach.

"Hey, get that thing away," I said, remembering all the crispy critter stories I'd heard about fire and synthetic sleeping bags. "Besides, you're supposed to clear a little place down to bare earth around it."

"Aw, you worry too m—" she began to say, but the stove had gone wild and flames were not only shooting up into the air but spreading along the ground through the pine needles, toward my nose. She kicked the stove a few feet away and turned it off, I poured coffee water on the fire with one hand and struggled to escape my sleeping bag with the other.

"Well, why didn't you tell me your stove wasn't safe?" Evelyn asked, when I finally quit cursing. We were going to have to reach an understanding about this coffee routine, I could see.

Courtesy of Jane's stove, we sat for an hour drinking hot coffee, trying to get warm. Though the sun was out, our small thermometers showed it was only 30°. We lit my stove again and it erupted into a three-foot flame that wouldn't die until Jane smothered it with a cookpot. Sitting among the snow and boulders, we played the trumpet and harmonica and munched sausage balls; then we slid over the glaze of ice to the truck, threw in the gear, and hit the road.

We stopped briefly to wander through one of Yosemite's meadows and across one of her bald granite outcroppings, but then, realizing that we were still far from Seattle and that Yosemite's main scenic attractions would be overrun with tourists on this Memorial Day weekend anyway, we reluctantly headed out of the Sierra Nevada down into the Sacramento Valley. Stopping at the first winery, we sampled their wares and made a valiant but unsuccessful attempt to convince them to donate the expedition's champagne. Then we drove for hours up the straight, flat valley past fields and farmhouses, spotting squirrel after squirrel perched (for what reason we never knew) atop pole after pole of a barbed-wire fence.

That night the six of us shared a motel room, which offered our first shower since leaving Dallas. Our bodies and clothes weren't the only things that had acquired strange smells. From the pickup camper wafted an unfamiliar scent that grew more disgusting by the hour in the California heat. We had no idea whether it was rotten food, mildewed mattress, dirty feet, or what. Each time someone opened the tailgate, she would sniff through the gear to ferret out the offending article, but to no avail. Jude finally concluded that her bluejeans were the source and sealed them in a plastic bag. We thought the mystery was solved, until Sue walked into the motel room with some of her gear and the rest of us dropped what we were doing and chorused, "What just came in? That's it!" We positively identified one of Sue's insulated boots as the culprit. Apparently it had been soaked in the great Las Vegas ice-chest upset and had fermented for two days in the hot camper. We banished it from motel room and camper, so Sue tied it up into her canoe on top of the truck.

The next two days were full of long drives around curving mountain roads, through wet forests, along ocean cliffs and beaches. We took full advantage of the CB for intercommunication: when Jude wasn't reading aloud some racy Southern novel, Jane and Evelyn were giving us an account of the plants and birds we were seeing, or I was making up stories about the cute hitchhikers we'd picked up at the last intersection. There were long philosophical discussions. Jane and Evelyn were quizzing me one day about whether I wanted marriage, kids, and such.

"Oh, I don't know about diapers or mortgages or china," I said. "I'd be happy just to find somebody who sleeps late on rainy Sunday mornings and who'll carry the tent if I carry the food."

On Wednesday morning as we sped the last few hundred miles into Seattle, Evelyn and I had an enjoyable and rambling talk about everything from income tax to relationships. I voiced the notion that every person is a composite of qualities that are admirable and enjoyable in some circumstances and irritating in others. Some of the same things that make someone seem earnest and creative and productive might also make her seem self-centered and disorganized and demanding. We were about to have three months in which to examine this phenomenon in action. I knew in my case, for instance, that the same concern for detail and organization that makes me reliable and thorough, also makes me aggravating if you're not in the mood for structure. By the same token, the wonderful unpredictability and disdain for convention that made Evelyn zany and fun-loving could at times be irritating; as, for instance, when six people were negotiating noon traffic in unfamiliar territory in two separate cars, communicating by CB, trying to find Twelve Baskets Restaurant in Bellevue, and Evelyn was prattling about prickly-pear jelly.

Which she was now doing. We suddenly found ourselves in the greater Seattle area, five days and 2,500 miles—or about halfway—toward our preliminary goal: the banks of the Yukon.

We did find Twelve Baskets, and they did have our nine cases of dehydrated food that they were generously contributing to the cause. We ate lunch at their open-air restaurant and realized that if their organic dehydrated food was anything like their organic restaurant food, we were in for a gourmet river trip.

The next two days whizzed by with a press conference at Twelve Baskets, a Seattle bus tour, packaging and shipping the Twelve Baskets food to Alaska, last-minute shopping at outdoor equipment stores, and replacing my defective stove valve, which we learned had been the cause of our unintentional bonfires at Yosemite.

On our last night in the Lower 48, we launched happy hour with a vengeance. Sitting in a bar awaiting a table in a big seafood restaurant, we watched ships come and go in Puget Sound, consumed bushelsful of shrimp balls, and downed beer and bourbon.

"Oh Janie!" cried Barbara, "try this Rainier beer, you'll love it!"

Jane customarily drank very little, especially not beer. But her curiosity got the best of her. "Well, maybe one," she smiled coyly as we ordered her one.

Soon we were all in love with Rainier beer and our conversation grew seemingly more witty with each round. Just about the time we started a contest to see who could curl our tongues or cross one eye or perform other anatomical tricks, the waitress dragged us away to the dinner we'd forgotten we came for.

"We're gonna eat seafood? Wonderful!" we stood up, knocking over a full glass of beer.

The clams and crabs and potatoes and chowder sobered us enough to reminisce about the first time we'd met each other, seated on the floor around Jane's wood stove almost seven months before.

"I thought Evelyn was *crazy*," said Sue, smiling. "Haven't yet decided if I was right or wrong."

We clamored for Sue's and Jude's life histories. Sue had grown up in Missouri, in a strongly religious family. We were amazed to learn that she almost married a theology student. But then she had determined to become a doctor. She had announced the decision to her family one Thanksgiving Day, and when they suggested that a future surgeon should carve the turkey, she obliged and nearly cut off her thumb. She had been one of only six women in her graduating class at the University of Missouri. She had married a fellow doctor whom she met in med school, and they had spent six years together in Texas and Colorado, before their divorce. She had no children.

Jude was born in Indiana. She grew up in Texas in a large, boisterous family where there was never a dull monent, and had remained there to earn her nursing degree when her family moved to Milwaukee. She had been heavily involved in all kinds of sports in college.

Then Jude dropped a minor bombshell. She hadn't fully decided to paddle the Yukon, she revealed, until after our campout on the Neches River in March. It was unthinkable that anyone among us had required any coaxing to paddle through America's last frontier. The rest of us had jumped instantly and enthusiastically at the first mention of the Yukon. We learned that Jude had initially refused Sue's invitation, but after seeing how much Sue wanted to go and after being slowly brainwashed by the Alaska literature Sue had placed strategically around the house, Jude eventually had become interested. It was one thing, said Jude, for Sue who was established professionally as head of her own firm to flit off to the Yukon for three months, but it was quite another for Jude, who was just beginning to go places in her career, to jeopardize her professional standing.

"You do whatcha gotta do," I said.

First thing next morning, upon her return from the coffee machine,

Evelyn tiptoed over sleeping bodies and backpacks and ice chests in our motel room and dropped on each of us a copy of the *Seattle Post-Intelligencer*. In it was the first story about ourselves we'd actually seen in print. The headline said, "Bears or no bears, six women will canoe down the Yukon." The article began, "Sue Sherrod is no bear fan, but she expects to see a lot of them over the next three months." The article quoted Sue as saying, "In December, when we were really getting into heavy planning, for two weeks I couldn't sleep because I was afraid of bears. At least now I've got all my worrying out of the way."

"You didn't tell us about that!" we teased.

"Johnson said the main dangers will be hypothermia and bears," the article continued. "Then there's the river itself, an icy, swift-flowing body sometimes clogged with debris, often more than a mile wide and filled with islands. But Judith Hammett, a nurse, believes they are ready. 'When you're prepared, you're not afraid,' she said."

"Right on, Jude," said Evelyn, settling back on the bed with her coffee. With a wave of her hand across the warehouse of gear that was our motel room, she added, "Good Lord, if we can't hack it for three months with all this crap we might as well give up."

Today was the Big Day—ferry-boarding day—and we launched into action. Sue and Jude and Barbara dashed to the washateria with our huge collective mound of dirty clothes. Wearing only a life jacket in the cool room, I shuffled my gear from duffel bag to backpack, and vice versa, trying in vain to compact it so I could easily carry it onto the ferry.

In an hour the laundry brigade stormed into the room and announced that a defective commercial dryer had just destroyed several hundred dollars' worth of Sue's and Jude's ultra-warm, ultra-lightweight polypropylene long underwear. Brimming with anger, they held up the shriveled garments, the legs of which were now about a foot-and-a-half long. Under cheaper and less immediate circumstances, it might have been funny, but when you're heading for Alaska in a few hours, the loss of a key component of your already-lean wardrobe is downright dangerous.

One last time, we threw the gear into the truck; Sue and Jude dropped the rest of us off at the Pike Street Market on the waterfront and drove on to an equipment store for more underwear. The others made for the open-air food stalls; I slipped off to a sitdown Mexican restaurant for one last enchilada and the only five minutes of peace and solitude (if I wanted to count this crowded tourist stop with mariache music) that I'd had in seven days and 2,500 miles. Since I had lived alone off and on for years, I was still having trouble coping with being thrust into a group of six women on a cross-country trip.

When we strolled back to the ferry dock, Sue and Jude had just returned with new underwear. The Alaska state ferry system had advised us months before that ferry passengers were allowed to board only with what they could carry in one trip. Canoes would be admitted *if* space were available, and it would "probably" be O.K. if we had "a few life jackets or paddles" in them. Any gear beyond the carry-on amount, they said, was freight and must be boxed and taken to a trucking company the day before, to ride to Skagway inside a truck on a ferry which might or might not be the same ferry we were on. It all sounded confusing, expensive, and liable to leave one sitting in Skagway for days waiting on one's gear. So now, nervous as cats, we conspired to make a half-ton of gear and two boats look like mere carry-on luggage for six women.

The key was to be inconspicuous, which wasn't easy with this bunch. We caused a minor flap with the entrance guards when we rolled into the dock area with two overloaded cars, neither of which was to board the ferry but both of which we wanted to park there while we unloaded. I had this gnawing feeling that Evelyn would do something crazy, Sue's wig would fall off, my knee would dislocate itself, or something else would draw attention to us and our gear.

We sought to park close to the loading area to avoid parading our excessive gear across the entire parking lot, so I set out to sweet-talk the head cop. "I'll bat my eyelashes," I told Sue and Jude.

Across the parking lot I strolled, dodging the hundreds of motor homes and tractor-trailer rigs and station wagons and jeeps and pickup trucks that stern-looking cops were ushering into position.

"Howdy!" I called in my best Southern drawl to a harried-looking older man who was whistling vehicles into a lane. "You're 'bout as busy as a New York traffic cop in rush hour!" I sympathized. He warmed up immediately, motioned me to safety near him, and asked, "Where you from, honey?" His name was Sy. I said we had a couple of canoes and a little gear and were wondering if we might pull up under the "no parking" sign for a teensy-weensy minute. He said that was a coincidence because some other women had just pulled in with canoes and a whole bunch of stuff in a great big orange pickup, and I had to admit they were me. So much for anonymity. He paused for an eternity to shout directions to a wayward truck, then, mercifully, Sy said we could park for a few minutes right at the loading dock.

I gave the signal, Big Orange rolled into place, and the six of us set upon the vehicle like flies on fresh watermelon. Ropes flew through the air, down came the canoes; Jude heaved bag after bag after backpack from the bed of the truck and we lugged them to the staging area. Then, Jude and Barbara sped away in the cars, severing some vague umbilical cord to civilization; Big Orange would spend the next three months in a field near Twelve Baskets in Bellevue and the Little Spook would stay with a friend of Barbara's in Seattle. The plan was for Jude and Barbara to return to the dock by bus in time to help us carry the gear onto the ferry. Jane and Sue and Evelyn and I hurriedly piled the gear in the boats, hoping it would appear less voluminous there. Once we had the gear tied in (a token gesture against theft), I surveyed the scene and tried to relax.

Hundreds of people milled around the parking lot and joined the boarding line. There was more gear in one place than one could imagine, and three-fourths of it seemed to be ours. Our plan to remain inconspicuous had failed miserably. Perhaps it was the two boats with "Bering Sea or Bust" on their sides. Perhaps it was our cowboy hats, or the mountain of gear that spilled from our boats, or our lack of menfolk. For whatever reason, a steady stream of people walked up to meet us and take our pictures.

We set up lawn chairs and soaked in the ambience. Strewn across the parking lot among the shuffling throng were shiny, new, brightly colored gear and old, dirty, grease-stained gear. There were bicycles and Mopeds and backpacks and duffel bags and sea trunks and suitcases and cardboard boxes. There were dogs and kids and bearded men in flannel shirts and teenage girls in shorts and dowdy women in pant-suits. All this was just in the foot-traffic line. Beyond, spread a sea of vehicles, each with windows taped, or wire grates in front of the headlights, or some other scheme to prevent inevitable breakage from gravel along the Alaska Highway.

In short, sprawled along that dock was every thing and every person of every age and size and condition imaginable. The scene was blissful chaos, and Evelyn was in her element. She flitted from clump to clump of people, mentioning in passing that we were about to paddle 2,000 miles down the Yukon River. Sue scribbled an article for the Dallas Downriver newsletter, Jane skipped off to phone her husband.

I fancied the scene a modern-day stampede, without quite the dimensions or the desperation of the Klondike Stampede of 1897-98. Perhaps Americans are becoming as covetous of the recreation and beauty of wild places like Alaska as the stampeders were for its gold. After all, here were six ordinary working women from Dallas, Texas, who'd left jobs and husbands to answer the lure of the North. When the early national parks of the West, like Yellowstone and Yosemite, were preserved for the public in the late 1800s, some believed that they weren't worth setting aside because they were too far away. "No one will ever go there," critics had said. Today, traffic is bumper-to-bumper through these scenic treasures now cherished by the nation.

In line beside us wiggled a lovable, eager flock of senior citizens who would ferry-hop and bicycle through the hamlets along the Inside Passage. Among them, beaming with excitement, were two older women wearing knickers and helmets. "Well, we could've taken one of those fuddy-duddy, plush cruise ships or air-conditioned bus tours, but that would've been too easy!" they exclaimed. We knew just what they meant, we said, shaking their hands.

Just then we discovered that I'd accidentally rendered useless Sue's and Jude's only water jug, three-gallon "Big Green," by leaving its cap in the pickup, but a quick call to Twelve Baskets caught Jude and she said she'd bring it with her. Meanwhile, rumor had it that they would open the gate to begin loading soon, so the four of us decided we'd better see if we could lift the canoes without Barbara and Jude. "One, two, three!" we synchronized our effort, lifting the canoe two inches off the ground for three seconds. Sue and Evelyn scurried off and soon returned with two Air Force guys who said they'd help after they loaded their van aboard the ferry.

Just as Kate the purser strode to the gate in her crisp navy blazer and skirt and officer's cap, and the multitudes began to surge and murmur in preparation for the race to get the best sleeping places on deck, Jude and Barbara rushed breathlessly into the parking lot. The cars were safely stored, they reported, but Barbara had unintentionally left her camera in hers, thirty minutes away. We'd worry about that later; right now we had to pull off our loading caper. We hoisted our packs. Evelyn, Sue, and Jude had never worn their new packs, and we all struggled to help them fasten buckles, adjust hipbelts and shoulder straps. Sue discovered that a bottle of lotion had leaked throughout one pocket of her pack. "Bear bait, bear bait," we chimed. Then Evelyn announced she'd wrenched something in her back; meanwhile, my pack was so overloaded I feared I'd reinjure my knee. Standing strategically between Kate the purser and our mass of gear, we asked if we could make one trip onto the ferry with our packs and then return for the canoes. "Go on," she sighed. She flung open the gate and we trudged with our burdens up the steep gangplank into the ship, up four narrow flights of stairs, and onto the top-deck solarium, where we staked out our sleeping quarters. The solarium was a big room sheltered on top and on three sides, but with an open deck at the end. Here we would sleep on the floor with a couple of hundred other lively characters for the 1,300-mile journey up the Inside Passage.

Back down to the boats we raced, where we discovered we had to wait in line to bring the canoes aboard. Barb dashed off to nab her camera and we awaited the final test of whether Kate the purser would buy the notion that the heap of gear it took us and several recruits to carry was non-freight. When the magic moment came, the five of us, plus two Air Force guys, plus a backpacker with a gorgeous mustache, staggered with one canoe a hundred yards up the gangplank onto the lower deck. A dock worker suggested we might put it under a semitrailer. We shoved it across the floor under the trailer up onto a mooring block. I could practically hear the aluminum hull, pressured with a good 700 pounds of gear, popping its rivets. Then it was back down to the parking lot ("Just one more quick trip?" we grinned at Kate), and up the gangplank we trotted with the second canoe. We shoved it into place, gave a victory shout, and shook hands all around. Now the only remaining element for successful completion of the caper—other than reuniting ourselves with Barbara and her camera—was making sure my huge duffel bag "Big Orange" (not to be confused with the truck of the same name), which weighed at least fifty pounds and stood four feet tall and contained a couple of thousand dollars' worth of film, tape recorder, spare camera, and clothing, made its way onto the ferry. We had left it and some of Evelyn's gear on a little motorized cart that we'd heard would drive onto the ferry.

It was now after six o'clock; we had been shuffling gear and cars and sweet-talking people since just after noon. We strode down the gangplank past Kate, to whom we gave a big smile, and headed for the nearest seafood restaurant. In an hour, after a little sautéed shrimp and ice cream, we strolled back up the gangplank; far above us on the top deck, Barbara waved her camera. Kate had let her back on board though her boarding pass was with us. Kate was a good ol' gal.

Finally aboard for good, I spotted Big Orange and was advised by the crew not to leave him on the deserted bottom deck in the cart because of the possibility of theft, so I strapped him onto my back and huffed and puffed up four flights of stairs, pulling myself hand over hand by the railing, praying my quivering knee would remain in its socket. When I reached the solarium, the others had a regular little camp set up, far enough back from the edge so rain couldn't get us and far enough from the heaters at the back so we wouldn't roast. We were in a giddy mood—all of us finally together, with all of our gear. Jane was reading a bird book, Barbara was doing Yoga exercises, Sue was reading a book called *Grizzlies Don't Come Easy.* Evelyn was prone, face-down on the deck, and Jude was sitting on Evelyn's legs and pummeling her back muscles. "This is the Swedish method," grinned Jude.

"My back hurts so much I really don't think I can stand up," moaned Evelyn.

As the last rays of sunlight glinted from Seattle's skyline, big engines rumbled beneath us and the 4,000-ton M.V. *Columbia* pulled away from the dock. A cheer went up from the solarium crowd, and we dashed to the rail to wave goodbye to whomever might be on shore. At 8:15 P.M. on June 4, 1982, the second leg of our long journey to the Yukon was officially under way.

I tried to imagine that I was one of the 100,000 adventurers who had boarded ships in San Francisco or Seattle in 1897, bound for Skagway or Dyea to walk over the Coast Mountains and float down the Yukon, or for Saint Michael on the Bering Sea to journey by steamer 1,700 miles up the Yukon to Dawson City and the Klondike River where the gold was. Crossing these same waters, men left their families and businesses. Mayors abandoned their towns, clerks locked their shops and boarded ships with what they had on their backs. Dentists and poets and prostitutes and cowboys and bankers and newspapermen and carpenters and all manner of humanity stood for days in throngs along this waterfront, waiting to pay a thousand dollars for a few square feet aboard anything that would float and was headed north. Few knew the first thing about gold prospecting, but they had heard Klondike gold was so plentiful you could pick it up by the handful from the ground. They believed they'd all get rich and escape, in a few short months, the grip of the nationwide depression.

In the North they would be called "cheechakos"—newcomers, tenderfeet who had yet to experience or survive their first winter among the snows. And thousands of them had pulled away from these same docks and waved gleefully to the thousands of others still waiting for a spot on a boat. "Hurrah for the Klondike!" they had shouted to each other across the widening waters.

Tonight we would slip through the narrow Strait of Georgia and up the protected Inside Passage behind Vancouver Island. Then, hugging the ragged coastline of British Columbia, we would churn steadily through the

Pacific for a day and a half and 900 miles before we would pass the Queen Charlotte Islands and the Canadian city of Prince Rupert and arrive at Dixon Entrance, the gateway to Alaska. Our first stop would be Ketchikan, Alaska, about thirty-six hours north of Seattle. Then we would wind for another day and 400 miles among the island maze of Southeast Alaska's panhandle, pausing briefly at Wrangell, Petersburg, Auk Bay near Juneau, Haines, and finally Skagway, the end of the ferry line, 1,300 miles and 60 hours from Seattle.

"Well, here we are, let's hit the bar," I said, as Seattle disappeared behind us. Evelyn was lying motionless on her sleeping bag.

"I think I'd better pass on that," she said, rubbing her back. I jerked my head with exaggerated concern; she must be dying if she refused a beer. She grinned and said, "I'll drink my beer right here from the ice chest." Though it was against ship rules to have alcoholic beverages in the solarium, dozens of bottles were being passed around the dozens of little parties erupting among the rough-and-tumble solarium crowd.

I went below, bought a beer, and sank into a chair in the glassed-in observation room. Almost too exhausted and relieved and numb to move, I stared out over the grey-blue water, at small waves rippled by a slight wind, at low, grey cottonlike clouds. After the third time I nodded asleep, I shuffled off to bed. Above me, electric rods on the ceiling blew strange ovenlike heat into my face and beside me, a fat, young drunk guy who'd passed out hours earlier slept in his shoes and clothes.

Next morning a thumping sound awoke me. Beside us, a bald, barrel-chested man in a white T-shirt was gleefully running in place and doing vigorous jumping jacks. Evelyn raised her head and groaned, "If I could move I'd kick the crap out of that man." She winced and pulled herself upright by a post near her sleeping bag; then, bent almost double and clutching her lower back, she hobbled slowly downstairs to the coffee shop. I limped down the steps, one by one, my knee still throbbing from yesterday's strains. We made quite a pair.

The six of us nibbled Twelve Baskets cornbread muffins and Pike Street Market cherries from our big plastic food bag and marveled at the snowcapped mountains and tumbling waterfalls that closed in on both sides of the ship. The islands were absolutely thick with trees. We could see glaciers high in the mountains in the distance. Sky, water, trees, mountains, and snow all seemed tinted with blue.

John Muir, the great naturalist, fighter for wild places, and founder of the nationwide Sierra Club, had made his way by steamer through these same waters in 1879, only twelve years after "Seward's Folly" had been bought from the Russians. Muir had just spent eleven years roaming the magnificent reaches of the Sierra Nevada and other ranges in the Lower 48, but after cruising the fairyland of the Inside Passage he declared that never before had he "been embosomed in scenery so hopelessly beyond description." (*Travels in Alaska*, page 13.)

I stood on deck, bundled against the rambunctious sea wind that

whipped my hair around my face, and became mesmerized by the
unfolding scenes of crisp blues, whites, and greens. The sunny weather
that lit up all these images, which was to hold through our entire voyage,
was highly unusual for the Inside Passage, where mist and fog and endless
grey days are the norm. I tried to imagine paddling a kayak day after day,
mile after mile, through these calm, sheltered blue waters, and camping
every night on one of the thousands of islands. I fancied that this magical
gateway to the Alaskan frontier had changed little since Muir first beheld
it more than a hundred years before. Muir had written:

> The islands of the Alexander Archipelago, with the straits, channels, canals,
> sounds, passages, and fiords, form an intricate web of land and water
> embroidery sixty or seventy miles wide, fringing the lofty icy chain of coast
> mountains from Puget Sound to Cook Inlet; and, with infinite variety, the
> general pattern is harmonious throughout its whole extent of nearly a
> thousand miles. Here you glide into a narrow channel hemmed in by
> mountain walls, forested down to the water's edge, where there is no distant
> view, and your attention is concentrated on the objects close about you—
> the crowded spires of the spruces and hemlocks rising higher and higher
> on the steep green slopes; stripes of paler green where winter avalanches
> have cleared away the trees, allowing grasses and willows to spring up; zig-
> zags of cascades appearing and disappearing among the bushes and trees;
> short, steep glens with brawling streams hidden beneath alder and dogwood,
> seen only where they emerge on the brown algae of the shore; and retreating
> hollows, with lingering snow-banks marking the fountains of ancient
> glaciers. The steamer is often so near the shore that you may distinctly see
> the cones clustered on the tops of the trees, and the ferns and bushes at their
> feet. But new scenes are brought to view with magical rapidity. . . . (Travels
> in Alaska, pages 14-15.)

Soon, we began to spot dozens of bald eagles. In the Lower 48,
they are endangered, their numbers critically low for survival of the
species, but here there was one perched around every bend on every dead
spruce tree. Jane explained that they prefer bare trees without foliage,
which offer less resistance to the wind, so that the eagles' perches are not
so buffeted by the wind. Jane and Evelyn birded for hours in the
observation lounge or on deck, spotting Arctic terns, ravens, glaucous-
winged gulls, and scoters. Before long we caught sight of our first
porpoises, their dark grey bodies arcing suddenly a few feet over the
water in the ship's wake. Like us, Muir had found the porpoises irresistible.
"A merry school of porpoises, a square mile of them, suddenly appear,
tossing themselves into the air in abounding strength and hilarity, adding
foam to the waves and making all the wilderness wilder. One cannot but
feel sympathy with and be proud of these brave neighbors, fellow citizens
in the commonwealth of the world, making a living like the rest of us."
(Travels in Alaska, pages 4-5.)

Killer and humpback whales also cavort in these waters and are one of
the highlights of the usual Inside Passage journey, but we were not fortunate
enough to see any. The only sighting on the entire cruise was that of a
ranger who thought he saw a killer whale surface for a mere instant before
we pulled into Skagway at the end of the cruise.

Over a picnic lunch, we sat in our lawn chairs in the solarium and voted on which actresses would play each of us in the movie that would surely follow our triumphant arrival at the Bering Sea. After much negotiation and debate, it was settled: Jane Fonda would be Sue, Candice Bergen would play Barbara, Katharine Hepburn would have a high old time playing Evelyn, Lilly Tomlin would play me, Elizabeth Taylor would be Jane, and Brenda Vacarro would play Jude.

Evelyn spent most of the day sitting on her sleeping bag, leaning against the pole, and reading from the cornerstone of her river library. For our reading matter on this voyage most of us had chosen things like *The Call of the Wild* or Robert Service poems, but Evelyn had lugged along a two-inch-thick, four-pound hardback volume of *The Hite Report on Male Sexuality*. It provided details of the sex lives of 7,000 men, ages 13 to 97. Evelyn joked that Hite had failed to include any Yukon men in her sample, and she suggested the Texas Women's Yukon River Expedition could contribute a supplementary report. Gary, the young Air Force guy who'd helped us carry the boats and with whom we'd been flirting for hours, finally grabbed the book and began reading aloud a particularly graphic passage that soon embarrassed him into silence. Then he sat on the edge of Evelyn's sleeping bag and they had a long, quiet, serious discussion, alluding at times to various sections in the book. We watched them from afar, and the longer they talked, the more our curiosity was piqued. Soon Barb was laying odds on whether Gary would be willing to dedicate his body to science and whether Evelyn would conduct some research of her own.

In the afternoon, we hit the only open sea passage of the journey. The ship began to rock ever so slightly, but enough to make me take to my bed. The M.V. *Columbia* is the flagship of the nine-ship fleet that comprises the State of Alaska's Marine Highway System used by 300,000 passengers and 70,000 vehicles yearly. The *Columbia* is 418 feet long and 85 feet wide, with a 65-member crew and space for 1,000 passengers and 180 automobiles. Staterooms are available, but they cost more than sleeping on deck, and we thought it was a lot more fun to be in the partylike atmosphere of the solarium. Though we had no beds or dressing rooms, we were free to partake of all the important amenities—bar, showers, dining rooms, observation decks, and lounges where they showed whale movies or Klondike Stampede movies. Besides, it was wonderful to bed down each night in the crisp sea air, among hundreds of sleeping bodies and ice chests and self-supported tents, by the light of a fiery pink full moon that seemed to follow the boat.

It was through these narrow straits and channels that hundreds of boats of every description, including South African mail boats and Chinese freighters and Indian yachts, had made their way north in 1897, weathering vicious gales and commonly loaded to many times their capacity.

Dozens of ships were hauled from the boneyards, where they'd rotted for years, and were heaved into the ocean with little or no repairs. Little better than floating coffins, these unseaworthy craft plied the ocean with bilge pumps running constantly. Greenhorn captains became lost or wrecked upon unseen reefs. At least one could face his task only after gulping down the entire stock of the ship's whiskey. Some passengers died of starvation, too seasick to eat; some were swept overboard by lashing waves. Some boats were so poorly loaded that they overturned in the first rough sea and went down with all hands. Greedy shipowners often sold duplicate tickets for every berth on a ship. But even if a hapless stampeder muscled his way into command of one of the narrow wooden boxes that served as beds, he was likely to relinquish it soon enough when the excrement from the hundreds of horses and dogs on the deck above him began to leak through the floorboards into his face.

Those ships that didn't wind their way through the maze of the Inside Passage braved the storms of the open ocean to Saint Michael near the mouth of the Yukon. Many sank en route. Most of those cheechakos who did manage to reach the forlorn outpost on the coast of the Bering Sea thought nothing but a quick ride by steamer then separated them from the Klondike's lasting wealth. Little did the battered souls know that they still faced 1,700 miles up the Yukon River, that freeze-up would trap them for the winter, that it would be ten months before they would reach the Klondike, and that, when they did, all the gold fields would be staked.

I stood for awhile leaning on the stern railing, smiling at the gulls that swooped and glided behind the boat, staring into the hypnotic wake spun out behind us. I was absently imagining paddling a kayak through those vicious currents churned up by our two 9,200 horsepower diesel engines, when from nowhere the thought hit me that three months is a long time. That, of course, was what a lot of people had already tried to tell me.

Upon reaching Seattle, we had already come as far north from Dallas as the distance from Miami to New York. The ferry would double that distance north, and the Yukon would carry us almost that distance north once again. Arriving in Whitehorse where we would begin canoeing, we would be on the same latitude as the southern tip of Greenland. Before we ever reached the river, we would have come as far as Bolivia is from Dallas, and after paddling all the way down the river to the Bering Sea, we would have traveled about the same distance as from Dallas to Tierra del Fuego, the southern tip of South America, hard by Antarctica. Then there would be the return trip. . . .

We had left Dallas just over one week ago, and already it seemed as though we'd been through so much. I knew it would get easier, though, when and if we ever got on that river. The question all the reporters had asked ran through my mind: Do you really know what you're doing? "Oh, not really," I thought, looking around at the glaciers and 800-year-old trees, "but we'll figure it out as we go."

After dinner, Evelyn and Jane and I stood for hours on deck watching alpine lakes and blue-grey forested slopes and creamy waterfalls glide past. At ten o'clock, we were still waiting for the sun to go down. As it dipped lower and lower behind the mountains, golden shafts of light washed across the glassy water. We were unusually quiet, almost reverent, and there settled within me a peace that grew deeper and more satisfying and relaxing with each passing mile of unmolested earth and sea and sky. I knew that in these waters and throughout those hills, fish were swimming, bears and deer were roaming the forest, birds were soaring over the mountains, young trees were growing up to give food and shelter to animals, and old trees were dying and rotting to nourish new trees—every creature was doing what it was supposed to do, and they were all thriving beautifully.

At 5 A.M. the second morning we were awakened by a crew member bellowing at the top of his voice the name of a man reportedly sleeping in the solarium. "There's a girl passed out in the passageway who's been asking for you," said the crew member. Our medical personnel, Sue and Jude, sat bolt upright, ready to administer emergency treatment, then deduced from the crew member's demeanor that the girl was just plain old drunk. By then I was wide awake, the sun was up high anyway, and we were leaving Canadian, and entering Alaskan, waters, so I got up.

Thirty-six hours out of Seattle, we pulled into the first Alaskan port at Ketchikan, a city built partially on stilts, that seems to tumble from steep, forested mountains. We took a quick bus tour to the Totem Heritage Center and the fish hatchery, then boarded the ferry and headed north again. In the afternoon, we pulled into Wrangell, perched on the tip of fourteen-mile-long Wrangell Island. We strolled down the gravel street into the chaos of their Salmon Days celebration, which, one resident explained, was held to raise money for their Fourth of July celebration.

The village had served as a base camp for some of Muir's explorations. When he wasn't wandering the "impenetrable" woods, living off hardtack, or paddling a canoe through masses of icebergs, he was counting tree rings or seeking other clues to nature's mysteries. The local folk thought him somewhat mad. "'What can the fellow be up to?' they inquired. 'He seems to spend most of his time among stumps and weeds. I saw him the other day on his knees, looking at a stump as if he expected to find gold in it. He seems to have no serious object whatever.'" (*Travels in Alaska*, page 21.)

At least one modern-day Wrangell resident had no more affinity for those of Muir's ilk than did his predecessors. Within ten minutes of our landing, Evelyn, who happened to be wearing her "Earth—love it or leave it" T-shirt, was ambushed in a bar by a drunk logger who was ranting about the "Sahara Club" and wolves. Never one to miss a good fight, Evelyn was soon shouting something about wolves having as much right to be in Alaska as loggers. I glared at Evelyn as if to say, "Don't you *dare* let on you know me," then stood outside nibbling smoked salmon strips and watching some girls screeching and doing a cancan dance in full red skirts that they kept flipping over their faces. Shortly, Evelyn tumbled from the bar at a brisk clip, laughing.

"You want wolves?!" the logger was weaving down the dirt road after her. "I'll give you wolves. I'll trap every damn one of 'em and you can take 'em back to Texas!"

Back on board, I scurried to the dining room to enjoy yet another shrimp dinner, to watch for whales through the big windows, and to read from one of the books in the Forest Service ranger's shipboard library.

I found myself trapped next to a table of elderly stateroom types, with which the ship was crawling. This odd species was prone to discuss for the longest times the most incredibly boring things, and always at shouting volume. They were usually griping about something—why wasn't dinner ready, why weren't we seeing any whales—or complaining to a spouse about having forgotten to mail a letter, cash a traveler's check, ad nauseum. They smoked in designated nonsmoking sections, saved seats for each other, against ship rules, in the crowded observation lounge, and chattered at the top of their voices during nature films. We had already voiced the hope, half-jokingly, that in addition to smoking and non-smoking sections, the ship should have designated shouting and non-shouting sections. This staid, inflexible, sedentary crowd, whose greatest enjoyment seemed to be worrying and fussing over every little detail, was the direct opposite of the solarium crowd. The latter included women and men and children of all ages who were content sleeping on the floor (amid the guitar or flute music one could hear at any time of the day or night) and being stepped on a few times each night as people went to the bar or the bathroom.

And now, as I finished my shrimp and tried to read about Alaska's glorious glaciers and sea lions and whales, I overheard a bizarre conversation that took place in all seriousness. I couldn't help overhearing it because every word was shouted. Civilization as we know it will end by the year 2,000, they nodded gloomily. And you know why? (I thought of nuclear war, poisoned air and water. . . .) Because we'll be a cashless society. Everyone will have only one credit card, think of it. (I figured I'd adjust easily since, to date, Sears was the only outfit that saw fit to give me credit.) Then one day "they" would take even that away, they shuddered. As near as I could make out, "they" were some people in Brussels. "They" already control the world. "They" watch you back while you're watching TV and "they" have already given you a number. I shared their concern about Big Brother, but I suspected that what really frightened them was their imagined loss of those precious credit cards. I found it vaguely disturbing that five grown people seemed to be saying that freedom and the very essence of our civilization are multiple credit cards, so I gulped my strawberry shortcake and beat a retreat.

Out on deck, I joined Evelyn to admire mile after untouched forest mile of Admiralty Island. For hours we had been passing this one chunk of wild earth, home to the Tlingit Indians, who have hunted and fished these rich forests and waters for more than a thousand years. Through the months in Washington, I had extolled Admiralty's wonders to dozens of reporters, for it was the source of violent Senate debate; now, for the first time, I was actually gazing at one edge of the place.

At the head of the Alexander Archipelago, Admiralty's million acres of forests, muskeg, beaches, meadows, lakes, and alpine tundra reach for ninety-six miles through the blue waters of the Inside Passage. Down the frigid, clear waters of Admiralty's sixty-seven streams, two million young salmon tumble to the sea each summer. In three years they will return as seventy-pound adults, to fight the current up the very stream in which they were born (scientists are still unsure how they know which stream is theirs), lay and fertilize the eggs of a new generation, then die. "The ultimate orgasm," nodded Evelyn gravely as we discussed the phenomenon.

Admiralty is the only large island in Southeast Alaska yet to undergo major logging or commercial activity. Her large expanses of natural habitat, plus her productive, unpolluted salmon spawning streams, support one of the finest grizzly bear populations in Alaska. More than 1,000 of the magnificent beasts roam the island the Indians call "Kootznoowoo," the Fortress of the Bears. And Admiralty is home to an equally phenomenal bald eagle population. With 893 recorded nests—more than one nest per mile of coastline—this one fantastic island hosts more nesting bald eagles than any single area in the United States.

Admiralty's only human inhabitants are the Tlingit Indians of the village of Angoon, one of the largest traditional Tlingit villages left in Alaska. The villagers have lived in harmony with the land and the waters and the animals for centuries, relying on the earth's riches for their survival. They know that to protect their traditional hunting and fishing way of life, they must keep the island home of the bears, deer, and salmon intact as wilderness. But one day they found out that the U.S. Forest Service saw fit to sell most of the island's commercial timber to Champion Paper, in the largest timber sale in the history of the United States. The Sierra Club sued the Forest Service, and after several years, Champion finally withdrew from the deal. Then the Angoon villagers and conservationists from throughout the nation fought for four long years to convince Congress—and finally succeeded with passage of the Alaska lands act in 1980—to set aside all of Admiralty as wilderness. In the meantime, a Sitka-based urban Native corporation sought to log part of the island, a proposal conservationists and the Angoon villagers are still fighting in court. As we sped past Admiralty's eastern coast, I wondered what the Tlingits at Angoon, twenty miles away on the western shore, made of having to send lobbyists to Washington to save the land they themselves had protected for a thousand years.

In addition to Admiralty, nearly every acre of land through which we had been weaving our way for the past sixteen hours, and through which we would continue to steam for another seven hours, was mine. I own it in common with every other citizen of the United States, for all fifteen million acres of it is federal land—the Tongass National Forest—part of our legacy from the Russians' sale of all of Alaska to the United States in 1867.

The Tongass includes 20,000 miles of tidal shoreline which is home to harbor seals, Steller's sea lions, sea otters, and millions of migratory waterfowl. The Tongass's 5,530 miles of salmon streams comprise one of the most significant fisheries on the North American continent. Through its forests and mountains rove timber wolves, marten, wolverine, and the rare glacier bear. In this lush rain forest live 800-year-old trees that grow 200 feet tall and 14 feet in diameter. Some apartments I've lived in would fit inside the trunk of one of these beings.

Congress passed the Wilderness Act in 1964, creating a system by which designated federal lands could remain in their natural state, to be used as wildlife and recreational resources with minimal human interference. Yet until passage of the Alaska lands bill in 1980, not one acre of Southeast Alaska's millions of acres of fjords and mountains and forests—the largest, most pristine national forest in the United States—had been protected as wilderness. In the meantime, the U.S. Forest Service had already permitted logging and related activities on three million acres. From the boat, I saw occasional clearcuts and immense rafts of logs pulled behind barges. On those rafts sprawled the fallen giants of these ancient forests that had never before known a chain saw, now most destined for pulp and sawlogs for Japan. For clearing huge swaths of my forest down to the dirt, the Forest Service extracts from timber companies but one dollar for every twenty dollars, according to economists, that I and every other taxpayer will shell out to grow comparable timber there. (As if one can replace an 800-year-old tree.) All this goes on despite the fact that the fishing and tourist industries, which depend on streams and vistas and habitat free from logging and mining, are far more important to Southeast Alaska's economy than logging. Southeast Alaska is but another scene of the same tired old battle that is fought every day throughout the Lower 48: multinational corporations and industry-sweet government bureaucrats versus campers, sightseers, hikers, commercial and sport fishermen, hunters, plants and animals, natural scientists, and the millions of people who'll never go there but who derive comfort and inspiration simply from knowing such wild places exist. When the deals were finally cut in Congress, after the most expensive, most widespread, most cohesive, and one of the longest efforts ever waged by America's conservationists, the score in the United States's last great pristine forest stood at industry—about two-thirds of the acreage; public—about a third. Congress is always free to preserve more—or less—anytime it wants. . . .

Yes, it was disturbing to know that probably more trees are piled onto rafts in Alaska in a single week than would fill an entire wilderness proposal in Texas's national forests, which are being logged and roaded and drilled ad nauseum. But at the same time, I felt exhilarated and awestruck by the vast untouched majority of what I was seeing. In no other part of the United States could I find even a fraction of the wild coastal ecosystem that I had witnessed for hundreds of miles here in Alaska. I longed more than ever to get off this boat and over those mountains and begin floating through this grandeur in my canoe.

Monday morning, June 7, the solarium swarmed into action in the bright sunshine at 5 A.M., for today was another Big Day. I took one last shower, not knowing when I'd enjoy my next one, and ate a big breakfast, for the same reason. We read a pamphlet about bears. "Alaska is bear country and you're in it," it began. It said to alert bears to your presence by singing or wearing bells as you walk; they'll generally avoid you if they know you're there, but they can be dangerous when surprised. If you do meet a bear, after taking all precautions not to, it said, help the poor nearsighted thing figure out what you are by waving your arms and making noise—any noise but a bearlike one. Don't run away with your back to the bear. If, during the eons you and the bear are eyeballing each other, he/she begins to make a "whoof" sound, do not become unduly alarmed. One "whoof" or so is probably more an expression of disgust and puzzlement, giving you the opportunity to make a graceful retreat, but a series of "whoofs" is a warning that a charge is imminent. Many bear charges are false ones, designed to scare away the intruder, which they are very effective in doing. But if you should find yourself the object of a charge that is not a bluff, said the pamphlet, go limp and play dead, maybe covering your neck and head with your arms if you get a chance. All of which may be hard to do, it added, if the bear is biting or clawing you, but it may save your life. For often, after one or two simple cuffs or nibbles, the bear has made his point and has no real interest in eating you—you are not his accustomed fare. Many bears may actually be repulsed by the smell of human flesh, the pamphlet comforted.

The ranger we talked to on deck added that we should take into our tents absolutely nothing that smelled—even something so unfoodlike as mosquito repellent or contact lens solution. The ranger reiterated various bits of bear-country advice we'd read. Cook and eat at least 200 feet from your tent. Never have food in or near your tent. (Barbara and Jane vowed they would never even carry the clothes they dined in into their tent.) If possible, tie all food into plastic bags and hoist them up into a tree, at least ten feet off the ground. If you can't tree your food, seal it in plastic bags and leave it as far as possible from your tent. Bears can smell fresh food better than dehydrated or freeze-dried food. Never camp near a game trail or bear trail. Grizzly trails are two well-worn lanes with trodden spots where bears step in the same footprints again and again. Never linger near a recent kill (you'll smell rotting meat), because a bear probably will be guarding it.

Suddenly, there hove into view, at the tip of a long narrow finger of blue water, a town nestled close against steep mountains with white snowcaps, beside a little river: Skagway, Alaska!

As thousands of Klondike stampeders had once waded ashore at this same hamlet, they, too, had thrilled to the sight, thankful they had survived a harrowing sea voyage. As the cheechakos rushed ashore, many discovered their gear had been ruined by the seawater in the ship's hold, smashed to pieces as it was tossed from the ship, or inundated by Skagway's swift thirty-foot tide. If he was lucky enough to avoid all such accidents, the stampeder was as likely as not to wind up having his gear stolen.

Standing in the tidal mud in his rubber boots, among the bedlam of shoving men, kicking horses, barking dogs, in a vast sea of crates and duffels and tents and picks and shovels, the bank clerk- or schoolteacher-turned-prospector might have gazed up at the heights of the mountains that swept down to Skagway's backside, toward the White Pass, which he might have been foolish enough to believe loomed as the last serious obstacle between himself and the riches of the Klondike.

Now, as the ferry docked, we began our own scramble ashore. Down four flights of stairs and up the long ramp into a gravel parking lot we staggered, then dumped our packs into Evelyn's care. She had carried her own pack, but thought unwise to strain her back further. I trudged back upstairs for Big Orange. It had been merely a great bother to carry the fifty-pound menace upstairs, but it was pure torture to my knee to bear the brunt of that weight coming *down* all those stairs. With our Air Force friends having disembarked back at the port of Haines, with the ferry behind schedule and anxious to off-load quickly, and with one-sixth of our crew out of commission, we now faced the unwelcome task of getting our half-ton of gear and two boats gracefully off the ferry and up to the train depot. All these thoughts flitted through my mind as I plodded up the steep off-ramp with Big Orange on my back, something inside my knee grating against something else with each step. Suddenly Jane and Barbara and Sue and Jude flew past, carrying a strangely empty canoe. At the top of the ramp I collapsed, huffing and puffing; I struggled free of Big Orange and quickly limped back toward the ferry to help carry gear, whereupon I saw another strange sight. Up the ramp chugged a big truck, its open bed enclosed with wooden sides, and atop its own cargo was piled all our gear. I couldn't imagine how our heavy gear had gotten over the ten-foot sides of that truck, short of a crane. ("When you're desperate, and you've got a free ride, the adrenalin goes to work!" Jane would explain later.) Alongside the truck trotted Jane, yelling, "Go on, go on, *please!*" to the driver. Behind the truck trotted a ferry dock worker, hollering something about freight and unions and about its being illegal for the driver to carry our gear even the four blocks to the train station. Killjoy. Jane won out, partially, convincing the driver to cart the gear at least to the parking lot, where she quickly threw the gear to the ground and the driver sped off before the ferry worker could catch up. Back on the ferry, Jude and Sue and Barbara and I grabbed the last canoe and dashed to shore, hoping the ferry worker wouldn't cause a fuss, and stopping only once for me to switch sides so the canoe wouldn't bump my bum knee and send me sprawling.

At the top of the ramp again at last, we witnessed a stranger sight yet. Grinning from ear to ear, Jane announced that she'd hired transportation to the train station. Wearily, we set down the canoe and said we didn't care how much it cost. Jane waved toward the street with a flourish.

"We love it!" we clapped and hooted, for there stood a horsedrawn carriage, complete with a driver wearing a Gay Nineties long dress, shawl, and bonnet.

The pony lady seemed infinitely patient and easygoing as we scurried to and fro with our gear; turned out she was actually dead on her feet because she'd spent the night hitchhiking the Klondike highway and had walked the last seventeen miles, stopping every few hours to build a fire to warm her hands. Jane and I heaved one carriage-full of gear onto the board sidewalk when we reached the train depot, then while Evelyn held the door I loaded the gear onto a pushcart to take it to the train platform. I heard laughter from the street and looked up to see Jane and the pony lady, with shoulders to the rear end of an old car, shoving to no avail with all their weight. The ponies had made too wide a turn and wedged their wooden trace beneath the car's bumper. I hobbled over and we all stared at the situation, bemused. I asked if the ponies couldn't just back up.

"Well, they don't know that one too well," shrugged the pony lady, adjusting her bonnet. Meanwhile, the baby pony, who wasn't pulling any load but was tied to his mother's halter, gazed at us with big brown puzzled eyes. Finally, the ponies made a quick sidestep and pulled the hitch free; Jane and the pony lady clopped away down the dusty street.

Soon the freight lady at the depot returned from lunch. Mercifully, she was happy to let us store our gear on the train platform overnight, at our risk, to let it travel at no charge (except for $30 for each canoe) if we loaded and unloaded it ourselves, and to let us switch our tickets to one day earlier than our reservation.

Before long, the ponies came plodding up the hill again. Tourists stared and took pictures of the quaint horsedrawn carriage with seven feet of yellow plastic canoe sticking out of it. By now some of the male workers at the train depot were caught up in the excitement of this bunch of women who were hauling all this gear to the Yukon, and they volunteered to help. At the height of the gear-shuffling, I rounded a corner to spot Jude bent over, eyes shut tight in pain, Big Orange crumpled beside her in the gravel. She had slipped on a rock or a rut and sprained her ankle, with the full weight of Big Orange on her back. After a few choice words for Big Orange, she was back up in the carriage heaving more bags to the ground. After passing Evelyn and Jude and me a few times as he carried gear to and fro, one of the dock workers asked gently if all of us ladies intending to float the Yukon limped.

Finally, the gear lay heaped on the train platform and we paid the pony lady $25 for her trouble. In addition, Jane had given the truck driver $10. "Well, that might have been a little high just for a two-block trip," said Jane apologetically, "but I figured since the poor man was about to be arrested. . . ."

To the Sweet Tooth Saloon we limped, where we ordered hamburgers, Cokes, and ice for Jude's ankle which was now quite blue and twice its normal size. Then those who could still walk dispersed to reconnoiter possible sleeping sites for the night. They returned with word that a hotel room for six would run $60 to $95, or we could stay at a campground about a half-mile through town for $4 per tent. We had considered sleeping on the train platform with our gear, but decided not to strain our good relationship with the railroad personnel. Besides, it turned out that the owner of the campground was sitting in the next room at the Sweet Tooth, so we made camping reservations there.

We finished a big bowl of ice cream to top off the celebratory lunch, then we hobbled down dusty, historic Broadway Street, enjoying walking the board sidewalks and poking into the many restored buildings with their false fronts, wooden floors, and high ceilings. Sue bought Jude a welcome-to-Alaska present—a carved wooden cane to spare her ankle. About three o'clock, the entire town closed up shop, donned gold rush costumes, and skipped along to the train depot to cheer around the bend an old steam engine being used for the first time in twenty-eight years. The Texas Women's Yukon River Expedition burst into several verses of "She'll be Comin' 'Round the Mountain," then we watched a glorious one-hour Park Service film at the visitors' center about the Klondike Stampede, and finally, at the appointed hour, shifted most of our gear for overnight safekeeping into the train station proper and packed what we'd need for camping.

We felt victorious and light-headed, much as we had when we'd finally gotten all our gear settled onto the ferry in Seattle. Our gear was all set for the last leg of our journey to the Yukon, and we even knew where we were going to sleep tonight, so we threw on our packs and waltzed down to Moe's Frontier Bar to celebrate. The next several hours saw round after round brought to the table of the six boisterous Texas women. It all started because Sue and I owed Barb two beers from a bet. On our last night on board the ferry, Gary, the Air Force guy, had finally been willing to dedicate his body to science, but upon learning that he had taken down his tent, Evelyn offered some lame excuse about having no lab. A true scientist conducts research under the most adverse circumstances, we had reminded her, but to no avail. So now, Sue and I owed Barb a beer each, for which we greatly ribbed Evelyn.

"That's O.K., Evelyn," said Barbara, "I was offering three to one odds, so you saved me six beers! Here, I'll buy you one."

Among the locals who were hunkered over beers at the bar, we made quite a stir, perhaps because we comprised most of the female clientele, perhaps because we were so loud, perhaps because our toasts grew more earthy with each round.

Moe's Frontier Bar was one of those wonderful dimly lit places where the smoke hangs low and the furniture is covered in black vinyl with a few knife slits, like you find in the down-home section of any city. It had the usual lighted beer-sign globes that hung over the pool tables, and the neon beer signs on the mirror behind the bar, and the juke box with lots of country-and-western songs. The ceiling above the bar was plastered with dollar bills that people had signed and pinned there. We wrote "Texas Women's Yukon River Expedition" and signed our names on a dollar bill and handed it to the bartender.

At eight o'clock it finally occurred to us we'd never eaten dinner, so we shuffled outside into the bright light, heaved our dust-covered packs onto our shoulders (they had this strange rule in the bar that you couldn't bring in your pack), stumbled across the street, slipped into a booth at a restaurant and ordered another round. Before long some of us were nodding into our chowder. Then Sue's "goose"—as she affectionately dubbed her problem-prone esophagus—began acting up from the liquor. Meanwhile, a dog raised its leg over Evelyn's pack outside on the sidewalk, and we all screamed and pounded on the windows. The locals in the restaurant hardly looked up.

Eventually we realized we'd better get to the campground or we'd pass out where we were. We hoisted our packs one more time and weaved down the dirt road, past cabins and one tepee. In the campground, we threw together the tents and collapsed inside them.

It had been an incredibly long, hard, zany day, and I had fallen in love with this crazy frontier town that seemed to welcome with open arms anything that might wander in. I was proud of this bunch of six Texas women who also took in stride everything from bending rules to spraining ankles. And I was relieved to know that after ten days' and 3,800 miles' travel, we were within one mere mountain range of the mighty Yukon. As I drifted into a weary sleep, I tried to imagine the dog-tired stampeders who must have slept on this same spot.

Skagway took its name from "Skagus," the Indian word for Home of the North Wind. In its day, this little town had been the very essence of wild abandon, vice, lawlessness, and heartbreak. As the cheechako slogged his way through the muddy streets, he was likely to witness anything, from a trained bear dancing down Broadway with his bearded Russian master, to a woman dashing through the crowds in a cart pulled by a yearling moose. Thousands of men, having abandoned their ascent of the mountains and slunk back in defeat to Skagway, wandered aimlessly with no means to return to Seattle. Inside one of the dozens of illegal and flourishing saloons and gambling halls, men drank and kept company with women called Mollie Fewclothes, the Virgin, or Ethel the Moose.

Skagway owed its existence to one William Moore, the kind of guy who would try anything. Once he brought a load of camels into the North in his sternwheeler steamship, convinced that the beasts were just the thing for North-country freight-hauling. When he was seventy-four, he trotted 700 miles through the snow over the Coast Mountains to relay the message that somebody named George Washington Carmack had just struck gold on a river called the Klondike. But even before that, Moore had believed that there would be a stampede of unparalleled proportions into the Yukon. Discovering the White Pass, which was lower and had a gentler slope than the nearby soul-crushing Chilkoot Pass that had long been the route to the Yukon, he dreamed that pack animals and eventually a train would negotiate his route. He waited to get rich from selling land and supplying the goods and services the prospectors would need when the Stampede reached him.

And reach him it did. Overnight, the cheechakos swarmed into the flatland, chopped down the forest, erected buildings, surveyed streets, declared a government—all while Moore protested that he was due some money because this was his land. They ignored him and built a new street where Moore's cabin had stood. Meanwhile, though, Moore made a fortune from tolls on the mile-long wharves he constructed, and eventually he won a lawsuit that awarded him twenty-five percent of the worth of every lot in his original townsite.

If and when the cheechako finally began his journey over the White Pass, he probably felt lucky to have escaped being fleeced of his entire bankroll in one of the ingenious con games or shot in one of the gun battles that rang through the streets at all hours of the day or night. At last, he was on his way up the Trail of '98, which he mistakenly believed to be an all-weather, all-year route suitable for pack animals.

As for six Texas women, after a glorious breakfast at the Sweet Tooth Saloon the next morning, we launched the third and final leg of our journey to the Yukon—a 110-mile climb over the Coast Mountains on the White Pass & Yukon Route Railway. Today, Lord willing, we would glimpse for the first time the river we had dreamed about and read about and planned over for so many thousands of hours.

The engine whistled and out of Skagway we chugged, aboard this narrow-gauge railroad that had operated continuously since 1900. We sat on benches and easy chairs, in a coach built in the 1920s. Clattering past one snowbank after another, we were thankful for the heat of the oil-burning stove next to us, with its stovepipe that disappeared through the roof. On we climbed, past gorgeous, tumbling waterfalls, around hairpin curves that hung 1,000 feet above canyon floors, over trestles that spanned deep gorges. Around every bend sprang into view more spectacular snowcapped mountains and meadows.

We were following the Trail of '98 over the White Pass. Known as the Dead Horse Trail, it was the scene of much that was shameful and disgusting, as thousands of men and women clambered over it in 1897-98 to reach the headwaters of the Yukon River. Three thousand horses edged onto the cruel trail in Skagway; but a handful lived to creep down the other side of the pass. Not only horses, but anything that could walk—oxen, sheep, even pigs—were whipped over the tree stumps and slippery jagged rocks and mudslides of the "trail." Jack London, who was there, wrote about it:

> The horses died like mosquitoes in the first frost and from Skagway to Bennett they rotted in heaps. They died at the rocks, they were poisoned at the summit, and they starved at the lakes; they fell off the trail, what there was of it, and they went through it; in the river they drowned under their loads or were smashed to pieces against the boulders; they snapped their legs in the crevices and broke their backs falling backwards with their packs; in the sloughs they sank from fright or smothered in the slime; and they were disembowelled in the bogs where the corduroy logs turned end up in the mud; men shot them, worked them to death and when they were gone, went back to the beach and bought more. Some did not bother to shoot them, stripping the saddles off and the shoes and leaving them where they fell. Their hearts turned to stone—those which did not break—and they became beasts, the men on the Dead Horse Trail. (The Klondike Fever, page 156.)

Many witnesses reported that animals actually committed suicide by flinging themselves over the precipices. The sliver of a trail that clung to the sides of the mountains was wide enough for but one animal, so any upset ahead caused the entire line to halt, sometimes for hours. The terribly overloaded animals stood in line, the weight of hundreds of pounds of provisions pressing upon their weary bones and flesh. One man saw a horse who could go no farther struck in the head with an ax and left where he fell. On the return trip that afternoon, the man saw the head of the horse where it had lain on one side of the trail, the hindquarters on the other, the body between having been ground into the earth by the thousands of feet and hooves that had passed directly over it. When a horse perished in a mudhole, its body was left there to furnish footing for the people and animals that followed.

At the summit lay the international border where the Canadian Mounties ruled. Each stampeder was required to bring over the pass enough provisions and equipment for one year—approximately one ton. The rule was the same seven miles west at the Chilkoot Pass, which was too steep for pack animals. Moving what he could carry in one trip five miles farther down the trail, then returning for another load, each stampeder moved his ton of gear up over the pass and down to Lake Bennett. All in all, it took him about three months, and 2,500 miles of walking under 65-pound loads.

On the White Pass Trail, most stampeders who led pack animals made a grim pause just short of the Mounties' station at the summit, for the Mounties would shoot on sight any animal that was visibly injured. The stampeder would remove the amimal's load and spread a blanket over its back to conceal the huge open sores that had worn into its hide from the load—a cruel load placed there by men who knew nothing of packing horses over mountain passes.

All along the trail lay the skeletons and rotting remains of hundreds of animals, as well as hundreds more barely alive. One night, a stampeder got up from his bed, wandered through the camp until he had shot out of its misery every last horse, then returned to his tent without a word. One young cheechako, whose father raised thoroughbreds in Kentucky, built a fire in the snow one night to boil a pot of beans and discovered with horror, as the heat melted the snow, that there lay directly beneath his supper fire a dead horse.

Over on the Chilkoot, it was the men who were perishing—men who had pushed themselves in the quest for gold until they, too, dropped to die in the snow. Seventy feet of snow fell that winter, but neither that, nor the high winds, nor the 50°-below-zero temperatures, stopped the human chains that inched over the mountain barriers. On through the avalanche weather of the spring of 1898 they pushed, and even when sixty-three men died in the Palm Sunday avalanche on the Chilkoot, those who still found themselves alive dug their outfits from the white depths and pressed on.

Amid this melee, railroad materials arrived at Skagway, and the vision that William Moore had had for a decade became a reality, as building commenced on the White Pass & Yukon Route Railway. Using nothing but horses, shovels, and black powder, men—some of whom lost their lives—blasted cliffs aside, bored tunnels through solid rock, erected bridges, hacked an incredible railway through the frozen earth. From sea level at Skagway, the tracks rose the 2,885 feet to the White Pass in twenty-one switchback miles. On July 6, 1899, the tracks were completed to the shore of Lake Bennett. From there the stampeder had an all-water route down the Yukon to the Klondike gold fields. On July 29, 1900, a brief twenty-six months from its inception, the White Pass & Yukon was complete to Whitehorse.

Finally six Texas women and the other passengers reached the White Pass. We were leaving the thin sliver of Alaska's panhandle and entering Canada—British Columbia. From these slopes trickled the waters that formed the Yukon River somewhere far below; we were almost home.

Soon the train stopped on the shore of big, blue Lake Bennett, where we piled out at what our young tour guide called the "eating house," and devoured a homecooked lunch of pot roast and baked beans.

In "The Trail of Ninety-Eight," Robert Service told the stampeders' thoughts upon reaching Bennett:

> . . . We landed in wind-swept Skagway. We joined the weltering
>    mass,
> Clamoring over their outfits, waiting to climb the Pass.
> We tightened our girths and our pack-straps; we linked on the
>    Human Chain,
> Struggling up to the summit, where every step was a pain.
>
> . . . Floundering deep in the sump-holes, stumbling out again;
> Crying with cold and weakness, crazy with fear and pain.
> Then from the depths of our travail, ere our spirits were broke,
> Grim, tenacious and savage, the lust of the trail awoke.
>
> "Klondike or bust!" rang the slogan; every man for his own.
> Oh, how we flogged the horses, staggering skin and bone!
> Oh, how we cursed their weakness, anguish they could not tell,
> Breaking their hearts in our passion, lashing them on till they
>    fell!
>
> For grub meant gold to our thinking, and all that could walk
>    must pack;
> The sheep for the shambles stumbled, each with a load on its
>    back;
> And even the swine were burdened, and grunted and squealed
>    and rolled,
> And men went mad in the moment, huskily clamoring "Gold!"
>
> . . . Thus toiled we, the army of fortune, in hunger and hope and despair,
> Till glacier, mountain and forest vanished, and, radiantly fair,
> There at our feet lay Lake Bennett, and down to its welcome we
>    ran:
> The trail of the land was over, the trail of the water began.

After lunch, we strolled up a rocky slope that overlooked the lake. At this spot ended both the Chilkoot and the White Pass trails. It was to this point that the cheechako—if he were lucky enough to have escaped death from meningitis, hypothermia, avalanche, or poisoning from the rotting horseflesh fed to him at the trailside "cafes"—slid on his shovel or his sled down the icy slope. Then he found himself obliged to wait several months until the ice broke up on Lake Bennett and the Yukon River, whose waters would carry him to his goal. Once again he found himself among the chaotic hordes, where 10,000 bickering men and women had thrown together the world's largest tent city. Now, instead of frantically gathering sleds and animals and grub and gear for an assault on a mountain pass, about which they knew nothing, they were frantically cutting timber and whipsawing logs into lumber and fashioning boats for a 550-mile float down a river, about which they knew nothing. They hurried to ready their boats to leap into the river at the first sign of spring breakup, to race down to Dawson where they believed there lay claims yet unstaked. In the meantime, though, some of the miners became sufficiently inspired to erect a tall wooden church with an impressive steeple overlooking the placid, mountain-ringed lake. But on May 29, 1898, when the ice creaked and groaned and began pushing its way down the lake toward the sea, the stampeders abandoned the half-finished church and launched 800 boats into Bennett. In the next few days, 7,000 boats would follow.

The church still stands, and as we peered at its dirt floor and unfinished insides, gazed down the length of the lake, and tried to envision 10,000 tents sprawled along these shores, the train's whistle signalled farewell. Barbara helped me hobble and slide down the gravel slope, careful of my knee. We hopped into the caboose just as the train pulled out, then walked through car after car until we reached our rather put-out-looking bunch of women.

"I wanted to see the church," I shrugged.

The tracks paralleled the narrow lake, and as we rumbled past I pressed my nose to the glass. A green Coleman canoe slogged through Bennett's waves. Little did we know then that a month later, and 700 miles downstream, that canoe and its owner would paddle into our lives in a big way.

Eleven miles down the length of Bennett, we crossed the border into the Yukon Territory.

I thought of the 7,000 boats that had so gleefully floated these waters in 1898. Many of the inexperienced boatmen lost their lives as their ill-equipped boats swamped in waves on the wind-whipped lakes or smashed into the black walls of Miles Canyon or the treacherous rocks of Whitehorse Rapids (now drowned by the Whitehorse dam). (Eventually the Mounties decreed that only experienced boatmen could run the rapids. For a fee, these men piloted boats through the whitewater while their owners hiked around the rapids.) Even if the stampeder survived a shipwreck, his food and entire outfit were likely to be ruined or lost in the waters. But onward he pushed, through tragedy, heartbreak, and sickness—a slave now to his overpowering dream.

It was a miracle not that one inexperienced, gold-crazed cheechako survived the incredible string of events that would take him to Dawson, but that thousands of others did likewise—all at the same time, on the same trails and waters.

And it seemed a miracle when, on that Tuesday afternoon, June 8, 1982—eleven months to the day since I had lain in the Utah sun on the edge of Joe Butler's rubber raft and dreamed absently about floating the Yukon—the White Pass & Yukon train lurched into Whitehorse, Yukon Territory. For there, a few dozen feet from the tracks, flowed our river—at last. It really was here, and so were we.

"Well, here we are," I smiled tiredly at Evelyn.

"The mighty Yukon," she raised her eyebrows and shrugged in mock nonchalance.

"Almost 4,000 miles from Big D," I sighed.

"As far as Bolivia," she chuckled.

It had been a rough 4,000 miles, not to mention the months preparing for this moment. But we had survived desert heat and ten-foot snows, runaway stove-fires, six-to-a-motel-room quarters for nights on end, 2,500 miles of CB chatter, celebrations in one high-class Seattle restaurant and one down-home Skagway bar, and one sprained ankle, one strained back, one dislocated knee.

Now we were ready to take on the Yukon.

Evelyn wandered across the muddy street, in her canvas boots, bear bells, and pink parka, into a log cabin with a neon sign that said "beer."

# PART II

Have you gazed on naked grandeur where there's nothing else
    to gaze on,
  Set pieces and drop-curtain scenes galore,
Big mountains heaved to heaven, which the blinding sunsets
    blazon,
  Black canyons where the rapids rip and roar?
Have you swept the visioned valley with the green stream streak-
    ing through it,
  Searched the Vastness for a something you have lost?
Have you strung your soul to silence? Then for God's sake go
    and do it;
  Hear the challenge, learn the lesson, pay the cost.

                              Robert Service, *The Call of the Wild*

# 5 klondike, here we come!

It was late afternoon, Wednesday, June 9, 1982. The past twenty-four hours since our arrival in Whitehorse had been one exhausting blur. Thankfully, going through customs had been a breeze. The inspector opened not a single bag or box, and we answered truthfully his questions about guns ("None"), liquor ("Forty ounces each"), and food ("We have some—we don't know just how much"). We weren't asked about the illegal fireworks Jude hid deep inside her duffel bag.

Then, Norman, the railroad worker with a star-shaped turquoise earring, had hauled our gear in his pickup truck to a clearing beside the river, which was strewn with old tires and bottles. This was where they piled the "rotten" snow in winter, and it was our camp for the night. The ground was still frozen and refused tent stakes. A steady stream of people came into camp, some of whom asked for liquor from whichever one of us was watching our gear. A few dozen yards from our tents, train engines rumbled and growled and hissed all night. When Barb and Jane went to the outfitter with whom, months before, they had reserved a canoe, they learned that all his canoes were downriver in Dawson; luckily, they found another outfitter with a canoe, albeit—as we would soon discover—one that leaked.

Whitehorse is the capital of the Yukon Territory, with a population of 14,814. We drank wine and ate Greek shishkabobs, called our families, studied river maps, obtained permits from the Mounties, ate pizza, purchased fishing licenses, toured museums, bought mosquito repellent and fishing lures and Coleman fuel, wrote press releases and shot publicity pictures, gave newspaper interviews, and finally, threw into the canoes a ridiculously huge amount of gear that included everything from lawn chairs to ukuleles to trumpets to the four-pound *Hite Report*.

At last I put on my life jacket and struggled with the zipper, feeling the nervous/excited "I've-got-to-pee" sensation I always feel when I get into a kayak or canoe. Two Whitehorse newspaper reporters smiled as if they thought we had not the slightest conception of what we were doing and there was no possibility that we'd ever reach the Bering Sea. The moment seemed mildly momentous.

111

"Well, ladies," I teased Evelyn, who didn't like to be called a lady, "ya think we oughta paddle the Yukon River?"

"Waitin' on you," Jude smiled.

## JUNE 9, DAY 1

Just after 5 P.M., I girdled the chaos of gear; Evelyn stuffed the wine bag into the bow. We heaved the three canoes into the Yukon and swung into the current.

The bare-chested newspaper photographer in gray sweatpants and running shoes waved good luck and we slipped from the grasp of White-horse and its noisy trains, its electric lines, its muddy streets.

"Yee ha!" I hollered. It reassured me that I knew what I was doing. In simple rapids that I know I can handle, I holler. In more complex water, I softly sing something like "Chantilly Lace."

Beside us sped foot-long chunks of ice. The Yukon had been ice-free but a few weeks; we wondered if Lake Laberge was yet navigable. Was it just the other day we had sweltered in steamy "Big D"?

I haven't properly launched a river trip until I've sung "Me and Bobby McGee," so around the first bend I inaugurated the voyage. It always seems to fit—singing about traveling and freedom and feelin' good. Besides, the tune has a good paddling rhythm.

High, grey cutbanks closed in. Books say the river here is 600 feet wide, the banks 150 feet high. All I knew was that it was *big*. Against the sheer wall ahead, Sue's yellow plastic canoe was a trivial speck. Gazing up at the crumbling cliffs, I recalled a warning: sometimes massive chunks calve off like icebergs from a glacier, and if you avoid being buried by them, watch out for their tidal waves.

As the bank blurred past, we appreciated the river's incredible speed—probably four or five miles per hour.

"Bald eagle!" Evelyn pointed to the unmistakable snowy head across the river. In the crown of a tall spruce presided the U.S. symbol over an eight-foot-high nest of dead branches. I quit steering and grappled with camera gear while the boat drifted sideways. Seen through a telephoto lens, the magnificent three-foot-tall bird with the seven-foot wingspan was still the merest dot; this river was *big*.

"Thwartation!" I commanded in mock military tone as we caught up with the others. "Thwartation!" they chimed, tying the canoes together side by side, thwart to thwart. We draped our feet over the gunnels, sprawled on the gear, gazed downriver and marveled that we were really here. It was pleasantly scary to be tied together, barely maneuverable, as we rushed down the Yukon.

Among the spruces on the left bank, white porcelain insulators revealed the old telegraph line that meanders all the way to Dawson. What messages had clattered their way over it during the Klondike Stampede?

We unthwarted. Barbara paddled shirtless in the golden afternoon light. Evelyn and I were still in the throes of adjustment, learning to paddle together and communicate as a team. When our boat thudded over a submerged rock, I reminded Evelyn—as bow person—to spot ripples indicating submerged objects. A long pause followed, then a steely voice said, "That instruction was superfluous." We paddled on in silence.

Deep green shadows now flanked the spruce-packed banks. In the distance rose blue-purple mountains sprinkled with snow. Through a break in the soft grey sky, a patch of turquoise pointed downriver. We strained to spot a moose or bear.

Soon we had our first false alarm: a blue oil drum in the shadows on the bank, which at first looked bearlike. Evelyn and I pulled out there for a pit stop.

I relished the familiar squatting on a gravel beach, although today my squat was somewhat modified. My swollen knee still wouldn't bend quite right. Once again, I was watching a river roll by with its little bubbles that always ride on rivers, squatting just right so my pants and shoes wouldn't catch the splatter. And suddenly the Yukon was real. When you don't have to hide behind something to pee, you know you're finally on the river, in the wild. The world seemed right.

Telephones and calendars and appointments and traffic jams were 4,000 miles away. And here I was, going about my business on the banks of the mighty Yukon. The *Yukon*, for God's sake. I looked at the boat, "Bering Sea or Bust" gleaming red on her side. There sat everything I required for the next three months and 2,000 miles. It seemed so simple.

Back on the river, Sue pointed with her paddle. There in the shadows, two brown shapes waddled down the bank and slipped into the water: beavers! Sue and I were elated; we'd never seen one in the wild. The beavers smacked their tails hard on the water and dived into its silver-grey depths.

A slightly silty Takhini River joined the Yukon. Just beyond stood a beaver lodge, a jumbled dome of sticks. Evelyn and I swung toward shore to sneak a glimpse, but no beaver. We pushed back into the current and I explained the finer points of a canoe maneuver called "ferrying," which involves pointing the bow upstream and paddling at a slight angle to the current. With it you can move laterally without slipping downstream; you use it to move directly across the river to land the boat or to avoid rocks and such. I wondered why in the world I was paddling the Yukon with someone who didn't know how to ferry. But I knew Evelyn had success-fully run the Guadalupe and dozens of other Texas rivers; she may not know the technical intricacies, but she gets there. I trusted her basic common sense, and I knew we'd do fine.

Downstream from the Takhini, we pulled out onto a big gravel bar. According to our topographical map, we had floated fifteen miles tonight—not too shabby (as Sue would say) when you don't put in until 5 P.M. On Texas's rivers, fifteen miles is a very full day's paddle. Two beavers played only a few yards from the island. Eventually, tails splatted, beavers disappeared.

Already, the trip was a success. Just being in a land where there hovered the *possibility* of seeing beaver, bear, moose, and bald eagles excited me enough to make well worthwhile the trip's expense, the lost salary, the months of planning.

Some of us untied gear while others, announcing our presence with bear bells tinkling and whistles blowing, roamed for signs of bear. The scouts reported no bear prints, bear scat, or animal kills, so we set up the kitchen near the boats. We emptied the boats and carried them twenty feet inland, but only a foot or so above the water level. There was nothing to tie them to, and I wondered if we were foolish to rely on the river's not rising more than a few feet. One book said an Alaskan sourdough canoeist, who always carried his boat as high as possible, spoke of ten-foot rises. We were skeptical; what flash-flooding tributary could swell the burly Yukon?

Jude quickly built a fire. Evelyn dumped big duffel bags of food onto the ground and crawled through the hundreds of little plastic bags. We pitched the tents on the other side of the gravel bar, with a clear view of kitchen and boats. Barbara and I buried the tent stakes to anchor them in the soft gravel. Then we all entertained ourselves by peeing a ring around the campfire to ward off bears.

To alert bears to our presence, Sue and Jane hung wind chimes on a downed spruce and a camera tripod.

With my usual sarcasm, I smiled, "Do you think a bear's gonna attack the tripod?"

Sue said, "You know Beth, I think you say things like that because you're angry."

I was dumbfounded. Granted it wasn't a great joke, but Sue had read some sinister motive into my attempt at sociability. "I was trying to make a little joke," I sighed, exasperated. "*Obviously,* I did not succeed."

Did Sue have a predilection for analyzing others' thoughts and motives, I wondered. If so, how emotionally draining on me might it become to feel as if the reasons for my every comment were being second-guessed? For now, I simply attributed her statement to exhaustion. The past twelve days and 4,000 miles had been rough on all of us. Sue smoothed things over a bit with a cheerful, "Of course, there's nothing wrong with being angry."

"I see a beaver!" exclaimed Jude. We laughed. She was pointing at Jane, naked from the waist down, who bathed at the water's edge. We were slightly amused at Janie's half-at-a-time bath, but she made a grand statement about innocence and freedom and wildness as she tiptoed over the rocks, flanked by mountains, tall green spruces, and gurgling river.

After dinner we relaxed and pondered the fire's coals. Evelyn heated water and took a "bird-bath" (under the wings and behind the tail). Then, still naked, she warmed herself at the fire's edge as we all sipped our tea. I couldn't help grinning at her thorough lack of inhibition.

Long after dinner, Sue and Barb and I lounged in the midnight sun's starless twilight, staring into the coals and ruminating about one thing or another. Dishes had been washed ("Leave no food smells for bears"), food bundled into its more-or-less airtight river bags, all garbage burned.

Gradually, we realized the sun was rising, not setting; we bolted for bed.

## JUNE 10, DAY 2

Slow and sunny, the morning was ripe for putzing. Jane and Jude threw their fishing lines into the water; on her first cast Jude's became a hopeless tangle. I journalized and photographed. Evelyn wrestled with the food.

In the clear, icy water, Barbara washed her hair then combed it before a hand-held mirror. There was a time when I rarely carried a mirror on a camping trip. But once, the morning after a particularly inspired tequila bash in the hot spring down in the Lower Canyons of the Rio Grande, I had chatted merrily through breakfast, unknowingly wearing dried vomit on my face. And after that I decided a mirror wasn't a bad idea.

So here we were, six women on a sandbar in the middle of the Yukon, 4,000 miles from home, cooking and humming and washing our hair like we thought we had good sense.

Sue duct-taped the battered hull of Jane's and Barbara's rented aluminum canoe that had leaked since Whitehorse. Her multilayered patch would hold superbly all the way to Dawson. Operating methodically on the upturned canoe, Dr. Sue looked quite the river-woman. She sported a leather cowboy hat with a feather stuck in the band, an oversized denim work shirt draped to midthigh, a big bear whistle dangling from her neck.

I spread my foam pad on the warm rocks and dozed, snakelike, in the sun. Eventually, we considered paddling down the river.

It was dawning on me that at last we were gliding down the Yukon. Beneath me now surged North America's fifth longest river, bigger and faster than any river I'd known. Sure seemed easy enough as we sped along. Like us, here, the Yukon commenced her trek as a neophyte confined to a quarter-mile channel between steep blue mountains. But by the time she had forced her way across the earth for 2,000 miles, she would grow to an incredible four-mile-wide veteran who ruled the vast delta wetlands. I peered over the gunnel at her moving energy. What kind of women would emerge at the Bering Sea after we had paddled 2,000 miles through America's last frontier?

We floated beneath a power line and past an expanse of bright pink-purple fireweed and small trees. In 1958, a tremendous forest fire raged here and threatened to engulf Whitehorse.

Through the water slipped another furry brown beaver's head, and I got several good pictures as we practically drifted into the overhanging branches under which he swam. Today, in the bow, I could photograph much more easily because Evelyn could continue to steer from the stern.

We thwarted, sang songs, munched peanuts from baby bottles. To commemorate our approach to Lake Laberge, Barbara read to us Robert Service's "The Cremation of Sam McGee."

There are strange things done in the midnight sun
  By the men who moil for gold;

The Arctic trails have their secret tales
    That would make your blood run cold;
The Northern Lights have seen queer sights,
    But the queerest they ever did see
Was that night on the marge of Lake Lebarge
    I cremated Sam McGee.

Now Sam McGee was from Tennessee, where the cotton blooms
    and blows.
Why he left his home in the South to roam 'round the Pole,
    God only knows.
He was always cold, but the land of gold seemed to hold him like
    a spell;
Though he'd often say in his homely way that "he'd sooner live
    in hell."

On a Christmas Day we were mushing our way over the Daw-
    son trail.
Talk of your cold! through the parka's fold it stabbed like a
    driven nail.
If our eyes we'd close, then the lashes froze till sometimes we
    couldn't see;
It wasn't much fun, but the only one to whimper was Sam
    McGee. . . .

Beneath us flowed the path of the most famous gold rush in history, a liquid
trail that whooshed 30,000 gold miners from the mountains down to the
riches of Bonanza Creek and the Klondike River. The Klondike! The word
had hit the sensational press like the ton of gold that sixty-eight ecstatic
miners dumped on Seattle's dock in 1897. Then all hell broke loose. All
over America, men and a few women dropped what they were doing and
got themselves up to the frozen gold fields.
    I lay back on the gear, closed my eyes, dreamed in the sun:

. . . And that very night, as we lay packed tight in our robes be-
    neath the snow,
And the dogs were fed, and the stars o'erhead were dancing
    heel and toe,
He turned to me, and "Cap," says he, "I'll cash in this trip, I
    guess;
And if I do, I'm asking that you won't refuse my last request."

Well, he seemed so low that I couldn't say no, then he says with
    a sort of moan:
"It's the cursèd cold, and it's got right hold till I'm chilled clean
    through to the bone.
Yet 'tain't being dead—it's my awful dread of the icy grave
    that pains;
So I want you to swear that, foul or fair, you'll cremate my last
    remains." . . .

The real story was that a steamboat named the *Olive May* got frozen
in for the winter at the head of Lake Laberge, just downstream from us
now. In a cabin near the boat, the Mounties discovered a prospector
dying of scurvy. A doctor arrived too late, and since the frozen ground

offered no burial, he cremated the corpse in the *Olive May's* firebox.

Returning to Whitehorse, the doctor recounted the bizarre incident to a bank clerk named Robert Service. And thus was born what would become one of Service's most famous poems. Service was a dreamer from England and Scotland who drifted into the Yukon just after the gold rush. His poetry would capture for millions the romantic hardship and humor of the North.

In Whitehorse's museum I had seen Sam McGee's cabin. The cremated prospector wasn't named McGee. But Service knew a Sam McGee and sought a rhyme for "Tennessee"—I never did get straight whether the cabin at the museum was McGee's or the prospector's. Service also changed the lake's name to "Lebarge," to rhyme with "marge." There's a story that one night, after closing time, bank clerk Service was writing poetry in the bank. Another employee entered, mistook Service for a thief, and fired a shot which, luckily for literature, missed the startled poet.

We neared Lake Laberge. The river widened to a half-mile and inexplicably seemed to move faster. Pilings for dikes that once controlled the channel for the old sternwheelers looked like an old railroad bridge. Still thwarted, we dodged mudflats and pulled into a strong back-ferry every now and then to avoid being swept into the pilings. As clouds rolled in on the gusting wind, we rigged Sue's groundcloth onto two upright paddles as a sail. It was pitifully ineffectual, but entertaining.

Lake Laberge was named for Mike Laberge, a French-Canadian, who in 1867 explored a proposed telegraph route to link Canada, Alaska, Siberia, and Europe. Backers abandoned the scheme when the first transatlantic cable was laid. Stationed at Fort Selkirk on the Yukon, Laberge learned from the Indians of a wondrous upstream lake. He dreamed of going there, and his friends dubbed it Laberge's Lake. He never got there, but the name stuck.

Somewhere around here were supposed to be the remains of Upper Laberge, an abandoned police post. And one map shows a wrecked barge and an Indian village. We probably took the wrong channel or the sandbars prevented our entering the correct one, because we saw nothing. Jane and I held our paddles up and braced the sail, while Sue, in front as navigator, shouted directions back to Evelyn and Jude and Barbara, who steered blindly. At first it was all pretty funny.

As we entered the lake, we recounted details we'd read. Ice remains on Laberge up to two weeks longer than on the flowing river, moving out anywhere from the end of May to the tenth of June. That was today. The lake water is never much warmer than ice. "To swim twenty yards in such cold water is a feat," says Richard Mathews in *The Yukon.* "A strong wind . . . can spring up without warning and whip the lake surface to a sudden frenzy of choppy five-foot waves. Many boats have been caught in the middle, or next to the cliffs in such circumstances, and gone down with all hands." (Page 140)

Beneath these waters lies the sternwheeler *May West,* hastily constructed on the beach at Saint Michael, on the Bering Sea, in 1897. A bunch of stampeders had reached the dark volcanic beach in late August and were forced to build the very steamers they thought they had booked passage on. In three weeks they threw together two boats, the *Seattle No. 1* and the *May West,* and set forth up the Yukon. But neither steamer got more than halfway to the Klondike before it was seized in the Yukon's icy winter grip. A "Suckerville" of shacks sprang up around the entrapped vessels. Of the 1,800 stampeders who attempted the all-water route from Seattle to Dawson that fall, a mere handful reached the Klondike that year, and those who did had to turn back because Dawson City had no food. The rest were stranded all along the Yukon's 1,700 miles between Norton Sound and Dawson. At any rate, the *May West* became the first steamer to reach Dawson after breakup the following spring. As she chugged into town at 4 A.M. on the eighth of June, 5,000 men and women thronged the waterfront. Her sixteen barrels of whiskey were sold at once in the bars, at a dollar a drink.

And they say on a clear day you can still see one A.J. Goddard's steamer beneath Laberge's waters. Goddard and his wife carried two sternwheelers in bits and pieces over the mountains in the winter of '97-'98. Each night there rang through camp the tortured screams of fellow stampeders dying from spinal meningitis. Goddard finally got one of his steamers down to the Yukon's fearful Miles Canyon and Whitehorse Rapids (now drowned by the power dam at Whitehorse), ran the rapids under his own steam, and did all right after that hauling stuff up and down the Yukon.

So here we were, duct-taping a groundcloth onto two paddles, bumbling into this thirty-one-mile-long lake. No doubt we looked as inept as the stampeding thousands who lurched through here in 1898. The folks in that spectacular flotilla, though, raced against each other, hell-bent for Dawson to stake claims (little did they know that virtually the entire Klondike was already staked) or to mine the miners' wealth. Everything imaginable bobbed with them down the Yukon—bank equipment and personnel in two boats, printing presses and staffs of two prospective newspapers in two others, 1,500 pairs of boots in one, a load of cats and kittens in another, eight tons of fruit and candy in another. All this and more the Yukon spat into Lake Laberge.

The literature warns to paddle on the lake's left side, sheltered from the storms that often blow in from the west. But it also says to avoid crossing open water. Forced by sandbars to the far right, we now faced a paddle of several miles across open water to reach the left shore. But because of the warnings and because we wanted to camp on Richtofen Island near the left shore, we decided to risk a dash across the open lake. We dropped the sail and, still tied together, tried to hug the sandbars along the southern shore as we worked our way to the left.

But the wind, now thundering from the hills on the left, flung us into open water; before we knew it, we found ourselves paddling a mile from shore in three-foot waves.

The boats thudded together, every third wave poured over the bows, the wind roared in our ears. Over the tumult, we sang and paddled in rhythm. "Oh Lord, won't you buy me a Mercedes Benz, my friends all drive Porsches, I must make a-mends. . . ." We tried to ferry on the wind, angling the boats so the wind would push us toward shore. We paddled with all our might, but we were losing; we were being swept straight down the middle of the lake.

Soon I was soaked from the waist down with icy water. Gripping the paddle, my stiff fingers hurt inside their soggy wool gloves. Singing stopped and the only sounds were an occasional rhythmic "Heave ho!" to synchronize our strokes, or a "Draw!" or "Pry!" command for the stern steerers.

We seemed to near the left shore, and we thought we saw signs of the government campground that is supposed to be there. But distances deceived; the mountains were so big they seemed closer than they were. Squinting at the elusive left shore was only slightly less painful than looking back at the two or three miles of rolling whitecaps that we faced if the wind beat us.

Waves sloshed over the gunnels, plopping into my lap or dashing me in the face. Besides that, we hadn't had lunch. This was getting less funny by the minute.

"Look, we've been paddling thirty minutes in this same spot!" shouted Evelyn, disgusted. "We're not gaining a thing." She had a point.

She wanted to abandon ferrying on the wind and make a dead run for the left shore. But this would put us broadside to the waves. A debate ensued and for a brief moment we rested our burning muscles.

That was the end of it. The wind sent us scudding across the lake. We tried to recoup, but had lost too much distance. We were exhausted, the wind had won.

We unthwarted, turned tail and rode the bucking water toward the rock-strewn right shore. To our dismay and relief, the two-mile passage took but a few minutes, and even in the big waves, our boats were so heavily loaded that they were really rather stable.

As we bashed among the rocks along the shore, Evelyn steered us broadside to the breaking waves. It was like trying to land in an ocean, with the waves shoving us onto the rocks. Water poured over the gunnel, the boat rolled. I swore. On shore, Jude waved us in, but Evelyn and I were busy shouting at each other about how to land a canoe. Finally I flung a rope to Jude and she pulled us in.

I was worried, for we were all cold, wet, hungry, and exhausted—ripe for hypothermia. When you lose more body heat than you generate, your temperature drops, you become disoriented and uncoordinated, your judgment falters, your speech may slur, and if things aren't reversed by warmth and/or food, you die. The first rule for river runners is that if your friends tell you that you're getting hypothermia, and you need to change clothes, you acquiesce. If you are getting hypothermia, your judgment can't be trusted. As soon as we hit the beach, we three bow paddlers, who were the wettest, stripped and threw on dry clothes. Then we all hurried to prepare food and shelter, keeping a subtle eye on each other for any evidence of hypothermia. Jane and Barbara checked for bear signs and found a tent site. Jude got a fire going in the whipping wind. Evelyn heated soup and tea water.

The gale lashed directly across the beach as we tottered over the rocks to set up camp. Being inherently uncoordinated and with the world's weakest ankles, I could barely walk on this disgusting excuse for a beach. It was nothing but rocks, rocks, rocks, and every one was pointed. It would have been funny, except that I feared wrenching my knee again. "Garden spot," I muttered. Evelyn, aware of my foibles, had kindly offered before the trip to carry the heavier stuff on rough ground. I was grateful, though I felt like a weakling.

The bedroom was a forlorn little strip of lumpy land, strewn with rocks, between the dense forest and the open beach. It lay at the high-water line where old grey lumber from God knows where had washed up. But it was preferable to the rocks of the beach or the mosquitoes of the forest. In the windstorm Sue's tent took to the air with Sue in tow. Sue swore, Barbara began to help; they snapped at each other. Meanwhile, I swore and wallowed among the rocks and boards and flailing ropes, outwitting one end of Evelyn's tent's A-frame as the other collapsed. "Three months of this?" I thought. Talk about togetherness, the three tents were so sardined that to get into or out of our shelters we had to do a little tiptoe rope-jig. Down on the beach at the campfire, Jude and Evelyn were arguing over kitchen duties. All in all, today had been a rough fifteen miles.

But before long, supper was ready, the fire's warmth penetrated our bones and soothed our spirits, and things began to look up. We could almost laugh at ourselves as we huddled on the "marge of Lake Lebarge," in the lee of our trio of canoes, the wind whipping the fire's ashes into our faces. Mercifully, the wind began to die.

Then came the mosquitoes.

## JUNE 11, DAY 3

Mosquitoes whined me into consciousness. The bloodsuckers hadn't bothered me all night, so why now? I jerked my head toward the doorway. Evelyn had just trudged off to gather wood and make her morning coffee, and where she had failed to zip the screen there yawned a three-inch mosquito flight path. I cursed and stewed, and when we were alone complained to Evelyn in a low-key way.

Thus ignited the War of the Zipper that would smolder 1,500 miles down the Yukon. My miseries were compounded midway through each night as Evelyn went outside to pee, left the screen agape, and we sat up killing the forty-two new mosquitoes. Her habit had to do with claustrophobia, I decided, or maybe simple masochism.

Just as when I went to bed, I felt exhausted. I suspected we were sleeping little, but who could tell because it never got dark. And at this point, we refused to keep time.

Nestled by the fire, I slurped tea and scanned the lake. Laberge is a glacier child, scooped from the earth by sheets of ice a mile thick. Around her hover mountains of limestone and granite.

Laberge begins about 3½ miles wide, puffs her chest to 5 miles, and cinches her waist in at 1½ to 2½ miles. You can see straight down the 31 miles of the lake.

Across two or three miles of choppy water lay Richtofen Island, a three-mile-long lump named for a prominent geographer of the 1880s. Supposedly, Richtofen sports beautiful campsites alive with wildflowers and birds. Sounded great but not worth risking a dunking in the storm-prone lake.

Girding for another day of battling the waves, Jude and Sue and I donned whitewater wetsuits. After the death-struggle to get into my full-length neoprene girdle, I vowed, as usual, to lose weight.

We shoved off and paddled steadily over the rollers. Though we were growing pretty casual about tossing around in them, we did try to stay near shore and within sight of each other.

Bald eagles abounded. Once three immature ones, their heads still cloaked in brown feathers, wheeled together through the sky.

We stopped where fresh drinking water gurgled from a steep creekbed lined with ice and snow. (Because the 14,814 citizens of White-horse dump their sewage into the poor Yukon, the water is not potable through this section.) After only three days on the Yukon, we seemed like rough-looking characters as we hit the beach and scrambled into a snow-bank in black wetsuits, cowboy hats, leather gloves, and knee-high boots. Jane found an old bear kill. A mass of long white hairs with brownish tips lay scattered on the beach. A fox? Nearby was a bear print. While the others hurried back to the boats, Jane and I nervously scanned the brush and blew our whistles.

Our rock-strewn lunch-spot was a craggy wonder, but if you hunkered behind the right crag you could find some peace from the wind. A driftwood fire blazed and soon Evelyn dished up hot macaroni and cheese. We munched figs. Afterward, Evelyn and Sue and I flopped onto our life jackets on the warm, slate-grey rocks. Despite the wind and the jagged bed, I fell fast asleep under my cowboy hat.

When I awoke, I clambered into the woods and took a dump (sounds better than "defecated," doesn't it?). Anyone who has spent a day in a wetsuit will appreciate the logistics, energy, and time required to relieve yourself while wearing one of those things. Normally the process offers little excitement, but it'll hold your interest if you do it in the forest while swatting mosquitoes on your backside and watching for bears. I hummed softly, a compromise between loudly alerting bears to my presence and not alerting them at all. It was pleasant to be alone, to walk the spongy earth, to ponder the secrets at the woods' edge.

After lunch we paddled into a sheltered cove, seemingly perfect for a campsite and a layover day. Barbara hopped out and sank ankle-deep in mud. Evelyn and I strolled through the silent spruce forest, sphagnum moss squishing underfoot. The woods-smell and eeriness of hiking in bear country were magical. Along the trail lay mysterious piles of chopped wood. Back on the beach, Jane squealed that two harlequin ducks were bobbing right in our cove. They were "lifers"—first sightings of the species—for Jane and Evelyn, and we cheered and peered through binoculars at the beautiful, delicately-painted creatures. On a nearby ridge, however, the scouting party discovered a game trail, complete with bear scat and paw prints. Suddenly the mystical cove lost its attraction and we left.

A huge ice shelf jutted onto the lake where a creek entered. The wind swept waves under the foot-thick shelf; I envisioned canoes being bashed against it and sucked under the ice.

Though we had come only nine miles today, we soon pulled out to make camp. A steep bank of rocks and moss, topped by a rolling hillside of poplars, offered some protection from the wind. Here we declared the kitchen. A washed-up wooden platform was a ready-made table. And we didn't much mind the empty oil drum that, like others we'd seen, had probably been left in some town or mining camp as litter and had been deposited here by flood-waters or moving ice.

As Evelyn and I unloaded the gear, we were startled to see a visitor talking to the others in the kitchen. He was a blond, heavy-set guy with a nice reddish beard and a big gun. He turned out to be David Gile, from New Hampshire, who was paddling solo from Whitehorse to Saint Mary's, one hundred miles from the Bering Sea. We had seen him put in at Whitehorse as we arrived. Now he was camped one ridge over and was taking a walk, hoping to shoot a rabbit. I bet the last thing he expected when he topped that ridge was a bunch of Texas women in black wetsuits. He chatted with us awhile then wandered off to find a rabbit.

We were developing quite a landing routine. Whenever we took out, we would deposit all kitchen and personal gear for the night on the first acceptably flat, unmuddy, and wind-protected spot nearest the boats. This was the kitchen-dining room. Then we would carry tents and sleeping gear to a practical place farthest from the kitchen. Jude and Evelyn would usually launch fire-building and cooking, while the rest of us pitched tents and tied boats. The scraggly trees generally were unsuited to holding several hundred pounds of food, so we sealed the dried food into water-proof river bags and left it in the kitchen. We placed rehydrated food in covered pots in or near the canoes, hoping that if a bear were attracted to the smell he would destroy only that food and spare the main stock.

After dinner, raising her cup of scotch, Janie offered a toast to the harlequin ducks. There developed a correlation between the number of toasts and the frequency with which our lawn chairs dumped us onto the cunning rocks. "Death traps," muttered Evelyn about the chairs as she squatted on a log.

Whenever we were too lazy to wash dishes right after supper, we loaded them into a mesh bag and flung them into the river, on the theory that bears couldn't smell through the water. Tonight, Sue tended the bag. I glanced up to see our biggest cooking pot bobbing down the lake, driven before the waves. Sue looked sheepishly in our direction.

"Hey guys!" she shouted. "I screwed up!"

Jude and Barb scurried over the rocks and grabbed utensils as they disappeared into the murky water. Sue and Jude shoved their boat into the lake and, paddling furiously and giggling, captured the fleeing pot.

We had a good laugh. Somehow, as the bag had sailed through the air and into the water, so did all the utensils. During the next week, we came to realize that half the expedition's spoons had been sacrificed to the river god.

I was the next-to-last one to shuffle off to bed, and after I crawled up the hillside through old lumber and brush, I gazed out over Lake Laberge, now forsaken by the thousands of boats that once raced down her valley.

> . . . Till I came to the marge of Lake Lebarge, and a derelict there
>   lay;
> It was jammed in the ice, but I saw in a trice it was called the
>   "Alice May."
> And I looked at it, and I thought a bit, and I looked at my frozen
>   chum;
> Then "Here," said I, with a sudden cry, "is my cre-ma-tor-eum."
>
> Some planks I tore from the cabin floor, and I lit the boiler
>   fire;
> Some coal I found that was lying around, and I heaped the fuel
>   higher;
> The flames just soared, and the furnace roared—such a blaze you
>   seldom see;
> And I burrowed a hole in the glowing coal, and I stuffed in
>   Sam McGee. . . .

I took one last glance at our boats. There stood Barbara at the water's edge, still tipsy and weaving on the rocks. For the pure-dee hell of it, she heaved one big stone after another out over the lake with an overhand throw. She hurled each one with her entire body; the rocks arced through the air and plunked into the rolling waters. Each time, her momentum carried her forward and she wobbled to avoid stumbling into the water. Looked like fun.

For me, the image will always speak of freedom and wilderness: a thirty-seven-year-old woman in red plaid knickers stands on an empty beach under the vast Yukon twilight, gleefully chunkin' rocks.

## JUNE 12, DAY 4

Today was a layover day and I slept past noon. I craved some time alone. I had been surrounded by people, day and night, for almost two weeks. The constant chatter, the dealing with others' wants and feelings, were draining me. I wanted some time to enjoy my own company, think my own thoughts, do nothing but ponder the pebbles at my feet. Several hours of talking to my tape recorder and sitting alone on a rock had me feeling amused and friendly and relaxed again. People don't sit on rocks enough.

After lunch, I pulled the canoe into the water, crawled in, hung my head over the side and washed my hair. As the waves pounded the boat, it was fun, in a perverse way, to pour that cold, cold water over my head. It took my breath away, stung my scalp, and gave me a headache, but it was a new experience. Then I stretched over the stern and swished my dirty clothes through the waves until my hands grew red and numb. I heated two cups of water in a pot, carried it to some big, black volcanic-looking rocks hot from the sun, and took a bath. I even shaved my legs as I sat naked on the rocks and gazed across Laberge to Richtofen and the snowy mountains beyond.

While chief cook Evelyn was away birding with Jane, Sue and I sneaked into the kitchen to remedy something that had bugged us for days. Evelyn had about eighty-three plastic jars filled with powders and bits of dehydrated food of every description. Scratched onto the top of many were words which might, or might not, reveal what lay inside them. Others offered no hint as to content. The white powder might be sugar, or powdered milk, or powdered cheese, or sour cream powder. The brown crystals might be regular coffee or they might be decaffeinated coffee. We had grown weary of opening several jars each time we wanted to make ourselves a hot drink. So we grabbed a fat felt-tipped marker (just happened to have one) and wrote on all the jars what was in them at the time. (Later, of course, just what Evelyn said would happen, did. As a jar became empty, it might be refilled with something different. Sometimes we crossed out the old word and wrote a new one, but after a few weeks we lost the marker or got lazy or something. It became a game to learn by trial and error that what said "coffee" was hot chocolate, that what said "whole-wheat flour" was sugar, and so forth. And of course, they changed; just about the time you learned that "coffee" was really hot chocolate, it had become empty and had been refilled with egg powder. Kept us on our toes though.)

Our cooking ensemble consisted of a wire grill (sturdy and big enough for several pots), a Teflon-lined skillet with a lid, a second Teflon skillet without a lid, a coffeepot with handles, and several aluminum pots that nested inside each other. In addition, we each had a plate or bowl or two, and a small aluminum pot or two, which could be used as mixing bowls or saucepans.

We grew attached to these items of comfort and survival. The smoke-blackened coffeepot, already a veteran of years of Sue's and Jude's campfires, would in the coming weeks take the worst beating, but we loved it the best. It was the symbol of our after-dinner relaxation and camaraderie. The first thing on and the last thing off each fire, it was always full of hot water for coffee, tea, or hot chocolate.

A few weeks down the river, its metal handles would fall off; Jude would stick them back on with pliers every few days. Further downriver, its glass percolator top would crack in two and fall out; we would discover that the pot heated water just about as efficiently with the hole open. Besides, you could add more water through the hole without removing the lid. Finally, over a thousand miles downstream, the metal bail would burn through; we would find a piece of wire lying nearby and a local villager would fashion a new bail. That coffeepot would have real character by the time it reached the Bering Sea.

Back in my rocky nook, soil was forming and I watched it. Tiny lichens lived in each crevice. Wherever the wind had put a few grains of sand, cute little flowers struggled for toeholds. Each scrap of vegetation worked its roots into the thin layer of grit, breaking the rock beneath into soil, which would support more vegetation, which would break more rock into more soil. . . . It was wonderful.

As usual, my efforts to photograph candid camp scenes failed; somebody was always half-naked, either changing clothes, bathing, or squatting.

Suddenly, the wind slapped Evelyn's beached canoe for a double roll across the rocks. This was a downright respectable wind we were dealing with. Carefully, we scrutinized the rocks that held our canoe lines; we sure would feel dumb to wake up canoeless some morning.

As Barbara and Sue and Jude enjoyed an afternoon cocktail hour around the campfire, there came a crashing sound from the woods. Sue and Jude lunged forward just as a dead tree half-a-foot in diameter thudded to earth inches behind their chairs.

Soon Evelyn and Jane emerged from the forest, excited from a day of birding, identifying wildflowers, and exploring. Near the ice shelf, they had found one old sod-roofed cabin and another with fences and a springhouse. An eagle had fished the creek, and as they followed the bubbling waters they wondered if they'd meet bears who also fished it. The best find of the day, though, offered a mystery. "We found fifteen empty wine bottles near the cabin," beamed Jane, "all buried neck down in the dirt!" We agreed with Jane's theory that each bottle was stuck in the earth by the couple in the cabin to commemorate something; maybe one bottle was so-and-so's birthday, one was the night they danced in the moonlight, another was spring breakup on the lake. . . .

Our biggest debate before the trip had been what kind of liquor to take. There's not much room in a canoe for three months' worth of liquor. Marijuana is lighter and smaller, but we had ruled it out. "As I told my kids when we backpacked through Europe," said Evelyn, waving her finger in the air, "I will not rot in a Turkish prison!" So we finally steeled ourselves for the worst and settled on taking mostly Everclear, supplemented by small personal caches of preferred liquor. Supposedly tasteless, mixable with almost anything, and ninety percent alcohol, Everclear would pack the most wallop for its bulk. I felt like an overgrown teenager when, after picking out the champagne for our end-of-trip celebration, I had to ask the store clerk for the Everclear.

Today, brave, young Jude finally mixed Everclear with hot chocolate and became the expedition guinea pig. The effects were immediate. I looked up from my journal to see Jude and Barbara stagger onto the rocky beach. Squatting to pee, Jude fell and plopped squarely into the puddle. Barb writhed in laughter.

They stumbled over the rocks toward the creek a half-mile away for fresh drinking water. They were gone for a long time, and Sue feared Jude would re-sprain the ankle just recovered from its Skagway injury. Somewhat less than sober herself, Sue borrowed the double-bladed kayak paddle to go after them. After several false starts when the surf whipped her canoe sideways and sloshed it back onto the beach, she finally muscled through the breakers and paddled upwind toward the creek. Sure enough, when the three of them thudded back into camp in the canoe, Jude's ankle was sprained and swollen.

The ankle injury couldn't dampen the layover day's party atmosphere, though. And besides, tonight was Evelyn's fifty-second birthday, the First Social Event of the Season. We followed a great mess of Cuban black beans, rice, squash, and onions with a loud chorus of "Happy Birthday." My present to Evelyn was a sign, scrawled on a piece of paper, with a string for hanging it on the tent. It said, "Do not disturb! Experiment in progress." With my gift, if, in keeping with her study of *The Hite Report on Male Sexuality*, Evelyn decided to undertake some "research" in Dawson or anywhere else, all she had to do to alert me to get lost was to hang the sign. We all laughed and clapped.

In Seattle we'd heard Jude's and Sue's personal histories, and now we pressed Barbara for hers. She had grown up in rural East Texas, had majored in music in college. She had taught music and outdoor education for sixteen years. One summer she had been a nightclub singer, a fact which seemed wonderfully exotic to me here on the lonely, windswept shore of Lake Laberge as Barbara stirred a charred pot on a campfire.

This evening I tried my arm at flinging the mesh bag. Full of dishes and pans, it was heavy. On the first try, it sailed about five feet through the air and—bang!—crashed in two inches of water on the rocks. Second try, bag sailed six feet through the air—bang!—landed in three inches of water on the rocks. O.K., by God, on the last try I hurled the bag and myself into the lake. The thing landed in deep water, but soon the pounding waves drove it ashore and there it sat for hours.

After dinner the others scuttled off to bed with Jude hanging on their shoulders.

I now faced the mesh bag, which was a big, gooey, greasy mess, congealed in the 47° water. As I dodged the waves on the slick rocks at the shore, I couldn't properly wash the dishes. So I dragged the boat down into the water, crawled into one end, and smeared the grease around in the lake. The waves splashed in, and when I finished, the boat was awash in grease and rice. To make matters worse, I was missing the lid to Sue's spill-proof glass, and I knew I'd be in for it. I searched in and under the boat, among the rocks and waves, finally found the thing back up in the kitchen under a pot. Ah, wilderness. . . .

While I fooled with the dishes in the twilight, lonely rhythmic waves bashed the shore. I had the sensation that someone was watching me. Was it a bear? Or maybe I had become so used to being with the group that I had grown skittish at being alone. I tried to imagine what the trip would have been like if I had chosen to tackle it by myself, in a kayak or solo canoe. I probably would have had a greater sense of danger, which might have been a good thing. But the trip would have been much less amusing.

I lay in the gravel and talked to my tape recorder, reflecting on Laberge. For two days, waves and wind reminiscent of the ocean had marched across the grey waters. Each night the wind had stolen what warmth the 50° temperatures might have offered us. I was glad I had brought my heavy winter parka. Under it I had worn T-shirt, long wool underwear, wool shirt, and wool pants.

A red glow slowly saturated the sky. It must have been very late, but I felt so peaceful I couldn't break the spell to go to bed. The clouds had mostly passed over, and purple streaks now hung near the blue mountains across the lake. Soon, brilliant bands of pink and orange dashed across the Yukon. When I finally trudged up the hill to the tent, an even better sunset graced the next cove.

## JUNE 13, DAY 5

When we awoke, something was terribly different. No wind, no waves, hallelujah! The lake lay dead calm. We charged down the hill, bolted breakfast and threw the gear into the boats. Jude still hopped over the rocks on one foot, her other stuffed into an unlaced tennis shoe.

Laberge was content, benign, and we were carefree ducks. Slipping through the flat, emerald water was wonderfully sensual. Paddles and muscles moved in satisfying rhythm. Peering through the still water to the rocky bottom two dozen feet beneath us, we seemed suspended in air. I felt giddy with only the merest slice of aluminum between me and those icy depths. It's pretty odd, when you think about it, that if you stick a piece of metal of the right shape into a river, it will perch atop the water. And fools will sit in that thing and go careening through the water and think it's fun!

The world was bathed in tints of blue. Blue water blended into blue-green spruce-covered slopes and the higher, barer mountains beyond. On the horizon hung blue-white snow.

Far across the water moved the dark head of a common loon. But he refused to voice his idiotlike laugh.

Huge grey lumps of rock lay on each side of us like big wads of whole-wheat dough, half-risen, with pockets and hummocks where some giant had pummeled and kneaded them and sprinkled them with a spruce-tree topping.

I'm a sucker for reflections. The real and the reflected merged, divided only by the red fleck of a faraway stern paddler chasing the blue fleck of a bow paddler. Much magic lay in the serene water, the cloudless sky, the sun's glint, and the canoes gliding through it all.

Jude and Jane fished from the boats. To me, it seemed pointless to throw in the line on blind faith; you could simply look around beneath the boat to see if there were any fish to be had.

Six-inch-long tornado tails—tiny spinning devils I'd never noticed—hung from the little whirlpools my paddle sucked down with each stroke. And, when I slung my paddle forward to begin each stroke, dainty drops danced onto the lake's surface and struggled to remain themselves before melting into the lakewater. In the wild I'm easily entertained.

In the echo chamber between the close cliffs, we couldn't control ourselves; gleeful soprano voices burst into "The hills are alive (ah-a-a-ah) with the sound of *mu*-sic. . . ." Then Barbara sang a rousing version of "Mack the Knife," complete with drum beats boot-stomped on the aluminum hull. She weaved and danced, as well as one can, sitting in a canoe. Gesturing and snapping gloved fingers, she spread her arms wide for the finale. Of course, she didn't paddle a stroke during all this.

"Now Barbara, I don't mind the singing," Jane said, in her sweet way, paddling harder to compensate, "but that stomping has got to go."

We pulled out to cook lunch on the shore, were driven off by mosquitoes; tried a rock out in the water, were driven off by mosquitoes; finally thwarted and had a floating lunch of delicious, cold, leftover black beans and rice. Thus began our culinary degeneration; by the end of the trip we wouldn't notice or care whether hot food was served hot or cold food cold, whether breakfast food was served in the morning or dinner food at night.

After lunch we paddled until I had to make a pit stop. I returned from the woods to find Sue and Jude napping out in the lake in their boat, Jane and Barbara snoozing on the warm beach rocks, and Evelyn snoring face-down on our gear. I, too, lay on the rocks, cowboy hat pressed hard on my face to keep out mosquitoes. Under the hat it was cozily warm and sweaty. Given more and more to gorging and then lying in the sun, we were certainly becoming reptilian.

We finally mobilized and paddled hard to finish the lake that day, though it meant a total paddle of about twenty miles on flat, dead water. Normally, I paddle on my knees to keep my body lined up for better power and comfort. But bending and putting weight on my injured knee brought a dead ache. I had to paddle on only one knee, which was irritating. It would be almost a month before my knee could fully flex.

We neared the end of the lake, and beneath us the current awoke. The lake became shallow; riffles warned of gravel bars just beneath the surface. When the wind and a few waves kicked up, we could no longer see through the water. Occasionally our paddles bashed into the rocky bottom which lay but a few inches beneath the boats.

We rounded a point, saw some cabins, and realized we were heading into the shoals where Laberge becomes the rushing Yukon. I turned for one last look:

> . . . And there sat Sam, looking cool and calm, in the heart of the
> furnace roar;

And he wore a smile you could see a mile, and he said: "Please
  close that door.
It's fine in here, but I greatly fear you'll let in the cold and
  storm—
Since I left Plumtree, down in Tennessee, it's the first time I've
  been warm."

There are strange things done in the midnight sun
  By the men who moil for gold;
The Arctic trails have their secret tales
  That would make your blood run cold;
The Northern Lights have seen queer sights,
  But the queerest they ever did see
Was that night on the marge of Lake Lebarge
  I cremated Sam McGee.

The Yukon looked like a puny creek as it poured from Laberge, but in ferrying across it we discovered a strong current of three or four miles per hour. It felt good after paddling all day on dead water.

Here lay the abandoned settlement of Lower Laberge. Blowing our whistles, we poked around the old telegraph station and sod-roofed cabins. The tinkling of our bells wafted through the forest as we scattered to explore this silent bit of history. A once-red truck—1940s?—slowly rusted, half-choked in green vegetation. Through the woods wound two parallel tracks over which someone had driven this truck back and forth to who knows where.

But it was the *Casca* that made me want to sit down and romanticize about this place. The old steamer lay half-buried in sand. Her weathered wooden hull blended into the muted greys and whites and browns of the beach pebbles. A forlorn widow, she reclined on one elbow and stared up the empty length of Laberge, shunning the river and its downstream adventures.

She was the first of three sternwheelers bearing the same name. After she was retired from steamer duty, she worked as a barge before being left here to rot. I could have crawled in the sand for hours, taking pictures of rusting bolts and scraps of wood, dreaming of the goings-on here at Lower Laberge and on the *Casca* as she danced the Yukon. But it was getting late and people were hungry. We hesitated to camp here near the buildings because bears probably had grown dependent on thoughtless campers' trash, so we ferried across the river.

The shore was rocky, but underneath, the ground became mud as we tromped back and forth. If we planted our feet and wiggled our bodies, a three-foot-square mud cake jiggled and quivered and slurped. Soon the fire, the grill and the cooks sank into the muddy ooze.

However, we produced spaghetti and tomato-and-corn chowder— just as a lone female canoeist appeared on the lake. We waved her over for dinner.

"Best offer I've had all day!" she shouted back. She ferried across the river through the riffle and slogged ashore in her waterproof boots. Those of us in the pro-lawn-chair faction clapped and cheered when she pulled from her canoe a full-sized lawn chair.

Her name was Sybil and she lived in a cabin on Lake Tagish, on the Yukon's headwaters above Whitehorse. She had the kind of easygoing grace and smiling shyness of people we would meet all along the river. She had blondish-grey hair, a slim, sturdy body, the kind of ageless sun-weathered face that made it difficult to tell whether she was thirty-five or fifty.

This was Sybil's fifth canoe trip on the Yukon. Once she shared company with Charlie Mayse from Fairbanks, one of the characters in a book we had read.

"One evening," she laughed, "Charlie had gone off to gather fire-wood, and I was sewing by the fire. As I closed the kit, I saw a brown furry shape bending over the campfire."

She shook her head. "It's interesting how the mind can play tricks when it sees something it absolutely doesn't want to believe. Instead of admitting that a grizzly was there in camp, the only thing I could think was, 'Now why would Charlie bring a bear suit just to impress me?' My mind insisted that it was Charlie and not a bear!

"It was really kind of funny; the bear had the most puzzled, curious look on his face as he poked around the gear at the campfire. It was as if he were thinking, 'Oh, so *this* is what they have in those things that float down the river.' Finally, I stood up in surprise, he stood up in surprise—a young grizzly. We looked at each other.

"I asked him to leave and he did; he ran off through the bushes. I yelled for Charlie, to warn him, wherever he was, that a grizzly was somewhere up there in the woods. Soon Charlie returned with an armload of firewood. I told him the story, but he didn't believe me. So I showed him the fresh pile the poor bear had left as he fled—he was as scared as I was—but Charlie still didn't believe me.

"But then," she grinned, "Charlie looked at his tent and said, 'Well, I guess you wouldn't have ripped my tent just to fool me.' Sure enough, that grizzly had taken a big swipe out of it with his paw as he ran past. Then Charlie believed me."

Sybil sat daintily in her lawn chair, in the oozing mud, wearing a white bonnet and a little green pouch tied around her waist. In the pouch she kept a whistle, money, and matches—her survival kit. "The money won't help you out here," she said, "but when you get rescued, you'll need it when you get to town. And you can't yell for long—your voice will give out and they can't hear you very far anyway—so that's why the whistle. I'm always very careful to tie up my boat, but you never know. A porcupine could chew the line to get the salt from my hands."

With her British-sounding accent, Sybil told us of her four years in the Yukon Territory. For five or six months in the winter, she goes into the bush to help friends who have a trapline. She keeps food ready and the cabin warm, does research for a book, and learns survival skills like snaring rabbits for table and dogteam. The trapline is 130 air miles from the nearest village, and the trappers see no one all winter. In early March, they take the furs into town and send them to a fur auction.

Since she was delighting us with tidbits of her life, we felt compelled to offer some sort of introduction to ourselves. "I know all about you," she grinned. "I read about you in the Whitehorse newspaper when I came through. I thought perhaps I'd meet you on the river."

We invited her to share our camp, but she cocked an eyebrow at our cheechako-chosen bog and winked that she'd opt for higher ground across the river by the *Casca*. She paddled over and set up her open-fronted canvas lean-to. Sybil didn't like enclosed tents, she said. "If I hear something, I want to see immediately what's coming through the woods."

## JUNE 14, DAY 6

It was obscenely early, maybe around 3 A.M., when Evelyn's southern twang penetrated my sleep. "Beth, I'm really in trouble," she moaned. In the dim light I saw she was serious. "I've got a terrible earache. It's killing me. I'm gonna have to hike out in the morning, find the highway, get to a doctor. I can meet y'all in Dawson."

This was a helluva way to start the day. I ignored her remarks about leaving the river, made a few sympathetic inquiries, and told her to take two aspirin, stuff the cotton from the bottle in her ear, wear my knit cap and we'd deal with it in the morning.

"I'll worry about this tomorrow," I worried, imagining Evelyn wandering senseless through the mountains for days. She was snoring again before I could get back to sleep.

The tough ol' gal was up hours before the rest of us, pawing through the food as usual. By the time I got up, she had taken some antibiotics, felt better, and grinned that she was sorry she had threatened to leave me. Though she could hear with but one ear for the next few days and felt a little "spacey," she remained in fine spirits. Though she exasperated me (and I her) at various times throughout the trip, I truly admired her hardiness and steadfastness, and the zaniness and stubbornness that went with it. Almost twice my age, she could outbackpack me any day.

Evelyn struggled with sourdough pancakes. Doughboy, our sour-dough starter who had come 4,000 miles with us in a plastic jug, was flaccid this morning; the pancakes never caked. The sourdoughs who nurtured their sourdough starters over Chilkoot Pass in the dead of winter must have known something we didn't, because we never could revive Dough-boy. Downriver, we jilted him.

When we cooked the dreaded powdered eggs two or three times a week, our great challenge was to overwhelm them with garlic powder, dried onions, dried potatoes, dried picante sauce, or whatever else we had lying around. We had brought very little meat, because dehydrated or freeze-dried meat is expensive and somewhat tasteless, so our menus were heavy on beans and eggs. Protein, protein. Some of us took the vitamin supplements that Sue had obtained.

Jane played a recording of owl calls. Sometimes this scares up smaller birds, owls' prey curious to spot their enemy. But we had no luck.

We heated water and scattered to bathe on the beach. Jane's and Barbara's daily baths amused us; I had never seen anyone bathe so often on a camping trip. We should have been tipped off, I guess, back in Yosemite when Jane had squatted in the snowbank, dipped water from the icy stream, and bathed in the pitch dark. That's hard-core. Now, just as I took off my pants, there hove into view a flotilla of canoes and rafts. I sat in my lawn chair, crossed my legs, and draped my pants over bare lap. The travelers waved and landed across the river to explore Lower Laberge.

Sybil paddled over as she left camp. She said she'd probably end up tonight at Hootalinqua, about thirty miles downstream, and would look for us. "Farther downriver," she said, "it's important that you agree each morning on a meeting place in case you get separated from each other." We nodded.

"You better just plan on it and be prepared for it," she said. "You'll be floating side by side, then when you approach an island, and there are hundreds, the current will pull one boat this way and the other that way. The current will be so strong you can't fight it, and you might end up on a sandbar if you do—so just be prepared. And don't try shouting, either, because no one can hear you through the trees and with the river's noise. You can yell till you're blue in the face. Once you get separated, because of all the islands and channels and so forth, you might not see each other for hours. So just go on and meet at the agreed-upon place." We thanked her and she paddled off down the Yukon in her bonnet.

In a little while, we, too, shoved into the blue-green water and floated a narrow channel. The current's speed was breathtaking, especially if we looked straight down through ten or fifteen feet of water to the pebbly bottom blurring past. It was hypnotizing. In the depths hung shredded pink fish guts.

Steep, sandy cutbanks, sometimes 300 feet high, rose to terraces of dark green spruce and lighter-colored poplar. In the distance, rounded hills with bald patches melted into a white cloudbank.

From Lower Laberge to Hootalinqua is known as the Thirtymile section of the Yukon. Our canoe bobbled easily through the occasional riffles and small rapids that had plagued the stampeders in their wooden boats. Somewhere in this stretch is Casey's Rock, which wrecked the boat and the entire outfit of an old prospector named Casey, who plied these waters alone in the days before the Klondike strike. Undaunted, Casey tramped back over the Chilkoot, bought another outfit, again crossed the mountains, built another boat, drifted again down the Thirtymile stretch. When the same rock once again ripped his boat to shreds and pitched his outfit into the current, Casey swam to shore, wandered into an empty prospectors' camp, found a gun and shot himself to death.

We were carefree, however, and relished floating through the middle of the Yukon Territory. The day was beautiful, crisp, and a little nippy only when the wind came up.

Once Evelyn and I pulled out for fresh water at a creek. It was fortunate we could spot creeks' ice shelves far ahead, because in the fast, wide river, we had to start maneuvers a half-mile ahead of where we wanted to land. If we failed to start our ferrying soon enough and overshot a creek, the only ways to get back to it were to paddle hard upstream against the current in the narrow eddies or to struggle along on the bank through the thick undergrowth; if we missed a creek we usually drifted on and hoped for another. We had agreed that whenever one boat stopped, the others would also, for safety, but today as Evelyn and I sidled up to the bank, our partners disappeared around a bend.

Oh, well, so you're left alone in the middle of the Yukon? We jumped ashore and spotted wolf tracks. We were thrilled, but knew there was little chance of seeing one of the shy creatures. Were they watching us? Evelyn trotted off through the brush with the water jug, while I photographed the paw prints. I was thinking she'd been gone too long just about the time I found some small bear tracks. Just as I started after her she reappeared, safe and happy.

The others were waiting for us around the bend; we paddled on together and soon stopped at a couple of cabins that had been a refueling station for the old sternwheelers. We carried cooking gear up the steep path through the forest and into the mosquitoes. For the first time, Jude and Jane donned "Shoo-Bug" jackets made of absorbent mesh impregnated with mosquito repellent. The jackets seemed to keep the mosquitoes at bay quite handily. We built a fire and boiled up a soup of leftovers, in the shadow of an old cart probably once used to haul wood.

The 200 sternwheelers that once ruled the Yukon burned a total of 300,000 cords of wood in their day, some devouring two cords per hour. Woodcutting at the camps, which lay about thirty miles apart, was a full-time job during the summer navigation season.

Peering through the windows of the decaying cabins, I imagined the lives of the lonely souls who chopped wood for those voracious steamers. I felt a kinship, too, with thousands of canoeists like me who had poked their noses into these same windows. There were two sod-roofed log cabins, one with a covered porch. Nearby rusted the runners of a dogsled. I walked through the poplars, down a path between the wildflowers, to the outhouse—a romantic one-holer, somehow picturesque as the afternoon light sifted through its cracks.

We paddled on and ran smack into a gorgeous bald eagle standing on a sandy bluff at the water's edge. He looked serene, but I fooled around so long trying to take pictures that he flew away over the river.

Later, we heard a terrible commotion behind us. Barbara screamed, "Jane caught a fish, Jane caught a fish!" Our chief fisherwoman had been trolling her line behind the boat all day.

We declared the ten-inch fish a trout, and grinning from ear to ear, Jane held him high to pose for pictures. We were pulled into shore in about a foot of water. Just as we opened our mouths to suggest that Jane hold him over the boat rather than the water, he dropped from the hook and ker-plunked into the river.

He sat there on the bottom, no doubt contemplating life's strange twists of fate, while Sue and Evelyn thrashed about trying to grab him. Then he was gone.

We couldn't help laughing. Even funnier, this trolled-up trophy would turn out to be the one, the only, fish we would catch in 2,000 miles!

The sun eased behind the mountains; the few clouds floating between patches of blue sky became tinged with purple. The river was a glassy liquid green, reflected from the spruces that had crowded shoulder to shoulder down to the water. Silently, we slipped through the rich light and dreamy shadows. It was probably eight or nine o'clock.

"Look!" whispered Jane. Barely visible in the shadows where the forest met the rocky beach, a porcupine sniffed among the leaves.

All along the river, trees and bushes bore the violent scars of spring breakup. Each year as the ice pushes and crashes down the river in great sheets and blocks, it rips the bark from the lower four feet or so of the trees. In some places, it flattens huge swaths of full-grown trees.

As the light faded, we met the valley on our right that brings the Teslin River to join the Yukon, and we spotted the abandoned Mountie post of Hootalinqua downstream on our left. We had come an amazing thirty-two miles, having put into the river well after noon and having stopped at least an hour for lunch.

There was Sybil's aluminum boat. We hopped out and talked to her as she ate pork and beans from a big blackened saucepan. She wore a napkin tucked primly into her sweater under her chin and a pink checkered scarf on her head. We swatted and danced and cursed at the mosquitoes, smearing Muskol or other repellents on our faces, but except for an occasional languid wave of her kerchief, Sybil ignored the humming cloud.

Apparently the mosquitoes could get pretty bad here, though. Frederick Schwatka, the U.S. Army lieutenant who was the first person to explore the length of the Yukon, said of the Thirtymile section during his 1883 expedition:

> . . . not a sign of any game was seen . . . the tracks of an animal are about the only part of it that could exist here in the mosquito season . . . had I obtained a fair shot, I honestly doubt if I could have secured it . . . for the reason that [the mosquitoes] were absolutely so dense that it was impossible to see clearly through the mass in taking aim. . . . I heard reports, which I believe to be well founded . . . that the great brown bear . . . of these regions is at times compelled to succumb to these insects. (*The Yukon,* page 143)

Hootalinqua means "where two big waters meet." The settlement sits on a wide bend, at a kind of cove, overlooking the confluence of the Teslin and the Yukon. In the cove tonight, the water was smooth and peaceful. Several cabins were there, slowly tumbling to earth. The flagstaff still stood atop the roofless roadhouse. I imagined a bunch of stern-jawed Mounties living here, policing the stampeding hordes the river had flung from between those hills.

Sybil led a gastronomic tour of Hootalinqua, showing us the not-yet-ripe wild gooseberries, cranberries, and strawberries. The purple fireweed was edible, too, she said, so we nibbled some. The smallest, youngest shoots were the sweetest. She said she always enjoyed young fireweed salad.

We asked if Sybil would mind our camping here. She said no, that whenever river runners camp at landmarks like Hootalinqua, they want to meet other river runners. We thanked her and felt glad that we weren't intruding. She would sleep in a tiny cabin near the water's edge, above whose doorway perched a bleached moose skull with antlers. Tonight, instead of emptying the boats and carrying them up onto the bank, we left much of the gear in them and simply tied them to a tree; that would be our procedure for the rest of the trip.

Over dinner, we discussed plans for the next few days. There was general frustration because we never knew what time the group would get the urge to get on the river each day. It was hard to plan our individual activities. Barbara and Jane were anxious to get to Dawson, having scheduled themselves on other adventures around Alaska in a few weeks. We discovered that they had always thought of Whitehorse to Dawson as a two-week trip, while I had considered it a leisurely three- or four-week trip. After all, these 460 miles were supposed to be the most historic and scenic of the entire Yukon.

We finally settled on what was to me a terribly regimented schedule, which meant we had to use a watch to tell time by. Ugh. But everyone else seemed agreeable, so I went along. I had chosen to do the trip with a group for safety and companionship, and accepting this schedule was part of the price of that decision. And after all, some frustration and tension over adjusting to each other were to be expected. Actually, I felt we were coping remarkably well, considering the strains of all the preparations and the 4,000-mile trip to Whitehorse. It was a fun bunch, and their company was worth having to live by a clock until Dawson.

In mid-discussion, Barbara accidentally dumped into her lap a whole bowl of soup. Swearing and laughing, she sprinted to the river to wash it off, as we chanted "Bear bait! Bear bait!"

We agreed that we would be on the river each day from 10 A.M. until 6 P.M., with a one-hour lunch break and other stops to take pictures, look at wildlife, poke around cabins, and such. On the river by ten meant breakfast at eight, and with that realization the others stampeded for bed.

I continued to sit alone for hours by the fire, sacrificing to the coals one little stick after another. Nearby, a clear stream gurgled from the hills into the river. The Yukon continued to roll past and the Teslin continued to pour in; there's something magical and comforting about the way rivers keep rolling, year after year. Every now and then a log drifted past. Two brown mice with white bellies and legs darted nervously around the woodpile. I listened to the birds and wondered if a bear was sneaking up behind me. The sky grew red; I whispered notes into my tape recorder. Snuggled into layers of wool, I blew smoke rings of frosty breath and inched my toes closer to the fire.

I was at peace, utterly. The movement of the river, the fluid notes of the stream and the birds' songs, the glowing and dimming of the coals: the changing sameness of the scene was sensual and rhythmic. This moment and a thousand others like it before and since were why I had come to the Yukon. I came to sit here by this fire and look out on this river and think whatever thoughts floated into my head.

It was getting lighter, the dusky night becoming dawn. So I went to bed.

## JUNE 15, DAY 7

We gulped oatmeal and Sue read aloud about Hootalinqua. On yonder island rested an old sternwheeler, the *Evelyn*, and there we headed.

Today, we straddled a different, more muscular Yukon. Glacial silt and raindrops and grains of earth from 13,900 square miles had tumbled 253 miles down the Teslin River and into the Yukon. The Teslin was the first of more than a dozen major rivers that would swell the Yukon between here and the Bering Sea. Accepting the Teslin's offering, the Thirtymile Yukon, a sparkling, once-slender innocent, spread out a half-mile wide and became a big, dirty old broad.

Suddenly, two objects loomed in midstream. At first they seemed downed trees, dangerous strainers that could trap canoes or people. Dead ahead, a cow and calf moose forded the Yukon, their powerful shoulders driving through the current. Flanked by dark green spruces and blue sky, the two brown shapes surged through the blue-green river. We drifted down upon them, cameras clicking. The Yukon basin supposedly grows moose bigger than those of lower Canada, Maine, or Montana; the record antler spread being 6 feet 5⅝ inches. Now, with surprising speed and quietness, but little grace, they vanished into the alders of Hootalinqua Island.

Babbling over the trip's first moose, we glanced up to see our island race past. We ferried hard across the current, dug into the island's meager tail eddy, and muscled upstream beneath the alder branches. We scrambled up the crumbling bank and, in wetsuit booties, life jackets, and bear bells, crashed through the woods in search of the *Evelyn*. Sure enough, a full-fledged sternwheeler nestled among the vines and saplings, her smoke-stack peering over the treetops. Built in Seattle in 1908, she had cruised the Tanana and the Yukon. A clearing, wooden tracks, and huge winches gave evidence of how she was dragged from the water for repairs and left forever. Beneath the curve of her graceful rotting hull, we gazed through the mosquitoes to the windows along her deck. What characters had waved their hats through those windows, and what sights had they witnessed as they steamed up and down the mighty Yukon?

As we explored, the Whitman College group paddled up. We had met them back at the ferry in Skagway, when they unloaded their boats as we unloaded ours. Although they had had to hike the Chilkoot Trail and paddle the headwaters lakes, they had already caught up with us. Now we learned that this year's Whitman leader had, several years earlier, led a group in which the camp doctor had been none other than our friend Richard O. Albert from Alice, Texas. Small world.

The morning breeze quickened our strokes as we paddled on down-river. Whizzing around the big snakelike bends, we grew complacent about the occasional riffles. Once, Evelyn and I were distracted by eating peanuts and ignored the situation until too late to redirect our course. We found ourselves in fast, shallow water; rocks zoomed just beneath our hull and little submerged boulders raised pillows of water all over the place. We dinged a few, but had no real problems and laughed about it afterwards.

The river grew bigger, the bends farther apart. We hadn't seen Jane and Barbara for a few bends. We couldn't imagine that they'd had any problems, but we back-paddled and finally began to ferry to the bank with a worried feeling that if they'd stopped for any reason, we could now be several miles downriver. At last, a tiny shape rounded the bend.

"You missed the biggest excitement of the trip!" shouted Jane when they caught up. Rolling their eyes and waving their arms, they spilled the details. As they had approached the riffle that Evelyn and I had bumbled through, they had meticulously followed our course. Somehow, they found a rock we hadn't, and the current pinned them broadside against it. They sat for a moment, looking at each other, wedged against the rock. The icy Yukon lapped at the gunnels.

"Barbara," Jane had said, "I've just got to get this fishing line in before we do anything else." Jane began to wind and Barbara began to scream; the line had wrapped around Barb when they spun in the current and now the lure had imbedded itself in her ear lobe. Jane reeled Barbara toward her; Barbara crawled on all fours over the gear and Jane removed the hook. Then Barb climbed onto the rock, wrestled the canoe free, and hopped in as the current caught them. They floated on down the Yukon— thinking all the while, no doubt, about our pact to keep each other in sight. Truth was, there wouldn't have been much we could have done if they had dumped, except shout encouragement and chase gear and people.

It was grey, cloudy, 50°; when the wind crept up the valley we needed gloves and wool hats. We drifted awhile, then pulled out to warm ourselves. Leaning back in our lawn chairs, we snuggled our toes close to the fire, gobbled potato soup and fresh-baked cornbread, and sipped hot chocolate. It's a rough life on the river.

Eventually we headed downstream and thwarted for the afternoon nap. If we were quiet and put our heads low, we heard the river silt dancing against the aluminum canoe. It made a "shhhhh" sound, like a finger nail drawn slowly down the length of an emery board. Sue took first watch. The sun had returned and I drifted to sleep. . . .

"Hey, guys, I think you better paddle," Sue apologized. We bolted upright and broke into a hard backpaddle to avoid bashing into the bank. A few embarrassed smiles, then quickly we resumed slumber position.

Now Jude was on watch as we drifted mile after mile down the Yukon. Jane fished. "Backpaddle," Jude whispered to Jane. Beneath my hat, I cocked an ear. Their paddles splashed as they stroked harder and harder. The sound of whitewater grew closer.

"Hey, y'all!" Jude sounded the alert. We were bound for a big, solid boulder that jutted out from shore. Around it swirled a great deal of water. We scrambled to unhook the canoes from each other, but saw we couldn't make it, then paddled madly to miss the rock. We pivoted around the rock, but there was no avoiding the huge whirlpool-like boils below it. Evelyn and I were nearest the surging eddy line; we knew we were in for a ride.

"Stay low, keep your balance," Sue and I muttered simultaneously. We spun into the boils with a good jolt, but in an instant we had rushed on downstream and were grinning sheepishly.

We decided this might be a good time to unthwart and paddle, though. Big boils continued to blub up suddenly from nowhere, some-times right under the bow. Sandy cutbanks rose from the river, with phalanxes of straight spruces marching down their crevices. Several game trails switchbacked down the steep slopes. Cheery white clouds splattered a blue sky.

I was fascinated by a canoe bow heading down a big, smooth river, by the vastness of the sky with its cloudy swirls and splotches. I would take hundreds of pictures of the bow of our canoe—sometimes with my feet propped on it, sometimes with a paddle shaft, sometimes with the lonely bow rope tucked under its elastic cord—pointing the way to the future, the unknown, the Bering Sea. It would amuse me afterwards to chart, through the pictures, the gradual and absolute deterioration of that clean white bow rope as it weathered three months on the Yukon.

Long before we expected it, there lay the abandoned village of Big Salmon. We had only a few miles in which to find a campsite before we'd end up there with dozens of other canoeists we wanted to avoid. As we flirted with sandbars and shoals, a debate erupted. Some wanted to camp on the left bank, others said there was nothing but mosquitoes and bushes over there, and we'd have to ferry like crazy to make it to the right bank to see Big Salmon in the morning. Meanwhile, we were barrelling toward Big Salmon. We finally ferried into a marshy creek on the right bank, but found no solid ground. We paddled down a few dozen yards and Evelyn scurried through the bushes up the steep bank into the woods, bear bells atinkle. Soon she crashed back down and announced this was her campsite choice. At the top of the rise, among the spruces, lay a small graveyard. The mosquitoes hummed and there were no clearings or level ground for bedroom or kitchen. I finally took a poll and we nixed Evelyn's choice, tumbled back into the boats, and paddled on in search of a home.

Again the left-bank-versus-right-bank argument was shouted between boats, while Evelyn grumbled into my ear that we never camped where she wanted. How was I supposed to "coordinate" a bunch that seemed to have no common ground? Barbara looked up from the map and announced that the creek in whose mouth we now sat was a cut-through to the Big Salmon River. All we had to do to find a nice quiet island campsite, she said, was paddle upstream in the creek a mile or two. Sounded like fun.

Soon the creek narrowed and the current flowed faster and faster against us. The tributary was not very deep and only about a canoe-length wide, but it was a powerful little bugger. The muddy banks offered little footing for tracking boats with lines. Besides, it was more fun to see if we could outwit and outpaddle the little devil. Barb and Jane got tangled up in a willow bush, so Sue and Jude tossed back their rescue line and pulled them upstream. I thought of Humphrey Bogart and Katharine Hepburn.

Evelyn and I managed to beat it around the willow and bash into the bank upstream. There we held the boat against the current by clutching clumps of grass one after the other until each uprooted. Hand over hand, we finally clawed our way into the Big Salmon River, where a perfect island campsite lay twenty yards away. Now Evelyn suddenly got her first chance to execute a critical ferry in fast current. As Jude shouted encouragement and I called instructions from the bow, we scooted right across without slipping downstream much and landed, to applause, alongside the others on the island's gently sloping gravel. We were tired. We'd been fighting currents and mucking around the forest for at least an hour past our scheduled disembarkation time. And today we had paddled not only thirty-five miles down the Yukon, but a mile or so *up* part of the Big Salmon.

The island was a quiet haven, flat and relatively mosquito-free. The only high ground for the bedroom was a little clearing among some trees. Trouble was, it was strewn with moose prints and droppings, like some favored feeding spot.

As we tromped back and forth between the boats and the bedroom, Jane spotted a semipalmated plover doing her broken-wing act. The mother bird does this to draw predators away from the nest.

"Hey y'all," said Jane, "watch out; there's a nest around here somewhere. It'll be right on the ground, and the eggs are really hard to see—they look just like little rocks."

We avoided the area, but soon Jane announced that we'd already stepped on the nest by accident and destroyed all three eggs. The speckled eggs blended perfectly with the greys and yellows of the beach pebbles. We felt awful and wondered if the poor mother, perhaps unaware that the eggs would never hatch, would keep hanging around.

Jane and Barb took a bath, while Jude and Evelyn threw together a casserole of dehydrated broccoli and squash, whole-kernel rye, and cheese powder. Sue dug out the scotch, wine, and bourbon and I spread out the music library.

We settled in for carousing as dinner bubbled on the fire. If you've ever wondered what it would be like to sit among six women on a Yukon sandbar and wait for dinner, here's a sampling:

JANE:       *(dragging a sittin' log from the woodpile)* I am getting off these rocks.

EVELYN:   Oh yeah, there's a lot about that in the *Hite* book. *(sound of tinkling bear bells as Evelyn stirs pot)*

BARBARA:  Let's sing a little song. Come on y'all, let's sing "The Rose."

SUE:         But you can only sing it when you're drunk and I can only remember it when I'm sober. Or maybe vice versa.

| | |
|---|---|
| JUDE: | I don't think we put enough rice in here. |
| CHORUS: | Right! |
| SUE: | Let's all do our school songs. . . . (groans) |
| JANE: | (jumping to attention, putting her hand over her heart, bursting into song) I wish I was in the land of cotton, old times there are not forgotten . . . |
| CHORUS: | (screaming) Look away! Look away! Look away, Dixieland. . . . |
| BARBARA: | I bet you were a cheerleader, Jane. |
| JANE: | I was! (howls, claps) |
| SUE: | I bet this is about as far from Dixie as we'll ever be. |
| BARBARA: | Oh, Beth has got the ka-zoo ready! |
| BETH: | Do I have any requests? (through kazoo hums tune to "When the Saints Go Marchin' In") |
| SUE: | (ad libbing) Oh when the Yukon, oh when she rolls, oh when the Yukon goes rollin' on, Lord I want to be in that number, when the Yukon begins to roll. |
| ALL: | (joining) And when Kazoo-Mama (my CB radio "handle"), begins to play. . . . |
| JANE: | (blurting it out just before the beat) When the Yukon Belle (Evelyn's CB handle) begins to cook! |
| ALL: | When the Yukon Belle, begins to cook . . . I want to be in that number. . . . |
| JANE: | (spreading arms and circling the campsite) When the Kittiwake (Jane's handle) begins to fly! |
| ALL: | Oh when the Kittiwake begins to fly. . . . (all collapse into laughter) |
| EVELYN: | You all can't imagine what that sounds like coming through one ear. . . . (sounds of pots and pans clanking as others serve themselves) Those are beans, but don't dig too deep because they're burned. |
| BARBARA: | Where's my fork? |
| EVELYN: | You know, those stringy things—once you know they're squash— aren't half bad. |
| BARBARA: | Has anybody seen my spoon? |
| JUDE: | (as others pick through food with puzzled expressions) It's rice and squash and broccoli. . . . |
| EVELYN: | Now ladies, I think we have to assess what we have left over after the first week. We have (holding finger in air with a flourish) fifteen pounds of peanuts. . . . (laughter and clapping) |
| BARBARA: | (in a wee voice) Where's my fork? |
| EVELYN: | . . . forty pounds of flour. I think we need to bake more bread around here. |
| BETH: | (tasting food) Wonderful! This is great. Is the rye the crunchy stuff? |
| CHORUS: | Y'all done good. Let's toast rye! |
| BARBARA: | (singing) Drove my Chevy to the levee but the levee was dry . . . |
| EVELYN: | Everybody eat up 'cause the beans burned and we're gonna throw 'em to the fish. |
| BARBARA: | . . . good ol' boys drinkin' whiskey and rye. . . . Let's hear it baby, for the Great Northerns! (whistles, clapping) |

SUE:         Y'all did good! Are we ever drunk. . . .

BARBARA:    Did somebody say you made some creme de cacao out of hot chocolate mix and Everclear? . . .

So here we sat, at the mouth of the Big Salmon River, where one Major J.M. Walsh, an ex-Mountie who'd been hired as the commissioner of the new Yukon Territory during the Stampede, had been stopped by snow and ice en route to Dawson and had waited out the winter. And it was just downstream, at the village of Big Salmon, where ten stampeders once spread ten  blankets on the bank and ended their partnership by dividing their outfit ten ways, including their large scow which they shredded into ten piles of wood.

The others staggered off to bed and I slouched in my lawn chair, watched the smoke from my breath, and listened to the river and the birds. When I finally crawled into bed, I heard great splashings in the river and tried to decide whether I'd prefer the moose to gallop across my stomach or my spine. I craned my head to investigate and discovered that a huge tree had floated too near the bank and had been pinned against the rushing current; its bobbing limbs sounded just like a thrashing moose.

## JUNE 16, DAY 8

Once again, breakfast discussion was schedules, deadlines, and mileage quotas. But it was a fine, sunny day and soon we paddled a few hundred yards down to Big Salmon.

Mud, mud, mud, always mud. With wetsuit booties and tennis shoes and Gore-Tex pants, I was merely annoyed, but as I squished into the goo I felt sympathy for those old miners and traders who'd lived in the stuff. They probably had but one pair of shoes—no dry tennies to pull from waterproof bags. Maybe they cursed the mud day and night, all up and down the Yukon. Of course, the mud came only in summer, like the mosquitoes, and folks probably felt no hardship. If one of them had found himself in Dallas rush-hour traffic, he'd probably feel sorry for *us*.

The college group's tents and canoes sprawled among the ruins of Big Salmon. One guy balanced on a rope strung about a foot above the ground between two trees. He gripped the rope with his bare feet, using a canoe paddle as a balance pole. He and two friends entertained themselves this way for about an hour.

Everywhere grew "chiming bells" or "languid lady"—living lavender bells that draped delicately from their stalks.

From gently waving grasses rose a weathered grey cabin whose roof had collapsed. I peered through the doorway into blue sky. In another cabin squatted an ancient black stove whose pipe pushed up through the roof; I imagined the soup that had bubbled on it, and the frozen toes that had toasted by that rusty black stove. In one corner leaned a frazzled broom, and dozens of recently emptied liquor bottles lined the shelves.

Quite Yukon-looking in her leather cowboy hat and knee-high lace-up boots, Sue posed in a doorway. What it must have been like to have awakened every morning, stoked a few logs into the fire, and gazed through this doorway across this river!

We stood beneath the eaves of a sturdy cabin with a sign on it that said "Big Salmon Trading Post and Village." One of the other canoeists took group pictures of the fearless Texas Women's Yukon River Expedition: Jane in white terry cloth sun-visor, nylon windbreaker, wool pants, rubber-soled hunting boots; I in blue Gore-Tex top and bottoms, an orange wool hat stuffed into my waistband, a grey wool sweater, tennis shoes and wetsuit booties; Evelyn in her "First National Bank of Muleshoe, Texas" farmer's hat, chamois long-sleeved shirt topped by a bright yellow life jacket, beige Gore-Tex pants, muddy canvas boots; Barbara in her fisherman's hat, red windbreaker, wool pants; Sue, in knit hat, dirty yellow life jacket, jeans, denim work shirt, rubber-soled boots; Jude, in leather cowboy hat, life jacket, Gore-Tex pants, one boot and one tennis shoe.

We waved goodbye, swung into the river, drifted past a naked woman soaping her hair in the 47° water; Jude hollered, "You've got guts!"

A headwind blew in and our paddles felt like lead in the water. Occasionally the mountains vanished and before us lay only tall spruces, shiny blue water, and friendly clouds. Once, we pulled into an eddy beneath the remains of a cabin that teetered on the edge of a high, eroded bank. Evelyn clambered up into the woods and returned with two handfuls of fresh rhubarb. "I guess they used to grow it here and now it's gone wild," she said.

We passed cutbanks so steep that no vegetation could get a foothold. As rocks and dirt clods slid down them continuously and plopped into the water, loud pops echoed up the valley.

Tons of water forced their way through the ugly jumble of a massive logjam where the Yukon had tossed full-grown trees against a little island. On the right bank stood an old gold dredge that had been hauled in and moved periodically to work the feeder streams. The others disappeared into the mosquito-thicket to see the dredge, while I relaxed in the boat.

On the river again, we heard whitewater roaring ahead, but saw nothing. Thoughts of uncharted waterfalls or perilous logjams always enter my head at times like this. Spotting a major hole where the Yukon heaved around a big boulder near the left bank, we steered a wide passage around the thundering mess.

Amid a blackened area of several hundred acres, a sign tacked on a tree said, "This was caused by your campfire. Is your fire out?"

Evelyn still could hear out of but one ear, which made for rather strained communications that went something like this:

(Beth, in bow): "Oh look, there's that old dredge way over there on the right bank. Do you want to go over there and check it out? We need to angle the bow upstream or we're going to overshoot it. Evelyn? . . ." (as dredge whizzes past)

As we paddled, I regarded my hands. A week of wind, sun, and grappling with ropes, sand, rocks, and bushes, had made them so dry, cracked, and raw that they stung. Did men ever have this problem? It was hard to believe the dryness in the air here in one of the continent's largest river basins, but our hands were proof. And we'd read that parts of the Yukon basin receive less annual precipitation than arid Phoenix, Arizona. My lips and hands had already sucked up the half-tube of Vaseline that I had expected to last three months.

A young guy was stuffing gear into a big kayak at the woods' edge, and we figured at last we'd reached Byer's woodcamp. He said it was about a mile farther downstream, and as we floated past we enacted with him the river ritual: "Where ya from? Where d'ja put in? When d'ja put in? Where ya takin' out? First time on the river? Well, see ya downriver." He had come from Anchorage for his annual Whitehorse-to-Dawson float. He was paddling a Klepper folding kayak that weighed eighty pounds (about the same as a canoe). I questioned him about it; there was one back in Dallas for half-price ("only been used once"). Supposedly ideal for Alaskan river travel, they break into two suitcase-sized parcels that you can easily take on a bush plane or a commercial jet. They are made of rubberized canvas and hold almost as much gear as a canoe. The drawback is that loading and unloading each day is more difficult than with an open canoe, and you get tired of sitting on your rump with your legs stretched before you all the time.

A rusty can atop a high bank was our only clue that several cabins of Byer's woodcamp stood up there in the woods. Grabbing the pot of soaking lentils from beneath Evelyn's seat, we hauled cooking gear up the sandy bank for lunch. The abandoned camp seemed lonely. Moldering clothes and old cans lay scattered on the ground, and a wall of grey clouds moved across the sky. We prowled the woods for firewood, then Jude and Barbara tackled lunch. Evelyn sprawled for a nap beneath her rain jacket on the grassy slope in front of a cabin. The rest of us scribbled in our journals, swatted mosquitoes, sipped hot chocolate, and anticipated hot bannock bread.

Barbara mixed the bannock: any ratio you feel like of whole-wheat flour, water, and baking powder, maybe a little salt. It's hard to ruin bannock. We baked bread and everything else in a skillet with a lid, set directly on the coals. When one side was done, we would turn over the bread (which was burning and stiff on the bottom and gooey and floppy on the top) and put it back into the skillet to cook on the other side. This was often a two-person job.

As Barb squatted over the fire and wrestled the bread, it leapt from the skillet, flew through the air, and landed gooey side down (what else?) in the dirt and sticks and leaves, precisely on the moldy sole of a long-abandoned shoe.

"Well, sonofabitch!" she sputtered and slammed down the skillet. She jumped up, hands on hips, stomped and snorted for a few seconds, then picked the thing off the ground, tossed it back in the skillet and stuck it on the fire. We grinned and shrugged. Jude patiently picked sticks and leaves from the dough. Evelyn slept through it all.

Finally the bannock was done and delicious, leaves and all. As we finished, two men with rifles stomped down the path. They were from one of the two motorized rafts that we'd seen traveling together. They had somehow misplaced their buddies. Both were stocky and in their forties; one was dark-haired, the other blond. Each sported a scraggly new beard. They hailed from Anchorage. They had run out of gas back on Lake Laberge and now faced several days of paddling their bulky rubber rafts until they reached gas at Carmacks. Secretly we delighted in their plight because we resented motors on the river. But they were friendly guys and we enjoyed chatting with them. They seemed amused and perhaps a little impressed by six women from Texas who'd never seen the Yukon, but were floating—*sans* motors—the same stretch as these rough-tough Alaskans.

We exchanged pleasantries with the two men as we sipped our hot chocolate. Suddenly, with a devilish light in her eye and working hard to keep a straight face, Jude blurted, "Evelyn, maybe these guys could help with your research on the river!"

The rest of us turned our faces and suppressed snickers, but with terrific aplomb, Evelyn said, "Yeah," and smiled sweetly. The guys nodded absently, probably thinking she was studying wildflowers or something. They waved goodbye, said they'd see us downriver, and strode off to find their partners.

We eased back into the river and thwarted; the others dozed while Evelyn and I took watch. The day was so peaceful that we shared an unspoken bond not to make a sound. We communicated with gestures and raised eyebows and smiles. It was fun, a secret world where the only noises were Jude's light rhythmic snoring and the gush of river silt on aluminum hulls.

After awhile, the others stirred and naptime gave way to visiting hour. Sue read to us from *The Yukon* about the gold discovery that had transformed the Yukon into an overnight racetrack.

George Washington Carmack was born in California where his father wound up in the gold stampede of 1849. George had come into the Yukon in the 1880s and married a pudgy Tagish Indian named Kate. He and two Indian friends, Skookum ("Strong") Jim and Tagish Charlie, had wandered back and forth from the coast to the Yukon for years, packing goods, cutting timber or catching salmon. Jim held the Chilkoot record for having lugged 156 pounds of bacon over the pass on his back in one trip. Around the town of Fortymile (downstream from present-day Dawson), which was the center of gold-mining activity in the early 1890s, Carmack was known as the biggest liar on the Yukon.

In May of 1896, Carmack sat amid the burned ruins of Fort Selkirk on the Yukon and fancied he saw a good omen in the morning star. He flipped a silver dollar in the air, and when it landed tails up, he knew Fate meant for him to go downstream. So down to Fortymile he went, and the night he arrived he dreamed of salmon with twenty-dollar gold pieces for eyes. "As

I reached out my hand to grasp one of the fish," he recalled later, "I awoke with a death grip on my right ear."

That meant Fate now wanted him to go salmon fishing, so he and Kate and Jim and Charlie set out for the Thron-diuck River, which was known as a good salmon stream. ("Klondike" was the miners' mispronunciation of the Indian word "Thron-diuck," meaning "Hammerwater" and so called because the Indians hammered stakes across its mouth to spread their fishing nets.) But the fishing was poor, so instead, Carmack's little band cut timber to sell in Fortymile. A man named Robert Henderson (who would turn out to be partly responsible for the Klondike strike) happened by and talked up some good gold prospects he'd struck about fifteen miles from Carmack's camp. Henderson made it clear that George was welcome to stake, but that he didn't want "any damn Siwashes staking on that creek." That anti-Indian remark would cost him dearly.

Later, Carmack and his two "Siwash" friends trekked up to Henderson's diggings and found them unimpressive. Once again, the two Indians were received coldly. But, following the prospectors' code, Carmack told Henderson he'd let him know if they spotted anything promising as they returned to Carmack's camp.

On the way back, they hunted along Rabbit Creek, a Klondike tributary, because their dried salmon had run out. Jim shot, butchered, and cooked a moose while waiting for Carmack and Charlie to catch up. Then he went to the creek for a drink and beheld more gold than he'd ever seen, just lying there. When the others arrived, he let them eat, then broke the news. Recalled Carmack later:

> Throwing off my pack, I walked down to the rim, and as soon as I reached it I stopped and looked down. My heart skipped a beat. After rubbing my eyes with the back of my hand to wipe away a misty film that enveloped the pupils, I reached down and picked up a nugget about the size of a dime. I put it between my teeth and bit at it like a newsboy who had found a quarter in the street. . . . Charlie grabbed the pan and the shovel, started down on the run, tripped and fell, and would have rolled into the creek if I had not caught him. I took the shovel and dug up some of the loose bedrock . . . I could see the raw gold laying thick between the flaky slabs, like cheese sandwiches.
>
> I walked back to the rim and set the gold-pan on the ground. Then as near as I can remember, three full grown men tried to see how big damn fools they could make of themselves. We did a war dance around that gold-pan. It was a combination war dance, composed of a Scotch hornpipe, Indian fox trot, syncopated Irish jig and a sort of Siwash Hula-Hula. (*The Yukon*, pages 152-153)

They got four dollars in gold from the first pan. In those days a ten-cent pan meant "paying" gold.

Carmack staked the two 500-foot claims allowed and renamed the creek "Bonanza." It was August 17, 1896. They filled a spent Winchester cartridge with gold and returned to Fortymile, telling groups of miners along the way about the strike. Carmack shuffled into Bill McPhee's saloon in Fortymile, downed two glasses of whiskey, and announced, "Boys, I've got some good news to tell you. There's a big strike up the river."

The news was met with predictable derision. "Strike, hell!" somebody shouted. With a smile, Carmack poured the gold flakes from the cartridge onto the scale on the bar. When the miners saw by the texture, shape, and color that it came from an entirely new streak, all they wanted to know was where he'd found it. By morning, Fortymile was a ghost town. Says Pierre Berton in *The Klondike Fever:* "Even the drunks had been dragged from the saloons by their friends and tied down, protesting, in the boats that were heading for the Klondike." (page 51)

Carmack never notified the Indian-hater Henderson of the strike, and Henderson happened along too late—after the entire creek had been staked. He roamed the Northwest for years in search of another Klondike, but he never got rich.

The strike changed the Yukon overnight:

Up and down the Yukon Valley the news spread like a great stage-whisper. It moved as swiftly as the breeze in the birches, and more mysteriously. Men squatting by nameless creeks heard the tale, dropped their pans, and headed for the Klondike. Men seated by dying campfires heard it and started up in the night, shrugging off sleep to make tracks for the new strike. Men poling up the Yukon toward the mountains or drifting down the Yukon toward the wilderness heard it and did an abrupt about-face in the direction of the salmon stream whose name no one could pronounce properly. Some did not hear the news at all, but, drifting past the Klondike's mouth, saw the boats and the tents and gesticulating figures, felt the hair rise on their napes, and then, still uncomprehending, still unbelieving, joined the clamoring throng pushing up through the weeds and muck of Rabbit Creek. (*The Klondike Fever*, page 51)

Still we drifted, tied together. The mountains ambled down to the river's edge. We passed a long ice shelf from which snow and ice crept up a spruce-lined crevice. Down it flowed a small waterfall.

We had come twenty-nine miles and it was getting late. The river was narrow between high banks and devoid of islands. We suspected the woods would be mosquito-ville, but we had wearied of island camping. Barb and I struggled up a fifteen-foot bank into a delightful poplar grove; the others waited below. It was wonderful to shuffle and stumble through spongy leaves and crunchy sticks for a change, instead of slurping and hobbling through mud and rocks. There was a clearing that would do for a kitchen, some small flat areas a few dozen yards away could pass for the bedroom, and there were no signs of bears. The only drawbacks were having to carry the hundreds of pounds of gear up that sheer bank and to leave the boats tied down at the water out of sight. We decided to go for it.

The beach became a loading dock as bag after bag after ammo can of gear was dumped from the boats. We planted ourselves along the shifting sandy slope and tossed gear from person to person. Jude, former soccer goalie, crouched at the top to catch all manner of flying life jackets and lawn chairs that bypassed the chain-gang and were simply hurled from the bottom of the cliff. We whooped and enjoyed the rhythm and challenge of the chain-gang routine, and soon all the gear lay scattered on the bluff.

There was something quiet and beautiful about the white bark of the poplars in the dim light. Beyond, the dark mysterious woods held bears or who knows what.

Evelyn rooted through the food while Jude and Barbara cracked firewood over their knees. Jane and Sue and I perched the three tents near the bluff's edge in the few rosebush-free areas. The delicate pink roses were beautiful but didn't do nylon tents much good.

Returning to the boat to get something, I stopped short at the sight of fresh deep tracks made by some odd beast moments before. With a glance behind me, I examined the deep gouges in the soft beach, then realized with a smile that Evelyn had made the holes while digging wild onions with the trowel.

Barbara and Jane patted out homemade whole-wheat tortillas on an overturned plate. I heated my little pan of bath water and carried it off behind a tree. Mosquitoes buzzed in my ears, and it was chilly without my clothes, but I enjoyed the sponge bath, and it was heavenly to put on fresh clothes. I swished the dirty clothes in the used bath water and hung them on bushes to dry.

We sat in our lawn chairs, sipped hot drinks, gobbled rice and beans, and watched rhubarb and tortillas burn. Tonight, even one of the soccer goalie gloves we used as potholders lost all its fingers to the fire. The food, once again, was delicious, but we began to grouse about the kitchen routine. Only Evelyn knew where anything was or what was to be cooked, or how much, so we felt helpless while she went through the cooking chores. We milled around, not knowing what to do, yet not feeling free to wander off and have some time to ourselves. The rest of us wanted a chance to cook and create different dishes, but we didn't want to offend Evelyn. Since Evelyn did the cooking, the rest of us were obliged to clean up. So, long after she had gone to bed each night, we would still be milling around, washing, stuffing things randomly into bags. What frustrated me most was that we carried two large, full duffel bags of food from the boats each night. If that much food had to be brought up, I thought, at least we could categorize the things, so that if your rhubarb was burning and your beans were boiling over and you were desperately looking for bell peppers, at least you had only fifty or sixty baggies to root through, instead of 120. It seemed like we spent half our lives dumping out the contents of duffel bags, later picking up all the little baggies of food and putting them back into the duffel bags for the night, then repeating the entire process the following morning.

The conversation turned to our garbage system. Theoretically, we had been burning all garbage so bears wouldn't be attracted to the kitchen. But in reality, the bowlful of beans somebody spilled, or the wad of used toilet paper, usually remained glopped onto some log, half-burned, in a corner of the fire. They weren't very appetizing to look at as you sipped your tea. And whoever happened to be sitting there last—usually me—was then faced with either rebuilding the fire and tending and coaxing it to incinerate the junk, or putting out the fire and leaving half-burned globs of food for the nearest bear.

We were all a little out of sorts, a little tired. But the delight of the evening, we agreed, had been those whole-wheat tortillas, each lovingly patted out and grilled on the fire. Only a few had fallen into the dirt before we ate them.

## JUNE 17, DAY 9

Evelyn had the water hot and the pancakes half-cooked when we got up at 7:30. It was that great kind of morning—damp and chilly—that makes you feel like you're out in the woods and it's a new day; the kind of morning when you know you're alive because steam rises from your pee as it hits the forest floor beneath you. (I'm always reminded of the old admonition not to hang around a pile of bear-crap if it's still steaming.) We wore parkas, except for Evelyn, who said she was hot all the time.

Strewn with fallen logs and all our belongings, the campsite was a wonderfully chaotic jumble. The stately poplars crowded close among us, their white, grey-notched trunks rising straight up toward the light that sifted to us in peaceful shafts through the dense forest.

As we munched pancakes and leftover beans and rice, there was the usual background chatter. I had concluded that no one in this bunch listened to anyone else; any remark had to be repeated four times. I theorized we were suffering from communication overload: we'd been subjected to too much input, too often, so we just tuned each other out.

The talk turned again to the state of the kitchen, and Sue said she'd forgo eating for one or more days so she wouldn't have to have anything to do with the kitchen. We shrugged and sipped our coffee.

Into yesterday's leftover lentil soup we threw some barley and wild onions and heated it to take for lunch. You don't need refrigerators for your leftovers. Sometimes for days at a time, we ate the same stuff from the same big pot. During the day it would ride somewhere in one of the boats and we'd nibble from it, then at night we'd haul it up the bank for supper.

We chain-ganged the gear down the precipice and were on our way, on schedule. We immediately thwarted and began visiting as the river sped us toward wherever. We talked about food again, and this time there erupted a full mutiny. People wanted a chance to cook; they wanted to do their share of the cleanup but have some time off. We devised a new system: Each day, one boat would have the day off with no cooking, fire-building, or dish-washing duties. Our eyes widened and we grinned at the prospect. The second boat would be fire-builders and dish-washers; the third would be cooks. We would rotate each day. Duty would begin with the evening meal, so that the same crew could wrestle from the bags the dinner food and put in a handy place what they'd need for breakfast and the next lunch.

The kitchen question settled, I pulled out the trumpet and played for an hour: "Misty," "If I Were a Rich Man," "North to Alaska." There was something exquisitely bizarre about sending the sultry notes of "Summertime" through the horn while searching the blurred Yukon spruces for grizzlies. From the sheet music, Barb and I sang all twenty-two verses of "Frankie and Johnnie," including a few I'd never known, like the one where Frankie tells the judge " . . . I never shot him in the first degree, I shot him in his trifling - - - - - - - , 'Cause he done me wrong,'cause he done me wrong." We pulled over for water, and while the others crashed through the alders to a creek, Barb and Jane and I lounged in the boats, twanged "Delta Dawn" at the top of our lungs, and blasted trumpet notes across the river to echo off the far bank.

Back on the river, Barb recited Robert Frost poetry from memory. Jane peered into the woods with her binoculars, mile after mile. "I'm trying to find you all a bear," she said.

At the Indian cemetery of Little Salmon, we tied the boats, rustled in our Gore-Tex pants along a path, and came upon one of the Yukon's stranger sights. Amid the poplars spread a "village" of tiny houses. These were the traditional houses the Indians made for the spirits of their relatives who were buried in graves behind the weathered grey fences. The houses stood about chest high, their windows knee high. Some were painted green or white, others were unpainted; some even had glass windows with little curtains. Tiny woodwork graced the windows and doors.

We strode down a dusty road into what was left of the village proper. In a clearing stood a church of thick, sturdy logs. Weathered into its face were the faint words "Little Salmon Mission." Sunlight slipped through cracks onto the mission's dark, bare, wooden floor. Who had trod this floor when Little Salmon was a thriving Indian village? Nearby, foot-tall grass waved from the sod roof of a cabin. Across the road, below the high bank, the Yukon rounded a bend and flowed onward through the mountains. Once again, I pondered what it must have been to look from your cabin's door every morning at this big old river and those big old mountains and to wonder what was happening upstream and downstream.

A family lived at Little Salmon; a woman hung clothes on a line. Beside their house stood a truck, and two horses rolled in the dust in the middle of the road. The people ignored us, so we didn't intrude on their privacy. We figured they were probably tired of the same old canoeists coming down the same old river with the same old tales and questions.

We paddled awhile until we happened upon a path on the left bank that led us to a group of abandoned cabins called Lakeview. From the high hill we could see the river and the mountains beyond. Flat-bottomed and fluffy-topped white clouds marched in formation across the blue, sunny sky. We built a fire and heated the soup while the wind kicked up dust, then we sprawled in the shade of a cabin that had fur and bear droppings on its floor. Evelyn thought a bear lived in the cabin, but we were too relaxed to move and figured the bear wouldn't return just now. Felt kind of like Goldilocks. We slurped our barley and lentil soup, nibbled cold bannock bread, and passed around the sticky dried apricot leather.

I rousted myself from my after-dinner stupor and took pictures of the cabins. On the wood-planked floor of one stood an iron bedstead with thin logs piled across it as a mattress. There was the standard oil-drum stove, blackened and rusty. I followed Jane and Jude, in their Shoo-Bug jackets, down a path that wound through skinny poplars. My usual impulse when walking through peaceful forests is to be as quiet as I can, but today, in bear country, I had a strange urge to hum or whistle. Actually, the rustling of our rain pants was deafening as it was.

Rounding a bend, we stopped short. "I thought that was a bear!" exclaimed Jude. We giggled nervously. Some canoeist's prank had worked; a rusted five-gallon can propped on a stick looked for all the world like a bear's head.

Back on the river, it was 70° and soporifically sunny. We thwarted. Somebody else was on watch, and I relished the half-secure feeling of lying back on the gear, my legs resting on a paddle laid across the gunnels, and floating down the Yukon. For a long time, the only sound was an occasional page being turned by whoever was reading. I was brought back to earth by the grinding gears of a bulldozer chugging up the road that had now swung near the river. Lifting my hat, I gazed at what were for me the two symbols of the loss of America's last frontier—the road and the bulldozer. I signalled my rather unladylike thoughts to the 'dozer and resumed my nap.

Later, as we floated, I wrote in my journal and contemplated my immediate "nest," my world for the next few months. Crammed into the bow before me were one ammo can with camera loaded with color-slide film, another ammo can with black-and-white camera, my water bottle, and my "waterproof" box with tape recorder. Beneath my wetsuit-bootied feet and their ragged, muddy tennis shoes lay a disintegrating spongy pad, black with mud, that padded my knees from the cold aluminum hull. My hands were by now very dry, wrinkled, and black with the dirt that had packed itself into every crease. They looked a lot like the spongy pad.

Evelyn read aloud some recipes for things like Eskimo ice cream, which had something to do with fish and oil, and Sue read passages from The Yukon. I photographed Barbara as she whittled a spoon from a poplar branch. We didn't notice it at the time—we were already acclimated to dirt and filth—but when I looked at the pictures months later, back in civilization, I would discover a woman whose face was smeared with soot, whose red life jacket was caked with mud, and whose leather gloves sported a slick black coat of dirt. Jane journalized, her head draped in a red bandanna. We rolled up our pants legs and sunbathed.

"Hey Janie," I said, "we ought to shave our legs, it's so warm out here." We finally decided the water would be cold and we'd shave off the goose-bumps and bleed all over everything.

Jude fished with a rodless reel. Her rod had snapped in two when she and Sue crash-landed into some willows, so now she just threw the line into the water and held the reel in her hand. It would have been entertaining to see her land a fish. Meanwhile, as we drifted, Evelyn peed over the side of the canoe. Dribbling down the aluminum, it sounded exactly like she was peeing into the boat, which amused us greatly. We'd had a long discussion some miles back about whether urine was pollution, but Dr. Sue had assured us that some famous statesman somewhere had lived to be a hundred by drinking a glass of his own urine every day. So we peed in the river.

"Oh, guess what?!" I exclaimed. "It's almost time for the Second Social Event of the Season, the summer solstice on June 21, the longest day of the year! I propose an All-Night Float." Everybody agreed. Jane and Barb planned a big floating feast. "Yeah," somebody said, "we can sing and play the ukulele and play cards. . . . " "And drink!" somebody interjected. Each boat began plotting sleeping accommodations for the all-night party 'neath the midnight sun.

The river carried us through mile after mile of high sandy banks and balding hills. Tongues of poplar licked their creases. By now we had mastered the strange art of ferrying three canoes tied together across a big, swift river. The trick was to start ferrying a mile or two above the problematic tree or riffle.

We snaked through scattered islands that offered poor camping; the land rose straight from the water, with five-foot-high undercut banks thick with spruce. The islands lacked sandbar heads or tails and they were undoubtedly alive with mosquitoes. The few places that seemed promising through binoculars were generally behind us before we could decide whether we wanted to unthwart and ferry madly to get to them. There's an old river saying that (1) the distance between you and a potential campsite when you spot it, and (2) the speed of the current, increase in direct proportion to (1) how late in the day it is, and (2) how tired you are.

Finally we grabbed a tiny gravel tip of an island at 7 P.M. We had come thirty-seven miles since breakfast, mostly drifting and having stopped for at least two hours at Little Salmon and Lakeview. Barb and Jane had calculated that we needed to cover twenty-five miles a day to get them to Dawson in time; at this rate, we could do that without putting a paddle in the water.

For the first time, Sue and Barbara wore their headnets. I was comfortable without one, for the Muskol liquid repellent I applied to my face kept the mosquitoes a few inches away. The new division of kitchen labor suited everyone, and Sue and Jude joked and sang as they used their evening off to clean out their boat, read, and putz. Jude threw some underwear into the fire; we asked no questions. Meanwhile, Evelyn was still deaf in one ear and kept looking off in the wrong direction every time someone called her name.

The others went to bed, and I marveled at the many colors of the beach pebbles. There were reds, pinks, and pale greens, beiges, greys, whites, some rose and browns, all smoothed and polished and rounded by years of battling the silty Yukon. They glistened in the evening sun. It was fun to crunch over them at the water's edge. Where had each pebble begun, where had it traveled, what had it experienced through the eons?

The evening and the sandbar were deliciously peaceful. A tiny channel broke away from the Yukon a few feet from me and gurgled around our campsite. Birds sang in the twilight. To shelter themselves from the faint breeze blowing against my back, hundreds of mosquitoes perched on my clothes in a curious fashion, along my shins and chest. As the sun set behind dark, ragged spruces across the river, its slanting rays made the river a glassy, shimmering swath. I wallowed in the damp gravel, with my nose to the ground, and photographed a lone canoe silhouetted against this golden glow. Was I really here, in the Yukon, watching rocks and sunsets? How did I ever get so lucky?

## JUNE 18, DAY 10

Evelyn and I were fire-builders this morning; we got up at 6:45. We were packed and ready to hit the river at 9 A.M., an hour ahead of schedule.

We paddled toward Carmacks, the only inhabited town between Whitehorse and Dawson. The morning clouds dashed a few raindrops to bluff us into and out of our Gore-Tex. Jane spotted another lifer, an old squaw duck, but Evelyn and I missed it.

Soon we spied Tantalus Butte, with its coal mine, that signalled Carmacks. Frederick Schwatka had named the butte during his 1883 expedition. He had written that "a conspicuous bald butte could be seen directly in front of our raft no less than seven times, on as many different stretches of the river. I called it Tantalus Butte and was glad to see it disappear from sight." (Exploring the Yukon River, page 74) (In Greek mythology Tantalus was some king who fed his son to the gods and was condemned to stand in water he couldn't drink, beneath branches of fruit he couldn't reach.)

We rounded a bend and confronted a sight that jarred us, after ten days of wild, open river: a huge highway bridge spanned the river. As the pincer-like structure gripped the mighty Yukon, it seemed to so insult her that I felt ashamed, but I couldn't dwell on it because we were swirling down upon massive concrete pillars that squatted in midstream. It was a little tricky to clear the pillars, cross the eddy line, and pull into the landing that lay just downstream of the bridge. As we did, the four rafters and the Klepper guy we'd met before welcomed us like old friends.

Around 300 people live in Carmacks, which has a post office, two stores, a gas station, hotels, taverns, and Royal Canadian Mounted Police and Forest Service stations.

Reaching Carmacks meant we had just paddled 202 miles down the Yukon; bent on celebrating, we strode down the gravel street in search of big-city adventures. At the RCMP office they counted heads and checked a form. Then we stormed the restaurant and swarmed into a big booth to wallow in food cooked by somebody else. While we waited, Jude and Evelyn and Jane scattered to do chores. They washed their rain suits at the washateria across the street and hung them to dry on the restaurant's window. The rafters said the shower wasn't much to write home about; the water wasn't very hot and only dribbled. Besides, we'd soon be crawling around in the mud again anyway. We called home and took turns washing our faces and hands in hot running water in the restroom.

Still we waited for the food. Now the college group had filtered into the restaurant. It was like old home week. Jude had turned around in the booth and was getting the lowdown on Anchorage Mexican restaurants from two vacationing couples from Anchorage. They'd read about us somewhere in a newspaper and were eager to help the six women from Texas who'd come to try their hand at the Yukon. Finally, there spread before me steak and eggs, coffee, and hot apple pie à la mode. Actually, I had tasted better, but it was the symbolic gesture that counted. My bill came to $11.75 Canadian (a dollar or two less in U.S. currency); I stuffed half the steak into my fanny pack for later.

We trudged a half-mile or so across the bridge to the post office. It operated only three days a week and this wasn't one of them. We bought stamps in the store next door, where apples were selling for eighty cents each. On the counter burned a mosquito coil whose incense-like scent filled the store. Cans of Vienna sausage and Campbell's soup, fishing lures, and boots lined the shelves. Jude bought up a big stock of spoons. The lady at the counter munched a sandwich of last year's salmon and said the mosquitoes were bad this year. A huge, Husky-like mutt with a sideways gait hung around the front door. As I surveyed the town from the bridge, I noticed that it was quite segregated—whites on the left bank and Indians on the right.

Back in town at another store, we undertook a food and Vaseline shopping spree. Meanwhile, we'd heard that the college group needed antibiotics. Sue offered help but they didn't seem to want any. The trouble had something to do with a throat infection that we figured belonged to that gal who washed her hair in the freezing Yukon.

Finally we mobilized to leave the chaos of the town for the peace of the river. I spoke briefly with the Klepper guy, who turned out to be Marshall Clymer, an instructor of T'ai Chi Ch'uan (which he described as a dancelike martial arts form) in Anchorage. He mentioned that as he drifted downstream, just after we'd seen him above Byer's Camp, he'd seen a black bear on the other shore. We swore and stomped; why didn't we ever see a bear? Did it have anything to do with the fact that we were always either asleep or singing at the top of our lungs? Marshall said he often paddled at night and slept during the day, said he saw more wildlife that way. We couldn't wait until our June 21 All-Nighter to test his theory.

We shoved into the water and immediately thwarted, to let Carmacks know we had a little class. We had passed our first big milestone. This was the last place between here and Dawson, 258 miles downstream, where we'd see much sign of civilization. I felt a sense of accomplishment, but also a relief to get out of the city confusion and back onto the river where we knew, more or less, what we were doing. Too, I felt a tingly nervous anticipation: twenty miles downstream lay Five Finger Rapids.

We floated through a bend where the river almost doubled back on itself, and Barbara read to us from an old newspaper she'd found about the Falkland Islands War. Up here, it seemed strange and utterly irrelevant.

As we passed the rafters, they claimed a sandbar we'd been eyeing for a campsite. The river banks loomed high and sheer; campsites were limited to the few sandbars in midstream. We figured that the big Whitman college crowd was on our heels and would beat us out of the next campsite, so we grabbed the first flat, open sandbar, though it rose only a few feet above the water. It was only 5:30, but then we'd started an hour early that morning, and we had already come a respectable thirty-two miles. As we unloaded the boats, sure enough, the Whitman flotilla rounded the bend. Nya, nya.

The wind raked across our unprotected home. Evelyn and I wrestled the tent into position and anchored it with big rocks we had collected around the sandbar. While we unloaded a boat at the water's edge, a gust of wind tossed Sue's lawn chair and life jacket into the campfire. Jude, former track runner, loped across the rocks to the rescue. The gear was a little melted but usable. By now the bath water was warm, and I took it to the edge of the island, ecstatic at having a whole big pot of water to myself. The trouble was that the "clean" clothes I'd "washed" a few nights before smelled just like the dirty ones I was taking off. And, of course, the minute I stripped down the wind stepped up its onslaught.

When I returned to the campfire, set for genuine homemade hamburgers, thanks to Carmacks' grocery store, I discovered a sad-faced crew of cooks and fire-builders.

"Hey, Beth!" Sue waved, "Come join us. The wind is blowing sand all over the meat patties and we don't know what to do about it."

Barbara added with a smirk, "So we decided to have a drink and think about it. . . . "

I grinned and shook my head. They looked well-settled and half-sloshed in their lawn chairs. Huddled behind an overturned canoe, we gabbed as sand swirled. No one seemed to mind or even remember that we hadn't eaten. Jane finished her first little plastic bottle of scotch and pulled a second from her pack. Evelyn was content; a neat little pile of empty beer cans from Carmacks now circled the tent, where she'd been reading for an hour. I pulled out my steak and gnawed on it.

Jane stood up and moved a few feet away across the sandbar, and when our usual "No peeing in the kitchen!" chorus had died down, Barbara said in a stage whisper, "You watch; tomorrow, Jane will casually start suggesting that we switch paddling partners for the day." We laughed, knowing that although Barb and Jane had paddled together for years, they considered themselves a less-than-expert whitewater team. "Then she'll offer money!" shouted Barb, grinning, her eyes smiling. "The closer we get to Five Finger Rapids, the more she'll offer." We guffawed. Barb leaned over to Sue, our best whitewater paddler, and advised, "Hold out for your best price!"

Jane returned. "O.K., Janie, we've been waiting a week now for your story; let's have it," we urged.

"Tell 'em about how you met Wesley!" said Barb. "I love that story."

Little Janie, the soft-spoken fifty-two-year-old grandmother, was full of surprises. She was the daughter of a Mississippi farmer and salesman. She had been out of college for awhile, working and dating around, when her father had introduced her to "this boy" Wesley, whom she liked pretty well.

"Well," she said, "Wesley played golf, and so did I. And I was pretty darned good," she shrugged. "He said I was the best lady golfer he'd met. Well, on our third date—our third date, mind you—we were playing golf. We were about halfway through the round; I don't remember which hole we were on."

She laughed, "He was doing horribly, kept slicing. He said, 'Jane, no one's ever affected my golf game like this. Will you marry me?' I said yes!" She shouted and clapped her hands. "And we've been married ever since! That was twenty-eight years ago. I don't even remember if we finished the round."

We rolled in the sand and screamed with delight.

Jane had gotten interested in outdoor activities a few years ago when her husband and youngest son were off playing golf tournaments. She had started birding with a neighbor on Audubon field trips, then backpacking, then had led long backpack trips for students to Big Bend National Park in Texas and to the Grand Canyon.

Then we started on my story. But before I could even get through my high school honors and tell how I used to drive around the West Texas plains through dust storms and tornadoes when I worked for the Girl Scouts, they wanted to skip all that and get right to every detail of my past, present, and future sex life. Just because Evelyn and I joked about sex and men all the way down the river, that was no reason for them to get so excited. But it was all in fun. I said I'd answer any question anybody had the nerve to ask. The discussion got progressively more detailed and interesting until we'd worked ourselves into a moderate frenzy.

"Watch out," sighed Barb, rolling her eyes. "Jane's gonna start missing Wesley now and hollering to get to Dawson so she can call him." Barbara grinned, knowing that after about six weeks Jane always became impossible because she missed Wesley so much.

Meanwhile, we were looking for some more water for our drinks. As we wrestled with Big Green, the water jug, our attention was drawn to its masculine-looking retractable spout with the cap that rested on the end, and somebody suggested we rename it the Sex Pot. Goodnight, ladies.

## JUNE 19, DAY 11

Five Finger Rapids dominated our thoughts. Sue, Jude, and I struggled into our wetsuits. Turning over in a canoe is no big deal—experienced whitewater canoeists are used to it—but the water runs five to seven miles per hour through Five Finger, and if you dump in that with a heavily loaded boat, you'd swim for a mile or more before you could get to shore. In 47° water, your body'd be right thankful for a wetsuit.

Every day we tied our gear into the boats, but today we took extra care. We adjusted the load to ride as low as possible. A half-a-bleach-bottle bailer poised amidships, and two big sponges lay at our feet. The spare paddles were more or less accessible. I'd paddle in the stern today, so Evelyn and I rearranged our nests accordingly. Meanwhile, Sue and Jude fussed at each other during one of their increasingly frequent morning spats over how to load their boat.

On the river, Evelyn and I placed within reach our nylon rescue bag with floatable rope. To rescue someone thrown into the water, you hold one end of the rope and throw the bag with the other hand; as the bag sails through the air, the rope unreels, and the swimmer grabs the bag as it reaches her. We recalled our attempts to throw it from the boat back in Dallas when the TV crew filmed us. Only Jude, the former javelin-thrower, had hurled it more than twenty feet.

Evelyn now picked it up like she'd never seen one before and stared at the rope loop at the bottom of the bag. "Well, do you throw this end or that end?" she finally said with a frown. It was embarrassing that she didn't know, but even worse when I realized I wasn't sure. We grinned at each other. This was a helluva time to brush up on basic canoeing safety, we thought as we roared down the Yukon toward Five Finger Rapids.

On we floated, through the Yukon's big boils. The dozen or more canoes of the Whitman group began to overtake us, making me nervous. I had paddled on rivers where lots of beginners stacked up at the top of each rapid, and it was no fun. You end up unable to maneuver into the right slot because people are in your way, or somebody overturns right in front of you and you have to dodge floating people and ice chests and canoes all the way through the rapids. The answer is to space yourselves far enough apart so that you each have time to read the rapids as you enter them, room to ferry back and forth, as necessary, and also to avoid bashing into the canoe in front of you if it suddenly overturns.

We had positioned Sue, the most experienced, in front, so the rest of us could follow her course. With Sue's experience and Jude's javelin-arm, they'd be best equipped to effect a rescue after they'd made it through and eddied out below. But this was a big river and that little throw-rope looked pretty feeble between the steep rocky shores that were a half-mile apart and 500 feet high. Barbara and Jane, the least experienced whitewater paddlers, would take the middle. Evelyn and I would run sweep. Sue and I would take what pictures we could with our telephoto lenses.

Rounding a bend, we picked up the rapids' faint roar. Just then, Evelyn decided she had to pee. She hung her rear over the gunnel, and while I leaned and braced with my paddle, I jokingly swore and she swore back and we decided it'd be about par for us to end up swimming the only rapids on the Yukon, not because the rapids outwitted us, but because we capsized while peeing! As we drifted toward that dull roar, straining to make out the details of the rapids, I admired the stampeders who'd rounded this bend eighty-four years before. What had they thought as they heard that sound? How had they felt as they swept down the current in their makeshift boats? Had they peed over the gunnel?

We knew that somewhere around the rapids is an old winch house that once pulled steamers upstream on a big cable through the right-hand channel. Everyone had said that was the channel to aim for. The river was supposed to run in five channels (like fingers on a hand) between four monstrous basalt hunks that everybody calls "flower pots." I had visualized the scene a dozen times.

The Whitman group waited in an eddy ahead of us. Now it was apparent that what I had thought was the whole river was but one channel, and into it the tiny specks of the Whitman boats now paddled one by one.

Then Sue and Jude swung into the current. I took pictures; Evelyn clung to a branch. Nobody said much. Soon Jane and Barbara pushed off. Just as Sue's canoe was so far away that it seemed a tiny yellow dot, it suddenly disappeared. Had they merely hit the drop or had they turned over? Binoculars revealed nothing.

Finally, it was our turn. We leaned downstream and carefully crossed the eddy line. As we paddled that interminable distance to the rapids, several thoughts went through my mind. I wasn't too concerned about the rapids, because of their tame description in books, but I was very, very respectful of the power of the river. Our boats were very heavily loaded, which would increase stability but would also increase our chances of swamping—filling up with water if waves splashed in. My partner and I had never run a serious rapid together. Capsizing meant possible loss or damage of equipment and a brush with hypothermia. Actually, these are the thoughts every serious river-rat always keeps tucked into her subconscious. It's wise and healthy to know the realities of rivers. But as we neared the flower pot, I put those thoughts behind me and concentrated on the matters at hand. We were here, we were now committed to running the rapids, and probably I had run rapids like them a hundred times.

Giving last-minute tips to Evelyn, whether she wanted them or not, gave me something to do. "Stay low, bail if you need to, keep your paddle in the water as much as possible so you can brace with it."

A forty-foot channel appeared between the massive brown boulders. The river surged into a tongue and there was a good roar as grey waters gushed through the gate. "Draw!" I yelled to Evelyn as we got sucked a little too close to the left rock face. We rushed past a turbulent eddy line behind the right "pot."

Ahead danced a series of "haystacks," standing waves across the current. We'd ship less water if we skirted them, but it seemed easier and more fun to blast headlong into them.

"Here we go!" I shouted. "Keep that paddle in the water!" We lined up, zoomed down a drop and hit the three-foot waves. We rode up the face of the first and plunged deep into the second. Cold water broke over the bow and dashed Evelyn in the face. A few cross-waves slapped at us, but we barreled through and had a good bucking ride.

"Yee ha!" we hollered. Five inches of water now wallowed inside our canoe, which we finally coaxed to shore. Excited and triumphant, we congratulated ourselves and bailed for ten minutes.

Later, we would learn that three German canoeists had drowned the year before in Five Finger.

In the excitement, we forgot that somewhere upstream from Five Finger are George Carmack's old coal mine and cabin, where he had had, of all things, an organ. Somewhere around here he had established a trading station. But in 1895, he left a note on his door that said, "Gone to Fortymile for grub," and never returned. He had gotten sidetracked by striking gold and launching the craziest gold rush in history.

According to the history books, Five Finger hadn't been a great problem for the stampeders, but a few interesting dramas had transpired here. One incredible tale dealt with stampeders who'd managed to get into Dawson just after the news had hit the West Coast. They scratched their way to the Klondike, as winter set in, only to discover there was no food. Turning in their tracks, desperate bands raced against starvation back up the frozen Yukon toward the passes, "rending their clothes, shredding their moccasins, and shattering their sleighs on the sharp blocks of ice that were sometimes heaped as high as twenty feet. As they stumbled on, they jettisoned their sleds, their food, their clothes, even their shoes, keeping only a single blanket apiece and a meager amount of provisions, with no shelter but a campfire to keep them from death by freezing." (*The Klondike Fever*, pages 184-185) During all this, it was fifty below zero.

Amid the fearful exodus traveled seventeen-year-old William Byrne from Chicago, who'd come to the Klondike with his uncle. "The elder man had worked the youth to exhaustion at pistol point until one night Byrne was too tired to remove his soaking moccasins. He awoke next morning to find both feet frozen. A doctor amputated his legs at the knee while the uncle rushed on. Byrne eked out the winter in a shack [near Five Finger], more dead than alive. The following spring he managed to make his way Outside, whereupon he announced that he would return at once to the Klondike on artificial limbs to dig for gold." (*The Klondike Fever*, page 185)

One droll brochure had said of the trip through the actual rapids: "If time permits, the canoeist will notice when passing through the right-hand channel that the rock walls are dotted with mud swallows' nests." Well, time didn't permit. We saw neither coal mine nor winch house nor swallows' nests, and I for one thought not a second about the seventeen-year-old amputee.

Around the first bend below the rapids, we pulled out for water where a clear creek poured into the Yukon. After having made it through Five Finger in fine style, it was a little embarrassing when Evelyn and I overshot the eddy at the creek's mouth and ended up quite a way downstream. The Whitman bunch was there, fly-fishing, happy over their successful run through the rapids. They were pretty casual about it all, as beginners are apt to be, and they looked at us like we'd overdone it a bit as we waddled in our full-length wetsuits. Evelyn spotted a toad among the grasses on the path. She insisted it was the northernmost amphibian in the world and that I take its picture. We stalked him on all fours, shouting "Here he is!" . . . "There he goes!" . . . and so forth. Jane and Barbara whizzed by in their canoe and hollered for us to grab Barb's life jacket that she'd forgotten on the beach.

We drifted six miles down to Rink Rapids. I hadn't understood from the literature that you miss *all* the whitewater of the rapids if you stick close to the right shore (you can't really see it as you're coming around the bend), but sure enough, that's what happened to Evelyn and me. The others plowed through the middle into what looked like some fairly squirrelly cross-waves, but they did fine, having nothing but a bouncy ride. Like Five Finger, Rink seemed more bark than bite. The rocks in Rink had given the old steamers a hard time, so the folks had simply blown some of the rocks to bits with dynamite, and that's what creates the smooth right channel.

We pulled out on a gravel bar, and Jude and Sue grilled the hamburger meat whose cooking had been postponed due to last night's Arabian sandstorm. We were in high spirits, having just run Five Finger and having spread before us *real* hamburger meat on *real* buns, with *real* onions. Then, for dessert, Sue and Jude produced Bananas Foster. I had to come all the way to the Yukon to experience this culinary marvel for the first time. They heated bananas and butter and brown sugar in the skillet, then set them aflame with Everclear. We felt like royalty at some elegant gathering, sitting in the middle of a Yukon River sandbar. And the cook, Sue, made quite a sight as she graciously served up the flaming concoction. She sat cross-legged in the sand, wearing a wetsuit whose peeled-down top (she had on a T-shirt underneath) flapped from her waist like a tail; her hair was now a cute inch-long furry mass, daily outgrowing the effects of the chemotherapy.

As we loaded the boats it began to rain, but the put-on-your-rain-suit routine worked and the rain stopped immediately. We rounded a bend and spotted the Whitman group lunching ashore. All they ever saw us doing was thwarting and goofing off anyway, so we decided to play up the image. Out came the trumpet from its sleeping pad, and as we drifted past—three boats abreast in thwartation formation—I blared "Acapulco 1922," "When the Saints Go Marchin' In," and "The Eyes of Texas Are Upon You," as the Texas Women's Yukon River Expedition sang and clapped. The shore crowd stood there, dumbfounded, their mouths agape. Some took pictures. We laughed all the way around the bend.

We drifted on, in the shadow of massive sandy cutbanks that absolutely dwarfed us. In places, sandstone bluffs had been carved into rippling "hoodoos" by the wind. Somebody suggested we have a contest to see which of us had ever made love in the most unusual place. Well, what else is there to do in the middle of the Yukon River when the fish aren't biting?

"One time my housemates in Washington, D.C., and I each nominated one or more places, but we weren't able to come up with anything too exotic," I confessed. "I had nominated on top of a car, but it had been a big Cutlass. One of my housemates beat that—claimed he'd done it on top of a little Volkswagen bug." The others looked skeptical, envisioning a

Volkswagen bug. Then there was silence as they scratched their heads and concentrated on their own nominations.

Sue related how, when she and her husband used to visit another couple, Sue's husband and the woman would always sit upstairs talking, while Sue and the guy would play ping-pong for hours in the basement, amid their spouses' joking accusations that no one could play only ping-pong for that long. "Well, one night we'd had a little wine and decided to play a trick on them," Sue said. "We took off all our clothes and just kept playing ping-pong. Eventually they came downstairs and we all had a good laugh—surprised hell out of 'em. But I guess I can't nominate on a ping-pong table since we didn't really do anything."

"Among my housemates," I continued, "the oldest person in the house—the 46-year-old union organizer from England—had won. She'd done it not *only* on top of a grand piano," I paused for effect, "but with a pianist from the London Symphony!" Squealing and applauding, we unanimously gave her the award.

No one was watching the map, and we spotted Yukon Crossing only as it slipped away behind us. A few buildings overgrown with poplars marked the place where stagecoaches had ferried across the Yukon on the run between Whitehorse and Dawson.

By now we were really revved up and began discussing various sexual variations: swingers' clubs, menage à trois, and so forth. Meanwhile, several good campsites slipped past; we always saw them at the last minute and were reluctant to interrupt the fascinating conversation to unthwart and ferry over.

All along this stretch, we observed a thin line of white, chalky rock known as "Sam McGee's Ashes." Volcanoes in the Saint Elias Mountains, far to the west, had spit this kind of rock throughout the valley. As we rode beneath the high banks we could see clearly the very shallow topsoil underlain with ash. They say because of the shallow soil, the cold winters, and the semiarid climate, trees don't grow very big in the Yukon's interior.

"Look at that," said Jude, pointing to a great cloudbank behind us. We were awestruck. Now I'm no gynecologist, but that giant, parted cloud spread across the sky was a dead ringer for what I imagined to be the view from beneath the stirrups.

"That's nothin'," said Jane, "look at that one!" We couldn't believe it, but five miles away, there towered the male cloud counterpart.

"Whoops, that jogs my memory," somebody said, gazing at the cloud. "I have another nomination." We laughed till we cried.

Finally, we faced the fact that it was getting late and we were tired. We came upon a nice island, piled out, had the firewood half collected and the tents halfway up, when Barbara started screaming from across the island. "Jane come here! Y'all come here!" She sounded fairly adamant so we ambled over.

She pointed ominously to the mud at our feet. There sat our first big—I mean *big*—grizzly print. It was about a foot long and very fresh. The claw marks sliced the soft mud. Our footprints sank a half-inch into the mud; the grizzly's were twice as deep. The line of pawprints marched down the length of the island near the shore. We stared a little, joked a little, looked over our shoulders a few times, took a few pictures. Then we threw the tents into the boats and boogied downriver as fast as our little paddles would carry us.

All suitable campsites had vanished from the river. The banks were steep; the islands thick with vegetation. On we paddled through the evening, realizing that we were approaching the abandoned Indian village of Minto, which had a government campground. We hadn't intended to stay there, preferring wild campsites to crowded, well-established ones, but we were getting cranky and decided to head for Minto.

A long-haired young man was standing on shore. We paddled over to him and discovered the Minto campground. He was from Holland, and he and his blond wife had come to float part of the Yukon. It was 10 P.M.; we had been on the river twelve hours. There ensued the usual enervating and temper-flaring procedure of reaching consensus on whether to camp here. I finally broke the tie and voted to stay. It had been a long forty-four miles.

We lugged the gear up a gravel landing to a flat, barren, dusty clearing lined with picnic shelters and Winnebagos (you can get here from the main highway). "Garden spot," we muttered. We could hardly drive tent stakes into the soil, yet there were no rocks to anchor the tent. I didn't care much; all I wanted was to get out of my itchy wetsuit girdle and into some dry clothes and get some food. Evelyn and I were on cooking detail. We were told there was no firewood, so we brought out the stoves. Jude couldn't get hers to work, so I went down the hill to the boat, jumped into the rocking thing from the steep shore, rooted around until I found my stove and fuel bottle, untied each, crawled out into the mud, trudged back up the hill again. By now Jude had hers going fine and I'd missed seeing Barbara's burst into flames.

Meanwhile, the disgusting mosquitoes flew into our eyes and noses, and if we talked or breathed they flew into our mouths and down our throats; we gagged and choked and coughed and spat. Minto was abandoned in 1954 after a series of unsolved murders. Maybe the mosquitoes'll drive you to it.

I was ready to murder Evelyn and she was ready to murder the rest of us. Here we were in the middle of a goddammed parking lot, dust was flying around, mosquitoes were killing us, there were millions of people and millions of Winnebagos driving back and forth, a helicopter was buzzing the campground with big loads of trash in a net bag, tents were falling down and stoves were exploding, Barbara's sleeping pad wouldn't hold air, there was no place to change clothes except in the pit toilet (where the bees lived), it was 11 P.M., and we were still waiting on dinner. And at that moment Evelyn wanted to discuss why we never camped where she wanted.

"Well, maybe there's a reason for that," somebody said. "It's because you pick dumb campsites." The mood was going downhill fast.

"All right," said Evelyn, "I move we let each boat pick a campsite, in rotation. Maybe the cooks should choose the campsite when it's their night to cook." I stirred the rice, blinked mosquitoes, and wished I wasn't here.

"You all," said Jane, "we're tired and we're in no shape to discuss this right now. Things will seem better and we can talk about it tomorrow." We agreed, and dinner was served.

## JUNE 20, DAY 12

All night long, a big dog had thudded around the tent on the hard-packed dirt. In the morning the hot sun drove us from the tent. Most of all, I resented having to go all the way to the pit toilet to pee.

Evelyn and I were in different solar systems this morning. We tried to cook breakfast, but somehow we weren't communicating. In the middle of a Mexican omelet, I had to go to the boat for something and asked Evelyn to mix the rest of the powdered eggs with those already scrambling. When I returned, the first batch was almost overdone and the rest hadn't been started. And she dumped a whole pot of rehydrated picante sauce into the eggs, though we had agreed to save half for the lunch macaroni. So now our prize-winning breakfast would be too spicy and our prize-winning lunch would be tasteless. I tried to be rational but I wanted to kick the dust and whine. This was the first time Evelyn and I had tried to cook together, and we found it wasn't one of our better team activities. Meanwhile, the mosquitoes buzzed and some guy (a nice man from New Waverly, Texas, who was camped nearby) traipsed in and out of our dining room to talk to Evelyn.

Evelyn and I were still on different planets when time came to load the boat. As usual, the others were completely packed and sitting in their boats twiddling their thumbs, while Evelyn and I were still fooling with our massive mess. Granted, most of it was mine. But it always embarrassed me to be last. Evelyn carried her bags down and left them for me to tie in. Invariably, she left the carabiners for her bags on the ropes that stretched between the thwarts, so that I had to dig them out from between the other junk to fasten the bags in. If she did leave the carabiners on her bags, she usually threw the bags into the boat in such a way that their carabiners were on the opposite sides from the ropes they were supposed to clip to. As I stumbled around, knee-deep in water, ankle-deep in mud, and wrestled the heavy bags, Evelyn gabbed with other campers up in the campground. I thought bad thoughts about my partner, myself, this campground, the campers and their Winnebagos, and the annoying schedule we were supposed to be keeping to get to Dawson.

I shouted up the hill to Evelyn that the packing might go faster if she helped. Now, Evelyn had done more than her share of carrying heavy gear and cooking and fire-building on the trip, and she was entitled to visit a few new-found friends if she wanted to, but I was in a snotty mood and I was gonna be snotty. At the root of my snit was probably that schedule. I was feeling rushed and incompetent, but if you don't have a schedule you never feel "behind," and if you don't feel "behind" you don't feel incompetent. Doing a three-month trip in daily quotas reminded me of what I call the macho backpacker whose only interest is how many miles and what climb in elevation he does every day, who races through the forest without a moment to listen to birds' calls or forest sounds or to photograph a wildflower the size of a bootlace eyelet.

Evelyn shuffled down the hill and stepped into the boat. Tension hung heavy. Jude smiled understandingly when I said curtly, "Let's paddle," ending any notion that we might thwart and visit.

I paddled like a fiend, enjoying my muscles and heavy breathing, gradually working off steam. Evelyn and I hadn't said a word, but I was sure she could feel the hostility. I felt sure, too, that she wasn't really at fault for anything; truthfully, there was nothing I felt justified in confronting her with. I knew that my frustration had as much to do with things in general as with Evelyn. I felt I had no right to try to change her behavior just to suit me; I just wanted to paddle it out.

The water spread smooth before us, rippled occasionally by a gentle breeze. To one side rose a smart cutbank topped by a crisp layer of green spruce-carpet. Ahead squatted pudgy grey rocks with spruce-lined folds. The sky was big and blue, with only a few clouds flung on the far horizon.

All along the banks were signs of spring destruction. Huge spruces, undercut by the ice's fury, lay toppled or about to topple into the water.

Soon enough, I was feeling good, singing "Me and Bobby McGee" in rhythm to long, powerful strokes. The sun was shining. We thwarted.

We talked about schedules, about packing boats. Jude observed something that made me feel better. "Beth," she said, "you've got it harder than anybody. You and Evelyn have never paddled together or camped together, and the rest of us have been with our partners for years. We're used to each other; we have a system worked out. You're also having to be the trip coordinator."

"And," Sue added, "at the same time you're trying to write in your journal because you have a book contract, do a lot of reading about the Yukon, take pictures, do nature study, be on 'vacation,' and still be among the first all-women's group to paddle the whole Yukon River—and all in three months." We grinned and shook our heads. "I'm not sure all that's possible at once," Sue said.

She had a point.

On we drifted. I told them my job as coordinator—as obtainer and enunciator of the group opinion—was made harder when they refused to state their opinions. I told them I hated blank stares when I asked a question. We agreed to cooperate.

Again Evelyn raised the question of the campsite selection. I cringed, fearing another outburst or, worse, that everyone would ignore Evelyn's remark. To my relief, the others listened and responded politely. It was a new day, just like Jane had said it would be. Evelyn brought up the subject in a low-key way, made her case, and let it go without forcing a referendum. "I would like to say, since we're discussing things," she said, "that I think sometimes you all purposely don't camp where I want to camp. I just want you to know that I don't like to camp on islands all the time—I get tired of islands. I want to camp sometimes on the shore, where we can walk in the forest and see some different terrain. I particularly like the poplar groves. And I would just like to say that I would appreciate it if you all would take into account the fact that Evelyn likes to camp on shore. That's all I'm asking."

Everyone nodded amiably, and that was that.

Now we entered a confusing series of islands. We were low on drinking water and looked for a creek that was supposed to join the Yukon somewhere around here. As we paddled, sharp-eyed Evelyn spotted the tiniest dots atop the mountain about a mile away across the river. "Dall sheep!" she sounded like a long-lost mariner crying "Land ho!" from the crow's nest. We smiled and stared through binoculars at the only solid white sheep in the world—found only in Alaska and the Yukon Territory.

Soon a basalt outcropping sprouted from the right bank like a care-fully mortared wall. It had been laid by a volcano fourteen miles away. Fort Selkirk was at hand.

Around the next bend we spotted log buildings on the left bank. From the right, at the end of the basalt wall, poured the Pelly River. We had come twenty-four miles in the morning's paddle.

It had been a day for sky. Our piddlings and paddlings, the little ripples on the river, and even the massive hunk of Victoria Rock that now rose in the distance were puny compared to the grand infinity of the sky. Deep blues and light blues washed a backdrop for the brilliant whites that swirled and drifted and puffed and creamed across the gigantic playground.

We trudged up Selkirk's high bank and were greeted by Danny Roberts, the stocky, taciturn Indian caretaker of the abandoned fort. With him was a young, bearded government guy connected with historical restoration projects, who explained that part of his job was to travel up and down the river visiting all the old sites. Rough life. . . .

So here we were at Fort Selkirk, founded by the Yukon's most famous explorer, Hudson's Bay Company's Robert Campbell. Campbell had grown up as a sheep farmer in Scotland. But a cousin's tales of the New World's boundless prairies, giant lakes and rivers, and the wild grandeur of the Rockies so fascinated him that he himself set out for the New World. The year was 1830; he was twenty-two years old. Working his way upward and westward as a Hudson's Bay farmer, then fur trader, then explorer, he made his mark by finding valuable fur-trading routes to the Alaskan Panhandle from the east side of the Rockies. He went on to discover the Pelly River, which he named after his home governor, then the upper Yukon River into which the Pelly flows. He named it the Lewes, after one of the Company's governors. (On some maps the portion of the Yukon above its confluence with the Pelly is still called the Lewes.)

Campbell spent two winters on the upper Pelly, during which he said he enjoyed

. . . the luxury of a bath in the river every morning. This practice I kept up until the ice got too thick. As the season advanced our cook would knock at my door to tell me the hole was made in the ice ready for me. I would then run down with a blanket round me, dip into the hole, out again, & back to the house, my hair often being frozen stiff before I got there. After a good rub down I would dress, & no one who has not tried it can have any idea of the exhilarating glow produced on the whole system by this hydropathic treatment. (*The Yukon*, page 50)

As I stood amid Selkirk's remains and surveyed the big Yukon on this warm summer day, I couldn't imagine jumping into it, even with the promise of a rubdown.

In 1848, Campbell established a trading post on an island, now eroded away, at this juncture of the Pelly and the Yukon. He named it Fort Selkirk after the English lord who had sponsored the colony where Campbell had first worked in the New World. In 1851, he went downstream to see where the big Lewes River went, and discovered, to his amazement, another Company fort, called Fort Yukon. Until that day, neither the Company nor its soldiers at the two posts suspected that both had overlooked the same river! Having solved the riddle, Campbell poled up the Porcupine River and up the Mackenzie, walked over the Rockies and ended up at Selkirk in mid-October to conclude his 3,000-mile summer experiment.

The following summer, Campbell and his men moved Selkirk from the island to the high bank where its remains now stand. When Campbell returned from Fort Yukon with a full supply of trade goods, Selkirk prepared to blossom into a full-fledged trading post with enough goods to buy all the pelts the Indians could tote in. (In those days, it was furs—not gold—that drew people to the Yukon.) But on August 20, 1852, twenty-seven Chilkat Indians on five rafts swung into the fort's landing. Long angered at Campbell for breaking their trade monopoly between the upper Yukon's Indians and the Russians and British on the coast, the Chilkats were in a fierce mood. For two days they rummaged through the fort's goods, stealing what they wanted. Campbell and his men holed up in one of the buildings until, after a brief skirmish, they escaped down the Yukon. When they returned, Fork Selkirk—the culmination of twenty-two years of Campbell's explorations and hard work—lay in ruins.

Campbell sent most of his men downriver to Fort Yukon, then he walked back over the Rockies to Fort Simpson. Denied a definite commitment by the Company to rebuild and reprovision Fort Selkirk, he snowshoed 2,000 miles to the Company's North American headquarters. Again he met indifference, so he snowshoed to Minnesota, took a train to Montreal, and pleaded with a Company governor who had supported his explorations for many years. But no one seemed to care about the little fort in the Yukon's wilds. Heartsick, Campbell finally gave up; he never again crossed the Rockies, never again saw his river or his beloved post. He continued working for Hudson's Bay until, after forty-one years with the Company, he was fired. He ended up cattle ranching in Manitoba.

So here I stood amid the wildflowers, where Campbell's little drama had played so many years ago, looking down upon the big, muddy Yukon.

Beyond the far bank, with its 450-foot-high basalt abutment, poured the Pelly that had swept Campbell into this place. I had visited lots of historical sites through the years—had walked, driven, and bicycled around and through battlefields, towns, forts, cabins, and mansions—but Selkirk was special. This time, I hadn't driven here in a car and stepped out to spend a few hours trying to take myself back in history. This time I had felt beneath me the same Yukon Campbell had felt, had ridden its ripples as he had, had wondered what lay around the next bend as he had. I had camped in the dirt and read beneath the midnight sun as he had. I felt a kinship with this now-peaceful fort and its quiet, crumbling log buildings in the clearing bordered by gently waving poplars.

Of course, I was eating dehydrated food packaged in plastic bags; I was riding a streamlined aluminum canoe; I was wearing the latest in synthetic gear; I had a pretty good idea what river I was on and where it flowed and that I would find few Russians when I got to the end; and I didn't much expect to be attacked by Indians or starve for lack of game. But I felt close to old Campbell. I liked him because he had put on his snowshoes and walked 2,000 miles across Canada, and I liked his little fort.

So did the others, and we decided to camp here overnight. We claimed a cabin, moved the boats down near some wooden steps that scaled the twenty-foot bank, and chain-ganged the gear. We felt like girls at a slumber party as we clumped around in our boots and staked out territories on the old cabin's wooden floor. Then we checked out the oil-drum stove outside near the picnic table. It was set vertically on the ground, with the bottom of one side cut out. You build a fire inside and smoke comes out the top through a hole. You put your pots on the top and they get hot fast. If you want to bake something, you stick the skillet through the bottom opening right onto the coals on the ground. Evelyn had the macaroni ready in a flash.

As we lunched, we plotted tomorrow's big All-Nighter. "I've got my nest all figured out," said Jane. "I'm gonna put my sleeping bag, rolled up, on the floor of the boat and pile up stuff to make it level with the seat, then I'll have big flat bed!"

"I'm gonna turn my nest around backwards," I said, "and figure out a way to set up my lawn chair." Evelyn rolled her eyes, but we all warmed to the absurdity of our undertaking.

"Yeah!" shouted Barb, imitating a half-drunk queen surveying the Nile as she fanned herself languidly with one hand, her other arm draped over her chair. "We'll cruise along like Cleopatra!"

Meanwhile, the Dutch couple we'd met at Minto arrived and set up camp near ours; the Whitman crowd pulled up and sprawled in the clearing for a few hours' rest before they would launch their own All-Nighter, and the four rafters from Anchorage pulled in, set up tents and chopped wood. River-rat city had sprung up in the clearing. The other Texas women trotted off to visit Danny and his wife at their cabin, while I crawled into my sleeping bag for an afternoon nap and some solitude.

As I snuggled into the rustling cocoon, I realized that I really wanted to be alone. Normally, I required a few hours a day of thinking my own thoughts; whole days had gone by without that, and I was building toward the need for another layover day. Today was sort of one, but camping amid forty other canoeists in a fort wasn't exactly my idea of communing with nature. There were even pit toilets here, too, with air fresheners in the pit marked "women." Somehow, though, they didn't bother me as much here, because I liked this place and I knew Danny had politely placed the little scented ornaments in there. At least there were no helicopters.

As I thought my thoughts, a big wet drop plopped onto Evelyn's sleeping bag on the floor beside me. I wiped it away and scanned the logs that supported the sod roof. It was sunny outside, no hint of rain. Whether the liquid was condensation or rat-pee I'll never know. . . .

When I awoke, the camp was astir with excitement. The entire Whitman crowd, the rafters, and our bunch were lined up with towels and soap and changes of clothes, with big grins on their faces. The foreman from the government restoration crew had offered the entire camp not only a shower, but a hot one! I grabbed my stuff and rushed to the end of the line.

Three stout spruce poles about twelve feet long had been tied together in a tripod. From them hung a fifty-five gallon oil drum, beneath which burned a hot fire stoked by bathers-in-waiting. Every twenty minutes or so, someone would holler and the government guy would come running from his tent in his big waterproof boots, clump down the steep stairs, and crank up a diesel pump at the water's edge. We would gather around the firehose that ran from the river up the bank, watch the bulge creep up the hose, and clap when the muddy Yukon poured into the oil drum. Another firehose snaked from the drum down into a little wooden house perched at the edge of the bank, and whoever was standing in there would get a shower. It sure beat craning your head over the end of a canoe. The only trouble was, if your turn came just after the drum had been filled, the water was pretty cold; if it came toward the bottom of the barrel, it was extremely hot. But it was definitely the highlight of the day.

Well, almost. Actually, tonight we were Entertaining. We had invited Danny and his wife, Abby, for dinner, and Barbara and Jane were now elbow-deep in whole-wheat flour, making tortillas. We milled around the yard of the cabin, chopped a little wood, set the table, and pointed out to Evelyn several research opportunities among the big canvas tents of the government crew across the way. A party atmosphere was abuilding. We joked with the Whitman folks and the rafters as they tramped back and forth across the clearing to the outhouse or the woodpile or the shower. Soon the Whitman bunch launched their All-Nighter, and we waved as they drifted down the Yukon into the golden sun.

Here came Danny and Abby. Abby was a large woman, her dark round face flanked by long black hair. She smoked a cigarette at all times, coughing frequently. She smiled and gestured often with her stocky hands. She laughed a lot and seemed glad to have a bunch of women to talk to; we enjoyed hearing her tales of life at Selkirk. As for Danny, we didn't know if it was because he had nothing to say to six women, if he was simply a very quiet person, if he got bored with cheechakos' questions, or if he truly was in pain from the sore throat he said he had, but for whatever reason, he stood thirty feet away the entire time, leaning against a rail, talking occasionally with the male rafters.

"Do you have an Indian name?" Evelyn asked Abby.

"No, I guess I was too young when they took me to school after my parents died. Maybe I was too young to get me an Indian name." Abby had been four years old. She said she forgot her Indian language.

Danny and Abby sat down with us at the picnic table and Jane and Barb served up Mexican beans, rice, and tortillas. The two Athapascan Indians seemed to like it all, and even bean-hater Jude dipped a spoonful of pintos onto her plate. The Robertses were the only year-round residents at Selkirk, their daughter having grown up and moved up the Pelly River to the highway. Danny and Abby had been married for thirty-six years.

We asked Abby what her favorite food was. "Fried chicken," she grinned.

We discussed the kinds of food we'd brought, the chum salmon that Danny fed to the dogs, food in general. "We never throw anything out," said Evelyn. "We had this leftover pancake with us that we'd been carrying down the river for three days—we finally ate it. . . . "

"Are there more beans?" somebody spoke up.

"Get 'em while you can, Danny, everything goes fast around here," said Barb.

Abby told us about dogsledding. "Danny is real good," she said. "But we have a Skidoo, too. We used to go all the time with the dogs. But then when I gained weight, he said, 'You get your own team.' So he trained me a team and I used to ride along with my own team."

I tried to imagine Selkirk in the winter, devoid of visitors, the Yukon a frozen ribbon, as Danny and Abby jounced behind two teams of dogs to visit their daughter up on the Pelly.

Later, after Danny and Abby said goodnight, Kalle, the Dutch guy we'd met at Minto, and his wife, Kosha, joined us for hot chocolate (bring-your-own cup) and Everclear, and the government foreman stopped by. Kosha and Kalle had hitchhiked to Carmacks, heard about renting a canoe, and decided to paddle down to Dawson.

At the other end of the table, Evelyn and the foreman discussed fur prices. He trapped in the winter, worked at Selkirk in the summer. I sewed a patch on my wool pants, whose pocket seam was ripping out. Jude and Jane laboriously spread lotion on their hands. Watching me sew, Jane confided that she couldn't wait to get to Dawson and throw away her woollies.

"You're gonna need 'em for Denali National Park and Mount McKinley!" we chorused. "You're gonna be cold up there, girl; you don't realize it."

"You all keep telling me that," she shrugged, "but I have yet to zip up my sleeping bag."

"Well, a friend of mine went to Denali in the summer," I said, "and it snowed on them—they camped *in the snow.*"

"Well, so did you at Yosemite," she said. She was right; it was no big deal.

My woollies had seen better days. It wasn't so much that the seam was ripping, it was more like the material was simply disintegrating. I had bought them used at the army-navy store six years before for about nine bucks, and since then they'd hiked their share of trails and knelt in their share of canoes.

The discussion at the other end of the table had turned to mosquitoes. "Well, Beth and I just murder 'em in our tent," said Evelyn. "The whole inside of our tent is bloody where we sqwushed 'em." We grinned proudly.

The foreman thanked us for the drink and said goodnight. "Thanks for the bath!" we waved after him.

I asked Sue about their afternoon tour of Danny's smokehouse. "Well, he had something hanging in there that was rotten," she said.

"Really?"

"And black," she made a face. "I don't know if it was a fish or what the hell it was."

"Why was he keeping it if it was rotten?" I frowned.

"I don't know," she said. "Anyway, he salts the salmon a little first—just for taste—then he heats up the smokehouse and dries the salmon and smokes them, to keep out the mosquitoes and flies and stuff."

"Maybe the rotten stuff is dog salmon," somebody suggested.

"Does this stuff really work?" asked Evelyn, struggling with the hand lotion. "It's like I've got cooking oil smeared all over my hands. . . . "

Kosha was concerned about bears. We told her about the great, fresh grizzly track we'd seen the night before and how we'd fled the island, just in case.

"Yeah," said Evelyn, grinning. "Apparently there're two kinds of bears: those that like to eat humans and those that don't want to have anything to do with us."

We all laughed, "But you don't know which is which!"

"You can't tell by the track," Sue joked.

"Except for that boot print dragging behind it. . . . " I shrugged.

Kalle and Kosha stood up to leave, and Kosha reeled slightly. "Everclear," we nodded knowingly.

It had been a day to remember. I looked downstream toward Victoria Rock that butted into the Yukon. The sun was a low glow in the sky. Somewhere downriver, I knew, floated and sang the Whitman bunch. I had spent part of the morning rehydrating picante sauce and talking to a man from New Waverly, Texas, about some wilderness proposals in Sam Houston National Forest near his home; I had spent the evening talking with two Athapascan Indians about dogsledding and with two Dutch people about hitchhiking in Canada; and now I was curling up on the floor of a cabin that had seen who knows what in its time. Had a friend of mine really said before the trip that he didn't think he could do something like this for three months because he'd get *bored?*

## JUNE 21, DAY 13

We had agreed we'd sleep late, so Evelyn got a few dirty looks when she rose at the crack of dawn, bear bells ajangle, and made coffee on the cabin stove. Ah, togetherness.

Outside our cabin door there spread a carpet of crisp white daisies. Campbell's log structures from the 1850s were mostly vine-covered heaps of rubble now. A mission had been built in 1892, and in 1898, the Mounties had headquartered their Yukon Field Force here to police the hordes that washed down the Yukon. In 1899, a Taylor & Drury store had come to the little clearing.

Shuffling through musty rooms, across rotting floorboards, I gazed at the peeling wallpaper and inspected the wood stoves. Someone had lashed together a crude rocking chair of split logs. The morning dampness brought out the rich brown color of the log church. White shutters covered the bell tower. The windows were real glass, and grey shingles topped the roof. A faded white door beckoned inside. Whose weddings and funerals had been held here?

You stand before a weathered cabin door, beneath a rack of caribou antlers, and slowly you turn the enamel knob. You peer into the darkness, across the wooden floor, and wonder who came and went and why, long ago, through this door.

Pale light filters through lace curtains. You study the roof logs, the heavy rafters. Who sat here, who wrote upon this dainty white table in the dim light that shone through thick glass?

I crawled among the wildflowers and grasses to photograph Selkirk. They say the clearing occurred naturally and was a well-known Indian trading ground before Campbell set up shop. Later, one Jack Dalton had forged a trail between the coast and Fort Selkirk, and over the summer of 1898, two thousand beef cattle had ambled into this clearing, bound for Dawson. Being from Texas where cows inhabit broad grassy plains, I found it hard to envision thousands of them plodding among the spruces of the Yukon Territory.

From beyond the far mountains, morning mist and rain-heavy clouds advanced down the valley. Struggling with them, though, came the sun and its own fleet of cheery white clouds.

On the high bank, I stood among the willows, where Campbell must have stood, and looked across the big river to the thick, green bushes. Massive natural basalt columns rose from the far bank. They say you can still see cannon balls imbedded in that wall, where Campbell's men lobbed them. On top of the wall stood a little army of poplars. Behind the abutment flowed the Pelly, and it was through that gap that one Inspector J.D. Moodie of the North West Mounted Police had washed into Fort Selkirk after almost fourteen months on an incredibly strange mission. When the Stampede erupted, his patrol had been sent from Edmonton, Canada, to find the best routes across the Rockies to the gold fields. He started out in September, 1897, to cover the 1,600 miles to Selkirk. It turned out to be a less than ideal route:

He and his men hacked their way through the wilderness, paddling, climbing, wading, and trudging, their clothes in tatters, their horses half dead, their packers constantly deserting them. . . . In one instance Moodie and his men had to chop their way through three hundred miles of fallen timber. At another point a forest fire almost wiped them out, and only an eleventh-hour change of wind saved them from roasting to death. Their ponies devoured poisonous weeds and expired on the spot. One of their guides went mad and vanished into the forest. Snow threatened to halt them for a full winter, but Moodie fought on . . . killing his packhorses to feed his sled dogs . . . . [in the end he] reached the Pelly. Down the great turbulent river he raced, in a canvas canoe until the sharp-edged ice floes tore into the sides and rendered it useless. He built himself a raft and kept on going, but it was too bulky and the ice in the channel blocked its passage. He spent four hundred and fifty dollars on buying a Peterborough canoe from another stampeder and plunged on, half starved, half frozen, his clothing caked to his body and his uniform in rags. The current grew fiercer, and the ice began to suck him under. He flung the canoe aside, donned his snowshoes, and plodded onward over the ice-sheathed boulders and through the fast-forming drifts. He would not stop for sleep, and when at last he arrived at Fork Selkirk, dazed with fatigue, Inspector Moodie had been on the move without respite for forty-eight hours. The date was October 24, 1898. (*The Klondike Fever*, pages 237-238)

By the time Moodie got to Selkirk, of course, virtually every inch of gold-bearing land along Bonanza and Eldorado Creeks had already been staked down at Dawson.

On the far side of the Pelly rose a huge ridge twice the height of the basalt abutment. It was rounded and grey, in contrast to the abrupt, dark basalt. Down it flowed streams of soft green poplars. We are small, indeed. This river, this abutment, those undulating hills, had been here for what to us is forever. People like Campbell, and Danny and Abby, and us, cruise through but for a split second. Our little adventures and excitements, our triumphs and defeats, must seem incredibly trivial to the river and the hills. Long after we'll be gone, the river will still be rolling by this little place that knew Indians and explorers like Campbell and a few Texas women.

The clouds flirting with Selkirk now ushered in a rainbow that arced from the Yukon's depths over magnificent Victoria Rock. As I strolled back into camp, refreshed by my few hours alone, Evelyn was returning from the woods where Danny had led her on a tour of the Indian cemetery. We kidded her for missing another research opportunity. She allowed that she'd really blown it; she could have done research on Yukon men and won the "place" contest in one fell swoop. "I think an Athapascan Indian spirit house on the Yukon would beat a grand piano without a doubt," she grinned.

We ate lunch, loaded the boats chain-gang style, and pushed into the river about two o'clock. Our All-Nighter was underway!

We battled an irritating headwind for a couple of hours as we wove through a smattering of islands between steep mountains. Then about 9 P.M. we pulled out on the left bank at a couple of cabins known as Selwyn. Sue and Jude rustled up soup and corn fritters that were a big hit. Kosha and Kalle paddled up and joined us for coffee.

Vines embraced the two long-abandoned cabins. The roofs had

collapsed and the walls looked ready to go at any moment. The world was so different up here away from the river. The minute I climbed the slope and stood in knee-high grasses, amid pink and white roses and purple chiming bells, surrounded by deep green furry spruces, I felt many miles from the wide-open river with its sweeping vistas. This was a close, intimate world, quiet and full of detail and maybe bears. I crawled through the flowers and mosquitoes and tested my close-up camera lenses. The evening light, with its slanted glowing rays, was magical. The place seemed like a great, thick rain forest, dense and lush.

Shortly before midnight, we slogged back through the mud, slithered into the boats, pushed into the river, thwarted up and poured a bit of Everclear. At midnight we offered one toast to the Yukon, sang "Summertime," and welcomed in the longest day of the year. At this moment, if tradition held, folks down in Dawson were tossing the first pitch of a sunlit baseball game. And others were partying atop Midnight Dome, a high mountain overlooking the city. Sue plunked the strings of her ukulele, and we accompanied with harmonica, kazoo, and belly-dancing cymbals.

"Look, look!" Jude whispered. A lone female moose stood nonchalantly on the rocky beach. We watched quietly. Then she trotted off into the bushes. "To moose!" we held up our cups.

Barb took watch; the rest of us wrote or admired the scenery. The sunlight dimmed now behind steep misty mountains, and although twilight remained, the temperature plummeted. We hauled out parkas, mittens, then sleeping bags, then bivy sacks; we wrapped ourselves in everything we had and got colder and colder as we drifted down the Yukon in our aluminum iceboxes. Once, Jane looked at her little thermometer and announced it was 35°. Rolling our eyes, we burrowed deeper among the backpacks and cooking pots and lawn chairs and ammo cans.

I had reversed my nest for the party, spread ammo cans and duffel bags and various things into a little bed, propped my lawn chair up where I could face the others and lean back and watch the scenery. But as the temperature dropped, as damp fog rolled in, as it got darker and darker, all I wanted was to sink deeper beneath the sides of the boat. Any little wind crept down my spine and froze my bones.

No one did any real sleeping, yet it seemed too cold to sit up and do anything. It was easier to hunker down and hope for morning.

Jane finally poked her face out of her cocoon. "You all, this is the pits."

We agreed and looked for a campsite. In the foggy dusk, the shores were barely visible. We finally pulled out and Barb and Sue tromped through the night to check out a spot, their dark figures disappearing down the beach. They reappeared to report that it was too muddy.

Back on the river, I took watch. I couldn't sleep anyway and my stomach ached from shivering so much. I figured I might as well sit up and create a little heat by paddling. It was 3 A.M.

"Fiord-type features characterize this portion of the Yukon River," a brochure had said, "with mountains rising steeply from both [banks], enclosing the river completely. . . . Campsites are limited to the shorelines with the best sites occurring at the mouths of small creeks that are usually infested with insects." Lovely.

Creamy, low-lying mist had rolled in. The damp, white fog thickened around each bend, just where I most needed to judge which channel to take through the islands. My fingers were surely dying of frostbite inside their mittens. But it was a wonderfully new and bizarre sensation to rudder an unwieldy three-canoe craft down a huge, dark river (visions of sea captains danced through my brain) in the middle of the night while five women lay crumpled and snoring.

The world was a silent collage of blue, white, grey. It was peaceful, with a tinge of mysterious excitement. The Klepper guy had said there'd be more wildlife at night, so I was counting on at least a million bears and two million moose to show up, but none did. We passed a few inhabited cabins as we drifted. I abandoned trying to read the map and simply enjoyed the feel of paddle and water and ferrying and judging curves and channels for the fastest current. We drifted past the silent Whitman College camp.

Once I heard churning water but could see only fog. Finally, squinting desperately into the grey dawn, I made out what appeared to be big waves, but I couldn't believe it. Five Finger was supposed to be the only rapid; based on that knowledge, I bore down into it and hoped for the best. When the sleepers and I reached the bottom of the bend, we hit some low standing waves but bobbled through easily.

At 6 A.M., we still hadn't found a campsite among the mountains that rose almost vertically from the water's edge, just like the brochure had said. Evelyn took watch; I shivered and curled in my sleeping bag like a Husky sleeping in a snowbank. My rest was shattered when Evelyn accidentally ran us into the shore.

"Prepare to crash," Sue mumbled, as our aluminum hull drove onto the rocks. I sighed and burrowed back into my bag.

"Moose!" someone whispered later. Big deal.

But the creatures were magnificent in their homely way. A cow and calf stood on the beach, their wary stares following us as we drifted past. Still we looked for a campsite. We were miserable.

"Land!" Evelyn finally announced, sighting a flat gravel tip of an island. We unthwarted, ferried over to it, gruntle-stumbled from the boats, threw together the tents, gulped a quick cup of tea that Sue and Jude had produced. Fork Selkirk lay seventy-four long, frigid miles behind us.

It was after eight o'clock now, and, mockingly, the sun was up full and hot. We stripped to T-shirts and crawled into the tents for a warm nap that lasted until past noon.

## JUNE 22, DAY 14

Slowly, we emerged from the tents and decided to make it a layover day. Sybil, whom we hadn't seen since we shared fireweed salad with her at Hootalinqua, paddled by and stopped for lunch. She insisted on making her own fire and cooking her own food, saying that she didn't want to use ours because we must have it all rationed. We assured her we had too much. As we chatted with her, we bathed or ate or fiddled with gear, enjoying the leisurely afternoon.

"How far down you goin' today, Sybil?" asked Jude.

"I'm not sure," she said, "because I'll stop and tell Linda that Sonny will probably be down sometime today. I just saw him at Ballerat Creek. Then I'll go down another eight miles and see Gerry and Jan. . . . "

Here was this dainty woman, squatting on a sandbar stirring her lunch over a campfire, out for a Sunday stroll down the Yukon to visit a few friends.

"How often do you get to see these people?" Jude asked.

"I saw Yvonne this spring—we had a good visit at my place. I saw Linda and Sonny fifteen months ago. . . . You just pick up wherever the conversation left off. It's almost as though you're resuming the same conversation, as though it's only been a few days since you've seen them. Nothing seems to change much; the children get older, but that's all."

We talked about Danny and Abby at Fort Selkirk. "We enjoyed visiting with Abby very much," said Evelyn.

"Oh, gosh, yes," Sybil agreed. She said Abby had had a couple of strokes within the past five years, one of which had laid her up at home for awhile. "They do not like to live in town," she said. "There's too much temptation to drink and waste their lives. Danny has a lot of respectability as the caretaker at Selkirk."

I considered the quiet life they had chosen and wondered how they must have felt when the hundred or so others who'd once lived at Selkirk began moving away.

"Can you trap during the summer, Sybil?" asked Sue.

"No, the fur's not prime," she answered, "and they are having and rearing their young. They shed their coats in the spring and they'll have a thinner coat in summer; and in early fall, for that intense winter cold— which they don't seem to mind at all—they start putting on thick, woolly winter underwear under all that. Then the outer fur is all glossy and nice, and with the thick, silky underwear underneath it, the furs are prime. Usually, later in November—from then on it's prime. Trapping legally starts November first."

Sybil stood up from her lunchpot. "I wonder if I have time to change before dinner?" she smiled.

"We'll stir your pot if you like," said Evelyn.

"I'll put it on simmer," Sybil said, moving it to the fire's edge. "I'll put it on the back burner and it'll be fine."

Sybil said the people along the river trap in winter and do odd jobs, like construction, in the summer. She said it's tough to make enough money on trapping alone. I still had a hard time imagining enough people in the world buying enough fur coats to support all these people up and down the Yukon. I pondered the unwilling and unpaid critters who serve as middle animals in this strange commerce between men on dogsleds in the Yukon and women with fur coats on the streets of Dallas or Paris.

A plane flew over, and as we sat in various stages of undress, we waved.

"We met a nice young man on the ferry who was going up to Fairbanks to fly on a fighter plane," said Evelyn, "and we told him to waggle his wings if he saw us on the river." Sybil looked aloft and smiled. Barb announced that canoeists were coming down the river, and we made halfhearted attempts to get dressed.

"Girls," Jane said ominously, "we are just this minute out of liquid soap." We booed. Dishes would have to be cleaned with sand until Dawson.

Sybil told of her friend Esa's sled dogs. "Sometimes old Booze, his lead dog, would want to go his own way," she said. "Then Esa would stop the team, smoke his pipe, and say, 'O.K., Booze, we're going that way.'

"Once he was working with Ringo. She had gotten some training, but Esa decided he'd put Booze back on again and see if he would behave himself a little better. But you have a spacing problem—you can't put Booze before or just after Sam or they'll start up this little feud again, so you have to space them in a certain way so those who get along best together follow one another. Booze was put directly in front of the sled as wheel dog. And he worked just fine back there; he seemed relieved not to have to make leader decisions. He didn't mind the sled right behind him. That was another problem; you had to keep away from the sled any dog that worried maybe the sled would hit him and spent too much time looking back, not keeping his line taut, not working properly, because the other dogs would have too much work to do if that one wasn't doing his share."

We asked about the verbal commands that mushers give their dogs. "You can use whatever commands you prefer for 'stop' and 'go,'" Sybil said. "They learn those very quickly. Esa says, 'Hey, let's go,' or 'O.K., gang' or whatever. It's a little more difficult to teach them to gee and haw, to right and left. Old Booze was stubborn; he didn't always gee or haw when you wanted him to, and this was going to be confusing for any new lead dog he was training. Esa didn't have time to train Ringo. She exhibited leadership qualities, so he put her in the front and away they went. Whenever she came to a fork in the trail, usually she could read his mind and she'd take the fork he wanted. If she didn't seem sure she'd slow down and enter one fork and look back, and he'd nod and say, 'O.K. Ringo,' or 'No, Ringo,' and she'd just cross over and take the right one."

Jude confirmed, as she'd suspected, that it had been Sybil who'd left the nice little pile of firewood we'd found at Selwyn when we stopped there for supper the night before.

"When was breakup this year?" asked Sue.

"It started to break up at Stewart on the fifth of May," said Sybil, "when I was there last spring. It was the next day or a little later that it broke up at Dawson. It starts out with cracking sounds, groaning; then when it separates into big rafts and they start moving, it has a sound of chandelier glasses chinking together, like tinkling glass or wind chimes."

We talked about the river in winter and about how Danny and Abby travel it. "The Yukon is the mode of travel," said Sybil. "To get from Danny's place to anywhere they want to go, they have to get on that river. He has the dogs and his Skidoo. In the winter, the Yukon is his highway."

I was now in the Yukon up to my knees, naked except for my wetsuit booties and tennis shoes. "How is it?" shouted Jude.

"Waaaah! I don't think I'm gonna wash my hair!"

"It's damned cold, no question about that," said Sue. "At least I got in up to my waist; get on down there!"

"Oh!" I shrieked, "I just remembered I just had a bath day before yesterday."

"Get on in there!" they shouted playfully.

I soaped up, rinsed quickly, then sat on the warm rocks at the water's edge and shaved my legs down to my wetsuit booties. The others had all sorts of lotions out and were giving their hands heavy-duty treatment. Except for applying an occasional soothing coat of lotion or Vaseline, I was toying with the theory that my hands would be better off if I just let the skin toughen, lotionless, in the sun and wind and sand.

Sybil spoke of Fort Selkirk and the Indians who had lived up and down the Yukon before the relatively recent era of canoe-tourists. "People left their cabins when they opened up the few roads through the Yukon," she said. "The river had always been the highway, winter and summer, and the sternwheelers used to run. When they opened up the highway to Dawson, and put the dam in, they took the sternwheelers off; those boats couldn't get through the dams, and the bridges weren't high enough for them to get under. So then the people had no way of carrying on the life that they used to have, no way to get their groceries and goods. It had been a good way of life.

"So then, people all wanted to get out where civilization was, for buying things, for getting jobs. They all moved out onto the roadside. It was too costly to load up their furniture, so they left it at Selkirk.

"Nine or ten years ago when I first started coming down," she said, "there were very few people canoeing compared to now." We told her that 900 had signed Danny's register in the last year. "As we made other trips," she said, "we noticed everything disappearing out of those cabins; now there's no furniture left, no books, no dishes. Danny couldn't keep track of everybody; in the meantime, canoeists would be walking off with whatever was in the cabins. Some of the cabins used to be furnished just the way the people left them."

Sybil told of a man back in the 1940s who took a load of trade goods up the Pelly to establish a trading post. "The moccasin telegraph being what it is," she said, "the Indians knew he was coming before he ever got there; they came across country, and they cleaned him out—traded for everything he had—before he even got established in his post. He had to go back and get another load and bring it up, and then they got the post built. So all those Indians that were living along the Pelly and the Macmillan and all through that country—when the roads were built they all moved out onto the road. They go over in there now to fish in summer or to trap in the winter, but that's about it."

"It's a whole way of life just gone, isn't it?" Sue commented.

Sybil told us about her life on the trapline in winter. We asked about cabin fever. "We had books," she said, "and I took knitting and little projects to do, things that wouldn't take up too much room on the plane. Sometimes we'd say, 'Well, I think there's going to be good weather Sunday, so we'll go out for a picnic.' And then toward the end I said, 'Gee, I haven't been anywhere for awhile,' so we hitched up the dogs, packed a big lunch, took off down the trapline trail, and I rode on the sled. We went down to one of the overnight camps where a lean-to tent was set up."

We smiled. I'm sure none of us could think of anything more romantic than to ride on a dogsled through the Yukon's winter scenery.

Sybil washed her dishes, then headed on down the river. We waved goodbye, saying we'd see her later.

The flat, sandy ground was ideal for the big mosquito-net dining tent and its stakes, and there were enough mosquitoes flying about to warrant putting it up, so as I napped in the sun on the warm rocks, the others struggled to erect the tent for the first time: "Wait a minute, that's got to be on top, doesn't it? . . . Well, let's see . . . That's upside down . . . You just lift up . . . I tried that . . . No . . . Wait . . . Is there something missing? . . . I got it . . . Here you go. . . . "

Eventually it was time for Evelyn and me to cook dinner. We made a potato quiche, which was a fair hit, and served it with milk shakes made from banana flakes and powdered milk, which weren't hits at all. Evelyn and I had our usual tug-of-war as we cooked; she adhered to a less-spice philosophy and I subscribed to the more-spice. We were doing fairly well, arguing in a friendly way, until she asked if I knew about relationships between ingredients. Well, O.K., she'd raised and fed two kids and cooked twenty years longer than I, but I wasn't a *complete* idiot; I'd lived twenty-eight years and I had cooked a *few* things in my time and by God I was gonna put more pepper into this quiche.

We enjoyed our first meal in the relatively mosquito-free dining tent and felt pretty pampered and relaxed, until the others got into a big argument about school discipline and dress codes that drove Jane and me from the tent.

## JUNE 23, DAY 15

It was a sunny day and, well-rested, we hit the river at 10 A.M. We stopped for water at Kirkman Creek, which flowed into the Yukon just below several inhabited cabins. It was great fun balancing on a log out over the creek so we wouldn't stir up the sediment. I stepped in accidentally, and mud swirled into the water jugs. We whooped at the millions of tiny flecks of "gold" that sparkled in the mud. We knew it was fools' gold, but here we were on the Yukon and we'd struck it rich.

As we drifted downstream, we passed a man and boy on the bank who were sawing wood; they ignored our greeting. We figured if we lived on the Yukon, we, too, would tire of interrupting what we were doing every time one of the hundreds of canoe groups passed by.

A few bends later we passed a cabin where Sybil's boat was tied. A young girl waved to us from shore. As we passed out of earshot, Sybil appeared on the front lawn and waved as if she hadn't seen us in weeks. We began to feel in some small way a part of the elongated little Yukon community.

Spring breakup had crammed a massive logjam into a little channel that would have taken us to the remains of the old Thistle Creek roadhouse. We hugged the right bank and wound between some islands, hoping to see remnants of the old settlement. We stopped once at a trapline cabin, then stopped again to inspect some modern machinery and pipes that were lying around, then finally pulled out for lunch on a steep, rocky bank. Over hot soup, we sat in the shade of the poplars and watched the river roll past.

After lunch we thwarted and drifted for several hours. I slept in the cozy aluminum-reflected heat. Soon we heard a small voice and splashing; Sybil had overtaken us and we invited her to thwart.

"I've been paddling like a Trojan," she said, "and you all have stayed ahead without a paddle in the water!" We laughed.

"Sometimes, though," said Jude, who was steering the three-canoe raft, "we get out of the current; we'll be just sitting still and we can see over on the other side where it's racing past."

"Ah, yes," nodded Sybil, "but then when you get over there, it's just the same, isn't it?"

"That's right!"

"You've been introduced to the Yukon blahs," said Sybil. "Wherever you are, you think the current's somewhere else."

We attached her boat to ours with a couple of bungy cords and drifted lazily. She brought out a bag of chocolate cookies she had baked in the sun on wax paper; we traded her a cold corn fritter from two nights ago. She talked of this year's unusually cold winter and the late spring, saying she thought parts of the Yukon may have frozen all the way to the bottom this year.

"I was visiting a family I know back there when you saw me," said Sybil. "They used to live in the old roadhouse when they first moved here, but then the roof fell in, so they built that cabin. They had quite a time this year when the ice went out. It jammed just near there and the water came up fast. They got the kids up on top of the chicken house, then they let all the animals loose—the chickens, goats and sled dogs. I think they had fourteen dogs. I think two dogs drowned. It was awful. The whole family spent the night on the roof of the chicken house, and the water came up to the windows of their cabin. A plane flew over the next day and saw them on the roof, with water up in the cabin and big chunks of ice all around, so they assumed he'd report it and someone would come soon enough to help. But he didn't report it. They'd left a pot of stew on the counter in the cabin, and the water and mud came up just that high. When they finally got off the chicken house the next day as the water went down, they were awfully hungry and they ate that stew. It was fine. Anyway, one way or another, neighbors up and down the river heard what had happened, and they came with food and clothing and helped them. Everything they owned was covered with mud—all their clothes, the insides of the cabin, everything."

We sat in wide-eyed wonder; the Yukon seemed so peaceful and helpful now as it sped us downstream without a care. Sybil said people on the river have a designated time each day when they go on the radio. "If you miss a day or two, nobody worries," she said. "They figure you've gone to Dawson or you're out trapping or something. But if you miss more than a couple of days—unless you've said you were going away—your neighbors begin to worry and they'll come over to your cabin to see what's the matter."

A big valley on the left indicated that we would soon hit the mouth of the White River. Up it somewhere, I knew, was a place called Snag that boasts the lowest temperature ever recorded in North America: -81°. Sybil watched some clouds far back in that direction and smiled.

"I rather like to see thunderstorms back up on the White as I'm passing by on the Yukon," she said, "because then you get one jolly good ride down to Stewart Island." We knew that the White poured tons of glacial silt into the Yukon, and we watched the water for signs of the merging. In *The Yukon*, Mathews describes the event:

> The White . . . plummets down nonstop from the St. Elias and Wrangell Mountains, among the highest and most heavily glaciated peaks in the continent. These glaciers pulverize rock to flour-sized particles which the White dumps into the Yukon. At first the parent stream refuses to accept this filthy donation, and the two rivers run parallel along a water edge sharp as a knife. But after half a mile the edge grows dull; the zone of intermingling— swirling billows of lactescence in the brown water—widens until, four miles below, it reaches from bank to bank. . . . [The White's] silt will henceforth be kept in suspension by the current of the larger river; and the Yukon will end as a great whitish blot spreading out into the Bering Sea. . . . The water is potable, however, especially if you leave a glass of it to sit overnight so that at least three fourths of an inch of sediment can settle out. With time and laziness you get used to drinking the river water as is, and soon enough the pellucid tributaries seem flat and tasteless—nothing to grit your teeth on. (pages 53-54)

Below the White's mouth, we rounded the tip of an island and came upon a beaver cavorting near the bank. We were still grinning over our good fortune when we realized that the wind had pushed us up into some sandbars and rock shoals. Quickly we unthwarted, and each boat began a futile ferry to reach the main current and avoid the shoals. I suspect the same little argument that took place in our boat was going on in the others: "Harder! . . . We need less angle, we're not gonna make it! . . . Maybe we could get through there. . . . No come on, we can make it. . . . We're not getting anywhere, the wind is pushing us into the . . . (sound of canoe hull grating into mud and gravel)."

Each boat got hung up at least once, but we squiggled through. Then we hit another bunch of shallows, each with a big, uprooted tree aground in the middle, and paddled through some eddies and boils and riffles. Something was odd about these riffles; we still couldn't quite tell which ones were simply the result of two currents merging and which meant shallow water flowing over rocks. The water was so murky we could see only an inch below the surface.

Sybil wore no life jacket when she paddled (I think we were the only group of canoeists who wore ours virtually all the time). She sat just back of midboat and used a regular single-bladed canoe paddle; she could move that boat along just about as fast with one paddle as we could with two.

Around a bend, we spotted the Stewart Island settlement. From our right poured the swift waters of the Stewart River, bearing several large floating trees. Says Mathews, "Though it drains an area larger than Switzerland and is just short of four hundred miles long, [the Stewart] is only the sixth largest of the Yukon's tributaries." (*The Yukon*, page 55)

It was among the sandbars and creeks of the Stewart where, in 1883, four men spent the summer prospecting and brought out about ten dollars worth of gold per man per day—the first "paying" mining that had been done anywhere in the Yukon basin. In the years that followed, more miners had trickled over the Chilkoot and down the Yukon and up the Stewart; its valley became the richest strike of that pre-Klondike era. In 1886 Jack McQuesten and Arthur Harper, the Yukon's longtime traders and promoters, abandoned their trading post at Fort Reliance, below present-day Dawson, and set up a new one at a ragtag settlement here at the Stewart's mouth. The Yukon had come into its own as a gold-bearing valley; McQuesten and Harper shifted their stock from fur-traders' supplies to prospectors' picks and shovels.

McQuesten then headed for San Francisco for more supplies. Meanwhile, Harper had interested two men in trying the waters of the Fortymile River, downstream from present-day Dawson. Sure enough, they struck good gold and the Stewart River bunch vanished downstream to try the new strike. Harper knew that as the news spread to the Outside, new hordes of miners would tumble over the mountains and down the Yukon on the spring breakup; he knew too that he must vastly increase his stock of food and equipment to save them all from starvation.

A steamboat man named George Williams and an Indian companion set out to carry Harper's desperate message through the winter snows. Their goal was the nearest outpost of civilization—John Healy's trading post on the tidal flats over the Chilkoot, five hundred miles away. The two men struggled on as their food ran out and their dogs died. Halted at the Chilkoot's summit by a raging blizzard, they dug a cave into the snow to wait and hope, their bodies sustained now only by a few grains of flour. When that was gone, the Indian carried Williams, who was near death by this time, down the mountain through the vicious storm and collapsed, at last, within the shelter of Healy's store. Pierre Berton tells what happened next:

> Williams lived two days, and the men who crowded around his deathbed had only one question: why had he made the trip?
> The Indian's answer electrified them. He reached into a sack of beans on Healy's counter and flung a handful on the floor.
> "Gold," he said. "All same like this!" *(The Klondike Fever,* pages 16-17)

As the years went by, mining boomed all along the Yukon. At one time the Stewart Island settlement, toward which we now headed, had a post office, a telegraph station, traders' cabins, and an Alaska Commercial Company trading post.

With George Carmack's big strike in 1896 at Bonanza Creek, the steady trickle over the mountains became an incredible flood of 30,000 gold-crazed souls who clawed their way down the Yukon however they could. Although the Chilkoot was their main path, there were several lesser routes, including the Stewart River. Some miners made their way down the Mackenzie, crossed the Divide, and floated down the Stewart into the Yukon. Others had started too late and were forced to winter over en route. Jack London had failed to reach Dawson before winter set in, and he was one of many who spent the winter of 1898-99 here on the Stewart. It was somewhere up this river that he gleaned the details for many of his hard-bitten tales of life in the North.

Once the Bonanza Creek strike was in full swing and everyone in the world knew of the Klondike River, this river (whose mouth we now negotiated), took up a new identity. Says Berton,

> Split-Up City lay at the mouth of the Stewart River, where the Yukon splays out into a confusing tangle of channels and islands and where a boat can be lost for hours or even days. The selection of the wrong channel led to endless recriminations, and the halves of boats lying all along this section of the river were mute evidence of a common disenchantment. *(The Klondike Fever,* page 286)

Indeed, we were now within a hard day's travel of Dawson City, and the fever to get to the gold fields must have been too much for many of the partnerships that rode these waters back then. We six Texas women and Sybil, though, found ourselves happily docking below Stewart Island's ten-foot cutbanks, climbing the convenient ladder, meeting Sybil's friend Yvonne Burian, and strolling across the very civilized mown lawn. We had floated thirty-four miles.

We fell in love with the place and decided to stay the night in one of the little cabins the Burians rent (for a modest $2.50 Canadian per person) to river travelers. Sybil's cabin perched about three feet from the vertical edge of the island. She said Stewart Island can lose up to seven feet of frontage land each year to the ice and floods. Our cabin nestled somewhat more securely back from the river near a grove of spruces. Yvonne's husband, Rudy, smiled behind the counter as we ogled the goods at the Burians' store. Devouring the store's crackers and cheese and soft drinks, we sprawled on the lawn, swatted mosquitoes, watched big fallen trees lumbering through the Yukon's grand, sweeping curve, and threw an ancient rubber ball to the Burians' little dog. Meanwhile, the Burians' son, Ivan, jounced around the island on a three-wheeled motorcycle with fat tires.

Jane and Barb learned the intricacies of the cabin's big woodburning stove, while Evelyn tried to teach me to split wood on the chopping block outside. She was an old pro, having heated her farmhouse for the past several winters with wood she had split. There was something rather gratifying about seeing a fifty-two-year-old woman in bear bells and a tuxedo T-shirt cleaving those big logs with one powerful stroke, as the Yukon rolled behind her in the afternoon sunlight. My efforts at splitting wood served only to entertain the others who were lounging in their chairs on the lawn. When they hollered tips like "Watch the wood, not the ax," all I could do was watch the tennis-shoed foot I figured sooner or later that ax was going to slice. I left Evelyn to her wood and tried water-fetching instead. The big hand-pump in the yard was broken, so the Burians invited me to use the pump in their kitchen sink. Their house was cheery and quiet. I pumped a few strokes and thought of a time when I had held my mouth beneath a pump on the screened porch behind a log cabin on an island in the Okefenokee Swamp in Georgia. Lugging the splashing bucket back to our cabin, I felt like a little wetsuit-bootied farmwife.

We dined on the lawn while Sybil told us more dogsled and bear tales. One spring a friend had agreed to bring Sybil to Stewart Island from Dawson by dogsled. But when she arrived in Dawson to begin the trip, she realized that they would each have their own team.

"But I've never done this!" she protested. Her friend had nodded toward the dogs, "It's O.K., they know how," and off they dashed down Dawson's snow-covered bank and out onto the frozen Yukon. Seventy miles and one-and-a-half days later, they arrived at Stewart Island. She said most of the time you run behind the dogs; if you try to ride on the sled going uphill, they'll look back and give you a dirty look. "You're like a team, you and the dogs," she said. "You have to help one another and be considerate of one another."

Sybil said we needn't worry much about bears. She said they'd had a few around her cabin, but had never had to shoot one.

"When I pull out to make camp on the river," she said, "I usually talk to the bears. I say in a friendly but firm voice, 'Hello, Mr. Bear, I'm going to stay here for awhile if you don't mind, and I'll clean up everything when I leave, and I won't bother you.' I think they don't like whistles too much. My friend Charlie said he thought a whistle would sound like a gopher and would attract rather than repel bears."

Sybil seemed to share our philosophy about bears, a philosophy that had helped us decide not to bring a gun. "Animals can sense the mood you're in," she said. "If you're carrying a gun and you get off in the woods and you're feeling a little cocky, thinking you're protected and all, you give off a hostile odor or vibrations or something. Bears can sense hostile people and they may react violently."

After dinner we joined Rudy in the little building that was his museum. For decades, he had collected everything from telegraph insulators to gold pans from the cabins and the creeks all up and down the valley. With obvious pride, he described to us item after item. There was a mastodon tusk; lynx, wolf, and marten skulls; an old wooden icebox; a complement of the kind of old irons that you heated on the stove; kerosene lanterns; rifles. . . .

"What's this great big skull?" I asked.

"Oh, that's a grizzly," Rudy said.

"Really?" we chorused.

"Good Lord, look at those teeth!" exclaimed Jane.

Evelyn and Sybil were involved in a long discussion about irons with detachable handles, irons that you filled with gasoline and that belched fire, irons that did this and irons that did that. . . . The only kind I had ever used (and I could probably count on two hands the number of times I had used them) had electric cords attached to them.

Rudy had catalogued just about everything in the museum. He was a small, wiry man with a slow, soft-spoken voice and a gentle manner. The Burians were the only ones who lived on Stewart Island now, but in times past it was a big stopping place for the steamboats. I looked around the grounds and pictured hundreds of gentlemen and ladies disembarking from a grand boat onto that grassy bank as they anticipated a fine evening meal in Stewart's roadhouse. Now there were only the silent Yukon, the Burians' neatly painted house, the outbuildings full of odd pieces of rusting equipment, and the sled dogs tied behind the house, each with a bare circle of hard-packed earth around his stake.

Yvonne was born in Dawson City. She met Rudy when he came to Stewart Island and bought the roadhouse. Before, he had been cutting wood for the steamboats on the Stewart River.

Discussion turned to mosquitoes.

"Yeah, they're worse this year," said Rudy. "Last year—and the year before, too—you could sit out anywhere and they wouldn't bother you. The thing is, this year the ice jammed and the Stewart flooded the flats here. Any time that happens we get mosquitoes."

"Well, they haven't driven me absolutely crazy yet," I said, knocking my knuckles on the wooden counter, "not like the mosquitoes in the Everglades." I judged all mosquito environments against the time my brother and I had been routed from our campsite by a vicious army of salt-marsh mosquitoes one May. At 5 A.M., we literally had ripped the tent from the ground, hurled the gear into my van, and burned rubber out of the campground toward anywhere but there. We hadn't stopped until we had cold piña coladas in our hands at Sloppy Joe's cantina ("Hemingway's Favorite Bar") in Key West.

I didn't know it then as we joked with Rudy in his museum on Stewart Island, but during our Yukon adventure I would add at least two more candidates to my list for all-time worst nights on a camping trip.

Just outside the museum door lay two, big, bleached racks of moose antlers, intertwined. "My sons found those," said Rudy matter-of-factly. "Two dead moose lying just like that with their antlers locked. I guess they got 'em locked when they were fighting and died of starvation."

Sybil led us down a path through quiet woods to a slough strewn with hulks of old barges. Here she had once spent a few weeks helping a crew of young people restore an old tug named the *Yukon Rose*. The *Rose* was gone now, floated triumphantly down to Dawson, but in the fading sunlight, amid the tall grasses and young trees that covered the other boats, Sybil smiled and told us of her good times that spring. We listened, twitching at the cloud of mosquitoes that hovered wherever we went.

"When the *Rose* was ready to launch, everybody on the island was here, it was such a big day," said Sybil. "When the *Rose* slid into the water, we all clapped and shouted. It was such a victory, until we realized we had actually done something you only see in comedy movies: we'd forgotten to keep the mooring ropes attached! There was a united gasp as she edged out into the current, starting for Dawson on her own. Somebody threw a line at the two young fellows on deck and soon the *Rose* was made fast. Quite a launching, eh?"

We said goodnight, strolled back into our cabin, spread our sleeping bags on the mattresses on the cots, and tried to sleep while mosquitoes buzzed our ears. Jude slept with her Shoo-Bug jacket over her face. Long after the others were asleep, I lay reading *The Call of the Wild* (copyright 1903) in the cabin's fading light. I hadn't read it since I was a child, but again I loved it.

I finished its last lines: "When the long winter nights come on and the wolves follow their meat into the lower valleys, [Buck] may be seen running at the head of the pack through the pale moonlight or glimmering borealis, leaping gigantic above his fellows, his great throat a-bellow as he sings a song of the younger world, which is the song of the pack" (page 102). And I thought of a pirate-policeman-hobo-prospector-turned-writer named Jack London from San Francisco, who'd headed for the Klondike with all the others in 1897, who'd spent a winter up the river at whose mouth we now slept, who'd most probably tramped upon this same island, and who published almost fifty books in the next seventeen years until his death at age forty.

## JUNE 24, DAY 16

We ate a big breakfast, swept out the cabin, and chain-ganged the gear down the bank. Sybil was chopping wood on the lawn. Since she'd be staying another couple of days to visit at Stewart, we didn't know if we'd ever see her again. It was a sad and awkward moment. We shared unspoken agreement with the invitation that Sue offered: "Sybil, come to the Bering Sea with us."

"I've considered it," she said. She had a faraway look in her eye, a bittersweet smile on her face.

"Really, we mean it," we said.

"Well, I'm supposed to visit my parents for a few weeks after I take out at Dawson," she said, gazing down the river.

"So visit them later," we said.

"No, I really can't," she said. "Well, maybe I could change things up a bit, visit them in the fall. No, I guess I better not. . . . Well, I don't know."

We hugged her goodbye and said we'd look for her in Dawson, where we'd try to change her mind. She stook on the bank waving.

On the river beneath the morning sun, we enjoyed dodging the mudflats and floating logs. I was happy to be paddling again after what seemed a long time; using my muscles felt good, and I hummed new melodies and thought up words for a song about the Yukon.

Every few miles, Evelyn and I would drift and chat. She gave her daily report on her readings from the *Hite* book. "Just about all the men admitted having run around on their wives," she said.

I nodded without surprise.

"And just about all of them thought it was O.K. if their wives didn't know about it—what they didn't know wouldn't hurt them," she said. "It was interesting how some of them defined their activities, though. One guy said he had never been unfaithful to his wife when they were in the same country. In other words, doing it overseas didn't even count."

The conversation continued in greater detail, around bend after bend, mile after mile, until somehow we ended up talking about shepherds and sheep on remote Australian ranches. Eventually we progressed from the topic of sex to food. We talked about the kinds of food we'd brought, the quantities, the cooking arrangement, and ended up discoursing on bodily functions.

"Yeah," said Evelyn, "I can really tell the difference between my usual diet and this whole-grain stuff!" I knew just what she meant. We joked about having to grab the trowel and dash into the woods, like clockwork, every morning right after breakfast.

"Sometimes," I confided, "I get in a hurry, what with swatting the mosquitoes and everything, and I miss the hole I've dug."

"That's nothing," she smirked. "The other day I dug a nice big hole and managed to hit it perfectly, but the pile was twice as big as the hole!" We finally embarrassed ourselves and put our minds back to paddling. Somehow we had missed seeing the ruins of the important settlement of Ogilvie, on an island across from the mouth of the Sixtymile River.

Here, in the 1890s, a conversation took place that would lead to the discovery of the Klondike strike. Here, Joe Ladue and his partner, Arthur ("Papa") Harper, had operated the Yukon's first post office, as well as a sawmill and a two-story trading post. They named the settlement for William Ogilvie, famous Canadian government surveyor who, a few years before, had established the boundary between Alaska and Canada.

Ladue had been one of the first to come over the Chilkoot, long before anyone knew anything about the Klondike River or Bonanza Creek. He had spent years prospecting, farming, sawing lumber, and trading. One day there wandered into Ladue's Ogilvie Post a Robert Henderson, the man destined to become known as the co-discoverer, with George Carmack, of the Klondike gold. Henderson was a Nova Scotian who had searched the world for years for gold. Believing that gold would be found all the way up the chain of the Rockies, he had come to the Yukon.

Here at Ogilvie, Ladue convinced Henderson that good prospects might lie on the Indian River, a downstream tributary of the Yukon. Henderson was discouraged by his recent lack of luck up on the Pelly, but since Ladue was willing to grubstake him, he couldn't resist charging off on yet another chase for gold. He spent two years panning the Indian River's tributaries. He found gold, but never enough to suit him. Meanwhile, he suffered snow-blindness from the constant glare and severe leg cramps from panning gold day after day in the freezing water. Once, on a little stream called Australia Creek, "he endured a harrowing experience when, falling across the broken branch of a tree, he was impaled through the calf and suspended over the rushing torrent like a slab of beef on a butcher's hook. For fourteen days he lay crippled in his bivouac; then he was away again . . . limping through the forests or traveling the shallow streams in a crude boat made from the skins of animals." (The Klondike Fever, page 38)

At length, Henderson crossed a divide alongside the Indian River, tried a new creek, and found a very good prospect that paid eight cents to the pan. He crossed back over the ridge and told about twenty miners who were working the Indian River. They joined him on the new creek, which he named "Gold Bottom."

In midsummer, 1896, Henderson poled his boat back upriver here to Ogilvie to resupply at Ladue's post. When he announced his news, everyone but Ladue jumped into his boat and headed downstream. When Henderson himself got back down to the mouth of the Indian River with his supplies, it was late summer and the water was too low for his boat, so he floated on down to something called the Thron-diuck River. He figured, correctly, that he if he poled up the Thron-diuck he would come upon his Gold Bottom Creek. It was on his way up the Thron-diuck that he met George Carmack, who was salmon fishing with his two Indian friends. And it was then that Henderson made his fateful invitation to Carmack to stake on his creek, while specifically discouraging the Indians. Drawn by Henderson's suggestion, Carmack had indeed gone over to the diggings, stumbled onto nearby Rabbit (Bonanza) Creek, and made the strike that would rock the world.

Meanwhile, back here at Ogilvie Post, on his little island in the middle of the Yukon, Ladue's promoter's mind was thrown into high gear by news of Carmack's strike. He registered himself a townsite where the Klondike met the Yukon, and he named it Dawson City after a government geologist. Within two years, Ladue's lots were selling for $5,000 a front foot on Dawson's main street.

As for William Ogilvie, the Canadian government surveyor after whom Ladue named the island settlement which we were now passing, he too would play a colorful part in the Klondike madness. As a surveyor, he would act as an evenhanded referee. He had been at Fortymile when

George Carmack unveiled the news of his strike at Bill McPhee's saloon, and it had been his sage observation ("Carmack must have found the gold *somewhere*") that sent many of the men up to the Klondike even when they doubted Carmack's word.

Ogilvie himself went to the Klondike, witnessed the richness of the strike, and sent the news in a message to his government by dogsled. William Moore, the seventy-four-year-old musher and steamboat man who had the mail contract for the area (who would found Skagway), hopped on his dogsled, overtook and rescued three stout young mushers who had already set out for the Chilkoot with the same message, and reached Juneau in the fall of 1896. He dutifully sent Ogilvie's message to the surveyor's superiors in Ottawa, where it was ignored. In January, the persistent Ogilvie sent another message by dogsled, and the next spring it was published in a little pamphlet and disregarded. In mid-June, Ogilvie sent yet another message by canoe, but by the time it reached Ottawa, two boats named the *Excelsior* and the *Portland* had landed on the West Coast with a ton of gold; the world's wildest gold rush was on in full swing. In fact, by that time, Ogilvie himself was on a brief trip Outside; he was one of the passengers on the *Excelsior*, but he was so publicity-shy that he disguised himself as a crew member to escape the reporters.

It was Ogilvie who resurveyed Bonanza and Eldorado Creeks, at the miners' request. Ogilvie had a rigid code against profiting in any way from his position as a public servant; the miners knew he couldn't be bribed, and they trusted his authority to rule on the claims. Each claimant was allowed 500 feet along a stream, but sometimes their haphazard measuring created oversized claims. When Ogilvie discovered these, the difference, called a fraction, was made available for staking.

One day Ogilvie and his assistant discovered such a fraction, a pie-shaped piece of earth eighty-six feet at its widest part. The assistant staked it, after learning that full-sized claims were all taken. Then, he tried to sell it, but found no takers. Finally he sank a shaft and found nothing. He sank another shaft and within eight hours had washed out $46,000 in gold. To this day, it remains, for its size, the richest piece of ground on earth.

In the afternoon, we thwarted and drifted through quiet sloughs between the many islands. Once, we spotted two gleaming bald spots far ahead and prepared to see our first glacier close up. But they turned out to be plain rock outcroppings that nudged into the river beneath a covering of spruces. We had lost track of where we were on the map, but figured we had come about forty-nine miles today and were now about twenty miles above Dawson, an easy day's paddle, so over to a big flat sandbar we ferried and set up camp for a last-night-on-the-river party.

Evelyn and I had the night off. After rolling trees over to our tent to anchor the ropes, I studied the shiny pastel rocks at the water's edge. Then we lounged around the campfire. The hot chocolate and Everclear stung my chapped lips. Lying in the sand, propped against a log, wearing her baggy green surgical suit, Jane filed her nails.

Finally we heard Evelyn's story, the last of the epic histories of our little

188 / YUKON WILD

group. She had grown up poor in rural East Texas during the Depression. She graduated from high school and started college when she was sixteen, then married soon after. She worked at various jobs and at one time ran her own employment agency before having her first child when she was in her mid-twenties. When she was a little girl, she suffered severe allergy problems and also caught malaria. When she was thirty-five, she had to have her thyroid gland removed. At thirty-seven, she had begun to go blind, then her eye trouble had disappeared as quickly as it had come. Later she found out she had breast cancer, had a mastectomy, and was still going strong now seven years later.

"One time, a year or so after the operation," she said, "I was worried. I had spent all weekend paddling the Brazos and felt kind of sore. I went to a physical therapist, this little slip of a thing who was going to try to help me find out if anything was wrong. The therapist held up her palm and said, 'Push on my hand,' so I gave her a little shove and sent her flying against the wall. She said she thought there was nothing wrong with my muscles.

"Another time," she smiled, "I was feeling kind of unhealthy again, so I went to my old family doctor. I said, 'Doc, something must be the matter; I can't run more than two miles without getting out of breath.' He looked at me like I was crazy and said, 'Evelyn, most women or men your age can't even run one block. It's probably not too much to worry about if you get a little winded after running two miles.'"

Evelyn told us about the ups and downs of her life as the mother of two daughters and wife of an insurance executive, and about her life now on the farm, where she continued constructing a house for her daughter out of scrounged materials, making jelly from the fruits of prickly-pear cacti, and occasionally hauling donkeys from septic tanks. Evelyn had grown wilder and less reverent with age, it seemed, so that now her freedom from inhibition and her lack of judgmentalness matched that of somebody half her age.

Jane and Evelyn saw some geese fly over and wandered down the sandbar to find them. Jude pulled out the illegal fireworks ("pyrotechnic devices") that she had smuggled into Canada and trotted off to launch them, stopping en route to hurl a javelinlike branch she'd found. Barbara taught Sue and me the words to a little ditty called "Blackberry Boogie" that she'd been singing all the way down the river. My favorite verse went like this:

Now we go through the briars a-walkin' hand in hand
Just pickin' blackberries just to beat the band.
He grabbed me for a kiss, I said 'You turn me loose—
Your lips are all blue from that blackberry juice.'
He hugged me once, he said, 'Don't you be coy—
You know I'm your blackberry-pickin' boy.'
He kissed me then I let out a sigh,
I said, 'Oh honey let's go to my house and we'll
Bake a pie. . . .

"Well, what are your thoughts here on the last night on the river?"

Sue asked Barbara, becoming serious.

"I've learned that it's very important for me to have a goal for each day, to know where we're aiming," said Barb.

"I'm just the opposite out here on the river," I said, thinking of that dreaded schedule. "Our whole lives are scheduled, predictable. In the city there are a few unknowns, but basically you can predict almost everything. You know that you're going to get up at a certain time, you're going to go to work, you're going to go when the light turns green and stop when the light turns red. It's so predictable. There are so many things you've got to do—appointments to keep, deadlines to meet, crises to solve. Out here I don't want to know where I'm going to sleep tonight until I get there; I don't necessarily want to know where I am on the map; I don't necessarily want to know what time it is or what day it is. I don't want each day to be the same, to go a certain number of hours or miles each day. Not only do I not crave having goals, I actively *don't* want to have goals out here. I just want to let things happen as they come."

Barb and I smiled and shrugged at each other, acknowledging and accepting a curious difference between us that, although vast, never hindered our enjoyment of each other's company.

Had I really just paddled almost 460 miles down one of the biggest rivers in North America, was I really drinking hot chocolate and godawful Everclear, and was a javelin-thrower racing across the sandbar as Roman candles zoomed into the midnight sun?

## JUNE 25, DAY 17

The morning dawned bright and warm. Giddily, we prepared to ride into the most famous city in the North. I glanced around. Into the rounded rocks of the gravel bar blended all manner of water jugs and life jackets and plastic food jars and cups and plates. Over on the tarp, as usual, Evelyn sifted through fifty to a hundred pounds of food whose little plastic bags gleamed in the sunlight. Wearing a cowboy hat, Dallas Downriver Club football jersey, panties and kneehigh boots, Sue served Jude's famous homemade cinnamon rolls. Jane cleaned her binoculars; Barbara read a paperback; Jude picked up the remains of last night's fireworks. We had become thoroughly comfortable with our nomadic life. We had proved what we knew all along—that floating down the entire Yukon was no different from camping out on the Neches River in East Texas for a weekend. You did the same thing, only more of it.

We pushed into the river and headed for Dawson. I looked forward to a change of scenery and some time alone in which I didn't have to check with five other people every time I wanted to stop and look at something.

We paddled for a couple of hours, humming and singing and feeling cocky. We whizzed past high, grey cliffs whose crevices were sprinkled thickly with spruce and poplar. After awhile we thwarted for a nibbling break and I sacked out in the sun under my cowboy hat. I was awakened by the strangest sound—a weird babylike cry that sounded like "Help me!

Help me!'' We looked at each other, then at the woods. Finally we spotted the tiniest head of a baby moose, thrashing and bobbing and bawling in the most desperate way as it was swept downstream a few feet away from an island cutbank.

Drawing our paddles to go to the rescue, we simultaneously realized that if Mother Moose found us messing around with her baby she could make a lot of trouble. Besides, what were we going to do if we caught up with the poor little thing, pull it into the boat?

We watched helplessly and listened to the awful crying. To our relief, the two-foot-tall moose reached solid ground, scrambled onto the island, turned around and glared at us with a "what-are-you-lookin'-at?" expression.

We paddled on, and I unveiled the only verse of my Yukon song that I had completed:

> Paddlin' down the Yukon River,
> For the Bering Sea we are bound.
> Strokin' along that big rollin' river,
> Oh, what a peace we have found. . . .

We tried to create more verses, but we hadn't come up with much when all of a sudden something stirred inside us. The hills ahead seemed vaguely familiar. Smoke rose from between two massive mountains at the far end of the bend; did Dawson lie below? Then there came into view two radio towers. Maybe we really had paddled 460 miles down the Yukon River. Then we saw conclusive proof: a thin horizontal scar on the left bank, high up on the hill—the highway, and straight ahead, a gigantic bald spot on the mountain—an old landslide.

We had reached that paradoxical place that meant attaining one goal and beginning another quest; at once culminating an unforgettable four weeks with friends we'd gotten to know better, and bidding goodbye to two of those same friends.

Pierre Berton describes how thousands of stampeders had ridden into Dawson on the same Yukon more than eighty years ago:

> . . . Eagerly the stampeders pushed on, traveling without sleep during nights as bright as the days, the tension rising as the miles ticked by until every man was taut as a watchspring. Each boat kept close to the right bank in case, by error, it should be swept right past the city, for no one quite knew where the city was.
>
> Then at last each in turn swung around a rocky bluff and saw spread before him a sight he would remember all his life. Roaring into the Yukon from the right was the Klondike River, of which he had heard so much. Beyond the river rose a tapering mountain with the great scar of a slide slashed across its face. And at its feet, spilling into the surrounding hills and along the swampy flats and between the trees and across the junction of the two rivers, were thousands of tents, shacks, cabins, caches, warehouses, half-erected hotels, false-faced saloons, screeching sawmills, markets, shops, and houses of pleasure. Here, in the midst of the encroaching wilderness, a thousand miles from nowhere, was a burgeoning metropolis. It seemed a little unreal, shimmering in the June heat, bathed in a halo of sunlight, blurred slightly at the edges by the mists that steamed from marshes . . . This was the goal they had

set themselves; this was the finish of the long trail north; this was where the rainbow had its end. They turned their boats toward the shore—a shore already thickly hedged by scores of other craft—and they debarked, still in a daze, yet inwardly exultant at having, after long vicissitude and much remorse and no little disillusion, set foot upon the threshold of the golden city. (*The Klondike Fever*, pages 286-287)

"Well, ladies," I said, "I think this calls for a celebration!" We thwarted and whooped and congratulated ourselves as we drifted through the last bend. Four hundred and sixty miles: I had probably just come close to doubling the total number of river-miles that I had paddled since I first set foot in a canoe five years before.

Suddenly civilization sped toward us in the form of a tugboat and a big wake; we unthwarted and scattered. We skirted the mouth of a small creek and realized it was the mighty Klondike. Dodging its shallow shoals, we ferried its current into an eddy at the city's edge. I felt light-headed, perhaps like thousands of others whose gripping struggle to this spot forever had changed their lives.

# 6 scarlet wallpaper, hot showers, and cold beer: the paris of the north

We slogged across a mudflat and up a high, rocky embankment into the Paris of the North. Leaving Sue to watch the boats, the rest of us swarmed through Dawson's gravel streets to obtain money, find motels, scrounge a place to keep our boats and gear for a few days, and return the rented canoe.

Evelyn and I slipped inside, just as it closed for the day, the Canadian Bank of Commerce on the waterfront, where Robert Service had worked in 1908-1909. I contemplated the businesslike tellers with their crisp suits and skirts and English-Canadian accents. Then I gazed somewhat self-consciously down at the muddy water squishing from the holes in my tennis shoes, at my balloonlike rain pants, and at the woman beside me who was wearing a tuxedo T-shirt and bear bells. Being a lady, I removed my cowboy hat. In seventeen days on the Yukon, my body had acquired a wonderful river essence—the smells, the gritty coating, the baggy clothes—with which I was so comfortable as to be oblivious of it, until I found myself queueing up at a marble counter behind a man who smelled of soap.

We traded traveler's checks for Canadian dollars, then stepped outside to consider where we might sleep tonight and where we would keep two boats and gear.

"Let's have a beer and think about it!" grinned Evelyn, as we raced to the nearest saloon.

A couple of hours and six-packs later, we were still lounging among the red velvet wallpaper and the chandeliers and, as it turned out, the four rafters from Anchorage. They kept buying us beers so we kept swapping river tales. We thought it hilarious that they had hauled down the Yukon things like battery-operated stereos and porta-potty seats (just the seats, no bags). On the other hand, they thought a trumpet and seventy pieces of sheet music were pretty strange things to bring on the river. In Anchorage, they worked in real estate, which seemed to be what those few souls who weren't in construction worked in.

"Now 'fess up," said Evelyn. "You all wouldn't let your wives come because you told 'em it was too rough out on the river, didn't you?" They grinned and hung their heads and said that rationale had been expressed. They said that not too many women do go down the river, and we allowed that as far as we knew, we were the first to paddle the whole river without men.

"You know, we're going to hold a press conference when we get to the Bering Sea," teased Evelyn, "and how much will you give us *not* to tell your wives and the whole world how easy it is floating down the Yukon every day without putting a paddle in the water?" We all laughed and ordered another round.

We had landed in by God Dawson City, and we simply had to celebrate the moment. For awhile, that overrode the fact that four women were undoubtedly sweltering and stewing in the hot sun down on the bank of the Yukon, waiting for us.

Finally we felt guilty enough to leave the impromptu party and staggered, giggling, over the wooden sidewalks, through the dusty streets, down the gravel embankment, and into two very angry women.

"Would you two like a beer?" Evelyn asked feebly, holding aloft a warm bottle. I sputtered and guffawed. Unmoved, Sue and Jude seemed in the mood for a confrontation.

"We're sorry," I said, my head spinning in the heat. "No real excuses; we just got tied up with the rafters at a bar. We shouldn't have left you waiting for us and we apologize."

"Jane and Barbara are staying across the river at the campground," snapped Jude. "The lady in the ice-cream shop said we could keep the boats in her yard, which is about a half-mile up the hill. There's a docking area by the ice-cream shop; we're going to paddle down there and carry our stuff up to her house. Sue and I are staying at the Eldorado Hotel; it's eighty dollars a night and I think we got the last room." With that they shoved off and paddled downstream.

Evelyn and I slid through the mud to our boat, which now overflowed with an extra lawn chair, ammo can, and several duffel bags that Jane and Barbara were leaving with us for the rest of our trip.

"I think we oughta think about all this—where's that beer?" I slurred. So we sprawled amongst the gear in the boat, in the hot sun, and guzzled warm beer. Our boat had congealed into the mud, but after falling to our knees several times we finally heaved it drunkenly into the river.

As we rammed into the landing a couple of hundred yards downstream, an older gentleman on the bank hollered in a Texas accent, "Hey, y'all wouldn't be from Dallas, would ya?" Oh Lord, I thought, now I'm gonna have to pretend I'm not totally blitzed on Canadian beer.

Here on the Yukon stood two couples from Killeen, Texas, who'd read about us in a Texas newspaper before they drove here and had hoped they'd meet us. They were running their car shuttle and were about to drive back to Whitehorse to launch their own trip down the stretch we'd just paddled. They had all kinds of questions about the river, the rapids, the camping, the mosquitoes. Conversing intelligently about such things was almost too much for me in my condition; all I could do was smile and weave and answer "no problem" to every question. But Evelyn—social being *extraordinaire* that she was—kept up a charming dialogue.

Here we were, dreading carrying through town two boats crammed with gear, and there these folks were—I observed—with two somewhat empty pickup trucks. They'd be delighted to help, they said, so the eight of us wrestled two loaded canoes onto the top of their camper shell, threw some ropes around them, and bounced through town to the ice-cream lady's cabin.

"Something always turns up," I shrugged at Evelyn. Why, if we'd drunk one less beer in the bar, we might have missed these nice folks and their trucks. As Evelyn and I stood on the tailgate holding the boat, we pretended we were the stars in a parade and waved—that big spreading-butter parade wave beauty queens always use—to innocent bystanders along the street.

In a flash we'd slid the boats up the ice-cream lady's muddy driveway onto her lawn and piled the gear under the eve of her cabin's porch. It would be safer here than down on the waterfront, where we'd heard that boats and gear had a way of disappearing. We waved goodbye to the Texans, Sue and Jude headed off to their hotel, and Evelyn and I rooted through our belongings, amid the mosquitoes that seemed to hang in a cloud around our cache. We finally got the right gear into the right packs and trudged through town, torn between whether to search first for food or for shelter. It was almost time to meet the others at the Midnight Sun Restaurant, though, so I saved a table there and downed beers and a Chinese smorgasbord, while Evelyn reconnoitered and found a motel two blocks away with a double room. That relieved our worries, generated by rumors we'd heard, that Dawson motel rooms were hard to come by. And at forty-five dollars Canadian, it was the second cheapest in town; the Klepper guy we'd met on the river had recommended it. It was called the Lucky Inn. We toasted each other and noted once again that something always turns up.

Jane and Barbara and Sue and Jude trooped in and we had a grand time toasting our arrival in Dawson, eating everything on the menu, and flirting with the waiters. Eventually we wore ourselves out and the party wound down. Evelyn and I hoisted our packs and lurched through the narrow doorway out into the midnight sun. Just outside, I got into a shoving and shouting match with a drunk guy who thought it chivalrous to grab my pack, throwing me off balance, as I staggered in circles grasping for its shoulder strap.

Moments later, Evelyn and I were the proud owners of a motel room—our own little wooden cabin that was clean, homey, and relatively mosquito-free. Simply furnished, its one extravagance was a television set. We were ecstatic at the sight of, let alone the experiencing of, the prefab shower with hot running water and two single beds—beds! (Actually, we found that both our backs hurt the next morning.) Reminding me of a life I had left four weeks ago today, the luxuries fittingly crowned the completion of not only the first leg of the Texas Women's Yukon River

Expedition, but also one of the most memorable months I'd ever spent. It seemed light-years ago that "six women with balls" had set out from Dallas, Texas, to follow a dream to the Yukon.

## JUNE 26-28, DAYS 18-20

So this was Dawson City, the crazy metropolis that sprang overnight from the muck where the Klondike River meets the Yukon River. Though it was in Canada, four-fifths of its residents had been American. Along these streets during Dawson's brief but passionate heyday—the twelve months between July, 1898, and July, 1899—30,000 characters rollicked in sin. A few rollicked in wealth as well. Says Berton,

> At first glance, this mélange of humanity seemed to be an odd and insoluble mixture of nationalities, races, and pursuits, yet it was really remarkably cohesive. Although the men and women who reached the Klondike came from every corner of the globe, and although their backgrounds were entirely dissimilar, they had one thing in common: they were there. Others, with weaker wills and weaker constitutions, had given up the struggle and retreated, but each of these disparate citizens had succeeded in what he set out to do. They were like war veterans who, having served their time in action, now found themselves bound together in a camaraderie born of fortitude. They were all part of a proud elite who, in spite of every vicissitude, had managed to reach their goal. (*The Klondike Fever*, page 373)

In those days the streets of Dawson were more mud than dirt; the center of town was a swamp. Dawson first bloomed from the mire as a tent city; but soon there rose log buildings chinked with mud, with sod roofs and windows of glass bottles, cloth, or thin wooden boards. The exceptions were the palatial gambling halls, saloons, hotels, and theaters that spared no expense in importing mirrors, expensive wallpaper—every luxury to provide an air of elegance in which the overnight Bonanza Creek and Eldorado Creek kings could part with their gold. Scattered among the lavish entertainment buildings and the ramshackle dwellings were banks, stores, barbershops, laundries, churches, hospitals. Several newspapers ran booming businesses, and there was telegraph—and even telephone—service.

The severe economic depression of the 1890s, the Klondike's placer gold capable of being mined by hand, and the era's sensational journalism glorifying the stampeders' trek through harsh climate and terrain set the stage for the world's most dramatic gold rush. However, few of those who milled about in Dawson during that wild year were actually rich. Some of those who were in the area in mid-1896 doubted the rumors of Carmack's big strike on Bonanza Creek, failed to stake a claim, and denied themselves a probable fortune. Others, of course—more from force of habit than belief in the news—dropped what they were doing, dashed to the new strike, and staked along Bonanza or Eldorado Creeks. Even then, some refused to believe their claims were worth much and quickly sold or abandoned them. The lay of the land wasn't right, they said—this was soggy moose pasture, not paydirt.

The only ones who had much of a chance to stake an extraordinary claim were those few thousand who happened to be mining along the Yukon at the time of Carmack's strike, or those few thousand who beat the Yukon's freeze-up in 1897 by leaving for the Klondike immediately after the *Portland* and the *Excelsior* steamed to the West Coast with their incredible cargoes of gold from the first year's diggings. From these two groups came the few hundred who became enormously wealthy. A peculiar characteristic of these few newly-rich, though, was that they delighted in parting with their money in the most immediate and ostentatious ways possible—ways that abundantly contradicted the Victorian mores of the era. The madly carefree mood permeated the little hotbed of hedonism that nestled among the frozen hills in this most unlikely corner of the world. For a brief moment in time, there was nothing like Dawson City.

Gambling was the preeminent sport. Fortunes were won and lost and regained in a night. Casinos themselves changed hands almost daily as their owners—inveterate gamblers all—wagered the very roofs over their heads. Men sat in poker games for days, taking their meals at the table. Around them, faro and roulette and other games of chance blazed twenty-four hours a day. One night a navigation company watchman named One-Eyed Riley—who customarily lost his wages at the faro tables during his midnight break—lit into a winning streak. Abandoning his job, he played through the night, betting the limit and winning at table after table in saloon after saloon. Behind him crowded a growing throng who watched the drama and made side bets on his luck. By morning, when the management at the Monte Carlo brought in a wizard dealer to try to break the streak, Riley decided to quit while he was ahead—with $28,000 in his pocket. He grabbed a dog-musher and paid him $1,000 to rush him away over the frozen Yukon before he could lose his incredible winnings. Seven hundred miles away in Skagway, Riley paused for a quick dice game and lost his entire fortune in three swift rolls.

Chasing women was the second most-practiced pastime, over-shadowed by gambling perhaps not so much by miners' preferences as their physical limitations. About one o'clock every night, when the last black-stockinged leg, red high-heeled shoe, and ruffled lace petticoat were kicked over the curly head of the last showgirl on stage, the women pranced down among the milling miners. And the real moneymaking of the evening began. A lonely prospector could buy drinks for the ladies who, of course, got a percentage of the bar take. Or, at a dollar per swing around the dance floor, he could dance with Daisy D'Avara, who wore a belt of seventeen twenty-dollar gold pieces; or little redheaded Cad Wilson, whose waist the biggest nuggets from Eldorado Creek encircled one-and-a-half times; or the picture of innocence—Flossie de Atley—who was only working as a dance-hall girl in the Klondike, she explained, to save money to care for her sick brother who lived in a sanitarium Outside; or the Oregon Mare who, among other quirks, whinnied like a horse when she danced; or the 170-pounder affectionately known as the Grizzly Bear, who was missing an eye. . . .

A miner could dance the night away, and in fact one Irishman named Roddy Conners spent $50,000 cavorting through the sawdust to Dawson's lively bands. He danced every dance, every night, except during rest periods when he paid to merely walk a woman around the floor. He danced and drank away between $500 and $2,000 every single night. Two sisters, popularly known as Vaseline and Glycerine, finally devised a shift system and, waltz by waltz, jiggerful by jiggerful, relieved the dancing Irishman of his entire fortune. He ended up, as did an astonishing number of Dawson's Bonanza and Eldorado kings, in a home for the indigent.

Or, a fellow could while away an hour or a night in one of the many "houses" of pleasure that were more often than not tents or shacks. If he was sober enough and short on funds, he could negotiate the narrow footbridge that spanned the Klondike River and stroll into the bargain-rate dwellings of the red-light district known as Lousetown.

Suddenly, the Paris of the North's fling with history was over. As quickly as they had come, and in numbers as great, the stampeders deserted Dawson in the summer of 1899. To a new strike they raced, to dig for gold on the beaches of a place called Nome, a couple of thousand miles away on Norton Sound just across the Bering Strait from Russia. In August, 1899, in a single week 8,000 people floated down the Yukon toward the sea. One was reminded of that crazy spring breakup in May, 1898, when that strange flotilla of 7,000 boats sailed down the waters of Lake Bennett for the Klondike.

A few stampeders remained in Dawson, suddenly smitten with the notion that this former moose pasture and scene of wild bedlam was the place to live and raise a family. Big commercial companies had bought up most of the individual mining claims, and they settled in to work the earth by the new method using huge dredges that churned the gold from the creeks with machine precision. The town dwindled to a steady population of several hundred. The now-solid citizens dismantled the wood shanties, filled in the swamp, leveled the streets, built board sidewalks, installed streetlights. On the bank of the Yukon sprang up proper Victorian and Gothic houses and substantial professional buildings. It was mostly among the remnants of this latter "respectable" period of Dawson's incredible history that we strolled today.

During our three days in Dawson, I attended to the usual duties that were becoming a routine whenever we stopped in a "big" town: going to the laundromat, calling home, calling the Dallas Museum of Natural History (our media contact), calling the Berkshire Traveller Press, writing and mailing a news release, mailing home pamphlets and books I'd collected and film to be developed.

In addition, Dawson provided a wonderful, lovable whirlwind of experiences:

At noon, the saloon was packed and pleasantly noisy. Short-skirted waitresses bustled to the tables with tray after tray of beer bottles for the mostly-male crowd. Behind the big wooden bar, the bartender with black string-tie, black sleeve-garters, and red-and-white striped vest fairly flew among his jiggers and whiskey bottles. I munched a grilled ham and cheese sandwich, drank a couple of Cokes, and watched a running marathon in the United States on the big TV screen in the corner.

The arrangement we adopted in Dawson was that each evening we'd get together as a group for dinner and whatever other trouble we could get into, but during the day we wandered individually wherever and whenever we wanted. At first, we had inquired about backpacking possibilities, but there seemed to be no nearby trails that weren't within sight of the city, and other hiking possibilities posed a transportation problem. So we settled on allowing a few days to explore Dawson, then heading downriver. After enjoying one night of bed and shower in our motel, Evelyn moved across the river to the inexpensive campground where Jane and Barbara were staying. A free ferry ran back and forth across the river every hour but one through the week. I decided to remain alone in the motel. It was worth forty dollars a night to sleep as late as I wanted without the interruptions of Evelyn's early-morning coffee fixings or the Battle of the Tent Zipper we still waged occasionally. Sue and Jude stayed two nights at their hotel, then moved to the campground.

Relishing the simple pleasure of being alone, without knowing or caring about what anybody else wanted to do, I relaxed in the saloon and scribbled gleefully in the journal I had neglected for days. But as I watched the crowd laughing and talking, it suddenly occurred to me that at this moment I would have felt lonely if there were not five friends of mine wandering around town somewhere. I needed and enjoyed my moments alone, but I was glad I had come with a group and looked forward to raising some hell with them in Dawson.

Amid my contemplations, I became aware that a big bug squatted on my bare forearm. I continued writing and absently brushed him off, more from habit than from irritation. It dawned on me that it was not normal for a bug to be in a saloon, and that most women would have shuddered and released some involuntary verbal outburst at the discovery of a bug on their arm while they were eating in a restaurant. I realized then that living outdoors on the river for seventeen days had already wrought subtle changes in my thinking. I felt much more at home with that bug than with the saloon's plush red carpet, the Coke with ice cubes, the glass tumbler, the red velvet curtains, or the giant TV screen.

In the Emporium, with its wooden floors and high ceilings, I searched among the rows of moccasins and hip-boots and hiking boots and found a pair of Taiwan running shoes for $23.95 Canadian. I needed a new pair to replace my old favorite tennis shoes that had suddenly sprouted huge holes. After I bought the new ones, though, they just didn't feel right. Throughout the rest of the trip, I would use them only as spares in camp whenever I felt the need for dry shoes; trudging through the mud to load and unload the boat, and tromping through the dirt streets of the various villages, I continued to wear the disintegrating old faithfuls.

It was Saturday night in the Paris of the North, and resplendent in our jeans and khaki pants and boots and tennis shoes, the Texas Women's Yukon River Expedition gathered at the fancy Eldorado Hotel for dinner before our big night on the town. Since I had no watch and had been napping all afternoon in my motel room, I was late.

When I arrived, I noticed Sue was in a sober mood. She'd received word that a friend of hers, about her age, who'd undergone post-surgery cancer treatment along with Sue, and who'd been there smiling and wishing us well as we left Dallas almost three months before, was dead. Once again, I thought angrily of all the proven cancer-causing chemical substances that industries put into the public's food and water and air every day, because federal agencies haven't gotten around to regulating them and because citizens haven't demanded vigorously enough that they do so. Once again, I thought how admirably stubborn Sue and Evelyn were for emphatically living their lives as they wanted, refusing to be beaten emotionally by the cancer that had defeated so many women.

I gulped down half my grilled salmon, then wrapped the other half and stuck it in my fanny pack as we dashed to the restored Palace Grand Theatre for an evening at the Gaslight Follies. The extravagant Palace Grand was the dream of a former Indian-fighter and rodeo king named Arizona Charlie Meadows. After making a small fortune, within four months of his arrival in Dawson, from publishing newspapers about the newly-rich Klondike kings, Charlie bought and wrecked two sternwheelers in order to incorporate them into the lavish false front of the great dance hall he was building. Part of Charlie's gala opening-night celebration in July, 1899, was a forty-person banquet, complete with a hundred-dollar bank note upon each plate. The Palace Grand hosted everything from wild west shows to opera. In those days, the actresses would help the management sell more champagne and wine to the wealthy patrons in private balcony boxes by making the rounds during intermission. On at least one occasion, when action on stage ground to a halt awaiting the overdue entrance of a certain character, the actress in question poked her tousled head from between the curtains of a balcony box and announced in an emphatic slur that her particular character "ain't a-comin' tonight."

Tonight, from our front-row straight-backed chairs, we enjoyed "The Truth Will Out," a musical comedy typical of turn-of-the-century drama, complete with villains and heroines and heroes and their laughable sidekicks.

During intermission, Jane and Barbara overheard a couple behind us discussing returning to Anchorage in the morning. Quick as a wink, Jane's Mississippi charm won her and Barb a spot in the bed of a pickup truck for the sixteen-hour drive to Anchorage. Anchorage and Denali National Park were Jane's and Barbara's next destinations on their summer explorations; they had been wondering how they'd get there, and now they knew.

After the good guys won out and the bad guys lost all at the good-natured conclusion to "The Truth Will Out," we and most of the audience strolled through the bright 10 P.M. sunlight to Diamond Tooth Gertie's

Gambling Hall, the only legal gambling hall in all of Canada. Inside the huge barnlike structure (formerly an Arctic Brotherhood Hall), hundreds of people crowded around gambling tables in the center, pushed their way back and forth to the bars, or staggered to and from the bathrooms. This was my kinda Saturday night. The six of us, plus the Gilberts from Anchorage, crowded around a big table at the very foot of the stage. A flock of cancan girls stormed onstage, and from our peculiar vantage point we felt a fine spray of spit as they sang and shrieked. I had more gartered legs thrust into my face than I'd ever dreamed I'd see. We recognized several of Gertie's dancers and musicians who'd just finished an evening's performance as actors and actresses at the palace Grand a few blocks away.

During each break, we ordered another round of beer and toasted Dawson or ourselves. Soon there strode among the throngs of half-drunk tourists and local gold miners a woman whose bosom was nothing short of extraordinary. It was Gertie, our hostess, welcoming the crowd before her appearance on stage. Even without her incredible physique, she would have been the center of attention in her white floor-length gown bedecked with lace and pearls and fringe, and in her outlandish white hat topped by a huge feather. At our table, looking quizzically askance at parts of Gertie's anatomy, Barbara and Jane and I had our picture taken with her. Gertie had obviously been through it all before and got a great kick out of it. She drew herself up unabashedly and threw back her head in a great laugh. When she took over the stage—which was the only way to describe her entrance—she belted out a rousing version of "Won't You Come Home, Bill Bailey?" which the Texas Women's Yukon River Expedition shouted along with her. It was one of the tunes from our river library, and only yesterday we had been practicing it as we floated down the Yukon.

During the next break, Barbara and Evelyn grabbed their beer mugs and waded into the mostly-male crowd, announcing that they were going trolling. "Good luck!" we called after them. At the next table sat two older women wearing "I got laid in Chicken, Alaska" T-shirts with pictures of chickens on the fronts. Soon there wandered over the Dutch couple we had last seen almost a week before, when we shared corn fritters with them during our dinner break on our All-Nighter on the Yukon. We welcomed them loudly, ordered another round, and pulled up two more chairs. The party was gaining troops. They, too, were trying to get themselves vaguely in the direction of Anchorage, so the Gilberts signed up two more people and two more packs for the great truck ride.

Like most of the people we would meet, the Gilberts were delighted to get to know new people and eager to help in their carefree way. They were both in their thirties, both from the Lower 48, and had lived in Anchorage only a few years. He worked in construction; she was a secretary. They had a nine-year-old daughter whom they had left with a neighbor for the weekend. Mrs. Gilbert had stayed home from work sick all day Friday, but when Mr. Gilbert walked in after work and suggested they spend the weekend in Dawson, she had suddenly felt better. So they had hopped into the truck and driven almost 500 miles to the Paris of the North, where they would spend less than twenty-four hours before it would be time to head back to Anchorage for work Monday morning. Tonight, Mr. Gilbert, in his green T-shirt with his cigarette pack rolled into the sleeve, seemed to relish the antics of the six Texas women he'd run into, the wild whirling and whooping of the cancan girls a few feet from his nose, the quiet Dutch couple, and the general good-natured roar of the place.

More and more locals were drifting in, but Barb and Evelyn returned from their trolling to report that no woman could compete for the fellows' attention with gambling.

Eventually, the rest of our crew decided to leave—the 9 A.M. truck ride would begin soon enough. We hugged Jane and Barb goodbye, wished them lots of good times on the rest of their trip, and invited them once again to float more of the river with us. I was just getting revved up when all the others drifted off to bed, so I stayed and drank a few beers with the bearded harmonica player, while trying to convince him to play "Me and Bobby McGee." Then, somehow, I ended up in the company of a young blond miner who told me all about how he'd been in Dawson for three weeks and was driving Caterpillars at a nearby gold-dredging operation. He had a car, he said, and it would really make him happy, he said, to show me the view of Dawson from atop Midnight Dome. It would be an interesting sight, I thought, but I was getting tired and besides, a smoky cigarette cloud hung around him. Suddenly the management announced last call for drinks, and I realized that the miner and I and a handful of stalwarts were the only ones left in the vast hall. I had done a necessary and memorable thing, something akin to duty as trip leader and a true Texan—*somebody* from the Texas Women's Yukon River Expedition had to close Diamond Tooth Gertie's on a Saturday night or we'd never live down the shame. The miner settled for walking me home through the 2 A.M. twilight and for a kiss on the front steps of my cabin. In the morning, all that was left of a Saturday night in Dawson was a hangover, a pile of my clothes, reeking of cigarette smoke, on my motel floor, and a fanny pack full of smelly salmon. . . .

I hunched over fried rice and an eggroll at a picnic table outside a Chinese carryout cafe. Around the corner ambled the big red truck that dribbles water onto the streets a few times a day to hold down the dust. I supposed Dawson's quaint refusal to pave the streets has more to do with problems of permafrost than with lack of funds or a desire to maintain the town's historical character, but whatever the reason, I enjoyed plodding along the dusty streets and nodding to the driver of the big red truck.

I bought a dish of ice cream, spread out my Alaska map, and drew a calendar on a page in my journal notebook. We had decided we wanted to get to the Bering Sea by September 1—to give Evelyn time to get back to Dallas for a Labor Day market, and to avoid the snows of autumn that might hover over the Yukon delta by that time. I now calculated that to reach our September 1 goal, we had to move down the river an average of only 24 miles a day, or 166 miles a week, for the next nine weeks.

"Piece of cake!" I thought to myself, for except for our time on the wind-ridden, flatwater Lake Laberge, twenty-three miles was the very shortest distance we had traveled in one day. And on that day we had been on the river only three or four hours. Most days, we had gone far more than twenty-four miles merely by drifting.

Of course, I knew from readings that the river would slow considerably between here and the Bering Sea and that we'd probably run into delaying headwinds and storms. But I also assumed that if and when we ever started paddling—as opposed to thwarting—our stamina would increase. Furthermore, I suspected that the rest of the river did not offer the wealth of historical sites scattered along the Canadian stretch that invited frequent stops and made for shorter paddling times each day. Armed with my new statistics, I was confident that as long as we kept a broad idea of how many miles a week we were traveling, we could finish the river by September 1 without the need for a strict daily regimen. I had in mind a general routine of paddling "hard" for three or four days, then goofing off for a day or two. Actually, I considered it criminal to float the Yukon without taking at least one entire day off each week—to do nothing but sit by the fire, read, nap in the sun, study wildflowers or birds, play the trumpet. . . .

In the afternoon sun, I perched on a narrow window ledge outside some forgotten, ramshackle wooden building. It was buckled, like all the others, from the permafrost beneath it that heaves and shifts with each freeze and thaw. In one hand I gripped a bean burrito, in the other a slice of pepperoni pizza, both purchased from an obscure window around the corner from the Midnight Sun Restaurant. I balanced a Coke on the ledge and shielded the delicacies from occasional clouds of dust kicked up by the wind or a pickup truck slowly chugging through town. Below me on the warm wooden sidewalk squatted a gorgeous Alaskan malamute and a black, matted mutt. Their intent eyes followed every morsel of food into my mouth, their paws inching ever closer toward my tennis shoes, their haunches tightening for a leap toward my lunch should the opportunity present itself. I told them that they weren't going to make me feel guilty, that I deserved this food, that these carryout items from Mexico and Italy were a symbolic remembrance of my American heritage—a thin tie with my homeland as I traveled the Yukon wilderness 4,000 miles from home. The canines were unmoved. Watching them warily from the corner of my eye, I pretended to ignore them and take in the scenery. I could see the headline: "Canoeist devoured in struggle with dogs over burrito." Some things are worth dying for. . . .

At ten o'clock on Sunday night, the sun dipped low toward the far, hazy hills. Sue and Jude and Evelyn and I squatted knee-deep in the cold, black, smelly waters of Bonanza Creek, panning for gold. Rosemary, the ice-cream lady, had invited us to the diggings of some friends of hers, and we had gladly accepted. Her friend Clara came along. Their friends, Al and Howie, "played prospector" in the summers, leasing three areas and sharing any findings with the landowner. Al was a fun-loving, middle-aged rancher from Alberta, Canada, with curly, reddish hair and a ready wit. As we had bounced along in a two-seater pickup truck, he had quoted from memory, with quite a flourish, both Robert Service's poetry and his own. Howie was fortyish, short, stocky, and tan, with curly grey hair and the cutest wide orange-and-yellow suspenders over his flannel shirt. He too spent most of the year in Alberta. Clara was sixty-five or seventy years old, with a sturdy, sun-weathered face and wind-blown grey hair. Though she claimed she was getting too old for it, she could skip over the piles of gravel and trudge up the mountainside more nimbly than the rest of us. She spent most of the year in British Columbia, as did Rosemary, when she wasn't running the ice-cream shop for Dawson's summer tourists. Rosemary was fortyish and seemed strangely cultured and well-groomed for this wild and woolly outpost in the Yukon. But we could readily sense that she and the others loved the isolation and the friendliness of this living museum of one of history's craziest moments.

Under the tutelage of Al and Howie and Howie's teenage son, we each shook two shovelsful of heavy black muck around in a big, green, plastic mesh basket called a "grizzly" that fitted inside a pan. We dipped and swirled and washed the mud out bit by bit over the rim, until there remained only a little inside the pan. Then we discarded the grizzly and swiggled the water some more. It was hard to believe that the water wouldn't wash the gold out, but our hosts assured us that gold was nineteen times heavier than water and would stay put in the pan. Finally a few minuscule gold flecks appeared in the mud. If they floated during the swishing, they were probably mica, but if they sat right on the bottom of the pan, they were gold. My pan ended up with two tiny flakes of gold, but they were so small that neither our host nor I wanted them, so we washed them back into the puddle in which we squatted. Evelyn found three flecks, one of which was easily seen with the naked eye, and though we suspected Al had put them there, he insisted she keep them. We put them in a little plastic film cannister.

Then we all scrambled about a half-mile through mud and piles of bulldozed dirt and rocks and spongy muskeg and scrubby trees up to the top of a mountain. Al and some of the others walked up the 30° incline of a small water pipeline that paralleled the steep mountainside. Half the top of the white calichelike mountain had been washed away by powerful blasts of water in a process called hydraulic mining. Bit by bit, the mountain would be fed through a dredge that shakes and washes the gold from the dirt—a mechanized version of our handheld grizzly and gold pan. Away from the mountain, as far as we could see, marched mile after square mile of nothing but the massive tailing piles spit out by these dredges. Whole valleys had been stripped of all vegetation and churned into gravel. Bonanza Creek and Eldorado Creek aren't really creeks anymore, for the bulldozers and dredges have changed their historical watersheds again and again. Now they are more like collections of black puddles than

204 / YUKON WILD

flowing streams. Dredges have worked over practically every cubic yard of earth in the Klondike Valley several times in the eight decades since George Washington Carmack did his "Siwash Hula-Hula" with Skookum Jim and Tagish Charlie somewhere around here on the bank of Bonanza Creek. We examined a small dredge that sat at the top of the mountain, then crawled into a cold, dark tunnel that Howie said was an old gold mine. We exited rather quickly when he explained that the dripping mud-and-gravel mixture that formed its walls was unstable permafrost, likely to cave in—sometime.

About 1 A.M., back down on the wooden porch at Al and Howie's camp, we sat in lawn chairs and drank iced tea. Around us were several Caterpillars, a house trailer, a screened tent, and dozens of piles of gravel and mud. Howie's son lit several mosquito coils that seemed to drive away the mosquitoes even here in the open air. Al showed us a tiny vial filled with gold flakes and water. For such a small thing, it was amazingly heavy; it was worth several hundred dollars at the current price of gold. Through my mind flashed images of those sixty-eight Bonanza and Eldorado kings who alighted from the *Portland* onto Seattle's wharf in July, 1897, struggling under the weight of bottles and kerchiefs and packing cases and caribou-hide pokes and trunks—all full of the incredibly heavy yellow metal.

Then we drove up to wander through the passageways of the awesome, now-silent monster known as No. 4 Dredge, which rests on Claim No. 17 Below Discovery on Bonanza Creek. Built in 1912, the thing was one of thirty-five bucket elevator dredges that munched the Klondike Valley between 1899, when the first one was brought in to work the mouth of the Big Salmon River, and 1959. They were powered by electricity, and this particular one drew its juice from the Canadian Klondike Mining Company's own hydropower plant on the Klondike River thirty miles away. No. 4 Dredge could, on one good day, devour and process 18,000 cubic yards of earth. Using seventy-five buckets that each held sixteen cubic feet of dirt, the dredge crept along in a pond of its own making, consuming earth with its continuous bucket-bearing chain in front, extracting ninety percent of the gold in the earth through its revolving screen washing plant inside, then expelling the gravel from its rear. No. 4 is the biggest wooden-hull, bucket-line dredge in North America. It is bigger than a sternwheeler: 140 feet long, 65 feet wide, 76 feet (the height of a 7-story building) tall. It weighs over 3,000 tons. Piece by piece, these giant machines were brought in by rail and steamer and then transported by dogsled and horse-teams to the particular creeks they would work. Comprehending the scope of this one dredge, which was but one of dozens, was as impossible for me as comprehending every other bizarre aspect of the world's last, great, frenzied gold rush that was still, apparently, drawing a few sourdoughs like Al and Howie.

I walked the decks of the restored sternwheeler S.S. *Keno* that sits on Dawson's beach. Built in Whitehorse in 1922, the *Keno* is typical of the sternwheelers that knew the Yukon during the Stampede, but none of the actual steamers then in use has survived. The colorful boats and their dauntless captains played a key role in moving stampeders and goods into the Klondike, and gold and passengers out of the Klondike. In 1898, between June and September, 12,000 tons of supplies docked at Dawson. Carpets from Brussels, evening gowns from Paris, expensive oil paintings, and fancy chamber pots were heaved onto the docks alongside beans, boots, flour, dynamite, coffee, and ton after ton of spirits. And with each steamer came another load of dance-hall beauties. In those days the wood-fired steamers had to stop every three or four hours to take on wood from the woodchopper camps that lined the Yukon's banks. It took one-and-a-half days to make the trip downstream from Whitehorse to Dawson, but four to six days pushing upstream against the current in the other direction. Anyone along the river could stop a steamer, to hitch a ride or to accept or offer cargo, simply by hanging a white flag from the bank.

It was not only the competition from the highways that eventually penetrated the Yukon region, but the highway bridges themselves, that brought an end to the sternwheeler era in the 1950s. The bridge at Carmacks was constructed too low for the tall ships. The *Keno,* part of the fleet that for years had brought the gold, silver, lead, and zinc out of the Yukon Territory, made her last trip in 1960 to her resting place on Dawson's waterfront. To clear the Carmacks bridge, she had to have her stacks hinged and part of her deck removed.

I sat among the willows and alders on the sloping lawn of a two-room log cabin, listening to an actor recite Robert Service poetry in the afternoon sun. Service lived in this cabin from November, 1909, to June, 1912, composing his novel, *The Trail of Ninety-Eight,* and his third and final volume of Yukon verse, *Songs of a Rolling Stone.* Here he rested each evening in a hammock slung on the front porch, beneath moose antlers that spread above the doorway. He printed his verses in big letters with pieces of charcoal, on rolls of coarse wallpaper. Then he pinned them on the cabin walls and paced to and fro—staring at them, reciting them. With him lived a cat he had rescued as a kitten on a frozen trail and a Siberian bearhound, said to be the biggest on the Yukon. "I would take supper about ten in the evening and smoke and talk till midnight," wrote Service. "Going home to my bright cabin I would read to the early hours, then sleep till eleven. I would exercise, bathe and descend to town for a leisurely breakfast, returning about three for a siesta. At five I would make tea and strum a guitar, after which I would go for a tramp on the mountain. . . . It was the bohemian life in the shadow of the Pole."

"Well, how's the trip?" Mother asked over the phone. "Is it like you thought it would be?" For the life of me, I could never conjure up a sensible answer to such questions. I could no longer remember how I had thought it would be, I knew only how it was. "It" was a river and sandbars and mountains and moose and eagles, and that's how it was. Truth was, it seemed irreverent to attempt to appraise the land through which we were paddling. It simply *was,* in its own right. Who was I to judge it? I realized that to me all wild lands and waters—from deserts to swamps to prairies to forests to jungles to barren alpine mountains to frozen tundra—were equally beautiful, inspiring, worthy of being experienced, and worthy of being.

Actually, it seemed far too early to be asked such broad questions. I felt as though the "real" trip were just beginning. We were just now leaving the popular stretch that teems with thousands of canoeists annually; now heading into an area with far fewer canoeing tourists, but far more villagers living and working on the river; and—I hoped—now abandoning a daily schedule to begin a casual river existence. And after all, we still had the whole of Alaska—the land that had sparked my imagination in the first place—to paddle across.

The one thing that I was able to articulate to the folks back home was that we sped farther downriver each day, with less effort than I'd dreamed imaginable. The speed of the river, the sunny weather, the lack of trouble with bears—it all seemed too easy and way too good to be true.

During the weekend, I toured restored buildings and museums, glanced at the Jack London cabin, browsed through bookstores and an occasional hardware store (just to tread on their creaking wooden floors and admire their ancient wooden nail bins), and watched films (during which I always choked up at least once) about the incredible hardships and hilarity of the Stampede. I strolled past shirtless men who listened to radios and hammered new planks into historical restoration projects; past shirtless men who hammered planks into modern residential cabins made of massive spruce logs and plate-glass windows. I spotted Evelyn emerging from a beauty salon next to a cabin with a big sign that said "Massages." Several times I tried to check in as requested with the Mounties, but I could never find them at their post, so I finally scrawled them a note indicating that the six Texas women had reached Dawson safely. From here on, there would be no protective police service that routinely kept track of river travelers; we were on our own across the breadth of Alaska.

Like the melting-pot of 1898, today's Dawson seemed to take in stride almost everything without batting an eye: a dogfight in the center of town was broken up by the swinging grocery basket of a woman wearing a long Mexican linen dress and thongs; a tour-bus crept along full of blue-haired ladies in pantsuits and paunchy men in leisure suits; a man in a top hat and long coat hustled over the board sidewalks with an open letter in one hand and a trombone case in the other; a horse and buggy for tourists was driven along Front Street by a thin young man with a flowing black beard and an earring; a giant dust-caked Winnebago eased up to the gasoline pump beside a motorcycle piled high with ancient bundles and a grease-stained backpack; Athapascan Indian boys reared up on their bicycles in the dirt driveway of a Chinese carryout; a drunk man passed out behind the bushes between an old cabin and a new restaurant; men and women dozed beside their packs on the lawn next to an old sternwheeler; women carried canoes past the Canadian Bank of Commerce. . . .

Through the writings of those who got themselves one way or another to Dawson during the Stampede, there runs a common thread. Whether they lost their feet to frostbite, their sweethearts to saner men who stayed behind, or their sanity to the bitter tragedies and disappointments and cruelties of the trail, almost every last one of them felt somehow enriched by the experience. This held true whether, like most of them, they failed to find gold at all; whether, like many, they found the gold but squandered it on pleasures of the moment; or whether, like a handful, they invested it wisely and stayed wealthy all their lives. For it was not what they found or failed to find in the Klondike, but the act of getting there, that changed their hearts and souls.

Of course, as the men and women scaled the icy summits of the Chilkoot Pass or the White Pass, or threw their flimsy boats into the teeth of Miles Canyon or Whitehorse Rapids, or struggled thousands of miles over glaciers or mountain ranges or rivers, they spent little time pondering the greater meaning of their endeavors; mostly they concerned themselves with surviving the next twenty-four hours. But long afterward, they would realize that simply setting foot in this sprawling camp in the shadow of the big scar-faced mountain next to the Yukon had infused them with an unshakable belief: determination alone had gotten them to the Klondike. Though most of them left Dawson for other adventures, they carried in their hearts the absolute conviction that they could surmount any obstacle they ever chose.

As for the four Texas women who now comprised our expedition, we still had 1,500 miles of the Yukon River to paddle. So at 5 P.M. on Monday, it was time to forget the cold beers and ice cream and showers and friendly people and other pleasures that Dawson offered, time to reunite ourselves with the open skies and sandbars and mosquitoes and spruce trees and mountains and moose and other pleasures and adventures that awaited us on the Yukon's flowing waters. We had run into Marshall Clymer, the T'ai Chi Ch'uan instructor paddling the Klepper, and he and a friend, who'd driven from Anchorage to pick him up, graciously helped us transport our boats and gear down to the waterfront in her jeep. Once again, something had turned up to make life easier. We thanked Marshall and waved goodbye to him, tossing into the jeep as a present Barbara's lawn chair that Evelyn refused to accept.

To our great delight, when we reached the waterfront, there stood Sybil! We hadn't seen her since Stewart Island, and there were hugs all around. She had paddled into Dawson a few hours before and had dropped by when she spotted our first load of gear on the landing. Again we tried to convince her to finish paddling the river with us, but she reiterated sorrowfully that she wouldn't have time, what with visiting her parents and heading back out into the bush soon for another winter on the trapline.

Knowing that this was probably the last time we'd see Sybil (unless she showed up on the dock in some village downstream, which we still hoped for), we found it hard to swing the boats into the current and head downriver. She stood quietly on the shore, her small hand held aloft in a static wave that bordered on a salute.

"Good luck!" her voice blended into the sound of paddles slapping against water.

Whitehorse, June 9, 1982. Left to right: Jude, Sue, Evelyn, Beth, Barbara, and Jane.

Jane pours and Evelyn shampoos her hair in water heated from the campfire.

Around the first bend below Hootalinqua, our first sighting of moose.

Sybil Brittin, who brings her lawn chair along on her canoe trips on the Yukon.

Jane peers inside one of the Indian "spirit houses"—built for the spirits of Indians who are buried nearby. Near the abandoned village of Little Salmon.

Riding the 40-foot channel between massive basalt "flower pots," Beth and Evelyn zoom down the drop and hit the 3-foot waves of Five Finger Rapids.

"Yee ha!" Beth (stern) and Evelyn (bow) holler as we plow through the haystacks of Five Finger Rapids. Evelyn just got a face full of 47° water, and 5" of the Yukon now wallows in the bottom of our canoe.

First big grizzly print

BETH JOHNSON

Left to right: *Sue, Beth, Evelyn, and Jude at Eagle, our first Alaskan town.*

*Sue, Jude, and Evelyn relax in the mosquito-mesh dining tent.*

*After a feast at Eagle's cafe, we head down-river to paddle across the entire breadth of Alaska—America's last frontier.*

*This is not a visitor from outer space— this is Evelyn, covered from head to toe against the mosquitos, washing wild onions.*

Two boats are "thwarted" while we celebrate completing half of the Yukon River—we think it's half, anyway.

BETH JOHNSON

Trapped by the wind and rain in an alder thicket, just below Russian Mission. Jude, Sue, Evelyn, and Dave played 5 hours of spades on a tree stump.

The first king salmon of the season, caught by Charley Kidd—what better fare for a 29th birthday?

Entering the village of Nulato, where we watched John Travolta on a flickering, makeshift screen.

Bing cooked pancakes, as usual. This was our last real camp on the river—a bear wallow at the mouth of a tiny creek.

# PART III

*I wanted the gold, and I sought it;*
  *I scrabbled and mucked like a slave.*
*Was it famine or scurvy—I fought it;*
  *I hurled my youth into a grave.*
*I wanted the gold, and I got it—*
  *Came out with a fortune last fall —*
*Yet somehow life's not what I thought it,*
  *And somehow the gold isn't all.*

*No! There's the land. (Have you seen it?)*
  *It's the cussedest land that I know,*
*From the big, dizzy mountains that screen it*
  *To the deep, deathlike valleys below.*
*Some say God was tired when He made it;*
  *Some say it's a fine land to shun;*
*Maybe; but there's some as would trade it*
  *For no land on earth—and I'm one. . . .*

*I've stood in some mighty-mouthed hollow*
  *That's plumb-full of hush to the brim;*
*I've watched the big, husky sun wallow*
  *In crimson and gold, and grow dim,*
*Till the moon set the pearly peaks gleaming,*
  *And the stars tumbled out, neck and crop;*
*And I've thought that I surely was dreaming,*
  *With the peace o' the world piled on top.*

*The summer—no sweeter was ever;*
  *The sunshiny woods all athrill;*
*The grayling aleap in the river,*
  *The bighorn asleep on the hill.*
*The strong life that never knows harness;*
  *The wilds where the caribou call;*
*The freshness, the freedom, the farness—*
  *O God! how I'm stuck on it all. . . .*

*There's gold, and it's haunting and haunting;*
  *It's luring me on as of old;*
*Yet it isn't the gold that I'm wanting*
  *So much as just finding the gold.*
*It's the great, big, broad land 'way up yonder,*
  *It's the forests where silence has lease;*
*It's the beauty that thrills me with wonder,*
  *It's the stillness that fills me with peace.*

  Robert Service, "The Spell of the Yukon"

# 7 king salmon, bearded strangers, and yukon skinny-dipping

## JUNE 28, DAY 20

Back on the river after our three-day hiatus, we were once again astonished at the Yukon's speed. We came upon the Indian village of Moosehide so fast that we began to doubt the maps showing it to be three miles downstream from Dawson. We peered unsuccessfully among the willows on the bank for any sign of abandoned Fort Reliance that was supposed to lie six or seven miles downstream. It had been one of the Yukon's early trading posts, established long before there was a Dawson City.

In a few hours we had drifted about twelve miles and felt far enough downriver from the motorboats and other hints of Dawson's civilization to pull out on a flat sandbar and set up camp. It was sad to have to find flat, dry spaces for only two tents instead of three; to heat tea water for only four instead of six. And, with Jane's and Barbara's cleansing influence removed, none of us heated any bath water.

Late that night, as I lay asleep, wind and rain whipped and pelted the tent. I must have felt a little guilty at not having pulled the boat up very high and not having tied it to anything very substantial, for a minor nightmare about boats floating away, walls of water, and logjams finally had me breathing so hard I woke up. Then I suffered mild heart palpitations when I sat up and saw only Sue's boat through the tent opening. But craning my head out of the screen and under the tent fly I saw, to my relief, that our boat still sat a few feet from Sue's, where it had been all along.

## JUNE 29, DAY 21

It was good to be back on the river where things were simple. We were free from having to fool with money and restaurants and motels and looking for restrooms every time we needed to relieve ourselves. Everything we needed was right here. My task for the morning was shoveling some of the filth from my canoe nest. With the trowel, I scraped a good inch of mud from the foam kneepad on the floor of the canoe. Meanwhile,

Evelyn created a tasty bannock for lunch that included leftover breakfast cereal, peaches, and pecans.

We shoved into the river about one o'clock. (Evelyn still wore the dreaded watch.) Soon, grey clouds crept over the river, struggling with the sunny blue sky that had been there first. Seeing the appaloosalike splotches reflected in the glassy, chocolate surface of the Yukon, beyond the dull, silver bow of our canoe, I was utterly captivated. Evelyn and I never lost our fascination with the sky—the endless swirls and changing blends of blues and whites and greys. It was a good thing, because there was plenty of it to see in 2,000 miles on the Yukon. The sky was so big—our view of it so unobstructed—that the wonder of it dominated even the river's magnificent, incomprehensible power and movement.

Eventually the sun beat back the clouds and we shed our shirts. We stopped to fish (with no luck) and to fill up our jugs where the clear shallow waters of Thane Creek tumbled into the Yukon's opaqueness. Already, there seemed to be a new, easygoing mood in the group. When Sue and Jude pulled out to fish, we pulled out after, with no thought of whether this would put us behind schedule. If they wanted to stop, that was reason enough for us; we were just as happy lying in the boat next to shore as floating down the river.

Then we pushed back into the river, thwarted, nibbled bannock and chatted, then napped. I was awakened by a motorboat's buzz. A man and woman cut their motor and drifted a few dozen yards away to visit with us. I zipped my life jacket to cover my bare chest. They were from Circle, about 240 miles downstream, and they were headed for Dawson for supplies and perhaps a night on the town. They said there was a couple living about 180 miles downstream, in a Park Service cabin in the Yukon-Charley River Preserve, who'd probably enjoy our company. We nodded. "Have a good one!" they waved as they motored upstream.

Late in the day as we attempted a landing at a high sand-dune island Evelyn and I fouled up our ferry, thudded over a bunch of rocks, and washed around the wrong side of the island; Sue and Jude disappeared behind the other side. We pulled out and I climbed up on top to see if they too had pulled out, but they were nowhere in sight. In the few minutes of our delay, they had floated two or three miles downstream. Now, though we paddled and they were merely drifting, it seemed we'd never catch them. In the narrow valley surrounded by steep mountains, distances were deceiving: though the mountain at the foot of the next bend seemed close at hand, the minute yellow speck of Sue's canoe against it proved it was actually several miles away. Things were so big up here that we tended to vastly underestimate distances. Evelyn and I remembered an old joke about women's overestimating distances because they've always been deceived by their lovers into believing that things six inches long are actually nine inches long. We assumed that after we'd spent a summer in Alaska, with its giant physical features, we'd encounter something that really was a foot long and would pass it off as a mere six inches.

As we considered the ramifications of all this, a gigantic boil welled up from nowhere, like some great whale, right beneath my bow. There was nothing to do but keep paddling as it sucked down into a five-foot-wide whirlpool that gurgled loudly beneath us. We were truly amazed and—after we'd successfully negotiated it—amused.

Finally, we caught up with our two cohorts and pitched camp on a steep, narrow beach. The nearby bushes might harbor mosquitoes or bears, and the ground was rocky, but it was getting late and there were no islands in sight.

After we'd finished dinner and several drinks, personality conflicts between Sue and Evelyn suddenly bubbled to the surface. After itemizing things about Evelyn that bugged her, Sue added that she and Jude were considering going on alone.

In the past, I had seen Evelyn take on people who had gotten up her ire, and I didn't relish seeing it again, although I figured she was entitled to respond however she wanted. Amazingly, she took the assault in stride. She responded matter-of-factly that she had signed on this cruise as part of a group, and that if her personality was unacceptable to the group, then she would do the group a favor and leave. She had thought perhaps she might be an asset to the group, she said, but she wouldn't want to spoil anyone else's trip down the Yukon.

I sat there stunned, feeling sorry for everybody. I thought of Jane's incredible wiseness a week or so before when Sue had suggested that we have a little encounter session and share our feelings about what we liked and disliked about each other. "Absolutely not," Jane had stated emphatically, leaving the campfire and ending the encounter before it began.

Pressed by the others now for an opinion, I admitted I'd been frustrated at times, so far, on the trip and said I thought it was mainly because of the schedule, which had just now been removed. I said I believed that after a few days of gelling into a cohesive unit, this smaller group would work out a routine and roles that were as agreeable and pleasant and entertaining as those of the larger group. I said that I thought it was far too early to judge the emotional success of the group and that I believed things would get better and work themselves out. I added that I thought some painful things had been said and that I hoped they had been given and received in a spirit of constructive criticism and respect for the other person.

I knew we each could and probably would get ourselves to the Bering Sea with or without each other, but I didn't particularly look forward to severing friendships and having to decide who would paddle with whom, who would get which gear and food, if we decided to split up. I crawled into the tent feeling weary and wondering how tonight's exchange could possibly have produced the slightest beneficial effect on anyone.

## JUNE 30, DAY 22

By the time we ate breakfast at half past nine, the sun was already deliciously hot. To my relief, nobody started a fight. In fact, breakfast-cook Jude went out of her way to attend to Evelyn's needs, politely offering her more coffee and food. Evelyn related how she had walked head-on into a porcupine right outside our tent at 5 A.M. when she made one of her nightly forays, and Sue and Jude seemed delighted by the story. Maybe Sue's approach had been right after all, I thought; maybe all it took to rid a group of ill feelings was the mere expression of those feelings, a catharsis that changed no behavior but made the complainers feel better. I couldn't believe life was really that simple, though.

We paddled through a canyonlike area. The steep left bank was a carpet of fir and spruce with a few bare spots of sphagnum moss. On the right rose rocky cliffs with their usual spruce-lined crevices. Every now and then a razor-sharp crag would slice down to the water's edge, perpendicular to the river. Creek after clear bubbling creek tumbled straight down the vertical cliffs and formed its own little gravel delta. Around them, beneath the shade of the spruces, a few small patches of snow still held out against the summer sun. But sightings of snow were becoming rare now; the white mantle was disappearing even from the distant peaks.

Soon some cabins, tucked back among the poplars on the left bank, tipped us off that we had reached the abandoned town of Fortymile. We trudged across a narrow, muddy beach, through a thin band of willows, and into a clearing full of thigh-high grass. Only with some difficulty did I switch my Texas mind from the snake-alert mentality that such grass always provokes to the carefree attitude I could adopt in snakeless Alaska. But once I succeeded, I could take my eyes off my feet and keep them on the nearby forest for bears. We poked around a somewhat modern-looking tin shed that harbored rusting machine parts, then after a mad dash back to the boat for more mosquito repellent, we ambled along the path toward what was left of the old Fortymile.

In 1886, up the little Fortymile River that meets the Yukon just below here, two men struck the gold that would drain the Stewart River settlement of its population and inspire the deadly dogsled journey of George Williams and an Indian companion through a Chilkoot blizzard. By late 1887, hundreds of prospectors were working the gravel bars all along the Fortymile and surrounding creeks. The town soon boasted six saloons, two blacksmith shops, two stores, several restaurants and hotels, a dressmaker's shop, a watchmaker's shop, a library, and even a cigar factory. There were also stills and an opera house where the few white women in the territory provided songs, dances, and other amusements for the miners. It was Fortymile that gave birth to a peculiar diversion known as the Squaw Dance. Occasionally, a band of Indian women would wander into a cabin and sit quietly in a row against the wall. The lively tune of a lone fiddle would pierce the air. Eventually a miner would grab one of the women, and together they would lurch around the room with dancelike movements. The others would follow suit; hours would pass with only the sound of shuffling moccasins and heavy boots and that lone fiddle, for the women and their partners spoke not the same tongue. After awhile, the women would tire and would silently creep away toward home. The men would drift off to their own cabins.

It was to Bill McPhee's saloon here in Fortymile that George Carmack raced in August, 1896, to report his rich strike on Bonanza Creek; the news emptied Fortymile overnight. Fortymile is the oldest town on the upper Yukon, inhabited until 1958. That was the year that its lone resident, an old prospector-turned-woodchopper-turned-trapper named Bill Couture, passed away. An SOS he had sent down the Yukon on a little raft was picked up fifty miles away at Eagle, and it produced a rescue ride for him to a hospital in Dawson, but he died anyway.

Today, the crumbling log buildings stood silently in the encroaching forest, offering only a hint of the wild times of almost a century ago. The only sound was an occasional whistle whose source we couldn't pinpoint. We knew there was a mine somewhere in this general part of the world, and we thought maybe one of the miners was hiking with a bear whistle. I strolled along a winding path that was paved with wood chips to combat the ubiquitous mud. Whose boots had crunched over these same chips through the years, I wondered. I poked my head into the old general store and the telegraph station and the two-story Mountie station. A sturdy log church with a tiny, wooden bell tower—Saint James Angelican Mission—nestled among the pale trunks of the poplars, its corrugated tin roof dappled with sunlight and shade. The entire scene was one of pastoral peace, belying the history of this place where crusty old miners sometimes lived for months at a time on nothing but flapjacks, and where scurvy and frostbite were accepted occupational hazards. With my closeup camera lens, I crawled among the wildflowers that populated every patch of sunlight offered by the young forest's partial canopy. The translucent pink petals of the exquisite wild roses cartwheeled around centers of yellow stamens. Pressing closer to them, all I could see was brilliant veined pinkness surrounded by the green blur of forest understory. Millions of tiny, purple chiming bells drooped in dainty clusters from their stalks. Some other, pink flowers hung from their long stems in a row like salmon drying on a smokehouse rafter. Once again, I was elated that I had gotten myself to the Yukon. I could think of nothing I'd rather be doing than sprawling flat on my back on the damp earth, blinking and blowing mosquitoes away from my face down here in the moist shade of the flowers and grasses where they thrived, craning to get just the right angle for backlighting and picture composition from the underside of the petals of a foot-tall flower.

My communing came to an end when Evelyn tinkled down the path with the request that I come quick to photograph a cat-sized furry animal that had just dashed into the general store. It was in the shadows under an old bed, she said, and would I please poke my camera in there and take its picture? Well, I didn't know if I would or not. Thoughts of rabies and tetanus went through my mind. And what if it were a wolverine? Though small, the wolverine is exceptionally fearless and has been known to bring down deer, caribou, and moose, and to give pause to bears. Feeling only slightly foolish, we each grabbed a stick and edged into the dark cabin, ready for a fast retreat. We spied the poor frightened critter under the bed, but it was so dark that we couldn't tell if it was a marmot or a young badger or a porcupine with weird-looking quills. It made no sound. Sue and Jude joined us and they, too, were perplexed. We finally declared it a marmot and attributed to it the whistling sound we'd heard before. We left it in peace.

As we untied the boats, I discovered a fresh, black-green pile of feces the size of a silver dollar, planted squarely on my foam-covered canoe seat. Then we spotted fresh, small paw prints along the beach, as well as muddy ones scattered over the clean clothes we'd spread in the boats to dry. Perhaps we had scared off a would-be grocery thief in the nick of time. I scientifically scooped up the neat little pile with my trowel, and the other members of the expedition passed the evidence hand to hand as we floated side by side down the river. Sue suggested that Evelyn's boat definitely deserved some sort of prize for being the first to undergo defecation in the line of duty.

On we drifted in thwartation formation, slurping our cold potato soup ("Vichyssoise, please!" exclaimed cook Sue) and beans. Gone were the days when we pulled out onto the bank to make a fire to cook hot lunches. Now it seemed more convenient and perfectly agreeable simply to pull our individual plates from their little stuff sacks, swish them in the Yukon to scrub off any leftover breakfast goo, turn around in our seats and get up on our knees (in the case of bow paddlers), prostrate ourselves on the gear across half a canoe-length with our outstretched plate in hand, and be served a ladleful of cold something-or-other from a pot beneath Evelyn's seat.

There was a brief flurry of excitement as Jude's rodless reel, which she had been trolling, caught something. She jumped as the reel pulled from her hands and we all screamed suggestions as she reeled in what turned out to be a trophy log. Then Evelyn spotted a flock of lifers—surf scoters— bobbing in an eddy near the shore. Throughout the day, and for many days to come, we were so eager to spot bears and moose, and our perception of distance was so skewed, that we swore each pile of driftwood was an animal until we came right upon it. Once, the changing angle between our boats and a midstream downed tree had us absolutely convinced until the last minute—even using binoculars—that a big black bear was swimming across the Yukon ahead of us.

During our post-lunch drifting period I ruddered the two boats, reveling in the blue, craggy magnificence of the Ogilvie Mountains far off to the north. It occurred to me that these mountains were really not so different from the Colorado Rockies. Why, then, did I feel a tremendous freedom, awe, and reverence such as I had never felt in the Rockies? For one thing, I supposed, I was experiencing these hills and valleys from a quiet canoe as it floated down a fairly undeveloped river, rather than from crowded hiking trails or highways, as I had experienced what little I knew of the Rockies. But more importantly, this land was simply wilder. Here, we could confront the scene around each bend with a pretty fair certainty that behind the next ridge lay no highway, no tourist town, no strip mine, not even a telephone pole. These ridges led my mind eagerly beyond them, imagining what bears and moose and porcupines were hanging around in them and beyond at this moment. But in Colorado, my mind had confined itself to pondering whatever immediate natural scene my eyes should happen to capture, for beyond the next hill almost certainly lay some human-made structure or scar. Here, I didn't have to turn my head and block out sight of a power plant or a highway in order to visualize what the land had looked like before white people and machines came; here, I could look right at it and see, now, what it had always looked like. It was infinitely more exciting to know that beyond the horizon lay wild land, instead of a Taco Bell.

As the others dozed beneath their hats in the sun, I heard whitewater ahead and saw a line of waves that, oddly, seemed to span the river. At the last moment we discovered we could skirt it to the right; still thwarted, we ferried hard out of its way. To our amazement, there was indeed a drop of a couple of feet on the left side, over which the river swooshed in a nice roll. It might have been fun to ride it in a single canoe, but perhaps a little too interesting for two canoes coupled with bungy cords.

We camped on an unusual bar whose shore began with the typical gravel and rocks, but whose center rose into sand dunes a few feet high. We were like curious kids in a new playground as we trotted over to examine these strange landforms that seemed quite out of place in the middle of the Yukon River. The other outstanding feature of our camp was a massive, downed spruce tree that lay in mid-island, deposited there by the last flood. Its root system, which rose eight feet into the air, not only provided a readymade woodpile of small logs and twigs that had lodged there but also made a nice windbreak for our kitchen fire. And either I was getting used to it or the rocks of late were smoother and rounder than those of our campsites a few hundred miles back. To top all that, Evelyn and I had the night off. All in all, life was easy. Everyone seemed in a good mood, and almost no hint remained of last night's personality conflicts. I waded into the Yukon up to my knees and—once I caught my breath—took sort of a bath, using the canoe stern as a soap-dish and towel rack. Then, still nude, I was inspired to sponge mud and marmot dung out of the canoe. By the time I got dressed, Sue and Jude had prepared an absolute feast of beef stroganoff, complete with a dessert of raisin bannock bread. It was almost embarrassing that life was so good—that we spent our days doing nothing but floating in the sun, eating, reading, occasionally strolling through the woods and eyeballing pretty flowers, and sitting on sandbars in lawn chairs, gazing at cozy fires while sipping hot chocolate. We had tried to tell all those reporters about it, but they could envision only hardship and all that conquering Nature stuff. Oh well, perhaps it was best to keep it a secret—more Yukon for the rest of us if word doesn't get out.

It was an evening for glorious pastels. A hint of dying pink sunlight washed over the river's rippled surface and danced among high, grey clouds that swirled up the valley. Beyond the purple hills at the river's bend, the slightest notion of pale blue hung on the far horizon. Beneath it all, looking pitifully insignificant but determined, rested a canoe that said "Bering Sea or Bust." Today, for the first time, we had spent an entire day without seeing or hearing any person or motorboat or airplane. I hoped for many more such days.

## JULY 1, DAY 23

As a minor sandstorm swirled into our dining nook, I baked a breakfast bannock of cinnamon and pineapples and a lunch bannock flavored with hot peppers and bell peppers and Mexicali spice, which we would eat later with the black-eyed peas I was cooking. No one seemed to mind or even notice that the cook's hands were filthy, for my hands couldn't possibly give half the body to the food that the morning sandstorm had provided. And no one seemed to mind that I vastly overestimated the potency of baking powder, the resulting bannock being a flat, dense little cake.

I repatched my wool pants where the pocket seam had ripped out for the second time, and I sewed up the side seam of Evelyn's tent sack. My jeans were riddled with tiny burnt holes where hot pebbles had landed after exploding in the fire. Everything seemed to be falling apart. But in the pantry arena, we had a different problem. If we reached the town of Eagle in a day or two as we projected, eighty pounds of food—at least two weeks' worth for four people—would be waiting for us at the post office. And yet, we still had with us about a week-and-a-half's worth of food for six—about seventy pounds. And another big batch was supposedly waiting at Fort Yukon, only two weeks away at the rate we were going. A combination of factors seemed to be conspiring to make our already-overloaded canoes absolutely overflow with food: (1) we were traveling farther each day, and thus reaching our food drop much sooner than expected, and (2) we were eating less than expected.

We paddled hard for a few hours through a series of islands, against a slight headwind. After lunch we thwarted and napped, as Evelyn took watch. It seemed a long time since we'd thwarted like this, and it crossed my mind absently that perhaps this was the first time that Evelyn had taken watch since she'd accidentally run us into the bank on our All-Nighter. Just about this time we hit the bank, and I bolted angrily upright, swearing and observing sarcastically that if Evelyn didn't want to do her fair share of taking watch, she could express it in ways other than crashing into the bank. She responded to my outburst by saying that running into the bank wasn't all that big a deal, which only exasperated me more. It was true that easing against a gravel shoreline in an eddy like this did no harm, but I worried that a pilot who wouldn't watch where she was going could just as easily run us into one of the many toppled spruces along the shore that could pin the boats and drown people. Just then the wind came up and it began to rain, so we unthwarted and paddled hard to warm up.

I used the exercise to paddle out my frustrations and to try to come to grips with the twenty-four-hour-a-day partnership into which Evelyn and I had suddenly immersed ourselves a month ago. As we'd both known before the trip, hopping into a canoe for a three-month trip with a casual friend would require a fair amount of acceptance and communication. Luckily, we seemed to share an unspoken commitment to let the other do her thing, no matter how seemingly weird, as long as it didn't really affect us. Time was on our side regarding the little things, I felt sure; if we could just tolerate each other long enough, our partner's irritating habits would surely become first amusing, then so expected and routine that we wouldn't even notice them. The sheet Evelyn always used inside her sleeping bag, for instance, and the nightly thrashing and rustling it seemed to generate, were on my threshold of becoming humorous; after all, she did meticulously keep her struggles confined to her three-foot half of the tent. And, though she awoke late one night in terror to discover she'd tossed and turned until she'd virtually mummified herself in the thing, she had courageously refused to wake me for assistance. Slowly, I was learning to accept and even find a measure of amusement in the fact that she would live with a disgusting amalgamation of mud and crushed beer cans lining her end of the canoe, that she would never learn to tie a bowline knot, and that she would until her dying day carry her pack *and* her two duffel bags all the way up to the tent every night, instead of retrieving merely the few things she needed from them and then leaving the bags in the boat. After all, these habits affected only her.

But, I was having a very hard time coping with those habits of hers that I felt adversely affected *me*. Bashing us into the bank, obviously, was a big no-no with me. And once, she had failed to fasten securely into the boat a small pack that contained half our emergency fuel supply for the cookstove. Then, there was the Battle of the Tent Zipper; granted, we waged it only occasionally now, but being awakened by mosquitoes even once a week was something I could do without. . . . At the same time, though, I was quite sure I probably did a million things that bugged her.

And she was really quite a good partner, overall. She did far more than her share of our cooking and hauling gear, she patiently cooperated with all my fidgeting and photographing in the bow, she tolerated my endless hours of singing the same verses over and over to commit them to memory, she gathered wood and started the breakfast fire almost every morning whether it was her turn to cook or not. It was her tent and boat that we were wearing out day after day on the Yukon. And whenever I did voice a complaint, she always said she'd try to do better, which was an honest enough answer. Actually, she was like a handy, floating reference library and tour guide; there was a good chance she'd know the names of, or would look up in one of the many books she'd brought, almost any tree or bird or flower I cared to know. And yet she didn't foist such information on me if I wasn't in the mood. Like me, she relished a few hours a day of paddling or drifting in silence, each of us enjoying our own thoughts; yet, when the time came to gab, she could, like me, certainly hold her own.

In fact, we were making progress, slowly but surely, in achieving a pleasant day-to-day coordination of our joint activities. From the middle thwart to each of our ends of the canoe had now been declared off-limits to the other partner—our own sacred, private nest in which we each tied or didn't tie junk, arranged or didn't arrange junk, according to our own whims. And, gradually, Evelyn was learning to mumble something or clunk her paddle across the gunnels or somehow signal me if she stopped steering in order to put on a layer of clothes or drink some water; otherwise, without knowing she'd stopped ruddering, I would continue blithely paddling along, enjoying my rhythm and power, only to realize too late that my efforts had served merely to turn the canoe sideways. And, though she didn't really like cameras or anything else that fell into the "gadget" category, she would gamely assist me with any of mine if I had the patience to ask her.

To achieve a peace of mind within our relationship, I knew I had only to continue to try to recognize and discuss with her those habits I felt I had a right to alter, and to appreciate the full humor in whichever of her quirks I thought merely odd. Discovering, day by day, the facets of her personality was actually pretty fun, and our camping routine had now evolved to the point that I no longer had to think about where I'd put my dry socks, but could turn my attention to relaxing and enjoying her company. I had learned long ago that people are beautifully strange and inconsistent, and it rather tickled me, daily, to observe that Evelyn was no exception. When asked before the trip what kinds of fabric she would take for the inevitable repairs to her clothing, for instance, she had replied that she wasn't taking any, she'd just cut off her shirttail or something; and yet, she had given a fair amount of thought to what kinds of measuring spoons (of all things) we should take for our baking (we decided not to take any and did fine). (Similarly, I was quite sure she herself found no small degree of mirth in the fact that I had given endless hours of consideration to what piece of hardware would fasten the gear into the boat, and yet I'd started out for a three-month trip with a stove that threatened bodily harm with every use.) And Evelyn would, with an unflinching flair, hold up her end of an argument, yet when it was over she was still your friend and would point out with glee the next bald eagle for you to enjoy.

My contemplations stopped short when we spotted some inhabited cabins along the left bank. We'd heard that a thirty-foot swath cut through the forest marks the international border between Canada and Alaska, but apparently we'd missed it altogether, for this line of cabins could only be Eagle village, an Indian settlement nine miles past the border. That meant we'd come a whopping ninety-nine miles in three days' travel from Dawson (not too shabby) and that we had finally crossed back into the good old U.S. of A., into our last frontier—Alaska! Congratulating ourselves, Evelyn and I nudged into the bank to wait for Sue and Jude, who had dropped far behind. We waved to some young Indian men who stood high above us on the bank. They asked the usual questions about where we had put in, how far down we were going. When we answered that we were bound for the Bering Sea, they seemed puzzled. Finally they realized we meant the end of the Yukon. "Oh, you're going to the mouth!" they exclaimed with a smile. They had apparently heard of the mouth but didn't know it was at the Bering Sea. When Sue and Jude caught up, we learned that Jude had been soloing the boat, turned around backwards in the bow and perched up on the bow deck so she could steer, with the stern facing downstream. Sue's elbow was bothering her. She diagnosed it as some type of tendonitis, perhaps from so many miles of J-stroking in the stern day after day. Observing Jude's bright yellow "Texas turkey" T-shirt, one of the Indian guys began singing a country-and-western song about Texas's being as close as you can get to heaven. . . .

We thwarted, broke out the Everclear, and began to celebrate with a vengeance Canada's Dominion Day (which happened to be today), our crossing the border, upcoming American Independence Day, and everything else we could think of. By the time we had drifted three miles down to what we assumed was the town of Eagle proper, we were feeling rambunctious and had stirred up half the sled dogs in the Indian village with our imitation wolf howls. Since it was late in the day and the post office would be closed, and since no logical campsites appeared along the sheer bank at the edge of town, we decided to camp on a flat open gravel bar halfway across the river from Eagle. Normally, we would avoid camping with no shelter under the gaze of a town; but we were afraid to float farther down to where the trees grew on the island, for fear the current would send us right past the town and our mail and eighty pounds of food in the morning. Even from the upstream tip of the island where we were camped, it looked to be an interesting ferrying job to make it into Eagle.

But we'd worry about that tomorrow. Right now, it was my turn to cook, but I was too soused to deal with it and the rest were too soused to remember we hadn't eaten. I said not to worry—that when the young men of Eagle (if there were any) caught sight of four women cavorting on this sandbar, they'd undoubtedly bring us pizza and ice cream and beer and all sorts of stuff in their motorboats. But none ever did. Somehow, a skilletful of popcorn, as well as chili and rice, got cooked, and we gobbled it. Then I sprawled in my lawn chair and blasted my trumpet in the direction of Eagle, while Jude set off firecrackers. "Hi, Eagle!" we shouted and waved occasionally, wondering if anyone was really watching or if anyone really cared what a bunch of women were doing out on the sandbar. Every now and then a volley of loud pops emanated from the town and echoed over the river. We assumed somebody over there was celebrating Dominion Day or an early Fourth of July or simply answering our firecrackers.

"No, I think they're shooting at us," said Evelyn offhandedly. "I read that they like to do that around here; they sit on the bank and shoot out over the river." I squatted, making a token effort to shield myself behind a duffel bag. "Oh, Beth," Evelyn shook her head, "at least go to the woods."

"I don't have time," I shrugged with a grin. "The woods are five minutes down the beach, and Everclear gives a three-minute warning, max . . . . If the citizens of Eagle get their jollies craning their necks to see somebody pee on a sandbar, then they better look quick 'cause here goes."

## JULY 2, DAY 24

During my somewhat restless night's sleep, either I dreamed it or I really awoke to an incredibly loud noise and looked out the tent door practically into the cockpit of a small plane as it flew toward us about ten feet off the ground. I didn't know which was odder—that I might have dreamed up something like that, or that I wouldn't put it past Eagle's pilots to buzz tents in the middle of the night. Only in Alaska. . . .

We executed an expert ferry straight across to Eagle. Then we crawled hand over hand up through the deep, shifting sands and roots and debris of the twenty-five-foot sheer cutbank until we stood, covered in dust, in Eagle's gravel street.

Evelyn asked if her hair looked O.K. and I said it looked about like it always did. "That's the nice thing about my hair," she smiled. "It always looks the same whether it's been three days since I combed it or not."

It was hot, so I took off the wool sweater I had worn for days over my T-shirt. That freed up the T-shirt aroma, the impact of which seemed more significant than usual here in town. In 562 miles on the Yukon, the Texas Women's Yukon River Expedition seemed to have acquired a certain river-woman veneer. Sue and Jude and I wore our cowboy hats beneath the bright sun. Sue's hair was now long enough that she felt no need to wear her wig in town. Jude wore her mosquito mesh jacket. Sue and Jude were in jeans and boots; I was clad in navy wool pants with a ripstop nylon patch on the hip, and tennis shoes. Evelyn wore her filthy cotton garden gloves that she always wore to keep the mosquitoes off her hands, her once-beige jeans that would never again be clean, and her long-sleeved chamois shirt with the growing rip over the left breast. We brushed ourselves off, stuffed our cameras and our money into our fanny packs, and prepared to encounter our first Alaskan river-town.

Trouble was, Eagle seemed like a ghost town. It was supposedly 9 A.M., but not a soul stirred. A small cabin that served as the office of the Yukon-Charley Rivers National Preserve was closed. The post office was silent. Maybe the wooden buildings and cabins were empty historical replicas and the people lived elsewhere? Maybe the whole town was hung over and sleeping off its Dominion Day celebration? Maybe this was Saturday instead of Friday and everything was closed? Finally Evelyn returned from a foray inland with the news that the time had changed two hours instead of one at the border, so that it was now only 8 A.M., rather than 9 as we had thought. Businesses would open shortly. "And!" she smiled devilishly, "there's a cafe!"

"Wah!" we chorused and started off at a trot to perform what was becoming a ritual when we hit any town. We strolled past poplars and an occasional barking dog. In one junk-strewn yard, a man wearing a pair of welder's safety goggles was settling his large frame onto the seat of a small tractor. I assumed the goggles were to keep the dust out of his eyes. From the cutout sleeves of his green T-shirt bulged massive tatooed arms. "Mornin'," we nodded.

"Howdy," he answered with a grin. "I saw you come in last night on the river and camp on the sandbar." We smiled sheepishly, wondering in what detail he'd seen us camp on the sandbar. "How far down you going?" he asked. When we told him all the way, he laughed and shook his head. "Well, I hope you gals make it, I really do," he shook each of our hands. "Now, I've met a lot of people coming through, going down the river, and I bet I've asked thirty of 'em to send me a postcard, and you know how many have?" He held his thick fingers in the shape of a zero.

"Well sir, we'll be the first!" Sue exclaimed, as we all nodded and smiled. "We guarantee!"

"All right," he grinned as he started his tractor. "Now I'm counting on you, you better make it to the end for me. Just send it to Sarge Waller, Eagle, Alaska!"

As he roared away, Evelyn slapped her knee and said that he was one of the characters in John McPhee's *Coming into the Country.* "We met somebody famous!" we smiled. Several of the people we would meet today had been immortalized in McPhee's 1976 bestseller that concentrated on people in and around what he called the bush community of Eagle. I considered Eagle itself to be pretty civilized, connected as it is to the rest of the world by a gravel road that is open in summer.

The cafe was a homey affair with red-and-white checkered curtains and tablecloths, a couple of pool tables, pungent mosquito coils burning on the counter, and a plastic lighted menu above the big grill that advertised everything in the world. We doubted that we could eat everything we wanted in one sitting, so we told the waitress we'd have ham and eggs ($7.40 U.S. currency) now and would be back in a few hours for pizza and hamburgers. To have someone else fix breakfast and to eat real eggs was divine, but I'd been away from soap so long that the faint hint of it on my juice glass seemed overpowering. We asked the waitress about possible nearby hiking trails. She looked blank, as if hiking had never crossed her mind and she'd certainly never seen it done. A handsome, grey-haired guy at the next table volunteered that if we hitched thirteen miles or so up the Taylor Highway we could backpack above timberline, which was pretty nice. He said no one hikes much around here because it's pretty rough country. He also said that the nearest bar or liquor store was 150 or so river-miles downstream at Circle and that it would take twenty-four hours floating to make it there—less if you paddled.

He, too, already knew we'd camped on the sandbar. "Y'all must have been setting off firecrackers over here last night, right?" I asked. "We heard some and figured people were getting ready for Fourth of July."

"Well, I didn't hear any firecrackers," he commented, sipping his coffee, "but my neighbor was drunk and was shooting out over the river, toward your sandbar. I was working on a house I'm building, and as I came out of the basement hole, a bullet whined through the air near my head.

I went over there and cussed him out. You guys oughta go over there now and do the same." He grinned.

He asked what we did for a living that enabled us to take off for three months. I kicked the others under the table. I had warned them not to speak a word of my past or present involvement with environmental organizations—especially not my role in passing the Alaska lands bill—if we wanted to make any friends in this town. For, judging by the hand-painted signs tacked on some of Eagle's buildings—including this cafe—the town liked to think of itself as a hotbed of anti-environmentalism. "Park Service not welcome," "I do not recognize Antiquities Act," "Antiquities Act illegal," proclaimed the signs. Sue and Jude and Evelyn described their occupations and we omitted mention of my livelihood.

The authorities under the Antiquities Act of 1906 were something that President Carter used in 1978 to permanently set aside fifty-six million acres of Alaska's federal lands—including the Yukon-Charley Rivers National Preserve, whose border lay just downstream from here—as national parks, wildlife refuges, and national forest wilderness areas. The pending Alaska lands bill that might have preserved these lands had just died in the waning hours of the Ninety-Fifth Congress in 1978, killed by the combination of delay by Senator Henry Jackson's Energy and Natural Resources Committee and filibuster threats by Alaska's then-Senator Mike Gravel. So Carter had invoked the Antiquities Act, he explained, to keep alive Congress's option to determine the fate of the lands; without his actions the lands could have been subject to mining entry, logging, and other impairments when their temporary protections expired in December, 1978. And, Carter explained, if and when Congress chose to pass a bill, they could change or undo the protections he had established. Congress eventually did pass a bill, in 1980. But some vocal Alaskans were mad about the whole thing, apparently feeling that—although the federal govern-ment had bought Alaska from the Russians in the first place; although the Natives' interest had been addressed with a settlement of 44 million acres; although the State's interest had been addressed with a grant of 104 million acres; although the entire state of Alaska contained far fewer people than a single city like Dallas; and although the American public now wanted its chance to preserve for future generations a significant chunk of the last frontier that they already owned—they were entitled to use the state's federal lands as their own private playground. And apparently there were a few such thinkers in Eagle, stirred up by the designation of the Yukon-Charley Rivers National Preserve.

"What do all these Antiquities signs mean?" I asked, to find out how this gentleman viewed things.

"Well, they tried to take all our (sic) land," he said. "Carter used this Antiquities Act to lock up (sic) all of Alaska. But then Reagan won the presidential election and the environmentalists—or conservationists or whatever they call themselves—accepted taking (sic) less land here in the Preserve and in other places because they knew if they didn't, Reagan would push for a worse bill. Anyway, they got that Preserve in here and now we can't use the land anymore." I failed to see his point, since the residents of Eagle and anyone else could freely roam about the Preserve to hunt, hike, fish, camp, and so forth, but I didn't press the issue.

We wandered through town and stopped briefly to talk with the Park Service summer ranger. She said there were no trails in the Preserve, that the country was pretty tough to hike in, but that it was better if you could get through the spruce and up onto some of the hills. This was beginning to sound familiar. I confessed in a whisper that I had worked for the Alaska Coalition, and she grinned. She said that people had taken down most of the anti-environmental signs and had begun to calm down as they realized that the land in the Preserve was pretty much as it had always been and that the citizens of Eagle could do pretty much what they always could.

A tall, thin, friendly middle-aged woman named Elva Scott led a couple of dozen tourists, including us, on a walking tour through a few of Eagle's historical buildings. Eagle had long been an Indian village, she said, then a trading post was set up in the early 1880s. In 1898, twenty-five miners incorporated Eagle City. The U.S. Army moved in and established Fort Egbert. A telegraph line was laid to Dawson. And it was from this little telegraph station in the middle of nowhere that the Norwegian polar explorer Roald Amundsen sent word to the world that he had discovered the Northwest Passage. His ship, *Gjoa*, and a crew of six had been gingerly plying the Arctic waters for two-and-a-half years when they finally met a whaling ship coming from the west, indicating they had at last found the passage. In September, 1905, their ship froze solid into the Arctic ice. Amundsen had heard there was a telegraph station at a place called Eagle somewhere south, so he snowshoed almost a thousand miles through the snow, walked into town as unobtrusively as any miner who might be picking up a few supplies, and sent a telegram. Only then did the folks of Eagle know who he was, and only then did the rest of the world, who'd assumed he was long dead and gone, know he was still around.

Eagle seemed to have had (and probably still has) a penchant for attracting unusual characters. There was one Nimrod Robertson, who used to go out and do a little mining and nature study, all the way up through his eighth decade of life. A distinguishing feature was the dentures he sported, made from the teeth of animals. One autumn he stayed out at his mine too long while awaiting some spiritual sign for him to return to town, and he ran out of food. He found rather unpleasant the thought of being eaten by animals after he starved to death, so he tied a bright red handkerchief on his pack and lay down in a frigid stream. Death came quickly, as did the ice that enclosed him in a neat little coffin until spring, when some of the folks of Eagle spotted that red handkerchief. They thawed him out and gave him a proper burial. The year was 1940.

As Mrs. Scott continued with the tour, explaining Eagle's historical schooling and courthouse and church facilities, a man ambled casually down the street with a rifle slung over his shoulder. Around the corner stood a two-story, white clapboard building that said, "Hardware, Automotive, Cookware, Camping—Eagle Sales and Service—Surplus Store—

Eagle, Alaska." Coca-Cola signs flanked it on either side. In front, between two poles, stretched a large grizzly hide. Along one side of the building were caribou antlers. Through the yard were strewn oil barrels, a greenhouse, and various kinds of machinery. At the end of the block where we were standing was the seventy-year-old town wellhouse, topped by its windmill, to which every household in Eagle comes to draw its water. Like many villages along the river, Eagle has electricity but no running water. The hassles of Arctic plumbing are apparently greater than the benefits of running water.

Today, Eagle has a population of about one hundred; Eagle Village has about fifty. And apparently every last citizen has a big picture window overlooking the river, and a pair of binoculars, and enjoys seeing what sort of riffraff finds its way onto that sandbar each summer. Mrs. Scott said that last night she had been in the middle of a hot bridge game when she had spotted someone playing a trumpet out on the river. She didn't mention what else she might have spotted. Oh well, it was fun to be famous, or infamous, as the case may have been.

As we walked into the post office, John Borg took one look at us and said, "Have I got mail for you!" Apparently it was obvious to everyone that we were just off the river and that we were from Texas. We took our letters down to the cafe, and over Cokes and pizza and ice cream, read aloud some newspaper clips we'd just received that had appeared in Dallas a month ago.

"Four Dallas women are about to embark on a trip that either appalls or enthralls those who hear about it," began one story in the *Dallas Morning News*. "They're proud, nervous, excited about their trip, an expedition that many people might talk about, but few would undertake. 'A lot of people won't give themselves permission to do things,' Ms. Edens says. 'You just have to let yourself do what you want to do.'" Beside the article was a picture of the six of us in Sue's and Jude's driveway, wearing shorts, sitting in lawn chairs and boats with all our gear, toasting each other with cans of beer. I remembered back to that afternoon; it seemed a century ago, and everything in the picture looked so *clean*.

"Four either very brave or very foolish women left Dallas Friday afternoon for an adventure. . . . " began the *Dallas Times Herald.* "'Who can hear the word Yukon without itching to dash off to Alaska, our last frontier, our last big wild place?' Beth remarked with a smile. . . . 'My son the lawyer made me get a new will,' Jane laughed. . . . 'My husband told the girls that if anything happened to me they weren't to bring my body back in a sack. I've told them I want my ashes sprinkled over Mount McKinley.' . . . The women try not to dwell too much on the possible dangers ahead of them. They laugh and joke about the grizzlies, canoes tipping over, and the prospect of getting lost in the marshlands. Sometimes, though, the laughter sounds strained. . . . "

In the cafe, a couple from California offered us a ride three miles up to the Indian village, so the four of us piled on top of each other in the car's small back seat. As we bounced down the talclike road, dust billowed through the open rear hatchback window. Eagle Village was a single rag-tag line of log cabins perched along the Yukon's high bank. Moose antlers adorned many of the doorways. A pair of snowshoes hung on an outer wall. Yards were strewn with everything from boat motors to aluminum canoes to baby carriages to snowmobiles. Two fish wheels sprawled on dry land on the high bank, awaiting the salmon run, which everyone said was late this year. Around them hung the smell of fish. A new community hall boasted the only washateria in this corner of the world. The white children of Eagle came here to attend school in the Indian village.

The lower beach was littered with soft drink, beer, and oil cans. A woman said the trash rides in on the ice every year, but somehow we doubted that, reasoning that, if so, it would be spread evenly all along the Yukon instead of having collected itself right here. In the shade of a cabin doorway, we chatted with some men who told of various supposed hazards downstream. All the way down the river, we would meet people accustomed to driving motorboats who considered things to be hazards that we hardly noticed in the canoe. A young guy wandered up and began shouting unintelligible things into our faces in a loud and friendly way. We couldn't tell whether he was drunk or crazy or speaking English. A friendly young girl with straight, black, shiny hair, wearing cut-off jeans, a tank top, and sandals, pointed to a page in a book about Athapascan Indians Evelyn had just bought. "That's me—Dorothy," she said. Evelyn asked for her autograph, and Dorothy printed her name in big grade-school letters across the page. The California couple with whom we'd ridden said they'd stay for awhile at the washateria, but we declined since our clothes had only 102 miles on them since Dawson. So in the 81° heat, the four of us began to walk the three miles back to Eagle.

Soon an open-bed truck zoomed down the road in our direction, and though he was already carrying eight people, the driver stopped and smiled and said, "Ride?" Evelyn and I, a hundred yards or so behind Sue and Jude, didn't hesitate for a moment. We climbed in among the Indians and leaned against the swaying wooden sides of the truck, smiling a silent greeting to its occupants as the wind whipped our hair into our faces. Sue and Jude laughed and hopped in when they spotted us. We ended up at the dirt airstrip, where most of Eagle and Eagle Village seemed to have gathered for the daily social event—the landing of the mail plane. They couldn't pick up their mail here (they had to go into town for that) but they enjoyed seeing what passengers came and went with the mail. Amid the hugs and kisses and excited conversations, our truck gained two more passengers who'd just flown in, and we all headed into Eagle.

I called home from Eagle's lone telephone beside the cash register in the store behind the post office. The conversation was beamed by satellite, which seemed to require shouting and thus enabled any customer in the store to know what the cheechako in the corner was telling her mother back in Texas. In addition, there was a delay of several seconds between the time either party uttered something and the time the other party heard it and could respond. And if the two parties happened to speak simultaneously, neither could tell that the other had spoken. The normal rhythm of conversation was utterly shattered, leaving one with the impression that the person on the other end was either mad or didn't understand or didn't agree with anything one said.

A woman happened by the post office as we dumped eighty pounds of food from badly battered shipping boxes into duffel bags. Noticing my Dallas Downriver Club T-shirt, she commented that she was from Texas, too. As we exchanged small talk, we discovered, much to our merriment, that I had sat in her husband's office at Sam Houston State University in Huntsville, talking with him about East Texas wilderness proposals, about four months before. Neither of us had thought then to mention to the other that we'd be on the Yukon this summer. He was Ralph Moldenhauer, a widely-known ornithologist at the university, and she was Marlene Moldenhauer, a junior high school science teacher. Ralph came out of the cabin across the street and we all had a good laugh about the coincidence. They were here for a month with their children Alex and Vicki, working with the Park Service in the Yukon-Charley as Volunteers in the Parks. Marlene was here to prepare a plant checklist for the Preserve and to make management recommendations; Ralph was conducting a bird survey. Evelyn and I asked Ralph about birds we'd see in the Preserve, especially the endangered peregrine falcons, for which it is famous.

"Well," he grinned, "you realize you scared one up right on the sandbar when you pulled in last night, don't you? A bunch of us were sitting on the bank with a telescope watching it until you scared it away."

"Uh," I dug my toe in the dirt, remembering the Everclear. "I think we were way too far gone for birding by the time we hit that sandbar."

Though we'd heard Eagle had no less than three bootleggers, it was officially a liquorless town. Therefore, we couldn't envision that there'd be all that much excitement to their Fourth of July celebration. On the surface, Eagle seemed a friendly but somewhat staid little community, at least compared to Dawson. And we'd already eaten just about everything on the menu of the only restaurant in town. So we voted to head downriver.

We gave some extra food to the pickup driver, and Evelyn donated some cookbooks to the town library. Then, down the bank we slid with our bulging food bags, which we tied in as best we could. Beside the boats was a flood gauge, reminding us of the wrath of the river that, during an energetic spring breakup, could bite giant morsels of earth from the high bank. In fact, in a place or two, the river had already nibbled away part of the road above us. Sometimes almost two hundred tons of glacial grist and eroded earth flow past this gauge, per minute. As Sarge and the Moldenhauers waved and took pictures, we shoved our own thousand pounds or more of solid material onto the Yukon's back and floated beneath the evening sun.

Little did Evelyn and I imagine then that, a thousand miles downstream from here, we would learn Jude had once figured that Eagle would be the farthest she and Sue would make it down the river before they would throw in the towel.

Feeling thoroughly delighted and refreshed by Eagle and all the characters we'd met, we drifted past monstrous Eagle Bluff and recapped the day's adventures. Sue and Jude noted that all the letters they had received closed with some wish for good luck and assurances that people were praying for us and thinking of our hardships. "Yeah, life's rough out here," I said, lying in the warm sun with my feet propped on the bow. An hour or two later, and ten miles downstream, we pulled out onto a gravel bar. Somehow Sue and Jude had the energy to boil all their clothes in a big pot on the fire, lean together some big logs into a tripod clothesline, and create a new dessert of cakes made from rice flour and peaches. We had been testing, with fair results, the theory that a thick coating of dirt on hands, face and body was the best protection against mosquitoes and wind-chapping, and after the third time the tripod collapsed and the wet clothes fell into the sand we suggested the theory might apply to clothes as well.

## JULY 3, DAY 25

"Wolves, wolves!" was the first thing I heard this morning. Sue and Evelyn raced across the sandbar; Jude and I burst from the tents. Squinting into binoculars, we picked up the shapes. Far across the river, hardly noticeable against the cream-colored sand, frolicked a dark shadow and a light grey one. They loped playfully across their sandbar, now poking around at the water's edge, now sniffing among the willows. Then they disappeared and we stared quietly at the spot where they had been, smiling over our great fortune at having witnessed the rare, wild, beautiful creatures. Our reverence was shattered when we noticed Jude was clad only in binoculars.

Jude had heard about a trail that led a mile or two inland to Ford Lake, and we were determined to get up into the woods and explore for the first time this land through which we'd been cruising for hundreds of miles. We looked forward to an overnight backpacking vacation from the river.

A mile down the river on the left bank, we spotted signs of the trailhead at a camp up among the spruces, so we beached the boats in the sticky, ankle-deep mud. Evelyn stood too long in one place, sinking unknowingly into the mud, and when she shifted her weight to catch the bowline I tossed to her, she plopped down in the wet goo squarely on her rear. We wondered whether it was wise to leave our boats, with all our gear, tied in full view of the river, but we weren't about to unload them and carry everything up the steep bank into the woods. Besides, even with one night's food and shelter and clothing removed, the boats still contained so much gear they were overflowing. They looked full, like we'd be back from a short break any minute. We hoisted our packs and groped our way up the slick bank.

Unlike the beach, the forest was thick with mosquitoes that attended us in a humming cloud. The air hung heavy, still, humid. The others donned headnets; I smeared extra Muskol on my face, neck, and bare arms. I had a headnet but preferred not to wear it if the Muskol would continue to keep the skeeters a few inches away from my eyes and nose. Through the filtered forest light, among tall paper birch and spruce, we strolled along a spongy, winding path that had been beaten down about a foot below the surface of the surrounding sphagnum moss. Immediately, we were captivated by the new environment. Evelyn identified new plants, Sue took pictures.

We came into a clearing and the trees shrank to skimpy, stunted spruces. Beneath our boots, the trail began to slurp. We found ourselves slogging through cold, melted permafrost. The bank muck oozed over our boot-tops, saturating our wool socks. My pants were soon soaked to the knee. The trail and everything around it was wobbly grass tussocks and sucking mud. Stumbling over the unpredictable terrain, I picked my way carefully, determined to avoid a sudden wrong stress, beneath the weight of the backpack, that might dislocate my knee. With one eye I chose each footstep, with the other I peered through the cloud of mosquitoes into the dark forest for bears.

It wouldn't have been so bad if the mud would have just let me take my foot back after each step, but it wouldn't even show that courtesy. Each step required a vigorous wrenching against the suction of the evil muck—the same kind of wrenching that had injured Sue's knee months before on the Lower Canyons of the Rio Grande. Whenever I tumbled into a vicious hole and was thrown off balance by the weight of the pack (which was often), I would slam into the prickly spruce boughs. The dead branches would give way and I would plunge face first into them, but the live ones would spring back and throw me to the other side of the trail. Once, my foot slid down the side of a hefty tussock and lodged among the roots beneath it, buried to the knee. My other foot could find nothing solid to stand on to gain leverage to retrieve the first foot, and I stumbled and thrashed and slopped in a wild semicircle. I didn't know whether to laugh or cry, but I didn't want to open my mouth for the mosquitoes. "Pretty rough country," someone had said.

So this was the stuff that generates all those trillions of Alaskan mosquitoes, the thin upper layer of permafrost that melts beneath the summer's sun. The water has nowhere to drain, trapped as it is by the permanently-frozen layer of earth beneath it, so it collects itself into hundreds of thousands of pockets and ponds and bogs, shallow and still and perfect for mosquito larvae.

Wet practically from head to toe, I was doing more crawling than walking. This was the infamous Alaskan muskeg, a hiker's horror, and it was winning. I felt like a fool, a worthless wretch. How in the world had all those explorers ever made trails and walked over all these mountains in this stuff? Then I remembered. They did it in winter, when ice-packed snow held the snowshoe and slid the sled, and there were no *mosquitoes!*

After a mile of torture, we stumbled upon the lake. "A red-necked grebe!" cried Evelyn gleefully, spotting another lifer. The rest of us weren't in the mood for birding. The lakeshore was nothing but cattails and spindly trees packed two feet apart. The ground was a lumpy wet slurry. Putting up a tent would have been a real challenge, but the mere thought of sleeping on the ground among the mosquitoes without a tent sent shivers up our spines. It began to drizzle.

We turned around and wallowed back up the path, trying several side trips in a vain attempt to locate some open ground, then slogged back almost to our starting point and followed another path along the riverbank. We came upon a rotting cabin, but a pool of stagnant water behind it was as close as we came to finding a lake in that direction. Beyond it spread an impenetrable alder thicket. It began to rain in earnest.

Someone suggested, in so many words, that this backpacking stuff was losing its glamour. We slogged silently back to the boats, threw in our packs, and retreated to the merciful mosquitoless middle of the river where we belonged. Though the skies were grey and a steady rain drummed on our cowboy hats, we were grateful to be out of those woods.

Thwarted, we floated past Calico Bluff, a famous thousand-foot-high landmark whose rock layers swirl in wavy patterns across its face. In the rain it wasn't too impressive, and we were more interested in jerky and apricot leather and getting our frozen red feet into some dry socks.

"The only good thing about that sorry excuse for a trail," grinned Sue, "is that it was so miserable it kept our minds off the mosquitoes." We agreed that our brief venture into the Alaskan back country had been a total disaster but that we were glad we'd done it. At least we'd gotten the itch to hike out of our systems, maybe for good. Perhaps at heart we were merely river runners, not hikers.

We floated about twenty miles downriver and as the rain stopped we pulled out onto an island thick with willows and alders, separated from the mainland by a thin spit of land. I was elated with the terrain. For the first time on the trip, the beach was flat, damp sand—with no rocks.

"Land, ho! We're talkin' regular ground, here!" I cried as I hopped out to check for bear prints. There was plenty of driftwood for fires, the firm sand would be great for tent stakes, and the mosquitoes weren't too bad since their main hangout—the thick bushes—was about forty feet inland. What more could a girl want? As I scouted, I spied half of a full rack of caribou antlers. "Wow!" I held them on my head, dancing up and down the beach. The others were green with envy. I tried to envision the animal who'd shed them here, probably a member of the Fortymile herd, which roams this general area during part of the year. Feeling only slightly guilty, I decided to keep the antlers, disregarding the usual wilderness rule to take nothing but pictures and leave nothing but footprints. Almost two months and 1,400 river-miles later, and 4,000 miles across North America, back in Dallas, the antlers would become a birthday present for my mother.

Evelyn's watch finally wound down; she tucked it away and forgot about it, as I applauded. We lounged in the dining tent, sipping hot chocolate, lingering over green spinach noodles and beef jerky. Jude and I crushed Evelyn and Sue in a heated game of spades, with our daring nellos and blind nellos. It could have been six o'clock or midnight; we didn't know or care which. The sun was back out, the distant blue hills and the rolling river were glorious, and we felt like queens in our royal lawn chairs.

Later, as Evelyn and I swatted the last few mosquitoes in our tent and rolled out our sleeping bags for the night, we simultaneously became aware of an alien presence in our cozy shelter. We almost always slept nude (clothes lasted longer between washings that way, and besides, it was hot), and now as we piled our clothes into a pillow shape and prepared to zip up our sleeping bags, we suddenly felt stings all over our bodies. The tent was full of no-see-ums, minute, black, mitelike creatures whose bites resemble those of mosquitoes. You turn to swat a mosquito when you feel a sharp sting and at first you see nothing, but then you spot the tiniest critter. Apparently our tent mesh wasn't small enough to keep them out, or else they had entered when we did. I smeared mosquito repellent on my face and shoulders and snuggled down into the hot sleeping bag, covering up as much of my body as I could. Either that did the trick, or it got too cold for the no-see-ums in the night, because I slept soundly. That is, except for the fact that I kept dreaming of frostbite, the thought of which probably occurred to me every time my forearm would burn and tingle as it came back to life after having gone numb from the way I slept on my shoulder. My arm did that every night, but maybe tonight its dream-inducing effects were amplified by the stinging no-see-ums and the remembrance of that freezing black muck Alaskans called a trail.

## JULY 4, DAY 26

"Happy Fourth of July and soon-to-be birthday!" Evelyn handed me a present. It was a printed sheet proclaiming 124 ways cucumbers are better than men, beginning with "A cucumber stays hard for a week, never gets mad if you complain of a headache, won't mind hiding in the refrigerator when your mother comes over," and ending with "will never make a scene because there are other cucumbers in the refrigerator, doesn't tell you it liked you better with long hair, and will never leave you for another woman, another man, or another cucumber . . . ."

Cook Jude absolutely outdid herself today, starting with cinnamon rolls for breakfast and ending with chicken enchiladas, complete with cheese sauce, for dinner. We were so content after the cinnamon rolls, the sky was so clear, and our campsite was so comfortable, that we decided to make it a layover day.

I crawled awhile on my stomach among the wet grasses and sand, taking pictures. Millions of glistening droplets of dew had transformed the low beach plants into a dazzling meadow that sparkled in the morning sun.

Evelyn dug up some wild onions for the lunch soup and washed them at the river's edge. As she went about her business, her entire body was clad in a protective layer against the mosquitoes. In her boots and baggy beige Gore-Tex pants and jacket, her garden gloves, and sun-visor hat—

over which she wore a big headnet that ballooned around her head—she looked like nothing so much as an astronaut. I rarely wore anything on my face or hands, and I didn't know why but the mosquitoes really didn't bother me as much as they seemed to irritate the others. The buggers didn't bite much, and I was fine if they would just stay out of my eyes and ears—which they did if I had on enough Muskol. The others had all given up taking their vitamin B1, but I continued taking my one tablet a day until the end of the trip. Perhaps it made my sweat smell a little funny (although that was hard to prove), but maybe it did indeed make me unattractive to mosquitoes as we'd heard it would. Sue and Evelyn wore their headnets a lot and were content enough. But even in a headnet, Jude had a rough time tolerating the beasts. All the way down the river, she would fidget and swear at the sight of what seemed to me only two or three mosquitoes in the air. Thankfully, the only times we had to deal with them were in camp; they rarely ventured onto the river.

Evelyn found several pools of water a few feet deep that had been stranded by the receding river, in which the silt had settled. They were also a few degrees warmer than the river. If you stood on a log and avoided stirring up the bottom sediment, she discovered, you could take a bath in clear water. Soon there were naked people and clotheslines all up and down the beach. We filled our water jugs with the clear water, boiling it in case the still pools harbored any unhealthy stuff. Almost all my various "waterproof" bags had failed in one way or another, so I spread out my gear to dry, including my entire stock of damp toilet paper. I scrubbed the caribou antlers in the river and set them in the sun to dry and air, but they still smelled a little strange, somewhat like a cross between a faraway dead dog and a faraway dead fish. Inside the water bottle in which I usually kept lemonade was growing a hefty coat of black mold, but neither the hot water and iodine tablets I put in the bottle nor the sand I shook around in it, removed the furry stuff very effectively. I decided to ignore it.

I strolled half a mile down the beach to my own little pool, waded in, took a bath, shaved my legs and washed my hair. Nary a mosquito stirred. It was all quite civilized and refreshing, the only detraction being that even in its small sun-heated pool, the water was still cold enough to sting my scalp. I washed my wool pants that still sported yesterday's dried muskeg goop, but by the time I swished them a little too vigorously and got the bottom silt all over them, it was debatable whether I'd gotten them cleaner or dirtier. Then I sat on the warm rocks, drying my hair and body in the sun.

I reflected on river life. As I'd hoped, we seemed to be gelling into a workable group. Decisions about lunch breaks and when to begin paddling each day seemed to be easier. Negotiations about when and where to camp each night were still a little wearisome but we were improving. Today, everyone seemed to be thoroughly content as she piddled and putzed with her equipment or read or played Scrabble. I was now so accustomed to Evelyn's one or two nocturnal visits to the nearest bush and her early-morning rising that I hardly awoke as she rustled to and fro. Evelyn and I had resolved our difficulty about trying to cook together by agreeing that when kitchen duty fell to our boat, we would take turns at handling both fire-tending and cooking solo. That meant that although we each worked hard on our own day, we could look forward to three whole days off afterward.

And Evelyn and I were becoming quite a team at outfoxing the mosquitoes into the tent. We would crouch together at the doorway. "Ready, go!" someone would say, and we'd each unzip one half of the screen door. One of us would dive through the opening while the other held up the screen behind her, then the second would dive in and we'd both zip the screen in a race to see whose zipper would make it to the top first. Only a few dozen mosquitoes got in that way. As we would chat and prepare our individual nests for the night, we'd murder them. Against the light-orange tent fabric, in the bright midnight sun, they were easy to see. And they seemed a lot more slow-moving than those feisty devils I'd battled in the Everglades. The dumb things would always light on the screen or the ridge line, and if you were careful and slow about the slaughter you could move methodically through their ranks without tipping off their brethren to the carnage. Evelyn preferred a direct assault with the heel of her hand, while I found more challenge and enjoyment in giving them a quick squeeze between my thumb and the side of the first knuckle of my forefinger, then watching them tumble to earth as I made sound effects. The key to the whole process was to do it slowly enough so that we created no rush of air to warn them of impending doom, and thus the nightly massacre took on a surreal balletlike quality. If we missed a few it didn't matter much; they usually spent the night hanging along the ridge, sleeping, I guess.

My hands were now adapting pretty nicely. During the first few weeks we had relied on lotions and creams to reduce the pain of their rawness and dryness, but now the protective layer of black grime that had worked its way permanently into the tiny creases of my toughening skin seemed to do the trick. Some of the others' skin had split open entirely, though, necessitating band-aids and gloves.

My knee no longer felt like it would slide out of its socket, and I could kneel on it for short periods in the boat. However, each day it seemed to feel more and more arthritic and produced a dull, aching pain whenever I tried to move it after remaining in any one position too long. Occasionally, as I walked, it would hold my weight but would send a sharp pain through my leg, as if something weren't lined up quite right.

I spent the greater part of the day luxuriating on my sleeping pad on the warm rocks beside my little pool, gloriously alone. Hour after hour I lay there, talking into my tape recorder, napping, watching tiny ripples spread by the feet of insects skating across the surface of the water. Every now and then bubbles rose from the floor of the pool, for what reason I never knew. It occurred to me that a bear could come ambling out of the dense alder thicket a few yards away, and that the others back at camp couldn't even see me because of a little rise in the ground between us. Ah well, one has to take one's pools where one finds them . . . .

The blues and whites of the sky and the greens of the shoreline spruces and alders were reflected marvelously in the pool. The wide, friendly river rolled away as always. My mood was such that I found every rock and piece of dirt and mountain enchanting. "Oh God, how I'm stuck on it all," Robert Service had said, and I knew just what he meant.

The immediate river valley and most of what I saw now and would see for the next three days was protected as the Yukon-Charley Rivers National Preserve. We had finally paddled into the first of five areas along the Yukon that I had worked to preserve and that millions of citizens had convinced Congress to act on; it was damn good to be here.

I knew that somewhere through these hills courses the Charley River, one of the clearest float rivers in Alaska, the last major watershed in the upper Yukon not impacted by mining. Near the Charley live the United State's main population of Fannin, and also Dall, sheep. All of it is protected in the 1.7-million-acre Preserve. Here the rivers have cut into the earth to reveal the most complete, unbroken geologic record known in North America where, if one had a mind to, one could study the rocks from 700 million years ago right up to the Fourth of July, in the year of our Lord nineteen hundred and eighty-two. Lying on my back, examining the folds and textures and shapes of the clouds and the mountains, during hours of blissful silence broken only by an occasional gull's cry or raven's squawk or distant airplane buzz, I felt almost one with the land. It aroused in me much more admiration than had Admiralty Island that I'd seen from the ferry. The difference lay not in the land, of course, but in how I had met each. In a canoe or on foot, you intimately acquaint yourself with waters and lands—touching them, smelling them, sleeping with them. Seeing them only through the window of a cruise ship or an automobile, though pleasant enough, is like conversing with them by long-distance telephone. It just isn't the same.

I tried to imagine I was a lizard, enjoying the easy life, basking in the sun. Of course, when a lizard got tired of basking and became hungry, she'd have to go run down some food, which would be a bit of a hassle. But then again, she wouldn't have to cook it, she'd just eat it cold. We humans have to fix ours. But then again, we don't have to run down every meal bodily. No, we have an elaborate system of getting by, a culture that allows four middle-class gals from Texas to scrape enough money together to buy three months' worth of food ahead of time. Considering that lizards and most other animals live from meal to meal, what these human animals could come up with was amazing. I decided that while lizards had the right idea about spending a lot of time lying on rocks, probably thinking nothing in particular, my condition was preferable because I could both lie in the sun and do a number of other things.

I joined the others in the dining tent. Two or three dark blue rainstorms had moved across the horizon during the day, from various directions. Now one finally hit us. It was short-lived and more wind than rain, though, offering only a few moments of excitement. First, the wind rolled Sue's and Jude's dome tent a dozen yards down the beach until the weight of its internal gear anchored it. Then a gust caught a nylon tarp we'd hung on one side of the dining tent and nearly blew the dining tent down.

The others played cards; I repatched my tennis shoes where the entire side was disintegrating, stitched my waterproof backpack cover where its drawstring was ripping out, and sewed my daypack's shoulder strap back into its seam.

"Shhh! What's that?" Sue suddenly whispered, looking up from her cards. Something big crashed methodically through the alders toward us. Wide-eyed, we stared silently through the mesh of the dining tent for a moment, eager to see what moose or bear might emerge. Then, simultaneously, the four of us began talking loudly, each having decided independently that seeing a wild creature in camp might not do it or us much good. The crashing sound stopped for a moment, then receded into the distance. We looked at each other and grinned.

Several sets of canoeists paddled by during the day. We waved and they waved back, too far away to converse. It took but a moment from the time they came into view until they disappeared around yonder bend, a few miles downstream. We were a little disappointed to see them, having hoped we'd left behind most of the river tourists at Dawson or Eagle.

Our after-dinner Fourth of July celebration consisted of trumpet tunes ("Bossa Nova" to "Zorba the Greek"), Evelyn's dancing solo on the beach, and four-part (more or less) harmony of every Mitch Miller oldie-but-goody from "Irene" to "Sweet Violets." Amid much joking about perhaps becoming the first group to paddle fingerless down the Yukon, Sue initiated a firecracker-throwing contest between herself and Jude and Evelyn, to see who could hold onto hers long enough so that it exploded in the air instead of on the ground. The others finally shuffled off to bed, Sue wearing only a shirt because her jeans were too bear-baited with spilled food. I wallowed briefly in the mud at the river's edge to capture on film an irresistible liquid golden ball of evening sunlight that floated on the most amazing horizontal purple cloud.

## JULY 5, DAY 27

The river had gone down six inches or so, which meant we had to drag the overloaded boats a dozen feet across the rocky flats at the water's edge before they would float. But with four of us tugging each boat, it wasn't too bad. The drop in water level also meant that the rocks we'd cleared easily when we landed two days ago now loomed just under the surface. The water was so thick with milky silt that it offered absolutely no clue to what might lie virtually on the surface. Between that and the wind's kicking up waves a few inches high all across the river, it made for an interesting day's start.

Around the first bend, though, high riverbanks thick with willows and alders blocked most of the wind, and we paddled along energetically, I whispering notes into my tape recorder as I stroked down the Yukon.

A floating stick caught my eye because it seemed to be moving of its own power. But I was so convinced that I was just witnessing another river illusion that I didn't even open the ammo can to get the camera until the stick was virtually under the bow. Only then did I realize that it was a ground squirrel, of all things, swimming for its life a quarter of a mile from shore in the middle of the Yukon. By then it was out of reach. Evelyn hypothesized that it had gotten accidentally dumped into the river when a section of the bank had crumbled off. That happened a lot around here, judging by the many giant dollops of tree-covered earth we saw resting at the water's edge. Quite a few logs floated in the river with us, never posing any problem as long as we were going the same speed as they.

Once, we were thwarted and munching peanuts, commenting on the funny-looking logs floating together near the shore far across the river, when Jude grabbed the binoculars and announced that the two logs were a mother and a baby moose. They swam across the three-quarters of a mile width of the river, passing less than fifty yards in front of us. The mother kept the baby on her upstream side so it would press against her and she could perhaps help it swim. They reached the bank, took one quick look over their shoulders at us, then clattered over the rocky shore and disappeared into the alder thicket.

The Nation River, where we had thought to get some drinking water, appeared on the right before we expected it; we found ourselves far from shore and too lazy to ferry over, so we drifted on. Two well-established camps were in the area. As we floated past, a floatplane took off from one, roared up the Yukon and into the air, then banked over the Nation and circled back over us. We hollered "Beer!" and waved our paddles; the pilot waggled his wings. (We never did learn whether there's an international hand-signal meaning, "Drop me a beer.") By then we spotted a slough on the left which probably led to the abandoned town of Nation, but we were too lazy to paddle over to that, too. Our fascination with old cabins was waning, our propensity to drift in the sun, waxing. We nibbled Mexican cornbread and stared into the grey waters for any sign of a fish fin; the Indians at Eagle Village had said that the first king salmon of the year had just then passed Circle and were expected 150 or so miles upstream in Eagle in two weeks.

Evelyn and I paddled over to where a silver motorboat with a green stripe, used by Park Service and U.S. Fish and Wildlife Service personnel, was beached. We were welcomed by a sandy-haired man in his thirties, who was barefooted and wore shorts, a T-shirt, and a Park Service baseball hat. We stood on the beach chatting with him while he followed, through a telescope, the movements of his two co-workers. They were perched high up on a nearby cliff face, counting and banding peregrine falcon chicks. The summer before, twenty-six nesting pairs of the endangered peregrines had raised seventy chicks in this preserve, making it the site of one of the highest peregrine concentrations in North America (the other three are in Alaska, too). The two guys soon returned to our beach in their own motorboat. The one who'd done the banding was covered in a thick coating of fine chalky dust, but he commented that while he was banding the chicks, the mother peregrine hadn't clawed him with her talons nearly as much as some of the other mothers had elsewhere. In their shorts and dust and mustaches, the guys seemed incredibly cute. But they had peregrines to band and we had a river to paddle, so we pushed on.

We caught up with Sue and Jude and slept and floated for a couple of hours among the massive bluffs that seemed to jump out of the river, until a sudden wind blew up. It churned the river into one-foot waves and whipped up whirlwinds of flying sand on the sandbars. The boats banged together and sent a spray of water splashing into our faces, so we unthwarted and tried to paddle against the freakish wind. Evelyn's cap blew off, and as we stopped paddling to cheer Jude on in retrieving it before it sank, a powerful gust of wind hit us broadside and tipped our boat a good forty-five degrees.

We paused at the mouth of Charley Creek and let the wind blow us upstream into its deep waters. The decaying vegetation on the creek bottom made the water appear a deep, awful brown, but when it entered our water jugs it was crystal clear. While Evelyn leaned over the side of the canoe and filled the jugs, I kept a wary eye on the high shoreline above us that had been severely undercut by the spring breakup. A twelve-foot-wide hunk of topsoil, complete with a spruce tree still growing from it, lay folded over the edge of the embankment, its supporting subsoil having been sloughed away. The twenty-foot tree, wavering slightly in the wind, arched over the creek at a forty-five degree angle a dozen feet above Evelyn's head.

Paddling back into the teeth of the wind, we aimed for a nearby island, but it turned out to be several miles away and already had somebody else's campfire smoke claiming it. So we pressed on. The slanted rays of the evening sun glistened golden on the water, the mountains and spruces ahead seemed hazy and blue in the distance, and I realized that I was relaxed and thoroughly enjoying myself despite the wind's whoofing in my ears and the waves' making my paddle feel worthless against the big Yukon.

Finally we grabbed a flat sandy island (again, few rocks!) in the shadow of monstrous Biederman Bluff, out of the wind. In the eight to twelve hours we had been on the river today, not more than two or three of which were spent paddling, we had come more than fifty miles. We congratulated ourselves and thanked the river. Then we devoured my homemade pizza, consisting of a whole-wheat and rice-flour crust topped by tomato sauce from tomato crystals, cheese sauce from cheese powder, rehydrated bell peppers and mushrooms, hot peppers, black pepper, thyme, and real garlic and onion. Not too shabby.

## JULY 6, DAY 28

The humming of eighty-seven mosquitoes on the tent screen greeted me on the morning of my twenty-ninth birthday. I spent an hour bringing what I considered a little organization to the hundred and fifty pounds or so of food we had in the pantry, categorizing our three big duffel bags into grains, everything else, and extras. The extras shared their bag with sacrificial things like alfalfa seeds, millet, and whole-kernel corn that we would just as soon give away or barter along the river. A fourth bag known as the spice sack held all our spices, odd dishes, and jerky or whatever else we might stick in it for lunch. Now I could rest easy at night knowing the kitchen was organized. Evelyn and Sue smiled and shook their heads as I prowled among the hundreds of baggies, muttering to myself.

We paddled around the first bend in the river and aimed for a clear side stream for drinking water, but Evelyn and I misjudged the river's speed, missed our ferry angle, and nearly washed into a salmon gill net stretched into the river. Though we'd planned only a quick stop, when we walked into the creek the sight of the clear gurgling stream caused us all to throw off our clothes and wash them and bathe in the icy water. We donned clean ones, hung the wet ones on the caribou antlers or lawn chairs or whatever was handy on top of the boats, and paddled on.

As always, it was a delight to be in the bow, free from much responsibility to steer. There was virtually no likelihood we'd run into anything out in the river, so I could stare off into space or even close my eyes as I paddled. I spread the sheet music to "Ol' Man River" in the bow before me and memorized its verses, singing them over and over and paddling in time. Far ahead, the mystical silhouette of Sue's and Jude's canoe eased across the Yukon's glassy surface toward pale blue mountains. An unbroken band of spruces stretched along the shore like a lone green finger pointing the way to whatever adventures lay around the next bend. The mountains had dropped back from the river's edge; the valley seemed wider, the sky bigger than ever.

Not a breath of air stirred and the sun beat down with a vengeance. The river's bends were so far apart that we seemed to be going nowhere until we looked to the side and saw the spruces blurring past, as ever. We thwarted and slept and read and journalized. Sue commented on what an utterly benign place the Yukon seemed to be. Jude lay on her back on the gear and sunbathed, shirtless. Three jets flew over in formation high above us. After some debate, we concluded that the loud pops we'd been hearing were neither the locals shooting at us again, nor a bear splashing for salmon, nor salmon leaping up and splatting upon the surface of the water, but big clods of dirt falling into the water from the undercut banks.

After a marvelous birthday lunch of cold pinto beans flavored with dehydrated barbeque sauce, cooks Sue and Jude unveiled a beautiful banana nut cake (how did they know that was my traditional and very favorite birthday cake?) made from dehydrated banana powder and topped with pecans. Like everything else, it had been baked in the trusty covered skillet. And like everything else, it had turned out fine without our having sifted or measured a single ingredient. They placed it on their drying laundry in the middle of the boat, stuck an inch-thick pink candle into its middle, and sang a rousing chorus of "Happy Birthday." I'd never had a birthday party in such grand surroundings, let alone a birthday cake served by a topless woman in a canoe in the middle of a mile-wide river; I was quite sure I'd remember this day.

We got dressed and peed quickly over the side of the canoe as we came upon the cabin where the Park Service couple lived. Colette Daigle-Berg and her husband, Bill Berg, met us with a smile and a wave as we trudged up the road with a skilletful of leftover birthday cake. They were about my age and were the first rangers to reside in the Preserve; they had arrived a week ago. They wore the crisp grey shirts and long green pants of the Park Service uniform, which they explained they were supposed to wear even in heat like today's. They lived sort of in the old two-story cabin and sort of in their little domed backpacker's tent in the yard.

Charley Kidd also lived in the cabin, although he was not connected with the Park Service. A long black beard hung from his face. A marten-skin sweatband held back his shoulder-length hair. A dirty blue T-shirt and jeans draped loosely from his lean frame. He wore jogging shoes. His front tooth was missing. He seemed to be about thirty years old, but it was hard to tell. Charley had just caught the first king salmon of the year in his gill net, and some strips of it now smoked on a grill above a fire that he poked with a stick. The flesh stood out fiery red against the blackened exterior of the ancient tea pot beside it. Grey smoke rose through and around the glistening strips, and we drooled as we photographed them.

Soon the salmon was properly smoked and Charley handed us each a huge piece that we ate with our hands. "Not too shabby," Sue smiled. Charley seemed much more impressed, though, with the hunk of birthday cake that he ate in one gulp than with a fillet of king salmon that would have sold for $15.95 in a Dallas restaurant. He lived mostly on king salmon (eating it fresh in the summer, dried in the winter) and the meat of wild animals, with peanut butter and rice as a backup if the fishing or the hunting was bad. Each of Charley's three sled dogs would consume between 150 and 250 pounds of dried chum, or "dog," salmon this year. Charley trapped in the winter and fished in the summer. Once a year, he explained, he paddled his canoe sixty miles downriver to Circle City to sell his furs and buy supplies. Then he would walk back along the bank to his cabin, pulling his canoe on a rope behind him. Each trip destroyed one pair of running shoes. Charley didn't believe in motors.

Charley stood up from the fire and went inside the cabin, an old wooden structure whose floorboards creaked and were rotted out in a place or two. In the shadow beneath its high eaves, the gaping mouths of baby cliff swallows stretched from the entrances of their mud nests. With a big knife, Charley sliced more flesh from the sixty-pound salmon that lay on a newspaper on a wooden table. Upstairs stood a big double bedstead of birch logs. On its mattress of young saplings lay a big, black garbage bag full of the rangers' belongings. Charley would tell us only that he was originally from Pennsylvania when we gingerly inquired into his background and how he came to be a trapper on the Yukon. We conjured up various fantasies that he was a well-to-do professor's son who'd rebelled against academe. He was obviously educated. He showed us his stack of National Geographics in the corner, and he expounded on various nutritional theories to which he adhered. He had lived here eight years, having worked initially at a gold mine up a nearby creek, where seventeen miners were now employed. He said food and luxuries come up the river by barge and then are trucked into the mining camp along the road that runs next to this cabin. The miners, he said, live in trailer houses with electricity. He said he preferred trapping and fishing.

I asked Charley what he thought about the designation of this area as a Preserve.

"Well, I don't like the government tellin' me what to do," he said, shaking his head and looking out of the window over the river. "But, if that's the only way to keep the mines and the roads outa here so there'll be some fish and some game left in this country, then I'm for it." From the high bank we saw, hanging thick in the valley, white smoke from a far-off forest fire.

Jude returned from our barter bag with a pound of Spanish peanuts for the rangers and a pound for Charley, who grinned a wide, toothless grin. Evelyn picked a few handfuls of wild lamb's-quarters from the clearing behind the cabin where they grew thigh-high, then slid into the skillet the quarter of a salmon that Charley had wrapped up in newspaper and insisted we take. We waved goodbye and pushed into the river.

I was awakened a few hours later by a man's voice. "Looks like you've got the right idea," hollered a solo paddler in a green Coleman canoe, referring to our nearly comatose method of making our way down the Yukon. We waved him over, stuck a bungy cord under his thwart, and floated with him for an hour or so. His name was Bing Ahlering. He was in his mid-thirties, with light sun-bleached hair that fell in his eyes, a scraggly month's growth of blond beard, and a deep tan. His eyes were a pale, piercing blue. He was wearing a pair of old, maroon polyester slacks, rolled up over the knee like shorts, and no shirt. For some reason I found fascinating his thick, hairy calves and his large, bare feet, whose toes wiggled a lot and which had spent some time in mud recently. His wide, tan shoulders and the wisp of short blond hair that crept down along the centerline of his tummy were pretty interesting, too. When you've seen nothing but female shapes for a month, you begin to look with new amazement at how men are built. Bing had hiked over the Chilkoot Trail in the snow in late May or early June, where he'd met up with a young German guy. They had paddled the headwaters lakes of the Yukon together as far as Dawson, when the German had to leave, and Bing had continued on alone, apparently making pretty good time with the two paddles lashed together kayak-style. He and the German had just put into Lake Bennett to begin their canoe trip when we had seen them from the window of the train the day we chugged over the Pass into Whitehorse; now here we were, more than 700 miles downstream, thwarting together.

Bing sipped water occasionally from a child's plastic sand bucket that he kept under his seat. He would dip it into the Yukon's murky waters and let the silt settle, drinking it without putting purification tablets in it. He kept a big windup alarm clock on the floor of the canoe in front of him. Its time bore no relationship to reality, though; he simply set it at whatever time ("Bing Time," he called it) he felt like each day when he got ready to paddle, then he would paddle until it said he'd paddled six hours, then he'd drift or pull out to camp. He also had a video camera mounted on a tripod sitting in the middle of his canoe and covered with a big plastic dropcloth like you buy in a hardware store. He seemed more mysterious and more entertaining by the minute, especially when he doggedly sidestepped the issue of what he did for a living. He said he was from Florida, more or less. He looked like a pretty rough character and spoke with a "dis, dat, dese, dose" street-fighter kind of accent, yet he smiled and talked of the thrill of seeing a moose up close. He knew at a glance all the birds that flew over, yet he had no binoculars. He had an expensive video camera, yet his 35-millimeter still camera had only one standard lens. About ten years ago he had paddled down the Mackenzie River across Canada (North America's second-longest river system), pulled his canoe up the rushing waters of the Rat River, portaged over the divide to the Porcupine River, and floated down it to Fort Yukon, following a century-old voyageur route of a couple of thousand miles. All that notwithstanding, he was a very unassuming, easygoing guy.

"You guys goin' to the Bering?" he asked, looking at the red lettering on our canoe. "Me, too."

He was the first canoeist we'd met who intended to paddle the whole river. Like us, he hadn't quite figured out yet how he'd get to wherever he was going next after he got to the Bering Sea, or what he would do with his boat, but like us, he'd worry about that when he got down there. We liked his style, and we sat grinning at him, sizing him up. He was probably doing the same to us. Probably the last thing he thought he'd run into today was four women from Texas who said they were going to paddle to the Bering Sea.

He smiled and said, "Well, what are you ladies gonna do for an encore next summer?"

"The Amazon!" I piped up, mostly joking.

"Hey, I've been wanting to do that," he nodded. I didn't know who was more surprised, him or me. And he was telling the truth, for he had done enough reading to rattle off some of the statistics of the world's greatest river system that flows through the world's greatest rain forest. He knew it was close to 4,000 miles long, was capable of handling oceangoing ships 2,000 miles inland, and was 30 miles wide for its last few hundred miles. And I had done enough reading about the Amazon to know he was right. I was amazed, impressed, and in love.

We pulled out to camp, and in a gentlemanly way he said he'd see us downstream somewhere tomorrow. "Stop by for coffee if you like; I'm in a khaki-colored tent," he said. "And feel free to wake me up if you don't see me moving around yet." He paddled away with a slightly bemused look when Evelyn said we'd wake him up with a trumpet reveille.

My birthday supper was grilled salmon, macaroni, corn, and a salad of fresh lamb's-quarters, sunflower seeds, and alfalfa sprouts, covered with lemon juice. I played my trumpet for as long as I could until my lip gave out; echoing across the river went the notes of everything from "If I Were a Rich Man" to "If My Friends Could See Me Now" to "Summertime" to "Saint Louis Blues." The day had been so wonderful, the people we'd met so gentle and full of life, and the sunset was so beautiful, I wanted to play my horn all night.

From the heights of Takoma Bluff, a thousand feet above the Yukon, a dark line of jagged spruces swooped down into the river. Beyond, across the river, rose a vertical wall of purple velvet mountains, hazy in the evening cast of the light. And beyond that hung the gigantic, golden, mellow ball of the sun. Through it all, this Old Man River, who must have known somethin' but didn't say nothin', just kept rolling along.

## JULY 7, DAY 29

"Where's Sue?" I asked casually as we lingered over a breakfast of salmon croquettes. Jude jerked her thumb downstream to where Sue was running her second lap down the beach. She'd finally decided that if we couldn't hike, she'd get some exercise one way or another. And Lord knows it hadn't really crossed our minds to paddle.

On the river, around the first bend stood a little khaki-colored tent, from within which came a surprised voice that expressed its appreciation at having been awakened by a trumpet reveille and a few strains of "The Eyes of Texas Are Upon You." As we drifted past, the tent said it would probably see us tonight in Circle City. We spent most of the day drifting, making up various wild answers to the riddle about who Bing really was and what he really did for a living. He was a professional photographer (maybe even the film producer I'd talked to before the trip, who was from Florida) who was secretly going to film the Texas Women's Yukon River Expedition; that had to be it. Why else would anyone canoe with a thousand-dollar video camera in his boat? No, he was on the lam from the law; maybe he was a drug-runner. Why else would he live in Miami? No, he must have been an alcoholic recovering from a long skid. He had said he'd take a Coke instead when we said we'd buy him a beer when we reached Circle, hadn't he? We amused ourselves this way for hours, making bets on whose theory would turn out to be right.

Once, I looked up from my journal and saw an amazing sight. A massive dump of unmelted ice and snow a hundred yards long and twenty feet high sprawled high and dry on a sandbar, pretty as you please, protected from the sun until mid-summer and who-knows-how-much-longer by a thick coating of mud.

Now that the vanguard of the king salmon run had made its way 1,300 miles up the Yukon to this point, we began to pass our first operating fish wheels. The curious-looking things creaked and groaned against the current as we paddled past. The fish wheel was invented by some white man, but for decades it has been the cornerstone of the Yukon Indians' subsistence way of life. Two giant wooden baskets are fashioned by hand and placed around an axlelike platform that reaches a dozen yards out into the river from the bank. Rotated by the power of the current, the baskets scoop up the salmon as they swim upstream and drop them into a big wooden box. During a mediocre salmon season, as this one would turn out to be in the Interior, one or two big salmon will end up in the box each day. The owner of the fish wheel simply goes out to the wheel a time or two each day, hefts the salmon out of the box, and brings them home. During a really good salmon run, though, the men (usually) must empty the box many times a day lest it overflow with salmon, and the women (usually) can barely manage to clean and cut the salmon for drying before the next batch arrives.

A vast blue rainstorm was chasing us down the Yukon, so we paddled hard the last few miles toward Circle, trying to beat it to shelter. We began to run aground on the shallow flats in the side slough that harbored the old gold-rush town, just as the first sprinkles started to riddle the water's surface. As we pulled into Circle's high sloping bank and makeshift camp-ground, who should be standing there next to his yellow canoe but David Gile, whom we hadn't seen since Lake Laberge, almost a month ago and almost 700 miles upriver!

"The bar opens in fifteen minutes!" he shouted as the rain began to pour. He pointed across Circle's only street to a long rectangular log building. On the door hung a red cardboard sign that said "Midnight Sun Saloon."

## JULY 7-9, DAYS 29-31

And that was where it all began. Though we had planned to visit Circle only long enough to check for mail, escape the rain, eat a restaurant meal if one could be had, and drink a beer, we still found ourselves there three days and as many hangovers later. The Midnight Sun Saloon and Cafe turned out to be the beginning, the end, and the essence of the little community that nestles in this obscure slough off the Yukon, and it had the same effect on us as that salmon stream where we'd planned to stop only for drinking water and had ended up taking a whole bath. Once you wade in, you might as well get on down!

Among my fond memories of wild, woolly Circle City:

The four Texas women sat around a small wooden table on a Wednesday night, drinking beer. I was wedged between Bing and David, enjoying looking at beards and trying to decide whom to be in love with most. The only reason we'd caught up with David in Circle was that he had been camped here for five days waiting for some topographical maps from Fairbanks or Anchorage or someplace. He'd started his trip with maps only for the Canadian stretch, planning to pick up the U.S. ones en route. But none were to be found along the river. Bing, on the other hand, had paddled the first 700 miles of the river with nothing more detailed than a highway map, and he intended to paddle the rest of the river that way. David was a tax accountant who had a habit of taking three-month leaves of absence. Once he had hitchhiked and backpacked across Canada. Last week he had celebrated his thirty-third birthday, so with the excuse of his and my recent birthdays, we began to order round after round of beer. David and Bing told us about all the wildlife—sandhill cranes, bears, foxes—they'd seen that we hadn't. David had panned for gold, caught lots of fish, hiked up into the countryside. Bing had met old trappers who'd invited him into their cabins. There seemed to be all sorts of advantages to being a lone paddler who didn't make as much noise as the four of us and who didn't spend so much time sleeping in the boats.

But we soon learned that there were advantages to being a foursome, especially if you were all women. When we floated into town, we were like an instant, movable party, and we were like nothing the locals had ever seen. Circle is kind of a hub of transportation in this part of the world, being at the end of the Steese Highway that goes to Fairbanks, and having an airstrip. It was full of men who were here on business, flying back and forth in airplanes surveying this and that for oil companies or Native corporations or whatnot. And sooner or later each one found his way into the bar. The only other women in the bar tonight were a few young girls with a church group that had rolled into town in two big vans, and they weren't much competition. Some guys were drinking and joking at the next table. They were obviously not from the river—they seemed so *clean*—and at first there lay between us a slight gulf of shyness.

But Jude broke the ice when she laid her fanny pack on the bar, pulled out her wallet, and told the bartender, "The ladies from Texas would like to buy the gentlemen from Alaska a round of whatever they're drinking."

So Joe and Sandy joined David and Bing and the four of us. We got rowdier and rowdier until at last Sue was asking Sandy if she could fondle his beard. "Only if the rest of us can!" we chimed.

Sandy was thirtyish, tall and thin, with medium-length blond hair and a large, curly, soft, reddish-blond beard. He had sparkling blue eyes and an ever-present grin. He beamed and said how much he loved Alaska, how great it was that the four of us had come up here to float the river, and how proud he was that his state could offer people this kind of experience. He was originally from the Lower 48 and had lived in Alaska a half-dozen years or so. He and Joe were land surveyors, and he said there was so much work to be done that he never had time to take long vacations. They were based elsewhere in Alaska, and they spent most of their time flying to all corners of the state.

More riffraff like us poured into the bar from the river, and it became apparent that the Yukon attracted quite a cosmopolitan crowd. Four long-haired Germans with scruffy beards, wearing ancient, baggy clothes and big boots, paddled up in two odd-looking, inflatable, orange canoes; they took a table in the corner of the bar beneath the TV set. A thin, wiry Canadian and a stocky one paddled up in one canoe, with an Irish setter and a big, golden dog. The thin one had a droopy mustache and a furrowed brow and looked a little like a heroin addict going cold turkey. The story we'd heard was that one of them had gotten arrested in Dawson and hauled away to the Whitehorse jail. The other one had gotten tired of waiting and finally sold his partner's clothing and equipment and headed downriver, missing his partner's return by only a few days as it turned out. When the second one got back into Dawson, he stole a canoe and also headed downriver. When he caught up with the first, they hid the stolen canoe in the bushes and continued on their way together, in their original canoe with their two dogs. We hoped they wouldn't go very far downriver; we didn't like having them around. They looked as if they might just steal all your food and, like everyone else, they had an arsenal of guns in their possession. But thankfully, they seemed to spend most of their time sitting on sandbars altering their consciousness by various methods. We figured at that rate it would take them two years to get to the Bering Sea.

"Hey, there's something weird coming down the river," somebody said, as he walked into the bar. What else was new, I thought. The bar crowd emptied out into the street and across the campground and we all stood on the bank, speculating on what the odd thing could be that had just rounded the bend. It looked exactly like a large pile of manure being paddled by two shovels, and it continued to appear so, even when viewed through binoculars, until it came within shouting distance of the bank. A bunch of logs was tied onto some huge half-inflated inner tubes, and on top of it all, two male forms were frantically stroking the Yukon with squares of plywood nailed onto two-by-fours. The whole town cheered and laughed and hollered advice as the current swept them right past us, even as they tried most valiantly to guide their bizarre craft to the shore. A half-mile below town, one of them leapt into the river with a rope and began swimming hard toward the shore. That brought a new roar of laughter from the crowd here on shore, for when the raft drifted far enough to tighten the slack in the rope, instead of the swimmer's pulling the raft to shore, the raft was simply pulling the swimmer down the Yukon. Amazingly, he somehow reached solid ground and appeared to be pulling the raft in for a landing.

Back in the bar, we smiled and ordered another round, knowing we'd meet the two Huckleberry Finns soon enough when they would undoubtedly come to the bar. An hour later two young, curly-haired, scraggly-bearded Germans—one of whom was soaking wet—wandered in with big grins on their faces. We bought them a drink and helped them celebrate their successful adventure. They were in the process of hitchhiking around Canada and the United States for a few months before they would start college in Germany in the fall. They had ended up in Eagle and had gotten the notion to build a raft and float 150 miles down the Yukon to Circle. They had never built a raft, had never been on a river, but they thought it'd be a fun thing to try. So they'd cut some logs and nailed them together. They found a couple of inner tubes on the beach which they stuck on for good measure. The paddles were an afterthought. They had launched forth, their packs tied in front; they even had a little bench about six inches above the level of the raft. Once the whole thing became waterlogged, the little bench was all that floated above water. The whole raft was about six feet square. Things had worked out pretty well, though, and they had made it from Eagle to here almost as fast as we had. The only problem, they grinned, was that they had to float throughout one night because they couldn't get the thing to shore.

At midnight on a Thursday night in the Midnight Sun Saloon, the shades were drawn against the sun. Bing, drinking his Coke, was buying rounds for the rest of us. The shots of peppermint schnapps chased with Olympia beer were going down smoother and smoother. Sue and Jude and Sandy had already called it a night; we were all still a little hung over from last night's celebration. David had received his maps and headed on downriver today. Dale, the stocky bartender with a black beard and curly, thinning black hair, finally got tired of bringing the bottle over to our table and just left it there, telling us to figure out later how much we owed him. Dale's tape deck was blaring Willie Nelson music in honor of the Texas women. He also had plenty of jazz and hard-rock cassettes behind the bar. Dale had been a professional river guide in California, rowing rubber rafts through the big whitewater of the West, but since he'd come to Alaska he hadn't found time to paddle rivers. Though he lived on the bank of the Yukon, he'd never floated any part of it. He lived in a plywood shack behind the bar. He worked pretty hard in the summers; tonight, between the tourists who'd driven in, the dozens of surveyors who'd flown in, the canoeists who'd floated in, and the locals who were here to begin with, he was kept busy mixing drink after drink and slamming beer after cold beer onto the bar. But in the winter, when the road was closed and the canoeists were gone, he opened the bar only two or three nights a week. In between, during the long dark days when the sun came up for but a few hours around noon, he would read and listen to his jazz tapes.

After his third schnapps and his third beer, Burt—the cook from the Midnight Sun Cafe next door, whose night off it was—burst from his chair and gave in to Evelyn's demands that he dance with her. And dance they did, nonstop, for the next two hours, while Bing and I laughed and applauded their antics. They frolicked in the available space among the tables, starting out with the Bump, moving into what Evelyn called "Ragu" dancing when Dale's steel-drum music began, on into a punk-rock dance called the Pogo, where you stand in one place and jump up and down for as long as you can, and winding up with a two-person bunny hop. Evelyn was wearing dirty white baggy shorts, canvas boots with black socks, a blue sweat-covered T-shirt advertising a Dallas bar, and hair she hadn't combed in three days. Burt was wearing red running shorts, shower thongs, and a maroon stretch pullover that accentuated his roly-poly figure. He had short dark hair that he greased lightly, and he was in his mid-thirties. Even with the front door open, the bar was hot; it made Bing and me sweat just to watch Burt and Evelyn swing madly around the room, scream with laughter, and fall into a table every now and then. Eventually, Burt carried a glass of icewater with him onto the dance floor, and at intervals he poured it over his own head or Evelyn's. Through it all, the local Indians and whites hunkered over their beers at the bar, taking little notice.

Burt's family—brothers, cousins, sisters, mother, and even grandmother who almost took us up on our offer to let her float down the river with us—all came from Kansas or thereabouts every summer to run the cafe and the trading post and the liquor store and the post office, which were all housed under one roof and pretty well summed up the total commerce of Circle. That is, except for the airstrip and the flying service, which they also ran.

Bing refused to dance even when dragged to his feet by the three of us. I tried dancing with one of the young Indian men, but that didn't work out too well because he was so drunk he kept falling into the wall. At 2 A.M., when Dale put on a tape of thirty-nine minutes of nonstop Beatles music, including all the oldies like "I Wanna Hold Your Hand," I could stand it no longer and went after Sandy. I marched outside and over to the long house trailer divided into motel rooms, beyond which the sun had gone down a few minutes ago and beyond which the sun was now rising. The first thing Sandy remembered upon awakening, he said later, was that he was halfway across the street, walking toward the bar with a cold beer in his hand, wondering how and why he'd gotten there. "Just dance!" I said, grabbing his hands and swinging him around the room. He did, joyously. He'd already gotten drunk once with us tonight and had gone home an hour ago to sleep it off, but he was always game for a party, and this one showed signs of continuing forever. For hours Burt and Evelyn and Sandy and I stomped and laughed and sang and banged into each other, stopping only to catch our breath between songs at the table where Bing happily kept our glasses full.

By 4 A.M., it was so unbearably hot in the bar that we danced out into the street and across the campground, shivering now in the cold air, swatting mosquitoes in time to the music, which we could hear clearly a block away. I decided that the only fitting way to end a night on the town was to go skinny-dipping in the Yukon, so Burt and Sandy and I threw off our clothes and plunged in. Burt somersaulted and Pogoed and cavorted like a great white whale, I sang thë entire version of "Faded Love" by Bob Wills and the Texas Playboys, and Sandy splashed and backstroked in a big circle talking about how great it was to be in Alaska. Evelyn stood on the beach shaking her head to our pleadings that she join us, her hands moving in a steady swatting motion against the mosquitoes that covered her bare legs and face and arms, and mumbled about hypothermia.

"Glory, glory, hallelujah!" Sue sang at the top of her voice, thumping the rope of a big washtub bass.

"Glory, glory, hallelujah!" Evelyn held her eyes to the wooden rafters and shook her black locks, banging a tambourine against her hip in a methodical, Salvation-Army rhythm.

Jude clanked two serving spoons against her thigh in rhythm, I blared my trumpet, Bing stroked a washboard, and Wendy the waitress from someplace like New Jersey played the kazoo and swayed to the music. It was a Friday night in the bar at the tiny hamlet of Circle Hot Springs, an hour by gravel road away from the Yukon and the town of Circle, and we were building up to the big finale of our "religious" set which had included everything from "Bringing in the Sheaves" to "Drop-Kick Me, Jesus, Through the Goal-Posts of Life." Burt slumped in a chair in the corner, resting his head on his chin and trying to forget his hangover. Sandy and Joe played pool; Sandy grinned and held up a beer after each song, but Joe was still a little miffed that he'd lost the first game to me by scratching on the eight-ball. Across the room, a couple of dozen locals and tourists ate pizza or hamburgers and looked askance every now and then at the unknown musicians who were making obnoxious fools of themselves. Above the pizza pickup window was a framed black-and-white photograph of two black bears which, upon inspection, revealed that they were copulating. The male bear, who stood more or less erect, was looking straight at the camera with an expression that, for all the world, said, "Well, what are *you* looking at!"

Today, Burt had driven us in a pickup truck two hours down the road to Eagle Summit, where we'd climbed among the wildflowers and mosses of the high rolling tundra, then we'd come here to swim in the luxurious warm waters of the hot springs in an Olympic-sized swimming pool. En route we'd run into an acquaintance of Burt's at a gas station. From the inside corner of her eye down to her chin ran a pink gash of scar tissue. More scar tissue covered her neck and arms. She and Burt chatted as he filled the truck with gas; we munched doughnuts and stared.

"Is that a bear-tooth necklace you're wearing?" asked Burt, pointing to the line of inch-long objects hanging from her neck.

"Yeah," she smiled, "but not the same one." She and her husband and a friend had been partying at their fish camp a few years ago, so the story goes, and shortly after they'd collapsed from their evening's merriment, a grizzly had come into camp. She and her husband were sleeping on the ground outside, the friend was in a tent; all three were dragged around, clawed, and chewed on by the bear. All three lived. She and her husband still live here, but they don't visit their fish camp much anymore.

At midnight we left the bar to head back to Circle. We had to double up on the small seat in the open back of the pickup. The warmth of Sandy's body as I sat on his lap with his arms around me seemed to be the only thing keeping me from freezing to death through the damp fog and rain and wind. An hour later, back in Circle, Evelyn and Bing and Sandy and I propelled our stiff, frozen bodies into Dale's bar to warm up with coffee. The longer I sat there talking to Sandy about his work, and the longer I looked into his smiling blue eyes, the more interested I became in exactly what it is that surveyors do with all those lines and flags and poles and boxes and things they carry through the woods. So about 3 A.M. we went over to the motel room he used as a temporary office and I learned a great deal about his instruments.

# 8 encounters pleasant and painful in the yukon flats

**JULY 10, DAY 32**

About noon, after one more giant breakfast buffet at the cafe and almost three full days after we'd stopped in Circle just to get out of the rain for a few minutes, we finally hugged Grandma and Dale and Burt and Sandy goodbye and pointed our weary bones down the Yukon once again. Fresh in our minds were the memories of three days of restaurant meals and hot showers. We were sorely tempted to continue carousing, but our bodies and our pocketbooks couldn't take any more. This river life was really rough. It seemed that the greatest obstacle to paddling the Yukon River all the way to the Bering Sea was not Five Finger Rapids, nor the mosquitoes, nor the grizzlies, but Circle City: if a paddler could just drag herself away from that Midnight Sun Saloon back onto the river, she'd be home free.

Thus we left the little village which had been the site of a big gold strike that brought 1,000 characters here between 1894 and 1896. At the time, it was said to be the biggest log city in the world. As in Fortymile, Jack McQuesten had a trading post here, too, with the town's thermometer: four liquid-filled vials in a rack. The mercury one froze at -38.4° F., the unwatered rye whiskey at -55°, the kerosene at -63°, and Perry Davis's Painkiller at -70°. As a dog musher prepared to leave town, he'd glance at the vial-filled rack. One driver said, "A man . . . started with a smile at frozen quicksilver, still went at whiskey, hesitated at the kerosene, and dived back into his cabin when the Painkiller lay down," (*The Yukon*, page 127) The miners had named their bustling burg, where every tenth house was said to be a gambling hall or saloon, after the Arctic Circle within which they mistakenly thought it squatted. But that invisible gateway to the land of frozen mystery actually lay fifty miles north, where we were headed.

David had paddled on after our first night in Circle, eager to hit the river after five days of awaiting maps. Little did we know then that it would be more than a thousand miles downstream before we'd see him again, or that we'd have so many strange tales to tell when we did. Bing was still in camp in Circle when we left and said he'd see us downriver. The four of us drifted, thwarted once again. Exhausted after three straight days of carousing in Circle, I spent the day lolling in the boat. My sole exertion was when I had to do a little wading to get the boat off some rocks at the head of a sandbar that we'd run into because we'd been too lazy to unthwart and ferry over into the main current. When we set up camp I was still so tired I went to bed without supper.

## JULY 11, DAY 33

So this was the Yukon Flats, a sprawling wetland empire 250 miles long and 80 miles wide, through the middle of which the Yukon makes its final lunge for the North Pole. The mighty river gets a fingertip just inside the Arctic Circle, then falls away in a grand sweeping curve to strut a thousand miles to the sea. Every summer the Flats becomes delivery room and nursery for two million baby waterfowl whose parents have flown from four continents to raise their young among its rich mixture of sandbars, 40,000 lakes, and 25,000 miles of streams, oxbows, and potholes. The Flats is said to be the largest and most productive solar basin anywhere in the Arctic. When the intense rays of the Arctic summer sun beat down upon its marshes and bogs almost twenty-four hours a day, this giant shallow pan rimmed by mountains produces an abundant plant crop to feed the hungry youngsters. In winter it hosts some of the 100,000 caribou of the Porcupine herd—the largest, healthiest, most viable herd left in the United States—as they await their annual spring migration to Alaska's Arctic Slope to give birth to their calves. The Flats also abounds in lynx, marten, otter, mink, and beaver. Native villagers who lived here depend substantially on the Flats' bountiful wildlife. And bird-lovers and waterfowl hunters throughout the Lower 48 can thank these and Alaska's other breeding grounds for millions of the geese and sandhill cranes and ducks who fill the autumn air with their high-pitched honking.

I was proud to have played a small part in helping protect 8.6 million acres of this marvelous natural Eden that straddles the Arctic Circle. But I felt just a tinge of sadness knowing that when the smoke had finally cleared from the Alaska lands battle in Congress, a great southern lobe of about 600,000 acres had been lobbed off the newly-created Yukon Flats National Wildlife Refuge and given to the State of Alaska for agriculture, land sales, and any other development the State might wish. Overall, however, the Flats Refuge, like the rest of the new Alaska lands act units, is largely whole. And thanks to the Act, the infamous Ramparts Dam proposal of the late 1950s and early 1960s is no more. The dam, conjured up by the U.S. Army Corps of Engineers in one of their wilder schemes to conquer Nature, would have drowned this entire miraculous basin under a lake the size of Erie. In addition to the deterrent of the Refuge, villagers in the Flats have selected millions of acres nearby for their subsistence needs under the Alaska Native Claims Settlement Act, and it is now highly unlikely that Congress would ever agree to flood both those Native village subsistence lands and the Refuge itself.

Looking at a map of the Flats is a little scary for a canoeist, for the blues of its watery maze are almost as numerous as the greens, meaning solid ground. It has large white patches with little drawings meaning "marsh." The Yukon's sloughs and countless islands and channels writhe across the sheet of paper in an intertwining jumble; place names like "Crazy Slough," "Deadman Island," and "Purgatory" add to the foreboding it arouses. Together, it seems to offer the canoeist mostly thick clouds of mosquitoes, slow current, boring scenery, and the possibility of getting lost and paddling for hours or days up dead-end sloughs. Ever since Dawson, people had been telling us that the Flats was the pits.

Not so.

It turned out that the mosquitoes were no worse here than anywhere else, as far as I was concerned. For at least half of the distance through the Flats, the current seemed amazingly fast. All we had to do to avoid going into a dead-end slough was to feel the current and follow it. True, we had no idea where we were on the map for days at a time, but we knew we were in the current that would take us somewhere eventually, and that was all that mattered. As for scenery, the immediate river view was about the same as it had been for weeks: cutbanks, spruce trees, willows, and sandbars. It was rather unvarying, true, but unvaryingly pleasant. The only real difference was that when we lifted our eyes from the immediate shoreline at which we were gazing, we noticed that the mountains were missing.

But that was O.K. because it offered us incredible 360° sweeping vistas of the sky and three-hour standing-ovation sunset performances. One night as we sipped our tea, the sun was trying to set in one corner behind a cloudbank, producing streaks of green and red and purple and pink and orange and yellow that were reflected in the still water of a slough. In another quadrant, ominous low clouds were rolling down the river in a thick, foggy procession. And directly across the river were rising, inch by inch upward from the spruces, two ends of a rainbow that strained toward a full arc they never quite made. Their efforts were mirrored in the rushing grey waters of the Yukon. (I swear all this is true.) Meanwhile, the sun had grown redder and dropped behind the clouds which rained on it in misty purple streaks. Finally, the sun sneaked just behind the spruces and created a crimson glow that you'd swear was a forest fire raging across the earth. The sun crept among the spruces for an hour, its rosy glow a dead giveaway to its whereabouts as it moved along the river, then it popped into view again for a beautiful sunrise. All the while, it was light enough to carry on whatever camp putzing we might want to do. Night after night, I sat sipping tea and watching the glorious atmospheric carryings-on of the Flats.

Today we had our usual cracked-wheat gruel with brown sugar for breakfast. We were a little slow rousting ourselves out of the tents; it seemed too soon to wake up and we accused Evelyn of waking us up at

4 A.M. Since she was an early riser and dedicated to her morning coffee, we had designated her as our human alarm clock. Whenever we heard her bear bells tinkling around the island, we knew we had about an hour to get things rolling toward breakfast and packing up the boats. So throughout the rest of the trip, however long Evelyn slept, that was about how long the rest of us slept.

We thwarted most of the day, the only trouble being occasionally getting blown into a sandbar by the wind.

## JULY 12, DAY 34

I was beginning to resent the dining tent that we seemed to be erecting every night now that the ground was mostly flat and free of rocks, for the world seen through a light green mesh just wasn't the same as one seen in the open air. But with it Jude was much more at ease from the mosquitoes, so almost every night we put it up. We had an elaborate entry and exit routine designed to keep out as many mosquitoes as possible; it involved standing at the doorway with one's lawn chair and book and supper plate and tea mug and announcing "Prepared to enter!", whereupon a partner on the inside would unzip the six-foot doorway, pull you inside while flailing the air with a Shoo-Bug jacket, then zip the thing back with lightning speed. Once dinner was ready, all the pots of food and hot water were brought into the enclosure, so if you wanted second helpings of anything, or if you wanted to socialize within reasonable proximity to the others, you had to spend some time in the thing.

Jude and Evelyn believed that if we took the particular channel on which we were camped this morning we'd end up in a dead-water slough; Sue and I thought otherwise. So Evelyn and Jude grabbed ropes and took on the role of a Humphrey Bogart pulling Sue and me—playing Katharine Hepburn, and hollering "Onward, Humphrey!"—through the water upstream in an Arctic version of *The African Queen*. When we got to the upstream end of the island the current began to push us into the sloping gravel headland, so I finally hopped out to help. Then the current began to tug the boat away from us, as Evelyn and I both waded knee-deep. I leapt toward the boat to throw myself across the gear, mostly to be funny, but missed and ended up dragging through the water briefly, then crawling on hands and knees to shore. I was soaked from the chest down; the others waited silently as I sat in the boat at the water's edge and put on dry clothes.

After a few hours of thwarting, we stopped at a fish camp to ask some Indians how far we were from Fort Yukon, and they said about twenty miles. A mile later we passed some Indians in a motorboat and, out of curiosity, asked them the same question. "About nine miles," they said. Soon we saw a high radio tower on the horizon that meant Fort Yukon was at hand, so we broke out a beer Evelyn had stashed away and celebrated having crossed the Arctic Circle. If Fort Yukon was truly seventy-five miles or so from Circle as the maps seemed to suggest, we weren't doing too badly to have made it there in two short days and one long day of doing nothing but drifting. To our surprise, when we rounded the bend to the city, there was Bing, tiptoeing barefooted across a gravel bar to greet us.

We'd been warned in Eagle and Circle that Fort Yukon was a bad place, where the canoes and belongings of cheechakos were often stolen. We'd been told that whites were not very welcome in this village of more than 600 Indians. And yet, we knew it was a major air destination for tourists who wanted to go somewhere above the Arctic Circle. When Bing told us that he and the Canadians (with the two big dogs) had already been invited not to stay too long on the gravel bar across from town where they were camped, we decided to make Fort Yukon a mail-only stop and head quickly downriver.

While the others trudged the half-mile to the post office to retrieve our four large boxes of food, I sat at the water's edge, watching over the boats and dictating my journal into my tape recorder. From the high bank, a sled dog tied to a stake sat puzzling over what I could possibly be doing, and a small dark-haired Indian boy popped his head playfully over the bank whenever he thought I wasn't looking.

Later, eating a chiliburger in the cafe on the first floor of a rambling old two-story wooden hotel, I learned many things: a group of college-age men and women from Colorado had just finished floating the Porcupine River, where they'd run into an Austrian couple who'd once floated the Amazon. The couple was staying in the cabin of a one-armed man, with whom Bing had stayed and helped sod his roof ten years before when he'd floated the Porcupine. The money that Bing desperately needed and had been expecting was not waiting for him here at the post office. One of the Colorado women and Bing had attended the same high school in Cincinnati.

I now had only $700 of the $1400 with which I'd left Dallas. And the rip in the front of Evelyn's shirt was now two inches in diameter and revealing more and more of what lay beneath. Fortunately, the chamois shirt was almost exactly the same color as her skin.

One highlight of our stop in Fort Yukon was when one of the men from the tourist bus saw Jude loading her boat and asked if we by chance knew about that expedition of Texas women who were planning to float the whole Yukon all the way to the Bering Sea. "We're it," grinned Jude. He'd seen us on TV in Florida and couldn't wait to get back home to tell his wife he'd met us.

But a better surprise, which sent us into fits of ecstasy and mild homesickness, was when we opened a care package from the Dallas Downriver Club to find a big bag of tostado chips and a jar of picante sauce.

We paddled downriver for an hour or so and camped on, of course, a sandbar.

## JULY 13, DAY 35

Morning dawned cold and damp from the gentle rain that had pattered on our nylon roof throughout the night. A low sky of dimpled grey clouds reminded me of October camping in Texas. We sat silently during breakfast, watching Arctic terns throw themselves headlong into the Yukon from a height of twenty feet as they tried to catch their own breakfast.

Out on the river, we revolutionized our paddling routines. After being blown by the wind or through our own carelessness into shallows near sandbars several times during thwartation, we realized the system wasn't working, but we were unwilling to give up our accustomed naptimes. So we split up the boats and designated one paddler in each to keep watch while the others loafed. Evelyn and I pointed the stern downstream and she read *The Mad Trapper of Rat River* that Bing had loaned her; I perched high up on the bow deck with my feet propped on an ammo can, facing downstream, and steered while reading and memorizing the words to "Shenandoah." It was a thoroughly pleasant way to spend the day, and we found that we could carry on our various activities without bothering each other, absorbed in our individual pursuits as we drifted ever toward the sea.

Jude spotted something big disappearing into the willows on the first sandbar she scouted for a campsite, and there were too many bear prints for our liking, so we opted for another one downstream. Sometime during the day, if our chief map-readers Evelyn and Jude were anywhere near on target, we crossed the Arctic Circle again and headed back into the subarctic zone. We'd reached the northernmost point of our journey and had begun our long slide toward home. Away, you rolling river.

## JULY 14, DAY 36

We sweltered in the morning sun, glad to be in the dining tent away from a horde of inch-long horseflies (Canadians call 'em deer flies) that had invaded the camp. We were five for breakfast, because Bing had come paddling down the river late at night and had accepted our invitation to camp over. We were jealous, though, that he had left Fort Yukon a full twenty-four hours after we had and had already caught up, with only three hours' paddling and two hours' drifting, according to the clock in the bottom of his boat. When he joined us he blew Evelyn's half-joking theory that his true occupation was being a bodyguard; that he had been sent by our families to watch over us on the river, but had dropped us like a hot potato when their second payment hadn't arrived in Fort Yukon.

We spent most of the day using the new one-on, one-off method, paddling beneath a glorious clear sky across glassy blue water. Much of the time I paddled shirtless. In his shy way, Bing was careful to paddle ahead where he couldn't see me. I hoped he wasn't offended, but I wasn't about to deprive myself of anything just because a man was around. Paddling shirtless also marked the first time I had broken one of our pacts, for I removed my life jacket. Sue and Jude had been drifting off and on for days without theirs. Though we put ourselves into some minimal danger by not wearing them, we were quite familiar with the Yukon's whims by now and felt perfectly safe. We were virtually the only paddlers who ever wore theirs anyway. Bing never wore one; his one theoretical safety feature was a twenty-foot rope that dragged at all times behind his boat, which he would supposedly catch if he fell overboard so he wouldn't lose his boat.

Every now and then a band of horseflies would find its way from shore half a mile or more out into the river where we were drifting. They really annoyed me until Evelyn initiated a contest to see who could kill the most with one swipe of the paddle through the air. Then it became fun to feel their bodies thud against the plastic blade of the paddle. A direct hit only dazed them and knocked them to the floor of the boat, though; we had to step on them for the final kill. Perhaps thirty-five days among the Yukon's mosquitoes had warped our idea of fun just a tad. . . .

What was really irritating, in an admirable sort of way, was that Jude could move their boat along faster, paddling solo, while Sue napped or read in the stern, than Evelyn and I could, paddling together. Bing, paddling non-stop as he always did, with his double-bladed paddle that afforded two strokes to our one, kept up with no problem. But as I paddled with a long, methodical stroke, enjoying putting my stomach and leg muscles into the effort, it was mildly distressing to see Jude's boat whizzing along a mile or two ahead with only Jude paddling. One's tendency in such circumstances is to assume that one's partner isn't paddling effectively. But perhaps our boat was somewhat more overloaded than theirs; perhaps our boat's design or hull material was slower on calm water; or perhaps Jude was simply one powerful paddler.

The five of us saw no person or motorboat throughout the day, passing only one empty fish camp. The warmth of the sun, the gigantic blue sky that spread in all directions, the silence except for the rhythmical splashing of paddles against water and the constant kittenlike calling of the mew gulls that wheeled overhead, all generated a fantastic feeling of peace and contentment. We passed within twenty feet of a large forked tree that was aground in the shallow water; upon it squatted fifteen Arctic terns. They all sat in a row facing the same direction, their bright orange beaks and black-capped heads statuelike. Immediately afterward, we came directly upon two Arctic loons bobbing near the shore. They were lifers for us, and we delighted in inspecting the delicate piano-key pattern of white on their heads and shoulders against the black of their bodies. Then, just as loons are supposed to do, they took a long running start across the top of the water with their big webbed feet—right in front of the bow—and took to the air.

That was reason enough for us all to celebrate, and with big smiles on our faces about the terns and the loons and the wonder of this great day in the Flats, the three boats thwarted for happy hour, breaking another safety pact of ours not to drink on the river itself. The first toast was to Arctic loons. I had bought the only bottle of peppermint schnapps in Circle; I pulled it out and began drinking straight from it. I gave my entire bottle of Everclear—which I'd hardly touched and the sight of which I could no longer stand—to Evelyn, who promptly began pouring it into a cup of lemonade. Sue and Jude still had their bourbon. As we all raised our cups or bottles with each toast, Bing would hold aloft his sand bucket of Yukon water and take a sip from it. Briefly, as we did almost every day, we tried to trick him into conversations that would reveal some hint as to what he did for a living, but he would grin and shrug and change the subject.

The bannock filled with peas and carrots that Sue had made for lunch didn't excite us much, and even Bing—who normally had a prodigious appetite—ate only a few mouthfuls. We dumped it overboard for the fish; Bing looked upstream and swore that behind us spread a trail of dead fish floating belly-up near each piece of bannock. Then he dodged the paddle blade that Sue swiped through the air toward him. As we floated and joked, we looked up to see that we were bearing down fast on a big downed tree, but Jude, who was on watch, insisted that she had things under control. We were getting pretty casual about this Yukon travel, for as we washed virtually into the thing at a good clip, all we did was smile and make bets on whether Jude could pull it off. At the very last second she leaned her entire body into a massive pry against the water and pivoted her end—which would have been the one that hit first—around the strainer, missing it by inches. We toasted her success and continued laughing our way to camp.

As we pulled the boats in for the night, Bing caused a major commotion when he spotted a black bear half a mile across the river. It was our first bear of the trip, and we were enormously excited. At first we didn't believe Bing; the thing looked more the size of a large hog. But once again, the Yukon's distances had deceived. The bear rolled and dug and played in a meadow of high green grass, completely oblivious to our presence. Soon it was joined by a second coal-black hoglike critter. The sands of our camp also held our first fox tracks and the large three-toed tracks of sandhill cranes. We lingered over Jude's lasagna, sang songs, and studied the subleties of the clouds and the sunset, whose pink tones somehow made the far mountains appear to be covered with snow. An owl glided through camp in the dusky late-evening light. There seemed to be no end to the wildlife the Flats would send our way, though we knew the real wonders lay up out of the river channel and across the boggy, pond-strewn highlands where huge rafts of ducks and geese were probably hanging around.

As he unloaded his boat, Bing pulled from his gear a big, long rifle case. We liked him thoroughly and trusted him, but we let it be known that the thing made us nervous.

"Oh, it's not loaded," he grinned, eliminating any notion that he might have been a bit of a trigger-happy macho-man. "In fact, I've never had it loaded," he shrugged.

"Well, this expedition is going downhill fast," Evelyn smiled and shook her head as she stirred a cupful of Everclear in which floated a huge glob of instant tea mix. "We said we weren't gonna have men and we weren't gonna have guns, and now not only are we with a man, but he has a gun!"

## JULY 15, DAY 37

But Bing was a great firewood gatherer, and this morning he delighted us at breakfast with his perfect pancakes. As he downed his sixth or seventh, he shook his head at the puny women who were dropping out after three or four.

Around the first bend we hit a hefty wind and one-foot waves. We also spotted something in the distance that looked like a town. It was the first thing we'd seen in some time that might clue us in to where we were on the map. A couple in a motorboat said it was Beaver, which we'd thought we must have already passed. It seemed to take forever to reach it as we battled the waves, but we finally slipped into a side slough and pulled up at its shore.

On the beach stood an Indian woman who was splattered with blood, cutting up giant salmon at a table and dropping the heads onto the rocks below. As a gentle rain began, we dug through our belongings for some money and our cameras and clambered up the steep bank to see what the town might offer. Bing volunteered to watch the boats; we were still a little uneasy after Fort Yukon and wanted to take no chances with losing our equipment.

Beaver seemed to consist mostly of a string of cabins along the waterfront. We strolled down the street, trying to imagine which cabin might be the post office and whether there was a restaurant anywhere. In the back of our minds was the question whether the village of Beaver harbored any residents who were as anxious for whites to leave as those Bing had encountered in Fort Yukon. To our relief, a woman stepped from a cabin, smiled, and said, "Want some fish?"

She was the woman who'd been in the motorboat and who'd been cutting fish on the beach. We stood with her and her husband behind the cabin, in front of the smokehouse where long strips of salmon hung from the rafters. She was an Athapascan Indian, and she explained the different subgroups of the Athapascans, which are scattered in western Canada and across most of Alaska. She and her husband had visited the Lower 48, including Texas, and we all joked together about how we missed Mexican food. We visited with an older woman who was cutting salmon. With her soft white hair pulled back from her round face, she reminded Evelyn of her auntie back in Texas.

I took some pictures of the bright orange salmon eggs that hung in a glob over a log tripod in the yard. They and the salmon backbones that hung beneath them would remain in the open air to dry for a few weeks and would be fed to the dogs. Like many of the other villagers we'd met, the couple politely declined to have their picture taken when I asked permission. I didn't really blame them; they lived here, I supposed, for a variety of reasons, none of which included being tourist attractions. I supposed I wouldn't like it if every time I sat on my front porch in Dallas somebody drove up and took my picture.

We filled up our water jugs at the village's wellhouse, checked at the post office for mail, bought a candy bar at the store, and headed back down to the boats. Bing explained that for half an hour he had been turning down a friendly invitation to fight with a wiry young man who seemed to be drunk and whose conversation was a broken record that went, "What's your name? Where ya from? Wanna fight?" Bing said he had smiled and said "No thanks, maybe some other time," at the appropriate point of the record each time. We'd heard that a load of liquor had arrived the night before; perhaps that explained why the village seemed strangely deserted this morning and why the young man was in a feisty mood. We were pleased that Bing and the guy had chosen such an amiable end to their curious encounter.

As we pushed into the river, we recalled writings about rural Alaska's growing alcoholism problems, and we wondered what that and Alaska's oil and population boom would mean for the future of the villages like Beaver that are scattered throughout the Interior. We'd heard that the villagers here had opposed (unsuccessfully) the opening to the public of the pipeline road, concerned that it would bring sport hunters from Anchorage and Fairbanks who could drive to the Yukon, launch their motorboats and in a few hours be up here hunting the moose on which the villagers depend. Writings had suggested that the villages are grappling with social change and disruption, that these are trying times for Alaska's Native peoples. And yet, the people we met in Beaver, and many others we'd meet, seemed incredibly peaceful and contented. They had a gentle, smiling way about them that left us with a feeling that the hundred or so residents of Beaver still have a way of life that many a heart-diseased urban executive might envy. We hoped that the designation of the Yukon Flats Refuge and the selection of Native lands around here would adequately preserve the resources upon which the villagers depend and, to the extent they want it, the way of life they have known.

Around the first bend down the river, we were hit head-on with a vicious wind that kicked up big, rolling swells three feet high. At first we whooped and laughed as we banged down into their troughs and the spray hit us in the face, but the battle soon lost its glamour and we pulled out. The island was unlike any we had camped on, with several broad, sandy terraces that culminated in a twelve-foot-high cutbank topped by poplars. In its middle lay a big lagoon. And there was even a big dead tree embedded in a high sand dune, on whose branches we could sit and bounce and play as we gazed at the Yukon and the far mountains.

We grilled the salmon the villagers had given us, and I served it with English peas and a kind of hush-puppy fritter. Bing even had some ketchup to go with the hush-puppies. We lounged for hours in the dining tent, the wind completely blocked by the island's high banks, wondering how each day could seem more wonderful than the last.

## JULY 16, DAY 38

Another day for sunglasses and cowboy hats it was, and we were rested enough from our half-day "off" yesterday that we paddled hard for the first few hours—a revolutionary concept in the Texas Women's Yukon River Expedition. Truth be known, it felt good, and I had learned the words to enough songs by now that I could sing for an hour or so without repeating any. Evelyn, who believed she couldn't sing on key or in rhythm if her life depended on it, paddled patiently behind me (she didn't have much choice, I guess), tolerating my endless singing.

We thwarted up for lunch and broke out the first packet of the Twelve Baskets food that had arrived in Fort Yukon. Their trail mix of cashews, carob chips, sunflower seeds, coconut strips, dates, raisins, and God-knows-what-all was a terrific hit, and we drifted along merrily munching our individual cupfuls and drinking lemonade.

At the mouth of a large creek, four women sprawled on a grassy bank. By the time we realized the group was all women, we were too far out in the river to pull over without a huge effort, so we merely drifted on, waving and exchanging a few words of greeting. We knew they hadn't come down the Yukon or we would have heard about them, and we wondered where in the world they had come from. Their two canoes looked almost empty compared to ours; we figured they must have been on a very short trip. When Sue and Jude ran into them later, while we were miles apart having our individual floating nap sessions, they learned that the women were from Anchorage, had put into Beaver Creek off the Steese Highway, and had floated into the Yukon. They would paddle down the Yukon to the oil pipeline haul road to complete their float trip of several hundred miles.

In the afternoon we thwarted and decided to have another happy hour to celebrate, for the third day in a row, the completion of half of our trip. We didn't know exactly where halfway was, and even if we did, we didn't know exactly where we were on the map, so we thought it best to celebrate several days running, just to make sure. Evelyn decided she'd have a lot more room to spread out and relax if she crawled into the bottom of Bing's boat, which was empty from his seat to the center thwart, so she stepped over into it and dozed beneath the video camera. Bing simply smiled and shook his head and lounged back against the stern deck, resting his feet on the mound of gear in our boat. We began to toast all sorts of things, most of which dealt with sex or bodily functions, until somebody finally suggested we change the subject. So Bing reeled off his repertoire of sacrilegious jokes, which reminded each of us of a joke . . . . Finally we had joked about or toasted just about everything that could offend almost anybody, and we were sure a bolt of lightning would strike at any moment. We were positive that yesterday's high winds had been caused by one or more of our off-color toasts from the previous day, and we fretted that we'd really be in for it tomorrow at the rate we were going.

We cruised among the islands, with no one watching or steering a course. "Anybody interested in thinking about a campsite?" I suggested.

"Aw, let's not worry about it and just camp on the first sandbar we run into—literally," said Sue, pouring another bourbon.

That sounded like a fine plan. Soon enough, the sound of canoe hulls grating against gravel woke us from our happy-hour daze. Jude tumbled out to pull the boats ashore on the barren sandbar and squatted to pee, as usual, the moment her feet hit the cold water. Doing so, her gaze fell on an oddly-shaped tree stump fifty yards away. Just as she was about to comment on how ugly it was, it began to trot toward us across the sandbar. Jude screeched rather emphatically that it was a male moose, and the rest of us splashed back through the shallow water to the boats for our binoculars and cameras. It was our first sighting of the male of the species, and he did seem big. He moved across the island just beyond its high center so that all I could see was a large brown head and a big pair of flared antlers bobbing over the landscape. Or at least after a few schnapps that's all I saw. He seemed quite unconcerned about us and finally eased into the alder thicket, disappearing instantly into its dense growth.

As we pulled into a terraced sandy beach just across a tiny slough from the sandbar to set up camp, a big thundercloud rolled down the valley. We wondered which particular joke or toast had caused our misfortune. Evelyn and I were becoming a precision team at getting our tent up. Bing had the firewood gathered and Sue and Jude had dinner ready in an instant. After several Everclear cocktails, though, dealing with the complexities of erecting the dining tent was too much for Evelyn. Jude helped me set it up, and by the time the rain started we were all settled comfortably under its canvas roof, eating a leisurely dinner. The zipper of the dining tent had now undergone several weeks of living in sand and being whipped briskly up and down, and though Jude had nursed it back to health several times, tonight it finally jumped its track for good. With a gaping six-foot hole, the dining tent was almost useless. Tonight would turn out to be the last time we used it.

Evelyn and I undoubtedly had been building up little hostilities against each other, and this evening marked a bit of a rift in our relationship. First, I wondered aloud to the group if the strategic hole in the front of her shirt might give the villagers a less than positive impression of the Texas Women's Yukon River Expedition; then I began accepting bets on how many days it would be before her breast would escape its confines entirely. She, in turn, declared to the group that the smell released into the tent when I removed my clothes each night was so potent as to wake her from a sound sleep. She said she'd sew up her shirt when I took a bath.

Touche.

## JULY 17, DAY 39

Well, I had been meaning to take a bath, I really had, as soon as we camped someplace where I wouldn't sink down to my knees in mud at the river's edge. Today's nearby gravel bar presented the opportunity, so I gathered my little cookpot and my soap and clean clothes and walked about a quarter of a mile through the moose tracks to the river's edge, swatting mosquitoes all the way. Just as I got undressed, of course, the wind came up and made me shiver, but at least it was preferable to the mosquitoes. I marveled over the fact that it blew downstream. (But sure enough, later, when our boats began paddling down the river it switched to a slight headwind.)

By the time the rest of us had gotten up, Evelyn had already taken a bath and washed her hair and put on a clean shirt. (Truce.)

We paddled most of the day, I resigning myself to seeing nothing but the stern end of Sue's and Jude's boat for another thousand miles, no matter how hard I paddled. Late in the afternoon a sudden cloudburst had us wiggling fast into our Gore-Tex. We kept paddling right through it, and I found that I was really quite comfortable with my head dry under its felt cowboy hat, my face pretty well shielded from the rain by the hat's brim, and my body covered head to toe in Gore-Tex and wetsuit booties. One odd thing about it all was that through the storm the sun kept shining brightly enough that I had to wear my sunglasses. Even weirder, the rain daunted the mosquitoes (who'd flown out over the water for the first time) only enough to make them take shelter under the brim of my hat right in front of my face!

The rain stopped a few bends down the river, though, and we pulled out onto a giant, flat gravel bar to camp. Bing continued drifting, with no explanation, and disappeared out of sight. We would learn later that he wasn't mad or anything; that was just his way.

As we began to set up camp, a monstrous alien structure rounded the bend. A three-story tugboat pushed a football-field-sized barge laden with all sorts of crates and bulldozers. When all you've seen for almost a thousand miles are canoes and small motorboats, it's quite a shock to have such a thing roar into your living room. We stood in silence, staring. It pushed upstream ever so slowly, the rumble of its massive engine almost shaking the gravel beneath our feet as it fought the Yukon's anxious current.

Although for the first time good firewood was scarce, we eventually had a big pot of Twelve Baskets chicken curry cooked up, and it, too, was a big hit. Throughout dinner, there echoed across the Flats the sounds of the barge's struggle.

## JULY 18, DAY 40

We had agreed we'd sleep in this morning, so I took the opportunity to walk up to the head of the island, think great thoughts by myself and dictate into my tape recorder. A steady breeze blew upstream. Semipalmated plovers marched their dainty legs across the narrow zone of mud at the water's edge. Gulls wheeled in the morning sun. It all seemed somehow more like the ocean than a river. As I squatted to pee behind the ten-foot-tall mass of roots of a giant spruce that lay prone on the sandbar, I found myself the subject of intense scrutiny by a big blue-black raven who alighted haughtily on the uppermost root. He blinked first.

Back in camp, Sue and Jude had picked up their self-supporting dome tent, moved it to the fire, heated bath water, and were now bathing within its confines out of the wind. It was certainly a novel way to take a warm, wind-free, mosquito-free bath and clean your tent simultaneously.

I thought about the bear-warnings the ranger had given us, including not taking even contact lens solution into the tents, and wondered what bears thought of the lingering smell of shampoo. Of course, every night I myself had been disobeying the ranger's admonitions against taking mosquito repellent into the tent when I took off my pants—with the ever-present Muskol in the pocket—and stashed them alongside my sleeping bag. But then, I figured the closed bottle couldn't smell any more like Muskol than I myself did. . . .

As we pushed into the river, Sue suggested that, since we were halfway through the trip, we thwart and have a little encounter session to voice our thoughts about how the trip was going and how we were getting along. I had been feeling that the group's honeymoon was over in a number of ways, and I figured it couldn't hurt to see what the others were feeling. I wondered why it was that Sue and Jude seemed to dislike layover days and seemed to want to race down the river as fast as they could, leaving Evelyn and me with the decision whether to paddle our brains out to catch them or to give up being concerned with what they wanted. Sue and Jude believed I purposely picked at least two bad campsites each evening when we began our search; I believed they conspired to keep us on the river at least two hours later than I wanted each night. They couldn't understand why I never voiced my opinions; I couldn't understand why, every time I voiced my opinion (such as saying I wanted to thwart near the bank so we could see wildlife in the woods, rather than in the middle of the river where we were too far from shore to see anything), they voted to do the opposite. They thought I had a weird sense of humor; I couldn't understand why they didn't laugh at my jokes. They wondered why the group never had much to say to each other anymore; I wondered why it was that every time I said something, somebody disagreed with it.

The details aren't important, for anyone who has been a party to a waning relationship—and we all have—knows that the causes are never quite rational nor easily explained. It suffices to say that the encounter session did little to erase a gulf that seemed to be growing between the two boats. In some ways, it laid the foundation for increasing the gulf. Just as the encounter drew to a close, we spotted the cabins of Stevens Village down a slough and unthwarted to paddle over to them.

The encounter did produce one immediate benefit, though, for as Evelyn and I voiced between us our reactions, we realized that we shared a common bond of aversion for such encounter discussions. From that day forward, the relationship between Evelyn and me grew more tolerant and open and supportive and comfortable. As I puzzled aloud over some of Sue's and Jude's criticisms of me, Evelyn advised, "Don't try to figure it out, Beth. Besides, who needs all this? I don't recall signing on for a 2,000-mile encounter. I signed on to paddle the Yukon River."

We beached the boats beneath the gaze of several sled dogs who whimpered occasionally at us from where they were tethered among the birches on the high bank. After chatting for a few minutes with some young, teenage Indian boys on the gravel landing, we asked them if our boats would be O.K. if left alone; they replied that no one would steal anything but whiskey. Among the randomly scattered cabins and high grass and flowers wound the usual gravel road. A tall, blond, older fellow with a Swedish accent was tending the garden in front of his cabin, and he introduced himself as Big Bad John of the Yukon Flats. He said his wife, an Indian woman, was in Fairbanks at the moment; his tone suggested that flying from the nearby airstrip to Fairbanks was like going to the corner grocery for a quart of milk. He talked of his garden and the long winters and the short but powerful growing season. He said he loved his cabin in the Flats but would probably spend this winter elsewhere; his hands couldn't take the cold anymore. He mentioned that the new schoolteachers who'd just moved into the village were from Texas, and he insisted that we pay them a visit.

Wandering toward the rectangular wooden schoolhouse, we wondered vaguely if they would resent an uninvited visit from a bunch of people they didn't know. But suddenly the door at the top of the wooden porch flew open and a middle-aged woman's high-pitched southern twang rang out, "Well come on (pronounced 'own') in!"

Priscilla and her husband had come from schools in Texas to try their hand at educating the Native villagers in Alaska, and they loved it. Her husband was away somewhere today, but Priscilla welcomed us in and told us all about their good times the past year or two at another village up the Chandalar River. She described with delight a Christmas day dogsled ride that the village's chief had given her as a present. She said that bouncing over the hard-packed snow at high speed had practically jarred her teeth loose, of course, but she'd loved every minute and would never forget the magic of the snow-covered winter landscape on that Christmas Day. With great affection she spoke of the friends and dances and parties they'd had, and she proudly showed us the handmade caribou leg-skin boots and fur mittens and parka ruffs the villagers had made for her family. It was clear that Priscilla was thoroughly in love with the North and its people. She projected that same air of unassuming contentment shared by so many of the others we'd met. Among them there seemed to be a common link—they were where they wanted to be. I hold a Texas teaching certificate, and by the time Priscilla had related an hour's worth of her tales I was ready to sign up for one of the the many one-teacher villages in Alaska. But I remembered that I was supposed to go back to Texas to save the world's environment for at least a couple of years.

As we chatted, we sat somewhat uneasily in our dirt-covered clothes on the new sofa and easy chairs that had just arrived by barge. The floor was covered with newspapers, awaiting carpet. Priscilla's daughter, Francis, and son-in-law, Martin, described with a warmth equal to Priscilla's their own brief experiences in the North. They had brought their two daughters, Shauna and Prissy (three years and one-and-a-half years, respectively), up to visit Grandma and Grandpa in the spring, in the other village, and had decided to stay through the summer and help with the move here to Stevens Village. Priscilla and her husband moved here for a job promotion, and they looked forward to settling in and beginning the new school year. The one-room school adjoined their cabin, and they shared a common electric generator with it. Martin was an electrician and had been hired for the summer to tend to the generator and the other physical needs of the school; he and Francis said they'd probably end up staying the whole winter here. As we talked, little dark-haired Prissy brought one after another Husky puppies from a box in the kitchen to our laps for us to hold, and Priscilla's elderly mother stood at the electric stove frying up a huge mess of salmon. Martin sat in his stocking feet, playing with Shauna, but when he saw through the window that the mother dog outside had escaped her mooring and dashed off to make trouble with the other dogs that squatted around every cabin, he slipped on his boots and took off at a run. The others hardly looked up from their conversation. We were vaguely interested in finding a telephone to call home; Priscilla said there was one in town, but nobody could remember who had the key to the building, so we dropped the idea.

It went without saying that we had to stay for Sunday dinner, so the four of us sat with the six of them and devoured the kind of sweetened Texas tea that I hadn't had in years, a vast bowl of macaroni and English peas, bread with butter, and a huge platter of king salmon deep-fried in batter just like southern catfish. Afterward, Martin showed us the salmon he'd gotten this morning from a friend's gill net; when he held it up its tail dragged the floor and its head was higher than Shauna's as she stood beside him. They gave us some dried salmon strips to nibble on the river.

Sue and Jude brought presents from the barter bag and also gave Priscilla their copy of a book called *Tisha*, the true story of a nineteen-year-old Colorado woman who went to the Alaskan wilderness in 1927 to become the new schoolteacher for the gold-mining community of Chicken. As we stood outside the cabin making our farewells, three long-haired Indian men strode quickly down the path in our direction. The leader wore dark sunglasses and a bandanna tied around his head, and he carried a rifle. We wondered if some of the racial tensions we'd heard about in Fort Yukon applied here, but as we stepped aside to let him pass, the leader said, "Howdy," with a smile, we said "Howdy" and smiled back. As we floated out of town, Priscilla stood among the tall purple fireweed on the bank, holding Prissy in her arms. "Wave bye-bye to the ladies," Priscilla instructed, and Prissy did.

Filled with a warm glow from the visit with new-found friends, I sang "Me and Bobby McGee" and paddled shirtless across the smooth, sun-drenched slough that reflected the rich greens of a willow-covered shoreline.

I was still paddling along in a daze sometime later when Evelyn asked casually if I saw that man standing on the shore. I replied that I hadn't and decided it would be a nice gesture to put my life jacket over my bare torso as we drifted past. We realized that the clear waters of the Dall River joined the Yukon here, so the four of us paddled up into the small stream for drinking water.

A stocky older man with short grey hair, two young men, and a big, black dog were fishing from a big, shiny motorboat, and as we paddled past we exchanged a greeting with them.

"We're gonna get some water," Evelyn explained by way of apology for our having possibly disturbed their fishing.

They nodded with a smile, then a few strokes later, a voice behind us said, "Forget the water, how about a cold beer?" Evelyn and I had never executed such a precision fast pivot in our lives, and the three men laughed at the speed and eagerness with which our two boats sidled up to theirs. "Gee," one of them said, "a few hours ago four women paddled by and we asked them the same thing and they didn't even stop."

"Good," laughed Evelyn, "Can I have their share?"

We joked and drank beer with the guys for an hour or so. They worked at a maintenance camp for the pipeline haul road, and they kept saying that there was plenty more cold beer back at their work camp and they'd be happy to take us there in their motorboat and truck. We said we appreciated the offer but were really kind of set on camping on the river tonight. They said that when they got through fishing they might go home and get the beer and bring it back upriver until they spotted us and have a little party. We said whatever they wanted to do was fine. During this exchange, a boatload of Indian men and one Indian woman pulled over to the shore without a word of greeting, strode quickly into the woods with guns, were gone for a few minutes, then hopped back into their boat with a box and roared away. We never knew if we'd witnessed a drug deal, a bootleg liquor pickup, a rape, or simply some normal activity of a Sunday afternoon near Stevens Village. The fact that everyone carried guns leant a somewhat sinister air to the most innocent pursuit. Finally, we extricated ourselves from the increasingly flirtatious discussion with the Dall River guys and paddled on.

Apparently the Yukon Flats didn't believe in long goodbyes, for it vanished abruptly and high, steep rock faces closed in on either side of us. Confined now to a mere quarter-mile channel, the Yukon made a sudden sprint for the sea. For the first time in as long as we could remember, the river had a shadow thrown rudely across its width. Our view of the sky was blocked by mountains, and once again they dwarfed the two canoes that had seemed so much more significant against the low horizon of the Flats. Cold air rushed through the rather ominous valley.

We began to feel tired, but the steep, narrow beaches had sprouted basketball-sized rocks. Every hint of a flat place for camping was already occupied by an active fish camp full of big, white canvas tents and barking dogs. To the river people, the dogs are as valuable for guarding the fish camps from bears in the summer as they are for pulling sleds in the winter. Every creek that tumbled from a cleft in the canyon wall had the white buoys of a salmon gill net stretched across its mouth. The whole scene spoke of salmon, bustling fish camps, and bears. Finally we pitched the tents in a narrow band of horsetails—foot-high green plants that were pretty and soft and full of mosquitoes—at the mouth of a creek. It made us nervous to sleep with fish camps close by on either side of us, and with a gill net a few yards away at our creek, but it was the only campsite to be had. By now we'd lost our party mood, and luckily the Dall River guys never showed up with the beer.

## JULY 19, DAY 41

My grumpiness over having been awakened a million times during the night by motorboats roaring through the canyon melted away with a rhythmic hour's paddling through the water.

Then, there loomed into view several miles ahead the gigantic grey lump of the Trans-Alaska Oil Pipeline, spanning the Yukon with its attendant structures and highway bridge and roads. It represented the outcome of a battle that Evelyn and I and thousands of other environmentalists had lost. We had sought to have the North Slope oil routed overland down the Alaska Highway to the U.S. Midwest and East, rather than to Alaska's coast at Valdez where its transport would be dependent on ocean-going supertankers and the environmentally-damaging spills associated with them. Recent moves to ship Alaskan oil to Japan had given credence to conservationists' fears that the oil would ultimately threaten the oceans and yet do little to lessen U.S. dependence on foreign oil. Though our outcries had probably caused it to be built with greater environmental safeguards, we held no affection for the big pipe that would carry a few years' worth of oil from Prudhoe Bay to the port of Valdez, where it would be loaded onto oil tankers. Only time would tell whether it would eventually disrupt the caribou's migration patterns or cause a major land or ocean oil spill. But here it was, so Evelyn and I entertained ourselves by standing up in the boat and good-naturedly shaking our fists at it and inventing a host of creative new curse words to describe anyone who had a part in promoting it. Sue and Jude looked at us as if we were crazy, as did a large group of Japanese tourists who scurried around on the far bank with binoculars and cameras; but we were having fun. When we pulled into a vast cleared field that served as a campground on the right bank, the Bing Ahlering welcoming committee awaited us as usual.

Evelyn and I paused under the pipeline to perform a solemn duty we'd promised to carry out months before. Trouble was, the darned pipeline was way too high off the ground and way too big to hike a leg over. We settled for peeing on one of its support columns; as we squatted in the high grass, recording the event on film, a station wagon full of Boy Scouts drove by and asked if we were with those women who were paddling the Yukon River. They wanted to congratulate us. Yes, we were, I nodded politely, buttoning my fly.

With the recent opening to the public of the pipeline haul road (the road, running adjacent to the pipeline, that was built to haul supplies for building the pipeline), this obscure place where the pipeline happens to cross the Yukon had now become a focal point of activity, a meeting place of two major transportation systems. It was crawling with canoe tourists, Winnebago tourists, truckers, oil-company geologists, government biologists, and fishermen in motorboats.

We ate the required restaurant meal and the required candy bar in a trailer marked "Kitchen" behind a gas station, asked briefly if any officials of the Yukon Flats Refuge were around for us to talk to (they weren't), then joined the groups of canoeists who had gathered by the river. One of the guys with the Colorado bunch we'd met in Fort Yukon (they were taking out here) had just returned from the town of Livengood with their car and a load of warm Olympia beer. Owing to Bing's efforts, there was a six-pack for us. The four Germans in the inflatable canoes had put in an order too, and we all stood in the hot sun congratulating ourselves on trips ending and continuing.

Then we pushed back into the river. Passing through the wide shadow of the pipeline ranked with leaving the Dawson beach as a milestone on the trip. For with the pipeline we left behind the last structure that would span the Yukon. For the next thousand miles all that would meet our gaze between the Yukon's banks would be its own waters and the big sky. And with the pipeline haul road, we left behind the last road that was connected with the rest of Alaska—Fairbanks, Anchorage—and the Lower 48. From here on, the only people we would meet on the river would have gotten themselves to where they were by water or by air or by birth. We drifted a half-mile or so ahead of Sue and Jude and Bing. As I lay in the boat with my eyes closed, listening to an occasional page turning in Evelyn's book or a wave slapping the boat as we drifted, my mood was one of confusion. It was still hard to believe that we had come so far so soon with so little physical discomfort. I was a little sad that our trip was probably halfway over. I hoped that we would begin to see more wildlife. I was a little disappointed that we were reaching so many villages with so little time in between alone to ourselves on the river, and yet I was thoroughly enjoying the variety and the craziness of the people we were meeting and the experiences we were having whenever we did enter these villages.

We had been thwarted for awhile and were just finishing singing "Clementine" for the third time—testing Sue's previous surgery with marine epoxy on the broken neck of her ukulele—when a big motorboat with a stocky man at the helm raced toward us. "Beer! Beer!" we hollered gleefully, for we thought it was the guy from the Dall River who'd said he'd find us and bring us some. But it turned out to be Paul Richards and Don Quan, two plainclothes "fish cops" (as they described themselves) with the Alaska Fish and Wildlife Department who'd heard we were looking for them. They had caught up with us to see if we wanted to report any "irregularities." We had actually been asking for the U.S. Fish and Wildlife Service personnel, but we were happy to chat with these two gentlemen anyway. We drifted with them for awhile, interrupted only every now and then when the wind blew us into the rocks on the shore, at which point Paul would start their big twin motors and ease our whole flotilla to the middle of the river. We talked about the regulations for the fish wheels and the gill nets. Their job was to patrol a section of the river, looking for violations of both sport or subsistence fishing laws as well as hunting regulations. And occasionally they might be called upon to enforce any other law, for they were state troopers and the only regular patrol in the area. Don drew circles on our maps indicating the bluffs where peregrine falcons nest and explained how we could make them fly out by clapping our hands when we got close enough to their bluffs. The fish cops explained where their camp was, about 130 miles downstream, and invited us to stop by for a steak dinner when we got down there. Then they started their motors, winked and tossed us a six-pack, and roared away upstream.

We drifted past a loud creek that gurgled down a steep rocky formation; it sent a rush of cold air out across the Yukon. Beside it stood a bald eagle who took to the air as we passed. A perfect line of black-bear prints lay along the length of the sandbar we chose for a campsite; after assuring ourselves that the island wasn't a regular highway for the critters, we set up the kitchen beside the tracks. Before long, Don and Paul cruised down the far channel and pulled out to camp on the other side of the island. They were mildly alarmed at first, for Sue was running down the beach as they pulled up—with a roll of toilet paper as it so happened—but when she made her second lap they concluded that she was neither being chased by a bear nor in any other distress.

They wandered over to our camp after dinner, and between Bing and the rest of us we rounded up some cups for their coffee. As we began to joke and to feel at ease with these two cops in our midst, what should Don pull from his pack but a full bottle of Bailey's Irish Cream!

"Have you ever tried—" he began, but his question was drowned out by the roar of approval that went up from the Texas Women's Yukon River Expedition.

Bing shook his head, smiled and said, "Oh no, here we go . . . ."

After the others went off to bed, Don and I sat talking for hours. He was a thin guy about my age who was rather quiet but who could be coaxed into describing some of his interests. It turned out he had done everything from teaching Outward Bound instructors to living in Baja California to teaching scuba diving off the coast of Mexico's Yucatan peninsula. Spanish had been my major in college, and wandering the back roads of Mexico was one of my favorite hobbies. Don also kayaked and did a lot of river-running. I was in love again. As we drank the last drop from the Bailey's bottle, we finally noticed the black bear across the river who'd probably been there for hours.

# 9 a broken bone, a wedding bash

## JULY 20, DAY 42

For hours Evelyn and I paddled as closely as we could beside the high bank, peering among the poplars for all the bears and wolves we knew must be in there. The only beast we saw was a squirrel, but the effort was a pleasant accompaniment to our rambling discussion about life and men and how we should go more often to the theater when we got back home. We rounded a bend and got blown by the wind into a cove; when we got within ten feet of the shore, a peregrine falcon sailed from the bluff above us, out over the river. Its dark streamlined body soaring against the cloudless blue sky made quite a sight, but it was exasperating to try to take its picture as the canoe rocked in one-foot waves. We had fun imitating its high-pitched cry. Unknown to us, but observed by Bing who was floating with Sue and Jude out in the river, a black bear had disappeared into the bushes as we had swung into the cove.

Late in the day, we came upon a fish camp where an older Indian man was spreading his fishing nets on the beach; Evelyn called out to ask if we could see them. Harold Woods welcomed us ashore and the four of us paddled over as Bing disappeared around the next bend. Our conversation naturally turned from fish to bears. Motioning to the rocky shore across the river, Mr. Woods said that was where he took his motorboat every day to dump the heads and guts of the salmon. We were mildly horrified, for we knew that feeding wild animals generally leads to the animals' associating people with food, which tends to promote the demise of backpackers and canoeists. We hated to envision what might result if we stumbled wearily onto some beach some night and camped, without realizing it, near somebody's feeding dump. We asked Mr. Woods if dumping the guts made the bears learn to feed there.

"Sure! We had thirteen there one night!" he said, somewhat proudly. His rationale, and that of most of the fish camps and villages in this stretch, was that dumping the guts across the river kept the bears mostly over there rather than in your own smokehouse. The people seemed to have the idea that it was illegal to dump the guts into the river, but as I recall the police officers we checked with said that was O.K.

At any rate, every now and then a bear would come into a fish camp. Mr. Woods began to describe the bears he'd shot in this camp, the dogs that they had nearly killed, and the bear who came to camp last night; as we listened, a mother bear and two cubs made their way down the steep hillside across the river toward the very spot we had been discussing. From this distance, they appeared as a black dot followed by two specks. When they reached the beach, the mother obviously told the babies to stay put in the bushes while she shopped at the salmon-gut deli, but one cub strayed onto the open beach and got a scolding.

"Ask them to come up for coffee and bring a cup, Uncle!" came a voice from among the poplars on the high bank. We climbed the steep wooden steps into the fish camp of Mary Jane Fate and her sister, Alice. The two Athapascan Indian women were quite beautiful, their shoulder-length dark hair framing faces of smooth brown skin. They were smiling and very gracious and somehow elegant in their jeans and cotton blouses. Their father had been a trapper, and they had spent their childhood along this area of the Yukon, at fish camps in the summers and out on the trapline in the winters. The two sisters were married to two white men—a dentist and a doctor. They all lived in Fairbanks most of the year. But for a month in the summers, the two women would come to this fish camp, to the woods and the river they knew so well; here they would cut up the salmon, then smoke or can it. We could tell they loved the river and vacationing here on its banks.

Their husbands were flying in at this moment in a floatplane, commuting here from Fairbanks after a day's work. The plane circled once to gauge the wind over the river, then glided onto the water right in front of the camp. It taxied to shallow water; Doc Fate hopped out in his hip waders and tied the plane to a stake as easily as one would beach a canoe. The two men joined us in sitting on the ground in the shade of the trees, drinking coffee, and swatting mosquitoes. Then they dashed off in a motorboat to set out the salmon nets, and the two women gave us a tour of their smokehouse and cabins.

Mary Jane showed us a picture of her college-age daughter, but it was impossible to believe Mary Jane was old enough to have a daughter that age. Mary Jane was president of the Rampart Native Village Corporation (one of the regional and village corporations established under the Alaska Native Claims Settlement Act), and she had helped found the Alaska Native Arts Center in Fairbanks. At the Center, their mother helped keep alive and bring about understanding of the Athapascan culture by teaching traditional skills such as the sewing of Indian garments of skin and fur. Mary Jane was a leader in Alaskan Natives' causes, and she was no stranger in the halls of Alaska's statehouse or the U.S. Congress. We talked for a long time about the changes that Alaska's Native people have undergone in recent decades. The two women served us their homemade bread and the jam they had made from the cranberries that grew around here.

When the men returned, we realized we were interrupting their dinner, so we said goodbye and headed downriver. All the way down the Yukon, it never ceased to amaze us how open and friendly and willing everyone was to invite a couple of boatloads of complete strangers into their living rooms.

A hundred yards away, an owl floated silently among the trees; then around the first bend in Hess Creek, a big bald eagle squatted on a dead snag in the water. We paddled silently a few miles up the clear, tea-colored waters of the creek, marveling at the multitude of bear and moose tracks that crisscrossed the muddy beaches. Our objective was to see wildlife; the small enchanted creek flanked by dense foliage certainly seemed the place for it. We tied the boats under the overhanging branches of a willow and sat quietly in them in the late afternoon light, covered head to toe against the mosquitoes. We spoke only with hand signals and concentrated on the sounds of the woods: the creek's current gurgled against our aluminum hull; a pair of belted kingfishers splashed loudly as they dived into the water for fish; somewhere nearby, ducks quacked; the general background whining of the mosquitoes rose a few pitches whenever one flew into my ear; with a quick "ush," somebody opened a beer can that had been cooling in the water; a bear bell tinkled as somebody shifted position; a water bottle glug-glugged as someone filled it in the creek.

Finally we could sit still no longer, so we paddled upstream farther. From his perch in a tree at the river's edge, a great horned owl, two feet tall, condescended to stare at us with piercing yellow eyes. Sue and Jude turned back and Evelyn and I continued up the creek. We tied the boat to a tree root and scrambled stealthily out onto some big chunks of bank that had sheared off into the creek. Everywhere my knee or tennis shoe could gain a foothold as I crawled up the slick, muddy jumble of grass and earth, there lay a bear print. We intended to make our way across the flat to spot the waterfowl we knew were up here somewhere, but as we reached the top of the bank and surveyed the meadow of high grass with a pond, surrounded by trees, we had a common reaction. We began to jingle our bear bells and talk loudly and giggle nervously; after a few seconds of giving token appreciation to the place, we beat a retreat back into the relative safety of the boat. This close new world seemed so much less predictable than the wide Yukon and its sandbars to which we'd grown accustomed; in that fact lay its magic and its scary excitement.

Around one more bend we tired of fighting the current and realized the sun was setting behind a mountain, so we floated silently back to the Yukon. Just before we reached it, we wheeled quickly at the sound of an ever-so-slight splash close behind us; Bing had earlier lined his boat up the same creek and was now floating behind us with a big smile, had been for a mile, and of course had managed to see a beaver and a moose! But then we'd eaten homemade bread and seen a mother bear and two cubs . . . .

Our camp for the evening was a high barren sandbar at the mouth of

Hess Creek that rose in terraces to a height of about twelve feet above the river. The only things on it were a huge dead spruce left there by high water, rocks, and the parallel tracks of an airplane's wheels running down its length. As we ate our chili and rice atop the huge mound of sand, it afforded a penthouse view of several miles of the Yukon. Now that we were back in the mountains and the summer was marching on toward fall, the sun was actually setting for a few hours each night. Dipping behind the mountains up the river, it transformed the wide Yukon into a silver swath flanked by black rounded hills. Above it all danced pink patterns in the twilight sky.

## JULY 21, DAY 43

The others had already been for a swim in the Yukon by the time I got up, but just as I got my clothes off to give it a try the sun went behind the clouds and a cold wind kicked up, naturally. I limited my endeavors to a quick bath.

By the time we began paddling, the wind had turned the Yukon into one- and two-foot waves, but we slogged merrily through them. I rather enjoyed the wind in my hair and guessing which of the waves would hit the bow just right so that it splashed into my lap. At least it wasn't raining, and I sang "I Was Born Under a Wandering Star" as the bow rose and plunged with rhythmic thuds into the troughs of the waves. A mile down, we spotted a strange white patch across the water and were sure there was a small rapid; reaching it, we realized it was the result of the tube of Jude's shampoo that Bing had lost during his bath, and we named the spot "Head and Shoulders Shoals."

We spent most of the day battling ever-increasing waves and rain, with only a few moments of excitement. Evelyn and I were reduced to subsisting on peanuts all day because Sue and Jude had disappeared miles ahead with the lunch. Later, when the wind blew Sue's hat into the water, she and Jude both reached over the side to retrieve it and nearly capsized in the big rolling waves.

Late in the day, the string of cabins known as Rampart came into view around a bend. We beached the boats on its rocky waterfront and spoke briefly with a California couple who had just come from the trading post and were heading on down the river in their double kayak. The others trudged up the hill into town; I tried to remember where I'd put my money.

"Beer or bourbon?" said Paul Beard with a wide grin when he opened his cabin door. I poked my head inside and laughed at the scene. Though I was but a few minutes behind the others, the Texas Women's Yukon River movable party had arrived and was in full swing. Everyone held up a beer can or a bourbon glass by way of greeting. Bing smiled and shook his head as if he expected an all-night dance to erupt. Boots and wet clothes were strewn about the one-room cabin, and everyone had stripped down to her bottom layer or two of clothing in the heat from the

Beards' woodstove. To walk into that warm, dry, friendly cabin after paddling twenty-four miles through a cold, wind-driven rain was like receiving an unexpected inheritance of a million dollars. And to be handed a cold beer, in addition, produced a contentment of indescribable proportions.

Paul and Penny Beard liked to party—loved to party. They'd known for weeks that we were coming down the river, for, what we dubbed the Mukluk Telegraph, apparently was pretty active in this part of the world, at least concerning the escapades of the four Texas women who'd been raising good-natured hell all the way from Eagle. And now the Beards delighted in setting a fresh cold beer or another glass of bourbon at our elbows just as we finished the one we had; in whipping up a Chef Boy-ar-dee pizza and setting it beneath our noses, though the Beards had already eaten; and in swapping tales of Northern hilarity with the four of us and Bing.

Paul was a tall, strapping man with just a touch of short grey hair left on his balding head. He wore a continuous, contagious grin and kept saying in his expansive voice how really, really *neat* it was that we gals were paddling the Yukon. When he was young, he and his father had paddled a thousand miles down the Columbia River, just the two of them. Penny was short and plump, with curly, blondish hair. In her deep, wisecracking voice, with a sly shake of her head and a twinkle in her eye, Penny could tell a good joke. Most of all, Paul and Penny loved to laugh, and as the five of us matched them joke for joke and wisecrack for wisecrack, the cabin rang with the roars of laughter and the pounding of fists on table or thigh.

The Beards were in their sixties. They were employed by the village corporation to run the store and post office that shared the one-room addition to the back of their cabin. They were among a handful of whites who lived in the Indian village of about sixty people. They had lived in Rampart a year or two; managing the store here was the latest of a long series of adventures that had taken them all over the West Coast and Alaska, and found them doing everything from managing hotels to running a kippered salmon enterprise. They had somehow found themselves in Alaska in the early 1960s and had stayed ever since. After a few bourbons, Penny loved to imitate the way the coon hounds Paul used as sled dogs down at Tanana had bayed as they raced through the ice fog on the frozen Yukon. Paul loved to tell the story about how he and Penny had taken a trip to Tahiti when he worked for Wien Air and could fly free. The day they were supposed to fly home, the two of them had enjoyed themselves so much in the bar that they missed their flight and ended up paying $1,100 in regular fare to get home in time to go to work the next day.

"Some afternoons on the town are more expensive than others," they shrugged and guffawed.

Penny joked about the small-town life of Rampart that they loved. "Up here," she said, "nobody puts on any airs. You can leave your cabin at forty below to go to the outhouse and wave to a neighbor with a styrofoam potty seat and a roll of toilet paper in your hand, and never think twice about it."

Their cabin was as cute and homey as it could be. Bright curtains hung at the windows, and Penny's oil paintings of flowers adorned the thick log walls. Shelves full of books lined one corner. Their water came from the fifty-five-gallon oil drum—also painted with flowers—that sat in the corner. Paul filled it from a nearby creek and carried it in his pickup truck. Since the cabin had no running water, we wondered at the fancy faucets that perched atop Penny's gleaming stainless steel sink. A friend had put them there, she said, because she kept losing silverware down the sink's drains. The Beards had electricity, when the generator was working, and it kept the lights on and the beer cold in the store's refrigerator. Before Penny had received her washer and dryer that came to Rampart on the barge, she used to mail her dirty clothes or send them with someone by motorboat seventy-five miles downriver to Tanana, where a friend would take them to the washateria and send them back upriver one way or another. All the while we talked, the Beards' fifteen-pound beige cat named Sam—the only cat we'd seen on the whole Yukon—jumped from one of our laps to another to be petted. At intervals, the villagers would knock on the door and Paul would take them through the cabin to the store—though it was officially closed for the evening—so they could buy a pack of cigarettes or a case of beer. One older Indian named Frank stood in the kitchen with us, enjoying our river tales.

Various rumors had been flying around town about illegal fish-selling or moose-hunting that supposedly had been going on, so when Paul Richards strode into the cabin—this time wearing his official Fish and Wildlife cap—Penny gave us a stern glance as if to say, "Dummy up."

We didn't know anything about anything anyway, but the Beards were visibly surprised at our air of familiarity with the Law when we chorused, "Hey, it's the fish cops!", poked Paul Richards in the stomach, and said, "How ya doin', Paul?" We explained to the Beards that the fish cops had camped with us on the sandbar; we joked that they had slept so late on the job that they were still wandering around in their pajamas when we had paddled away.

Paul grinned, puffed out his chest with his hands on his hips, and in a mock macho tone said, "Fish cops don't wear pajamas."

As if on cue, the four of us raised our glasses and shouted a toast "to nude fish cops!" This party was heading downhill fast. Paul and Don declined our invitations to stay, saying that they had to go chase some bad guys somewhere, but they repeated the invitation to drop by for dinner when we paddled by their camp downstream.

Then, surveying the five of us, Paul added, "If you come this weekend you're gonna have to behave a little bit—the boss'll be there." When our roar of disapproval died down, he said, "Well, just a little bit" and walked out the door.

After several beers it was imperative that I find the outhouse, so Paul Beard handed me a roll of toilet paper, slipped his slippers onto my stocking feet, and propelled me out the door of the cabin. I lost his huge slippers two steps down the gravel road and continued hobbling in my wool socks through the mud and the rocks in the gentle rain. I staggered around the corner and stood puzzled, in my white longhandle shirt and my socks and my army-navy wool pants, with my roll of toilet paper, staring at a young Indian man who sat on the porch of a cabin with a big sign that said "Leaping Lee's Saloon." God, I love Alaska, I thought. The Indian smiled and nodded toward the outhouse and I dashed inside, pausing only to note with amazement that it had a bona fide doorknob.

Finally it occurred to us that we'd been drinking with the Beards for five solid hours, that we could hold no more liquor, that our stomachs hurt from laughing so much, and that we had no idea where we were going to sleep tonight. Paul told us about a flat sandy beach about a quarter of a mile below town; we concluded that even as drunk as we were we could get the boats that far. Led by Frank, we stumbled out into the cold dusk, hugged and kissed the Beards, promised to see them tomorrow, and shuffled down the dirt road to the boats. Evelyn and I became enmeshed with a small herd of Husky puppies that playfully bit our hands and bounced and tumbled under our feet, all without making a sound. We finally got the boat into the water, beating back one final puppy who still had his paws over the gunnel trying to get in the boat, and made our way through the waves to the beach. Somehow we got the tent up in the roaring wind and I tumbled in. Behind me, the screen zipper jumped its sand-encrusted track for the last time, trapping me inside and Evelyn outside. I passed out to the sound of her bear bells roaming the beach . . . .

## JULY 22, DAY 44

"We think Jude's fractured an ankle bone, and I'm gonna walk into town to see if there's an X-ray machine around here," was the first thing I heard this morning. It was Sue, shoving very strange tidings into my hungover brain. Somehow, in my own drunkenness, I'd missed Jude's slipping on the rocks at the water's edge and severely twisting her ankle last night. They told me that she happened to be carrying Sue on her shoulders at the time. Sue said she'd given Jude some painkillers, that Jude was sleeping soundly and was willing to continue the trip if they could get an X-ray or a cast or something. This was a helluva way to start the day. I rubbed my eyes and looked around the tent at the mass of wet, muddy clothes and shoes. Something seemed to be missing; it occurred to me that it was my partner.

"Where's Evelyn?" I moaned.

"I don't know," came Sue's voice again through the solid flap of the tent. "I think she slept under a tarp in a fishing boat." Sue's footsteps faded away as she trudged up the hill toward town; I zipped my sleeping bag over my face and went to sleep.

Throughout the day, the wind blew furiously, flapping the tent into a now-billowing, now-sagging accordion. The sheet of plastic that Bing kept over his tent next door whipped about, sounding like small machine-gun shots. When I finally emerged from the tent to find some aspirin, I discovered that the entire stern end of our boat—which we'd halfheartedly pulled up onto the foot-and-a-half-high bank—was full of water from the waves driven into it by the wind and the motorboats. The pot of Cuban black beans that Evelyn had been soaking for days under her seat lay submerged and forlorn, as did a host of other gear that bobbed in the water at the ends of nylon cords.

I poked my head into Jude's tent. Sue had taped Jude's horribly swollen foot—not the one she'd sprained twice on this trip but the one she'd broken during her college track days—and the patient was having a high old time playing cards and taking painkillers. There was no X-ray machine in Rampart, Sue had learned, but there was one seventy-five miles or so downriver at Tanana, if it hadn't yet been dismantled and flown to Fairbanks with the rest of the hospital that was due to be moved by August 1. The plan was to paddle downriver whenever the waves died down enough to get on the river, and in the meantime there was nothing to do but wait.

I headed into town for aspirin and candy bars. En route, Evelyn passed by me with a grin, flanked by three men each shouldering a case of beer. The whitecaps on the river looked a little like the North Sea during a storm anyway, so I guessed a beach party was as good a way as any to pass the afternoon.

I called Mother from the phone inside the community hall where a bunch of kids sat watching game shows on TV. I told her about the broken foot and said that all our food boxes had arrived intact. She asked if anything exciting had happened, other than the broken foot.

"Well, right now I'm looking out the window at three black bears who are playing with a big, pink pile of salmon guts across the river," I said. There was silence, then a faint laugh.

I bought a bottle of schnapps and a six-pack of beer and wandered back toward our camp. Two Indian girls rode bareback on a pony through the muddy street. Men down on the waterfront were cutting up salmon and hanging them on racks to dry. Three Indian guys with their heads buried in a jeep engine looked up as I passed. "Howdy," one grinned.

By the time we had finished eating the salmon Bing had found and cooked for us, it seemed as though every male in the village of Rampart was drifting into our camp, each with a case of beer. Somebody built a big fire and threw horsetails onto it to make a smudge pot; sitting in the smoke with watering eyes was preferable to breathing the mosquitoes that hovered in a thick cloud. The four Germans paddled by and we waved them over. Somebody brought a pair of crutches from the clinic, so Jude was now mobile. Paul and Penny strolled down the hill with a case of beer, lawn chairs, and a bottle of bourbon. Pickup trucks rolled into the clearing, motorboats zoomed up to the beach, and from each poured more Indians and more refreshments. Everyone we met seemed to have the same last name—Evans—and we finally lost all track of who was whose cousin or father or brother or in-law. Before long, one of the Germans was throwing massive quantities of horsetails onto the fire and doing a kind of solo waltz in his big boots around the smudge pot. Leaping Lee (of saloon fame) was lying in the grass on one elbow, with one eye shut, whispering sweet nothings into the ear of whichever one of us happened to sit next to him. Sue was interviewing one of the Germans, through an interpreter, about his pants which were in fact nothing but a conglomeration of patches. The pants had owned him since he was seventeen, he said proudly, and he was thirty-two now; the pants had taken him hiking in the Swiss Alps, canoeing down various rivers, and all sort of places.

A sexy young Indian woman named Marge strode into camp in a pair of designer jeans and knee-high, high-heeled boots, and wherever she went there hovered a cloud of eight to ten men. Suddenly, the German who hadn't been able to speak English to us for several hundred miles initiated a lively conversation with Marge. A very funny, very friendly Indian named Manny set a huge battery-operated tape deck on the beach; he and Marge began dancing to the disco music that blared from it. Through it all, six black bears worked in shifts on the big pile of salmon guts across the river, interrupted only by the gulls that flew in at every oportunity to steal a pink morsel or two.

About midnight, the hostesses began to drift, one by one, into our tents, exhausted; the party continued unabated. Evelyn was the last holdout, outlasting even Bing, who'd taken on the role of chaperone; she was last seen stepping into a motorboat with Frank—who was just sober enough to stand behind the wheel—clutching a pot of warm bath water as they roared away down the Yukon.

## JULY 23, DAY 45

Paul Beard had said the quantity of beer (not counting whiskey) that the fifty or so residents of Rampart ordered for the eight-month period between the last barge run before freeze-up and the first run after breakup each year was 1,800 cases; this morning they all appeared to be lying, empty, in our camp.

Evelyn and I took down our tent in preparation for paddling downriver, but by the time we'd eaten breakfast the wind had come up and turned the river into a rolling ocean again, so we spent the day waiting, tentless. Everything I owned was wet either from the water in the boat or from the water that had seeped into the tent during the all-night rain. And it was raining yet. I spent part of the day dictating into my tape recorder, under the shelter of the trees where all the mosquitoes had come to get out of the wind.

Finally I retreated to the community hall. Evelyn found some logs and built a fire in the stove; I slept in front of it across three folding chairs. We wrote in our journals, ate crackers and cheese, stared out the windows at lines of grey clouds marching down the valley, drank Cokes, read stories about the Mad Trapper of Rat River, talked to the villagers who wandered in. It was the kind of day that made you think the sun would never come out again, the wind would never again stop blowing nor the rain pouring, and you'd spend the rest of your life between the four wooden walls of this room.

Once, the rain let up for a few moments. Evelyn and I tiptoed in our wool socks down the muddy path through the tall fireweed to the community outhouse. With our filthy Gore-Tex down around our ankles, we sat silently beside each other on the two-holer bench. We observed without a word that there was no toilet paper. We swatted mosquitoes in the darkened plywood structure. We breathed through our mouths to minimize the stench that hung in the air from our own clothes and the accumulation of community excrement that lay a few feet beneath us. "Well . . . here we are," I sighed. We began to laugh, and we laughed and laughed until we couldn't stop.

## JULY 24, DAY 46

The morning brought more rain and clouds, but we were all determined to go *somewhere*, regardless of weather. Jude wrapped a wool balaclava around her swollen foot, put it in a stuff sack, propped it on the gunnel, and, with Sue, pushed off into the cold, grey Yukon. Bing paddled with them. Evelyn and I were set on getting down to a big Indian wedding dance at Tanana, which Manny had said would be the biggest party one the Yukon.

"They'll welcome you with open arms," he'd said, when we noted that we knew neither the bride nor the groom. "You'll fit right in," he'd said, when we protested that all we had to wear were the filthy baggy clothes we had on. So we hopped into Frank's motorboat and headed for a Saturday night in the big city with Frank, Manny, Marge, and Marge's younger sister.

Frank was a carpenter, a thin Indian, whose face and hands showed the wrinkles of the forty-odd years he'd spent working off and on, up and down the Yukon. He'd just bought a new $12,000 motorboat, and sitting on its floor we jarred through seventy-five miles of heavy waves at full throttle, the speed of the boat increasing the chill of the air and the sting of the raindrops on our faces. We stopped every few miles so Manny and Frank could light another cigarette out of the wind; we stopped once to drink more beer, warm ourselves, and have some coffee at the cabin of Frank's sister, Effie; then we stopped to let the women go ashore to pee; then we stopped again so Marge and her sister could clamber up a muddy cutbank into the woods on an island to hide a case of beer for the return trip home.

Marge had grown up in Rampart, finished college in California, and would start law school there next fall. She was full of life, grace, and mischief. "Par-ty!" she would sing-song at intervals, stretching her hand around the corner of the steering cab so Evelyn could put another beer into it. Manny lived mostly in Fairbanks, but apparently spent much of the salmon season in Rampart. He was thirtyish, with medium-length dark hair, an open grin, and a burn scar on the side of his face. He and Marge had joked with us and made us feel very welcome in Rampart that night at the beach party. He said it was fun to have people come down the river so they could meet them, and he assured us that from Rampart on down, all the Indian villages would welcome whites. He said there was no racial tension here. And it was because of his good-natured encouragement that Evelyn and I were now bound for an Athapascan Indian wedding in Tanana.

"City lights!" exclaimed Manny as we rounded the bend above Tanana. Sure enough, a few electric light poles stood above the muddy streets of this Indian village of almost 400 people. Tanana's taxi service was a red station wagon that sputtered and rumbled and was missing a window, but it was a welcome sight to convey all of our beer and our backpacks the few blocks up to Frank's cabin. Evelyn and I grabbed our towels and soap and dashed to the shower-washateria in hopes of improving our appearance to some extent and enjoying the first hot shower we'd had in two weeks. We hadn't felt the need to avail ourselves of the showers in Fort Yukon or Beaver, but now we felt a calling. We reached the building just as the manager locked the door. They were closing an hour early, she explained, because the whole town was going to a big wedding.

By then we were starving; we prowled the streets, found everything closed, and finally wolfed down the lone can of fruit cocktail that comprised Frank's pantry. Frank's cabin was just big enough for two single beds and a woodstove and a bucket of something I preferred not to investigate. The smoke from his cigarette hung heavy in the air. There were no lights because the electric company had turned off his electricity. I preferred the mosquitoes and the fresh air of Frank's front yard, so Evelyn and I erected the tent in its high grass. We never did get straight just where it was that Frank actually lived; he seemed to be a resident of Rampart and Tanana and his sister's cabin and a number of other places.

We missed the wedding ceremony because Frank didn't like weddings and we weren't aware that it had started yet, but we slogged through the mud to the front of the Episcopalian log church just in time to see the bride and groom leave after the ceremony. Everyone stood in the street beside the river and threw rice as the couple walked down the wooden steps—he in a dark suit and running shoes and a baseball cap; she in a long white dress that dragged in the mud, a cigarette dangling from her lips. We ambled over to Frank's brother's house and quickly devoured the leftover fried chicken they offered us. Frank never seemed to eat, only drink. Finally we all piled into a pickup truck and lurched through town, picking up passersby en route, to the large, one-room, log community hall that Frank had helped build.

Inside, hundreds of elderly people and toddlers and everything in between milled about, eating moosehead stew and other items from a long table. The women wore long or short dresses, mostly with running shoes underneath. We felt incredibly dirty in our muddy wool pants and T-shirts and hair that had spent the better part of a week under a knit hat. The men wore their usual jeans or khaki pants or flannel shirts or whatever they happened to be wearing. We all sat in rows of folding chairs around the edges of the vast hall, chatting among ourselves and watching children playing in the center of the room. Women brought wedding cake on paper plates and champagne in plastic glasses. Frank and the other men passed a bottle among themselves in the back row. Tanana was officially a "dry" town, where one could not legally buy liquor, but, like every other such place, there were bootleggers aplenty.

Fights—mostly harmless—erupted, the initiators of which were usually too drunk to inflict any real damage. One huge man was physically removed from the hall several times by teams of men, then he finally slunk back in and gently began positioning all the chairs he'd knocked down back into their proper places. Meanwhile, Evelyn and I found that we could sit in no one place very long before whatever man happened to be sitting beside us got too far out of line in his eagerness to welcome us to Tanana and Alaska. But the women were protective and friendly and watched our maneuvers with some amusement. There were but fifteen or twenty whites in the entire crowd. The beer cans circulated, children screamed and played tag and raced around the room, people stood in groups visiting, one old man danced an Indian dance by himself in the center of the room. Through it all, Ronnie and Linda smiled at the head table behind their wedding cake, opening the hundreds of presents piled in a corner, holding each one aloft for all to see. No one was watching.

This continued until about midnight, when Frank announced that he was going home to take a nap until the dance started. Evelyn and I looked at each other and giggled, for Bing had been to some of these Indian dances before and he'd made us promise to leave by one-thirty in the morning because that was when the fights started.

At two o'clock three young guys took the stage and began to beat out country-and-western songs and hard-rock songs on electric guitars and a drum set. The lights dimmed and hundreds of shadowy figures, young and old, began to do the Twist or the two-step or disco or whatever they felt like to the music, kicking the occasional beer can or sticky paper plate or crushed champagne glass out of their way. After a few reconnaissance forays to ascertain that we were women beneath our bulky clothes and boots, the young men began to ask Evelyn and me to dance. We trod through the debris out onto the slick floor and bumped and banged among the crowd. Some partners were very graceful and gentlemanly; others were so drunk they kept falling into us and sending us careening into someone else.

They all tried to converse to some extent, but it was next to impossible in the throb of the band music. Some were pretty direct in their approach to courtship, and once Evelyn was left standing alone on the dance floor in mid-song when she answered a question in the negative. But it was all terrific fun to stomp and holler and wonder what strange thing might happen next. Evelyn and I were sweating and smelling like wet dogs in our wool longhandles, but all the men kept on their heavy wool or leather jackets.

Meanwhile, the younger women had shed their dresses for jeans, and the party really began to take off. Every half-hour or so, Marge or Manny would come by to say hello and make sure we hadn't happened into something we couldn't handle; each time we'd wave and give the thumbs-up sign. Finally I had to go to the bathroom badly enough that I was ready to brave my way through the throngs of men who stood at the doorway and in the street; luckily an old Indian woman asked me to go with her. We weaved through the crowd and walked in the light rain across a grassy field to a two-holer outhouse with a star and moon cut into the door. Inside, we swatted mosquitoes and talked about weddings.

As we pushed our way from the cold night air back into the furnace of the dance hall, I looked back over my shoulder at the Yukon, whose surface was smooth for the first time in days. Somewhere upstream, I assumed, were Bing and Sue and Jude, no doubt sleeping on some sandbar. Back inside, the band was playing "Help Me Make it Through the Night" and Evelyn was twirling around the dance floor cheek to cheek with Frank's nephew Bobby, his big boots stepping lightly among the beer cans, her bear bells jangling from her hip.

## JULY 25, DAY 47

At 9 A.M., the next morning when we began to stir, the electric bass of the dance band was still throbbing across town. We never knew just when the dance ended, but we were probably well on our way back to Rampart in Frank's motorboat with a load of hungover passengers when it did. It was another tortuous, jarring ride over the waves, entertaining only because one young guy was still so drunk that he refused to wear anything more than a lightweight denim jacket over his clothes. The rest of us were freezing in the cold wind and the spray from the waves, but he rode the whole way without a whimper, his head banging directly on the plywood floor of the boat. As we neared Rampart, Frank ran out of gas; he and Manny shouted to a boat ahead of us and they loaned us enough gas to get to a nearby fish camp to fill up from an oil drum.

Back at Rampart, the wind was blowing, the skies were grey, a light drizzle was falling, and everybody from Leaping Lee to Paul and Penny was pleading with us not to get on the river; but, as we had at Circle, we felt that we'd never get past Rampart if we didn't take some affirmative action. So about 7 P.M., Lee helped us roll the boat into the water, carried Evelyn to the stern in his arms so she wouldn't get her feet wet (though we were already soaked head to foot), and shoved us down the Yukon.

A few miles later, we were sitting in the rolling waves under a pouring rain, floating sideways and eating peanut butter and wet crackers, when we looked up to see our first and only grizzly of the trip.

On the shore, sitting on his haunches, unconcerned with the rain, a light brown bear looked at us for a moment. All the other bears we'd seen had been coal black. And he was a little lanky compared to the roly-poly black bears we'd seen. Not particularly big, he could've been a young bear. Or, once again, distance could have been deceiving us. The grey, pouring rain obscured all but a brown bearish outline. Suddenly he shook himself and loped into the willows.

We paddled for a few hours and made camp on the flat, cementlike sands of Garnet Island, sixteen miles downstream from Rampart. Since nothing else was handy, we used our two loaded backpacks to tie up the boat, pulling the packs as high up on the beach as possible.

## JULY 26, DAY 48

The breakfast fire succumbed to the rain just after the coffee water steamed, so we put into the river and drank our coffee and tea as we drifted. Paddling an hour or so through misty morning fog and steep mountains brought us to the camp of Frank's sister, Effie; she'd said to stop by, and nothing seemed more inviting now than a few moments of warmth and another cup of hot anything. We had no idea what time it was and hoped we weren't showing up at five in the morning. She came to the door in her nightgown when her little yapping dog announced our arrival; she said it was nine o'clock and she should've been up anyway. The warmth of her cabin was exquisite, and she showed us how to put our wool mittens and socks and hats to dry on the racks above her wood stove. Then, without a word she set before us a huge bowl of oatmeal, a platter of dried salmon strips, and a can of Vienna sausage, which for some reason made our eyes light up. All the while, she kept hot coffee coming from the pot on the stove, and as we talked she mixed up a wad of bread dough and set it aside to rise.

Effie Kokrine was in her sixties, grey-haired, short and stockily built. She had raised eight children in one-room cabins like this up and down the Yukon. Her husband had trapped and fished and done carpentry work. Year after year, she had cut up salmon and dried it and sewn the skins of the animals into moccasins and mittens and hoods. Her husband of forty-four years was dead now, and Effie lived most of the year in Fairbanks, but in the summers she was here at her cabin, cutting the salmon. Her son Bobby lived just downstream.

"You eat that salmon like a white woman!" she kidded Evelyn good-naturedly, showing us how to zip the dried salmon strips between our teeth so that we gleaned every morsel from the skin. She said her children were scattered all over Alaska now, but they could communicate with her over the "Trapline Chatter" program on the radio in which people in the bush send messages to each other. Once, she was here alone at her cabin on a Saturday night when the news came over the radio that all her children were together in Fairbanks and were thinking of her. "So I went outside and I got a beer to join the party!" she smiled.

Effie said she'd had severe arthritis at one time and could hardly walk, but she'd gone to the Philippines to a special place run by some kind of religious outfit where they performed surgery and took out the stuff that was causing her pain. She said they performed the surgery without an incision, simply putting their hands on the painful area and removing a white mass of bad stuff. Then they wiped their hands on a towel and were ready for the next patient. Effie said she didn't know or care exactly how it worked; she knew only that at one time she could hardly walk and now she could hike around the hills and cut up salmon with the best of 'em. Of course, every year or so she would go back for remedial treatment.

Around the room were scattered wolf skins and fox skins and pieces of moosehide from which Effie planned to sew garments. From a support log near the table hung pieces of beadwork that she would sew into the uppers of moccasins. She made a fair amount of money with her sewing and she always had more work than she could handle. Evelyn and I decided to give ourselves a present and put in an order for a pair of moosehide moccasins that would wrap around the ankle. We each stood on a sheet of notebook paper in our socks and Effie drew an outline around our feet. She said she couldn't start them until the fall; we said that would be fine. We asked her to make up a picture that had something to do with a canoe for the beadwork on the top of the foot. She said the cost would be $75 per pair (we knew that was the going rate) and we could pay when they were finished.

Effie said she'd seen Sue and Jude and Bing pass by yesterday afternoon, and that reminded us that we needed to head on downriver. Besides, our things were now dry above the stove. We made one last trip to the outhouse, piled on all our various layers of winter clothes and rain gear, and pushed back into the river. Effie stood on the bank waving, her tiny, one-pound white dog, Socks, poking his head out of his customary place in the pocket of her coat.

We paddled steadily through a day that dealt us everything from sunshine to cold rain, but thankfully, not much wind. As instructed, we paddled to the left through the stretch known as The Rapids where the motorboat drivers claimed big boils could be felt, but we made it through with hardly a bounce. Nibbling when we felt like it, sleeping for a few minutes when we needed it, we found that we could continue seemingly forever without tiring, and late in the day we noted with amazement that we were already nearing Tanana.

We entered a side slough just as an airplane took off from the tip of an island at its entrance and two cow moose wandered out of the woods along its shore. We drifted silently down upon the moose, coming ever closer as I madly clicked away with my camera. Every time the shutter clicked they would look up from the low willows they were nibbling and stare out into the river; if we sat absolutely still they would return to their business. Finally we were within twenty yards of them. One took a quick step into the water in our direction, at which point Evelyn began to backpaddle. Throughout the encounter, a steady rain poured upon my camera, but I figured closeup moose pictures were hard to come by.

We were still congratulating ourselves over our good moose fortune when we reached the end of the island and realized we'd passed Paul's and Don's camp, where the steak dinner awaited. We were too far downriver now to reach the camp without ferrying to shore and crashing through the woods for a mile or so, pulling the boat upstream behind us with a rope, which seemed the only thing worse than missing a steak dinner. We paddled on, with much wailing and gnashing of teeth, through the rain.

Just before seven o'clock we paddled into familiar Tanana, past the scene of the wild dance whose empty champagne glasses and beer cans still littered the street, and down to where Bing's green boat and Sue's and Jude's yellow one were tied to a cable. Sue's tent was perched at the top of the cliff, but no one was in sight. We slithered up the rain-slick clay embankment and into the ankle-deep mud of Tanana's main street. Looking and feeling like very wet dogs, still clad in our warm life jackets, we slid into the store just as it was closing. I shook the water from my cowboy hat and removed my soaked balaclava. I'm sure my hair was standing straight up. Mary, the store clerk whom we'd met at the dance, said we could have whatever we wanted but the store was closing and we'd have to come back tomorrow to pay. We heated four small pizzas in the microwave oven and ate them and an ice cream bar and a Coke under the eaves of the front porch. When we asked about our cohorts, Mary said she'd seen somebody coming up the bank on crutches an hour before.

We finally connected with the gang, who didn't believe at first that we'd really come down here to the dance, gone back upriver, and paddled back down so quickly. They hadn't expected us for two more days, and they themselves had arrived only at two-thirty this morning. The difference lay in the fact that during the two full days they had paddled, the river had been covered with choppy, windblown waves; during the one day it took us to get here, we'd been blessed with smooth water that made for fast paddling. We piled our gear into the pickup of Roger Maynard, a thirtyish white guy who was the local constable, and he drove us a mile through town to his cabin where we could sleep on the floor.

Jude's foot had been X-rayed, and the doctor at the hospital had said he believed there was no fracture. But there was some debate over the hard-to-read X-ray, and Sue diagnosed a hairline fracture of one bone. At any rate, Jude was hobbling on crutches with no cast, taking a quick step· on the foot every now and then as she hopped around Roger's cabin. They had accidentally missed the fish cops' island too, and we moaned over our misfortune to Roger. He said there was no way to radio them.

"We could drop them a message in a bottle," he mentioned casually, and we smiled at the joke. He returned from the bedroom with a plastic vitamin bottle. "No, really, who wants to be my copilot?" he asked. I volunteered to fly with him to drop the message and Evelyn volunteered to donate to the inevitable, ensuing party the bottle of Bailey's Irish Cream she'd bought in Rampart.

Roger handed me a memo pad. "To: Nude Fish Cops," I wrote. "From: Texas Women and Bing. Subject: Bailey's. Message: Sorry we missed you. We've got the refreshments if you'll bring the dinner. We're at Roger's."

Roger and I drove to the airstrip. Into his two-person plane he threw his survival gear—an eighty-pound backpack with a shotgun strapped to its side. Then he began checking out whatever it is that pilots of small planes always check out. I stood beneath the wing, out of the rain, in a cloud of mosquitoes, thinking what a wonderfully bizarre set of circumstances had brought about my first ride in a small plane. We taxied down the gravel runway through puddles of water. Strapped into my seat, staring at the back of Roger's broad shoulders and short military-type haircut, I was just thinking (or hoping) that here was a person who could fly anything and hike anywhere and handle with ease any emergency in the North, when he said, "Where's the bottle?"

"I thought you had it."

We taxied back down the runway and up into the field where the planes were parked; I ran to his pickup and got the message bottle, and we tried the whole thing again. The takeoff was less scary than expected and I found myself banking at a sharp angle over the Yukon; the big river looked incredibly muddy from up here. We followed its bends until we spotted the fish cops' island, then we dived toward the river to buzz them and make them come out of their cabin. As we whizzed by almost at ground level we saw them standing in their boat. Roger held up the bottle to let them know we'd drop it on the next swing. I grinned and waved. We flew high into the air, banked and coasted directly over their boat as Roger dropped the bottle, then we banked again and circled by one more time to get their answer. It was a definitive "yes" as they held their arms straight into the air.

"That's Mount McKinley," Roger said a few moments later, pointing to a large white mass that I had thought was a huge cloudbank. It was approximately 150 miles away and monstrous even at this distance. Below us spread rolling hills, an occasional pond, and the mighty Yukon.

"What took you so long?" the gang said, when we walked back into the cabin and began peeling off our clothes. Don and another fish cop, Ken (Paul was in Fairbanks), had come downriver in their motorboat and were already halfway through their first cup of Bailey's by the time Roger and I got back to the airstrip, filled his plane with fuel, and drove back to his cabin. Don and Ken were out of steaks and had arrived only with malt liquor, so Sue cooked up a bunch of our dehydrated cabbage and pinto beans. Jude hopped around, I cleaned my trumpet valves with Roger's gun oil, Evelyn scrounged up a wire whisk and a stainless-steel bowl to substitute as a tambourine, Sue tuned up her ukulele, Bing donned the finger cymbals, and Roger pulled his banjo from its case. We spread my sheet music on the floor, Roger threw in his own music books, and we all began to sing and clap and generally carry on. Don and Ken smiled, shook their heads, and drank their Bailey's.

At 3 A.M., Bing and I were still talking to Roger after Don and Ken had left and the others had gone to bed. Roger said with a grin that he'd heard we were coming and knew we'd cause some kind of wild ruckus in town; he figured the best thing to do was contain the ruckus in his own house where he could keep an eye on it. We had a long rambling discussion about the Indians of the area, including their alcoholism (though no liquor could legally be bought in Tanana, alcohol-related health problems and violence were commonplace) and how they related to Roger and other whites. Roger mentioned that Rampart, where we'd just spent three days in one big, happy beach party, was considered by law enforcement people in the area to be a bit of a rough place for a white cop to set foot in. We found that hard to believe. He then told about a time when he had to bring in a rough character from Rampart who allegedly tried to run down a female cop in Fairbanks with his car. As he described the incident, we realized he was talking about Manny! We all shrugged and smiled at each other. Maybe four women floating down the river were more welcome than cops.

It had been a long day. I had paddled a canoe fifty-nine miles through the rain, flown over the Yukon to drop a bottle to some fish cops, seen Mount McKinley, and played my trumpet and partied for about five hours. I spread my sleeping bag on the floor and went to sleep.

## JULY 27, DAY 49

Long before we awoke, Roger had left to fly to Fairbanks where he had to testify in a trial. We made breakfast and tried to put his kitchen in order. He had a gas stove and electricity and telephone service. His cabin was really a modern frame house, complete with wall paneling and carpets. The only thing a little odd was that he had no running water. Neither did anyone else in town. They all showered and washed clothes at the one central building, which I suppose was served by a well or water pumped from the Yukon. Roger kept some five-gallon jugs full of water in the kitchen. Like Penny Beard, he had a modern sink, but no water came from its faucets. He told us to pour used dishwashing water into what he affectionately called the Yuck Bucket. His bathroom contained a sink, a mirror, and a large plastic chemical toilet that contained no water or chemicals and served mostly as a throne upon which to sit. Somehow, trying to wash vinegar and grease out of frying pans and using a toilet with no running water all seemed a little dirty and a great deal of a hassle. We preferred to be out on a nice, clean sandbar where we could properly bury our waste where it would have no odor, where we could rub some sand in the pans to clean them, and where we could rinse them in the good old river. Of course, we were sure that when it was forty below outside, Roger's Yuck Bucket and bathroom throne would seem like pretty handy things to have.

The main projects for the day were washing our bodies and our clothes and picking up yet more food boxes at the post office. With the new arrival, each boat was probably burdened with a good 150 pounds of food. Evelyn was determined to wash every last possible scrap of material she owned, so she tended her washing machine and dryer wearing only wetsuit booties, a T-shirt, and a plastic garbage-bag skirt. The hot shower was heavenly, though it was one of those into which we had to keep feeding quarters every few minutes. I couldn't remember the last time I'd washed my hair, but I strongly suspected it had been eighteen days ago in Circle.

It was late in the afternoon when we finished all the chores, and the weather was still cloudy and damp. I was sick of being in towns where every time you wanted to change clothes or pee, three motorboats drove past, but my suggestion to get on the river today was voted down with the promise that we'd get an early start in the morning.

We crawled into the tents we'd set up on a narrow strip of land between the road and the river. For hours, a flock of kids across the street laughed and screamed as they played "tent," inspired by our example. The three-wheeled, motorized mud bikes that everyone seemed to own roared up and down the street, a few feet from our bedrooms. I had finally gotten to sleep when I was awakened by the violent dieseling of a car engine and noxious exhaust fumes a few inches from our tent. Addressing our three tents, a drunken man slurred a long, soft oration about white people and sissy tee-pees and a bunch of other stuff I couldn't make out. The upshot was that he thought it would be a good idea if we got the hell out of town.

# 10 birds, bears, and yukon sun dogs

## JULY 28, DAY 50

We concurred with the gentleman's suggestion to leave the city lights; first thing the next morning, at last, we were back on the open river.

Among the first set of islands we somehow lost Bing. Then, as we sought to take a shortcut through a side slough, we tried a last-minute ferry across river and got caught up in a series of shoals. Evelyn and I launched an all-out shouting and swearing match at each other as our boat dragged and thudded over rocks and among tree snags; all the while we kept paddling and floating backwards into the slough. Not five minutes later we spotted the first bald eagle we'd seen in some time.

"Oh, look!" said Evelyn.

"Wow!" I said.

Truce.

We paddled throughout the day in on-and-off rain and waves. At one point we found ourselves a mile or more ahead of Sue and Jude, which was indeed a rare circumstance. Thus, for the first time, it became apparent that our flatwater keel sliced through the wind-driven waves, holding us on course and allowing us to make good progress, while their whitewater hull slowed their progress as it allowed their boat to toss slightly on top of the waves. During the rest of the trip, although we could never keep up with them on smooth water, we could outdistance them with ease in moderate to heavy waves. But Sue was having other troubles today as well, for she'd picked up some kind of stomach virus. We pulled out early to let her recuperate.

The rest of us crawled into the tents out of the mosquitoes and the rainy mist and napped, while Evelyn soloed our boat up a tiny slough that bisected the island. She sat alone on the beach in the wind, thinking of home. She had learned when she called home in Tanana that her daughter had just been released from a five-day stay in the hospital for minor, but unexpected, surgery. Jude had learned that her grandmother, who'd been sick for some weeks, had died. Our thoughts were turning to friends we'd left, Sunday morning newpapers over coffee and pancakes, cheese enchiladas, and the families who always sounded so relieved when we called.

## JULY 29, DAY 51

A strange addition to our camp gear leaned against the canoe at the water's edge: a pair of crutches. But we also had another supplement. Paul Beard had insisted that we take Penny's rifle with us, and Sue had accepted it as a loan. We all knew that our level of understanding of the contraption made it almost useless if anything were to happen, but Sue faithfully carried it, wrapped in plastic garbage bags, from the canoe to her tent every night. The small wooded island we'd chosen as last night's camp also marked the first time we'd camped really close to our kitchen, except in towns. All our pacts seemed to be crumbling.

After breakfast, Evelyn and I paddled into the mainstream of the current and began drifting, brushing our teeth and washing a few odd clothes or dishes over the side, as we did every morning. We could perform these water-related duties better here on the river than in camp, because we wouldn't get our feet muddy, would be out of the mosquitoes, and could be floating downriver at the same time.

Ahead rose the ominous, grey, four-story-high mud cliffs known as the Palisades or the "Boneyard." Vast sheets of mud and dirt perched vertically above the river, waiting to fall on canoeists. Hundreds of tusks and skulls and other bones from woolly mammoths and other prehistoric creatures lie within the slimy layers  of these giant walls, new ones constantly exposed as huge sections of earth shear off and plunge into the river. We drifted within a few feet of the awesome banks, pressing our luck, but drawn to the danger. It was hard to say which would be more exciting, spotting a mastodon tusk or getting buried in a mud avalanche.

The rains had turned the five-mile stretch of the Palisades into a web of tiny, rushing creeks that cascaded and splattered and slurped and dribbled over the mud. All along, we could hear the plops of small clods smacking into the water. The whole thing looked like it might suddenly ooze into the Yukon. Sue's and Jude's yellow canoe looked like a plastic party toothpick next to a three-bedroom-two-bath-sized glob that had toppled into the water. From the cliffs drifted a dank, odd stench of newly exposed earth that maybe had lots of dead things in it.

At first we floated silently, caught up in the eery effect of the Boneyard, our paddles poised to outrun any tumbling ten-ton block or its tidal wave. But then we got a little cocky and began screaming, banging our paddles on the gunnels, and singing in high pitches to try to cause an avalanche. With a devilish look in her eye, Jude pulled from her bag a compressed-air Freon horn. She'd brought one to scare away bears but this was the first time she'd found a use for it. She pointed it at the cliffs and pushed its button. We covered our ears as its high, loud blast echoed across the water. But the Boneyard wasn't accepting any dares this morning; we neither saw any tusks nor buried ourselves under a landslide.

Floating close to shore around the next bend, still marveling at the mystery of the Boneyard, Jude spotted a calico-colored fox sniffing among the grasses on a flat muddy bank.

"A bear!" shouted Evelyn, seconds later. Sure enough, a small, black one trotted up the shore toward us. Silently, we drifted downstream and toward shore as he splashed along the bank, moving upstream. We were now so close that he could hear the clicks of our camera shutters; he stopped and squinted across the river. The only things moving in our canoes were Sue's and my thumbs as we cocked the film-advance levers of our cameras, and Jude's and Evelyn's clandestine swivel of the wrist as they ruddered the boats with their paddles. Now Sue and Jude were twenty yards from him. They sat still, holding their breath; he stood very still on all fours, staring right at Sue, trying to determine whether the floating object posed a threat. His light brown muzzle wiggled as he sniffed the air for a clue. Suddenly a loud splashing erupted as Jude decided they'd pressed their luck far enough and leaned into powerful, rhythmic backstrokes. The bear shrugged and loped away up the beach.

Before we could reload film, we came upon two Canada geese, our first of the trip, shuffling among the willows at the water's edge. Then, another fox emerged, this one a brown color. All these animals seemed to be heading along the shore in an upstream direction; we decided one rather interesting meeting would erupt when this mob convened somewhere upriver.

As we drifted, still smiling and shaking our heads over the incredible string of wildlife we'd just witnessed, we spotted our first sandhill cranes of the trip. Two grey lumps stood up from the sandbar into which they blended, walked about nervously for a few minutes on their spindly, two-foot-tall legs, then lifted into the air simultaneously. With slow, graceful beats of their wings, the two shapes with their six-foot wingspans powered across the distant blue-green hills and up into the grey afternoon mists. It was amazing to think that these two beautiful creatures might spend next winter thousands of miles away on the Texas coast.

Such was our introduction to the Nowitna National Wildlife Refuge, established under the Alaska lands act—a wetland haven of muskeg, willows, marshes, and sloughs that is the summer home of 110,000 nesting ducks and 52,000 nesting and migrant geese. It is also a waystation for 220,000 birds on their fall migration. It stretches from the Yukon's left bank across a wide basin to the flanks of the Kuskokwim Mountains, fifty miles away. We would paddle through it for three days.

Sue was all smiles after our wildlife rendezvous, but soon the cold, damp afternoon and her stomach cramps got the best of her. We pulled out onto an island strewn with low willows. We built a little platform of logs to ease the loading and unloading of boats in the shin-deep mud at the water's edge; Jude crab-walked (or crab-hopped, I should say) the gunnels from the stern to the bow, hopped on one foot over the wet logs, and hopped over to the kitchen where she was relegated to fire-tender duty by her somewhat immobile status.

A fine, rainy mist was falling—not enough to keep the mosquitoes off the beach. The sky had been grey, either getting ready to pour or resting up from a recent downpour, for as long as we could remember. We settled for a quick-cooking meal of commercially-prepared freeze-dried chicken and rice. Sue and Jude sat beside each other in their lawn chairs, bundled in their blue parkas with a Shoo-Bug jacket draped over their heads—Jude wearing a boot and a tennis shoe, Sue holding her stomach—sharing a plastic bag of rice in the rain. They had a faraway, somewhat disgruntled, look in their eyes, like they wondered just why it was that they were here. We were accustomed to enduring rain or mosquitoes as we sat around camp, but not both at the same time, so after dinner we took to the tents.

Evelyn and I were both propped up on our elbows reading, sometime later, when we simultaneously looked at each other from the corners of our eyes.

"Did you hear something?" I whispered. We listened, holding our breath. There came a distinct sound like someone—a big someone—drawing in three, long, deep breaths.

"Something is out there," declared Evelyn, her expression a mixture of excitement and concern. Quietly, she unzipped the tent flap and poked her head into the night. She crouched motionless on all fours. I waited an eternity, her naked white posterior all I could see of the outside world.

"It's Bing!" she cried.

"You guys want some bear meat?" came his matter-of-fact voice through the night. He'd spent two days with a trapper at his camp, and a young bear had threatened them by parading into camp so many times that the guys had finally shot it. Bing now had a bear ham, which he was carrying around in a skillet in the bottom of his boat. He'd pulled quietly into our camp some time ago, thinking we were asleep; he'd rigged up a lean-to with his poncho and some logs and had gotten a fire going, all without our hearing a thing as he walked barefooted on the beach. What had tipped us off were the three long sighlike tugs of his plastic boat hull across the smooth sand as he pulled it up for the night. He was lucky Sue hadn't shot him.

## JULY 30, DAY 52

We made a pressure-cooker out of the pot with the bent lid and boiled a big hunk of bear meat in the morning mist. Bing sat on a log, barefooted as usual, sewing up his old green sweatshirt where the neck ribbing had finally separated from the front, from shoulder seam to shoulder seam. As he sat cross-legged, one could see through the crotch of one pair of his pants, which had split out for several inches, into the crotch of the second pair of pants he always wore, which so far was still intact. He wore the two pairs for warmth and also to minimize the chances of a mosquito's proboscis finding its way into thigh or butt. (That very event had happened to me, through my wool pants, several times as I sat in my lawn chair.) The hems of both pairs of Bing's polyester pants had long since come undone, and they dragged in the dirt around his muddy feet. His red knit cap had ridden up on top of his head, and a few long strands of blond hair stuck out at odd angles from beneath it.

Beside him lay a crusty, fossilized animal's hip-bone he'd found in the Boneyard. Altogether, as he sat there licking the end of a thread and squinting to run it through a needle, he was quite a sight. He smiled as we applauded his progress across the neck of the shirt. I suggested he would get so carried away with his new hobby that he might even sew up the crotch of his pants; he peered earthward between his legs with a grin, shook his head and said he wanted to save some projects for rainy days in the tent.

Bing gave us some bear meat to take for lunch and we paddled downriver, leaving him to his sewing and saying we'd see him later. The fare for the day was again wind-driven waves and occasional rain, but today the skies also offered an unexpected pleasure: sun dogs. That's what Evelyn called the spectrum of colors that lined the bowlike valleys around almost every bend. In the changing patterns of distant falling rain and mist and shifting clouds and shafts of sunlight, the yellows and oranges and greens of the sun dogs appeared and grew and disappeared against the grey hills and green spruces. Every now and then a sun dog would become a rainbow, rising from the Yukon's grey waters, then evaporating before one could point it out to one's partner. At the height of the sun-dog migration, we thwarted and drifted and ate bear meat, which tasted like extra-greasy pot roast with tiny black hairs on it. The boats began to bang together in the waves too much for thwarting, so we drifted individually for awhile. I fell sound asleep.

Once, trying to cut between two sandbars, we wandered into shallow water. Evelyn and I got through, poling the boat with our paddles and dragging bottom only once. But as I looked back at Sue and Jude I had to laugh. Jude was steering turned around in the bow, her swollen foot propped on the gunnel. Sue was doubled over, half-asleep, wearing a headnet against the gnats that had swarmed onto the river when the wind died; she was facing Jude and barely able to sit up, let alone paddle, in her pain. At that moment they dragged bottom, so Jude got out, hopped in the water on one foot until they floated free, then shoved the boat into the current and slid onto the seat. Nothing much seemed to slow them down; Jude kept up with us, though she was the only one paddling. We had told them we could lay over for a few days so they could both mend their injuries, but they had wanted to push on.

A young gull soared overhead. A pair of Arctic terns zoomed toward us repeatedly, veering off at the last minute. Two bald eagles lifted from a dead snag among the spruces and floated along the tree line.

Rounding a bend, we found ourselves in low waves again. On the far shore at the next curve lay some barrels, a road, a silent cabin, and Bing's green boat. The river was two miles wide at times and filled with so many islands that it was not unusual to lose sight of each other for days, and we were now growing accustomed to happening upon him. He had pulled out to warm himself with a quick fire before pushing on, but we wanted to find a campsite. The floor of his boat was littered with the curled cylinders of old birch bark that he collected for starting fires; he tossed us some bark and some boullion cubes for Sue as we said goodbye.

298 / YUKON WILD

Around the next bend, the wind swept up the narrow valley with a vengeance; the skies unleashed a pelting rain. We crashed through big rollers and whitecaps, rather desperately scanning the shoreline for a campsite. For miles there was nothing but a two-foot cutbank packed with trees, against which the waves smashed and were tossed into the air. Once or twice, the combination of the high, irregular waves and sudden gusts of wind produced the sensation of a canoe rolling out from beneath me, which I had experienced many times in my life, but keenly desired to avoid just now. Clouds overhead swirled into an ever-blackening mixture. We finally bashed into a steep, rock-strewn beach crowded by a thick forest of alders and spruce.

"Garden spot!" we shouted to each other over the roar of the wind and the dashing of waves against the rocks as we prepared to batten down the hatches for the night. Big logs rode in on the waves and thudded against their brethren in a slim eddy. Heaving in unison, the four of us lifted the stern of each boat to jam a log under it, hoping that would get it out of the water so the waves wouldn't drop into it all night. Evelyn and I put up the tent near some bushes, where the wind whipped it with only moderate violence. Wet and shivering, I crawled in with most of my books, prepared to hibernate for the duration. I was hungry, but not enough to go out in that mess. Snuggled into the warmth of my sleeping bag, I read about wolf packs and sled chases and love in the frozen North in *Tisha*.

But Evelyn, ever one for a challenge, was determined to get a fire going. Bing paddled up, and together they found a clever (albeit only thirty feet from our tents) niche in the alders, built a fire, cooked vegetarian chili, and sat there for hours drinking tea and ruminating about whatever one might ruminate about in an alder thicket during a gale.

## JULY 31, DAY 53

The crashing of the two-foot waves against the rocks, the grey skies, the grey waters, the cold wind, and an occasional gull struggling high overhead brought to mind November on Chesapeake Bay. Sue was still sick, and no one was in any hurry to paddle anyway, so we crammed ourselves around the fire in Evelyn's smoky little den and drank tea. At least it wasn't raining, and after awhile I rather liked the roar of the wind in my ears and its coolness on my face. I walked up the beach, sat on a four-foot-thick tree that the Yukon had long ago deposited there, and talked into my tape recorder. Once I squatted to pee, gazing absently out over the grey, choppy Yukon. I happened to look beneath me, where the byproducts from my morning tea had filled to the brim the sandy cloven hoofprint of a large moose; God, I love Alaska, I thought.

Evelyn entertained us for awhile by performing her beer-can-crushing act, which was always a hit. On top of an empty can placed vertically on the ground, she would balance on one foot; then, as she reached down and tapped the sides of the can gently with her two index fingers, the can would collapse suddenly into a dense, convenient-to-transport mass of aluminum two inches in diameter and no more than an inch thick. After she had crushed all available cans, she and Bing wandered down the beach and up a creek in search of some hot springs that were supposed to be there. They came back with a report that there were a lot more mosquitoes and bear prints along the alder-lined path than there were hot springs.

Finally we tired of sitting around and Sue felt well enough to travel, so we packed up and launched into the waves. The sun came and went, the rain came and went; on we slogged. Bundled from head to foot in wool and Gore-Tex of varying degrees of dampness, rising and falling in waves bigger than many a rapid I had run, I reflected on our familiarity with the old river. I was at ease enough now that I thought nothing of taking my camera from its ammo can, turning around and, perched high up on the bow, taking a picture of Sue and Jude—all in two-foot waves. Our boat truly seemed so overloaded that it was like a comfortable old barge that nonchalantly wallowed through almost anything, and the weight of our bodies was so little compared to the weight of the gear that we could shift around without causing the slightest rocking of the boat. Often we would stand up in the boat in the waves to undo our pants (at which point Bing always rolled his eyes and looked elsewhere); we would sit on the gunnel and hang our rears out over the water to pee, leaning forward and grasping the opposite gunnel so we wouldn't fall in, while our partner leaned slightly in the other direction. Seven weeks ago in Canada it had seemed daring to do this, even while we were tied stably to another boat; now we did it in individual boats on the high seas and paused while we were hanging over the side for a quick river-water half-bath.

And as long as the rain wasn't stinging directly into my eyes, I didn't mind the waves and the rain. I would sing for hours, hypnotized by the irregular, jiggling energy of the waves, stopping only to add or subtract clothing as the weather dictated or to sponge the accumulated rain from the bottom of the boat. I knew Evelyn was back there patiently steering, peering from beneath the brim of her Muleshoe National Bank hat for some new bird, as content in the cold and the rain as she was anywhere else. And that's what enabled us to continue enjoying ourselves; it was as if we had an unspoken pact that neither would decide she was miserable if the other wouldn't.

About nine miles above the town of Ruby, within sight of the high rock face that rose from it, we pulled out for the night onto a smooth terraced beach. Sue was feeling a little better, but now Jude wasn't feeling so well. They seemed to have some sort of lingering flu, with intermittent diarrhea, upset stomach, and general aching. Long after dinner, I sat in my lawn chair, watching the river roll and the pink rays of the sunset dance upon a high, white cloudbank beyond a distant mountain range. It was so cold I could see my breath, and the dampness of the air made the chill sink into my feet. I marveled that I still had the energy to notice or delight in that fiery cloudbank, but I did.

## AUGUST 1, DAY 54

As we paddled toward the village of Ruby, I tried to imagine how this stretch of the Yukon looks in winter when the mushers zoom over the hills and out onto the Yukon at Ruby during the Iditarod race. All the way down the river we'd been hearing about the famous Iditarod, the 1,000-mile sled dog race from Anchorage to Nome held in early March every year. It is a reenactment of a real race when relay teams of the best mushers rushed serum from Anchorage to Nome during a diptheria epidemic in 1925. Today, however, it is not a relay; each musher makes the entire race, or tries to. Sue and Jude had seen a documentary on TV about Susan Butcher, who lives 140 miles northwest of Fairbanks; she had come in nineteenth in 1978, ninth in '79, fifth in '80 and '81, and second this year.

Somehow the day before, we had lost Bing again as we were paddling, and now we found his little tent perched on the rocky beach at the edge of Ruby. Together, we strode into town in search of the hot breakfast a couple of passersby had said we'd find at the roadhouse. Jude could now move along at a pretty good clip through the main mud street. Along the beach bobbed a row of motorboats. Each stretch of the river seemed to have its own characteristic motorboats, and these were long open ones that would hold plenty of fish. Their wooden cabs with plastic curtains would shield the driver from the rain. The ones up at Rampart and Tanana had been entirely open, the only thing between the driver and the stinging rain being a windshield. Walking through town, we passed sturdy cabins and flimsy shacks, a house trailer with a commode sitting on the front porch, twenty Huskies tied to twenty stakes beside twenty doghouses in a yard, a boarded-up trading post. The owner of the roadhouse didn't feel like making any breakfast this morning, so in a rather disappointed mood we paddled on downriver. Bing stayed to pack up, saying he'd see us later.

My mood became more foul during my after-lunch floating nap, when my feet, propped up on a paddle stretched across the gunnel, got so cold that I couldn't properly sleep. I was clad in wool mittens covered by Gore-Tex outer mittens; a wool balaclava that extended down into my shirt, topped by the hood of my Gore-Tex rain jacket and my cowboy hat; wool longhandle bottoms, wool pants, Gore-Tex pants; wool longhandle shirt, T-shirt, wool sweater, wool outer shirt, Gore-Tex rain jacket, life jacket; wetsuit booties and tennis shoes. If this was August 1, I wondered what September 1 would bring. Yet truly, if we paddled, we stayed pretty warm.

Alaska was beginning to lose its enchantment for Sue, who commented while we were drifting that she wondered why anyone would want to live here among the mosquitoes and eat salmon, salmon, salmon. Meanwhile, Evelyn plotted how she could return to spend a winter somewhere on the Yukon to witness freeze-up and breakup.

Late in the day, just below where we'd spotted a porcupine with silver-tipped quills waddling among the alders of a rocky beach, we grabbed the only moderately flat spot to be found between all the fish wheels that lined the bank. Because bears had been known to rob the catch-boxes of fish wheels, and because we assumed there would be some fish-related smells around the things, we liked camping near them no better than camping near the fish camps, where the salmon was cut up and dried.

Several motorboats zoomed by; we nodded to the occupants.

## AUGUST 2, DAY 55

Sue's project for the morning was culling, subject to group debate, a hundred pounds of food from our pantry to ship back home. We would ship it along with the two big boxes that would be waiting for us in Galena, and that would still leave us a hundred pounds or so for the final 600 miles on the river. This was the case even after we had foisted all kinds of food on Bing all the way down the river; Evelyn pointed out that he was the perfect traveling companion, because he could always be counted on to eat anything you didn't want, and yet he wouldn't drink your beer. We had run into more restaurant meals and shared more dinners with friends than we'd anticipated, and we were reaching our destinations sooner than expected, which left us with a vast food excess.

Cooking detail now included drying the wool socks and gloves and tennis shoes that were always draped on a log near the fire, most of which now had a few black, singed places on them. As Jude hopped among the rocks, she would give the eggs and onions and potatoes and picante sauce a stir, then turn over a sock, then pour somebody a cup of tea, then hold a glove over the smoke....

As we paddled through a slough, a fox disappeared into the willows along its edge. The leaves of a few trees were already turning yellow for the coming autumn, and the grey skies looked almost wintery; maybe it was time to be thinking about getting to the sea, before snow started to fly.

There was always an air of excitement whenever we hit a town. We never knew if we'd be shot at, proposed to, danced with, fed pizza or Bailey's Irish Cream, asked to leave town, or all of the above. We had declared Galena to be three-quarters of the way to the Bering Sea; it represented the attainment of another milestone and the beginning of the home stretch. We also knew there was a U.S. Air Force base in Galena, so there was no telling what the next twenty-four hours might bring as we crowded into Galena's beach among the fishing boats early in the afternoon.

As usual, Bing was standing on the shore waiting for us, with the lowdown on food and services to be had in Galena and an update on which canoeists were ahead of us, which were behind us, and which had disappeared altogether. David Gile had headed downriver just this morning; a woman soloing 600 miles from Circle to Galena had finished and taken out already; the Germans in the inflatable canoes were taking out here; some Swiss guys were staying here awhile to do odd construction jobs to earn some money to continue their trip; a French couple we'd heard about all the way down the river, but had never met, had headed on down a few days before; two Austrian guys were somewhere ahead of us; and the two sinister Canadians hadn't been heard from in a long time.

We wandered through town. The usual dogs slunk along, dodging the usual pickup trucks and three-wheeled fat-tired motorbikes. The usual puddles lay in the usual mud and gravel streets. But Galena offered a few different sights. It seemed more modern than the other villages, and somewhat more tacky. There was more plywood and corrugated tin and plastic than there were old logs. Snowmobiles sat on top of the gently sloping roofs of some of the buildings, for what reason I couldn't imagine. Attached to their engine compartments were rifle holsters. A sign saying "Iditarod Headquarters," tacked on a small building, hinted at the commotion that stirs here when a pack of mushers slides into town off the frozen Yukon, well into the two- to three-week sled dog race.

On the side of a long, low, windowless log building was a faded wooden sign that said "Yukon Inn Saloon and Hotel." From the open entryway drifted cigarette smoke, country-and-western jukebox music, and the sound of a cue ball breaking a game. Skirting the mud puddle at its door, we stepped inside.

A thin, balding man named Hobo had a cigarette in one hand and a beer can in the other and a big smile on his face, as you knew he always had. He was half-sloshed, as you knew he always was, but then it was his bar so he could do what he wanted. And what he wanted was to buy the four ladies from Texas and their friend from Florida a beer, so we let him. He liked it so well he did it again, and again. Hobo had been waiting for weeks for the movable party to arrive, and now it was shifting into high gear, once again.

The fifteen people in the bar—mostly Indians and mostly men—looked as if they'd been there all day. Some played pool, one or two leaned on the jukebox and stared motionless at its song titles, a few hunkered silently over their beers at the bar. Most sat nodding in their chairs or passed out across the tables. The other inebriated folks with whom we'd been associating during the past weeks had at least been mobile; these were comatose.

We swapped beers and wild tales and congratulations and risqué toasts with Hobo throughout the afternoon. Periodically, he would excuse himself from the table to go unstop a toilet or sign somebody's check (as near as we could make out, he was some sort of bank, too) or handle some other crisis. He had a cabin across the street but spent most of his time here, watching over the bar.

Evelyn had launched into her standard array of descriptions about our river exploits, which she delighted in telling and which everyone along the river delighted in hearing, but which I'd heard before, so I directed my attention elsewhere. A lean, mean-looking Indian, with a mustache and shoulder-length black hair pulled back by a bandanna headband, stared at me intently. One never knew in these situations what background of racial tensions you might have walked into. But when he pulled up a chair beside me and said with a nod and a smile that he knew a good woman when he saw one, I was relieved that his stare had denoted not scorn but merely lust.

A big grey cat sauntered up and down the long wooden counter, between the beer cans. A thin older woman slumped in a chair, a cigarette dangling from her hand, her eyes closed and her black hair a wild, disheveled mess. When Freddy Fender burst into "Wasted Days and Wasted Nights" on the jukebox, her eyes flew open and she rose from her chair as if propelled by some ejection mechanism connected directly to song No. J24. With a kind of dance-stagger she made a beeline for our table. Smiling and spreading her arms like a nightclub singer, she careened into the table and into our faces and shouted a wondrous beer-breath rendition of "Wasted Days and Wasted Nights." At first we were taken aback, not quite knowing whether the performance was in mockery or appreciation of the Texas singer's popular hit, but Hobo simply smiled and shook his head and deftly spun her toward her table. Every twenty minutes or so the entire performance would be repeated, after which we would clap and hold our beers aloft and she would bow and stumble off to save her strength for her next set.

It was unbearably hot in the bar, so I removed the red T-shirt that I wore over my white longhandle top. But the smell that drifted from the long johns when I did so was quite unacceptable, so I put it back on.

A messenger finally brought the two giant pizzas we'd ordered from a nearby plywood shack whose sign said "Pizza, Donuts." The Germans came in to celebrate the end of their river trip and we drank a toast to them. Sue and Jude went to set up camp in the back yard of Twilight and Jim Billings, a Texas couple who ran the store. Evelyn was pacing her beer-drinking and waltzing with the bartender.

I wedged onto a stool between two patrons at the now-crowded bar, borrowed somebody's eight-inch hunting knife, and began methodically carving my initials into the wood in one of the few tiny spaces where someone else hadn't carved theirs. A young man struck up an idle conversation and offered to pay my way back to Alaska after my canoe trip if I would live with him.

"Why, that might cost about a thousand dollars," I grinned absently, carefully digging the knife into the wood.

"One paycheck," he shrugged. He had a car and a cabin and he wanted to make me breakfast in bed—fried chicken or whatever I wanted.

Now why would he want to do all this when he didn't even know my name, I asked, blowing the sawdust from the "B."

"Because you're beautiful," he answered, with soulful eyes.

I laid down the knife and surveyed my muddy wetsuit booties, my spacious Gore-Tex pants, the grimy grey cuffs of my white long johns protruding from the T-shirt that sealed in the long johns' smell, and I had to laugh. But it had been a long day—we had paddled more than twenty miles down the Yukon before we ever walked into this bar, and it seemed like we had been in here forever—so I declined the fried chicken and stumbled through the dusk with Evelyn.

We set up our tent on the riverbank, among the oil drums and salvaged lumber behind Twilight's house. Bing paddled off down the river; I collapsed into the tent and began murdering mosquitoes. Then Evelyn and her bear bells jangled back over to the bar for one more fling around the dance floor.

# 11 mooseburgers, northern lights, and a hurricane

## AUGUST 3, DAY 56

By 1 P.M., we had shipped excess food back home, bought gloves to replace those whose fingers had burned or rotted off, mailed film, read letters from home, called museums and publishers and parents and newspapers, given a radio interview by phone, filled our jugs with water, eaten a big breakfast at the hotel, and were back on the river. In less than twenty-four hours since we'd hit town, we'd done all this and still danced a fair portion of the night away at the local watering hole; we were getting this village routine down to a fine art.

The one thing we didn't do was accept Hobo's offer of a hot shower in his cabin. Taking a shower was not particularly inviting if you had no clean clothes to go with the clean body, and we didn't want to stay among the barking dogs and rumbling airplanes and boats and cars long enough to wash and dry our clothes. Besides, we'd just done all this less than 200 miles back in Tanana, seven days ago; there was no sense getting carried away. In addition, I had suspected for years that one reason I run rivers is that I like to be dirty; I intended to relish my condition for awhile.

Air Force planes flew overhead as Galena slipped behind us. When the ice jammed below here for more than twenty-four hours during breakup in 1945, the Yukon flooded and practically destroyed the air base. A squadron of B-17s went to the rescue, hurling 168,000 pounds of bombs on the ice-dam. The dam broke and the Yukon continued toward the sea.

We paddled in moderate waves and calm side sloughs, sunshine and clouds, off and on, throughout the day. Once, a motorboat, skimming the water at full speed, changed course to head straight for us. It would have been a little embarrassing to have survived the Yukon's storms and rapids and mosquitoes and broken bones, only to be done in by a fishing boat; we waved our paddles in the air so the driver could see us. On he came, purposefully, veering away only at the last minute to race by a few feet away from us. We pivoted the boats and braced with our paddles to ride out the wake he dumped in our lap. Ah, wilderness.

The mountains had dropped back from the river's edge and once again we paddled beneath the tremendous open skies we had loved in the Flats. For the next several hundred miles we would paddle mostly through low, willow-lined banks, with occasional nearby bluffs or distant mountain ranges to draw our interest. There was hardly a dull moment visually, though, because that vast sky was always stirring up some amazing cloud formation or other, somewhere within view.

Much of what we would see along the left bank for the next six days would be the Innoko National Wildlife Refuge, established by the Alaska lands bill. Like the Nowitna and the Flats, this refuge is one of the key solar basins—representing the most productive habitat for nesting waterfowl and other waterbirds—in the central interior Yukon region. And like the others, its statistics are beyond comprehension: 100,000 nesting ducks, 20,000 nesting geese, 225,000 migrating birds. We saw few of them on the river; they preferred the ponds that dotted the muskeg flats above and beyond the river channel, whose mucky, mosquito-ridden reaches we had lost all desire to penetrate. But it was reassuring to know that all those birds were out there somewhere, happily taking care of business; we were content to glimpse a few of them as they flew over the Yukon or paddled quiet sloughs.

Late in the afternoon we entered one of the weirdest river bends I'd ever seen, on the Yukon or anywhere else. With nothing but swampy lowlands to turn it, the Yukon made a giant curve for no apparent reason. About halfway through, it ran head-on into giant Bishop Rock and was forced to reconsider the whole thing, then spun off the face of the bluff and swirled on its way. In the process it made a giant eddy. We got caught up in the eddy, half-intentionally. We enjoyed the strange sensation of speeding upstream on its current and addressing all the boils and frothing eddy lines that spread about us. All the while, a bunch of kids at the village of Yistletaw that lay in the shadow of Bishop Rock screamed at the top of their lungs. They were too far away for us to tell whether they were gleeful or concerned about what we were doing in the eddy, whether they were inviting us to join them or ordering us to stay away. Meanwhile, a plane landed on the shores of Bishop Rock Island. And a voice from across the river on our left shouted, "Hey, you're goin' the wrong way."

It was Bing, racing downstream with his paddle resting on the gunnels, the illusion of his speed magnified by our drifting upstream in the eddy. We finally decided we'd be in the one-mile recirculating eddy till freeze-up if we let it have its way, so we paddled out, feeling like we'd just stepped off a carnival ride.

Bing was just starting for the day, so he drifted on when we pulled out to camp. The mosquitoes weren't too bad, but the gnats were out in force. Back in Rampart, as we had stood in the smoke at the beach party cursing the mosquitoes, Manny had told us that mosquito season was almost over. When we had sighed with relief, he had grinned and said, "Then come the gnats, and they're worse." Manny was right. The gnats seemed more apt to fly into noses and mouths and eyes than the mosquitoes, and insect repellent rather seemed to attract them. They were too quick even to give you the fleeting pleasure of killing a few. When I took a bath in the river, they lined up along my bare, wet legs. Every now and then one would bite and I would brush it off, but I didn't think much about it.

As I sat in camp, putting on dry shoes, I took stock of my body and immediate life-support systems, which seemed to be the thing to do now that we were but a brief 600 miles or so from the Bering Sea. My hands were now covered in black creases and toughened to the extent that a swipe of my finger across my face produced a nick on my cheek. From the tops of my wetsuit booties to my knees, my legs were a mass of red blistery bumps where the mosquitoes bit me during the times I hiked up my pants to wade back and forth to load and unload the boat. I rarely felt them bite, and the bumps didn't itch much, so I felt it better to endure them than to go around with wet pants-bottoms all the time. Little did I know, though, as I pondered all this, that the gnats that had bitten me tonight were White Socks, the infamous black gnat with tiny white feet. You don't feel its bite but it soon raises a red welt that itches with incredible intensity.

My water bottle had all sorts of permanent black stuff on its bottom and sides, and in it floated various brown vegetation bits that we accepted as normal in our drinking water. My one bar of soap was now a thin sliver that showed signs of breaking in two any day, but with any luck it would make it another 500 miles. The insulated cup from which I drank spiced tea now offered spiced tea when filled with mere hot water, so imbued was it with the flavor. The white polyurethane rope that had gleamed in the sunlight on the bow back on Lake Laberge now camouflaged its filthy self in the dull grey tones of the aluminum canoe. All in all, I supposed I looked like I'd been living on a river for eight weeks, and it felt good. It was a sunny evening for the first time in two weeks; I gazed at the shifting pinks of the sunset and the purple clouds reflecting on the water with a sense of sadness that our trip might be over in a few short weeks. In no time we'd be back in hot Dallas with roofs and walls blocking our view, with no flowing water or mountains or sunsets to stare at over dinner.

Sue and Jude were in a giddy mood, celebrating the beginning of the home stretch. Sue stumbled through the food. Wearing her headnet, Jude stood knee-deep in the river and took a bath. They joked and talked into their tape recorder, splashing and clanking pans and making a tape to send home to a friend. We congratulated ourselves on having made it three-quarters of the way to the Bering Sea, and Jude mentioned casually that she never thought they'd make it this far. She said she thought she and Sue would have had their fill of river life by Eagle. It was clear, even more so than before, that Sue and Jude were intent on getting to the Bering Sea and finishing the river. Evelyn and I, meanwhile, were mostly intent on being wherever we were; we knew we'd get to the Bering Sea soon enough.

In Rampart, the zipper on the mesh flap of Evelyn's tent had died, and ever since we'd been using the solid flap. As it turned out, that worked fine, because it had been cold enough and wet enough that we needed the solid flap anyway. But I hadn't known that in Rampart and had asked Mother to mail my tent from home to Galena. I now had it, and Evelyn and I decided we'd sleep in the Bishop Rock Hilton tonight by putting up both tents. We chuckled at the luxury of having a whole tent to ourselves in which to spread out our clothes and books. For the rest of the trip, whenever there was space and soft ground enough, unless we were dog-tired, we'd put up both tents. Thus, the Battle of the Tent Zipper drew mostly to a close; now, if Evelyn left her tent flap open for the mosquitoes or the gnats or the rain, that was her very own problem.

## AUGUST 4, DAY 57

It was a sunny day, and we paddled. The river was the color of a White Russian cocktail; milky clouds of water swirled and blended on its surface. We bypassed the village of Koyukuk, with its big tanks and scattered houses, at the mouth of the Koyukuk River; we were too lazy to ferry the mile or so across the river that visiting it would have required. As we swatted and gulped gnats and an occasional horsefly, Sue read to us from *The Yukon* about the Yukon's tributaries. The glacial ones help stabilize the water level throughout the summer. Just about the time the snow-fed tributaries, such as the Koyukuk, have dumped most of their spring melt into the Yukon and are dwindling to their summer low, the summer sun reaches the high mountain glaciers, and they melt in earnest to take up the slack. In winter, when the glaciers are frozen, they no longer contribute their grist; the Yukon flows clean and clear—under five feet of ice. But in summer, hundreds of tons of silt flow past a given point each minute.

No wonder the river looked like a White Russian. And no wonder everyone standing on the bank in Circle, when the German had jumped into the Yukon, had figured the silt would coat his jeans and he'd sink like a rock. We drifted on, marveling over the big, old Yukon and unaware, at that moment, that slipping away from us around that bend was a place called the Last Chance Liquor Store. It was our last chance to buy liquor legally on the Yukon River.

We floated miles behind Sue and Jude for most of the afternoon. After we nibbled our beef jerky and our sticky apricot leather and our peanuts, I watched ahead and read a non-fiction paperback about a guy sailing a boat up the Amazon River. Evelyn snored, lying flat on her back on an ammo can, her feet propped on a thwart, her face covered by her rain jacket to ward off the gnats. Then she took watch while I slept under a sweater in the warm sun, to the canoe's gentle rocking. Later, she steered facing downstream in normal fashion; I sat on top of a couple of ammo cans, turned around to face her and backpaddled, so we could talk. These long afternoon conversations that followed our naps were becoming routine, and we enjoyed them thoroughly. We were talking about a reggae club that we wanted to visit in Fort Worth, when Nulato came into view.

In the mid-1800s, this little village had been the farthest-inland Russian trading post, the most important one on the Yukon. It had also witnessed a series of bloody skirmishes between the Upper Koyukon and the Nulato Koyukon Indians. Today, Nulato was pretty peaceful. We missed the required candy bar because the store was closed, but we heard that the movie *Urban Cowboy* was playing at the community center and that they served machine-popped corn and soft drinks there. We decided that nothing could be more deliciously strange on a Wednesday night in Nulato, Alaska, than watching John Travolta honky-tonking in Pasadena, Texas, on the silver screen. So we trudged a mile and a half up the dusty road to the community hall. Jude's foot was now healed to the point where she could make the field trip.

En route, we passed ancient log shacks that sagged from years of battling the permafrost's heaving and the Yukon's ice-jam flooding. The Yukon threatens these cabins more each year as it eats its way into town, and slowly the people of Nulato are abandoning them and moving into HUD (Housing and Urban Development) houses a couple of miles inland. The process has split the village geographically, and it was odd to stroll past the familiar faded shacks and Husky puppies and laundry flapping on a wire, then through a half-mile of open fireweed meadows and muskeg flatlands, then into a subdivision of spruce-lined streets and three-bedroom redwood homes with plate-glass windows.

Fashionably attired in cowboy hats and fanny packs and Dallas Downriver Club T-shirts, we stood in line for popcorn and Cokes and settled into folding metal chairs along with about forty teenage villagers. Numbers counted backwards on the screen, ushering in the feature presentation. Pieces of cardboard blocked most of the outside light from the windows. Mosquitoes were few. The projector in the center aisle clickety-hummed. The movement of John Travolta's mouth and the sound of his words were only slightly out of synchronization, but between that and the noise of the projector in my ear and the strange Texas accents of the actors, old John had danced his way through the first reel before I understood a word. I wondered what the Indians made of it all, but they laughed and whistled in all the right places. Whenever it was time to change reels, which was often, the whole crowd would bolt for the back of the room and buy a Coke from the machine. Two boxes of popcorn and two Cokes (each) later, when the good guys won out and the bad guys were thrown in jail and Travolta finally rode the mechanical bull to everyone's satisfaction, we ambled back to our boats through the dusk and the mist that rose from the muskeg.

To cap off our night on the town, we paddled silently a few miles across Mukluk Slough's smooth water, bathed in a mystical evening light. By the time the barking dogs and the rumbling pickup trucks had slipped behind us, it was getting too dark to see, so we grabbed a soggy grass-covered spot at the river's edge. As we slipped the tent stakes into the mushy ground we danced from one foot to the other to avoid sinking to our shins. By the time our shoes had slurped around the tent a few times, the campsite resembled a nice hog wallow. Evelyn and I dived into the tent and began murdering mosquitoes in the fading light. We joked that we'd have to sleep with our arms and legs outstretched or we'd ooze, tent and all, down into the muck, never to be seen again.

"Oh my God," sighed Evelyn as she happened to look out the tent door. The most amazing, huge, full orange moon had jumped onto the horizon from behind the line of spruces across the river. As it surged into the deep blue sky, its reflections spread, foot by shimmering foot, across the Yukon. It was the first real moon we'd seen in weeks, and here it was, gigantic, smiling squarely into our tent door. For some reason it brought to mind John Travolta's hairy chest, and I felt a little lonely.

## AUGUST 5, DAY 58

First thing next morning, we slogged to the boats and paddled across a slough to a relatively dry island for a breakfast of beans and rice. As we began paddling for the day, a barge rounded the corner and passed us, its roar vibrating the boats in the water. It had passed us a few times, coming and going, in the last few weeks; it never failed that when it rounded a bend and came into view, one of us happened to be hanging over the side of the canoe with her drawers down.

There was still a good current by Lower 48 standards, but the Yukon had slowed compared to her speed a thousand miles back in Canada. She no longer whisked us thirty miles a day while we slept and read. Now we had to paddle for our thirty miles a day.

Shirtless in the morning sun, I studied the intricacies of a five-mile-long island on our left. With their hints of fall colors, the willows and poplars took me back to a quiet afternoon years ago on Georgia's Suwannee River. But a glance at the spruce trees oozing down the folds of the rocky hills on the right bank brought me back to Alaska. The Innoko Refuge's river bluffs are another of the four major peregrine nesting areas in North America. Sure enough, as we paddled close under a cliff we flushed out a peregrine falcon, her curved wings slicing the cloudless sky.

Given glassy water and sunshine and our mood for mild exercise, Evelyn and I were hitting our stride as a paddling team. In the mornings we usually kept to ourselves, each thinking our own thoughts and enjoying the rhythm of our strokes. If the weather stayed the same long enough for us to avoid stopping every few minutes to add or subtract a clothing layer, we could paddle for hours without a break. Thus, long before we thought we'd see it, there lay the village of Kaltag, announced by the grave markers and crumbling picket fences that nestled among the willows upstream.

The store was already closed and Jude wasn't in the mood for the smell of dead fish that permeated the beach, so she and Sue drifted on downstream. Evelyn went aboard the big docked barge to talk with its captain about odds and ends, including how one might ship one's canoe back to Dallas, Texas, from the Bering Sea. I strolled along the narrow street at the top of the sheer high bank. An old man and a young boy sat on a bench, quietly gazing out over the Yukon. More than a mile wide here and glassy blue in the afternoon sun, the big old mama completely dwarfed Sue's and Jude's canoe and the huge barge and the vast lowlands that spread around us. She brought to mind the words to "Moon River" I had memorized as we paddled today. "Two drifters, off to see the world, there's such a lot of world to see—we're after the same rainbow's end, waitin' 'round the bend, my Huckleberry friend, Moon River, and me . . . ." The only drawback had been finding a paddling rhythm that matched a waltz.

At the foot of the barge's gangplank, I called to Evelyn; at the sound of my voice, a young Indian girl who was walking the beach stopped in her tracks.

"Are you a girl?" she asked in the forthright way that children have.

"Yep," I answered.

"I thought you was a boy," she said matter-of-factly. I was only partially wounded, for I could see how someone in my baggy clothes and cowboy hat might appear so. In the same offhanded tone, the young girl went on to express her hope that her mother would return home from Fairbanks soon, where she'd been taken because she might have to be in jail because she had shot a gun. She hadn't hit anybody but she was drunk, so it might be awhile before she came back. As Evelyn and I pushed into the river and waved to the girl and her brother, who had been crawling among our things in the boat, the little runny-nosed boy smiled and said we'd better go on down the river or he'd shoot us. (Later, we heard that when the parties in Kaltag got a little wild the usual outcome was a shooting spree. There was a portage route to Norton Sound on the Bering Sea from Kaltag, and once when a paddler had left his canoe in Kaltag to investigate the trail, the villagers had shot it full of holes.)

In the afternoon light, the smooth surface of the Yukon shone silver. The effect of the three-foot, slow, loping rollers that the barge shoved beneath us as it rumbled past was absolutely mesmerizing. We drifted for an hour or two, philosophizing as usual, and finally ended up an amazing forty-eight miles from the day's starting point on a smooth island beach that Sue had found. A perfect line of tracks told how, not long ago, a mother black bear and a cub had strolled the beach at the water's edge. For the first time, the gnats drove me into my headnet as I sat around the fire. Late that night, a big white moon and two hints of stars hung in the evening sky.

## AUGUST 6, DAY 59

A motorboat buzzing through our slough during breakfast was the only thing that detracted from Jude's incredible homemade cinnamon rolls beneath a gorgeous, sunny sky. We joked over the fact that although we had paddled between 22 and 48 map-miles each of the three days since we'd left Galena, the people in the three villages we had passed all said they were 500 miles from the mouth of the river.

The better part of my last three nights in the tent had been spent scratching the dozens of red White Socks bumps that covered my legs, and in smearing on Sue's cream that quelled the itching for a few hours; I was no longer very interested in bathing on the beach in the gnats. So today as we drifted I added bathing and hair-washing to the ever-expanding list of activities that we performed out on the open water in the canoe. Out here, bathing was much more pleasant, and certainly no more difficult, than staggering around in the muck at the water's edge. I took off my shirt, leaned over the gunnel, dipped the cold water over my head with a cookpot, and soaped up; Evelyn leaned the other way and steered. Since the silty rinse water itself was the consistency and color of slightly diluted skim milk, it was hard to tell if I had gotten all the soap out. My hair didn't feel exactly squeaky clean afterward, but it was the thought that counted. I gave my torso a quick once-over with the washcloth for good measure.

We paddled silently, enjoying. The sun soaked my bare skin. My head and eyes were cool enough under the shade of my dear old, grey felt cowboy hat, which had now been wet and stuffed into its ditty bag so many times that its brim flopped down around my ears. Low blue hills rose ahead, reflected in the river's glassy surface. Clouds came and went. The rolling movement of my arms and shoulders and torso as the paddle and I moved the canoe through the water felt dancelike, and good.

This was self-indulgence at its best. You know you're on vacation when you wake up from your afternoon nap and you're in the middle of the two-mile-wide Yukon River. I woke up slowly, gradually, gently, trailing a finger in the cold water and rubbing it on my eyes to shake off the heavy sleep of the sun's warmth. I scanned the hills and bends for clues to whether I'd been asleep for half a mile or five miles. There was no clue to time, partly because the sun seemed to move little during the day, but mostly because more than a month ago we had ceased winding our only timepiece.

Today, we saw neither motorboat nor airplane. We passed no villages. The only sounds were our own paddling or snoring, a page turning in a paperback, a gull's mewing, the faraway rumble of a thunderstorm, an occasional breath of wind playing with my hair. Sometimes before I take a big trip, I look forward to having the time to contemplate the answers to life's big questions. But a good trip is when you're so much at peace that you cease seeking the answers and forget there ever were questions.

Today, floating down this river through these rolling hills, I forgot the questions.

## AUGUST 7, DAY 60

I awoke to the gobbledy-clucking of sandhill cranes as they danced on the upper end of our island. As we drifted past the lower tip of the nine-mile-long island, Bing came paddling around the other side. It was always a pleasure to run into him, for he would paddle up with a big smile and some new tale of a fox or a sandhill crane or an old trapper he'd run into. We drifted with him and exchanged all the news since we'd seen him three nights ago.

It was another sun-drenched day. Late in the afternoon when the steep western shore was hidden in shadow, I was dozing in the bow half a mile from shore when I heard a loud pop. I peered from beneath my hat toward the shore; the glare on the water obscured all but the hazy outline of a fish camp nestled into a cleft in the rocks. Bing was paddling close to shore, barely visible in the shadows. Sue and Jude had drifted on the other side of a sandbar and were out of sight. Another pop echoed between the cliffs as something made the water jump halfway between us and shore.

"Hey, I think we'd better paddle,"said Evelyn. The water jumped again and somebody, still unseen, shouted something. We weren't too worried about ourselves, for we figured that as obvious a target as we must have been out in the sun in our slow-moving canoe, if whoever was shouting and shooting had wanted to hit us, he already would have done so. But he seemed to be saying something to Bing, and we didn't know what might happen between the two of them since they both had guns. Perhaps the cultural quirks that kept the guy on shore from shooting women didn't apply to men. Bing and the guy had some sort of casual conversation as Bing paddled past, and the guy kept shooting out into the water as if we'd never been in his range. We paddled steadily toward the next bend, in case he decided to change his aim. Just as we reached the huge bluff at the point, he switched to some sort of cannon-like gun whose blasts resounded through the valley; we paddled faster still. When Sue and Jude joined us, we shrugged and said we thought it was about time for happy hour.

"So you've just paddled fifty miles down the Yukon and it's hotter than hell and the gnats are so bad you have to wear your headnet even out on the river, and now someone's shooting at you? Drink some more!" we shouted, mimicking the gleeful way that Manny back at Rampart had altered the message of an Alaskan anti-alcoholism TV commercial.

## AUGUST 8, DAY 61

We had pulled out before the agreed-upon island last night when we spotted a small rocky beach that looked like it might be the last flat place for some time; in doing so, we had lost Bing again.

This morning, we paddled close to the bank, looking for clear drinking-water creeks. Most of the small willows along the shore had turned bright yellow; they were beautiful but reminded us that fall was imminent, and we still had almost 400 miles of river to paddle. We finally found an ice-cold creek and waded in to get our water.

The minute we resumed paddling, a frisky headwind dashed waves against the boats. We battled these for awhile, Sue and Jude sticking close to shore while Evelyn and I tried to cut off some distance by making straight for the next point across open water. About halfway across, though, the wind began sending three-footers under and into and occasionally over the bow. As I turned to shout to Evelyn that I thought we'd better run for the lesser waves near shore, I saw looming behind her the biggest, blackest mass of thunderheads I'd ever seen. Hearing my very ladylike words of surprise and commentary, she too spun to confront the storm and concurred that we were in for an interesting afternoon. The weirdest part about the whole thing was that the giant blue-black storm was chasing us downriver, gaining on us minute by minute, while a headwind was trying to blow us upriver. It made no sense; the headwind should have kept the storm off our tails. We figured that in the end, the two forces would probably collide and produce one helluva rainstorm, right over our boats.

We thrashed madly ten miles through the bouncing waves and the spray to the village of Grayling, which offered the first flat beach not already claimed by a fish camp. We thudded onto the rocks just as the villagers rushed to the beach to make sure their boats were covered and securely tied to ride out the storm. Bing had arrived shortly before and was there to greet us, as usual. Evelyn raced to the store, Sue and Jude and I raced to get our tents up, Bing climbed into a big sewer pipe that was lying on the ground. The heavens launched their downpour just as I tossed the last of my necessities into the tent for the night. As I skated through the mud street to the store, I poked my head into Bing's metal pipe and gave it a few slaps to send the echo through his ears.

"Mother always said I'd end up in a sewer," he grinned. As the rain drummed on the outside of the pipe, he lounged against the curved inside, reading a book.

The store was just closing for the day, and they were out of my standard Three Musketeers bar; I settled for an Eskimo Pie and two Hershey bars, which I downed posthaste. The store clerk pointed us to the home of Lance and Beth Hughes, friends of friends of mine in Dallas, with whom we'd corresponded. Evelyn and I slogged down the winding road and through somebody's back yard to an oblong plywood box with a corrugated tin roof. A wooden sled leaned against the front wall, and a sign over the door said "Lance and Beth Hughes." We hesitated before the door, feeling that we might be intruding. The people at the store had told us that Beth Hughes had been in Fairbanks all summer taking a college course, that she had just entered the hospital to have a baby, and that Lance was at this moment awaiting a flight out of Grayling to join his wife. Perhaps he was in no mood to welcome two strangers whose only connection with him was that his wife's old college roommate had married a guy who had an old high school friend who was now paddling a canoe down the Yukon River. We knocked.

Eventually Lance came to the door, looking a little harried. He took one look at the two dripping women in a cowboy hat and a Muleshoe

National Bank hat and said, "I don't believe this. Come on in, take your shoes off, hang on a second."

He was in the middle of a long-distance phone call to Beth in Fairbanks, and as we stood dripping on his floor and ripping off our clothes in the heat of the cabin, he told Beth, "You won't believe who just walked in."

Lance was around thirty, with longish dark hair and a mustache. He and Beth were two of the approximately ten percent of whites in the village of a couple of hundred people. They had decided about three years before, when they were living in Florida, that they wanted to live a simpler life, in Alaska. They agreed they'd go wherever one of them could get a job; Beth had gotten one as a teacher in Grayling, so here they were. While she taught, Lance did various carpentry jobs and trapped and fished. As he fed us coffee and salmon strips, he showed us pictures of some four-foot-long salmon he and his friends had caught. He brought out some furs he was taking to Fairbanks to sell, and showed us which ones he would keep so Beth could make him a parka hood. His packed bags lay in the middle of the floor, next to the wooden cradle a friend had made for their first child. In the center of the room was a large oil-drum wood stove. Near it were the usual rows of books. A rocking chair helped bring to mind a picture of long winter evenings spent near the comfort of the stove, with a good book. An odd complement to the rather rustic appearance of the plywood cabin was the pre-fab, walnut-stained, formica-topped, kitchen counter-cabinet combination that sprawled along one wall.

Every few minutes Lance went to the window to scan the skies for a clue to whether his plane would venture into Grayling in the bad weather. He was remarkably calm and gracious, considering the circumstances of our visit. He admitted with a grin that he never thought we'd really do the trip and would certainly never make it this far down the river. He hinted that some of our questions of nine months before—such as whether whales ever swam into the mouth of the Yukon—had made him think we had no business being on the river in the first place. (We were told when we got closer to the mouth that in not-so-distant times past, an occasional whale did swim up into the wide deep river; but today, with the many motorboats and people living along the river, they seldom come in.)

On the way to the outhouse, Evelyn and I discovered a small pig in a corral behind Lance's house. It seemed strangely out of place. For some reason, during the entire time I was in the outhouse, I took great delight in imitating in the back of my throat the pig's muffled grunts; maybe the Hershey bars and sixty-one days on the Yukon were beginning to take their toll.

Lance reached into his big electric freezer and gave us some moose steaks and ground moose meat wrapped in butcher paper. He said he'd join us later if his plane didn't come in today.

Two hours later, when I awoke from my nap in the tent, a party was brewing on Grayling's rocky beach, for today was Sue's forty-first birthday. Jude and Evelyn launched the birthday feast by mixing Lance's ground moose meat with tomato paste and pouring it over store-bought hot dog buns for a mooseburger Sloppy Joe. Sue tended bar and played a tape of a graceful, hymnlike song called "Roll, Yukon, Roll" that she and Jude had composed. Bing was there, ever feeding logs into the fire. We were joined by Lance and several of the villagers. The faithful coffee pot with its missing percolator cap and its bent handles was kept busy all night. We capped off the birthday dinner with a marvelous lemon cake that Jude made from a mix she'd bought at the store; we devoured it amid appropriate oohs and aahs and the singing of "Happy Birthday." We sat for hours drinking hot chocolate in the on-and-off rain, the four Texas women clad comfortably in Gore-Tex and the Indian guys oblivious to the weather in their blue jeans and flannel shirts.

We talked of the Iditarod, and the guys gave Bing the name of a dog-trainer and breeder in Anchorage who might let Bing work for him in exchange for loaning Bing a team to run in the next Iditarod. The only time Bing had handled a dog team had been one afternoon ten years before during his Mackenzie River trip, but knowing him the way we did, we could easily see his entering a 1,000-mile race the next spring, in his quiet way.

Just before bedtime, the sky began to clear and the moon struggled to peek from the clouds above the far bank. A few stars twinkled in the darkening sky.

"Hey, northern lights!" Bing pointed.

Sure enough, a faint swath of white light appeared beside the moon. We sat in quiet admiration of our first glimpse of the aurora borealis. Slowly, the mysterious lights began to move across the twilight sky, quivering, alive. They played hide-and-seek for awhile, spreading higher above the river and along the bank, dancing among the fading clouds. Putting their fingers in their mouths, the two Indians whistled loud piercing notes into the sky. They said the lights would dance faster if you whistle. We tried it, with no results. Smiling, they said the lights only dance faster for Indians.

We complimented them on Grayling's fine beach with its great view of the river and the moon and the northern lights—a perfect place for a birthday party and an evening around the campfire with friends.

"Grayling Beach—best place on the river for northern lights!" they exclaimed. "It's also the last beach," they grinned and shook their heads. "From here to the mouth, you're camping in mud."

## AUGUST 9, DAY 62

We launched into the mild waves of a cold grey morning, leaving Bing on the beach to catch us later. We waved to Lance's plane as it circled overhead shortly after we got on the river. When we reached the first point of land seven miles downstream, the wind slackened somewhat and Evelyn and I stopped to drift. But the waves tossed me about in the boat just enough to keep me awake, and I had to blow my nose every five minutes from the head cold that had been worsening over the last few days. My throat was getting sore, and it rained off and on. The middle of the Yukon was a helluva place to try to get some rest, I thought to myself.

Soon we drifted within sight of the village of Anvik, the place where, in 1834, white men first laid eyes on the Indians of the Yukon, and vice versa. It was into this village that the Russian explorer Glazunov had wandered after snowshoeing from Saint Michael on the Bering Sea to the frozen Anvik River and down its length to its junction with the mighty Yukon. At Anvik, which meant "Place of Louse Eggs" in the Athapascan tongue, the Russians first caught sight of the Yukon, which meant "River of Rivers."

We missed the Place of Louse Eggs, with little regret, because it came up unexpectedly and we were too far out into the current to bother. Sue and Jude had floated into town briefly, but rejoined us when they saw we were drifting on. By the time they caught up I was feeling so sick that we pulled out on the first flat sandbar below town.

There was something about the sandy island, with its low willows and the sun's sparkle on the water, that reminded me of the Caribbean, and I suggested as much to Jude. She looked at me as if she thought my cold had brought on hallucinations. We stood on the beach squinting to blur the willows into palm trees in our imagination; the effort was only partially effective.

I put up my tent and collapsed into it for a nap; Sue and Jude started a fire for the moose steaks we'd been carrying in a pot under Evelyn's seat. But a terrific rainstorm blew in unannounced. I could hear muffled shouts across the sandbar. Burrowing deeper into my sleeping bag, I tried to forget the whole thing. Rain lashed the tent with machine-gun ferocity. I watched the whole nylon roof strain at its poles from the weight of the water. Flashes of lightning pierced the grey afternoon through the green walls of my tent. Tremendous claps of thunder ripped through the roar of the rain and rumbled for seconds through the valley. It was surely the end of the world, I thought, between nose-blowings and pondering the physics of lightning and aluminum tent poles.

Finally I peered outside and gasped at the sight. So heavy was the rain that it was impossible to distinguish between run-off on the flat sandbar and the river's water. The entire world was grey pelting water. I could barely make out our aluminum canoe staked to a very forlorn-looking stick that Evelyn had driven into the sand; I decided the river hadn't risen to my tent door yet because the rope between the stick and the canoe didn't seem to be moving. The line of spruces across the river was all but obscured, so that the river looked as wide as an ocean. The only things not covered in rushing water were our three little hummocks of sand on which we'd perched our tents. Sue and Jude had abandoned the kitchen. Evelyn was undoubtedly in her tent.

I lay back down, drew my sleeping bag up around me, and groaned.

There was no telling how long we'd be tentbound. I was very thankful I happened to have my little cookpot with me so that later I could avoid going outside for any reason. My nose ran, my body ached. I could scarcely sleep for the itching from the White Socks bumps that riddled my legs and forearms. Some of the bumps now sported open sores where I'd scratched them in my fury. My forefinger had finally split open along one of thousands of dirt-filled creases etched into the tough skin. It was precisely along this painful red gap that I must grab things like tent zippers and canoe ropes. My hands looked like those of a ninety-year-old woman—a deep, dry, brown from the sun, the fingernails and wrinkles black. I could remember neither my last bath nor the last time I'd washed this snotty handkerchief. I was hungry. It hurt my throat to swallow, and when I coughed a rib felt broken. It was too dark to read.

Mother always said there'd be days like this.

## AUGUST 10, DAY 63

We hunkered in our nylon cocoons until the next morning, which dawned cold and windy, but sunny. Bundled in their parkas, Sue and Jude fried the moose steaks with some Stove-Top Stuffing they'd bought in Grayling. I was feeling somewhat better but a little disjointed after more than twelve hours in the tent.

We paddled through moderate waves and occasional rain throughout the morning, then Evelyn and I stopped to drift in the tossing waves when the sun finally came out in the afternoon. Bing came paddling from between two islands where his canoe and his tent had completely blended into the willows and the sand. He said that when the sudden storm had hit the river yesterday he'd taken shelter under a big rock shelf that jutted out from a bluff. He had made a fire, read a book, watched the rain sweep across the Yukon, and wondered what he'd do if a bear took shelter under the same shelf.

We paddled with Bing and Sue and Jude through the afternoon. At one point I grabbed Bing's trailing rope while Jude distracted him, and we took great delight in being given a free ride by his paddling. He finally noticed that he was unwillingly towing a half-ton barge; he sprinted with paddles flying and, disgustingly, could keep up with Sue and Jude, even while towing Evelyn and me!

The sun was back, and the snow-white gulls once again gathered on the sandy island tips. Against the dark green spruces, the sun's late-afternoon rays silhouetted in gold the drops of water that flew from Bing's kayak paddle. The immediate river environs were the same as always: islands, spruces, willows. But just beyond, along the flanks of the nearby mountains, treeless tundra now replaced spruces. I wasn't quite sure why, but it seemed to be another sign that our trip was ending.

Sue spotted a perfect sandy beach along the left shore. There was a ready-made woodpile of logs left in the trees by high water. I made two pizzas and we wallowed in them as the sun set across the river. Everyone commented on how truly pizzalike were the crusts; it wasn't until the next morning, as I watched Bing make his raisin bannock, that I remembered I hadn't used any baking powder whatsoever, thus discovering by accident the secret to perfect pizza crust.

The others drifted to bed. The night grew quite cold and dark and a few stars began to appear. Relaxed by the hypnotic warmth of the fire, Bing and I dreamed aloud about the Amazon and the Nile and Australia and Nepal. We talked about the guy in the book who was attempting to sail a boat in the lowest water (the Dead Sea) and the highest water (Lake Titicaca) on earth. Bing had given a lot of thought to sailboats and knew just the size and the cost of the one he would buy to sail around the world. It wasn't such a far-fetched dream; the guy in the book mentioned that thousands of people are doing it at any given moment, and I myself knew someone who was doing it then.

"I figure when I get older and hiking or canoeing is a bit much for me," Bing said, "I'll turn to sailing. After I learn how to do it, I'll sail around the world."

## AUGUST 11, DAY 64

I awoke with a mild start; all I could see outside the tent door was greyness. A thick magic fog hung in camp and on the river, snuffing any thought of an early launch. When I got up, Bing was tiptoeing barefooted around Sue's and Jude's tent, with the biggest grin on his face. He tiptoed all the way to the water, walked in it a few minutes down the beach, then returned to the campfire with a normal stride. His little prints did look remarkably like a black bear's—enough so to fool Jude when she first crawled from the tent. When her typical (unprintable) exclamation of surprise pierced the damp morning air, we all had a good laugh.

Bing's raisin bannocks, prepared lovingly in the charred coffee cans that he used as mixing bowls, were a tremendous hit; we lolled in our chairs, stuffed the sweet bread into our mouths, drank tea, and waited for the fog to rise. Soon it did and we paddled seven miles down to the village of Holy Cross.

For some reason—perhaps because he had no money to buy anything—Bing drifted on, while we pulled our boats onto the gnat-infested beach. A pickup drove by and the driver waved us in; as we hopped into the back I sat unknowingly on a tow-sack full of dead salmon. "Bear bait, bear bait," the others droned, out of habit. The gnats were ferocious, even in town. The air was still and hot, and the smell of dead fish seemed to hang over everything. Loud engines rumbled somewhere. Hammers rang against nails. Kids stared at us. All in all, Holy Cross didn't invite a week's stopover. We took shelter from the gnats in the store, where we bought a few things and learned that David Gile had left town only two hours before. Here, as everywhere, he had acted as our advance press agent by telling everyone we were coming. We marveled at his faith, for it had been more than a month since he'd seen us.

We went to the city hall to use the phone. There was a message that a reporter who'd been planning to paddle with us during the last week wouldn't be coming; her editor had decided against it. Evelyn called a Fort Worth columnist who'd urged her to do so at various places along the river. I called an Alaskan airline to find out how and when and at what cost we could fly out of Emmonak, which seemed the logical village on the logical fork of the river at which to end our journey. The city clerk was a Mr. McGee, a friendly sort in his fifties who was formerly of Fort Worth, Texas. He and Evelyn reminisced about the city they both used to call home. As we left, he asked Evelyn to call his mother in Fort Worth when we got home and let her know that he had a new girlfriend and thought this one would work out well.

The gnats followed us onto the glassy Yukon, and I was finally driven into my headnet for the first time out on the water. I began to rant and rave, and Evelyn began to question my mental health.

"Mosquitoes you can deal with!" I screamed. "You can take'em on one by one, swat by swat, on an equal basis. Horseflies you can stun with your paddle then sqwush 'em when they fall into the boat. But gnats!!! They fly in your ears and your eyes and your nose. What are they even doing, anyway? What do they get out of this? They're not getting blood— nourishment for their breeding cycle or whatever the hell it is that mosquitoes do. Are they eating our sweat? They're serving absolutely no damn purpose other than to drive us crazy!!!!"

I paddled on, imprisoned in my green-tinted headnet that reflected the afternoon sun to such an extent that I could barely see. We passed a flock of sandhill cranes resting on a beach before we saw them, by which time it was too late for pictures.

Finally, we pulled out onto a beach that had little wood but plenty of mosquitoes, gnats, and no-see-ums. The only places of relative comfort were in the tent or in the campfire smoke.

As we set up camp, a motorboat with a young man and a boy pulled into our beach. "It's women!" cried the little boy as the motor died. Julian Demientieff and his nephew, Dean, from a fish camp across the way, stepped onto the beach "to check us out," they said with a smile. They stood around the campfire with us, spraying "Off" on themselves. Julian was about twenty and wanted to visit Texas. He invited us to visit his eighty-seven-year-old grandmother at the fish camp in the morning for coffee, and we happily accepted the invitation.

Julian took Evelyn for a ride in his boat across to a clear creek so she could fill our jugs with water. Moving slowly up the creek, they motored through the half-rotted carcasses of dozens of salmon who had spawned and died. They kept inching farther upstream, trying to find a less-graveyardlike spot to collect water, until the creek narrowed so, and the bushes grew so thick on either side, and the bear tracks became so abundant, that they decided a little carcass-flavored water would do just fine. They filled up quickly and motored merrily back to our camp.

I was learning many things these days. I learned that it didn't much matter if two million gnats came into the tent with you at night, for they wanted netting more than they wanted you. Those that came in would line up along the inside of the screen door, facing outward, while those on the outside would line up facing inward, and they'd stay put all night. I learned that if you scratched open the red White Socks bumps, they merely stung rather than itched, which was infinitely preferable. Of course, then they were a little tender where your tight-fitting long-john cuffs rubbed against them all day....

## AUGUST 12, DAY 65

After breakfast, I requested half an hour to sit in my tent and talk to my tape recorder; Sue and Jude paddled on while Evelyn and I took our time in camp. On the maps, the four of us had agreed upon a probable island for the night and said we'd see each other this evening. A few hours later, when Evelyn and I paddled over to the Demientieffs' camp, Sue and Jude were just leaving.

Frances Demientieff was eighty-seven years old, and she seemed delighted to visit with four women who were paddling canoes down the Yukon River. Her two granddaughters said she'd been up since early that morning, keeping the coffee hot and watching the river through binoculars, hoping we wouldn't bypass her camp by mistake. She was an Athapascan Indian who'd been born in a village far up on the Koyukuk River, but who'd come to Holy Cross to attend the Catholic mission school at an early age. She never saw her parents or her family again. Just a few years ago her children had finally chartered a plane and she had flown into the village she hadn't seen in eighty years. With a twinkle in her eye, she told of the time she and the other girls at the mission had slipped some tobacco past the watchful eyes of the nuns. Frances had been too young to understand the proper use of the substance, had swallowed it, and had become violently ill. She laughed as she described the hard time they had had explaining the sudden illness to the nuns.

She wore wire-rimmed glasses. Her white hair was pulled back into a bun. She had on a cotton dress and tennis shoes. Her brown face and hands were wrinkled, but she was quick and active. She smiled a lot and waved her hand in the air when she laughed. At her side, the coffee water steamed on top of the oil-drum stove. The cabin's walls and tables held the rosaries and pictures and other items of the Catholic faith. Between the two beds along one wall, blankets hung from wires. On the beds sat Frances's two granddaughters, and Julian, when he would wander in occasionally; they would all smile at the good time their grandmother and the two white women were having. We chatted away, eating salmon strips and drinking coffee.

Frances said she thought we were so brave to paddle the river and asked if we were afraid of the bears. The granddaughters began to giggle.

"Is it true that you have some little bitty bells to scare away the bears?" Frances asked, barely able to control her laughter. "Julian tried to tell us you had some bells, but we didn't believe him."

Evelyn stood up and jangled her bells from the string on her waist where they hung, and the room erupted into laughter. The grand-daughters rolled on the bed, Frances covered her face and rocked back and forth. We laughed with them until we were all crying. The more we thought about it, the funnier it did seem that the only thing between us and the bears for 2,000 miles on the Yukon River was a string of five tiny jingle-bells.

Frances said she was afraid of the bears sometimes, even with the protection of the walls of her cabin. She told of an Indian woman named Big Mary who would go into the berry patch every year, but the bears never bothered her because she would talk to them.

"Now listen, you," said Frances, imitating Big Mary, "I'm not a-gonna bother you so don't bother me. I'm just gonna pick a few berries and I'll leave all the rest for you." And the bears never bothered Big Mary. "But never say animals' names when you're talkin' to 'em," Frances told us, shaking her finger. "They don't like it when you call 'em wolf or bear or something like that."

Somehow we got onto the subject of kissing, which reminded Frances of her now-deceased husband. He was half-Russian, half-Indian, and he had blue eyes. The first time she saw those blue eyes, she said, she knew she would marry the guy. She nodded and said he was a good man—a bonus to having blue eyes. All of which reminded Evelyn of a line from the movie *On Golden Pond* when a young smart-aleck tells Henry Fonda that he likes to "suck face," meaning "kiss," and Henry Fonda repeats it to his wife, Katharine Hepburn. Again the cabin was in a female uproar, Frances laughing the loudest. The granddaughters told us they'd just heard on the radio that Henry Fonda had died; the news brought a moment of sadness and the realization that while we were up here playing around on the Yukon, the world carried on.

Frances was well known in the area for her beadwork and had embroidered a stole that was presented to Pope John Paul II when he visited Alaska in 1981. As we walked back to the boat, she showed us a small shrine that she maintained on a hillside near her camp. She and her family lived in Holy Cross most of the year, but they came here to the fish camp in the summers. I hopped on the back of the three-wheeled motorbike and Dean drove me over the uneven terrain to the boat; I just knew the two of us would fall over and I'd break a leg. As we stood at the boat, Frances kept telling Evelyn and me how brave we were, how grateful she was we had come to visit, and how her prayers would go with us. She had never seen the mouth or the headwaters of the river on which she'd spent most of her life.

"What's its name?" she asked, looking fondly at the boat. "Bering Sea or Bust," she repeated slowly, a little puzzled. She marveled over the amount of gear we had in old "Bering Sea." She was the first of many of the Natives along the river who would express an interest in buying the canoe. "Maybe I'll buy that thing for my grandkids to play in," she said. We waved goodbye, paddled out of the big eddy at her front door, and drifted for a long time, smiling and reliving the incredibly warm, friendly few hours we'd spent with Frances Demientieff. It was mind-boggling to us, and probably to her, that at the time she was born, George Carmack was on the verge of starting a gold rush that first brought the word "Yukon" to Americans' attention, and by the time she had lived to be eighty-seven, middle-class women were paddling canoes down the Yukon for fun and relaxation.

"Cuban black beans tonight!" we hollered to Bing as we rounded the first bend and spotted him taking down his tent. We knew they were his favorite. He'd been waiting for some ever since our last batch had been drowned when the canoe filled up with water on the beach at Rampart. Evelyn had cooked them for awhile before we broke camp this morning, and they just needed a few more hours.

"Sue and Jude already told me!" he shouted back. "See you in a little while!" Soon he joined us and we paddled side by side and talked. He said Sue and Jude had passed by a couple of hours before.

We had set ourselves an ambitious goal of about fifty miles on the river today, if we were to meet Sue and Jude at the agreed-upon island. It was 1 P.M. when we left Frances, so we had our work cut out for us. We paddled steadily the entire day, with only a fifteen-minute break or two for nibbling. It rained off and on, but at least most of the time there was no wind. As we paddled, we talked with Bing about his plans for the future. He thought he might stay in Alaska, might check out that possibility of helping to train racing dogs. After he paddled to the Bering Sea on the Emmonak channel, he thought he might paddle upstream and take another channel to Saint Michael. He'd heard there was an old guy there who'd quit his job in New York and paddled and portaged his way across Canada and down the Yukon to Saint Michael; Bing wanted to meet him. He also wanted to track down an old friend he'd heard was living in Anchorage. Or, he might go straight back to Florida, or maybe Cincinatti, where his family was.

Later in the day we passed a few deserted-looking cabins. I was reminded of a story we'd heard concerning a middle-aged man somewhere along the Yukon who routinely advertised in some Lower-48 magazine for female companions and routinely paid $1,000 for them. We got the impression that the practice was not all that unusual on the Yukon. The last one who'd come up to join the man had been in her twenties, and everybody had thought it would work out fine—she'd stayed all winter with him in his little cabin beside the frozen Yukon. But then, toward the end of the winter, they'd taken to shooting at each other and that kind of ended the affiliation.

By the time we reached the last bend before the agreed-upon island, it had been raining softly but steadily for hours, I'd sung every song I knew four times over, my fingers were numb with the cold, and the three of us were getting a little punchy. As we rounded the bend, a wind started up and the rain fell more heavily.

"Hello Mudda, hello Fadda, here I am at Camp Granada," the three of us began to chime, repeating the old song by comic Alan Sherman about summer camp misery that had become our theme song lately. We smiled as we sang it, but it had a certain ring of truth. The rain drummed on my hat. "Take me home, oh Mudda Fadda!" I pulled my outer mittens over my soggy wool gloves. "Take me home, I hate Granada!"

We quit paddling and drifted, hunkering down into our clothes, wishing a cabin would show up on the bank. There would be a nice empty one with plenty of firewood piled beside a big stove, we told ourselves. Better yet, there would be one occupied by a big, friendly family, and they'd invite us in. Yes, that was it. They'd have coffee on the stove and would just be sitting down to a meal of . . . . We debated what would be best for them to be sitting down to a meal of, but we agreed that they would have plenty of it and would insist that we join them.

"I think I remember why people have houses," Evelyn lamented, looking at the dreary skies.

"It all comes back to me now," I nodded glumly. We entertained ourselves by jokingly wailing and boo-hooing for a few minutes, as Bing shook his head and smiled. The rain let up just long enough to coax us into trying to make it to the island for the night. We could see it just ahead, but we forgot that distances deceived and it was really six or seven miles away.

Evelyn donned another layer of clothes and we paddled. The wind worsened, the waves grew, darkness settled, until finally we realized we could barely see the shoreline, let alone spot Sue's and Jude's beige tent. Bing had said he thought he saw a tent on a lone sandbar in the middle of the river, but we couldn't believe that they would have camped on the barren low-lying bar with little wood or shelter. It was hard to see much of anything in the rain, and we began to edge toward the right shoreline to make camp. I finally grabbed the binoculars and tried to determine, in the pouring rain and the bobbing boat, what it was out on the sandbar. Sure enough, a case could be made that it was a tent. By now we were directly across from it, which meant that to reach it we'd have to ferry across a mile of one-foot waves in near-darkness, but for some reason we decided to do it. Evelyn had taken off her glasses because the rain coated them too much to see anyway; now, she had to set our ferry angle with absolutely no idea where we were headed. We faced upstream and, as I paddled with long, hard strokes, I tried to devise hints for where she should aim the boat.

"Don't you see the tent over there?" I shouted above the noise of the waves.

"Nope."

"Well, see that big downed tree on the sandbar?"

"Nope."

"You do see the sandbar . . . ."

"Nope."

"Do you see Bing's orange poncho flapping in the wind—surely you see that?"

"Kind of."

"Aha, the gull overhead—I'll let you know when he's right above where we want to aim. Surely as a birder . . . ."

"Nope."

"Don't you see him right above that hump on the horizon—you do see the horizon?"

"Sort of—is it kind of straight and long?" We began to giggle hysterically. So you're trying to ferry, with a blind bat at the helm, in a rainstorm, across a two-mile-wide river, toward something you're still not sure you even want to get to . . . .

About that time we crashed into the sandbar anyway, pretty much where we wanted to all along. And sure enough, the object at the far upstream end, about a hundred yards away, was a tent. Sue and Jude had already given up on us and turned in for the night; they poked their heads out of the tent and waved.

Evelyn and Bing and I quickly unloaded gear and set up our three tents in the fading light and worsening rain. I was so cold and wet that I didn't take time to find extra clothes or my flashlight; it was now getting completely dark at night, but the phenomenon had been so gradual and so inconceivable that for days we'd been refusing to admit it. By the time I stomped the last tent stake into the sand and threw myself inside my little shelter, a severe wind was blasting down the valley. Evelyn and Bing trudged through the rain and the darkness to the lee of the huge downed spruce tree that lay in the middle of the sandbar. They were determined to make a fire and eat Cuban black beans in the rain and wind; I was convinced they were insane.

Snuggled naked inside my sleeping bag (synthetic ones generally keep you warmer that way), I soon realized I was being physically buffeted by the billowing side panel of the tent. If this were true, I groaned, it meant that the stakes had pulled out on that side and that the fly was no longer keeping the water off the tent itself. I poked my head and arms out of the sleeping bag and felt around in the dark to investigate. Not only was the side of the tent plastered against me, but the roof was inches from my face, meaning the front stake had pulled out, too, and there was nothing to hold up the tent. The entire length of my sleeping bag was soaking wet. If I went outside to restake the damned thing, I'd only get wetter and colder, and I'd probably never be able to find the stakes in the dark. Maybe the wind would die soon and I could go to sleep in peace. I lay back down.

But the wind didn't stop; I realized my sleeping bag was getting wetter and I was getting colder. Thoughts of hypothermia went through my mind. We had been paddling hard for fifty miles in the rain and wind, with only some peanut butter and crackers to sustain our energy. I was tired, hungry, wet, and now cold—the four perfect factors for hypothermia.

But lying here getting wetter wasn't the answer. I sat up, fought my way through the nylon cloud to the front flap, struggled with the sand-encrusted zipper (wincing where it dug into the open red gap on my forefinger) and opened the door into a freezing face-full of blowing rain. In a second, the whipping wind stole all the heat from my naked torso. I shrank back, held the flap closed, pushed against the apex of the A-frame with my full weight—straight-arming the thing as the wind bucked me back—and thought for a minute. The wind had shifted 180° and increased its ferocity many times in the space of a few minutes. I had tried to walk in forty-mile-an-hour dust storms in Lubbock, Texas, and I could tell this storm could match them gust for gust. This was getting serious. Unless the tent stakes would stay in the ground, the tent would lie on top of me and would not be waterproof; my only protection in this gale would be a sleeping bag.

"Come on, Johnson," I said aloud, as I shivered and breathed in quick involuntary jerks like I do whenever I jump into icy water. "Either get back into the sleeping bag or get outside and do something." I threw down the flap, lunged out naked into the freezing wind, found the whipping front stake cord which, thank God, still had its stake attached, and jammed the stake into the soft sand, cursing it. I recoiled into the tent and fought with clenched, chattering teeth and frozen fingers to get the zipper back up.

I found the sleeping bag in the dark and threw my wet body into it. Now I was really shivering, even in my usually-warm bag. I blew on my hands to warm them. When I couldn't stop shivering, my thoughts returned to hypothermia. I also thought about our boats being carried away if the waves washed up on shore or if the river rose. I thought about the wetsuit in the boat that I might have to wear tomorrow because almost all my clothes were wet. I thought about how very exposed we were on the barren sandbar, and how low it was. If the water rose just a couple of feet, we'd have to make a run for shore, which probably wouldn't be successful because the waves would swamp us or turn us over. I thought about one December night when I'd been this cold and wet, and how we'd taken hot chocolate into the tent (didn't have to worry about bears in Texas). The hot chocolate had helped some, but what had helped even more had been my warm, friendly, bearded tent mate. . . . No such luck here on the Yukon. Oh, well, I decided that my cramped, soggy quarters would be even more miserable with two people's gear thrown in here, and the wet-dog and I-need-a-bath smell that hung in the tent was pretty disgusting to foist on myself, let alone somebody else. I thought of the words to "Help Me Make It Through the Night" that Evelyn had been learning to sing. I remembered that somebody said once that you're not on a really memorable trip unless, at some point, you wonder what in the hell you're doing there. Well, that's just what I was wondering; our Yukon trip was hereby successful. I thought again about why people have houses, as I tugged my wet wool balaclava down around my shoulders and guessed how long it would be before my tent ripped to shreds and I'd be left lying in the sand.

Still I shivered. Five minutes of not being able to stop shaking seemed serious, so I began to talk to myself aloud again.

"Are you shaking because you're cold or scared?"

"Both."

"Well, you better do something. Put on your wet wool longhandles, dummy."

"O.K., O.K."

The wind roared and bashed the sides of the tent against me. I struggled madly, on the verge of tears, to find my long unders by touch in the dark, figure out which were the tops and which were the bottoms, and get them on. I finally succeeded and zipped the bag back over my head. Still I shivered. Now the wind was physically tossing me off my sleeping pad.

I reached up and found the roof in my face; the front stake had pulled out again. This tent was not going to remain erect in this soft sand, it was clear. The choices were to go to the boat and bring heavy gear to anchor the tent stakes, or to take shelter in someone else's tent. I figured if I left the tent to go get some gear, it would blow away altogether into the river and be gone forever. I considered making a run, tent and all, for Sue's and Jude's three-person tent. Peering out my back window, I could see nothing but darkness; their tent was so far away and the visibility so low in the rain that I thought I might get lost trying to find them. I struggled to my front door and peered out. Evelyn's and Bing's tents, barely visible a few yards away, seemed upright. It seemed proper to try Evelyn's first.

I struggled into my Gore-Tex and my shoes and rolled out of the front door into the wet sand. I pushed all the gear—trumpet, sleeping bag, clothes—to the rear of the tent, zipped the front flap, grabbed the tent in my arms and pulled it out of the ground in the few places it was still staked. I began to crawl, dragging the heavy nylon jumble. The wind struggled to tear it from me; I knew that if I stood up, the tent and I would probably take to the air across the sandbar. Crawling around in the wet sand like this, wrestling a bucking tent, seemed pretty ridiculous, but I didn't want to lose my tent and I was shivering too much to laugh.

"Evelyn!" I called through the wind when I reached her door. "My tent won't stay up! Can I come in?"

"Come on in!" came the wide-awake reply. "I'm sittin' here holding up the back end of mine!"

I dumped my tent in the lee of hers and struggled with the zipper. "See if you can restake that back stake before you come in," she requested in a serious tone, when I got the door open. I could see nothing; she was only a voice. I threw one of her heavy bags onto my tent to weight it down and crawled behind her tent. I tried for a few moments to catch the whipping end of the rain-fly to find either the rope or the stake, but by then I was shivering so uncontrollably and my cold hands had so little movement or feeling left in them that I realized I was useless. I did find and restake one corner rain-fly rope, but the key one was still Missing In Action.

I crawled back to where my tent lay heaped in the sand, struggled with it interminably, finally got it open, and dragged my sleeping bag and pad out of it—breathing in quick jerks all the while. I threw the gear into the puddle of water on the floor of Evelyn's tent and collapsed on top of it. I took off my Gore-Tex and my shoes, showering water and sand throughout the tent, and crawled into my sleeping bag.

"Free room and board if you hold up your corner of the room," came the voice from the far corner of the tent. Still in my bag, I sat up against one pole of the A-frame, while Evelyn sat against the other. We leaned with our weight and the wind bucked us. In a few moments, feeling a little more secure and warm with Evelyn's tent and company, I began to see a tiny bit of humor in the whole situation.

"Well, here we are," I sighed. "If we hypothermiate I guess we can do it together."

"Here we are," she laughed weakly. "I was just sittin' here thinking— as I held up my house around me—that I guess leaving this world in a blaze of glory in a hurricane on the Yukon's as good a place as any."

"Hey, you know, this is just like a slumber party, we get to sit up and talk all night," I said. "Only difference is, we *have* to sit up to hold up our house and we *have* to talk to make sure the guests aren't freezing to death." We snickered.

"I wonder about our boats," I said. "We didn't pull them up very far."

"Yeah, the waves sound like the ocean," she said. We could hear them crashing on shore, probably filling up our boat with water, as they had at Rampart. "Did you tie the boat to anything?"

"Well, I drove a little stake into the sand, which I'm sure would pull out in an instant if the boat began to float away. But then," I muffled a laugh, "I tied the leftover end of the rope to Bing's tent, so remember, if he hollers it means our boat's heading for the Bering Sea without us." We found that extremely funny.

Evelyn uttered, with a flourish and a great deal of satisfaction, her favorite string of swear words, copied from her daughter. I sighed my typical, long, low expression of dismay, "Oh Lord. . . ."

Evelyn asked with a snort, "Hey, how will we know if we're getting hypothermia and getting delirious?"

"It would be pretty hard to tell," I guffawed. "We probably already are and are too far gone to know it . . . . By the way, did you eat the beans?"

"We got a fire going, we really did," she said proudly. "But the rain kept putting it out, so we finally forgot it."

"I think those black beans should be banned from this expedition," I suggested. "The last time you cooked 'em Jude broke her foot and now they've caused a damned hurricane."

We found enough things to giggle about until I finally stopped shivering. She said for me to lie down to sleep while she held up the tent, then after awhile we'd switch. I amazed myself by falling sound asleep, in wet underwear, in a wet sleeping bag, on a wet sleeping pad, on the wet floor of a tent. Sometime in the night, the wind died enough for Evelyn to go out and find the missing tent rope and restake it. It held. We slept.

## AUGUST 13, DAY 66

Finally, the rain and wind stopped for a few hours. People crept from their tents to survey the damage and recount their various tales of disaster and adventure. Our boat was filled with water, gunnel to gunnel. Every piece of equipment floated in it or lay in the sand beside it, still tied to its thwart. The boat was half-buried in sand where the waves had driven the beach up against it. Three feet away, Bing's boat was unburied and had only three inches of water in the bottom. Old Bering Sea or Bust was a truly forlorn sight. Staring at the floating mass of gear, we knew this was where we would put every piece of waterproof baggage to its ultimate test. When all was said and done, when every piece of soggy stuff had been dragged from the boat, we would learn that the $5.99 used army-surplus ammo cans—which, luckily, housed the cameras—were the only things that were waterproof. The $12 guaranteed-airtight box that held the tape recorder was not; the $42 plastic duffel bag that held the camera film was not; the $25 vinyl bag that held the books and the toilet paper was not . . . .

At the height of the storm, we learned, Sue and Jude had awakened to find themselves being crushed and smothered by the ceiling of their dome tent, whose fiberglass poles had been smushed flat by the wind. The stakes had pulled out and nothing but the weight of their bodies was keeping the tent on the ground. They had sat up on their elbows, holding down the edge of the tent with their hands as the roof beat upon their heads. They had switched on their tape recorder and added some fairly exciting footage to the tape they were making for a friend.

Bing had gotten a little wet in his fifteen-pound dome-shaped canvas mountain tent, but other than that he had been fine. He said with a grin that he kept expecting it to be dragged into the ocean by our boat whenever it headed out to sea.

Sue and Jude made breakfast. We huddled in our parkas. We dubbed this miserable beach "Camp Granada," and throughout breakfast, one or the other of us would burst into some favorite line of the song, usually, "Take me home! I hate Granada!" Sue and Evelyn helped me set up my tent, and we anchored the ropes with backpacks and ammo cans. I spread all my wet things inside to dry. The rain began to fall, the wind began to blow. I crawled inside and stayed there for the next twenty-four hours, reading, sleeping, blowing my nose, and occasionally venturing forth to reposition the backpack when the wind tugged it across the beach.

## AUGUST 14, DAY 67

There was a new twist to Granada's dismal scene this morning: a sandstorm. From the ground to our knees there hovered a brown flurry of stinging bits of grit. The wind was so strong we had to ferry against it with our bodies, moving laterally between our tents and the forlorn kitchen tree, which was the only scrap of shelter on the sandbar. When we hunkered over our breakfast mush with our backs to the wind, shielding our bowls from the blowing sand, our bodies created eddies; the sand swirled around our shoulders and back into our faces and bowls. Now, not only was my handkerchief wet when I had to drag it out to blow my nose every few minutes, but it was caked with sand.

At least the sun was shining.

Eventually, the wind calmed to a mere gale and we decided to make a run for it. Feeling none too peppy from my cold, I had my doubts about the whole thing. There was still a good three-foot chop on the water, and the nearest island lay a mile downstream. I put on my wetsuit.

Sue and Jude helped us empty the water from the boat and we launched forth. A few dozen yards offshore, we knew we were in for a rough ride. The waves came at a slight angle to where we wanted to go, and that made the boat wallow. Every now and then the waves came at angles even to themselves, which also made things difficult. As I plunged down into each trough, staring at the crest of the next wave, which was sometimes as tall as I was, my only hope was that we'd hit it just right so it wouldn't topple into the boat; one or two waves of that size could quickly dump enough water into the bow to swamp us. The rollers got so big they evoked images from *Kon-Tiki*, which I hadn't thought of in years; I wondered if we'd lost our minds to have gone out in them. Once I swear we rode up the face of and, luckily, over a five-foot wave.

At last, we made it to the lee of an island, paddled down a shallow slough, and crossed over to another island, working our way toward the right shore where we thought we'd get out of the wind and where we knew Russian Mission lay, sooner or later. The four of us pulled out to survey the rest of the river from an island; Bing paddled on across open water, his green bow rising and falling several feet with each wave, his paddle blades flying furiously through the air. Sue climbed over some high dunes and around a slough and returned with the report that the last channel was no worse than what we'd just gone through. And far down the river, Bing's boat still appeared to be upright. We decided to go for it.

We made it through the last stretch with relative ease, but by the time we reached the mere one-footers near the shore, my head and throat and overall body felt so bad that my paddle seemed like a forty-pound lead weight. Sue gave me some pills and I lay down while we drifted.

A few miles later, we rounded a high point and spotted the boats and buildings of the Eskimo village of Russian Mission, which was comforting, if for no other reason than that there were other human beings around. Even if they did have a tendency to shoot at us . . . .

And who should be standing on the beach smiling and waving his hat like a long-lost friend, but David Gile! It had been a month and a thousand miles since we'd seen him. We thought that with our forced layover at Granada he'd be too far ahead for us ever to catch him, but he'd waited out the same storm on the beach here at Russian Mission. He was amazed we'd caught up.

"At the rate you guys were going back at Circle," he smiled, "I thought I'd never see you again."

"We began to paddle," we grinned. There were smiles all around as we began to tell him of our adventures of the last few days.

"Wait, wait," he said, "I want you to come on up and meet the people who've been hosting me."

"Hosting you?"

David opened the door of a house trailer and out came a rush of warm, dry air—reward enough for our having paddled eight miles on the high seas today. When Laura Walter took care of somebody, she really took care of 'em. She sat us on chairs and laid a plastic bag of cold leftover chicken on the table. We set upon it like a pack of famished wolves and practically had it devoured before she could bring the homemade bread and real butter that went with it. Then, merciful angel, she asked which flavor of herb tea we'd like, and whether we'd like *honey* in it! Between bites, we mumbled "Oh my God" and thanked her again.

Laura and a dozen or so other young whites worked for the federal Bureau of Indian Affairs. They had lived together throughout the summer in a couple of house trailers in this, the first Eskimo village we'd come to on the river, conducting historical and archaeological surveys of Eskimo burial sites throughout the Yukon Delta region. They all ate together in this one trailer. It had running water that came out of the faucets in the sink, and it had a toilet that flushed when you pushed the handle. It had a refrigerator and a gas stove. It had an oven. It had some kind of heating system. It had a TV and a washer and a dryer.

But mostly what it had was food. Laura was the full-time cook, and she was trying her darnedest to get rid of all the food during the last week of the summer-long operation. We were willing to give our all to help her. Laura would set one major meal under our noses before we'd properly completed the last. This went on for hours, as we watched tennis on TV, talked to Bing and David and the various crew members who wandered in, sewed up wetsuit booties, and tried to bring my tape recorder back to life after its all-night swim on Camp Granada (the $70 gadget never regained consciousness).

After we'd gorged for several hours and darkness began to settle, we all trooped up the hill to the school building to watch a documentary about the Eskimos of Russian Mission. Then Bing and David went down to the beach to sleep in their tents; the four of us went to Laura's house. We had turned down hot showers 150 miles back in Grayling and almost 400 miles back in Galena, but now, eighteen days since our last hot shower in Tanana, Laura had no trouble talking us into making use of her bathroom with hot running water.

How fickle was life on the Yukon, I smiled to myself. A few hours before, I had felt sick, everything I owned had been wet and muddy, and I was filthy. But now, by the time I lay down to sleep on Laura's warm, dry floor, Sue's pills and Laura's food had cured the aches in body and soul. I was clean (I'd even shaved my legs between the open sores), I was dry, and most of my clothes were likewise.

"Laura," I muttered as we all said good night, "I'm good for another thousand miles."

# 12 bering sea or bust!!!

## AUGUST 15, DAY 68

The first order of business was to attend a service in the Russian Orthodox church here. Beside a small graveyard on a hillside in town stood a plain wooden building topped by Russian Orthodox crosses. We stepped inside cautiously, bundled in our parkas against the morning cold and wet, careful to keep a knit hat or scarf on our heads, as women are supposed to do. The sounds of our boots echoed heavily on the wooden floors of the empty building. We were the first ones there, except for an older woman who knelt before candles in the corner. Along one side of the room was a single, low, backless wooden bench; along the other side, the same. The woman clued us in that we were sitting on the men's side, so we moved.

Three Eskimo priests in long black robes entered and began all sorts of chants and prayers and readings, interspersed with the shaking of incense from bells. We thought we heard bits and pieces of Russian and English and perhaps Eskimo, but it was all pretty hard to tell. People drifted in until, eventually, a couple of dozen adults and assorted babies and young children crowded onto the benches. There was a constant standing up and sitting down of the congregation, each movement accompanied by a great shuffling of boots on wood. Beside me sat Marsha, one of the women from the Bureau of Indian Affairs crew. Her long black hair fell from under her blue bandanna over her Gore-Tex parka, and she looked a little more elegant than I in my green army-navy shirt and blue wool pants. She wore a long patchwork skirt. Crossing her legs, she revealed giant rubber fishermen's wading boots. Beside her, three Eskimo women with tiny babies also wore long skirts, from which also peeked big boots or tennis shoes.

It being only mid-August, the two big oil-drum stoves hadn't yet been lit; we could see our breath throughout the service, and everyone sat with hands tucked in pockets. This was a relatively new church, but all around its walls and ceilings were the icons and gold ornaments of the original church, which had been built here in 1851. It had been the first

Russian mission on the Yukon, established in the same village as the Russian-American Company's fur-trading post, which was established here in 1836 or 1837. The village was then called Ikogmut. The old church with its blue onion dome still stands, but it is no longer used for services. During the service, a small boy crawled on the floor and played with a plastic sports car. Electric light bulbs brightened an otherwise grey morning. A vacuum cleaner with a long snakelike plastic hose stood in the corner. Beneath their robes, the priests wore Dingo boots.

After the service, there was time to squeeze in one more of Laura's huge hot meals before getting back on the river. As we washed dishes afterward, David came striding into the trailer holding my caribou antlers, with an apologetic look on his face. He'd rescued them from the boat where two dogs were fighting over them; the bigger dog had managed to get a good gnawing start on one end. Evelyn and I shook our heads and smiled; in every village we'd beaten back the dogs, who for some reason always wanted to make off with those antlers above everything else in our boat. To us, the antlers gave off only a faint, slightly dead-animal odor, but the dogs must have thought otherwise. Several times we had to sleep with the things in our tent, to guard them from attack. David set them in the corner by the door and they dripped blood (from the dog's mouth, we supposed) all over Laura's floor.

The one thing I needed to purchase to ensure a happy final two hundred miles or so to the Bering Sea was dry toilet paper, but the trading post had not a single roll. Laura gave me a roll and we launched forth into the cold, grey drizzle that fell on the Yukon. The BIA crew stood in the mud shaking their heads and taking pictures, saying how crazy we were to go out in weather like this. It was definitely cold, but there was no wind; we had the feeling that if we stayed one more hour in that warm trailer with all that warm food and good company, we'd become permanently addicted and could never face the open river again.

The four of us paddled with David; Bing stayed behind for awhile to finish drying some clothes. At first we bantered back and forth between the boats, singing bits about "rollin' on the river" from the rock song "Proud Mary," and generally trying to bolster our interest in paddling. But within minutes of our launch, the wind began to whisper up the valley into our faces. Little waves slapped the bow. Then the wind cleared its throat and burst into an impassioned, sustained oration that sent David's bow spinning upstream and had us hanging onto our hats and washing against the shore. Soon David had to pull out, and shortly we did the same, less than an hour and only three miles below today's starting point.

We decided this garden spot was second only to Granada for lack of amenities, but it was the only flat, clear place to be had. We heaved the boats up onto a one-foot muddy cutbank to get them out of the waves. The main shoreline was another three feet higher, where you'd sink to your knees and lose your tennis shoes in the suction mud if you dawdled. We set up the tents in the scanty shelter of a line of willows, automatically tying the ropes to the trees and weighting tents with backpacks and ammo cans. Waves crashed ever more loudly against the straight high bank, rain dripped off the brim of my cowboy hat, mosquitoes bit my backside as I squatted and tried to keep my toilet paper dry: another day, another dollar.

I was in the mood to hunker down and sleep forever. I crawled into my tent, ready to relish the depressing circumstances of our forced layover which were made all the more ironic by the fact that Laura's food and her warm, dry trailer lay almost within shouting distance. Every now and then someone's lonely wail, "Laura!", would drift across our muskeg flat.

Just about the time Sue and Evelyn ventured forth to cook, Bing and David paddled up. We spent the rest of the afternoon and evening in an extremely pleasant niche in an alder thicket. The leaves were just thick enough to keep the brunt of the rain off of us, and high water had deposited just for us a quarter-acre pile of logs, within reach of our campfire. Between that and the full bottle of peppermint schnapps that David pulled out of his boat, we did all right.

## AUGUST 16, DAY 69

All day long, waves thudded against the shoreline, wind whipped the Yukon into an ugly chop, rain fell with varying intensity from forlorn skies. But in our niche, Bing mixed pancake batter in his old bent coffee cans, David opened a can of bacon he'd found in his boat, Evelyn simmered a big pot of lentil soup, and we sat around the fire all day like we had good sense. Whenever somebody got bored, he or she would drag a few more logs from the woodpile and saw them into firewood, rearrange them into better furniture, or build a walkway across the mud with them. How strange and wonderful it seemed that an environ-mentalist, a gift salesperson, an anesthesiologist, and a surgical nurse from Texas; an accountant from New Hampshire; and a drug-runner or whatever he was from Florida were happily sitting here together in the rain all day on the Yukon, thrown together by nothing more than our peculiar love for long canoe trips through wild land.

My book about the Amazon was now soggy mush from the Granada hurricane; I spent the day reading another paperback about sailing a boat through the Greenland icepack. If I read fast enough, the pages didn't get too wet. The others played five hours of spades on a tree stump.

Long into the night, David and Bing and I sat around the fire drinking hot chocolate and talking about the Amazon (David said he'd always wanted to do the Amazon, too, but, like Bing and me, the only problem he foresaw was that he knew nothing about camping in jungles) and about some of our more memorable hangovers and parties in college. Bing let it slip that he'd gone to college in Ohio, which added a tiny piece to the puzzle we still tried to solve occasionally about what he did for a living. (The next morning, with a teasing smile, he denied having said anything about college.)

As I trudged toward my tent through the mud past David's tent, knowing he had two guns in there, I called out half-jokingly, "Don't shoot, I'm not a bear."

"I know," came a voice through the darkness. "Bears don't wear Gore-Tex."

## AUGUST 17, DAY 70

When I awoke, something was very different; a strange silence hung over the land. No wind! No waves! It was 6:30 A.M. by David's watch; we threw down the tents, gulped some breakfast, heaved the boats into the water, and paddled like Olympic racers (more or less). It was extremely cold; I wore my wetsuit in case I got more lapfuls of cold water over the bow as I usually did when the wind came up.

We were tired of sitting around tents and campfires, so for the challenge of it, and also because we knew it could take us weeks to go the mere couple of hundred miles to the Bering Sea if we failed to utilize the windless days, we paddled hard and steadily throughout the day. We practically left David standing still; even Bing, the paddling automaton with the double-bladed paddle, seemed to appreciate the few short breaks we took.

From here on to the Bering Sea, we'd be paddling through the giant Yukon Delta National Wildlife Refuge, a 13.4-million-acre collection of lowland lakes, sloughs, and ponds. (Actually, it began a few miles above Camp Granada.) An astounding 100 million shorebirds and other water-birds raise their young here each summer. Today, paddling through the last of the major directional changes the Yukon makes across Alaska, we turned northwest and began our final swing to the sea. By now, we had paddled across half of the Pacific time zone and the entire breadth of the Alaska-Hawaii time zone, and today we began paddling across the Bering time zone. By day's end, when we grabbed a tiny beach across a slough from the village of Marshall, after ten hours on the slow delta current, we'd come almost sixty miles farther toward the Bering Sea. It was our finest hour.

The evening would prove to be David's finest hour. Tonight, Evelyn and Sue and Jude introduced the heretofore-low-key New Englander to the speciality of the house, which they'd perfected in 1,800 miles of Yukon bartending. They'd christened the innocent-looking concoction a Yukon Sun Dog, and it was the only Everclear-related brew that wasn't too revolting to drink. To make it, you mix two parts Tang or red Kool-Aid with one part Everclear and a hint of grit (very important for authen-ticity—if you're on the Yukon it'll find its way into your drink auto-matically, but if you try a Yukon Sun Dog at home you'll have to throw in a dash of sand).

Before the second course of the evening's dinner feast was properly served, David was falling backwards off his log; the rest of us weren't far behind. Our mobility became so hampered by the Sun Dogs that we finally relaxed our no-peeing-in-the-kitchen rule; this expedition was losing all semblance of civility. Bing smiled and shook his head and sipped his tea, knowing he was in for another long night as chief fire-tender and chaperone. At least the whole village wasn't here on our beach this time. A mother grizzly and cub had been, though, very recently. The open part of the beach was so small that our five tents had to be set up within a few feet of each other and very near the campfire and food. But grizzlies weren't much on our mind tonight; we entertained ourselves for hours just watching David succumb to the Sun Dogs.

Finally, after he'd lost one-on-one poker to both Sue and Jude and was thus selected to wash dishes, David grabbed all the pots and Bing's coffee cans and headed for the river's edge. He miscalculated somewhat and walked into the water up to his knees, hiking boots and all. He staggered in the mud, falling now into his boat, now onto his hands and knees. As he thrashed and scrubbed and chased errant pots as they escaped down the Yukon, he swore and laughed maniacally and shouted to the world that this was the first time in his life he'd lost a poker game. And now, he'd lost to not one, but two, women. And now, they were making him wash a bunch of paint cans. He implored the heavens to tell him where was the justice in the world. The outbursts were interspersed with the sounds of huge boots being extricated with great force from ten inches of suction mud. All the while, periodic involuntary squeals burst from his mouth and echoed across the water.

Some of us, staggering to our tents or attending to our nightly toiletries, laughed so hard we couldn't catch our breath; we stopped in our tracks and lay on the sand. Evelyn suggested that a little dishwashing music was in order, so I pulled out my trumpet and the David Gile aquatic floor show shifted to high gear. I growled out a few stripper numbers; David gyrated his hips (as best he could with his feet cemented into the mud) and scrubbed to the music. At the appropriate points, he would swing a plate over his head and toss it landward or pound on his canoe in bass-drum fashion with a serving spoon.

Thus, we came to know a wonderful and somewhat unexpected side of David that brought new pleasure to our already agreeable relationship. Afterward, Evelyn and I would declare that he was the funniest drunk we'd ever seen. And that was saying something.

## AUGUST 18, DAY 71

It was another grey morning; Bing's pancakes were frying in a skillet, awaiting the Vermont maple syrup that David happened to have. A loud groan from David's tent indicated that he was still among the living. He had enough sense of humor left, even with his hangover, to note that when he had stumbled into the tent, he had meticulously laid his muddy boots outside the door on the ground (wouldn't want to get the tent messy), but had forgotten a minor detail like zipping the mosquito netting. How anyone could have slept soundly through the night as the main course for the mosquitoes was beyond us. True, there weren't as many of the insects as there used to be, but there were still plenty by Lower 48 standards.

We were losing interest in exploring every village, so we decided to bypass Marshall and push on down the river. Somehow, David summoned the energy to join us. We paddled for hours in moderate waves and seemed to be getting nowhere, according to the map. More yellow willow leaves lined the banks. A few fish camps were still occupied, but many seemed to be shut down for the season. We'd long since paddled through the tail end of the king salmon run. The dog salmon and the silver salmon were still coming in, but they seemed to generate less activity among humans than the kings. Here in the delta, there were no more fish wheels; people used mostly gill nets, and we were seeing fewer and fewer of them. The mountains had disappeared altogether. There were still some spruces along the bank, but mostly the world was grey, choppy water and grey, low-hanging skies.

Maybe it was time to get to the Bering Sea. To me, the thought seemed premature. Where were the endless days of lying in the sun? I could remember only one or two self-imposed (as opposed to weather-imposed) layover days in camp, although, truthfully, we'd had our share of lazy days in the boats. Where was all the time to practice my trumpet? I'd learned the words to plenty of songs as I paddled, but I'd learned very few on the trumpet. I hadn't made a dent in my reading library. But somehow, I knew the end was at hand; there was simply no more river left to paddle. Fall was closing in and big storms could begin to sweep up the delta any day. Jude and Sue now seemed so anxious to get off the river that they thought of little but paddling, and to suggest a layover day now was to suggest a rainy day in a tent; I'd just as soon paddle.

Late in the day, Evelyn and I stopped paddling and drifted. We nibbled our lunch and gabbed. We'd long since given up racing to the Bering Sea; as usual, the others paddled on and soon disappeared down a long open stretch of the river. After relaxing for thirty minutes or so, we began to paddle. Soon, tiny specks on the horizon indicated we were gaining on the others, and when a small wind kicked up, we gained faster. As usual, our keel and perhaps the bargelike load we were carrying helped us slice through the waves.

Far ahead, the others were hugging the right shoreline around a giant curve. Evelyn suggested that with the river being more than a mile wide here, we could cut off a mile or two of distance if we made straight for the next point of land around the inside of the curve.

"O.K.," I said, "but let's cut to the other side fast in case the wind starts up." The shifting clouds overhead looked fickle, and the river was big. When we got halfway across, sure enough, the wind began to stir up two-footers, and we tossed about in the heavy chop. We made it into the relatively calm waters in the lee of the point of land, just as the wind really began to rip across the water. We continued paddling casually, staying within a couple of dozen yards of shore in case we had to pull out. By now we figured we'd passed the others because we'd cut off the distance around the curve, and we knew that the wind was probably dashing huge rollers into their shore. Straining to see through the binoculars as our boat rocked in the waves, I thought I saw a yellow and green speck near each other against the far shore, and another yellow speck a mile or so behind them. For miles along their shore there was nothing but a five-foot, crumbling, earth cutbank covered with dense spruces; if the others had to pull out because of the waves, they were going to have a hard time finding a landing. It was with no small degree of mirth that we discussed the accidents of weather and timing that had brought Evelyn and me—who mostly goofed off and didn't really care when we reached the Bering Sea—to relatively safe waters, a mile ahead of the others, and had kept Sue and Jude—who no longer kept our boat in sight behind them and were bent on setting mileage records every day—from making any headway this afternoon.

We would learn shortly that at that moment they were rolling uncontrollably in the vicious waves, taking on water, and being blown upstream if they stopped paddling for an instant—all with little hope of a place to pull out for the night. We also learned that when they spotted a distant aluminum canoe ahead of them near the other shore, so inconceivable to them was it that it might be us that they thought they'd come upon the long-lost French couple we'd heard about, or perhaps some mystery canoe the Mukluk Telegraph had missed. So long had it been since they'd looked behind them that they never knew we'd caught up with them and crossed the river. As the wind began to die, so curious were they as to who was in the new boat that Bing braved the still-high waves and paddled a mile across the river, only to discover that the mystery boat was only old Bering Sea or Bust with old Beth and Evelyn.

But the others had had quite a harrowing and tiring afternoon, and we pulled out early on a flat, muddy beach covered with grizzly tracks. We'd still made thirty-five miles for the day, which wasn't too shabby, considering the others had been blown upstream for an hour or two. Somehow, we'd lost David in all the excitement; we assumed and hoped he had safely pulled out somewhere and would catch up tonight or tomorrow.

Evelyn threw together some Chinese fried rice, with eggs and peas and garlic and onions, all of which for some reason sent us into fits of ecstasy.

## AUGUST 19, DAY 72

I knew the odds were that as I stripped off my clothes at the water's edge this morning to take a bath, either an airplane would fly over or a boat would come by. One did, right on cue, and it was David. We all ate breakfast together, then began paddling in calm weather on what would probably be David's last day on the river. He wanted to take out at Saint Mary's, where transportation connections were easier to the rest of Alaska, but we were still trying to talk him into paddling the final hundred miles of the river with us. We were all in a pretty gleeful mood—even more so when two whistling swans flew overhead around the first bend.

As we neared the village of Pilot Station, about ten miles from the day's starting point, I happened to be teaching Evelyn how to sing "Faded Love," the fiddle classic by Bob Wills of Turkey, Texas. She had written the words on a notebook that lay before her on her backpack. I would paddle and sing, looking ahead, and whenever we got far enough off course to warrant a J-stroke on her part, I'd holler "Steer!" on an upbeat; she'd take the corrective action without looking up as she continued reading and singing. This went on for a mile or two as we rounded the bend into the village; it produced a crazy zigzag course that probably had the villagers wondering what oddball bunch of cheechakos was pulling in now, but she had the whole song memorized by the time we eased into the beach. We had been so caught up in the hilarity of her endeavors that we hadn't noticed a huge ship behind us that whizzed downstream just after we landed on the beach; we wondered how close we'd come to being run down during our music lesson.

I was too lazy to teeter across the logs over the mud into town, so I lay in the boat in the sun. The others stayed in town just long enough to relieve Pilot Station of its entire supply of chocolate-covered doughnuts (two boxes) that had sat in a box on a shelf for who knows how long. The Eskimo village looked like all the others we'd passed—log cabins, plywood shacks, mud—except that from it sprouted a tall wind generator with long, sleek blades.

Evelyn and I realized we'd acquired a certain river mentality of immediate gratification when we could not restrain ourselves from gobbling the entire box of stale doughnuts, plus a candy bar each, before we'd drifted out of sight of the town. Then, with a sudden burst of energy, we sprinted through the water singing "Faded Love"; our chocolate-doughnut-powered canoe overtook even Sue and Jude. As quickly as the energy had arrived, it disappeared, giving way to giddiness. Evelyn happened to comment that the two gallons of breakfast soup that stood in our big, charred cookpot this morning had looked exactly like the slop she used to dump over the fence for the hogs when she was a little girl on the farm, and with that, we lost all rational composure. Throwing down our paddles, we giggled. Bubbling to the surface of our minds came all the insanity of seventy-two days on the Yukon, and we laughed, gloriously, uncontrollably. We screamed and guffawed about one thing or another for about ten miles, sometimes laughing so hard that we had to lie back on the gear for fear of falling overboard. All the while, dozens of motorboats raced at top speed, one after another, down our slough; their wakes only sent us into further hysterics. By the time we reached the end of the slough, they were racing back the other way; we never did figure out whether we'd happened into the middle of the annual Pilot Station fishing-boat race or whether the bootleg-liquor plane had just arrived twenty miles downriver at Saint Mary's.

"Oh, Evelyn," I gasped, crying with laughter and trying to catch my breath, "how would I have survived without you? You're the only person I know who can appreciate the full humor of all this." (A new roar of laughter erupted from the back of the boat.) "By the way, do you think we were this crazy before we got here or did the Yukon do this to us?"

Lying on her back on her ammo can, Evelyn kicked her feet in the air and spread her arms wide. "Who cares??!!" she boomed to the heavens.

Through the weeks on the river, our friendship and communication had deepened immeasurably. Evelyn's bizarre and unfailing good humor helped sustain us. She could recognize something truly comical—like being forced to sleep sitting up holding a tent against a hurricane—when she saw it. There's nothing worse than seeing something funny and having no one with whom to share the laughter, and, mercifully, we saw humor in the same things. The foundation of our increasingly comfortable paddling and camping partnership was our common belief in tolerance and acceptance of others—without judging. We recognized that each of us did things that bugged the other, but we believed that it was easier, healthier, and more legitimate to enjoy the overall person as she was—oddities and all—without trying to change her quirks and mannerisms to suit the other's whims. And, we were on the same wave length in our commitment to experience to the fullest whatever or whomever might be around that next bend. Thus it was, for instance, that although we'd arrived at Effie's cabin hoping for coffee and vowing we'd stay for just one cup because we had to paddle down to Tanana and catch up with Sue and Jude, we were still sitting there with Effie an hour and a half later, enjoying—with no worry that our partner was anxious to leave.

I had decided long ago that there were two kinds of people in the world: those who need to grow and expand, to confront new people and new situations and the confusion and challenge that go with it; and those who need to contract, to feel "in control," to experience only what they already know, to shrink from new people or situations, to judge or mistrust others, to seek the familiar. Happily, Evelyn and I both fit into the former category, and that helped us understand each other.

For weeks, it had been clear to me that Sue's and Jude's humor was not ours, and vice versa. Their goals on the river were not ours, and vice versa. The relationship between the two boats had become one of benign neglect, but for whatever reason, each boat had decided to retain at least a marginal affiliation with the other. There was a certain sadness in that realization, of course, and I wondered if such a split was the result of our four particular personalities or whether it was inevitable in any expedition of this length. The way to know would be to do a dozen or so expeditions of this length and tally the results . . . .

Finally, just about the time we could laugh no more and were beginning to wonder if we'd really lost our minds, we spotted our crew pulled out on a flat, open, grassy place just upstream from the mouth of the Andreafsky River where Saint Mary's lay.

"David got to pick the campsite since it's his last night on the river," grinned Jude.

"Garden spot, David," we smirked sarcastically, sinking to mid-shin in the mud at the water's edge and tossing our gear up the four-foot cutbank.

"That's nothing," he laughed, "wait till you get up here." The entire bank was like a bowl of Jello that had just been taken out of the refrigerator; the longer it sat in the air and was played with, the mushier it became. Within minutes, the circle we had tromped around the fire was a slurping mud-hole, seemingly bottomless. Sue and Jude and I took refuge in our squatty lawn chairs, moving them occasionally whenever they sank so deep that the mud began oozing up through the mesh of the chair seats. Evelyn and Bing balanced on two logs beside the fire. Evelyn stood with a Sun Dog in one hand and the words to "Faded Love" in the other and serenaded the audience in honor of David's last night on the river. Sue led us in Mitch Miller oldies. Every now and then, either Bing or Evelyn would slip on the rain-slick logs and stumble toward the fire or back into the woodpile, at which point the other one would rescue his or her partner from a fall. Somehow, in the middle of it all, they were still able to crane their heads backwards to try to identify some new gulls that flew over.

Meanwhile, David, in his big boots, was stuck fast in the mud as he squatted beside the fire. Whenever he would attempt to shift positions to grab some pot that was boiling over, he would flounder, lose his balance, and do a crazy, staggering dance over the fire and us and anything else that happened to be in his way. The merriment continued as we awaited the big feast David was preparing as his goodbye present to us and himself. He had been telling us for days that it would be a surprise; sure enough, it was, to us and him, because the labels describing the contents of the foil pouches he was boiling had long since been eaten away in his food duffel by leaking salmon juice.

By the time the first set of logs under Bing's and Evelyn's feet had sunk into oblivion and they had laid another set on top of them, the surprise feast was ready. Some of us got sweet-and-sour pork, some, beef stew, some, barbecue; we exclaimed over the thrill of it all. Out of self-protection, David went slowly on the Sun Dogs. After his reminiscences of some of his experiences in paddling the whitewater of New England's small, rocky streams, he and I agreed to get together sometime in Missouri or somewhere else and float some rivers.

## AUGUST 20, DAY 73

During breakfast, a young Eskimo man drove up in a motorboat, tossed us a fresh, twenty-pound silver salmon, visited a few minutes, then went on his way. David and Bing each shamefully posed for pictures with the fish, smiling like triumphant fisherman as they held up the fish and their fishing rods. We hadn't been able to convince David to come to the Bering Sea with us, so after we slithered to the boats with all our gear, we each hugged him goodbye and wondered whether we'd ever see him again.

The four of us drifted on, while Bing and David paddled up the Andreafsky River to Saint Mary's. Bing, who was penniless at this point, would charge David's airplane ticket on his credit card and receive the cash with which David had planned to pay for his air fare. Then Bing would catch up with us.

For the first time, the tundra had come right down to the river; the high, rounded hills along the right bank were treeless and brown and reminded me of the Great Plains. Several flocks of sandhill cranes flew over, all headed south. Yesterday, we had unfurled the last of the twenty-three topographical maps that had pictured our course down the Yukon. We had just said goodbye to someone we'd first seen the day we arrived in Whitehorse, eons ago. Every sign pointed to an imminent end to a fun adventure and yet, a successful completion of a quest; together they produced a bittersweet feeling.

Evelyn and I drifted in our usual lackadaisical fashion, keeping an eye out for Mountain Village. As she had been doing for weeks, every time Evelyn saw four or more white gulls sitting on a sandbar near us, she thought she was seeing small houses off in the distance. Well over a mile wide here, the river did tend to distort things, but Evelyn never seemed to catch on. Today, she steered us right into a sandbar—talking all the while about how the big building in the center must be the community hall or maybe that cannery we'd heard about—before she realized she was looking at three gulls and a swan. I laughed till I cried.

Soon we arrived at the real Mountain Village, our last stop before the very last village on the river. Anchored off its waterfront were oceangoing fishing trawlers—another bittersweet sign. Our thoughts also turned to the possible problems of incoming and outgoing tide and high winds that we would be facing in the final few days of paddling. We pulled old Bering Sea or Bust up onto the littered tidal flat of Mountain Village and trudged into town. Stopping to talk to two Eskimos who were building something beside the river, we learned that Sue and Jude had left an hour before, carrying a box. We grinned, knowing that was the champagne we had shipped here (illegally) to ourselves three months before. We bought some crackers and ham spread and candy bars at the store and ate them in the rain, sitting on a pile of lumber. Though we still had at least twenty pounds of wholesome food in the boat, buying something at the store in each village and chatting with the locals who always gathered there had become a mandatory ritual. As we sat there, a guy running for state representative walked over and said hello; we told him he could count on our votes. I called the airline that flew from Emmonak and made a reservation for our flight at the end of our trip. I had no idea when we'd really reach the Bering Sea—storms could hold us up for days—but I estimated that the earliest we'd be ready to leave was in three days. I made a reservation for the following Monday. It all seemed so sad.

Back on the river, we battled a headwind for a few hours until we came across Sue and Jude in the agreed-upon slough. They'd found a dry sandy beach that was exceedingly welcome after the campsites we'd had lately. There were even some low willows to break the wind if a storm should arise. We unwrapped the four bottles of champagne and drooled over them. With amazing restraint, we each kept our own bottle sealed, saving it for our final moment of glory at the Bering Sea. In Mountain Village, Sue and Jude had finally run into the French couple, who were selling their canoe and leaving the river. The couple had confirmed the story we'd heard that a bear had stuck his head into their tent one night and they'd scared it away with a flashlight. The only paddlers on the river now who were planning to finish the river, besides Bing and us, were two Austrian guys who we heard were ahead of us. Four Swiss guys were behind us, but they were planning to portage over to the Kuskokwim River to finish their trip.

There were a few letters from home, which reminded me of all the hassles I faced when I returned. All my belongings and work files were scattered in my parents' garage and attic; I'd have to find an apartment, get a phone installed, pay deposits on gas and electricity, remember whatever it was I used to do for a living and find whatever shoes and clothes I used to wear . . . write a book. . . .

Our thoughts turned to the immediate future. "You know," Evelyn observed, "the only thing we *can* do now is finish this river. The next possible take-out is the last village, and it's all downstream between here and there. We're gonna do it; we've paddled the whole Yukon River." She was essentially correct, but we reminded her that we still had seventy miles to go and that three or four hurricanes could strike between here and Emmonak.

It was a night for reflection, though. There was Evelyn over there, wielding a hunting knife against the pink flesh of a big salmon on a log at the edge of the water, still wearing her life jacket from the day's paddling and squatting in the water in her wetsuit booties, just as comfortable as a housewife in the suburbs trimming T-bones on her cutting board. There was Sue, wearing only panties, stirring a pot of boiling clothes on the campfire, squinting into the smoke. Jude commented on the new muscles that lined Sue's shoulders, and Evelyn swore that my shoulders, at which she'd been staring for almost two thousand miles, were now bigger. There was Jude, breaking firewood with the foot that had been so swollen and bruised a few weeks before. Our pants hung from our hips, not merely because they'd stretched over the weeks, but because our bodies had converted fat to muscle. I'd lost the inches I'd been trying to lose ever since college, and the "Yukon Spa" was the most pleasant way I could think of to have done it. Sue's hair was now several inches long, full of curls and full of life, free from the effects of the chemotherapy and radiation.

After dinner, we addressed post cards to many of the people we'd met on the river—including Sarge Waller in Eagle, who had said he was counting on us to make it to the Bering Sea and to send him a card. We knew that in the hectic rush at Emmonak we'd have little time for such details, and we wanted to be sure to say goodbye properly to all our new friends. We also wrote a goodbye-and-thanks message from the Texas Women's Yukon River Expedition to all the folks along the Yukon, to be read over the "Trapline Chatter" program on the radio.

Late in the evening, the grey clouds opened up and the sky grew a brilliant red behind a big, rounded bluff far off in the distance. Its light danced on the Yukon's slightly rumpled surface. In the air hung a farewell sadness.

## AUGUST 21, DAY 74

During breakfast, Evelyn and Jude studied the maps. As usual, they agreed upon a probable goal for the night, an island about forty miles downriver. We no longer attempted to travel together during the day; each boat was free to set its own schedule. They picked a route through the many islands that would keep us out of open water and get us into the channel to Emmonak, the shortest of the three channels to the ocean. The river would become almost four miles wide at one point today, and with the wind's tendency to sweep across the treeless, mountainless delta and turn the river instantly into a wind-driven ocean of waves, we didn't want to be in the middle of it any more than necessary. Then Sue and Jude set out on the elaborate route Jude had chosen through some sloughs to avoid the main channel; Evelyn and I sat on the beach, took pictures, and lingered over our tea.

After an hour or so we, too, got on the river, opting for the main channel because navigation would be simpler and the current might be faster. Soon enough, the same old waves kicked up, but they were manageable and we were used to them. They made paddling a little frustrating, though, because our strokes lacked that feeling of movement and rhythm that we enjoyed on smooth water.

"I'm glad nobody's paying me to do this ten hours a day," I joked. "Whatever they'd pay me wouldn't be enough. But since I've imposed it upon myself, it's O.K."

Soon we saw a curious sight: Sue and Jude coming out of a side slough (we had assumed they were far ahead), paddling upstream around the tip of an island. We never knew if they saw us, and we stopped paddling and started drifting and gabbing as they rounded the island and headed downstream. We found it mildly humorous that once again we'd goofed off and they'd paddled diligently, and here we were at the same place. We'd taken to the open river because we were too lazy to fool with navigating the protected sloughs; we'd come out fine and they apparently had gotten a little fouled up. Soon we came upon them again, and this time they were sitting up in the woods. We didn't know if they were having a fight, praying for guidance in map-reading, or taking a serious potty break; it turned out they had only stopped to put on their long underwear which was just now dry from last night's washing. We drifted on, bouncing in the increasing waves and practicing the words to "Help Me Make it Through the Night." They overtook us and paddled on at full speed; we continued an idle discussion about where we might be on the map.

We drifted close to shore in the main channel, in waves that were becoming substantial. "Left side," I matter-of-factly gave the signal as I hung my rear over the left side. Evelyn leaned nonchalantly to the right and stared at the map, as we continued to roll in the waves.

"Let's eat," I suggested, as I stood up to fasten my pants. I turned around to face her and perched up on my ammo cans, swaying with the waves in a movement that felt a lot like riding a horse. "What's for lunch?"

"Well, let me see!" Evelyn exclaimed with mock interest, crawling forward and peering into the plastic gallon lunch jug. "Why, we have beef jerky, figs, and damp peanuts."

It was, of course, the same stuff we'd been eating for lunch every day for as long as I could remember. "Somehow that doesn't excite me," I said.

For some reason this statement hit Evelyn with the same comic force that her observation about the hog slop had hit me a few days before, and she began to laugh. Our laughter fed on itself once again, until we were crying and holding our sides.

"Here we are," I smiled, "just munching our little lunch as if nothing out of the ordinary were happening, peeing over the side, and sitting up high and turning around backwards—all while we're wallowing in waves probably bigger than Five Finger Rapids. We've come a long way in our paddling skills—or maybe I should say our peeing and eating skills."

"Yeah, about two thousand miles," she laughed. We decided to open the can of Spam that we'd bought in Mountain Village and had been hoarding for a big feast tonight; we couldn't resist eating it now and figured we'd worry about dinner when dinner-time rolled around.

"Seriously, though," said Evelyn, stuffing a cracker into her mouth, "we are totally comfortable with this old river. We're ready to take on and welcome with open arms *anything* that might lie around that next bend—anything." She smiled and held her arms wide.

"Oh, Lord, are we ever," I smiled and shook my head. "On the Yukon, there's no tellin' what might be around that next bend. It could be anything from a grizzly to a rainbow to an all-night Athapascan beach party." Evelyn shrugged a little sheepishly, remembering how she'd outlasted even our self-elected chaperone, Bing.

"Well, whatever it is, we're ready for it," she said. "You know, some people just aren't that way, though. They think something bad's gonna happen. When my brother-in-law kept trying to convince me to take a gun before the trip, he finally said, 'Why, what would you women do if you were paddling along and looked back to see that you were being overtaken by a boatload of Eskimo men?'"

I blurted my own punch line, "We'd probably holler and tell'em to bring beer."

"That's just what I told him!" she screamed with laughter.

Every few minutes during our discussion, as we tossed in the waves, I'd motion to her that we were about to crash into the fallen logs along the cutbank as the wind drove us into shore; she would set her cracker on her backpack and pick up her paddle, and I would do the same, and we'd paddle out a few yards. During all this, the waves prevented us from making much headway downriver, but eating in the boat was preferable to fighting the mosquitoes on shore.

"Anyway," she said, "we're really gonna do it. You really can paddle two thousand miles down a river if you just put your paddle in the water, stroke after stroke, day after day."

"Well, it's like we tried to tell everybody all along," I said. "It's really not that big a deal; the river does most of the work if you'll just get on it day after day. Now backpacking two thousand miles, like the Appalachian Trail, that would be work."

"Even that," said Evelyn. "If you just do a little bit every day, eventually you'll finish whatever it was you wanted. You can walk around the world if you just get out there and do ten miles a day." When she put it like that it did sound easy.

"Well, you're right, like that woman who walked across the entire Australian desert with some camels," I said. "She did something like fifteen or twenty miles a day; if you didn't have a pack you could work up to that pretty easily. Why, Robert Marshall—the founder of the Wilderness Society who explored a lot of the Brooks Range in Alaska back in the thirties—used to hike up to seventy miles a day, in the mountains. 'Course, the poor man died from a heart attack when he was about forty years old; I don't know what that says about walking. . . ."

"I think that's what this trip has brought home to me the most," Evelyn said. "You really can do anything you want if you just put your paddle in the water one stroke at a time. You've just got to be willing to invest the time and to give yourself permission."

"And the money," I added.

"Well, no," she said, "if you've got the time, you don't need so much money because you could stop and work along the way, like those Swiss guys who stopped to build that log house in Galena to get money."

"That's true," I said. "'Course, you *know* what this means if we let this out of the bag, don't you? Neither we nor anyone else will ever have any excuse for not doing something they claim they want to do." We shrugged and frowned in mock guilt for having discovered the terrible secret. "Yeah, from now on," I said, "whenever I get myself in some fix, I'll just remember that I really had grabbed up three friends and we really had paddled the Yukon River, even though none of us had ever seen it and the longest previous river trip any of us had done was two weeks. Then I'll think, go for it!"

"Go for it!" Evelyn toasted with her Kool-Aid bottle. "Whatever it is, go for it!"

We spotted a clear-water river entering the Yukon and paddled up into it for fresh drinking water. The water had so many suspended solids in it that it looked brown in the jugs, but we hauled it in and shrugged. Then, out of the wind and in the sun on the slow-moving little river, we couldn't resist taking a quick nap. In the middle of the river in the boat, we both lay back, covered our faces against the sun and the gnats, and fell sound asleep. When we awoke, we had drifted into the river's marshy shoreline, and we had no idea if we'd slept for thirty minutes or two hours. We grinned at what hedonists we were becoming. We speculated that Sue and Jude were who-knows-how-far downstream, battling the waves in their race to get to the Bering Sea. And here we were snoring in the sun.

"Look at that, would ya?" I said as we paddled back into the choppy Yukon, for here came Bing, paddles churning as ever. He'd already caught up with us, though he'd left Mountain Village only this morning. He now had a few hundred dollars from the airline ticket transaction and was feeling rich.

"Guess what else I've got," he wiggled his eyebrows. "David gave me a whole bunch of food." Since David was prone to carry things like maple syrup and sweet-and-sour pork, this news sent us into loud, gleeful chants.

"I told ya if we gobbled that Spam for lunch something else would turn up for dinner," I reminded Evelyn.

We paddled with Bing for an hour or two, until the waves began to tire us out.

"This is losing its glamour," I finally said. "I don't see the point in wearing ourselves out. What's the big deal about beating our brains out to get to the Bering Sea? Besides, there aren't too many campsites along here—the shore's straight up and we can't cross to the other side 'cause the waves are too big. Let's grab the first flat spot we see."

We felt some mild interest in catching Sue and Jude, but not enough to go out of our way to do so. Just then, Bing spotted a campsite possibility where a tiny creek joined the Yukon. We paddled into a wind-protected (which meant mosquito-infested) cove and pulled out onto a minute patch of land surrounded by thick alders and willows. The mud was knee-deep at the shore, and the grass was waist-high on the land, but the high ground was flat and not all that muddy because of the high grass. We didn't know it then, but this would be our last real campsite on the river. Ducks quacked on a pond at the end of the clearing. I set up the tent where a bear or moose had matted down the grass (comforting thought), while Evelyn and Bing tended the fire and planned a huge feast. I felt exhausted now that I had a chance to sit down; we'd come a hard twenty-five miles today, fighting the waves all the way.

Bing cooked up gallons of rice, filling all his paint cans—as David had affectionately dubbed them—with the white stuff. Then he grinned and pulled out a whole plastic tub of butter that David had given him. We hurrahed and thanked the Lord for Bing and David and butter. Evelyn lectured Bing on how unhealthy it was for him to eat mostly rice all the time, with few vegetables, and how it was quality rather than quantity that determined good nutrition.

"Well," Bing shrugged, "if I'm gonna die of malnutrition, at least I'll go with a full stomach." We couldn't much doubt whatever it was that kept him going; he could paddle rings around us.

By the time Evelyn and Bing had stumbled and joked and tossed food around the campfire for awhile, their good humor began to bring back my energy. Two or three bowls of rice and a cup of tea helped further.

"I wonder where Sue and Jude are?" I said, looking out of the mouth of our cove and across the waves to the setting sun.

At that moment, they were having a helluva bad time. Sue would later describe the evening in *River Runner* magazine:

> What a predicament for me, a relatively fearless whitewater canoeist, to be in. I have been in some incredible rapids in a canoe (on Hell's Canyon of the Snake, Middle Fork of the Salmon, Rio Grande), but there was always an end to it. A place that would be safe at the end, no matter how big and bad the rapid. Who said big rivers, with fast current but few actual rapids, aren't exciting? I am scared. There seems to be no end, no answer.
>
> We are tired, bone weary. But there is no way we can rest. For either of us to put our paddle down even a few seconds means the wind takes the upper hand, wrenches us around broadside and begins its destructive work of dumping wave after wave of frigid Yukon River water over our gunnels. . . . Swamping is not far from our minds. How cold would that water be? How long would one have before hypothermia rendered one senseless?
>
> For that very reason we hug the shore, in hopes we could swim if we had to. The waves seem a little smaller and less angry near shore—or is it just a feeling of comfort we get from being near it? Of course there are dangers here, too. Those rocks look mean. And a particularly characteristic feature of the Yukon is its tendency to undercut its banks, rendering them likely to fall in great hunks, with a sound like a cannon shot, into the river.
>
> Even if we remain upright, what are we going to do when the sun goes down? It is going to set around 10 P.M., about 45 minutes from now. The shore ahead shows no sign of changing for the five miles or so we can see. We've already tried to stop three times. The shore slopes up about a 60° angle, up some 15 feet to what we hoped was land, but it was solid, no, very unsolid, tundra brush, muskeg swamp, and mosquitoes. Impossible even to sit down, let alone pitch a tent.
>
> Surely we can't let it whip us now. We have only two to three days to go 'til the end of this . . . journey. In fact, that's another problem. If we don't cross the river soon . . . at least to an island half way across, we will miss our particular chosen route to the Bering Sea. . . . After nearly 2,000 miles of paddling, often in weather like this, we are looking for the best and quickest way out. . . .
>
> As if by magic, and just in time, the wind dies, the waves calm. We can ferry across the current to the island which at least is sand instead of swamp. Something solid, if wet, on which to pitch a tent and fall into sleeping bags, too tired to even bother with dinner, again grateful to and humbled by the river. (Vol. 2, No. 1, Winter, 1983, page 17)

"Oh, I can't eat another bite," I smiled, leaning back on a log. "Hey, look, the waves have calmed down. The wind must have died on the river." We lay down in our bear wallow and slept soundly.

## AUGUST 22, DAY 75

In the morning, a magic fog hung in our clearing. Bing made pancakes, and we gloated as we smeared butter on them. By the time we finished breakfast, the sun had burned away the fog and made the dew sparkle on the high grasses.

Out on the river, we made a quick crossing almost four miles over to the other side, lining up to hit the channel to Emmonak. Just after we reached a relatively small side channel, we saw that the wind was already kicking up waves in the main channel. We paddled steadily and chatted with Bing, stopping about once an hour for five minutes to nibble food or lie back in the boat.

It was a sunny day, and I marveled over the bigness of river and sky. I was going to miss this old river, this living creature that in its time had carried all manner of beings and inanimate objects to the ocean. Now it had carried us and would leave us, as it had left all the others, at the doorstep of the sea, like abandoned children. I would miss the feeling of movement that had pervaded every aspect of my life on the river. Back home, I always felt static. Events and triumphs and defeats and crises moved around and through and past me, but I myself was in one place, dealing with things in a fleeting second as they moved past on a sort of conveyor belt. On the river, though, the tables were turned. People's villages and animals' habitats and the daily natural and human events of the different sections of the river were carrying on as always, but *I* was moving through *them*. I was on the conveyor belt. And I was always going somewhere. There was always that next bend, beckoning.

The river had her moods, to be sure, but she was my friend and I would accept her every quirk and whim, for that's just how she was. Besides, she would have her way. She *would* have her way. She ruled this country, and every creature here knew it.

Here, the Yukon was so wide, its points of land so low, that she herself seemed an extension of the ocean, or vice versa.

> The Yukon, like all rivers, arises [in the sea]. . . . There, and in the sun. For forty million years the Yukon has come down to empty into the sea, yet it has never arrived nor ever been emptied. The sea itself and the sun have made the journey interminable: the sea that supplies the water, the sun that raises it up by evaporation to renew the river at its sources. This ceaseless journey is given form by the earth's convulsive inner turmoil, and by the river itself, which sculpts the land that forms it. For the river holds nothing it can touch inviolate. It washes down the loose Quaternary gravels of the Kaiyuh Flats where salmon fishing camps stood the year before, and it abrades the hard Pre-Cambrian schists of Rampart Canyon that are older than life on earth. It erodes the debris of Tertiary volcanoes and the remnants of Eocene peat bogs; it rifles the Pleistocene graves of woolly rhinoceroses and giant ground sloths, and the Carboniferous embalmments of semitropical forests. Down to the sea the Yukon carries the slow wreckage of the face of the earth; back to the sea whence come all land forms and all life. (*The Yukon*, page 3)

"Bing, we want you to know that we think you've been a perfect gentleman all along on this cruise," Evelyn was saying, as we paddled side by side. "Nevertheless, we've thoroughly enjoyed your company."

Bing grinned and shook his head, "Wouldn't want to bite off more than I could chew."

We talked about relationships. Bing had never been married. He had sort of a girlfriend in Florida. Upon questioning, he revealed that, like so many outdoorsy men we knew, he had a girlfriend who didn't go for camping or canoeing at all. He hadn't really invited her to come down the Yukon with him, knowing that she wouldn't come.

"Well, where did that put your relationship when you told her you were going to Alaska for four months?" I asked.

"Well, if she doesn't understand. . . ." he shrugged, as if to say that anyone who didn't understand his need to go to the river didn't understand him very well in the first place and perhaps wasn't worth losing any sleep over.

"Yeah, if they can't take a joke. . . ." Evelyn added.

"You know, what I wonder," I said, "is if I'd been really involved with somebody a year ago, whether I'd have ever gotten such an uncontrollable urge to do this trip in the first place. Would it have ever crossed my mind to do this, or would my creative, crazy energies have been channeled instead into his interests, enjoying myself day to day with him? Would my interests have subconsciously begun to follow his? Would the kinds of dreams that were out of bounds for him have become subconsciously out of bounds for me? Probably not, I guess; the guy I more or less lived with for five years stayed home while I went to Mexico three different times for six weeks each, and once to California. Well, whatever forces helped bring me here today, it's worth it."

"Amen," said Evelyn. Bing nodded.

The barge went past, and a bright red fox with a white-tipped tail loped from the alders into the grassy clearing at the water's edge, scrutinizing the strange noisy beast as it headed upriver. We paddled on, past fish camps whose white canvas tents had been removed for the season, leaving nothing but lonely frame skeletons.

"Well, what's it gonna be next, Beth, the Amazon or the Nile?" asked Evelyn. "I still say the Nile because there aren't as many deadly critters in it."

"Oh, it probably comes out even," I said. "On the Amazon you've got your crocodiles and anaconda snakes and electric eels and piranhas—"

"And don't forget the ants that eat up wooden boats and the tiny fish you were reading about that swim up your urine and into your guts," Evelyn rolled her eyes.

"And the headhunters—I'm sure there're still some of them there, and now there's a big gold rush and there's all this violence over claim-jumping," said Bing.

"Well, O.K., so you've got all that on the Amazon, but the Nile has hippos; I think most of it is cities and dams and stuff, anyway," I said. "Besides, don't get me started; I have to keep my mind on paying off this little jaunt before I get hooked on the next one." We smiled.

"Lord, we're never satisfied, are we?" asked Evelyn.

"I hope not," I said. "I've always thought there was something grossly dissatisfying about being satisfied. The guy I used to live with always got so exasperated with me because I was constantly talking up some new project or place to go or something. He was always just happy and easygoing, content with whatever came along or didn't come along. I envied him in a way. But we had two different philosophies; he was always satisfied and waiting for things to happen, and I was always thinking too much and dreaming up things to make happen. Some people just float wherever the current takes 'em; others kind of like to steer a course."

We were now seeing lots of fishing boats that were bigger and deeper than those upriver. They looked to be twenty feet or longer, and their gunnels stood four or five feet above the water. As we ventured into the main channel to cross to the right bank for the final Emmonak channel, a fishing boat pulled alongside us and drifted for a few minutes to chat. A man and a young boy from Emmonak said that Sue and Jude were a couple of hours ahead of us. The man offered to buy Evelyn's canoe; she had already decided that shipping it up the Yukon and the Tanana River to Fairbanks by barge and then trucking it all the way to Texas would cost far more than it was worth. We'd been hoping all along that, somehow, somebody would show up to sponsor our trip at least to the extent of paying for the return of both canoes to Dallas—they had incredible sentimental value by now—but nobody ever did. Another man upriver had expressed mild interest in buying Evelyn's canoe; Evelyn told this fellow that if the other one didn't come through, he could have old Bering Sea or Bust for $200. He didn't bat an eye, said he'd let his kids play with it and maybe use it to hunt seals among the ice floes.

He said Emmonak was only twelve miles farther, so we paddled hard, stopping but briefly to visit with an Eskimo family who paused in their motorboat on their way to Saint Mary's for a wedding.

At last, we rounded a bend on a narrow channel and spotted Emmonak, a village of more than 500 people, whose waterfront was strewn with oceangoing ships, barges, small boats; all manner of confusing things. Immediately, everything seemed noisy, and we knew we were in for an evening of hassling with logistics—where would we sleep, would the boats be safe from theft, how would we get back from the Bering Sea tomorrow, how and when would we sell the canoes and ship the gear home. . . .

But the cluttered waterfront and the wooden shacks of Emmonak represented the achievement of ninety-nine percent of our goal—all that was left was the actual paddling to the sea tomorrow. This was it, the last village, the last outpost of civilization on the Yukon, the end of the river, and I meant to let them know about it. Drifting into shore, I pulled out the trumpet and played "The Eyes of Texas Are Upon You" till my lip hurt. Some passersby on the high bank waved and stopped in their tracks; others seemed to think such goings-on were quite ordinary. Sue and Jude waved and gave a victory signal from shore; success was in the air.

We paddled down to the end of town where Sue and Jude had left their boat in the thick tidal mud below a twelve-foot sheer bank. Their tent perched at the edge of the bank, where they could keep an eye on the boat. "Garden spot!" we groaned, observing the layer of smelly trash—dead fish, old boots, tin cans, lumber—that we had to negotiate to carry our gear up the bank. That was after we negotiated the knee-deep mud at the river's edge. But this campsite was as good as any, for the entire waterfront was that way.

After paddling more than forty miles today, Evelyn and I were tired and hungry. We passed up a dance at the community hall, but did manage to gobble down a cheeseburger at the cafe. We ended up sharing dinner with a traveling boat-motor salesman, who then introduced us to the village policeman, Kenneth Paul. Ken agreed to meet us at the sea tomorrow at 1 P.M. to bring us and our boats twelve miles back upriver to Emmonak in his big fishing boat.

"I signed on to paddle to the Bering Sea," explained Evelyn, "but I never said a word about paddling back *up* the Yukon."

Even here at the very mouth of the river, there was still enough current to make paddling against it a chore. One o'clock was the latest Ken could pick us up before he had to go fishing or something. That meant we'd have to hurry to paddle the twelve miles before he got there, but we were willing to give it a try in order to get a motorboat ride back upriver.

The night would turn out to be second only to Granada in discomfort, and not nearly so funny. The air was deathly hot and still and muggy, but we had to enclose ourselves in our sleeping bags because the tent was full of biting no-see-ums. We had to sleep with the smelly caribou antlers because the local stray dog had a terrible longing for them; I'd had to beat him back several times as I carried them between the boat and the tent. We must have been camped in the local necking spot, because throughout the night, we could hear whispers and laughter and conversation in the bushes behind our tents. All night long, dogs barked; as I recall it was mostly the same dog, with the same yapping bark. And the final blow, we had to set Bing's alarm—with real time, instead of Bing Time—for 7 A.M. so we could get up in time to do all our chores and still paddle down to meet Ken at 1 P.M. I'm not sure I slept at all that night.

## AUGUST 23, DAY 76

It was almost a relief to be rudely awakened by the alarm clock and told that it was time to fight the dogs for the caribou antlers and struggle through the mud with our gear; at least we no longer had to endure the no-see-ums. Today would be our day of triumph, but it would also be one of our longest, toughest, and strangest of the whole trip.

We paddled upstream a hundred yards and pulled into the bank below the yard of the man who would buy Evelyn's canoe. He'd said we could leave our gear for the day, if we were careful to stay out of reach of the Husky chained under the "Bad Dog" sign.

The 500 souls of Emmonak dispose of their garbage mainly by tossing it over the bank each day. The tide brings it back in, of course, and the accumulation lies rotting on the tidal flat below the cutbank. We struggled over the broken bottles and rusty cans, over the logs and scraps of lumber, with bag after bag of our gear, into the man's back yard. With each layer of baggage that we removed from Bering Sea or Bust, forgotten pieces of our own trash came to light. There were pieces of beef jerky, soggy mosquito coils, mushy pilot crackers, charred Spam cans—all covered in a layer of grit, as were the hundreds of feet of rope and all the duffel bags we heaved onto the bank. Every piece of gear was damp and reeked of one odor or another. We couldn't remember the last time we'd cleaned out the boat; it had seemed useless since a new layer of mud was deposited each time we got in. With a flourish, Evelyn gathered up the crushed beer cans that she had placed one by one throughout the trip on the floor of her space in the canoe. She had used them as a kind of island to keep her feet out of the mud and water that lay in the boat.

By the time we hauled our gear to shore (leaving in the boat only some food, sleeping bags, and tents as emergency gear in case we didn't make it back to Emmonak today) and grabbed a quick cheeseburger in the cafe, it was 10 A.M. Our three boats shoved off for the Bering Sea, paddling feverishly to make it the twelve miles to the ocean in three hours so we'd get there by the time Ken did.

Actually, we had our doubts that Ken would come. We'd seen him this morning in the cafe, where he would hardly acknowledge our greeting. We couldn't tell if he was shy, mad about something, or whether that was simply the Eskimo way. He had seemed so casual about our agreement last night that we wondered whether he'd said he'd pick us up just to get rid of us. We dearly hoped he'd come, because we'd heard that the peculiarities of the outgoing tide at the mouth could cause real problems for canoeists. One Japanese expedition, we were told, had been rescued near death after they were swept out to sea. We assumed there was little solid ground for camping near the mouth if we did have to stay over, and we knew from experience there would be little cover to block the windstorms that could rage through the delta. We'd been warned that much of the mouth was deep mud at low tide, which could strand boats and swallow canoeists who tried to step out into it. Even the topographical map was covered with large areas of tiny black dots with the word "mud." But if all else failed, we'd been told, there was a big fish camp on the left just before the ocean, and the man who lived there—who happened to be Ken's father—usually came into town in his motorboat once or twice a week.

As we rounded the first bend below Emmonak, all three boats pulled over to an island with the same goal in mind. After sixteen hours or so in Emmonak (where there didn't seem to be a public restroom—outhouse or otherwise—to be had, even in the cafe, and where the frequency of river and main-street traffic precluded anything longer than three seconds of privacy behind a bush), we were in desperate need of certain wilderness amenities. We each raced through the mud and up into the high wet grass, clutching a roll of toilet paper.

That chore completed in record time, we jumped back into the boats and sped through the smooth water, discussing our next problem. **We** were determined to celebrate with champagne at the ocean, but we'd heard that Emmonak was one of several Eskimo villages that coped with its alcoholism by outlawing not only the sale of alcohol, but the possession of it, by anyone. And who had we linked up with to bring us back to town in his motorboat, but the local cop?

"Well, if I get arrested, it'll be worth it," said Sue, eyeing her champagne bottle. "Actually, I think I'd be rather proud to have as the one item on my criminal record that I'd been thrown into an Eskimo jail on the Yukon River for consuming a fifth of champagne."

"So you've just paddled two thousand miles down the friggin' Yukon River, and you're about to be swept out to sea, and you pop the cork on a bottle of champagne that you've been waiting three months for, and you haven't had anything but Everclear to drink in the last five hundred miles, and now the local cop is bearing down upon you with a motorboat and handcuffs?????" hollered Evelyn.

"Drink some more!!!!" we bellowed.

The sun was hot, the sky was clear, the water was glassy calm—a glorious day for paddling into the Bering Sea. I thoroughly enjoyed the warmth on my skin, my new muscles that had developed during the last thousand miles or so since we first began paddling, and the way the bow sliced the flat water. In my mind, I'd said most of my goodbyes to the river yesterday. This was really it: nothing but flat spongy tundra and muskeg, the delta, the mouth, the sea, the end of the Yukon. Our journey was over; there was no more river left to paddle. I watched the little whirlpools that my paddle sucked into the Yukon's waters with each stroke, as I'd watched them for eleven weeks, and I knew this would be the last time I'd see them for awhile. I sang "I Was Born Under a Wandering Star," which has a fine paddling rhythm.

We paddled as hard and fast as we could, cursing the land that appeared around each bend where we'd hoped the open ocean would be. Finally, at 1 P.M., just past a large fish camp, there it lay—a wide gap between two low points of land, beyond which we could see nothing but water.

"That's it, this'll do, where's that champagne!!!" we whooped, as we drifted between some sandbars. For the last time, our three boats thwarted up. Evelyn and Jude popped the plastic stoppers on two bottles of champagne; we filled our cups and held them together with Bing's sand bucket in a toast.

"To the Bering Sea!" we smiled and began taking pictures.

"My God, look where we are!" somebody exclaimed. We looked up and realized the outgoing tide had caught us. We'd drifted extremely fast around an island and were headed out to sea with amazing speed. We slammed the stoppers back into the champagne bottles, unthwarted and ferried to a place where the current couldn't catch us. Sue and Jude headed over toward the fish camp; Evelyn and Bing and I coasted into a mud flat where we could take pictures with the open ocean as a backdrop.

By now we'd given up on being retrieved by a motorboat; it was already 1:30 P.M. Bing waded into the water and took pictures of Evelyn and me with my camera; we posed in the boat with caribou antlers, champagne bottle, handshakes, and so on, guzzling champagne all the while. The trumpet sent a champagne version of "When the Saints Go Marchin' In" across the open water. Then I waded ashore and took pictures of Bing with his video camera. We were only halfway through the champagne and the pictures when we realized that Ken had been waiting at his father's fish camp all along and was now zooming to pick us up.

There was no time to relish the moment, reflect on what we'd just done, look at the ocean, or even sober up; in a flash Ken had hauled Sue's and Jude's canoe into his big fishing boat and landed on our beach. Evelyn hid the champagne bottle in her pack and we threw our gear and Bing's boat into Ken's boat. Without a second thought, Ken tied Bering Sea or Bust behind his boat and gunned his motor.

In an instant, the Yukon was gone from beneath us; we would no longer feel her rhythms beneath our canoe hulls as we had felt them for two thousand miles. Now, we would interact with the river only through the vibrating hull of a high-speed motorboat or through the window of an airplane, and in a few hours even that would be gone.

Ken was a good ol' boy after all; apparently quietness was just his way. He'd intended all along to pick us up, and had even given us extra time when he realized we hadn't reached the ocean by one o'clock. Undoubtedly, he'd watched our drunken antics from the fish camp and, mercifully, he saw no harm in a bunch of women having a few nips of champagne after they'd paddled their silly canoes all the way from Canada. Ken stood stoically at the back of his boat, steering nonchalantly through the sandbars as we raced along at what seemed breakneck speed. All the while, Bering Sea or Bust danced back and forth in our wake, playfully riding at the end of her rope.

"She likes it!!" Evelyn looked back and grinned.

We huddled between the other two upturned boats, playing with a Husky puppy and talking to Ken's sister, who'd come along to meet the crazy white women and their friend.

An hour later, we were back in the mud of Emmonak, unfastening the last carabiner on the last ammo can, handing Bering Sea's bow rope over to the man in exchange for the two hundred-dollar bills he pulled from his pocket. But there was time only for one sentimental pat of her gunnel by way of farewell and thanks, for we had a plane to catch in a few hours.

We raced to finish all the last-minute errands. Sue left her canoe with someone who would ship it upriver to Roger in Tanana on the next barge (which would be next spring—this season was over); he'd sent her $350 for it. She and Jude sold the dining tent, our lawn chairs, and some of the cooking gear to the man who bought Evelyn's canoe. They shipped crutches and rifle back to Rampart. We gave away most of the leftover food. Evelyn and I stuffed ninety-three pounds of gear into two duffel bags and lugged them to the post office, where we shipped them to Dallas for about $40. That still left paddles, two ammo cans, caribou antlers, two extremely heavy backpacks, and two daypacks that we'd carry onto the airplane. At the post office, not a single congratulatory letter or card awaited us. Had no one thought we'd make it this far?

I checked in at the airline ticket office, which turned out to be someone's living room. They'd never heard of our reservation and the afternoon flight (with room for only five people) was already booked, but they'd send another plane in a few hours. That gave us a little extra time to linger over yet another cheeseburger at the cafe. I called home for the first time in three weeks and learned that my father was scheduled to enter the hospital in two days for unexpected surgery.

We strolled across the airport runway, which was essentially one of Emmonak's gravel streets, and sat with our gear on the dusty field. Beside us ran the river. We had already been racing in our boats or on land for one reason or another for almost twelve hours today, and we were tired. We felt jubilant and triumphant, but in a quiet way; already, I felt lonesome without the river. Bing was there, and the thought that in a few minutes we would part with him, too, was sad.

"Well, Bing, so where do you go from here?" I asked.

"I'm gonna paddle about twenty miles back upriver, then cut across a slough I heard about, take that over to the other channel, and paddle back out to Norton Sound. Then, a hundred miles or so through the ocean to Saint Michael." He grinned.

"You're crazy," I said.

"I know," he shrugged. "None of us would be here if we weren't, would we? Really, though, it won't be hard. I figure if I stay in the eddies, paddle hard, take breaks—and maybe I'll have a tailwind now—it'll be fine. I figure two days max to reach the slough, then unless I get lost, no problem. Besides," he grinned, "I have a map now—Jude gave me her last topo of the mouth."

We talked about all the other canoeists we'd met on the river. No one in Emmonak had heard of the two Austrian guys, so we assumed they had either taken out or we'd gotten the story confused with the Swiss guys or the French couple. The river people said the canoeists hadn't started paddling the river recreationally until the late 1960s. If this was a typical year—in which five people had paddled the whole river—that meant we were probably among an elite band of less than one hundred people now living who knew the river by canoe as we knew it. Thousands of people, of course, had traveled the river all the way up and down during the Stampede, but they did it mostly in wood-fired sternwheelers. And everyone else today does it in motorboats.

"Well, come on, Bing, now's your last chance to tell us who you are— we're off the river, so it's O.K.," I said idly, knowing he wouldn't tell. He smiled and shook his head.

"It's not that big a deal; I'll write you guys later," he said.

"I know, you're really King Solomon," joked Evelyn. All the way down the river, we'd heard of a character calling himself King Solomon who, every now and then, would escape from some Alaskan mental hospital, make a crude raft and float down the Yukon, determined to paddle across the Bering Sea to Russia, raise an army, and return to fight for Jesus. Sooner or later, King Solomon would always be captured and rescued, always near death from hypothermia and starvation, hanging onto a few half-submerged logs and still muttering about his army, and he would be taken back to the hospital. The people telling us the story always did it with such a smile that we never knew whether it was true or merely something the river people liked to tell the cheechakos.

"Yeah," Bing smiled, "I was gathering up a pretty good army—first you guys and then David—and now you've all deserted your leader. Guess I'll have to paddle to Russia after all."

"What will you do without us?" Jude asked. "No more broken bones. . . ."

"No more happy hour on the river where we crash into stumps. . . ." said Sue.

"No more beach parties," said Evelyn. Bing rolled his eyes. "You won't have anybody to chaperone anymore."

"Gee, maybe I'll get some sleep at night," Bing grinned and shook his head. He petted the town stray dog, a big German shepherd who spent most of his time slipping into the cafe behind unsuspecting customers.

"Why don't you take him for company?" Jude suggested. "He'd love it; he doesn't belong to anybody."

"He'd sure be easier to chaperone than you guys," Bing smiled.

Then, suddenly, our little plane was there, our gear was crammed inside, Bing was giving each of us a long, crushing, wonderful bear-hug. Then this gentle, happy, utterly decent man with the scruffy beard and the tangled sun-bleached hair and the tattered polyester pants, whom we would and had trusted with our lives on and off for more than a thousand miles, was gone—waving with all his might, in his old green sweatshirt, disappeared into the cloud of dust stirred up by the propellers of our plane.

"Can you swim?" the pilot was asking as we left the runway and flew straight over the river. He delighted in banking at steep angles to circle the delta and head for Saint Mary's. We screamed mildly, half with excitement, half with fear. Wedged into the tiny plane with all our gear, we could hardly move. Beside us sat a small Japanese man, whose luggage consisted of one small bag. He was buried beneath Sue's massive backpack, with a tight smile on his face.

Beneath us in the evening sun spread the thousands of ponds and creeks and sloughs and bogs of the Yukon delta, none of which we'd seen from the river. Here she was in all her majestic, glorious, wild bigness— the Yukon valley, the living force that dominates a third of the subcontinent of Alaska, the natural entity whose name means River of Rivers, in a state whose name means the Great Land. Here beneath us sprawled the valley that had, in all probability, served as the dry, glacier-free corridor through which the first Americans wandered from the Bering land bridge and down into the heart of the Americas, during the last Ice Age. This magic basin was most likely the first major American river known to humans. And Alaska was the American land first touched by humans, and yet it is now the last vestige of America to escape overwhelming alteration by humans. Tens of thousands of years ago, those nomadic hunters came here for food—for physical survival—and now, people come from Texas and Florida and New Hampshire and Germany and Switzerland and France to renew and challenge themselves within its wild glory—for emotional and spiritual survival.

We had come for a combination of reasons not easily articulated or understood even by ourselves; I knew only that I needed to be here. Perhaps the desire of four, working, middle-class, college-educated women to spend months of preparation and thousands of dollars, and to abandon their jobs and families, in order to endure months of muddy feet, gritty food, mosquitoes, wind, rain, and the murky water of the Yukon says something about humans' profound need for wilderness experience. And we were not all that unusual; true, few people paddle the whole river each summer, but thousands paddle as much of it as their work schedules permit. Millions more come to Alaska to hike or hunt her trailless back country, to fish her pristine streams, or simply to glimpse her untouched trees and glaciers and mountains from a ship or airplane or tour bus. And of course, many millions more find enjoyment and peace in the scraps of Lower 48 wild areas that we as a nation have fought to protect. The valley beneath us was but one portion of natural ecosystems throughout the country—big and small—that together comprise our natural heritage. Together, their wildness represents a national treasure whose value is incalculable, whose essence is irreplaceable.

I gazed through the plane window at the sandbar where Sue and Jude had finally found refuge from the waves the last night on the river, at the clear little river where Evelyn and I had dozed in the sun in the canoe. I wondered if there would ever come a time when the child—young or old—who dreamed in the bathtub of paddling a canoe or hiking through unknown wild lands, as I had dreamed a year ago, could *only* dream. Would there come a time when the child in each of us could go nowhere to find that dream? Would there come a time when most of the wild lands were gone—those left, overrun with ever-growing numbers of hikers and motels? Would there come a time when no one could paddle face to face with a moose or a bear in Alaska, or an American alligator in a southern swamp? Would there come a time when I could no longer roll gleefully down a ravine through crackling beech and magnolia leaves on a wintery afternoon—but, instead, only through the rows of a pine plantation?

I knew that at this moment there were pending before local, state, and federal governments hundreds of water projects that would destroy rivers and their ecosystems. Most of the projects could survive no thorough economic scrutiny, have no rational economic justification.

And yet, year after year, they are authorized. There are dams built to provide drinking water in regions where supply already outstrips projected demand, flatwater recreation in areas where reservoirs already abound but flowing rivers are scarce, and flood control where no one lives in the floodplain anyway. There are dams built to generate excess electricity, even though more electricity than would be created by the dams could be saved through simple education and pricing incentives, at a fraction of the cost and without the loss of river ecosystems. There are levees bulldozed through bottomland hardwood forests, rivers turned into vast ditches, and whole ecosystems drowned under reservoirs, so that new shipping concerns can be subsidized at the expense of existing railroads, one group of farmers can be shoved off their land to benefit another group of farmers, and the people who make money by building these projects can benefit at the expense of the public. The whole pork-barrel system is paid for by every taxpayer. The taxpayer also pays for the two agencies that conceive and push almost all of it through Congress—the U.S. Army Corps of Engineers and the U.S. Bureau of Reclamation. The whole thing never made any sense to me, and even less now as I looked down on the mighty Yukon from the window of a plane.

Somewhere several hundred miles east of us at this moment roared—as it had roared for millions of years—the awesome, terrifying, challenging, magnificently powerful whitewater of the Susitna River's Devil Canyon, not far from Anchorage. But at this moment, even those giant wild rapids—the biggest kayakable water in North America—were under the lustful gaze of the Alaska Power Authority. It wants to drown eighty-two miles of the Susitna and 50,500 acres of wilderness with two dams to bring hydropower to a state that already has immense oil, gas, and coal resources, to bring a massive centralized energy system to a state suited to the flexibility of smaller systems, to promote hydropower before honestly evaluating alternatives of conservation, wind and tidal power, and geothermal sources. All this it wants to do to provide more electricity than anyone can project will be needed—in a state whose entire population could fit into Dallas, Texas. Ludicrous as it is, though, the scheme is no more absurd than the Ramparts Dam the Army Corps wanted to thrust into the middle of the Yukon, drowning several hundred miles of the Yukon Flats—one of the most productive waterfowl breeding areas on this continent. Nor was it more ridiculous than the Corps's age-old yen to make Dallas-Fort Worth into a seaport by turning 550 miles of the Trinity River and 100,000 acres of wildlife habitat (including rare bottomland hardwood ecosystem) into a 335-mile ditch with dams, locks, and reservoirs, for oceangoing barges.

Looking down at the miles upon miles of still ponds, low willows, and those damned, wonderful tussock meadows and permafrost bogs like the ones that had humbled us on our little backpack trip, I strained to spot a moose or a wolf or a grizzly happily munching whatever they might be dining on tonight. A few ducks and geese sat on the ponds. The critters couldn't know that their delta homes are threatened by possible oil spills from offshore oil drilling. They didn't know their homes are at the mercy of the U.S. Department of the Interior, or that there is such a thing. They couldn't know that the Yukon basin is threatened by possible oil and gas drilling, possible construction of transportation corridors for oil and gas, and by state inholdings that could be developed. Unknown to them, a giant controversy was brewing now over the Reagan Administration's low funding and its peculiar, possibly illegal implementation of the ecosystem protections set forth by Congress in the Alaska lands act, and that conservationists would inevitably sue the government over the whole mess.

It occurred to me that all these creatures and these vast acres of earth couldn't elect anyone to Congress to represent them. They were out here minding their own business, unaware that at this moment and forever more they were at the mercy of bureaucrats, congressmen, presidents, judges, and people like the four women flying in an airplane above them on this Monday night. Together, we held the fate of these beings and the land and waters they roamed in our hands. Somebody had said once that in a democracy you get what you deserve—the outcry or lack of it by citizens determines our course as a nation.

Suddenly, I felt very tired. I thought of all the mailings and phone campaigns on environmental issues I'd have to do in a few weeks when I returned to work. I thought of all the battles we'd lost in the past and those we'd lose when I got home. But, I supposed, staring at the dear old Yukon, the only thing worse than fighting and always losing would be not fighting at all; the only pain worse than the slow, burning one of defeat would be the guilt for not having tried.

Through the window, the Yukon suddenly seemed small, not at all like herself. Seen from the air, through a pane of glass, already she was fading from memory; the life we'd known for seventy-six days down there among her sandbars already seemed a little unreal. That's the trouble with rivers, I thought as we banked away from the river and flew inland to Saint Mary's. Running them is like making love: the memory is pleasant but meaningless compared to the real act. And the mere memory is never enough; you've got to do it again.

"I bet you bush pilots end up carrying some pretty strange cargoes, don't you?" Jude was asking the pilot.

"The weirdest are the bodies," he said. "Once I had one in a body bag—no casket—just me and the body. When you change altitude it makes the air in them expand or something and they groan. It can be pretty weird when you're flying alone in the darkness in the middle of the night, and a dead body behind you starts to groan."

We touched down on the runway among the barren hills of Saint Mary's, lugged our filthy gear into the airport, hassled with combining gear into parcels to be shipped as easily and cheaply as possible, paid for airline tickets, and tried not to feel too self-conscious among all the clean Eskimos who were gathered in the one-room airport to fly to Anchorage. When all the logistics were settled, Evelyn and I trudged outside behind the dumpster to polish off the half-bottle of warm champagne she'd been carrying around all day.

"Well, here we are," I observed, squatting to pee into the mud.

"Yeah, it's finally come to this," Evelyn smiled. "Here we are like a couple of winos in the alley behind the Safeway store, sharing straight from the bottle."

"I beg your pardon," I zipped my pants and took a swig of the flat pink stuff. "This is *champagne* we're drinking." We began to giggle with the giddiness that came from having slept little last night and having been on the run for fourteen hours already today.

Then, all too soon we were on a 727, drinking cold beer, zooming through the darkness toward Anchorage, and the Yukon valley was gone. All too soon, we were waiting, dog-tired, for our gear at the baggage terminal. All too soon, I was struggling with coins and Yellow Pages and telephone in a booth in a hot airport, trying to find a place to sleep for the night. Sue and Jude happened onto the last room in one hotel and said they'd see us tomorrow, inviting us to join them, if necessary. It was clearly harder to find a hotel room in Anchorage—at any price—than to paddle the Yukon River. Who could all these people be who wanted to spend a Monday night in Anchorage, Alaska? Finally, at 1 A.M., after an hour and a half of hearing "no" on the phone, I was ready to laugh or cry uncontrollably and was too tired to tell which.

"I can't handle this," I whimpered to Evelyn, when she stuck her head in the phone booth.

"Come on," she said, grabbing me by the arm. "What we need is something really decadent."

We trudged to the coffee shop with our backpacks and our ammo cans and our caribou antlers, and we each ordered a hot fudge sundae and a cup of coffee. When I finished that one, I ordered another and sat pouting over it, feeling like a homeless puppy. Why couldn't things be simple like they were on the river?

"Something will turn up," Evelyn drew herself to attention and held her finger in the air. "Do not worry—I will find us a place to sleep." She marched away and I played with my ice cream.

Sure enough, in a few minutes she returned, smiling. She'd talked to a waiter who talked to a cashier who suggested a hotel that had a room where there might be a no-show if we waited awhile. . . . Finally, we got the go-ahead and caught a cab and rode—terrified at the speed—in a car on a paved road for the first time in three months. Finally, we rode an elevator up inside a building, stuck a key in a doorknob, and dragged all our gear into a hotel room. Inside, it was criminally hot. We ripped off our jackets, T-shirts, long underwear tops; we threw open a window and stuck our heads into the cool darkness. Below us twinkled city lights.

I collapsed on the vinyl couch and wrestled a mud-caked wetsuit bootie from my foot. "Well, here we are," I sighed.

"Here we are," Evelyn threw herself onto the couch, propping her boots on the coffee table with a thud. "Think I can take off my bear bells now?"

I smiled tiredly. It was about 3 A.M., twenty hours after we'd crawled out of an insect-ridden tent into the tidal mud of an Eskimo village five or six hundred miles from here, to paddle our canoes to the Bering Sea.

Evelyn winked, pulled a warm Olympia beer from each pocket of her jacket, and popped the tabs. "We did it!" she held her can to mine.

"We sure did, didn't we?" I smiled. We began to laugh.

# epilogue

The wondrous insanity didn't stop then, of course. The next day there were radio and newspaper interviews to do and plane reservations to make. Sue and Jude would stay in Alaska a few days to sightsee; Evelyn and I would take a flight out that night.

Evelyn and I spent five hours in the Anchorage airport bar waiting for our flight and seeing how much trouble we could get into. "Guess what we just did?!" we'd grab the sleeve of anyone who happened by and looked as if he or she might appreciate the answer. We sat at a little table with our two ammo cans and our caribou antlers, and we toasted every person and animal we'd met on that river. We never quite figured out whether it was our drunkenness, whether it was because we'd been around small Indian and Eskimo men for three months, or whether the Yukon had permanently altered our sense of perspective, but every man in that bar seemed so *huge*.

There was Clyde, the horny Cajun who said he was from someplace called Bayou Lafourche (the pronunciation of which was good for three toasts itself), Louisiana, who'd just come off of twenty-eight days on an offshore oil rig and had twenty minutes to kill before his flight to New Orleans. So drunk were our ears, so drunk was his mouth, and so Cajun was his accent that he had to ask if we shot that reindeer—pointing to the antlers on the table—three times before we realized he was speaking English. We were having such a good time that Clyde's friends surrounded the table and tried to impress upon him that he was about to miss his flight. Clyde waved them away and concentrated on the matter at hand, which seemed to be me. I finally laughed, looked him in the eye and responded in slow, distinctly-enunciated syllables to his unasked question, "Clyde, there's not time." He blinked and frowned, tried to focus his eyes on his watch, looked at me, looked back at his watch, raised his eyebrows questioningly.

"If you're gonna do somethin'—" I shook my head.

"Do it right," we nodded together.

"Aw, you're right," he stood up to go, knocking over our table and sending beer bottles and shot glasses and caribou antlers flying onto the carpet. He stumbled across his bags and into Evelyn's lap, where he engaged her in a three-minute French kiss while tilting her back in her chair. I took the opportunity to order another round. Then he circled the table, grabbed me in his arms, and explored my ear with his big, warm, wet tongue for a few minutes; I squealed and got the hiccups, Evelyn straightened her hair and tried to look dignified.

Then Clyde was gone, blowing kisses and loping out the door thirty seconds before flight time.

There were various lesser characters who'd heard about us on the radio and wanted to buy us drinks. We obliged.

There was brawny Lucy with the hard muscles ("Here, feel 'em!"), who was the only female roustabout among several hundred men at Prudhoe Bay. The only thing Lucy could do faster than toss down shots of Jack Daniels was tell dirty jokes, at the punch lines of which she always elbowed our ribs or shoulders. Lucy was en route to California for a two-week vacation where, among other things, she would race outrigger canoes in the ocean.

Around midnight we stumbled onto an airplane, spearing only a stewardess or two with our antlers. We harrassed a traveling elevator engineer until we landed someplace in Canada in the middle of the night. The only thing I would remember about it later was that a rabbit had run from a hole on the grassy airfield just as we touched down. By then our walking hangovers had hit us, and we slept on some chairs with our ammo cans and a warm bottle of champagne, until they told us to get on another plane. After a few hours we felt well enough to drink some coffee and eat a breakfast roll and wonder what country we were in.

It occurred to me, as I looked down on the clouds, that our trip was over. Perhaps some eloquence was in order.

"Well, thanks, partner," I mumbled, picking absently at the largest of the scabs on my shin. Evelyn looked as if she'd be sick.

Finally we touched down at Dallas/Fort Worth International Airport, where my parents had been telling everyone at the gate for an hour what their daughter had just done. We marched off the plane in all our filthy glory, presented my mother with the partially-chewed antlers, then strode outside into the 102° heat for a terrifying ride on LBJ Freeway. At Evelyn's house in Dallas we uncorked the second bottle of champagne that she had carried from Emmonak, three-fourths of which spewed in a tremendous foamy geyser over the ceiling and light fixtures.

"To the Yukon!" we smiled and sipped our drinks, beneath the champagne rain that dripped for some time.

\*       \*       \*

Bing paddled a hundred miles or so, mostly in the ocean where he saw whales, to Saint Michael; he arrived there two weeks after leaving Emmonak. There, he met Tom, a biochemist who in 1972, at the age of 51, had paddled out of New York City, up the Hudson and the Saint Lawrence and the Great Lakes, etcetera, etcetera, until he finally got himself to Saint Michael in 1981. Bing also met the man who took the legendary King Solomon into custody somewhere in the Yukon delta; the King was real and, when taken to Fairbanks and put back on medication, "was perfectly normal," according to Bing. When Bing left Saint Michael in early October, the temperature was 18°F., a foot of snow lay on the ground and more was falling, and some eighty-mile-an-hour winds had blown into town.

Bing turned out to be Dr. William Ahlering, D.V.M., a race-track veterinarian who had treated thoroughbred horses in the professional horse-racing circuit for thirteen years. He followed the action between Florida and Kentucky, moving with the season. He also owned and bred thoroughbreds on a 100-acre farm in Ohio. When Bing returned from his summer vacation and the race-track crowd realized he was neither dead nor in jail, he eased back into what he called the race-track game. By the time he returned from the Yukon, his girlfriend had found another companion. Bing began planning an '84 Canadian canoe trip.

David Gile stopped over for a few days in Fairbanks, where he happened to get a little drunk and happened to get in a little barroom brawl and happened to get taken to jail for a little while. He routed himself through Dallas on his journey home so he could say "Hi," but realized when he got there he'd shipped all his phone numbers and addresses on to New Hampshire, so he spent the entire time at the airport trying to remember our last names. He returned to his accounting practice and his whitewater paddling in the mountains of New Hampshire and began planning an '84 canoe trip.

Sybil Brittin spent another five months on the winter trapline, seeing only her partners and their dogteam and wild creatures during the entire time. A hungry grizzly prowled around their cabin for six hours one day; to avoid having their dogs killed or themselves ambushed for their meat supply in the cabin, the trapper held a flashlight along the barrel of his rifle and brought down the bear with one shot. Sybil made a solo dogteam run of twenty-three miles in December and another of forty miles in March when she went to the end-of-trapline tent camp for her annual picnic. Although the temperature dipped to -67° once and stayed at -45° for long periods, Sybil said overall the temperatures were reasonable. Someday soon, she said, she'd put together her old folding single-seat kayak and paddle the lower half of the Yukon River beyond Fort Yukon, the farthest she'd gone.

In the spring of 1983, as the Yukon flexed her muscles to carry the winter's ice and snow to the sea, she took part of the bank and the little cabin, perched in the Burians' yard on Stewart Island, where Sybil always stayed when she came to visit.

In the fall of 1982, two pairs of beautiful, handmade mooseskin moccasins arrived by mail from Effie Kokrine. The smell of campfire smoke that permeated the house when I opened the box took me back to a cold, wet morning before a warm fire in a dry cabin on the Yukon, where oatmeal and Vienna sausages meant a breakfast feast beyond belief. Beaded into the uppers of the moccasins were two figures in cowboy hats paddling a silver canoe through the blue waves of the Yukon, with green mountains along the far shore. Along one side was the word "Alaska," along the other, "Bearing (sic) Sea." Effie noted in her letter that she was headed for two weeks in the Philippines and that Frank had been working near Fort Yukon, but had come to town and forgotten to go back.

Beth Hughes gave birth to an eight-pound-plus baby boy in Fairbanks, a surprising five weeks after we left Grayling. They named him Dan.

In late 1982, the trains of the White Pass & Yukon Route Railway stopped running, at least temporarily. Falling ore prices had shut most of the area's mines, and lack of freight made it uneconomical to operate the railroad. Someday, Whitehorse residents say, prices will go up, the mines will reopen, and the trains will roll.

We heard that by the end of the 1982 summer, a new washateria with showers was built in Eagle, and the lone telephone in Eagle's store lost its quaint prominence as telephones were installed all over town.

Within a few months of our return from the Yukon, the "Country Meals in a Pouch" line of dehydrated and freeze-dried foods made by Twelve Baskets, which had served us so well on the river, went out of business.

By one day, in Seattle, we had missed meeting Verlen Kruger, a 61-year-old plumber from Michigan, and his 30-year-old assistant Steve Landick, who were paddling the third season of their Ultimate Canoe Challenge that would take them 28,000 miles by paddle and portage all over North America, including *up* almost half of the Yukon and the entire Mississippi. We had corresponded with Verlen before our trip; he had kindly advised us and put us in touch with two women who had canoed the Yukon across Alaska. We learned that Verlen had swamped in his solo canoe in the ocean off Coos Bay, Oregon; had been rescued, wearing nothing but his undershorts and shoes, by Steve and the Coast Guard helicopter; had arrived at the hospital with a body temperature of 91°. But he recovered in a few hours; a fisherman found the canoe eight miles out at sea two weeks later with most of the gear still in it; and Verlen and Steve continued on their merry way.

Jane and Barbara backpacked through Denali National Park and finally got to see plenty of grizzly bears. Jane flew to the Pribilof Islands for several days of sea-cliff birding and seal-watching, then she and Barbara wandered around Alaska's Glacier Bay National Park and down to Washington State to hike through Mount Rainier National Park. Barbara drove back across the country with her mother; Jane drove back with her husband, Wesley. They ambled into Dallas a few days before Evelyn and I did, just in time to begin the new school year.

Sue and Jude stayed a few days in Anchorage, visited Denali National Park, where they got to see the Mountain make a rare appearance from behind its veil of clouds, flew to Seattle, hopped in Big Orange, and drove 2,100 miles back to Dallas, visiting friends along the way. They arrived in Dallas in mid-September; by early October they were back at work as an anesthesiologist and a surgical nurse. They started collecting information about African safaris.

Evelyn sold plenty of crystal perfume bottles and other stuff at her September market. Soon afterward, she built a cinder-block prickly-pear jelly factory at the farm, which now belonged to her as part of the agreement from the divorce that was suggested shortly after our return from the Yukon. For some reason she bought a big map of Canada and tacked it prominently on her wall.

The newspaper stories that appeared after our return illustrated a dramatic difference between the two boats in our reactions to the trip. "I really think we got out because the river said, 'You've been through enough hell. Go ahead,'" Jude was quoted as saying in one story. "Toward the end I was tired of the river and was ready to be home again." Sue was quoted as saying, "The weather was terrible [toward the end]. We couldn't navigate the delta and couldn't find a place to camp. I was hysterical. I was convinced we were goners. . . . I never felt so vulnerable to weather before. The wind cut right through our clothes. I never want to see a large, flat river again. I enjoyed it, I've seen it now, and that's enough. I'm going back to whitewater rivers."

"Actually, the trip was a lot easier than we anticipated," I was quoted as saying. "There were obstacles, but not huge ones. . . . Evelyn and I were just happy as larks most of the time. We didn't mind the dirt, the mosquitoes." Evelyn was quoted as saying, "The toughest part of the whole trip was finding a hotel room in Anchorage after we came off the river. I had a marvelous tan until I took a bath. . . . If somebody said let's go back and do it again right now, we're ready. I loved it."

\*       \*       \*

By the time I rented an apartment and bought a typewriter to write a book, I was in debt to the full limit of my mother's Mastercard account, my credit at the bank, and my mother's own bank account. I calculated that with luck, I'd have it all paid off in two years. My share of the leftover dehydrated food and the five pounds of beef jerky that Evelyn discovered in her freezer when we returned held me over for several months until I could afford groceries. By the time my White Socks sores had healed into tiny purple scars, I had relearned that there's a thing called a refrigerator into which you can put the leftover soup instead of leaving it in the open air all day. Gradually, I relearned the concept of thinking beyond the present moment. But at first, my mind couldn't shake the passive state into which it had lapsed on the river; I seemed to be able to deal only with whatever happened to be under my nose at any given moment.

The Canadian Embassy threw a party and presented us with congratulatory plaques from the Minister of Tourism. A professional adventurer whom we ran into in Dallas said she'd refer a sponsor to us next time she came across one whose needs didn't quite fit one of her projects. (I could imagine her, fanny pack in hand, making her rounds in the "expedition biz.") We never heard any evidence to indicate that any other women traveling without men had paddled the length of the Yukon in muscle-powered craft before us. Women and men from around the country wrote to sign up for our next expedition, propose blind dates, or ask about Gore-Tex. The venture seemed to spark the imagination of an incredible variety of people. Young and old, they would get a wistful look in their eyes and say, "Here's to you." Their enthusiasm redoubled my commitment to save wild places, not only for the sake of the earth's ecosystems, not only for people like us who need wilderness, but for the millions who derive inspiration simply from knowing that such places are there, still, challenging people like us, still.

For the next year I juggled my life between working full time as executive director of the Texas Committee on Natural Resources and writing a book, neither of which I'd ever tried before. It was a rough year. My paddles and life jacket lay neglected in the closet. I could no longer remember whatever it was that I used to do besides sit at the typewriter. My apartment became a ridiculous jumble of books, maps, files, cassette tapes, typewriter ribbons, and thousands of pages of rough drafts. Scattered among them were beer cans, pizza boxes, dried-up chicken bones on paper plates, dirty coffee cups.

Then, one hot summer afternoon, more than a year after we'd headed to the Yukon, I typed the last page of the final revised draft of the final revised draft. "Ta-da!" I yelled to the pizza boxes and took a bow. I couldn't remember ever feeling this tired. I went to the refrigerator, opened a beer, and ran a tubful of hot water, as I do whenever I'm recovering from some mess I'm in or dreaming up a new one to get into.

I slid down in the steamy water up to my chin, closed my eyes, and began to dream. . . .

*There's a race of [folk] that don't fit in,*
  *A race that can't stay still;*
*So they break the hearts of kith and kin,*
  *And they roam the world at will.*
*They range the field and they rove the flood,*
  *And they climb the mountain's crest;*
*Theirs is the curse of the gypsy blood,*
  *And they don't know how to rest.*

Robert Service, "The Men That Don't Fit In"

(my apologies to Mr. Service for taking liberties of gender with his otherwise eloquent poem)

YUKON RIVER GUIDE AND LOGISTICS SUMMARY
by Beth Johnson

I. Introduction, Exhortations, and Listing of Conservation Organizations.
If you've ever dreamed in the bathtub (or hoped your children will), and
if you've gained some moment of pleasure from the words I've written, I'm
grateful and flattered.  In return, let me respectfully implore you to do
yourself and the earth a favor:  Join an environmental organization.  Your
dollars will hire people to represent your interests (and the interests of
other species who have no governmental representatives) before local, state,
and federal governments.  Following is a selected list of citizens' environmental organizations:  (1) Texas Committee on Natural Resources, 4144 Coch-
ran Chapel Rd., Dallas, TX 75209  (214) 352-8370, membership $10/yr.  (2)
American Rivers Conservation Council, 323 Pennsylvania Ave., SE, Washington,
D.C. 20003, (202) 547-6900.  (3) Center for Renewable Resources/Solar Lobby,
1001 Connecticut Ave., NW, Suite 510, Washington, D.C. 20036, (202) 466-
6880.  (4) Defenders of Wildlife, 1244 19th St., NW, Washington, D.C. 20036,
(202) 659-9510.  (5) Environmental Action Inc./Foundation, Rm. 731, 1346
Connecticut Ave., NW, Washington, D.C. 20036, (202) 833-1845.  (6) Environ-
mental Defense Fund, Inc., 444 Park Ave. South, New York, NY 10016, (212)
686-4191.  (7) Environmental Policy Institute, 317 Pennsylvania Ave., SE,
Washington, D.C. 20003, (202) 547-5330.  (8) Friends of the Earth, 1045
Sansome St., San Francisco, CA 94111, (415) 433-7373.  (9) The Izaak Walton
League of America, Inc., 1701 N. Ft. Myer Dr., #1100, Arlington, VA 22209,
(703) 528-1818.  (10) National Audubon Society, 950 Third Ave., New York,
NY 10022, (212) 832-3200.  (11) National Parks and Conservation Association,
1701 18th St., NW, Washington, D.C. 20009, (202) 265-2717.  (12) National
Wildlife Federation, 1412 16th St., NW, Washington, D.C. 20036, (202) 797-
6800.  (13) Natural Resources Defense Council, Inc., 122 East 42nd St.,
New York, NY 10168, (212) 949-0049.  (14) The Nature Conservancy, Suite 800,
1800 N. Kent St., Arlington, VA 22209, (703) 841-5300.  (15) Sierra Club,
530 Bush St., San Francisco, CA 94108, (415) 981-8634.  (16) The Wilderness
Society, 1901 Pennsylvania Ave., NW, Washington, D.C. 20006, (202) 828-6600.
Alaskan Organizations:  (17) Alaska Center for the Environment, 1069 W. 6th
St., Anchorage, AK 99501.  (18) Anchorage Audubon Society, SRA Box 429-B,
Anchorage, AK 99507.  (19) Arctic Audubon Society, Box 82115, Fairbanks,
AK 99708.  (20) Denali Citizens Council, Box 41, McKinley Park, AK.  (21)
Friends of the Earth, 1069 W. 6th Ave., Anchorage, AK 99501.  (22) Juneau
Audubon Society, 1280 Fritz Cove Rd., Juneau, AK 99801.  (23) Kenai Penin-
sula Conservation Society, Box 4231, Kenai, AK 99611.  (24) Knik Kanoers
and Kayakers, P.O. Box 101935, Anchorage, AK 99510.  (25) Kodiak Audubon
Society, Box 435, Kodiak, AK 99615.  (26) Lynn Canal Conservation, Inc.,
Box 118, Haines, AK 99827.  (27) National Audubon Society, 308 G St., Ste.
219, Anchorage, AK 99501.  (28) Northern Alaska Environmental Center, 218

Driveway, Fairbanks, AK 99701. (29) <u>Sierra Club Field Office</u>, 243 E. 5th
Ave., #205, Anchorage, AK 99501. (30) <u>Sitka Conservation Society</u>, Box
2158, Sitka, AK 99835. (31) <u>Southeast Alaska Conservation Council</u>, Box
1692, Juneau, AK 99802.

I present the following about the Yukon and expedition-outfitting with
reluctance, for by making it any easier for you to run rivers, I am contributing to the degradation of the very area that I am suggesting you
visit. My only justification is my hope that as the ranks of those who've
experienced wild areas grow, so will your commitment to protect wild
places. It is only right that as you gain personal pleasure and solitude and peace from visiting wild places, you should spend an equal amount
of time or money working to protect those and other places so that others
can enjoy the same level of wilderness experience that you have.

II. <u>Yukon River Characteristics Summary</u>. The following is based on my
limited readings about the river and on my one-time, eleven-week experience in 1982, which may or may not be typical of the river in other years:

<u>General</u>. The Yukon is very, very big and very, very flat. Except
for wind-driven waves, you can count on only one day with whitewater rapids.
However, even the Yukon's flat waters move with astonishing speed, and
Five Finger Rapids' waves and some wind-driven waves were bigger than any
others I had paddled in an open canoe. As to what extent the Yukon offers
a "wilderness" experience, she's Saturday-night hell-raising in a bar, and
Saturday-night bear-watching on a sandbar, and everything in between. The
days in which you will pass no villages or canoeists or motorboaters will
be few and far between, yet the river is so big that such encounters aren't
too bothersome. Scraps of what you'll encounter <u>on</u> the Yukon I would consider wilderness, and very much of what you'll observe <u>surrounding</u> the Yukon is wilderness. If you want a three-month float down an undammed river
with very little development along its shores and very little traffic on
its waters, I don't know where in North America you'd go....

<u>Section I, Whitehorse to Dawson</u>, 460 miles June 9 to June 25, 17 days.
<u>Water Characteristics</u>. Starts out clear, unglaciated, gradually clouds un-
til a milky color. Lake Laberge on calm sunny day is clear, magical.
Thirtymile Section between Laberge and mouth of Teslin is shallow, quite
a few riffles. Throughout Section I, huge boils common, very interesting.
<u>Scenery</u>. Big, steep, snow-capped mountains crowd close to river; chang-
ing, pleasant scenery. Numerous historical structures--early explorations, Klondike Gold Rush era, sternwheeler period, and traditional Indian cemeteries. <u>Degree of Wilderness Character</u>. To some extent between
Whitehorse and Laberge, and especially for 75 miles around Carmacks, highways crowd close to river, detracting from wilderness character. This is
the only section where a highway parallels river for substantial distance.
Few locals use motorboats here; occasional recreational boaters do.

Hundreds, possibly thousands, of recreational canoeists float this stretch each year. <u>Wildlife</u>. We saw 6 beaver, 1 porcupine, 7 moose, numerous bald eagles and other birds, no bears. <u>Hazards</u>. Hug the shore of Lake La- berge. Get off lake immediately if wind builds. Riffles of Thirtymile no problem if you can read water and know to lean downstream if you hit a rock. Just paddle through the big boils, stay low, and with a heavily- loaded boat you'll be fine. Neither floating trees/other debris, nor sweepers protruding from shore, are any problem if you are alert. Five Finger Rapid is high Class II or low Class III at the level we ran it: waves three or more feet high, with a wide clear channel (take the right- hand one) obvious without scouting, some maneuvering required, irregular waves capable of swamping an open canoe. Know something about big water and eddy lines, stay low, take rescue precautions; it is a serious rapid not so much because it is difficult to run but because if you do capsize you and your gear are going to be in cold fast water for a mile or more before you can get to shore. Hundreds of beginners make it through with- out mishap each year; we also heard that at least two people drifted into the wrong channel (reportedly asleep in their canoe), capsized and drowned. Be cautious, serious and sensible, then go for it. By hugging righthand shore of Rink Rapid, you'll miss all whitewater except very low standing waves; the whitewater in the middle looked like large, irregular waves with a few souseholes, but those of our group who ran it had no problem. We ran Five Finger and Rink on day 11 of our trip, almost exactly halfway between Whitehorse and Dawson.

<u>Section II, Dawson to Pipeline Haul Road</u>, 552 miles, June 26 to July 19, 24 days (including almost 3 in Dawson). <u>Water Characteristics</u>. Big, wide river, big boils until Eagle. Occasional sandbar may hang you up in the Flats if you're sleeping. Contrary to popular notion, river flowed plenty fast through Flats; we did 263 miles in Flats in 7½ days, average 35 miles/day, with moderate paddling. <u>Scenery</u>. Steep mountains line riv- er Dawson to Eagle. Eagle until just above Circle--nearby mountains and rocky bluffs with nesting peregrine falcons provide grand scenery rivaling Canadian section. As river divides into several channels through the Flats, you'll feel you're on a smaller river. Many islands and smaller channels heighten illusion of river speed. Mountain ranges usually visi- ble in distance rather than at river's edge in Flats. Unobstructed view of river and sky offered magnificent pageants of clouds, distant rain- storms, and sunsets. Below Stevens Village the Flats disappear suddenly, giving way to narrow rocky canyon that continues to Pipeline Haul Road. Abandoned gold-mining town of Fortymile provides pleasant glimpse into pre-Klondike history; Eagle has restored turn-of-the-century buildings with a delightful walking tour; Circle has historic atmosphere but not as well restored or explained as Eagle. <u>Degree of Wilderness Character</u>. We

saw 1 motorboat, no canoeists or villagers between Dawson and Eagle (4-day trip). Several canoeists between Eagle and Pipeline Haul Road. Motorboats few between Eagle and Circle, numerous between Circle and Pipeline Haul Road. Numerous planes fly out of Fort Yukon daily. In this section on July 17 (day 39 of our trip) we first encountered the barge. Roads touch river at Eagle, Circle, and Pipeline. Despite traffic, I remember this stretch as fairly wild. Charley River, protected in Yukon-Charley Rivers National Preserve, is one of most pristine float rivers of upper Yukon. Vast Yukon Flats also protected as refuge. Thus, most of this section protected. Wildlife. We saw 1 porcupine, 3 moose, 2 wolves, numerous birds, first black bear of trip on July 14, day 36, just above Beaver (mile 876). Hazards. If you hear gunshots in Eagle, don't worry; they'll probably miss. If you have slightest notion of how to read current, there's little chance of dead-ending in a slough in Flats; don't worry if you don't know where you are on map, just follow current and you'll get somewhere sometime. Again, floating trees and shoreline strainers--no problem. Don't run into salmon gill nets stretched a few dozen yards into the river from bank.

Section III, Pipeline Haul Road to Galena, 328 miles, July 19 to August 2, 14 days. Water Characteristics. River sometimes 2 miles wide, occasionally shallow with sandbars. Scenery. From Pipeline to Tanana, steep mountains quite nearby. Tanana to Galena much like Flats--flat or slightly rolling hills, occasional range in distance. Awesome, fascinating Palisades below Tanana. Side trips up Tozitna or Nowitna River, or other clear slow-moving tributaries offer glimpse of wildlife and different river environment. Delightful rainbows and sun dogs in Kokrines Hills above Ruby. Several-day trip through Nowitna National Wildlife Refuge is only protected area in this section. Degree of Wilderness Character. Because Pipeline Haul Road is last road connecting with rest of Alaska, very few recreational canoeists on this stretch. However, quite a bit more motorboat traffic between villages. Occasional barges. Numerous Air Force planes at Galena. The largely protected stretch of 130 miles between Tanana and Ruby is nice, wild, should be savored. Wildlife. We saw 1 porcupine, 3 foxes, 2 moose, 1 owl, many geese/bald eagles/peregrine falcons/sandhill cranes, at least two dozen bears (including our only grizzly of the trip). Last bear seen July 29, day 51, two days below Tanana (about mile 1,220), although we continued to see fresh bear prints to Bering Sea. Hazards. As always, practice standard safety procedures for bears. It rained heavily or lightly, with frequent high winds, during some part of each day in this stretch. Winds created substantial, choppy, irregular waves, reducing progress to a minimum. We had 2 layover days due to impossibly high waves.

Section IV, Galena to Bering Sea, 615 miles, August 3 to August 23, 21 days. <u>Water Characteristics</u>. River widens until, at one point a few days above Emmonak, 4 miles wide. Current feels slow but by paddling rather than drifting we averaged our highest mileage on this stretch: 29 miles/day including layovers. Interesting hydraulic situation and magnificent eddy at Bishop Rock below Galena. <u>Scenery</u>. Mostly flat surrounding terrain, occasional distant mountain ranges. Most of at least one side of river protected in Innoko or Yukon Delta National Wildlife Refuges throughout this stretch. Treeless tundra on nearby mountain ranges at low elevations visible below Nulato and again near Mountain Village. You'll reach first predominantly-Eskimo village, Russian Mission, 230 miles from mouth of Yukon (August 14, day 67 of our trip). All villages upstream are Indian, below are Eskimo. Some points of historical significance in Nulato, Anvik, Russian Mission, dating to early Russian settlement. We saw our only northern lights at Grayling, August 8, day 61. <u>Degree of Wilderness Character</u>. Numerous, closely-spaced villages only a day or two apart, abundant motorboats. Exception is 3-day Kaltag-Grayling stretch, should be relished as last real solitude you'll have. Despite the traffic, though, land's bleakness/stunted trees/awesome river size/frequent grey weather and wind lent a very wild atmosphere. <u>Wildlife</u>. We saw 1 fox, many sandhill cranes, a few peregrine falcons. <u>Hazards</u>. Two- to four-mile river width invites sweeping wind and rain with high rolling waves. Minimize river crossings so you won't be caught in middle in waves. Flat campsites (w/out cutbank) few in delta, dry sheltered ones rare, much of last few days is 15-foot sheer slopes topped by mosquito-ridden muskeg. Mosquitoes mostly gone by time we reached this section, but occasional hordes of gnats were vicious. Force of river always overpowers current of in-coming tide, even at mouth, so downstream progress still easy. Take care at mouth, though, that combined force of out-going tide and river doesn't sweep you out to sea.

III. <u>Odds and Ends</u>.

   <u>Boat Considerations</u>. Rental/shuttle is easy from lakes/Whitehorse down to Dawson. Several outfitters available (write Tourism Yukon, listed in this Guide). Barb and Jane paid about $200 U.S. for 17 days incl. canoe, life jackets, paddles, shuttle, Whitehorse to Dawson. Below Dawson, no standard shuttle/rental arrangements. Below Dawson, since no roads parallel river, you can run your own shuttle but it'll be long; put-ins/take-outs at Bennett, Whitehorse, Carmacks, Dawson, Eagle, Circle, Pipeline Haul Road. Below Pipeline, only route out is by air. Freight charge per 17' canoe on Wien Air from Emmonak to Seattle in 1982 was $580, more than some canoes are worth. Instead, you can sell canoe (easy to do) at Bering Sea. To begin trip, you can bring your own or buy a canoe in Skagway (if White Pass & Yukon Railway isn't running, you'll have to have your own car or hitch ride with a truck over the mountains to Bennett or White-

horse).

What kind of craft? Foldboats or inflatable rafts easy to ship, but
I think inflatables are worrisome around snags and rocks and wind drag is
greater than on a canoe. Foldboat or solo canoe fine, plenty of room, for
one person--somewhat harder to pack than 17' open canoe. Seventeen-foot
canoe plenty big for two people and gear for three months, plus one to
three months' food. If soloing anything, double-bladed paddle is best.
I strongly suggest flatwater keel if doing the frequently-windy section
below Pipeline; whitewater keel not necessary for any of the Canadian rapids.

Boating Season. If doing whole river, put in as soon after June 1 as
possible. River/lakes probably ice-free by then, and that will give you
plenty of time to reach Bering Sea before winter weather starts. Three
months/100 days plenty of time to paddle whole river, under weather conditions like 1982 (however, in one book two canoeists were on river for
99 days and still had 300 miles to go).

Budget. A wild approximation of what I spent, in 1982 U.S. dollars,
not counting equipment: (1) Transportation (see detail this section) $961.
(2) Lodging (4 nights en route Seattle, $20; 2 nights Seattle, $10; 1 Skagway, $2; 3 Dawson, $90; 1 Stewart Island, $3; 1 Anchorage, $30) total $155.
(3) Restaurant food, spirits, incidentals, en route (5 days to Seattle,
$50; 3 days in Seattle, $50; 3 days on ferry, $60; 1 day Skagway, $30; 1
day Whitehorse, $20; all along river 12 days, $250; 1 day Anchorage, $40)
total $500. (4) Food to ship to ourselves, total $300. (5) Shipment
costs, food to river/gear back home, by U.S. mail, total $70. (6) En-
tertainment, books, incidental equipment en route, total $100. My total
cost, except equipment: $2,086.

Customs Regulations. Contact Canadian consulate in your city, or
write (see info sources, this Guide). Prepare to pay 15.7% of cost of
food you bring into Canada and to have gear searched, but you may not be
subjected to either. They're serious about handguns/modified rifles/modi-
fied shotguns prohibition. Re-entry into U.S. in Alaska very informal
(good idea to keep receipts of any Canadian purchases); you're allowed
$300 worth of Canadian-purchased articles for personal use without paying
U.S. duty. No passports/visas required for U.S. citizens.

Drinking Water. 100 iodine tablets for treating 100 quarts are more
than enough if you get water at clear side streams. We treated water only
once when we filled up at small creek downstream from a settlement. Sometimes we got water from settled-out pools on islands and boiled it. Bing
drank directly from Yukon with no problems from glacial silt, but we
didn't; plenty of side streams if you plan and watch a little.

Experience necessary. First prerequisite for doing whole river is
that you be thoroughly comfortable mentally with camping in all kinds of
weather; second, minor prerequisite is knowing how canoes behave in moving

water. Beginners have done it fine; experienced sourdoughs can also happen
into wrong set of grizzlies or storm conditions and die. Wind-driven waves
in Canadian lakes and on open stretches in lower Yukon are no laughing matter. If you know basics of whitewater paddling, Five Finger Rapid no problem, but exciting. All in all, if after careful, honest thought, you think
you're ready, you are.

Insurance. I felt the $100 I paid for three-month theft/accidental
destruction insurance on my gear, and hospitalización on myself, was well
worth it.

Maps. The following topographic maps cover the Canadian stretch from
Whitehorse to U.S. boundary, each at 1:250,000 scale and $2.50 cost (plus
$.50 handling per order), available from Canadian map office (see info
sources, this Guide), check payable to Receiver General of Canada (listed
here are map number, map name, and year of publication): 105D, Whitehorse,
'79; 105E, Laberge, '58; 105L, Glenlyon, '79; 115I, Carmacks, '74; 115J
& 115K, Snag, '71; 115-O & N (E½), Stewart River, '63; 116B & 116C (E½),
Dawson, '74. Total Canadian map cost, $18.00.

The following maps for the entire U.S. section may be ordered from the
U.S. Geological Survey (see info source), alphabetically, check payable to
U.S. Geological Survey, all contour edition, state of Alaska, 1:250,000
scale, $2.00 each: Beaver, Charley River, Circle, Eagle, Fort Yukon, Holy
Cross, Kwiguk, Livengood, Marshall, Melozitna, Nulato, Ophir, Ruby,
Russian Mission, St. Michael, Tanana, Unalakneet. Total U.S. map cost
(no handling charge), $34.00.

Take maps so that you can hike out to a highway or make it to a
village for emergency reasons. Maps not available on river; order ahead
and allow six weeks' delivery time.

Mosquitoes. From June until August billions thrive in hundreds of
thousands of ponds atop impenetrable permafrost. Seem to slack off in
August, making way for gnat armies. They are fact of life like sand in
food and other delights that make a river trip a river trip; relax and enjoy. Headnet a good idea (though Bing never wore one); repellent a must
and I vote Muskol (with highest percentage of Deet). Supposedly, taking
orally 50 milligrams of vitamin B1 per day the week before your trip, and
10 milligrams/day on the river, makes you unattractive to mosquitoes. I
took B1, wore Muskol, and mosquitoes were no big deal.

Permits. Fire-building permit required by Royal Canadian Mounted Police; pick up at Whitehorse office when you sign in with expected itinerary,
for safety's sake. No other permits required in Canadian stretch (unless
fishing/hunting, see info source this Guide).

As of August, 1983, no permits required from federal agencies managing
preserves/wildlife refuges through which you will paddle in U.S. section.
No U.S. agency like Mounties with whom to sign in for safety's sake.

Portages. None on whole river if starting at Whitehorse. If starting above Whitehorse, portage around Whitehorse dam (usually easy to solicit aid of local pickup truck on nearby highway). Above lake formed by White-horse dam, an old dam with self-operating locks is easy to negotiate w/out portaging.

Safety. Most serious concerns are hypothermia (from a capsize) and bear encounters; each requires caution but neither should cause undue worry. Try to avoid capsizing, yet be prepared in case you do: Tie all gear into boat; have stove, matches, firestarter jelly readily available; wear life jacket; have rescue rope available.

Spare paddles and boat repair equipment are standard for wilderness trip. Each boat should be self-sufficient, not dependent on others for maps, food, shelter, first aid, in case of separation for any reason.

If hurt seriously enough to require medical attention, best bet is to wait on river for next motorboat/canoe to relay word at next village/ highway crossing. Mounties no longer routinely patrol Canadian section.

Animals other than bears pose no serious threat if left alone and treated with caution. Never feed (directly or indirectly) wild animals, as it endangers all campers and erodes animal's ability to live in wild.

Treat river risings (if any), strainers/sweepers, floating debris, and boils with caution, but they're no big deal if you're knowledgeable about canoeing.

Lightning is a real concern anytime you're the only thing arising from a two-mile-wide flat water surface. We never had any problem, but Thomas McGuire in 99 Days on the Yukon was struck by lightning while sitting under a spruce tree on shore during a rainstorm; after a few days in Tanana's intensive care unit, he was fine.

Transportation. Here's what we did: (1) Dallas to Seattle, 5 days, 2,500 miles. Drove cars, camping out/staying at Motel 6's (under $20/ night nationwide). My share of gas/ice/beer: $120. (2) Seattle to Skag-way, Alaska, 1,300 miles, 2½ days. Took Alaska Marine Highway System (ferry), $155/person sleeping on deck, canoes/gear free. Reservations strongly advised, accepted after Dec. 1 for following summer's ferries. (3) Skagway to Whitehorse, Yukon Territory, Canada, 110 miles, 1 day. Took White Pass & Yukon Route Railway, $60/person plus $30/canoe, gear free. Reservations suggested. Lack of mining activity closed this line in 1983; I don't know if it will reopen. Yukon Stage Lines (bus) oper-ates Skagway-Whitehorse service, $41/person (I've heard they don't carry canoes). (4) Emmonak to Saint Mary's, 100 miles, 1 hour. Took Wien Air Alaska (they serve or subcontract to just about every village), $43/person (gear, except canoes, free). From Lower 48 call toll-free 800-562-5222. (5) Saint Mary's to Anchorage, about 500 miles, 2 hours. Flew Wien, $140/person plus small fee for gear if more than a few pieces per person.

(6) Anchorage to Dallas, about 4,000 miles, 1 day. Several routes on several airlines available. Ours $443/person. Total transportation cost, per person, Dallas to Whitehorse, Emmonak to Dallas, $961.

Weather. In three months' time, 2,000 miles, everything from 85° days with no wind and clear sky to wind-whipped rain throughout a 35° night; take clothes for it all. I believe layering of wool and Gore-Tex beats reliance on new thin "miracle" fabrics. We had rain 1 day between Whitehorse and Dawson (June 9-25), 7 days between Dawson and Pipeline (June 26-July 19), 11 days between Pipeline and Galena (July 20 to August 2), and 9 days between Galena and Bering Sea (August 3 to August 23).

Wilderness Ethic. Leave no litter (including cigarette butts!) or other garbage in camp. Instead of burying garbage, dump it in current; river's big enough to absorb it, and a cleaner camp will help prevent wild animals' associating humans with food. Carry with you any slowly-biodegrading containers. Garbage disposal is great problem for the villages; any cans that you use will add to the problem and will end up dumped out behind the village or in the river.

Don't pick wild plants unnecessarily or use macho outdated "woodsman" techniques such as trenching around tents/digging fire pits that de-wilderness the land for the next camper or animals. To dispose of human waste, dig a 6-inch-deep hole as far as feasible from water; use little toilet paper and burn it. Never take cultural artifacts such as old mining tools that others will enjoy seeing. Don't vulgarize your own wilderness experience and everyone else's by carving on driftwood, trees, rocks, or other parts of the scenery. The caribou antlers and one palm-sized rock were the only things other than photographs that I stole from the Yukon; in the Lower 48 I would have left them there because natural areas are too heavily traveled to withstand everyone's taking away part of the scenery. If other groups are around, don't impinge on their wilderness experience by making lots of noise.

Better environmentally to cook with liquid fuel and cookstove rather than wood fire: Burning wood robs soil of nutrients gained from decomposition of wood, pollutes air, reduces natural scenery of down logs/driftwood. Admitting that, we chose to use wood fires because we disliked having much flammable fuel in boats, because we wanted to eat whole-grain (long-cooking) preservative-free foods that would have used up lots of fuel, because driftwood was abundant and Yukon not heavily traveled by recreationists, and because fires helped warm us each evening. In Lower 48, luxury of a wood fire is almost gone; many rivers and trails would be nothing but end-to-end fire pits and devoid of downed wood if everyone made a fire.

IV. Some Sources of Information. Canada: (1) Canadian Map Office; Dept. of Energy, Mines and Resources; 615 Booth St.; Ottawa, Ontario; Canada; K1A 0E9, (613) 998-9900. [Ask for free index to maps.] (2) Director

of Wildlife, P.O. Box 2703, Whitehorse, Yukon, Canada, Y1A 2C6, (403)
667-5229. [for hunting/fishing regulations, also excellent pamphlet "The
Bear Facts"]  (3) Klondike Visitors Association, Box 389, Dawson City, Yukon, Canada, YOB 1GO.  (4) Parks Canada, 400 Laurier Avenue West, Ottawa,
Canada, K1A OH4. [info on Dawson historic sites, Chilkoot Trail, etc.]
(5) Revenue Canada, Customs & Excise, Box 4520, Whitehorse, Yukon, Canada,
Y1A 2R8.  (6) Royal Canadian Mounted Police, 4100 - 4th Ave., Whitehorse,
Yukon, Canada, Y1A 1H5. [Ask for "Yukon River Travellers' Guide" and other
info.]  (7) Tourism Yukon, Government of Yukon, Box 2703, Whitehorse, Yukon, Canada, Y1A 2C6, (403) 667-5340. [maps, general info, Whitehorse canoe outfitters list, & other useful info]  (8) Yukon Archives, Box 2703,
Government of Yukon, Whitehorse, Yukon, Canada, Y1A 2C6. [Write for old
steamer maps of Yukon River.]  (9) Yukon Stage Lines, Ltd.; Main St. at
First Ave.; Whitehorse, Yukon; Canada; (403) 668-6665. [bus service Skagway to Whitehorse]  (10) White Pass & Yukon Tours, 419 Queen Anne Ave.
North, Suite B1, Seattle, WA 98109, 800-426-9865. [Owns White Pass & Yu-
kon Railway.]  Alaska: (1) Alaska Dept. of Highways, P.O. Box 1467,
Juneau, AK 99811.  (2) Alaska Division of Tourism, Dept. of Commerce &
Economic Development, Pouch E, Juneau, AK 99811, (907) 465-2010. [excel-
lent "Worlds of Alaska" magazine & other info]  (3) Alaska Railroad, P.O.
Box 2344, Anchorage, AK 99510.  (4) Klondike Gold Rush National Historic
Park, National Park Service, P.O. Box 517, Skagway, AK 99840.  (5) Nation-
al Park Service, U.S. Dept. of the Interior, Alaska Area Office, 540 W.
Fifth Ave., Room 202, Anchorage, AK 99501.  (6) Skagway Convention and
Visitors Bureau, P.O. Box 415, Skagway, AK 99840.  (7) State of Alaska
Dept. of Fish and Game, Subport Bldg., Juneau, AK 99801. [hunting/fishing
regulations; good pamphlet "The Bears and You"]  (8) State of Alaska Dept.
of Transportation and Public Facilities, Division of Marine Highway Sys-
tems, Pouch R, Juneau, AK 99811, (907) 465-3946. [state ferry info for
Inside Passage and Gulf of Alaska]  (9) U.S. Customs Service, P.O. Box
7118, Washington, D.C. 20044.  (10) U.S. Fish and Wildlife Service, U.S.
Dept. of the Interior, 1011 East Tudor Rd., Anchorage, AK 99507. [Ad-
ministers Yukon Flats, Nowitna, Innoko, and Yukon Delta National Wildlife
Refuges along the Yukon.]  (11) U.S. Forest Service, Box 6128, Juneau,
AK 99801.  (12) U.S. Geological Survey, Branch of Distribution, Box 25286,
Federal Center, Denver, CO 80225. [Ask for free map index to Alaskan maps.]
(13) U.S. Heritage Conservation and Recreation Service, 1011 East Tudor Rd.,
Suite 297, Anchorage, AK 99507. [info about recreational Alaskan river-
running]  (14) Yukon-Charley River National Preserve, Box 64, Eagle, AK 99738.

V.  Food Summary.

   How Much.  We assumed food for 90 days for 4 people, or 360 people-days,
plus 20 days for 2 people (Jane and Barbara from Whitehorse to Dawson), or
40 people-days, for a total of 400 people -days.  In reality, we lost 62

people-days because the 4 of us were on the river only 76 days and Jane and Barbara only 17. We lost another 72 people-days from unanticipated meals in restaurants, food given by friends, food eaten in village stores, and skipping meals. Thus, we ate from our food stock 134 people-days less food than we had planned, or about one-third less than our total assumed food of 400 people-days. If you're doing the whole river, I'd plan on 100 days, perhaps adjusted slightly downward if you plan to visit village cafes. Make your best guess, then don't worry about it. If you take too much, give some away; if too little, buy some in river stores.

Although there is a store in every village, I would again take with me/ship most of what I wanted. Stores have a limited variety of canned, dry, and fresh goods, but virtually no dehydrated/freeze-dried food. Prices were up to double that of Lower 48. Very little in easily-biode-gradable packages, few whole-grain/preservative-free/low salt/low sugar foods. By bringing/shipping your own food, you have to hit only your re-ceiving-point villages during regular work hours; if relying on frequent purchases of the more-bulky store goods, you commit yourself to arriving during store hours. Although we paid up to 50¢ per pound to ship food to ourselves (depending on size and weight of box), all in all it probably cost no more than buying expensive food in village stores. Our food all arrived intact and we had a greater variety than what was available in village stores. (Note, however, that Bing bought all his food in stores as he went down the river and was quite satisfied.)

Weights, Prices. Evelyn calculated the quantities appearing next un-der "Kinds" based on 400 people-days, assuming 2 cups of food equals 1 pound. One cup/person for breakfast, 2 cups for lunch, 3 cups for dinner, totalling 24 cups/day for 4. One hundred days, then, equals 2,400 cups or 1,200 pounds of fresh food (not counting drink mixes, spices, incidentals). Assuming reduction of food weight by dehydration, then adding weight of packaging and incidentals, we calculated total food weight at 600 pounds (200 pounds/month or 50 pounds/week). (Harvey Manning in Backpacking: One Step at a Time states that careful planning and use of some dry/dehy-drated food means 1.5 to 2 pounds/person/day [600-800 pounds for 400 people-days].) Evelyn calculated that we could purchase the following kinds and quantities for about $3/person/day, 1982 dollars, or $300/person for the entire summer.

Kinds. Because of last-minute contributions of free or discounted dehydrated/whole-grain foods from Twelve Baskets, Arrowhead Mills, and friends, what we took was not what's on the following list and it's im-possible to calculate how much and what was substituted since packaging/ food mixtures didn't correspond to our fresh food list. I believe the end weight, however, was the same as we had planned. I offer the follow-ing list as a planning tool. Foods on it were chosen because generally

preservative-free, low-salt/sugar, and can be purchased organically-grown.
Most were dry initially (beans), could be dehydrated easily by us in our own
dehydrators, or could be purchased commercially dehydrated. (C. = cups;
# = lbs.) Vegetables: Alfalfa seeds for sprouting. Bell peppers, 50.
Black beans, 4#. Black-eyed peas, 4#. Broccoli, 50 C. Cabbage, 12 heads.
Carrots, 50 C. Celery, 6 bunches. Chick peas, 2#. Corn (giblet), 50 C.
Green beans, 50 C. Green peas, 50 C. Lentils, 4#. Lima beans, 4#. Navy
beans, 4#. Okra, 50 C. Onions, 100. Parsley, 3 jars. Pinto beans, 4#.
Popcorn, several pkgs. Potatoes, 52#. Split peas, 4#. Tomatoes, 150 C.
Yellow squash, 75 C. Zucchini, 50 C. Fruits: Apples, 100. Apricots, 100.
Coconuts, 12. Dates, 50. Figs, 50. Lemon concentrate equivalent to 50
whole. Peaches, 100. Pineapples, 12. Prunes, 50. Raisins, 12#. Strawberries, 12#. Grains: Bisquick, 10#. Corn meal, 10#. Cream of Wheat, 100
C. Flour (whole wheat, rice, rye, buckwheat), 30#. Grits, 50 C. Macaroni, 13#. Malto Meal, 100 C. Masa, 10#. Noodles (spinach, whole wheat),
13#. Oatmeal, 100 C. Rice (brown long-grain), 13#. Spaghetti, 7#. Tabouli (cracked wheat), 2#. Tapioca, 6 boxes. Wheat germ, 1#. Nuts: Al-
monds, 10#. Cashews, 10#. Peanuts, 50#. Peanut butter, 2 gals. Pecans,
10#. Pumpkin seeds, 1#. Sesame seeds, 1#. Sunflower seeds, 1#. Walnuts,
10#. Meat, Poultry, Eggs: Beef jerky, 13#. Boullion cubes, 4 jars.
Chickens, 13. Chili, 5 qts. Eggs (powdered), 400 equivalent. Salamis,
13. Dairy Products: Cheeses (sealed in paraffin), 13. Dry milk to make
100 qts. Beverages: Hot chocolate mix for 100 qts. Instant coffee for
for 1,200 C. Instant spiced tea for 100 C. Instant tea for 800 C. Kool-
Aid for 200 C. Lemonade mix for 200 C. Sanka for 150 C. Tang for 400 C.
Miscellaneous: Baking powder, 1 can. Baking soda, 1 box. Banana flakes,
several pkgs. Black pepper, 1 box. Cheese powder, 2 cans. Chili powder,
2 boxes. Cinnamon, 2 boxes. Cooking oil, 4 qts. Garlic cloves, 2 pkgs.
Hot peppers, 3 jars. Oleo margarine, 4 bottles. Oregano, several jars.
Peanut butter powder, 1 can. Picante sauce, 2 large jars. Salt, 1 box.
Sour cream powder, 1 can. Sugar (white and brown), 8#. Thyme, 1 box.
Tomato crystals, 1 can. Vanilla, 1 bottle. Vinegar, 4 bottles.

Comments on Kinds. We should have eased up a little on our no-chemicals
rule and taken some instant soups, commercial granola bars, instant potatoes,
M & M's, or other foods that were ready-to-eat or quick-cooking, for windy/
rainy days when cooking was difficult or for long days when we were too
tired to cook.

Some of us took multi-vitamins to avoid a vitamin deficiency that
could develop over three months if we had failed to plan a balanced menu.
Since we had so little meat in our menu (hard to preserve without artificial
chemicals), we wondered whether we'd be getting enough fats. (One book
quotes an Alaskan nutritionist saying that at normal activity and temperatures of 68° to 77° F., today's standards suggest 2,800 calories per "man"

per day, of which 9% is protein, 41% is fat, and 50% is carbohydrates. Another book states that a balanced 1,500 calorie diet [to maintain good health for a robust individual of average size engaged in moderate activity in a temperate climate] would typically include 17% protein, 4% fat, 79% carbos. A third book says the National Research Council says 1% fat is adequate. I have no idea why the vast discrepancy.) We discovered that whenever we hit a restaurant or store, we stuffed ourselves with anything greasy or sweet, but who knows whether our bodies really needed that stuff.

Fruits were always gobbled up fast and really brightened our lunches; take plenty. The Illes Spice Company in Dallas contributed sample bags of dehydrated spices from Mexican flavorings to Worcestershire sauce and barbeque sauce. Those, plus things like cheese powder that we got from backpacking stores/survival companies, really enabled creative cooking. Take plenty of spices. Next time I'd take fewer peanuts and a greater variety of other nuts. We took Neo-Life dehydrated, nitrogen-packed scrambling eggs, seemingly the best-tasting and most reasonably-priced of brands available. They're fine for baking, fair for using in quiches, and barely bearable as scrambled eggs; mix rehydrated bell peppers/picante sauce/onions/potatoes with them and they're not half bad. They're a significant source of protein. [Fair warning: The strange-smelling sawdust-like stuff called "pre-cooked" or "instant" eggs might be good to soak up automobile grease in your driveway but that's about it; kitty litter would serve as well and taste better as "eggs."]

Don't worry about measuring or sifting ingredients. For bannock bread, for instance, just grab a jar that looks like any kind of flour, another of baking powder, another of sugar (if you want it sweet) or salt (if unsweet), shake some of each into a pot, stir in a little water, scrape it into a skillet and set it at the edge of the fire for awhile.

If dehydrating your own foods, your 600-Watt dehydrator would use 42¢ worth of electricity at 1982 Dallas springtime rates over a 10-hour period (usually enough for one batch); 875-Watt dehydrator would use about 61¢.

Some Sources of Dehydrated/Freeze-Dried/Organic Foods. (1) Apache Meat Processing Co., Inc., Apache, OK 73006, (405) 588-2186 [beef jerky]. (2) Arrowhead Mills, Box 866, Hereford, TX 79045, (806) 364-0730. (3) The Frontier Food Association, Inc. (Long-Life Foods), 7263 Envoy Court, Dallas, TX 75247, (214) 630-6221. (4) Illes Spice Company, 5527 Redfield, Dallas, TX 75235, (214) 631-8350. (5) Neo-Life Co. of America, Hayward, CA 94545. (6) Oregon Freeze Dry Foods, Inc. (Mountain House), P.O. Box 1048, Albany, OR 97321. (7) Your local backpacking/canoeing/sporting goods store, health food store, survival store.

Packaging. Use Seal-a-meal bags, best if sealer makes at least a ½-inch thick seal (if not, make two seals). Cut bag ½ in. away from seal. Continuous-roll bags best, can cut to variable size. The more air in bag

when you seal, faster food will spoil. Properly-sealed and dehydrated
vegetables and fruits will not go stale/spoil/rehydrate prematurely during
a three-month trip, even if you dehydrate them a few months ahead. Our
jerky lasted OK except for a little mold toward the end; I don't know about
other meats. Seal-a-meal bags were more durable than some of the commercial
plastic-and-foil pouches whose seams came undone after being subjected to
dampness/grit/jostling in our 50-pound food bags.

We packaged our own dehydrated stuff into meal-for-four sized bags.
Left commercially-dehydrated vegetables or drink mixes in lightweight cans
in which they came, then put them into plastic jars as we opened them on
river (burned cardboard-ish cans except for tin ends). Left flour/sugar/
salt in its original thick paper sack/box, then sealed that into a Seal-a-
meal bag. All containers were then put inside big "waterproof" durable
Bill's Bags, sealed at night because of bears and during day to thwart rain
or waves. This double sealing prevented stuff from getting wet even if a
little water got into Bill's Bags. The only thing that consistently leaked
out of its container no matter what we put it in (including "leak-proof"
screw-top bottles from backpacking stores) was liquid cooking oil; perhaps
we should have put the oil bottle inside a bigger plastic jar.

Our labeling system had its flaws but we didn't starve. We labeled
contents of each Seal-a-meal bag on piece of paper, taped flat against
inside of bag, but flour, etc. worked its way in front of paper, obscuring
label. Though it may rub off, probably simplest and best to label with
felt-tipped marker directly on outside of bag. Probably best to label
plastic jars (into which other stuff is dumped as necessary) with different
colors or numbers; as contents change each week, you just relearn what
colors/numbers signify.

When ready to cook, we spread a 7-feet-by-9-feet nylon tarp on ground
and dumped contents from grain bag, everything-else bag, and spice bag onto
it. Then we saw at a glance what our portable grocery contained. By not
having package sizes and menus planned down to every meal, we had tremendous flexibility and allowance for creativity in what we cooked.

Shipping. If doing the whole river, I'd take a month's worth of food
with me to start, ship a month's worth to Eagle (we arrived on day 23 of
our journey), and another month's to Galena (we arrived there 32 days out
of Eagle, and arrived at Bering Sea 21 days out of Galena). That keeps
everything even, simplifying your calculations. Since you're supposed to
pay duty on food you ship into Canada, and since we also heard that regula-
tory hassles prevented some river-runners from receiving their shipments
in Canada, we didn't ship anything there. Everything we shipped arrived
intact in Alaska, but pick sturdy boxes and tape them extensively. (Fort
Yukon, incidentally, is not a logical place to ship to because, unlike all
other river villages, its post office is ½ mile from river.) To send food

or anything else to yourself or anyone else who's canoeing the Yukon, put
the person's name, town, state, zip code (as shown on "Yukon River Data
Chart", this Guide), and write "hold for pickup until (date)." I've heard
that postmaster may charge minimal daily fee for holding packages, but we
were never charged.

Call your local post office for restrictions/packaging requirements
for shipping to Alaska (specify it's for Alaska). They'll throw out anything that leaks or smells. Parcel post is cheapest; allow two to three
weeks' delivery from Texas to Alaska. Insure packages (the kind of insurance with a number) so can be traced or cost (up to $100) refunded.
Cheapest to put as much weight as possible (up to limit) in each box.
Sample rate (1983): 20 pounds for $9.95, Texas to Alaska. We spent about
$134 to ship food to ourselves along the river (no record of how much
weight that accounted for), some of which was shipped from Texas and some
from Washington State.

VI. Equipment Summary.

Following is a listing of all personal gear (that I can recall) that
I took, plus some common items for Evelyn's and my boat. Prices are
approximate 1982-1983 retail. Most weights are exact, except in case of
lawn chair/canoe/other incidental items I no longer have.

A. Camera Equipment, total approx. weight 33#, cost $2,145.

Ammo can I, 12"x6"x6" (containing equip. listed below), 4# empty, 11#
w/equip. listed, $6 used. The only thing I found truly airtight, water-
proof. Glued blue closed-cell polyethylene foam pad to inside surface,
used pad as partitions betw. lenses. Take extra lens caps; you'll lose
them overboard. Paint outside of can white to reflect sun, make easy to
see in river/on shore. Equip. listed here will fit tightly in 1 can. ●
Minolta SRT 101 camera body, $209 incl. lens listed next, loaded w/color
slide film. Manual. Worked fine. Motordrive would have been good to have
w/bird-in-flight pics, but subject usually too far away. Motordrives require lots of batteries. ● 55 mm f/1.7 Minolta lens. Rarely used exc.
w/flower pics w/close-up rings. ● 28 mm f/2.8 wideangle Vivitar lens, $88.
Great for river w/mountains & sky, also for in-camp scenes. ● 75-205 mm
f/3.8 zoom Vivitar lens, $200 incl. teleconverter listed next. Useful for
nearby canoes/people, animals on nearby shore. ● Teleconverter 75-205 2X
matched multiplier in padded case. Not powerful enough for anything across
river, makes lens too long for shots from bobbing boat, usually not enough
time to add it to lens for wildlife pics. ● Filters (3 UV-Haze, 3 polar-
izing) in hard plastic cases; 3 close-up filter rings in padded case, total
$86. Always have some filter on lens. UV for grey days; polarizing fan-
tastic for blue skies w/white clouds, esp. w/wideangle lens. ● Rubber lens
shades. Rarely used, difficult to fit into ammo can on lens. Make sure
wideangle shade doesn't show in edge of pics. ● Air brush, lens cloth in

plastic bag. Several rolls of my pics were marred by two parallel scratch-
es from pieces of grit. Should have taken time to crawl into tent, out of
wind/rain/sand, once a wk., to brush out inside of camera. ● Desiccant
Silacagel, 3 packets. To absorb moisture that gets into ammo can while
open in mist/rain. From camera stores. ● Minolta pocket 8 X 20 binoculars w/padded case, $100. Never could see too well out of them; small
size a great plus, tho. Kept around neck, tucked dry under life jacket.
Total cost equipment in Ammo can I (most purchased on sale)--$689.

Ammo can II, 12"x6"x6", (containing equip. listed here), 4# empty, 10#
w/equip., $6 used. Usually after I took 1 series of pics w/color film,
subject was gone or I was too lazy to take black & white pics (this can).
● Minolta XG-M camera body, automatic, loaded w/black & white film, $209
incl. lens listed next. ● 50 mm f/1.7 Minolta lens. ● 28 mm f/2.8 wideangle Minolta lens, $118. ● 75-205 f/4.5 zoom Minolta lens, $180. ● Teleconverter 75-205 2X, $59. ● Minolta pocket 8 X 20 binoculars w/padded
case, $100. Total cost equipment in Ammo can II--$672.

Miscellaneous. ● Electroflash, 8 oz., $75. Never used. ● Film canis-
ters (about 100) @ 1 oz., total 6#, $440. Leave film in its plastic can,
put inside "waterproof" bag, inside bigger "waterproof" bag. I used 57
rolls (36 exp.) color slides (incl. trip to river); 4 rolls black & white.
Would have used more if more layover days, less if not trying for natl.
mag pics. Suggest 2/3 Kodachrome 64, 1/3 Ektachrome 400. Ektachrome very
blue but necessary on dark days. ● Film development mailers (Kodak), 50,
2.5#, $234. Safest way to ensure that exposed film doesn't get wet or
lost; friends back home can examine developed film to alert you to camera
malfunctions. ● Tripod, telescoping (21" collapsed), 3#, $35. Carried
inside 2 coated nylon stuff sacks to keep out sand. Great for self-timed
camp scenes, sunset shots w/zoom lens.

B. Clothing, total approx. weight 27#, cost $746.

Feet. ● Socks, 1 pr. terrycloth sport anklet, 2 oz., $2. Rarely
wore. ● Socks, 1 pr. thin Wick-Dry liner, 2 oz., $2. Excellent for hik-
ing, under wool. ● Socks, 1 pr. orlon knee socks, 2 oz., $2. ● Socks,
2 pr. 100% wool, 6 oz., $12. Indispensable. ● Wetsuit socks (booties),
1 pr., 5 oz., $23. Wore every day under tennis shoes--love 'em! Ripped
seams periodically, ripped material itself after 67 days; I sewed them
up w/needle & thread, which held fine. ● Tennis shoes, 1 pr., 1.5#, $15.
Wore every day. They were 1 yr. old before trip; disintegrated rapidly
on Yukon's rocks. ● Boots, 1 pr. ankle-high canvas, 2#, $24. Rarely
wore, canvas never seemed to dry & didn't fit right w/wetsuit booties.
Evelyn wore hers every day. Sue/Jane/Barb took L. L. Bean Maine Hunting
Shoe, 6" or 12" high, loved them. ● Boots, 1 pr. ankle-high leather hiking, welt-soled, 3#, $80. Rarely wore because we rarely hiked, but they
were good when we did. Summary: Next time I'd leave home sport anklets

and canvas boots, add 1 pr. wetsuit socks & 1 pr. tennis shoes.

Legs. ● Underwear, 2 prs. cotton, 2 oz., $2. Brightly colored so not to lose in sand/on bushes. ● Longhandle pants, Duofold brand, 40% wool, 50% cotton, 10% nylon, 8 oz., $13. Indispensable. ● Belt, nylon, 1" wide, metal ring buckle, 2 oz., $3. Useful when weight loss created baggy pants. ● Shorts, 1 pr. cotton knit (no pockets), 4 oz., $2. ● Shorts, 1 pr. khaki, w/front & back pockets, belt loops, 10 oz., $14. Wore on hot days on river/in town, rarely in camp (mosquitoes). Belt loops handy to tie things to. ● Pants, 1 pr. khaki w/reinforced knees (patches I put on before trip), w/front & back button-flap pockets, 15 oz., $14. Dry quickly when wet, pockets useful, can roll into shorts. ● Pants, 1 pr. U.S. Navy, 100% wool, w/front & back pockets, 1.5#, $10. Indispensable, wore every day. ● Rain pants, 1 pr. Gore-Tex, by Kelty, w/drawstring waist (I put slide lock on it), no pockets/zippers, huge cuffs (for boots), 9 oz., $60. Indispensable, wore every day because kneeling or sitting on wet boat floor/seats. I installed thin shock-cord closures into cuff hems so they wouldn't flap when I walked or let underneath pants get wet. Lack of pockets no problem and kept weight of pants down. After sitting/kneeling all day on wet surfaces, dampness would eventually seep through rain pants, wool pants, and longhandles, but not too bothersome & still better than sweating in conventional rainwear. I highly recommend Gore-Tex. Be sure to get size big enough for over 2 prs. pants. Summary: Next time I'd leave home cotton knit shorts.

Torso. ● Halter top, 1 cotton knit, 2 oz., $3. Used once as part of swimsuit. ● Longhandle shirt, Duofold brand, 40% wool, 50% cotton, 10% nylon, 9 oz., $13. Indispensable. ● T-shirt, heavy cotton/polyester blend, 6 oz., $8. ● T-shirt, lightweight cotton/polyester blend, 2, 10 oz., $10. ● Shirt, 1 long-sleeved cotton workshirt w/pockets, 8 oz., $10. Rarely wore. ● Shirt, 1 Army 100% wool, long-sleeved, w/collar, button-down pockets, 1.5#, $6 used. Indispensable. ● Sweater, 1 crew-neck pullover 100% wool, 13 oz., $20. Indispensable, wore every day. ● Dickey, 1 orlon turtleneck, 5 oz., $6. Never wore. ● Rain jacket, 1 Gore-Tex, "Stowaway" style by The North Face; w/shock cord (slide-locked) drawstring closures on hood, neck & bottom openings; zippered outside & inside pockets; zipper & snap front opening; Velcro closures on cuffs; waist-length; seam-sealed, 13 oz., $120. Indispensable. Style & features perfect, light weight wonderful yet plenty warm, never "leaked," I never sweat even when paddling all day in it. Hood handy to draw tightly over balaclava. Held up superbly in 3 months' daily use. Zipper tabs a little too small if fingers stiff in cold weather; I always used snaps instead. ● Wetsuit, full-length "Farmer John" style by Seda, w/padded knees, 5#, $78. Could save your life or at least make it more comfortable in Five Finger & Rink Rapids, as well as choppy wind-driven waves. Wore 5 days during trip,

w/T-shirt or longhandle top underneath, wool sweater over. ● Parka, 1
Polarguard fabric (100% polyester), w/60%-40% unquilted outer shell, by
The North Face; zipper & snap front closure; detachable hood; Velcro-
closure top-entry (w/flap) or side-entry pockets; shock-cord (slide-
locked) closures on hood, neck, waist, 2.5#, $130. Indispensable. Used
only a few days but thankful I had it. Have had mine 6 yrs., still warm
& in great shape. Zipper broke first month but snaps do fine. Synthetic
fabric a must for river-running where rain/waves will eventually wet
everything you're wearing & everything in your "waterproof" bags. Summary: Next time I'd leave halter, cotton workshirt, dickey home. Wool
& synthetics (as opposed to cotton) are a must, insulate even when wet.
Layering is key to warmth; if outer layer Gore-Tex you're in comfort city!
I believe selection of clothes is key to your happiness/misery on river.

Head. ● Cowboy hat, 1 grey felt; w/nylon-cotton chin-strap of bootlace material, w/slide-lock closure, 6 oz., $10. Indispensable. Light-
weight so not hot in sun, sturdy enough to keep rain off completely (I put
seam-sealer in holes punched to install chin-strap). More comfortable
paddling when a broad brim like this protects your eyes from wind-blown
rain. If cold, I wore balaclava (plus sometimes rain jacket hood) under
cowboy hat (chin-strap kept everything in place). ● Mosquito headnet, 1
to fit over brim of cowboy hat; homemade (netting available in Army-Navy
stores, use smallest mesh available) w/drawstring & slide-lock closure at
neck, elastic closure around hat band, 2 oz., $3. Rarely used, but in-
dispensable (others used theirs all the time). Brim of hat kept net away
from face, but it still drove me crazy. Used more for gnats than mosquitoes. ● Balaclava, 1 100% wool, w/bill, 5 oz., $5. Indispensable, used
every day, kept head warm & wind off neck. Very versatile--can roll up
into a hat if not cold enough for neck portion. Slept in it many nights.
● Balaclava, 1 orlon, 2 oz., $5. Used if wool one got wet. Summary:
I'd take all these again.

Hands. ● Gloves, 1 pr. vinyl palms w/mesh back, by Northwest River
Supply, 2 oz., $5. Provide some warmth, great grip on paddle. ● Gloves,
1 pr. cotton/polyester blend, 2 oz., $2. Brought to keep mosquitoes
off hands, but Muskol worked fine instead & didn't impede my grip. Evelyn
wore hers at all times, though. Sue/Jude used buckskin gloves. ● Gloves,
1 pr. 100% wool from Army-Navy, made as inserts to outer mittens, 3 oz.,
$5. Pretty warm even when wet, but hard to grip paddle w/them. ● Mittens,
1 pr. flannel-lined, w/nylon outer shell, vinyl palm, 4 oz., $7. Useless
when wet. ● Mittens, 1 pr. Gore-Tex outer, to fit over other gloves/mit-
tens, 5 oz., $22. Couldn't grip paddle w/them at all, and didn't need in
camp because could put hands in pockets. Summary: Next time I'd leave
home cotton ones, flannel-lined ones, and big outer mittens. Would take
extra pr. wool, plus maybe wetsuit gloves. Vinyl paddling ones a must.

General comments on clothing. You can scrutinize & agonize & go high-tech like I did; or you can grab a couple of cotton sweatshirts, some old polyester pants, and a $4 plastic poncho and be on your way, like Bing did. How comfortable you want to be is the important question. There is a greater risk of hypothermia w/cotton clothing, and you'll spend longer drying it out each time it gets wet.

C. Entertainment, total approx. weight 12.5#, cost $333.

● Bb cornet, wrapped inside sleeping pad, 2.5#, $250. ● Blues harp, key of G; double-row harmonica, key of C, 6 oz., $20. ● Books, 6 paperback, covers coated w/clear contact paper to resist water/tearing, 6#, $18. ● Finger cymbals, 4 brass, 4 oz., $10. ● Kazoo, 9" (or was it really 12"?) tin, shaped like a trumpet, 2 oz., $3. ● Playing cards, 1 deck, 3 oz., $2. ● Sheet music, some coated w/clear contact paper, 70 (?) songs, 3#, $30. Summary: All in all, perhaps a bit much, but what's a few more pounds? Had I been alone or had we had more layovers in camp, I'd have used all much more.

D. First Aid, total approx. weight 2#, cost $41.

First aid kit in "waterproof" 8½"x6½"x3" guard box, (containing equip. listed here), 1# empty, 2# full, $12. ● Hand lotion (as unperfumed as possible) in leak-proof plastic screw-top bottle. ● Sun-tan lotion (unperfumed) in leak-proof plastic screw-top bottle. ● Vaseline, 1 plastic tube. ● Film can full of aspirin & sinus pills. ● 1 coil of snare wire. ● Visine, ½ fl. oz. plastic squeeze bottle. ● 5 yd. x ½" roll adhesive tape. ● Pepto Bismal tablets in zip-lock bag. ● Di-Gel tablets in zip-lock bag. ● Potable Aqua brand emergency drinking water tablets (100 tablets to treat 100 qts.), active ingredient Tetraglycine Hydroperiodide. ● Moleskin, three 3"x4" sheets. ● Sterile gauze pads, seven 2"x2". ● Waterproof matches, Seaway brand, 100. ● Scissors, folding. ● Fingernail clippers. ● Toenail clippers. ● Campho-Phenique brand first aid gel, 1 tube (.2 oz.). ● Lomotil anti-diarrhea tablets. ● Whetstone. ● Emergency/survival handbook in zip-lock bag. ● Tweezers, pointed, 1 pr. ● Bandaids, 20. Total cost first aid supplies--$23. Summary: I consider this a bare-bones personal first aid kit, designed as a supplement to the extensive one w/antibiotics, painkillers, etc., that Sue carried for all of us.

● Ankle brace, elasticized, 1 oz., $3. ● Knee brace, elasticized, 2 oz., $3.

E. Kitchen Equipment (Personal), total approx. weight 7#, cost $123.

● Water bottle, 1 qt. plastic, w/stopper & screw-top lid, w/loop for tying into boat, 4 oz., $3. ● Water bottle, 1½ qts. plastic, w/stopper & screw-top lid, w/loop for tying into boat, 4 oz., $3. More brittle plastic loop broke. ● Water jug, collapsible, plastic, w/screw-on valve-spout, 2½ gal. capacity, 7 oz., $4. Material didn't puncture, but sooner or later valve will leak. Much handier than rigid containers. Recommend 2

per boat, so you won't have to find side creeks for water so often. ●
Personal kitchen 12"x12" coated nylon drawstring stuff sack, containing:
aluminum Sierra Cup, insulated cup, 2 stainless steel spoons, tongs for
gripping pots, 5" diam. x 2½" depth aluminum pot w/handle & lid, 5" diam.
x1½" depth aluminum plate (slope-sided), 6"x12" terry cloth towel, all-
purpose liquid camp soap (4 fl. ozs.) in plastic screw-top squeeze bottle,
1 brightly-colored plastic trowel in small stuff sack, hunting knife in
holster. Total stuff sack 2#, $15. ● Fuel bottle, Sigg aluminum, 1 pt.,
plus 3 1-qt. Sigg aluminum fuel bottles, total 19 oz. empty, $20. We
took 1 gal. fuel capacity per boat, had virtually all left at end, but
safe to have it for emergencies. ● Stove stuff sack (6"x12" coated nylon
drawstring, lined w/foam rubber) containing: 1 Svea backpacker's stove,
100 Seaway brand waterproof matches, 2 Optimus mini pumps, 1 pour spout
for fuel bottles, aluminum pot nesting over stove, total stuff sack weight
1.5#, cost $60. Matches (even if waterproof) should be inside screw-top
container inside another waterproof container. Waterproof matches eventually become mushy if wet and won't strike. ● Tarp, 7'x9', nylon with
grommets, 1.5#, $18. Great for dumping food onto.
F. Office Equipment, total approx. weight 8#, cost $171.
● Journal notebook, looseleaf w/vinyl cover, 4½"x7", 8 oz., $7. Used in-
delible ink; good thing because journal got wet even in "waterproof" vinyl
pouch inside "waterproof" Phoenix bag. ● Tape recorder, mini hand-held,
Sony Cassette-corder TCM-121, 1#, $152 (incl. tapes, listed next). ●
Cassette tapes, 26, 2¼"x4¼", Sony, 60 mins. ea., & several sets of batteries, 5#. Used 12 tapes in 65 days on river before recorder was ruined. ●
Guard box, through Colorado Kayak Supply, O-ring sealed, ABS plastic, w/
gasket; I glued blue closed-cell polyethylene foam inside as padding; box
housed tape recorder, 1.5#, $12. Contrary to advertisement, cannot be
carabinered into boat without alteration because there's no attachment
loop; I drilled holes through hinge bracket & fastened chain handle.
Much more serious a flaw is that box leaked twice--once in heavy rain &
once in a swamping--ruining tape recorder latter time. I think these boxes
are a waste of money.
G. Personal Equipment, total approx. weight 14#, $216.
● Bandanas, 2 red cotton, 2 oz., $4. Great for a variety of things. ●
Bathroom coated nylon stuff sack, containing: stainless steel 3"x4½" mirror; toothbrush in plastic holder; mesh drawstring bag (so as not to lose
soap bar in river while bathing) & coated nylon stuff sack (to keep soap
off other stuff), to fit 1 bar soap; terry cloth 5"x5" wash cloth; 1 rat-
tailed comb; 1 hairbrush; 1 small tube Colgate toothpaste; 1 razor w/2
blades; 20 yds. waxed dental floss; 1 plastic bottle containing 100 tablets
vitamin Bl; 1 plastic bottle containing 100 tablets multi-vitamins; 3 mos.
birth control pills. Total stuff sack 1.5#, $45. ● Pocket knife, 2 oz., $2.

● Lawn chair w/short legs, 2.5#, $15. A luxury but well worth weight/space. Short legs put ground at perfect foot-stool & coffee-table height. ● Mosquito repellent, 1 plastic screw-top bottle (2 fl. oz.) Muskol (95% Deet), plus 1 plastic screw-top bottle (2 fl. oz.) Repex (95% Deet), 6 oz., $10. Both will eat paint off various surfaces, so you wonder what they do to your skin, but if you hate headnets they're wonderful. One bottle Muskol lasted entire trip (a very few drops will keep mosquitoes inches away). Repex seems to dry out skin terribly. ● Stuff sacks of coated nylon w/drawstring closures (slide-locks), homemade to fit various articles (about 16 sacks), 1#, $13. Material available by the yd. at backpacking stores. Useful for keeping sand/water off gear, organizing gear. ● Sunglasses, 1 pr. mirrored, 2 oz., $5. A must on very sunny days when glare on water causes headaches. ● Sunglasses strap, homemade of wetsuit material, fits onto eyeglasses earpiece (commercially available as Croakie brand), 1 oz., $3. ● Tampons, 18, w/paper (not plastic) covers, 9 oz., $1. You can't waterproof them enough, but try. ● Toilet paper, 4 rolls, 1.5#, $2. ● Traveler's checks, credit card, driver's license, etc., 10 oz. All village stores will cash low-denomination traveler's checks. Didn't hear of anybody having anything stolen, but I wouldn't want to take cash. ● Towel, 1 cotton/polyester terry cloth, 17"x25", 6 oz., $2. Big enough (wind usually dries you off anyway). ● Whistle & bear bells on ¼" nylon cord, 6 oz., $2. Wore around my neck outside shirt to jangle or be grabbed quickly, if on land; wore inside shirt or in pocket in boat. ● Duct tape, 1 roll, 5 oz., $2. Essential part of aluminum-hull repair kit; useful for a million other things. ● Fishing tackle, 8 oz., $5. ● Fishing rod & reel, breaks down into 18" case, 2#, $60. ● Firestarter jelly, Fire Ribbon brand, 1 (6 oz.) tube, matches, 10 oz., $2. Works great! Excellent safety item. ● Flares, aerial signal, 4 red, 4 oz., $10. Safety measure for signalling each other or others; might have scared away bears if necessary. Never used. ● Flashlight, 6"x1" Tekna II, waterproof, 4 oz. (w/batteries), $11. ● Mosquito coil, 7 oz., $2. Incense-like substance, effective in driving away mosquitoes, readily available in river stores. I'd rather smell fresh air and have a few more mosquitoes. ● Repair kit in 6"x8" Velcro-closure pouch, containing: 2 Water Sports International vinyl repair kits (tubes of liquid & vinyl patch come w/Bill's Bags); one 4-oz. tube of Shoe Saver brand shoe patch liquid for rubber, leather, vinyl, canvas articles; one 1½ oz. tube of Plastic Wood cellulose fiber filler (to fill in leaks around loose or replaced canoe rivets); 2 extra flashlight bulbs; one 6" Velcro strip; one spool heavy-duty white thread; 2 safety pins; 2 rubber bands; ten ¼" metal screws, w/washers & nuts to replace canoe rivets; 5 buttons; 3 snaps; three 9" pieces of shock cord; several ft. nylon cord; several feet of elastic; 6"x24" piece of mosquito netting; 1 scrap nylon webbing; 1 scrap seam tape; one 12"x12" scrap coated ripstop nylon; one

4"x4" scrap <u>coated canvas</u>; one 12"x12" scrap <u>khaki material</u>; spare <u>Svea</u>
<u>stove parts</u>, w/directions; one 5"x6" hemmed <u>denim patch</u>; one empty plastic
dental floss container containing metal <u>thimble</u>, 2 spools <u>thread</u>, several
small <u>safety pins</u>, several sizes <u>needles</u>, <u>straight pins</u>. <u>Total repair kit</u>
<u>weight 14 oz.</u>, cost <u>$15</u>. Shoe Saver didn't work; may have been too cold or
wet. ● <u>Space blanket</u>, <u>2 oz.</u>, <u>$5</u>. Never used, but is essential for safety.
H. <u>Shelter, total approx. weight 14#, $413.</u>
● <u>Plastic groundcloth</u>, heavy duty, 6'x8', <u>1#</u>, <u>$5</u>. ● <u>Tent</u>, 2-person, North
Face A-frame, <u>5.5#</u>, <u>$250</u>. Seam-seal it. Held up well in wind/rain, but
14 stakes are a pain on Yukon's often-rocky ground. Sue's 3-person dome-
shaped North Face tent much roomier and, w/only a few stakes, set up much
faster. ● <u>Sleeping pad</u>, "Therm-a-Rest" brand, 21"x6', foam-filled air
mattress, <u>2.25#</u>, <u>$48</u>. Very warm; makes rocks disappear. Worked beautiful-
ly for 76 days on river, but was punctured by airline on flight home and I
still haven't been able to properly patch it. They offer fair padding w/
an air leak, tho. ● <u>Sleeping bag</u>, PolarGuard filled, by Camp 7, mummy
style, <u>4#</u>, <u>$110</u>. Synthetic fibers are a must on river where there's al-
ways a chance your bag will get wet; bag is your last line of defense
against hypothermia when all your clothing has gotten wet. True to its
advertisement, I was warm in this bag even when it and I were wet inside
and out. W/exception of some unravelled stitching and a broken zipper,
both of which were fixed by Camp 7, mine has lasted fine for 6 yrs. <u>Sum-</u>
<u>mary</u>: Next time I'd take separate tents, for privacy and ease of drying
things out on storm-bound days (what's another 5 or 6 pounds?).
I. <u>Transportation, total approx. weight 109#, cost $723.</u>
● <u>Backpack</u>, Nanda Devi Expedition style by Lowe, internal frame, w/2 detachable pockets, w/homemade coated nylon drawstring rain cover, <u>5.5#</u>,
<u>$154</u> pack, <u>$31</u> pockets, <u>$13</u> cover. Great! Internal zipper converts it
from a 2-compartment backpack to a 1-compartment duffel bag handy for
canoeing. Fits into boat much more easily than frame pack. Indispensable
for any overnights away from river. ● <u>Canoe</u>, Lowe-Line aluminum, 17', 3
thwarts w/flatwater keel, <u>80#</u>, <u>$250</u>. Plenty of room for gear for 2.
Seats very low; big-footed people would have trouble getting feet under
seats to paddle on knees, also freeing feet in whitewater capsize. Keel
& aluminum hull made slow, heavy work (compared to ABS) dragging it a-
shore, but keel made paddling easy in wind/waves. Permanent pads glued
onto seats & knee area on floor very useful to keep out cold, provide
padding. ● <u>Carabiners</u>, 10 ultra-light, <u>1.5#</u>, <u>$26</u>. Great for fastening
gear into boat securely, quickly. We permanently tied ropes between
thwarts, kept a carabiner on each big piece of gear and just clipped
carabiner onto nearest rope as we put gear in boat. I keep all gear
tied into boat, on river or shore, at all times. ● <u>Compass</u>, <u>4 oz.</u>, <u>$6</u>.
Not essential to navigate on Yukon itself, but you'll need it if you

hike overland for any reason. ● Daypack, water-resistant nylon w/vinyl-covered bottom, 1#, $15. Useful for village trips. ● Fanny pack, w/Velcro belt fastener, by The North Face, 5 oz., $17. Useful for camera gear on village trips. Once, Velcro belt came undone; I caught pack just as camera headed toward earth. ● Knee pads, 1 pr. rubber w/web straps, 1#, $10. Great to leave in bottom of boat and kneel in (unfastened). ● Maps, topographical, 24, 3#, $52. See discussion under "Maps" under "Odds and Ends," this Guide. ● PFD (personal flotation device), Extrasport brand, w/front zipper (I attached whistle to zipper), short-waisted, U.S. Coast Guard approved, 15½ lbs. flotation, 1#, $40. Wear it. So comfortable that you'll forget you have it on; acts like a vest for warmth. ● Paddles, 2 standard Mohawk metal-shaft, plastic 8" blade and plastic T-grip (they float), 4#, $27. T-grip is only thing I'd use. Wood might have been warmer and lighter, but be sure to get wide blade. ● Paddles, 1 pr. spare (an 8' kayak break-down paddle w/2 T-grip inserts), 6#, $42. Too short to use effectively as solo double-bladed canoe paddle, but fine as spares. ● Rescue bag, homemade, w/floatable rope, 2#, $28. Essential. ● Ropes, assorted nylon cords & polyurethane ropes, incl. 50' rope on bow & stern, 2.5#, $10. 50' bow rope handy, longer handier. Always tie boat to something. Polyurethane bow/stern ropes can help in rescue. ● Sponges, bailer, 1.5#, $2.

J. Waterproofing, total approx. weight 8#, cost $144.

● Ammo cans, 2 (see discussion under "Camera Equipment"). ● Bill's Bag (brand), 3.8 cu. ft. capacity, 13"x16"x32" packed full, PVC-covered Dacron material, w/2 padded shoulder straps, orange, 3# (empty), $45. This bag size too heavy for me to carry when full. Material did not puncture, straps did not rip away. Orange color easier than blue to find stuff inside. It allowed water inside during heavy rains/partial or total swampings. However, I'd still take it next time because I think it's most well-made and durable flexible bag on market. ● Guard boxes, 2 (see discussion under "Office"). ● Phoenix #2 Dry Bag, 18"x22½", clear vinyl w/fold-over lip secured by twist locks, 1# (empty), $25. Material did not puncture, grommets did not rip out, clear vinyl makes easy to see what's inside. Good size for daily odds & ends you need often. It allowed water inside during swampings. When air cold, vinyl too stiff, metal twist locks too small & stiff, for me to close properly. Sometimes got condensation inside. ● Duffel bag, w/drawstring closure, of water-resistant nylon, 3' tall, by Seda, 1# (empty), $20. This is outer shell of bag intended to be used w/vinyl zip-lock bag inside (which will split immediately). We used as semi-waterproof catch-all for stuff like lemonade cans that was sealed itself. ● "Stuff Sack" by Northwest River Supply, 2, 20"x14", PVC-coated w/Velcro closure & Fastex buckle, 1# (empty), $23. Handy, durable, leaked. ● "Tuff Sack" by Northwest River Supply, 1, 20"x14", PVC-coated nylon w/Velcro closure & Fastex buckle, 1# (empty), $15. Heavier, sturdier, than "Stuff Sacks." Sleeping bag will fit directly into this bag. It leaked. ● Vinyl pouch, 2, w/Velcro closure, 6"x8", 4 oz. (empty), $7. A real joke. With 5 days, Velcro tab had separated from vinyl, w/gap that admitted water. Zip-lock bags last longer. ● Vinyl pouch, 2, w/Velcro closure, 12"x12", 6 oz. (empty), $9. Same joke as above. This size handy as see-through container to keep some rain off map of the day. Summary: Ammo cans great for a few things, but too bulky/rigid for canoe if keeping everything in them. Bill's Bags fine as outer covering, but stuff inside needs to be well waterproofed with another "waterproof" container.

K. General Equipment Summary. Our boat carried approximately 121.5 pounds of my gear, 80 pounds of Evelyn's, plus 33.5 pounds of common gear, totalling 235 pounds. At times, 100 pounds or more of food was also in boat, bringing total gear and food weight for boat to at least 335 pounds. With our added body weight of less than 300 pounds, total weight carried by our boat was well within recommended maximums for any 17' canoe. (As film and cassette tapes were used, they were shipped back home, lightening load.) Total 1982-1983 retail cost of items listed in this Equipment Summary: $5,055.

L. Some Sources of Equipment. (1) Barry's Camera Co., 11171 Harry Hines, Dallas, TX, (214) 241-0582. (2) Camp 7, 1275 S. Sherman, Longmont, CO 80501. (3) Coleman Company, Inc., Wichita, KS. (4) Colorado Kayak Supply, Box 291, Buena Vista, CO 81211. (5) Early Winters, Ltd., 110 Prefontaine Place S., Seattle, WA 98104. (6) High Trails Canoe Outfitters, 12421 N. Central Expressway, Dallas, TX 75243, (214) 661-3943. (7) International Mountain Equipment, Inc., Box 494, North Conway, NH 03860, (603) 356-5287. (8) Kelty Pack Inc., 9281 Borden Ave., Sun Valley, CA 91352, (800) 423-2230. (9) L. L. Bean, Inc., 2091 Main St., Freeport, ME 04033. (10) Lowe Alpine Systems, 802 S. Public Rd., Lafayette, CO 80026, (303) 665-9220. (11) Mesquite Boat Works, 3124 Caribbean, Mesquite, TX 75150, (214) 279-1602. (12) Minolta Corporation, 101 Williams Dr., Ramsey, NJ 07446. (13) Northwest River Supply, P.O. Box 9186, Moscow, ID 83843, (208) 882-2383. (14) Recreational Equipment, Inc., P.O. Box C-88125, Seattle, WA 98188, (800) 426-4840. (15) Southwest Canoe and Trail, 2002 West Pioneer Parkway, Arlington, TX 76103, (817) 461-4503. (16) The North Face, 1234 Fifth St., Berkeley, CA 94710. (17) Your local backpacking/canoeing/sporting goods/ Army surplus store.

YUKON RIVER DATA CHART BASED ON TEXAS WOMEN'S YUKON RIVER EXPEDITION, JUNE 9 - AUGUST 23, 1982

+ = yes
- = no
? = I don't know

| TOTAL MILES | POINT OR VILLAGE | MAILING ZIP | POPULA-TION | MILES BETW. | TRAVEL DAYS | grocery store | a telephone | public shower/laundry | drinking water | cafe/restaurant | bar | liquor sold legally | rent cabin/motel/hotel | medical clinic/hosp. | police | road connection | scheduled air service |
|---|---|---|---|---|---|---|---|---|---|---|---|---|---|---|---|---|---|
| 0 | Whitehorse | YT, Canada | 14,814 | ---- | ---- | + | + | + | + | - | + | - | + | + | + | + | + |
| 202 | Carmacks | YT, Canada | 311 | 202 | 8.0 | + | + | + | - | + | - | - | ? | + | + | + | - |
| 258 | Minto | abandoned | 0 | 56 | 1.5 | - | - | - | - | - | - | - | - | - | - | + | - |
| 282 | Fort Selkirk | no mail | 2 | 24 | .5 | - | - | - | - | - | - | - | - | - | - | - | - |
| 390 | Stewart Island | no mail | 3 | 108 | 3.0 | + | - | - | + | - | - | + | - | - | - | - | + |
| 460 | Dawson | YT, Canada | 697 | 70 | 2.0 | + | + | + | + | + | + | + | + | + | + | + | + |

TOTALS FOR SECTION: 460 miles, 17 days on river, incl. 2 layovers (1--high wind on Lake Laberge, 1--rest). Averaged 27 miles per day incl. layovers; 31 miles per day actual paddling.

| TOTAL MILES | POINT OR VILLAGE | MAILING ZIP | POPULA-TION | MILES BETW. | TRAVEL DAYS | grocery store | a telephone | public shower/laundry | drinking water | cafe/restaurant | bar | liquor sold legally | rent cabin/motel/hotel | medical clinic/hosp. | police | road connection | scheduled air service |
|---|---|---|---|---|---|---|---|---|---|---|---|---|---|---|---|---|---|
| 562 | Eagle | AK 99738 | 110 | 102 | 4.0 | + | + | + | + | + | - | - | + | - | - | + | + |
| 713 | Circle | AK 99733 | 81 | 151 | 5.0 | + | + | - | + | + | + | + | + | - | - | + | + |
| 789 | Fort Yukon | AK 99740 | 619 | 76 | 2.5 | + | + | + | + | - | + | + | + | + | - | - | + |
| 876 | Beaver | AK 99724 | 66 | 87 | 2.5 | + | + | + | + | - | - | + | + | + | - | - | + |
| 976 | Stevens Village | AK 99774 | 96 | 100 | 3.0 | + | + | + | + | - | - | - | - | - | - | - | + |
| 1,012 | Pipeline Hl. Rd. | no mail | ? | 36 | 1.0 | + | + | - | ? | + | - | - | - | - | - | + | - |

TOTALS FOR SECTION: 552 miles, 24 days on river, incl. 5 layovers (2--sightseeing. Dawson; 1--rest; 2--sightseeing, Circle City). Averaged 23 miles per day incl. layovers; 29 miles per day actual paddling.

| TOTAL MILES | POINT OR VILLAGE | MAILING ZIP | POPULA-TION | MILES BETW. | TRAVEL DAYS | grocery store | a telephone | public shower/laundry | drinking water | cafe/restaurant | bar | liquor sold legally | rent cabin/motel/hotel | medical clinic/hosp. | police | road connection | scheduled air service |
|---|---|---|---|---|---|---|---|---|---|---|---|---|---|---|---|---|---|
| 1,077 | Rampart | AK 99767 | 50 | 65 | 2.0 | + | + | - | - | - | + | - | + | - | - | - | + |
| 1,152 | Tanana | AK 99777 | 388 | 75 | 1.5 | + | + | + | + | - | - | + | - | + | - | - | + |
| 1,282 | Ruby | AK 99768 | 197 | 130 | 4.5 | + | + | + | + | - | - | + | - | + | - | - | + |
| 1,340 | Galena | AK 99741 | 765 | 58 | 2.0 | + | + | + | + | - | - | + | - | + | - | - | + |

TOTALS FOR SECTION: 328 miles, 14 days on river, incl. 4 layovers (2--high wind, Rampart; 1--attend dance; 1--X-ray, wash clothes, shower in Tanana). Averaged 23 miles per day incl. layovers; 33 miles per day actual paddling.

| TOTAL MILES | POINT OR VILLAGE | MAILING ZIP | POPULA-TION | MILES BETW. | TRAVEL DAYS | grocery store | a telephone | public shower/laundry | drinking water | cafe/restaurant | bar | liquor sold legally | rent cabin/motel/hotel | medical clinic/hosp. | police | road connection | scheduled air service |
|---|---|---|---|---|---|---|---|---|---|---|---|---|---|---|---|---|---|
| 1,372 | Koyukuk | AK 99754 | 98 | 32 | 1.0 | + | + | ? | ? | ? | ? | ? | ? | ? | ? | ? | + |
| 1,395 | Nulato | AK 99765 | 350 | 23 | .5 | + | + | + | + | - | - | - | - | + | + | - | + |
| 1,436 | Kaltag | AK 99748 | 247 | 41 | 1.0 | + | + | ? | ? | ? | - | - | ? | ? | ? | - | + |
| 1,576 | Grayling | AK 99590 | 209 | 140 | 3.0 | + | + | + | + | - | - | - | - | + | + | - | + |
| 1,596 | Anvik | AK 99558 | 114 | 20 | .5 | + | + | + | + | - | - | - | - | + | + | - | + |
| 1,642 | Holy Cross | AK 99602 | 241 | 46 | 1.5 | + | + | + | + | - | - | - | + | + | + | - | + |
| 1,722 | Russian Mission | AK 99657 | 169 | 80 | 2.0 | + | + | + | + | + | - | - | + | + | + | - | + |
| 1,784 | Marshall/F. Led. | AK 99585 | 262 | 62 | 2.0 | + | + | ? | ? | ? | - | - | ? | ? | ? | - | + |
| 1,830 | Pilot Station | AK 99650 | 325 | 46 | 1.5 | + | + | ? | ? | ? | - | - | ? | ? | ? | - | + |
| 1,850 | Pitkas Point (St. Mary's) | AK 99658 | 88 (384) | 20 | 1.0 | + | + | ? | ? | ? | - | - | ? | ? | ? | - | + |
| 1,868 | Mountain Village | AK 99632 | 583 | 18 | .5 | + | + | ? | ? | ? | - | - | ? | ? | ? | - | + |
| 1,943 | Emmonak | AK 99581 | 567 | 75 | 2.5 | + | + | + | + | + | - | - | + | + | + | - | + |
| 1,955 | Bering Sea | no mail | 0 | 12 | .5 | - | - | - | - | - | - | - | - | - | - | - | - |

TOTALS FOR SECTION: 615 miles, 21 days on river, incl. 2 layovers (1--high wind, "Camp Granada"; 1--high wind, island below Russian Mission). Averaged 29 miles per day incl. layovers; 32 miles per day actual paddling.

TOTALS FOR RIVER: 1,955 - ? miles, 76 days on river, incl. 13 layovers (5--high winds, 2--rest, 6--sightseeing/medical/laundry). Averaged 26 miles per day incl. layovers; 31 miles per day actual paddling.

There is wide disagreement about the length of Yukon River, depending on what book you're reading, what point it considers to be river's source, which channel into Bering Sea it measures, none of which is usually specified. I've seen estimates 1,979 mi. to well over 2,000 mi. Mileages above were computed from combination of existing references and my personal whim. Above mileages bear rough relationship to topographical maps (mileages expressed to us by river residents were usually 20% higher). Services listed (some of which changed after our 1982 trip) are as they exist, to best of my knowledge, in August, 1983. I present above info with something of an apology to residents scattered along the Yukon. In demystifying (to some extent) the logistics of floating the river, I have reduced villages on paper to convenience stops for canoe-tourists (a role Yukon's people may well loathe), and I may be encouraging annual onslaught of precisely the kind of Lower-48 yahoos that people live on the Yukon in order to avoid. So, canoe-tourists, please remember, these are private people and you're paddling through their front yards; give them some privacy. On the other hand, virtually all of the land you'll be paddling through is public land owned by State of Alaska or federal government, the Yukon is a public waterway, and much of the land alongside it is protected precisely for the benefit of canoe-tourists and native wildlife--so you have a right to be there.

# bibliography

1. YUKON RIVER

Albert, Richard O. *The Yukon Experience.* Privately published, 1982, by Richard O. Albert, M.D., 310 No. Wright St., Alice, Texas 78332. $25 each.

Cantin, Eugene. *Yukon Summer.* San Francisco: Chronicle Books, 1973.

Mathews, Richard. *The Yukon.* New York: Holt, Rinehart and Winston, 1968.

McGuire, Thomas. *99 Days on the Yukon, An Account of What was Seen and Heard in the Company of Charles A. Wolf, Gentleman Canoeist.* Anchorage: Alaska Northwest Publishing Company, 1977.

Satterfield, Archie. *Exploring the Yukon River.* Seattle: The Mountaineers, 1975 and 1979. [A guide to the Upper Yukon]

Sherrod, Sue. "Canoeing the Yukon—From Whitehorse to the Bering Sea." *Ms. Magazine,* Volume XII, No. 2 (August, 1983).

_____. "Yukon River Trip." *River Runner Magazine,* Vol. 2, No. 1 (Winter, 1983).

Tryck, Keith. *Yukon Passage: Rafting 2,000 Miles to the Bering Sea.* New York: Times Books, 1980.

2. KLONDIKE STAMPEDE

Berton, Pierre. *The Klondike Fever.* New York: Alfred A. Knopf, 1977.

Martinsen, Ella Lung. *Black Sand and Gold.* Portland: Binford and Mort, 1956.

Satterfield, Archie. *Chilkoot Pass, the Most Famous Trail in the North.* Anchorage: Alaska Northwest Publishing Company, 1973.

3. ALASKA, CANADA

Armstrong, Robert H. *A Guide to the Birds of Alaska.* Anchorage: Alaska Northwest Publishing Company, 1980.

Crisler, Lois. *Arctic Wild.* New York: Harper & Row, 1958.

Fejes, Claire. *Villagers, Athabascan Indian Life Along the Yukon River.* New York: Random House, 1981.

Freedman, Benedict and Nancy. *Mrs. Mike.* New York: Berkley Books, 1968.

Heller, Christine A. *Wild Edible and Poisonous Plants of Alaska.* University of Alaska, Cooperative Extension Service, 1953.

London, Jack. *The Call of the Wild.* New York: Pocket Books, 1963. (1903 by the Macmillan Company)

Marshall, Robert. *Arctic Village.* New York: Quinn and Boder Co., 1933.

McPhee, John. *Coming into the Country.* New York: Bantam Books, 1979.

Miller, Mike, and Wayburn, Peggy. *Alaska, The Great Land.* San Francisco: Sierra Club, 1974.

Mowat, Farley. *Never Cry Wolf.* Toronto: Bantam Books, 1979.

Muir, John. *Travels in Alaska.* Boston: Houghton Mifflin Company, 1915.

Murie, Margaret E. *Two in the Far North.* Anchorage: Alaska Northwest Publishing Company, 1957.

North, Dick. *The Lost Patrol.* Anchorage: Alaska Northwest Publishing Company, 1978.

————. *The Mad Trapper of Rat River.* Toronto: Macmillan of Canada, 1976.

Service, Robert. *Collected Poems of Robert Service.* New York: Dodd, Mead & Company, 1907.

Specht, Robert. *Tisha.* New York: Bantam Books, 1976.

Wayburn, Peggy. "Bear Etiquette: What to Do if You Meet *ursus arctos horribilis*" [excerpt from *Adventuring in Alaska*]. Sierra, 66:48-9, July/Aug. 1981.

Young, Ralph W. *Grizzlies Don't Come Easy: My Life as an Alaskan Bear Hunter.* Tulsa, Oklahoma: Winchester Press, 1981.

4. HOW TO

American National Red Cross. *Canoeing.* Garden City: Doubleday & Company, Inc., 1977.

American National Red Cross. *Standard First Aid and Personal Safety.* New York: Doubleday & Company, Inc., 1973.

Bridge, Raymond. *The Complete Guide to Kayaking.* New York: Charles Scribner's Sons, 1978.

Evans, Jay, and Anderson, Robert R. *Kayaking.* Brattleboro, Vermont: The Stephen Greene Press, 1975.

Manning, Harvey. *Backpacking: One Step at a Time.* New York: Vintage Books, 1973, revised 1975.

McNair, Robert E. *Basic River Canoeing.* Martinsville, Indiana: American Camping Association, Inc., 1968.

Narramore, R.E., and Nolen, Ben M. *Texas Rivers and Rapids, Vol. VI.* High Trails Canoe Outfitters, 12421 N. Central Expwy., Dallas, Texas 75243, 1983.

5. SOME USEFUL PERIODICALS

*Alaska, the Magazine of Life on the Last Frontier,* published monthly by Alaska Northwest Publishing Company, Box 4-EEE, Anchorage, Alaska 99509. $18/yr.

*Backpacker,* published bi-monthly by Ziff-Davis Publishing Company, One Park Avenue, New York, New York 10016. $16/yr.

*Canoe, the Magazine of Self-Propelled Water Travel,* published six times a year by New England Publications, Inc., Highland Mill, Camden, Maine 04843. $12/yr.

*Outside,* published monthly by Mariah Publishing Corp., Continental Bank Building, 1165 N. Clark St., Chicago, Illinois 60610. $12/yr.

*River Runner,* published Feb., April, June, Aug., by Juniper Publications, Inc., Powell Butte, Oregon 97753. $9/eighteen months.

6. SOME HELPFUL BOOKSTORES (Write for their catalogues)

Alaska Northwest Publishing Company, Sales & Shipping, 130 Second Ave. So., Edmonds, Washington 98020.

Alaskan Book Shop, 4617 Arctic Blvd., Anchorage, Alaska 99503.

Baranof Book Shop, 100 N. Franklin St., Juneau, Alaska 99801, (907) 586-2130.

The Book Cache, 436 W. Fifth Ave., Anchorage, Alaska 99501.

Dedman's Photo Shop (Alaskan Books, Photographs & Gifts), Box 417, Skagway, Alaska 99840, (907) 983-2353.

Mac's Books, 203 Main St., Whitehorse, Yukon, Canada Y1A 2B2, (403) 667-2358.

(See also listing of environmental organizations, most of which publish useful periodicals.)

7. UNRELATED BOOKS REFERRED TO IN TEXT

Davidson, Robyn. *Tracks.* New York: Pantheon Books, 1980.

Hite, Shere. *The Hite Report on Male Sexuality.* New York: Alfred A. Knopf, 1981.

Jones, Tristan. *The Incredible Voyage: A Personal Odyssey.* Kansas City: Sheed Andrews and McMeel, 1977.

_____. *Ice!* Kansas City: Sheed Andrews and McMeel, 1978.

# index